SCEPTICAL ESSAYS ON HUMAN RIGHTS

D1450513

Sceptical Essays on Human Rights

Edited by
TOM CAMPBELL, K. D. EWING,
and
ADAM TOMKINS

OXFORD
UNIVERSITY PRESS

OXFORD

UNIVERSITY PRESS

Great Clarendon Street, Oxford OX2 6DP

Oxford University Press is a department of the University of Oxford.
It furthers the University's objective of excellence in research, scholarship,
and education by publishing worldwide in

Oxford New York

Athens Auckland Bangkok Bogotá Buenos Aires Cape Town
Chennai Dar es Salaam Delhi Florence Hong Kong Istanbul Karachi
Kolkata Kuala Lumpur Madrid Melbourne Mexico City Mumbai Nairobi
Paris São Paulo Shanghai Singapore Taipei Tokyo Toronto Warsaw

with associated companies in Berlin Ibadan

Oxford is a registered trade mark of Oxford University Press
in the UK and in certain other countries

Published in the United States
by Oxford University Press Inc., New York

© The Several Contributors 2001

The moral rights of the authors have been asserted

Database right Oxford University Press (maker)

First Published 2001

All rights reserved. No part of this publication may be reproduced,
stored in a retrieval system, or transmitted, in any form or by any means,
without the prior permission in writing of Oxford University Press,
or as expressly permitted by law, or under terms agreed with the appropriate
reprographics rights organization. Enquiries concerning reproduction
outside the scope of the above should be sent to the Rights Department,
Oxford University Press, at the address above

You must not circulate this book in any other binding or cover
and you must impose this same condition on any acquirer

British Library Cataloguing in Publication Data

Data available

Library of Congress Cataloging in Publication Data

Sceptical essays on human rights/edited by Tom Campbell, K.D. Ewing, and Adam Tomkins.

p. cm

Includes bibliographical references and index.

1. Civil rights—Great Britain. 2. Human rights. I. Campbell, Tom, 1938–
II. Ewing, K.D. (Keith D.) III. Tomkins, Adam.
KD4080.S29 2001 342.41'085—dc21 2001039744

ISBN 0-19-924669-6
ISBN 0-19-924668-8 (Pbk.)

1 3 5 7 9 10 8 6 4 2

Typeset in Ehrhardt
by Hope Services (Abingdon) Ltd
Printed in Great Britain
on acid-free paper by
T.J. International Ltd, Padstow, Cornwall

Acknowledgements

Unlike many edited collections of essays, this book is not a volume of conference proceedings. The specially commissioned chapters in this book were written to be read rather than heard. However, we did hold a small workshop in London in September 2000 which most of the contributors to the present volume were able to attend (including most of the international contributors), and at which the shape of the individual chapters, and the book as a whole, were discussed.

The editors would like to express their deep gratitude to the School of Law, King's College London, for providing a generous grant which facilitated this workshop. The editors would also like to thank John Louth and all at OUP for their support of and commitment to this project.

TDC
KDE
AT

Contents

List of Contributors

James Allan
Associate Professor of Law, University of Otago

Richard Bellamy
Professor of Politics, University of Reading

Tom Campbell
Professorial Fellow, Centre for Applied Philosophy and Public Ethics, Charles Sturt University, Canberra

K. D. Ewing
Professor of Public Law, King's College London

Sandra Fredman
Professor of Law, University of Oxford, and Fellow and Tutor in Law, Exeter College Oxford

Judy Fudge
Professor of Law, Osgoode Hall School of Law, York University

Conor Gearty
Professor of Human Rights Law, King's College London

Jeffrey Goldsworthy
Professor of Law, Monash University

Colin Harvey
Professor of Constitutional and Human Rights Law, University of Leeds

Chris Himsworth
Professor of Administrative Law, University of Edinburgh

Saras Jagwanth
Senior Lecturer, Department of Public Law, University of Cape Town

Martin Loughlin
Professor of Public Law, London School of Economics and Political Science

Maleiha Malik
Lecturer in Law, King's College London

Aileen McColgan
Reader in Law, King's College London

Alan Norrie
Edmund Davies Professor of Criminal Law and Criminal Justice, King's College London

Richard Rawlings
Professor of Law, London School of Economics and Political Science

Wojciech Sadurski
Professor of Legal Theory, European University Institute

Adrienne Stone
Senior Lecturer in Law, Australian National University

Adam Tomkins
Fellow and Tutor in Law, St Catherine's College, University of Oxford

Mark Tushnet
Carmack Waterhouse Professor of Constitutional Law, Georgetown University

Neil Walker
Professor of Law, European University Institute

Table of Cases

N. United Kingdom and Ireland

O. United States of America

Table of Treaties and Legislation

F. Croatia

G. Czech Republic

H. Estonia

I. European Community

Treaties and Legislation

O. Israel

P. Italy

Q. Lithuania

R. Moldova

S. New Zealand

AC. United States of America

AD. Yugoslavia

1

Introduction: On Being Sceptical about Human Rights

ADAM TOMKINS

Human rights have played a central role in the rhetoric (if not the reality) of international relations—from the United Nations down—ever since the mid-twentieth century. But over the past two decades human rights have additionally come to enjoy an ever more dominant position in national constitutional or public law. This has been as true for Canada and New Zealand as it has been for Poland and Hungary. One of the last countries in the common law world, and one of the last countries in Europe, to allow its domestic legal system to embrace human rights is the United Kingdom. At the turn of the millennium, however, human rights are beginning to be paraded as a central pillar of even the UK's rapidly changing legal order. After years of argument, Parliament in 1998 at last enacted legislation to 'bring rights home' as the government rather jingoistically put it. The Human Rights Act 1998, which came fully into force in October 2000, gives effect to a unique form of 'domestic incorporation' of (most of) the substantive provisions of the European Convention on Human Rights, a treaty which the UK had been bound by (but only as a matter of international law—and not therefore within the UK's own domestic legal system) since the Convention first came into force, in 1953. The Human Rights Act is, loosely, the UK's Bill of Rights, the UK's approximate equivalent of the Canadian Charter on Fundamental Freedoms (1982), of the New Zealand Bill of Rights Act (1990), and of the constitutional texts of countless emergent democracies from the Baltic States of north-east Europe to the turbulent but thrilling polity of the new South Africa. Human rights law is a global phenomenon to which, it seems, the UK is no longer immune. This book is a critical examination, by an international array of legal and political scholars, both of the global phenomenon and of the UK's—somewhat belated—participation in it.

The Human Rights Act 1998 was one of the most widely celebrated statutes to have been passed by Parliament in many years. Nowhere were the celebrations more pronounced or more intense than among communities of lawyers. The celebration has taken many forms: from the self-congratulatory back-slapping of Tony Blair's Lord Chancellor[1] to the publication of an enormous pile of both academic and practitioner-oriented literature which seeks to explain, to expound and to expand lawyers' lawyerly understandings of the manifold changes which this legislation is

[1] See e.g. Lord Irvine of Lairg, 'The Development of Human Rights in Britain under an Incorporated Convention on Human Rights', [1998] *Public Law* 221.

assumed to necessitate. This volume has as one of its principal objectives the task of offering a set of alternative perspectives. The authors of the essays collected here find little to celebrate, and much to be variously cautious of, sceptical about, or otherwise disturbed by, in the Human Rights Act. In the clamour for liberal self-congratulation, and in the rush to explain how the UK has at last brought rights home, there has been little space for dissent, for critique, or even for doubt. This book provides a little of that space, although we all recognize that we have far from filled the gap. More on that below.

Clearly, in a book to which twenty-one authors have contributed, a variety of views will inevitably be expressed, but in an attempt to steer towards at least a degree of coherence, the following 'mission statement' was used in the development of this book:

New Labour's constitutional reform programme, particularly with respect to the partial entrenchment of the European Convention on Human Rights through the Human Rights Act 1998, has been widely welcomed by the public, by political activists, by senior judges, and by academic and practising lawyers. There are, however, very considerable doubts about the wisdom of these developments within the British democratic tradition which remain unanswered. This collection of essays explores these reservations and considers how they may be taken into account in the implementation and use which is made of the important and largely irreversible changes which are taking place in the UK's constitution. All the participants endorse the importance of human rights within any democratic system of government, but question whether the primary responsibility for the articulation of these rights ought to be taken away from the normal political processes of representative government. Specifically, the extensive shift of political authority to the judiciary which is involved in the Human Rights Act is critically examined and other ways of specifying and promoting human rights in more democratic forums are considered. Particular attention is paid to the priority which should be given to economic and social rights within the new constitutional settlement. Overseas contributions illustrate the pitfalls of importing other constitutional models.

I. What is scepticism?

In his recent introduction to the classic work on scepticism, Sextus Empiricus' *Outlines of Scepticism*, Jonathan Barnes writes that ' "sceptical" contrasts with "credulous" or "gullible": if you are sceptical, you tend not to accept what others say, not to believe what you hear, not to trust what you read. A sceptic is essentially someone who doesn't believe things.'[2] Barnes then refines this philosophically (as opposed to linguistically): 'you are sceptical with regard to a given proposition if and only if, having reflected on the matter, you neither believe it nor disbelieve it.'[3] Some might prefer to call that being agnostic, or even indifferent, rather than being sceptical, and it is not what Sextus Empiricus would have called scepticism either,

---

[2] J. Annas and J. Barnes (eds.), *Sextus Empiricus: Outlines of Scepticism* (Cambridge: Cambridge University Press, 2000), xix.
[3] Ibid.

as Barnes goes on to acknowledge. For Sextus Empiricus, a sceptic was 'essentially a searcher, someone who continues the inquiry'. Barnes explains:

the Greek word for 'sceptic' means something like 'inquisitive', 'investigative' . . . If you undertake any inquiry [according to Sextus Empiricus] one of three things will result: you will hit upon a solution to the problem, you will determine that it is impossible to hit upon a solution, or you will continue the search . . . A sceptic, according to Sextus, is one who continues the search.[4]

Perhaps there are some commentators who believe, now the UK has incorporated a bill of rights into its law, that continuing the search for better government, for fairer administration, or for more justly composed and enforced laws, is either somehow futile or otherwise unnecessary. But certainly no contributor to this volume would advocate abandoning the search, or even dimming the lights. In this sense, we are all sceptics. But for us, scepticism is not taken as having only this technical meaning.[5] Scepticism here is not the antonym of gullibility: rather, it is meant in contrast to celebration. Instead of welcoming the Human Rights Act, the authors of the essays in this book express caution, concern, and doubt. They are dubious, mistrustful, and questioning as to the likely effects of the Human Rights Act. Some would say that this is nothing more than what should in any event be expected of the scholar: that our natural, almost automatic position on anything, practically, should be to raise concerns, to think again, to pause for thought, to quibble, dissent, reargue, reappraise, reconsider; that if and insofar as we could claim to have anything of much practical utility to offer society, that this would be it; that this is the very essence of academic scholarship—its *raison d'etre*—to adopt, and express, as thoughtfully and authoritatively as we can, our positions of scepticism.

Be that as it may, it certainly has not been the case that (until now) the Human Rights Act has been subjected to a great deal of sceptical or critical analysis. Indeed, it has been extraordinarily widely welcomed, not least by a good number of the senior judges whose power has been so considerably enhanced by its passage and subsequent coming into force.[6] Leading barristers—set to play a vastly inflated role in the UK's polity as a result of the Act—have joined the judges in these celebratory festivities.[7] By contrast, until now it seems that the principal task assumed by

---

[4] Ibid., xx.

[5] Indeed, the philosophers are of remarkably little help in exploring the question of what it means to be sceptical. As another commentator on Sextus Empiricus has written, philosophers have deprived the word 'scepticism' of its meaning, making 'a rather empty but highly charged swear word'. See P. P. Hallie's, 'Polemical Introduction' to his *Selections from the Major Writings of Sextus Empiricus* (Indianapolis: Hackett, 1985), 3.

[6] See e.g. Lord Cooke of Thorndon, 'The British Embracement of Human Rights' (1999) 4 *European Human Rights Law Review* 243, and Lord Irvine of Lairg, n. 1 above.

[7] See e.g. Lord Lester of Herne Hill, 'The Art of the Possible: Interpreting Statutes under the Human Rights Act', (1998) 3 *European Human Rights Law Review* 665. Practitioners have also engaged themselves in the rather more important task of writing books for the non-specialist lawyer which explain what the Act, and the ECHR, set out to do: representative of this literature are Lord Lester and D. Pannick, *Human Rights Law and Practice* (London: Butterworths, 1998), and S. Grosz, J. Beatson, and P. Duffy, *Human Rights: The 1998 Act and the European Convention* (London: Sweet and Maxwell, 1999).

academic commentators has been neither overtly to welcome nor to dissent from what the Human Rights Act will do, but rather merely to seek to understand and explain the Act's likely impact in a variety of legal fields. For a constitutional lawyer, this is fascinating reading, and humbling. The literature in the academic law journals reads like a series of reminders of that most powerful of (constitutional) rules: the law of unintended consequences. The Human Rights Act came into being because of a protracted campaign by *constitutional* reformers, some of whom were public lawyers, and some of whom were political journalists.[8] And yet it is an instrument which is unlikely to have a profound effect on the UK's constitution.[9] Its effect will be felt elsewhere. It is not constitutional lawyers who will be rewriting their syllabuses in the coming years as much as the family lawyers,[10] criminal lawyers,[11] commercial lawyers,[12] employment lawyers,[13] planning lawyers,[14] and even the land lawyers,[15] who are to bear the brunt of the Human Rights Act burden, not only in the classroom but also in practice. This is not to say that public lawyers have been silent on the Human Rights Act. On the contrary, there has been a considerable literature, on two issues in particular: first, on the Act's likely impact on judicial review proceedings,[16] and secondly, on the question of the extent to which section 6 of the Act will enjoy horizontal as well as vertical effect (that is to say, on the question of the extent to which the Act will bite in proceedings between 'private' parties *inter se*, where no 'public authority' is party to the proceedings).[17]

---

[8] See M. Foley, *The Politics of the British Constitution* (Manchester: Manchester University Press, 1999), ch. 4.

[9] This point was fully argued in C. Gearty and A. Tomkins, 'Constitutional and Human Rights Law', in D. Hayton (ed.), *Law's Future(s)* (Oxford: Hart, 2000).

[10] See H. L. Conway, 'The Human Rights Act 1998 and Family Law', (1999) 29 *Family Law* 811 (pt. 1) and (2000) 30 *Family Law* 30 (pt. 2); and S. Barnett, 'Compatibility and Religious Rights: The Human Rights Act and the Children Act', (2000) 30 *Family Law* 494.

[11] See the special issue of the *Criminal Law Review* devoted to the Human Rights Act, containing articles by A. T. H. Smith, A. Ashworth, S. Sharpe, and S. Uglow: [1999] *Criminal Law Review* 249–99. As if that were not enough, see also R. Buxton, 'The Human Rights Act and the Substantive Criminal Law', [2000] *Criminal Law Review* 331 (and the reply by A. Ashworth at [2000] *Criminal Law Review* 564), and K. Kerrigan, 'Unlocking the Human Rights Floodgates?', [2000] *Criminal Law Review* 71.

[12] See Sir N. Bratza, 'The Implications of the Human Rights Act 1998 for Commercial Practice', (2000) 5 *European Human Rights Law Review* 1, and M. Smyth, 'The UK's Incorporation of the ECHR and its Implications for Business', (1998) 3 *European Human Rights Law Review* 273.

[13] See G. Morris, 'The ECHR and Employment: to Which Acts does it Apply?', (1999) 4 *European Human Rights Law Review* 496, and Sir G. Lightman and J. Bowers, 'Incorporation of the ECHR and its Impact on Employment Law', (1998) 3 *European Human Rights Law Review* 560.

[14] See D. Hart, 'The Impact of the ECHR on Planning and Environmental Law', [2000] *Journal of Planning and Environmental Law* 117, and M. Redman, 'Compulsory Purchase, Compensation and Human Rights', [1999] *Journal of Planning and Environmental Law* 315.

[15] See J. Howell, 'Land and Human Rights', (1999) 63 *Conveyancer and Property Lawyer* 287.

[16] See M. Supperstone and J. Coppel, 'Judicial Review after the Human Rights Act', [1999] *European Human Rights Law Review* 301, and K. Steyn and D. Wolfe, 'Judicial Review and the Human Rights Act: Some Practical Considerations', (1999) 4 *European Human Rights Law Review* 614.

[17] M. Hunt, 'The "Horizontal Effect" of the Human Rights Act', [1998] *Public Law* 423; N. Bamforth, 'The Application of the Human Rights Act 1998 to Public Authorities and Private Bodies', (1999) 58 *Cambridge Law Journal* 159; Sir R. Buxton, 'The Human Rights Act and Private Law', (2000) 116 *Law*

The present volume should be seen as complementing the more technical and practitioner-oriented literature which already exists. Law students certainly, and academics and practitioners additionally, will be required not only to understand the narrower, more technical legal problems which are posed by the legislation but also to see that there is a bigger legal and political picture which the passage of the Human Rights Act significantly and profoundly alters. Our project is an attempt accessibly yet authoritatively to paint that picture. Yet, in seeking to place the Act in its constitutional and political settings, our contributors do not shy away from the complexity of the law. Putting the law in context does not mean painting with such a broad brush that important points of detail are missed. Rather, it simply means that the detail of the law will be but one part—and not the entirety—of the material with which we are concerned. This collection includes hard-nosed black letter legal analyses of some of the most difficult points of law which the Act raises (see especially the essays in Part II of the book, as described further below). We make no apology for that. But the book also contains essays which seek to lift the reader's attention from the legal text of the Act so that the enormity of the change in the UK's polity which the Act prefigures is not lost in a mire of technical bafflement.

II. The structure of the book

The essays in this volume are grouped into three related parts. The essays in Part I, 'Scepticism and Human Rights', concern the general issue of the various reasons why we might be sceptical about schemes such as that adopted in the Human Rights Act to incorporate judicially enforced human rights norms into binding law. This is not an exclusively legal problem, of course, and our contributors to Part I are not all lawyers: indeed, the section includes contributions from noted political theorists, Richard Bellamy and Tom Campbell. Bellamy contrasts the limited liberal legalism of human rights law with a fuller, perhaps neo-republican, notion of active citizenship, suggesting that by reducing citizens to empty rights-holders we fail to give adequate weight in our polity to the democratic values of participation, engagement, transparency, and belonging, alienating the governed and diluting the richness of the relationship between government and people to one of little more than plaintiff versus defendant. Campbell, by contrast, focuses on what judges can do even with a 'weak' bill of rights, how practices of interpretation can (and will) be used gradually to enhance the judicial role still further, thereby reducing the importance, and the power, of what Americans tend to refer to as the elected branches of government.[18]

Quarterly Review 48; Sir W. Wade, 'Horizons of Horizontality', (2000) 116 *Law Quarterly Review* 217; and N. Bamforth, 'The True "Horizontal Effect" of the Human Rights Act 1998', (2001) 117 *Law Quarterly Review* 34.

[18] As if it is appropriate for any branch of the 'government' to be unelected.

The essays by Martin Loughlin, K. D. Ewing, Neil Walker, and Jeffrey Goldsworthy all complement, in various ways, the arguments put by Bellamy and Campbell. Loughlin, building on his recently published work exploring the changing nature of the relationship between law and politics[19] discusses the role of incorporated rights in the broader processes of legal and political change which permeate contemporary western constitutionalism. Ewing considers the constitutional imbalance left by the passage of the Human Rights Act, with liberal civil and political rights now taking such precedence in the UK over social and economic rights, and considers the options for reform towards (re-?)establishing a happier equilibrium. Goldsworthy focuses on orthodox constitutional doctrine—the sovereignty of Parliament and the rule of law—and considers in detail the now rather frequently made argument that the two are somehow mutually incompatible, and that the former ought to give way to the latter in the form of an entrenched and judicially enforced bill of rights. Goldsworthy concludes that on analysis, it transpires that neither 'thin', formal conceptions of the rule of law nor 'thicker', substantive conceptions of the doctrine require any such thing, and indeed, on the contrary, that such a move 'might actually detract from the rule of law'. Finally, Walker argues that even though many of the traditional arguments against rights—such as that of Jeremy Waldron in his *Law and Disagreement*[20]—take place in the context of theories about the constitutions of nation states, the fact that this context in Walker's analysis no longer reflects the (whole of the) reality of what he calls 'postnational' and 'meta-constitutional' plural arrangements does not mean that the arguments are no longer valid; merely that they call to be recast. We can still be sceptical about rights even in the postmodern, fragmented, undemocratic era of the European Union and government by multi-nationals.

In Part II, 'The Impact and Implications of the Human Rights Act', the principal purpose of each essay is to take a hard look at the detailed way in which a certain area of law is likely to be affected by the Act. While it is our hope that all the essays in the book will be accessible to lawyers and non-lawyers alike, it is in Part II that the most narrowly legal concerns will have greater prominence. It is also in relation to Part II that the most difficult editorial decisions have had to be made. As the literature surveyed above indicates, Part II could sensibly have included contributions on family law, criminal evidence, civil procedure, commercial law, planning law, and administrative law, in addition to (or instead of) any of those topics which we have selected. There is clearly room for a whole book of essays on the theme of Part II, but this is not that book. Rather, for us, the point of Part II is not to be an encyclopedia of all the big and little bits of law which are to be affected by the Human Rights Act. Instead, it is to be read as a kind of case study of the broader constitutional and political concerns outlined in Part I, and while case studies

---

[19] See M. Loughlin, *Sword and Scales* (Oxford: Hart, 2000).
[20] J. Waldron, *Law and Disagreement* (Oxford: Oxford University Press, 1999).

should be representative, they are never complete. We have made our selection based on two criteria: first, we wanted essays in this section of the book to tackle areas of the law which have been rather passed over in the existing literature (there is already much more written on all of the topics listed above than there is on any of the topics we have selected); secondly, within those fields which have not been widely scrutinized through the prism of the Human Rights Act we wanted a sample from both public and private lawyers. The result of all this is an arresting series of eight often alarming and sometimes downright disturbing pieces, each of which points to various incongruities, rough edges, nonsenses, or limitations imposed by the Human Rights Act in the fields of devolution, labour law, discrimination, tort law, criminal justice, and minority protection law.

The final part of the book, 'The Experience of Elsewhere: Reasons to be Sceptical' comprises a series of essays offering an international or comparative perspective on the UK legislation from a variety of standpoints ranging from post-communist eastern Europe to South Africa via North America and Australasia. The 'elsewhere' of Part III is primarily the common law world, or at least representative samples of it. There is some reference to Europe—but not the familiar Europe of the EU. This is in part because all EU countries have ratified the ECHR (and so in this sense it is not really 'elsewhere') and partly also because the relationship between EU countries and human rights, and the relationship between the EU itself and human rights, are already extensively covered in existing literature.[21] It would be easy to dismiss Part III as being merely another opportunity for the pessimists to list the reasons to be dismal about the prospects which bills of rights offer. But this would be a mistake. The essays in Part III do not constitute a chronicle of failures, although our respective authors do of course point to a number of instances where bills of rights have not lived up to all that was promised of them. The principal aims of the essays in Part III are to instruct us in the UK as to what we might expect; critically to compare the new British arrangements with those of other leading common law jurisdictions; to warn us of the potential pitfalls which lie ahead, as well as to identify surprises or alternatives; and to inform us of the ways in which political processes have coped with or matured under the juridification of constitutional rights-talk. In the common law constitutional world, the UK has a particularly special relationship with Canada and the USA, and with Australia and New Zealand, and all four of these jurisdictions are discussed here. But less familiarly, Part III also includes two more unusual and in many respects more unnerving essays, on South Africa and on post-communist eastern Europe. These are both regions of the world about which we in the UK know too little, and yet they are both areas which have been repeatedly prayed in aid of the liberal celebration of rights[22] and constitutional

---

[21] On the former, see C. Gearty (ed.), *European Civil Liberties and the ECHR* (Deventer: Kluwer, 1997) and on the latter, see P. Alston (ed.), *The EU and Human Rights* (Oxford: Oxford University Press, 1999).

[22] See e.g. B. Ackerman, 'The Rise of World Constitutionalism', (1997) 83 *Virginia Law Review* 771.

reform; so it is of particular interest (and, we hope, value) to be able to include in this collection sceptical yet progressive voices from South Africa and Eastern Europe.

III. Sceptical of what?

The essays in this book illustrate a healthy variety of scepticisms. We are not all sceptical of the same things, and we are not all equally sceptical. Perhaps the least sceptical view presented here is that of Sandra Fredman, who argues that we should be sceptical of scepticism, that the judiciary might well find themselves in certain circumstances more, not less, constrained by the existence of the Human Rights Act, and that while the passage of the Act marks a catalogue of missed opportunities, there is nonetheless the potential in the Act to develop positive, social democratic values, despite the 'liberal, individualist, and property oriented notion of human rights' which the Act propagates. Just as there are differences of degree, so too are there differences of what it is we are sceptical about. Three broad variants of scepticism are detectable in these essays. First there are those who express scepticism about rights. Here we find arguments about the appropriateness of casting the relationship between the individual and the state in terms of rights. Secondly there are those who are sceptical of the wisdom of having rights enforced by judges, or at least by the judges which we presently have. Here we find arguments about the politics of the judiciary, and about the limitations of using the adjudicative mechanisms of litigation in seeking to have rights protected. Thirdly there are those who express scepticism as to the content of the specific rights which are enshrined in the ECHR (and thereby the Human Rights Act). Here we find more specifically focused legal arguments as to the limitations of those rights which do find their way into the Convention (and the Act), as well as arguments lamenting what is omitted from the Convention.

These strains of scepticism are not mutually exclusive, and a number of contributors exhibit a combination of them. Neither are these three broad varieties monolithic, in the sense that each can helpfully be further broken down. A good number of different reasons can be identified, for example, in support of the proposition that we should be sceptical of rights (our first category of scepticism). First, rights-talk is inherently antagonistic, and encourages litigation. Secondly, human rights law imagines a paradigm in which there are two parties (the individual rights-holder and the public authority), a model which squeezes out any room for the *res publica*, for the public interest, along with any third party interests which, in the absence of their being 'victims', find it incredibly difficult to get into or otherwise be heard in court. Thirdly, human rights law reduces the relationship between the citizen and the state to one of regulation by quasi-contract—a bill of rights is a list of the clauses in the contract of good governance. The state will be allowed to tax you, to coerce you, to imprison you, to impose restrictions and constraints on you, and you will tolerate (and indeed support and protect—even be prepared to die for) the political, regulatory, military, and economic coercive power of the state on condition that the state respects your rights. Not only does this result in the state being portrayed in unambiguously negative terms, seemingly denying the good that the state is in a unique position to provide in terms of housing the homeless, healing the sick, educating both young and old, and providing welfare for the disadvantaged, and so on, but it also imagines that the individual wants nothing more than to be left alone, that freedom from government, rather than participation in government, is the goal. It also apparently—and dangerously—imagines that any political grievance can be successfully remedied by filing a lawsuit.

Fourthly, human rights law is insufficiently sensitive to the hegemonic power of its own discourse. Rights are an incredibly powerful rhetorical tool, and they get everywhere, strangling other devices, stymieing alternative developments. Adrienne Stone makes this point in her essay in the context of recent developments in the Australian High Court. The discovery (or invention) by that court of an implied right in the Australian constitution to freedom of political speech has led the court, Stone argues, to focus so sharply on arguments based on constitutional rights that it has ignored or sidelined other arguments, based on the common law perhaps, which in her analysis could (and should) have been developed more effectively, but were stymied—or trumped—by rights. Similarly, but more broadly, locating the task of enforcing rights in the courts can lead to the suffocating of alternative avenues for dispute resolution. What fate awaits ministerial responsibility, or the Parliamentary Commissioner for Administration (the ombudsman) after the Human Rights Act?

That there is life beyond the courtroom, but that institutions such as Parliament, ombudsmen, and others are likely to find it more difficult to make their scrutineering voices fully heard in the new post Human Rights Act legal order, connects with the second category of scepticism which manifests itself in this book: scepticism about judges. Why should it be the unrepresentative, overwhelmingly white male upper-middle-class judiciary of the UK's creaking courts who enjoy the emancipation that will come to them with the Human Rights Act? There are two questions here: why give power to *these* people, and why *not* give it to others? Even if the reasons for being sceptical about rights can be overcome, and we decide that we do properly want rights-talk to play a greater role in our polity, why give the job of talking that talk to the judges? After all, what have they done to show either that they deserve, or that they are the appropriate body to enjoy, this newfound role of constitutional referee?[23] By inflating the power and responsibility of the judiciary, the

---

[23] Compare e.g. the respective contributions of the courts, of the Press Complaints Commission, and of the Broadcasting Standards Council in the arena of protection of privacy. Similarly, compare the respective contributions of judicial review and of ombudsmen to the development of practices of better administration. On the former see S. H. Bailey, D. J. Harris, and B. L. Jones, *Civil Liberties: Cases and Materials*, 5th edn. (London: Butterworths, 1995), ch. 8, and on the latter see C. Harlow and R. Rawlings, *Law and Administration*, 2nd edn. (London: Butterworths, 1995), esp. chs. 12, 13, and 15.

influence and contribution which could be offered from other less well-dressed, but perhaps better-suited, institutions has been sidelined and overlooked.

Among those whose essays in this book demonstrate this particular variant of scepticism are Mark Tushnet and James Allan. Tushnet's argument concerns the institutional design of federal government in the USA and its inability to deliver on the promise of rights, at least in part due to what he calls the 'authoritarianism' of American (and especially US Supreme Court) judges. Allan's argument is, if anything, even more uncompromising than Tushnet's. He concludes his essay with the following warning:

Once a constitutionalized Bill of Rights is in place, giving judges power to strike down legislation and so, undeniably, to have huge social policy-making powers, the judges end up deciding *controversial questions of social policy* over which sincere, honest, intelligent, well-meaning people disagree—questions about where to draw the line when it comes to abortion, privacy, police powers, free speech, religious practices, who can marry, how refugee claimants are to be treated, and much else. The judges do not end up stopping vulnerable minorities from being imprisoned because of their race or protecting those with (or even without) distasteful political views from being hounded into unemployment and pariah status. In any imaginable scenario in which the elected legislators would contemplate the sort of things almost everyone today (in the absence of an external threat, when times are good) would consider wicked, the judges too would contemplate the same measures. There is no special moral goodness or acute ethical perspicacity inhering in judges that the rest of us lack.[24]

As to the third and final category of scepticism exhibited in this book, namely scepticism about the specific content of, and omissions from, the ECHR and the HRA, this really speaks for itself, and little needs to be added here. Clearly the rights protected under the terms of the ECHR are partial—in two senses. They are incomplete, in that there are many, many other social or political goods which we might want to be protected, or at least respected, in our polity but which do not find their way into the Act—an argument persuasively and forcefully made by Keith Ewing, Sandra Fredman, Aileen McColgan, and Maleiha Malik, as well as others, in their respective chapters. But they are also partial in the more profound, and more disturbing, sense in that they represent a particular political—and party-political—vision of what it is that society should privilege and prioritize. In the ECHR, and thereby in the HRA, for example, we find the paradigmatic right of liberal political theory (freedom of expression) but not the core of republican philosophy or deliberative democracy (freedom of information, open government, and guarantees of full participation). Property is protected for those who possess it, but the homeless have no right to be housed. Religious freedom is protected, but not the right to an adequate standard of health care. And so on, and on. Social and economic rights are nowhere to be seen in the new liberal order: only a select few rights have been 'brought home' in the Not-Very-Many-Human-Rights Act of 1998.

---

[24] See Allan, Ch. 20 below, 389 (footnotes omitted, emphasis in original).

Nowhere in the present volume is the argument made that this unhappy state of affairs should remain—even the least sceptical voices here have significant suggestions for reform. But the question is still open as to what should be done. It seems there are two options: either more rights (economic and social) or fewer rights (repeal of the 1998 Act), but which one of these alternatives we should be the more sceptical about is a question which will, for the time being, have to wait.

Part I

Scepticism and Human Rights

2

Constitutive Citizenship versus Constitutional Rights: Republican Reflections on the EU Charter and the Human Rights Act

I. Introduction

Constitutional rights are standardly justified on the grounds that they reinforce citizenship. They guarantee citizens certain entitlements linked to their basic interests in security and welfare, promoting their autonomy by providing the preconditions and stability needed for them to act and plan their lives. As such, their advocates argue, they are both the foundations for and above the exercise of political citizenship through the normal democratic process. Citizens who voted to curtail certain civil or political rights would be literally undermining the very possibility of citizenship. Whilst it is true that any political system entails certain rights, however, it is also the case that citizens disagree about the nature of the polity and the role of the state within it. These disagreements are intimately related not only to different views about the basis, character and extent of rights, but also to disputes over the character of citizenship—both who are citizens and what can be expected of them. These debates are continuous, arising in all policy decisions, be they about welfare provision, education, defence, criminal liability, or the conduct of the economy. Far from resting on a settled constitutional consensus, this chapter will argue that politics is a constitutive process through which citizens struggle to promote their interests by ensuring that the character of the polity is such that it recognizes their evolving ideals and concerns. Indeed, the capacity to discuss these issues and resolve them through appropriate political mechanisms is itself a mark of a citizen's autonomy. Citizenship so conceived operates as 'the right to have rights' rather than as a given set of rights.[1]

I am grateful to Miriam Aziz, Alan Scott, Jo Shaw, Adam Tomkins, Jim Tully, Neil Walker, and audiences at Royal Holloway College in London, the EUI in Florence, and the University of Innsbruck for their comments on earlier versions of this paper. Research was supported by an ESRC Grant L213 25 2022 on 'Strategies of Civic Inclusion in Pan-European Civil Society' and a Jean Monnet Fellowship at the EUI in Florence.

[1] I borrow this phrase and some of the inspiration behind my argument from C. Lefort, *Democracy and Political Theory* (Cambridge: Polity, 1988), 37, who takes it in turn from Hannah Arendt. See too Jeremy Waldron's parallel notion of political participation as the 'right of rights' (*Law and Disagreement* (Oxford: Oxford University Press, 1999), ch. 11), a phrase he borrows from William Cobbett, although I distinguish my view from his below.

Thus, a potential tension exists between constitutional rights and the constitutive character of political citizenship. This tension grows the more pluralist a political community happens to be. For pluralism tends to fuel demands for more differentiated decision-making that grants increased political autonomy for particular regions or groups to ensure that their interests and related views on rights get taken into account in collective decision-making, or that even allow them partly to withdraw on certain issues and to formulate their own positions. As Neil Walker and Chris Himsworth note respectively in their chapters on the EU and Scottish devolution, this tension is manifest in the conflict between the dispersal of sovereign power occurring within both Europe and the UK, on the one hand, which fosters the political autonomy of citizens to control the processes affecting them in ways they deem appropriate to their ideals and interests, and the entrenchment of rights through the new EU Charter of Fundamental Rights and the Human Rights Act, on the other, which tends to promote a unitary conception of constitutionalism whereby all must abide by a uniform set of standards. This chapter contends that if we take the constitutive character of citizenship seriously, then we must adopt a quite different and more political approach to constitutionalism from that stemming from constitutional rights.

Instead of constitutions being seen as establishing a just foundation and framework for politics, they have to be conceived as institutional mechanisms for preserving the civic freedom of citizens to negotiate different views of rights and justice and reach collective agreements that avoid mutual domination. I shall relate this political view of constitutionalism to republicanism.[2] The historical source of a political constitutionalism, the republican tradition viewed conflict as inevitable.[3] Rather than regarding conflict as the sinister product of self-interest, to be overcome through a consensus on rights, republicans sought to employ these conflicts to protect liberty and foster solidarity. They advocated a balanced political constitution that so mixed the various contesting parties that they were obliged to engage with each other. The aim was the production of laws embodying norms of fairness and equality every bit as compelling as those desired by advocates of rights-based constitutional settlements, but which had a flexibility and attentiveness to the particular circumstances and peculiar complexion of the demos that these often lack.

The chapter proceeds as follows. Section II explores the constitutive function of citizenship. Struggles for citizenship and between citizens are shown to entail redefinitions of the subjects, spheres, scopes and styles of politics that lead to a continuous reconstitution of the polity and hence of the rights of its citizens. Section III investigates the norms generated by these practical exercises of citizenship and

---

[2] P. Pettit, *Republicanism: A Theory of Freedom and Government*, 2nd edn. (Oxford: Clarendon Press, 1999) and R. Bellamy, *Liberalism and Pluralism: Towards a Politics of Compromise* (London: Routledge, 1999).

[3] See R. Bellamy, 'The Political Form of the Constitution: The Separation of Powers, Rights and Representative Democracy', in R. Bellamy and D. Castiglione (eds.), *Constitutionalism in Transformation* (Oxford: Blackwell, 1996), 24–44.

their relationship to the standard packages of citizen rights. The latter are shown to require the former in order to resolve the conflicts between and within them. Meanwhile, the struggles over citizenship find their constitutional rationale within a neo-republican view of politics. Section IV then suggests how this neo-republican analysis might be applied to the EU and the UK. Both are shown to be contested polities which have begun to develop political structures that can be harnessed to the republican scheme of promoting constitutive citizenship practices that foster and promote civic freedom. In each case, attempts to implement a rights-based constitutionalism risk undermining progress in this direction in ways that threaten the legitimacy and hence stability of the resulting settlement.

II. The constitutive role of citizenship

Historically, the processes of state-making, constitutionalism, and the development of citizenship have gone hand in hand, reflecting not only external pressures, notably war, but also internal political struggles amongst citizens themselves. Most normative citizenship theorists and many legal and political scientists have discounted these factors. They have either seen them as a matter for historians and political sociologists or fallen back on an implicit teleology derived from a Whiggish reading of Marshall,[4] whereby an expanding set of citizenship rights forms part of the natural evolution of modern democratic societies. Their focus has been on various ideal models or typologies of just, democratic societies.[5] However, liberal democracies are far from converging on a single model, though many of their procedures and norms share certain affinities. At least part of this diversity is to be attributed to the various ways in which struggles between citizens have played out. Though these struggles have been geared towards securing justice for those involved, only a Panglossian optimist would regard them as moving towards a consensus on justice. Rather, they have been debates about justice—debates, to be sure, that might well assume that an objective and ideal account ultimately exists, but which arise because citizens disagree over what that account might be and have no common basis for determining whose version is right.

It is sometimes alleged that such disagreements result solely from the presence of injustice, the product of self-interest, ignorance, or bad faith by one or more groups within the polity. Wittingly or unwittingly this is often the case. However, disagreement also arises because human beings value a variety of goods which different people prioritize and order in divergent and occasionally incompatible ways. This perspectival diversity stems not just from different experiences, backgrounds,

[4] T. H. Marshall, *Citizenship, Social Class and Other Essays* (Cambridge: Cambridge University Press, 1950).
[5] e.g. D. Held, *Political Theory and the Modern State* (Cambridge: Polity, 1989), ch. 7, and T. Janoski, *Citizenship and Civil Society: A Framework of Rights and Obligations in Liberal, Traditional and Social Regimes* (Cambridge: Cambridge University Press, 1998).

and social positions, but also from the ways in which the sheer complexity of many political issues renders the relevance of different facts and considerations dependent upon rather than independent of the views of the discussants. Many contemporary rights- or justice-based constitutional theorists acknowledge the 'fact of pluralism' yet seek to circumvent it. Thus, John Rawls accepts the significance of what he calls 'the burdens of judgement' when seeking to adjudicate between different comprehensive conceptions of the good,[6] but argues that they should lead to a consensus on common principles of political justice that limit what we may legitimately propose for or impose on others in the name of our inevitably contentious beliefs.[7] Unfortunately, for reasons explored more fully in the next section,[8] the right proves as controversial as various views of the good, as debates over abortion, affirmative action, the death penalty, taxation, and welfare amply demonstrate.

If no collective agreement were ever necessary and we could each simply go our own way, such disagreements would be like academic quarrels about these same matters: challenging, provocative, diverting, and occasionally frustrating, but not an issue of life and death. However, what Rawls (following Hume) calls the 'circumstances of justice'[9]—namely the conditions of moderate scarcity, limited altruism, and unavoidable social coexistence—mean that some common rules are necessary. The benefits from collective action within a shared framework range from the security of the person and property to environmental protection and public health. The difficulty is that we disagree about the character of the framework, what should be pursued under it and even the best way to implement those policies we do agree to. Jeremy Waldron has coined the term 'the circumstances of politics' to describe the resulting condition of having to reach agreement in the face of such disagreements.[10] The upshot of this predicament is that citizens search not for a just consensus but for a politics that shows equal respect for their different views in the ways common decisions get deliberated and decided. Waldron believes that majoritarian voting satisfies this goal because of its procedural fairness.[11] But he takes as given that all relevant views are adequately represented and that we can agree on forms of respect without invoking controversial views of justice. By contrast, I shall argue that disagreements about the nature of justice inevitably spill over into debates concerning who is recognized as worthy of respect and how their beliefs are represented. Disagreement enters into the form of politics, therefore, producing an ongoing political constitutionalism whereby a polity is continually reconstituted more appropriately to recognize, respect, and represent the opinions of its members—often producing modifications to majoritarian rule, as in federal and consociational systems, or even calls for secession. Herein lies the constitutive role of citizenship.

  [6] J. Rawls, *Political Liberalism* (Chicago: Chicago University Press, 1993), 56–7.
  [7] Ibid. 36–8.
  [8] See too Bellamy, *Liberalism and Pluralism*, ch. 2.
  [9] J. Rawls, *A Theory of Justice* (Cambridge, Mass.: Harvard University Press, 1971), 126–30.
  [10] Waldron, *Law and Disagreement*, 107–18.   [11] Ibid.

We can analyse this phenomenon via the ways political recognition, respect, and representation get mediated through four intersecting dimensions of the polity: namely, the sphere, subjects, scope and styles of politics. The *sphere* of politics refers to where politics takes place. These borders involve not only the external frontiers of the polity but also its internal administrative divisions. These tend to be both territorially and functionally defined, with different functions usually mapping onto different territorial units and occasionally cutting across them. They are also frequently subdivided into more localized units that implement and inform central decisions. There are also demarcations between the political and non-political areas of life, as in attempts to distinguish a public from a private sphere. The *subjects* of politics concern the definitions of rulers and ruled, or who decides for and over whom. Even in a democracy, where the designated demos are potentially both governors and governed, the criteria for voting can be different from those for standing for election. Meanwhile, no polity identifies citizens simply with those physically present within a relevant sphere. Citizenship is standardly associated with certain capacities and commitments that only a subset of these will possess. The *scope* of politics has to do with its aims and the claims it makes upon people within its designated spheres. Different areas of political life may warrant a greater or lesser degree of intervention and be more or less demanding than others. A politics aimed at ensuring non-interference and forbearance will have a very different character and impact from those of one demanding positive action. Finally, the *styles* of politics relate to the ways politics is undertaken as a result of the various types of formal and informal consultation and influence that the political system allows. These may range from voting as determined by the electoral system, through membership of political parties, unions, and various lobbying organizations, to consultative meetings, letter-writing campaigns, demonstrations, direct action, and even—in extreme circumstances—terrorism and civil war.

These four dimensions of politics are clearly related, with the character of each influencing that of the others. Thus, the boundaries marking the sphere of politics will partly, though not entirely, determine its subjects, scope, and styles by creating certain constituencies and designating which areas are political or not. Recognizing a region as a legitimate sphere of politics by granting it a degree of political autonomy may be tied implicitly or explicitly to recognition of a national minority as a subject of politics. Giving them a degree of self-government, however, will also lead to acceptance that the claims of language or culture fall within the scope of politics, and that new styles of politics may be necessary to allow certain minority groups to participate according to their particular linguistic and cultural traditions. Similarly, if the scope of politics consists simply of upholding negative rights, then its legitimate sphere, subjects, and styles will differ from a view that includes positive rights. For example, it is more likely that the economy will be treated as a largely private sphere, employees not recognized as political subjects, and certain styles of consultation, such as workplace democracy, deemed inappropriate. And so on. When citizens struggle to be recognized as political subjects, therefore, they are not simply demanding access to a pre-constituted set of political rights. For that recognition will invariably have profound consequences for the other dimensions of politics and hence for the very constitution of the political. Moreover, struggles between citizens over any of the other dimensions, such as the appropriate scope of politics, will equally have constitutional consequences for how we conceive its sphere, subjects, and styles.

Because political disagreements invariably turn on the definition of one or more of these dimensions, citizenship has performed a pivotal constitutive part in the transformation and re-formation of political communities across all four of these dimensions. In the nineteenth century, for example, nationalist movements played a significant role in defining the sphere of politics as the nation state. Frequently tied to revolutionary and democratic movements, these struggles for national self-determination also served to make 'the people' the subject of politics and in the process altered both its scope and forms. Similarly, later struggles to extend the franchise to women and workers have not only expanded the subjects of politics but, as we noted above, inevitably changed its sphere, scope, and styles. Though the United States constitution is sometimes treated as the archetypal rights-based document, establishing the republic on 'self-evident' just constitutional principles, its true foundations lie in 'we the people'. As Bruce Ackerman has shown,[12] citizens have transformed it through successive waves of constitutional politics, from the extreme case of civil war, through the Depression years that gave rise to the New Deal, to the civil rights movement of the 1960s. In all these cases, citizens have been struggling to construct a framework within which their concerns will be recognized and respected. Yet that has not been simply a matter of getting noticed under the established rules but, as we have seen, has inevitably meant challenging those rules as well.

Three features of these constitutive citizenship struggles need emphasizing. First, some commentators grant that such constitutional moments occasionally arise, but like Ackerman regard them as exceptional, with 'normal' politics occurring within the framework set by the last constitutional struggle.[13] To some degree that is inevitably true. Revolutions are rare, and even then attempts to start totally anew prove impossible. The constitutional ship is necessarily rebuilt at sea, with modifications in one area being realized through the established practices in another. Nevertheless, this is a more incremental and everyday process than Ackerman and others allow, with momentous transformations usually the cumulative result of a gradual alteration in public opinion produced by numerous small shifts within debates on a variety of particular issues.

Second, past struggles by workers, women, and ethnic minorities (and occasionally majorities) are sometimes contrasted with current struggles over gender and multiculturalism.[14] The former are typified as struggles for inclusion within the established framework—as demands that the cooperatively produced benefits and

---

[12] B. Ackerman, *We the People: Foundations* (Cambridge, Mass.: Harvard University Press, 1991).
[13] Ibid. 3–33.   [4] N. Fraser, *Justice Interruptus* (London: Routledge, 1997), ch. 1.

burdens of political community be shared more equitably. In sum, they are struggles for a fuller realization of justice. By contrast, the latter are characterized as struggles to be recognized as different and to enjoy an exclusive status. They seek a more diverse rather than a more equal society. Certain critics go so far as to vilify them for promoting injustice by seeking to entrench the very inequities and hierarchies that past groups struggled to overturn. The foregoing analysis, however, suggests far greater continuity between the two.[15] Like contemporary struggles, those of the past involved demands for recognition as well as distribution. They sought not only admission to, but also a reconstitution of, the political community and the forms of justice and equality it inscribes. Thus the enfranchisement of women brought with it an enlargement of the sphere of politics to include the domestic arena, a corresponding extension of the scope of politics to include issues such as sexual harassment and marital rape, and demands for new and less confrontational styles of politics. Like past struggles, those of the present are for a more inclusive and equitable society. However, once again these demands involve reconceptualizing how political goods are produced and distributed. As we saw, the struggles of workers and national minorities entail parallel transformations of the sphere, scope, subjects, and styles of politics.

Third, and most importantly, it is impossible to say a priori what the 'best' conception of these dimensions and their relations to each other might be. Any criteria we might come up with will not only have to be tailored to varying and highly contingent circumstances in ways that are impossible to specify in advance, but also will be subject to diverse judgments and interpretations by citizens themselves. Indeed, divergent priorities and values may lead groups to propose different criteria. Meanwhile, as one group alters the ways in which it is recognized by others, that has knock-on effects both for the ways these others are recognized and for how they recognize themselves. Thus, new struggles are spawned as identities, ideals and interests change in response to the new structures, producing in their turn further struggles for new forms of recognition. Consider, for example, how in recent times gains in certain domains by the feminist movement have given rise to 'post-feminist' discourses, on the one hand, and a reappraisal of masculine gender, on the other, fostering a further spate of political dialogue and change. The process of reconstituting the polity is a continuous one.

This section has endeavoured to show how the need to find agreement in circumstances of disagreement produces struggles over how different groups are recognized, respected, and represented which are directly related to the ways the polity is constituted. Hence, citizens are not ready constituted by a pre- or supra-political constitution; they seek to constitute themselves, and thereby the very shape of politics itself. In the next section I shall describe how these struggles disturb rights-based constitutionalism but can nevertheless be harnessed to promote a form of political constitutionalism.

[15] J. Tully, 'Struggles over Recognition and Distribution', (2000) 7 *Constellations*, 469–82.

III. Two models of constitutionalism, citizenship, and rights

Constitutionalism can be divided into two broad families: the juridical and the political. Though they share certain elements and have been intertwined historically, they operate different and not entirely compatible logics—not least in the ways they conceptualize the relationship of citizenship to rights. Juridical conceptions of constitutionalism concentrate on the legal mechanisms for controlling the abuse of power and protecting individual rights. Their aim is to secure a just framework within which citizens and the government can legitimately act by constraining what may be matters of political dispute and decision. The constitution defines citizenship and regulates citizens' struggles. To a broad extent, therefore, this view assumes a consensus on the four dimensions of politics.[16] By contrast, more political conceptions see constitutionalism as the various political practices through which citizens constitute their relations with each other. Instead of aiming at or assuming a just ordering of politics, this approach focuses on the ways citizens continually renegotiate the dimensions of politics in order mutually to determine the rules and institutional processes governing their collective life. This striving for reciprocal recognition guards against groups or individuals being subjected to another's will. A condition of civic freedom rather than a substantive conception of justice provides the primary rationale of politics. For freedom from oppression and domination are best secured through participation in framing the collective arrangements and public goods which provide the context for autonomous choice and development.[17]

As noted, the juridical and political conceptions coexist within most constitutional democracies, the historical product of the roles played by the political languages of liberalism and republicanism respectively in the evolution of Western states. Thus, written constitutions standardly specify the components of the political system as well as containing provisions for the juridical protection of rights. If the second aspect prevails over the first, however, the political system will be designed in accord with the official understanding of justice and operate as an imperfect procedure for its realization, thereby justifying the occasional judicial overturning of purportedly unconstitutional political decisions. If the first aspect prevails, though, the legal system will play a more subordinate role. Since arbitrary rule is a prime source of domination, the court's protection of institutionalized rights and the formal properties of the rule of law will remain essential. But the definition of those rights and the guarantees of their fairness derive from the capacity of the political mechanisms and procedures to preserve civic freedom.

---

[16] R. Dworkin, 'Constitutionalism and Democracy', (1995) 3 *European Journal of Philosophy* 2–11, and Rawls, *Political Liberalism* both exemplify this position.

[17] For different versions of this thesis see Bellamy, *Liberalism and Pluralism*; Pettit, *Republicanism*; C. Sunstein, *The Partial Constitution* (Cambridge, Mass.: Harvard University Press, 1993); and M. Tushnet, *Taking the Constitution Away from the Courts* (Princeton, NJ: Princeton University Press, 1999).

These two views of constitutionalism give rise to two different perspectives on citizenship, which I shall explore in turn. Juridical conceptions define citizenship by rights. Table 2.1 outlines three of the main models.[18]

The libertarian and the social democrat reflect two versions of liberalism and provide the main contemporary rights-based positions. The communitarian model is often aligned to the republican and contrasted to these. However, I shall argue that it has more in common with them than the neo-republican account described below. I wish to focus on five features of these models, with the first two remarks directed at the rights-based conceptions alone, the last three at the communitarian as well.

Table 2.1

	Libertarian	Social democrat	Communitarian
Legal rights (liberties and immunities)	Formally equal negative liberties	Formally equal negative liberties, though certain immunities for reasons of substantive equality and linked to social rights to defend their equal worth	Equal, though often restricted to exclude other groups
Political rights (powers)	Protective, limited	Protective and informative, limited	Stress on public service and participation
Social rights (claims)	Few (mainly insurance and compensatory) or none	Broad range, including enabling and distributive as well as insurance and compensatory	Usually extensive
Civic rights (powers)	Few (consumer) or none. Strict divide between state/civil society, public/private	Workers and consumers. Need for state to regulate and balance civil society	Usually workers and consumers (corporatism). State and civil society closely related
Duties	Of respect, with duties subordinate to rights	Of concern and respect, with duties being corollary of rights	Rights product of the general duty to uphold and pursue the values of the community

[18] For a fuller discussion see R. Bellamy, *Rethinking Liberalism* (London: Continuum, 2000), ch. 9.

First, the two rights-based conceptions offer not only contrasting but conflicting and incompatible views of rights. Certain accounts of citizenship rights assume that one can simply add on new rights to come up with a maximal package that incorporates all legitimate points of view. However, this is not the case. Thus, libertarians claim that the taxation required to support the welfare and social policies desired by social democrats would necessarily conflict with their understanding of market freedoms and the system of property entitlements on which it rests. Social democrats necessarily accept that as true. Consequently, they offer an alternative account of coercion and interference that includes certain structural effects of a free market, such as the creation of discrete pockets of unemployment and the vulnerability of the poor and the uneducated to exploitative contracts. Libertarians, though, would deny that the social democratic position is an improvement on theirs because it reinterprets aspects of the rights they favour as part of a fuller set of rights. In their view, there is no justification for the additional rights since the social democratic reinterpretation of coercion is mistaken.[19]

Second, this problem cannot be circumvented by seeking a more minimalist set of negative liberty rights, such as the standard civil rights, as libertarians sometimes imagine. Theoretically, upholding negative liberties imposes no costs on others and creates no clash between such rights. Rights to non-interference simply require that we leave others alone. In practice, though, they need to be secured via a police force and the courts. The resulting costs can be as burdensome as welfare provision and may involve as many clashes with other negative rights. An official secrets policy, for example, usually has to be balanced against rights to freedom of expression and privacy. Meanwhile, different interpretative standpoints can lead to divergent views on when, if at all, interference takes place even amongst adherents of the negative position, leading to competing opinions on whether negative rights ever conflict. Such disputes surface when deciding whether an exercise of property rights might produce negative externalities damaging the property rights of others, as when people complain about noisy neighbours or the effects of fishing upstream on the fishing rights of those below. Indeed, similar issues arise with any attempt to designate a certain set of rights as 'basic' or 'absolute'. Thus, to take the strongest case, banning certain punishments as 'degrading', such as torture or the death penalty, might lead to more crimes being committed and thereby produce more rights abuses than they prevent. Implementing such policies, therefore, involves an implicit calculation that fewer, or no more, equally important individual rights will be damaged because of a resulting rise in the number of murders and acts of violence. For example, it is standardly argued that these methods have no greater deterrent effect over other less brutal forms of punishment, that there is a danger of people being wrongly convicted, and so on.

---

[19] For this debate see R. Plant and N. Barry, *Citizenship and Rights in Thatcher's Britain* (London: Institute of Economic Affairs, 1990).

Third, and following on from this last observation, rights cannot be isolated from collective decisions of a utilitarian or communitarian nature. Rights are sometimes claimed to protect the individual from tyrannous majorities by 'trumping' decisions made in the name of the public interest or common good.[20] However, such social considerations are intrinsic to how we define and interpret rights. Indeed, rights are generally valued not because of their worth for particular individuals per se, for whom they may be of no interest and burdensome, but because of their contribution to certain collective goods and the more diffuse benefits that result from living in a community where they exist.[21] For example, journalists and politicians apart, few individuals personally make use of freedom of speech. However, all benefit from a society which enjoys this right and the role it plays in protecting against the abuse of power, disseminating information, and so on. These factors come into play when interpreting or resolving conflicts between rights, as in US debates over whether pornography counts as 'speech' or when considering possible limits to freedom of speech in cases such as incitement to racial hatred or the diffusion of state secrets.

Communitarians acknowledge this collective dimension to rights and consequently stress the primacy of upholding community values. But sociological and perfectionist versions of communitarianism overestimate the homogeneity of communities and the degree of agreement on the good life. As a result, they end up downgrading the role of politics in parallel ways to rights-based theories. Thus, the former seek to segregate politics to a bounded political community, the nation state, where 'language, history and culture come together . . . to produce a common consciousness'.[22] The latter espouse a form of ethical naturalism that suggests that all values can be ordered within a full vision of how the good society will foster human interests.[23] Though communitarians give more weight to political deliberation than rights-based models, both versions hold that such deliberation assumes and promotes consensus on the good through explicating shared understandings, thereby abstracting from the very circumstances of dissent that make politics necessary. Indeed, they are apt to treat division as suspect, the product of factions and sinister interests. Where they endorse judicial review, this too is seen as the explication of supposedly common community values.

Fourth, and in this context most importantly, all three of the aforementioned sources of conflicts between rights or interpretations of them are related to disagreements over the four dimensions of politics. As Table 2.2 reveals, each of these models of citizenship assumes a different view of the sphere, appropriate scope, subjects and styles of politics. Yet these are far from settled, with political debate

---

[20] R. Dworkin, *Taking Rights Seriously* (London: Duckworth, 1985), 91, 199–200.

[21] J. Raz, *Ethics in the Public Domain: Essays in the Morality of Law and Politics* (Oxford: Clarendon Press, 1994), ch. 3.

[22] M. Walzer, *Spheres of Justice: A Defence of Pluralism and Equality* (Oxford: Martin Robertson, 1983), 29.

[23] J. Raz, *The Morality of Freedom* (Oxford: Oxford University Press, 1986), 215.

turning on precisely how they should be interpreted. As we have seen, room for conflict exists even between proponents of the same model. The problem with either rights-based or community-based conceptions of citizenship, therefore, is that they rest on agreement on precisely those issues citizens most disagree about.

Finally, none of these models has adequate political resources to cope with the disagreements that, for the reasons rehearsed above, inevitably arise. As we remarked, communitarians take consensus as the basis, logic, and outcome of deliberation. Even if the first two elements held in theory, however, practically decisions often have to be made long before all the parties have managed to agree. Meanwhile,

Table 2.2

	Libertarian	Social democrat	Communitarian
Subjects	All autonomous agents capable of entering legally recognized contracts, particularly in the economic sphere	All autonomous agents capable of entering legally recognized contracts, including social and political spheres	Cultural and national groups
Spheres	Political sphere a narrowly defined public framework for social interaction. Political discussion and intervention, if not regulation, inappropriate within a broad private sector.	Political sphere a more broadly defined public framework for social interaction. Political discussion and intervention, if not regulation, inappropriate within a narrower private sector.	Political sphere the nation state
Scope	To protect the natural negative freedom and formal equality of individuals	To foster autonomy by preserving the broader negative freedom and more substantive equality of individuals and classes	To preserve communal self-determination and group solidarity
Styles	Constrained maximization to achieve mutual advantage via market trading	Constrained maximization to achieve mutual benefit via pluralist bargaining	Collaborative pursuit of shared goods

dissent frequently arises precisely because disputants do not share common experiences or a normative framework. Real politics must provide procedures for conciliating conflict in the face of continued disagreement. Rights-based theorists also assume a pre-political consensus, in their case produced by constitutionally trimming the areas of value disagreement from the political agenda. The residue supposedly comprises far more tractable interests that can be traded and modified in mutually beneficial ways. However, we have seen that disagreements over the right and the good remain, being intrinsic to most policy decisions. Nonetheless, rights-based theorists are correct to fear the consequences of settling such disputes by political or economic horse-trading. Amongst purely instrumentally rational agents, the interests of others will only be acknowledged if concessions are necessary, whilst the collective interest is liable to be sacrificed to the personal whenever free-riding or defection appear possible. Moreover, interests may remain in play connected to ideals and identities that people are unprepared to trade. In sum, this style of politics makes majoritarian tyranny and myopia all too likely. Of course, constitutional courts are invoked to guard against these dangers. Yet if there is no clear 'right' or 'principled' answer, as I have suggested, then their deliberations will not differ in kind from those of citizens. Indeed, they may be worse. The judiciary possesses a narrower range of experience than is available within a legislature, is comparatively poorly placed to consider the resource and other implications of a particular decision for the total package of government policies, and lacks the electoral legitimacy of political representatives.[24]

A political approach to constitutionalism attempts to overcome these difficulties by establishing practices through which citizens may agree on ways to disagree whilst making mutually acceptable decisions in areas requiring collective action. In the republican original of this thesis, the body politic is assumed to contain conflicting classes whose interests need to be balanced and mixed by dividing and dispersing power.[25] Such balancing and mixing serves to check the adoption of purely self-serving positions and promotes a propensity to heed the views of others and take account of them in collective decision making.[26] Traditional devices have included creating two legislative assemblies with different forms of representation and election, separating the legislature from the executive, and forms of federalism ranging from regional autonomy to self- governing functional associations. In other words, multiple spheres, subjects, scopes, and styles of politics are employed to secure the mutual recognition of diverse groups.

As we noted, the underlying rationale of this system was to avoid domination by encouraging civic freedom. The crux is Rousseau's dilemma in the *Social Contract*: how can one be subject to the collective rules required for social life without being enslaved by the will of another.[27] As with Rousseau, the answer lies in taking part

[24] Sunstein, *Partial Constitution*, n. 17 above, 145–9.   [25] Bellamy, 'The Political Form' n. 3 above.
[26] Bellamy, *Liberalism and Pluralism*, n. 2 above, ch. 5.
[27] J.-J. Rousseau, *The Social Contract and Discourses* [1762], ed. and trans. G. D. H. Cole (London: Dent, 1973), bk. i, ch. 4, 174.

in a regular form of collective self-determination that assures that decisions are not products of the arbitrary will of particular individuals or groups but reflect the general will. This response is often believed to work only for relatively homogeneous and simple communities, and is rejected as anachronistic today. This objection is certainly justified in the case of those communitarian and deliberative democracy theorists criticized earlier, who do assume that a common good or universal principle must underlie and provide the goal of self-government. By contrast, the neo-Roman and Renaissance republican tradition I am drawing on makes no such assumption. On the contrary, these thinkers regarded conflicting conceptions of the right and the good as the norm. Instead, they conceived the political process as a dialogue through which agreed positions are constructed rather than discovered.

The key to this view is the injunction 'to hear the other side' (*audi alteram partem*). As Quentin Skinner and James Tully have shown,[28] dialogue was valued within humanist culture precisely because moral and political concepts were regarded as capable of being applied and interpreted in a variety of ways, so that any case can be described and evaluated from numerous and differing perspectives. The purpose of dialogue was to weigh these different points of view and find an accommodation between them. The dialogue neither assumed nor aimed at consensus in the sense of finding a fact of the matter or set of general principles underlying or common to all their positions. Instead, the disputants exchanged interpretations in order to find connections, draw contrasts, and construct compromises that build on these comparisons. To 'hear the other side', therefore, disputants must drop purely self-referential or self-interested reasoning and look for considerations others can find compelling, thereby ruling out arguments that do not involve a degree of reciprocity and mutual respect. They must strive to accommodate the clashes of preferences and principles associated with pluralism by seeking integrative compromises that view the concerns raised by others as matters to be met rather than constraints to be overcome through minimal, tactical concessions. In line with the classic logical principle *omnis determinatio est negatio*, the upshot is a negotiated compromise built upon multiple affinities and analogies between the views in play. Gradually an evolving practice of coexistence develops, founded not in the application of common abstract principles but in the experience of collectively reasoning about and making numerous particular decisions.

This culture of dialogue can be likened to a scheme of procedural justice within which different substantive conceptions of justice are discussed.[29] For justice to be done it must be seen to be done. Thus, the openness of the dialogue is crucial, both in terms of the accessibility of the proceedings and their transparency. Citizen involvement guards against false negatives by trying to give all voices a hearing, and against false positives by allowing proposals to be contested. Dialogue also pools

---

[28] Q. Skinner, *Reason and Rhetoric in the Philosophy of Hobbes* (Cambridge: Cambridge University Press, 1996), 15–16; J. Tully, *Strange Multiplicity: Constitutionalism in an Age of Diversity* (Cambridge: Cambridge University Press, 1995), 115–16.

[29] S. Hampshire, *Justice is Conflict* (London: Duckworth, 1999).

perspectives, so that laws can be attuned to the complexity and multiplicity of individuals, situations, and social relations with which they will have to deal. Thus, rights get defined, refined, protected, and respected through various political processes, which allow them to be tailored to particular contexts through primary and secondary legislation and more specific rules and regulations.[30]

Debate about rights and debate through and about the polity's constitution are intimately related in this schema. For the struggle for rights is part and parcel of citizen struggles to avoid domination by securing political forms that provide adequate recognition of their evolving and diverse concerns and circumstances. It is commonly objected that these political processes and forms must themselves imply rights.[31] At one level that is undeniable. Clearly, any political practice institutionalizes a set of rights detailing who can participate, how, when and why. However, these do not reflect underlying general norms common to all legitimate democratic systems but are the products of citizens organizing themselves so as to be able to contest the ways the polity is structured. For example, workers' interests have been furthered more from their becoming unionized than as a result of the recognition of their rights per se. Indeed, the mobilization of workers has been crucial not only to those rights being recognized in the first place but also to how effectively they have been implemented. Moreover, because workers' rights have to vie with the property rights of capitalists and the interests of consumers, amongst other values, their defence and extension necessarily remains an ongoing political struggle. Nor are the norms governing the conduct of these struggles themselves constituted by prepolitical rights. Instead, practice leads citizens to develop various dispositions of civility, tolerance, and reciprocity which facilitate their ability to hear and learn from others and live with difference. These appear in some form within most accounts of disputation and public reasoning, though their modes vary between cultures. Both fuller and less rigid than any set of principles or rules could ever be, such qualities can no more be acquired from a book of rules than a sense of humour. They develop through practising citizenship and having to engage with others in conditions where the circumstances of politics apply. Moreover, they evolve and are enriched as the dimensions of politics get reinterpreted through new voices entering the dialogue and current ones changing.

Such a system resembles a democratic, common law *Rechtsstaat*. It contrasts with the two commonest versions of democratic politics associated with modern conceptions of constitutionalism—legal positivist notions that insist on the absolute authority of the author of the law, standardly the legislative assembly, and principled rights-based notions that seek to respond to the dangers of majoritarian and executive tyranny created by such views. Given the role that citizenship practice has undoubtedly played in the making of modern states, these theories have clearly

---

[30] Pettit, *Republicanism*, n. 2 above 'Postcript'.
[31] J. Cohen, 'Procedure and Substance in Deliberative Democracy', in S. Benhabib (ed.), *Democracy and Difference: Contesting the Boundaries of the Political* (Princeton, NJ: Princeton University Press, 1996), 95–119.

never accorded totally with reality. However, they do constrain the available possibilities. The next section argues that within both the EU and UK contexts, they will exacerbate rather than placate the legitimation problems of these different unions. To remedy these requires encouraging the modest developments of European and British citizenship practice that currently exist.

IV. Citizenship practice and rights in the reconstitution of Europe and Britain

Few would deny that within both the EU and the UK all four of the dimensions highlighted in Section II are currently matters of greater or lesser contestation So far as the EU is concerned, its sphere both in terms of territorial extent and range of competences remains at best uncertain and at worst a matter of deep dispute. Similar doubts and discussions surround the designation of its subjects, both actual and potential. Though European citizenship is currently restricted to nationals of member states, for example, certain entitlements of the Union are enjoyed by resident third-country nationals and other 'legal persons' as well. The scope of the EU is likewise much debated, with some seeing it solely in terms of removing trade barriers whilst others extend this logic to a whole range of common financial, fiscal, welfare, security, and other policies. Finally, discussion of the styles of EU politics ranges over such disparate issues as the introduction of qualified majority voting in the Council of Ministers and the establishment of European-wide political parties, to the direct election of the President of the Commission and the opening up of the comitology process to all through more freedom of information.

If we turn to the dramatic constitutional changes currently occurring in Britain, we see a similar pattern. Thus devolution and the extensive privatizations of the 1980s and 1990s have dramatically altered the sphere of the British state both territorially and with regard to its competences, though in each case the changes are ongoing and still disputed. Parallel, and often related, debates surround the issue of subjecthood. Should Scots be equal citizens to the English at Westminster, for example, or ought the granting of their own Parliament in Edinburgh result in a reduction of political rights in certain areas? To what extent are the clients of privatized services to be treated as mere consumers rather than citizens? How far is talk of Britishness appropriate in a multicultural as well as a multinational polity? Likewise, the scope of politics continues to be a central issue dividing the political parties. Notwithstanding its ideological shifts, New Labour still distinguishes itself from the Conservatives in allowing for a more interventionist state. The form and extent to which state regulation and control are either legitimate or practical within a globalizing market economy, in which many previously state-run utilities are now owned by foreign multinationals, have become increasingly pressing questions. Finally, the styles of politics are under discussion as never before with a commitment to consider changes to the electoral system, the possible extension of devolution to English regions and the introduction of elected mayors, the possible consequences of reform of the House of Lords and new provisions for freedom of information, and the desire to introduce a rights culture with the HRA.

As we saw, struggles and changes in any one of these dimensions produces often unintended consequences for the others. This is particularly the case in the way political debates within the Union and its member states invariably interact. Most domestic struggles have a European dimension and vice versa. For example, the whole devolutionary agenda has been greatly facilitated by the existence of the EU and has had knock-on effects, often of a problematic kind, for European regional policy. More generally, there is an increasing proliferation of multiple spheres of politics, from the domestic to the workplace, to the regional, state, and supra-state level, with individuals and groups possessing a somewhat different subjecthood in each and adopting a correspondingly different style and view of the scope of politics. As I remarked in the last section, the balancing and mutual interaction of these spheres is what fosters civic liberty and allows the recognition of evolving claims. Before sketching how they might be employed as part of a republican constitutional scheme in Europe and the UK, I wish to turn to their implications for constitutional rights.

These struggles have two aspects that render the rights-based project problematic. On the one hand, they are (as we saw in Section III) debates about the nature of rights. On the other hand, they are also debates about who has the right to decide the range and character of the rights we have. In other words, they are debates about the modalities whereby, and the domains within which, citizens exercise their 'right to have rights'. Both the European Charter and, in a more limited way, the HRA ignore these issues. Instead they threaten to constrain ongoing debates about both aspects, replacing an emerging pluralist polity with a unitary system.

Thus the Charter of Fundamental Rights of the European Union takes its cue from the Treaty of European Union as amended at Amsterdam (Article 6, formerly F) and is explicitly premised on the member states and 'peoples of Europe' sharing a 'spiritual and moral heritage' centred on certain 'common' and 'indivisible, universal values' and the supposedly unproblematic 'principles of democracy and the rule of law' (Charter, Preamble).[32] Though the diversity of their political and constitutional 'cultures', 'traditions', and 'identities' is acknowledged, this is alleged to pose no difficulty (Charter, Preamble). First, these are supposedly variations on a core set of fundamental principles (Charter, Preamble). Second, the Charter applies to the institutions and decisions of the Union, which allegedly complement and provide an additional layer to the domestic arrangements of the member states (Charter, Articles 51–3). To the extent that the EU and member state levels interact, the principle of subsidiarity will ensure the Charter's implementation and fine tuning will also be in large part a domestic matter.

---

[32] References are to the English version of the Draft of 28 Sept. 2000.

Both these assumptions are misplaced. With regard to the first, we saw in Section III how the possibilities for reasonable disagreement over rights extend even to the most basic provisions. Constitutional democracy has developed in quite different ways and under very different pressures within Western Europe, whilst in the East the differences are even more dramatic. Thus, the Italian constitution reflects the presence of Communist and Catholic traditions, the reaction against fascism and the experiences of the resistance which are largely foreign to Britain and which played out in quite different ways in the writing of the postwar German constitution. Likewise, the French constitution reflects a revolutionary republican tradition that accords a constituent power to the sovereign people which is absent or considerably weaker in other constitutions. Meanwhile, immigration and the resulting multiculturalism makes talk of a single European 'spiritual' and 'moral' heritage problematic. Thus, differences in their civic cultures and the extent and nature of immigration have produced important variations amongst the member states in the interpretation of rights to freedom of thought, conscience, and religion, discrimination and freedom of expression. With regard to the second assumption, we noted above how the EU interacts with—indeed, is in part a manifestation of—the changing political dimensions of the member states. The economic and associated legal and social regulations stemming from the EU are not discrete. They affect core functions of government policy and the State's very *raison d'être*.

Because of this complexity, the Charter is likely to prove far more problematic than its proponents assume. Although the ECJ has consistently asserted the supremacy and direct effect of European law, this has never been entirely accepted when it involves constitutional essentials peculiar to the member states. Indeed, as the decisions of the French Conseil d'État in *Nicolo*, the German Federal Constitutional Court in *Internationale Handelsgesellschaft* and *Brunner*, the Italian Constitutional Court in *Frontini* and *Granital*, and the House of Lords in *Factortame* all indicate, member state courts have consistently grounded the validity of Community law, including its claims to supremacy, in the domestic legal order.[33] When the two seem to collide, therefore, a constructive constitutional dialogue has got under way. Despite some posturing by both sides, mutual accommodations have always been found and outright conflicts sidestepped. Most importantly in this context, the ECJ has come to recognize a patchwork of rights

---

[33] *Nicolo*, [1990] 1 CMLR 173, Case 11/70, *Internationale Handelsgesellschaft* [1970] ECR 1125, 1134, [1974] 2 CMLR 540, *Brunner* [1994] 1 CMLR 57, *Frontini v. Ministero delle Finanze* [1974] 2 CMLR 372, *SpA Granital v. Amministrazione delle Finanze* [1984] 21 CMLR 756, *Factortame Ltd v. Secretary of State for Transport* [1990] 2 AC 85. These cases have been crucial to the evolving constitutional pretensions of the ECJ. They reveal how it has been forced by challenges from the constitutional courts of the member states to gradually assert the supremacy and direct effect of European law and its competence to decide such issues. However, these claims have not as yet been accepted in their entirety by any national constitutional court, although certain concessions have been made. Space prevents a full discussion of the details of these cases here, but for a useful outline see P. P. Craig and G. de Búrca, *EU Law: Text, Cases and Materials*, 2nd edn. (Oxford: Oxford University Press, 1998), pp. 264–94.

claims and has generally been sensitive to national peculiarities.[34] This is not to say that there are not difficulties. In *Cinéthèque*, for example, the ECJ tried to distinguish its role in ensuring the compatibility of community law and rights and the role of national courts in upholding rights within domestic legislation.[35] But as *ERT* revealed, that distinction becomes problematic when a domestic rights-based judgment becomes the basis of a derogation from fundamental Treaty rules.[36] Similar problems emerged in *Grogan*.[37]

These difficulties are evidence not of a lack of human rights protection within the EU, however, but of its strength. The Charter simply adds an unnecessary further tier which lacks the subtlety and flexibility of the current system of negotiation. Instead, it is a highly conservative document which gives a status quo approach. The articles on citizenship are particularly telling in this respect (Charter, Chapter V, Articles 39–46), since they now appear to raise to the status of Fundamental Rights what has been a limited policy reflecting the lowest common denominator of what can be achieved given existing institutions and member state sensibilities. For example, the key right on the present account is the right of citizens to define their rights and hold accountable those empowered to defend and serve them. In its place, however, we get the far from fundamental shadow of this essential entitlement—the right of every citizen of the Union 'to vote and stand as a candidate in elections to the European Parliament in the member state in which he resides, under the same conditions as nationals of that State' (Charter, Article 39.1)

Of course, this chapter has argued that such a flexible system of rights negotiation ought to be carried out by political rather than juridical bodies. The European Parliament (EP) might be thought the appropriate place for this. Yet its legitimacy as a proto-European legislature is weak. Indeed, its attempt to gain that legitimacy through promoting the Charter and enshrining its place within it is a testimony to that weakness. It is now commonplace to acknowledge that no European demos exists.[38] Support for the EU is largely mediated through its being beneficial for national, regional, and other interests rather than because of a straightforward allegiance to the European idea.[39] Similarly, the EP is thought by most people to represent national views rather than pan-European interests per se.[40] Put another

[34] e.g. Case 4/73, *Nold v. Commission* [1974] ECR 419, Case 36/75, *Rutili v. Minister for the Interior* [1975] ECR 1219.

[35] Cases 60-1/84, *Cinéthèque v. Fédérations nationales des cinémas français* [1985] ECR 2605.

[36] Case C-260/89, *ERT v. Dimotiki Etairia Piliroforissis* [1991] ECR I-2925.

[37] Case C-159/90, *SPUC (Ireland) Ltd v. Grogan* [1991] ECR I-4685. For a fuller discussion of these points, see Bellamy, *Liberalism and Pluralism*, n. 2 above, 205–6.

[38] D. Chryssochoou, 'Europe's Could-Be Demos: Recasting the Debate', (1996) 19 *West European Politics* 787–801, and J. H. H. Weiler, 'European Neo-Constitutionalism: In Search of Foundations for the European Constitutional Order', in Bellamy and Castiglione, *Constitutionalism in Transformation*, n. 3 above, 110–13.

[39] When asked in a recent poll how they describe themselves: by nationality only, nationality and European, European and nationality, or European, respondents divided 45%, 40%, 6%, and 5% respectively (Eurobarometer Report 48, Mar. 1998). Thus there is little evidence of a European demos or a shared political culture.

[40] Its noteworthy that in a 1989 Eurobarometer poll, 59% preferred the idea that the EP be organized around national criteria rather than the current political ones.

way, a European demos only exists through its links with various other demoi. This relationship has been conceived in the following ways: as an additional and complementary civic identity; as an overarching civic identity within which others—the national and the regional, for example—are nested; or as interacting and occasionally conflicting with other civic identities.[41] Though national governments favour the first and Eurocrats the second, it is the last that best captures the actual situation. For though the EU does add to and reinforce many aspects of national and sub-national governance, the various cases referred to earlier indicate that it also rivals, conflicts with, and potentially shapes these too. Yet it is the first and especially the second position that would be necessary for any common Charter or unitary legislative body to have legitimacy. As Weiler has pertinently remarked, in the absence of a unified European demos, asking the European peoples to accept legislation by majoritarian voting in the European Parliament would be like expecting the Danes to acknowledge the legitimate authority of a German Bundestag to which they had been granted voting rights.[42]

A parallel problematic arises for the introduction of the HRA within Britain's increasingly devolved political order. As in Europe more generally, there was a growing sense that the United Kingdom contained multiple yet interacting demoi. One of the main arguments in favour of devolution was that the constituent nations of the UK had different political cultures and not simply different interests. In Scotland, for example, it was argued that there was far greater support than in England for a broader scope for politics within an extensive public sector. There were also distinct legal, educational, and religious traditions and institutions. Yet, as Chris Himsworth details in his chapter, the HRA risks undercutting some of that diversity by allowing potential interferences in areas of Scots private law and administration, for example, previously untouched by UK or English decision-making. Moreover, Acts of the Scottish Parliament are treated in effect as secondary legislation and so as open to challenges in a court at any level, rather than, as is the case with the UK Parliament, being liable solely to a declaration of incompatibility by a superior court. As a result, the Scottish Parliament will not have the luxury afforded to Westminster of either avoiding innumerable threats of court action disrupting the legislative process and executive action or being able to make a considered case to have tailored rights to the pecularities of Scottish circumstances in ways consented to by the Scottish people.

It is hard to avoid the conclusion that the HRA will serve as a mechanism for constraining devolution and reducing the competences of the Scottish Parliament and executive within an increasingly centralized system. Not that this attempt will succeed. For the HRA simply adds yet another level of judicially protected rights that is in potential conflict with the European Convention and the Charter. It would not be impossible to imagine a situation in which a policy touching a possible area of EU

---

[41] J. H. H. Weiler, *The Constitution of Europe: 'Do the New Clothes Have an Emperor?' and Other Essays on European Integration* (Cambridge: Cambridge University Press, 1999), 344–8.

[42] Weiler, 'European Neo-Constitutionalism', n. 38 above, 111.

competence elicits different views of its consequences for fundamental rights from the British legislature, a domestic court, the ECHR, and the ECJ. Yet there are neither judicial nor, more importantly, political mechanisms for discussing these differences.

Far from enhancing citizenship and democracy, therefore, the European Charter and the HRA represent a juridical and justice-based form of constitutionalism that conflicts at numerous points with a political and freedom-based form of constitutionalism centred on the constitutive activity of citizens. Moreover, they do so at the very moment that the EU and the UK have begun to establish the political framework needed for such a republican framework to flourish. Indeed, they can be seen as counters to such a development.

The existing structures of the EU, for example, reflect to a remarkable degree a situation in which there are multiple European demoi, with progress in integration requiring dialogue between them and the various ways in which they debate the changing dimensions of the proto-European polity. Thus, there are multiple channels of political representation for different sorts of political subjects: member states in the Inter-governmental Conferences and Council of Ministers, national political parties in the EP, selected functional interests in the Economic and Social Committee (ESC), and sub-national territorial units in the Committee of the Regions. In addition there are an increasing number of national and transnational interests, professional and campaigning associations, and firms located in Brussels, many of which play a part in the formal decision-making process through the obscure process of comitology. Though states retain a primary role in high politics and control the integration process through the Treaties, they are increasingly subjected to both informal and formalized input from a wide range of other actors. At the Amsterdam IGC, for example, some fifty 'public interest' organizations came together at the initiative of the International European Movement to form a Civil Society Forum running parallel to the official conference.[43] Hundreds of NGOs also submitted written observations as well as participating in the European Parliament's public hearings with 'civil society' both prior to and following the IGC. Meanwhile, the EU's institutions have begun to develop a degree of autonomy which has encouraged a variety of sub- and trans-state organizations to deal with them directly. As a result, decision-making has become diffused across several tiers of government with ill-defined and shifting spheres of competence.[44] In the area of social policy, for example, Articles 136–9 TEU have produced a major diffusion of democratic decision-making away from centralized public bodies to private actors operating *in situ*.[45] These charge the Commission not merely to consult

---

[43] D. Curtin, *Postnational Democracy: The European Union in Search of a Political Philosophy* (The Hague: Kluwer Law International, 1997), 56–9.

[44] G. Marks, L. Hooghe and K. Blank, 'European Integration from the 1980s: State-Centric v. Multi-level Governance', (1996) 34 *Journal of Common Market Studies* 341–78.

[45] See the judgment of the Court of First Instance in Case T-135/96, *UEAPME v. Council* [1998] ECR II-2335.

but also to promote 'social dialogue' between workers and employers so as to produce agreements on issues such as parental leave that can be transformed into EU
legislation.

This diffusion of power provides the basis for the sort of political dialogue republicans advocate and that seems all too necessary in a system trying to balance
regional, sectoral, state, transnational, and supranational concerns. Both Neil
MacCormick and Paul Craig, for example, have argued that just such a republican
rationale informs the sharing of legislative authority between the EP, Council, and
Commission.[46] Thus, Craig argues that though the extension of co-decision
procedure rightly reflects the EP's standing as the only directly elected European
body, it is nonetheless appropriate that the power of legislative initiative rests with
the Commission.[47] On the one hand, this arrangement recognizes the need to
accord due weight to the Council given that the democratic legitimacy of the
Community remains largely state-based and grounded in an international agreement. On the other hand, it also acknowledges the legitimacy of the Commission's
powers as guardian of the Treaties and the most likely body, given the
Community's current stage of development, to direct policy towards fostering the
collective goods embodied by the Treaties rather than sectional interests.

Of course, as Craig emphasizes, there is no denying the shortcomings of these
arrangements from a republican perspective either. For example, Philippe
Schmitter has made proposals on representation within both the EP and the
Council which would create a consociational system that would guarantee and
improve on the current balance in decision-making power between large, medium,
and small states.[48] He and Weiler also both suggest grafting a referendum on key
legislative proposals onto elections for the EP in order to generate a Europe-wide
public sphere, to counteract the current tendency for voting to reflect national
rather than European issues.[49] More important, the role of national parliaments and
regional assemblies remains inadequately addressed, as do the concerns of a whole
series of non-business interests—from the unemployed, through ordinary consumers to the proliferating public interest movements, including transnational
coalitions of these group. Here too, however, proposals for improvement are legion.
These range from the frequently mooted suggestion that the EP be recruited from
selected members of national legislatures to demands for the right to form Europe-
wide organizations at the EU level rather than those organizations being subject to

[46] N. MacCormick, 'Democracy, Subsidiarity, and Citizenship in the "European Commonwealth"',
(1997) 16 *Law and Philosophy* 331–56, and P. P. Craig, 'Democracy and Rule-Making within the EC: An
Empirical and Normative Assessment', (1997) 3 *European Law Journal* 105–30. See too R. Bellamy and
D. Castiglione, 'Democracy, Sovereignty and the Constitution of the European Union: The Republican
Alternative to Liberalism', in Z. Bankowski and A. Scott (eds.), *The European Union and its Order: The
Legal Theory of European Integration* (Oxford: Blackwell, 2000), 169–90.

[47] Craig, 'Democracy and Rule-making within the EC', ibid. 116–19.

[48] P. C. Schmitter, *How to Democratize the European Union . . . And Why Bother?* (Maryland: Rowman
and Littlefield, 2000), ch. 4

[49] Ibid. 36–7 and Weiler, *The Constitution of Europe*, n. 41 above, 350–1.

the legal and tax regime of a particular member state; the provision of more formal rights of consultation by such measures as broadening the ESC into an 'associative parliament'; granting citizens opportunity structures for a direct input in the legislative process via a right to initiate referenda, and the passing of an American-style Administrative Procedure Act to ensure the participation of all interested parties in the framing of regulations; and finally, increasing transparency and freedom of information, often through the use of new information technology.[50]

In many respects, these measures can be assimilated to the earlier analysis of the constitutive character of citizenship. The actions of public and other interest groups reflect the emergence of a new trans-European subject of politics. This development, however, is not occurring within a settled political framework. For in the process it is bringing about the creation of new styles and spheres of politics whilst expanding its scope. The demand for new rights of association, participation, and access is part and parcel of the creation of new types of governance that supplement, cut across, and occasionally subvert and supplant current systems of representative democracy in order to create a European public sphere. Yet these innovations should not be read in a teleological manner as heralding an 'ever closer Union of European peoples' or a deepening consensus on liberal democratic values. For the key to this new form of politics is dialogue and negotiation between a widening range of actors and agencies. The aim is not to achieve some pre-established goal but to set up a process within which different voices can be heard and their concerns taken into account. The central dynamic is the further dispersal of power to preserve freedom from domination and promote reciprocity and compromise.

In some respects, the most interesting aspect of the Charter is the process whereby it came into being, involving as it did a wide consultative process with a broad range of actors. However, the final decisions rested with the delegates of the member states who were under pressure to produce at the very least a definitive declaratory Charter. Would it not have been infinitely better had this process been an ongoing discussion between actors of equal standing focused on making particular decisions—in other words, had the convention been a legislative body engaged in the never-ending business of determining the rights implications of the multiple rules and regulations determining our lives? If such a body can draw up a Charter, surely it is best equipped to interpret, update, and implement it. It would certainly have been a less rhetorical and anodyne document had this been the case.

We can be briefer in discussing the UK. Devolution is much more recent and as yet incomplete, whilst the HRA has been only just implemented. Here too, however, the potential exists for the creation of a mixed commonwealth via the dispersal of

---

[50] See D. Curtin, 'The European Union, Civil Society and Participatory Democracy', in *Collected Courses of the Academy of European Law* (Florence: EUI, 1996), pt. 5, for a summary. Craig, 'Democracy and Rule-Making within the EC', n. 46 above, 119–24, draws out their republican potential. For parallel arguments in the US context see M. Seidenfeld, 'A Civic Republican Justification for the Bureaucratic State', (1992) 105 *Harvard Law Review* 1511–76.

power and the development of a pluralist polity.[51] The chief deficiencies of the current arrangements arise from the attempt to treat the jurisdictions of the devolved assemblies as discrete rather than as interacting both with each other and, most importantly, with Westminster. As a consequence, the devolved institutions neither operate negatively as mutual checks nor positively as a means for promoting a balanced dialogue. Reform of the House of Lords must be regarded as a disgracefully wasted opportunity. Once again, the potential exists to have a second chamber that adds a different perspective—for example, through being elected by a different system to the House of Common or by including representatives from different bodies—such as the regional assemblies, and so on. Instead, the current proposal is to have it mirror as closely as possible the views of the executive and Commons. In these circumstances, the attractions of the HRA are certainly greater than they would be under a genuinely republican scheme. Yet the declared purpose of repatriating rights, of having a system in which they were made relevant to the views of the British people, has been lost in the process. As Colin Harvey shows in his chapter below on Northern Ireland, when dialogues about rights are allowed they can have a transformative effect in how conflicting parties view each other. Moreover, they allow the participants to see the rights as theirs, as a collective decision that reflects the political constitution of the society concerned. By excluding citizens from such processes, by trimming principle from politics so it becomes a purely aggregative mechanism for promoting dominant interests, rights-based constitutionalism creates the very dangers it purports to avoid.

V. Conclusion

Citizenship is frequently identified with mere membership of a given system and possession of the entitlements that follow. However, the most important entitlement is the leverage such membership gives for changing its terms and conditions. Though citizenship activity is conditioned and often facilitated by prevailing structures and the norms they embody, it also challenges and seeks to modify them. For the demands of existing and aspirant citizens alike involve implicit and often explicit reinterpretations of the general shape of the polity. However, there is no necessary telos towards an ever-expanding and fuller system of rights that is to be regarded as somehow more just or better than what went before. Rather, citizenship practice is a continuously reflexive process, with citizens reinterpreting the basis of their collective life in new ways that correspond to their evolving needs and ideals. The role of constitutionalism lies in promoting the civic freedom for such activity to unfold in ways that avoid dominating others. As we have seen, this is best achieved through the dispersal of power and the promotion of dialogue over common rules and arrangements.

[51] I discuss this issue more fully in Bellamy, *Liberalism and Pluralism*, n. 2 above, ch. 7.

The EU and UK offer especially fertile ground for such an approach. Their boundaries, competences, membership, and character are all in the process of negotiation. What remains as yet undeveloped are precisely those structures necessary to ensure that the resulting accords promote rather than diminish the freedom of citizens. Endowing citizens with rights will not remedy this situation if these reflect highly contestable visions of Europe and Britain which those citizens might wish to debate and dispute. An active citizenship requires citizens having a say in the constitutional dialogue so that they can shape these unions for themselves. As we have seen, the potential exists for this to happen. However, in each case the result of opening up to citizens will be the start rather than the end of the constitutionalizing process. The results are likely to be arrangements that are increasingly flexible and diverse, but which enjoy both greater legitimacy and efficiency through being closer to the people whose lives they govern.

3

Rights, Democracy, and Law

MARTIN LOUGHLIN

This essay has three main objectives. The first is to outline the main issues of debate which surround the question of whether or not it is desirable to seek to protect fundamental rights in constitutional documents. For the purpose of clarifying these issues, I shall focus especially on those liberal philosophies of government which have been influential in shaping the discussion. The second objective will be to assess the potential juristic significance of this exercise, an exercise in what might be called the positivization of natural rights. Here, my argument will be that these theories of government can help not only to clarify matters of political debate but also to understand the character of the consequential shifts which are likely to be effected in legal discourse. These theories therefore enable us both to identify the language through which government seeks to justify its activities and to expose the political underpinnings of those adaptations to the style of legal reasoning and judgment which are likely to follow. Finally, and most importantly, I will try to assess whether the institutional protection of designated rights will set us on the road towards finding more effective, enlightened, and responsive modes of governing. This aspect of the essay is the most tentative: the issue it raises is not a matter of philosophy but is a complex political question which can only be addressed in specific institutional contexts and in the light of local conditions. And in the British context, where human rights legislation has recently been introduced, I shall suggest that there are reasons for doubting that the course we have taken should be seen as a progressive development.

I. The antagonism between democracy and rights

What legitimates the legal order of modern society? This question assumes a particular importance within liberal political philosophy. After the dissolution of hierocratic notions of authority, two main schools of liberal thought emerged. One school has sought to resolve the question of legitimacy in democracy; the other answers it by appealing to individual rights. The legal order is justified either as an expression of the will of the people, and therefore as an articulation of the principle of self-government, or because it ensures an equal protection of the fundamental rights of citizens. The two schools of thought reflect different, and potentially opposing, philosophies of government

The democratic justification for the legal order is underpinned by the principle of popular sovereignty. A body of free and equal citizens comes together, generally through a representative assembly, to enact rules to promote the general welfare. The business of government must be conducted within the framework of these rules (hence the idea of government under law) and officers of government are accountable to the people through their representatives and as a consequence of periodic popular elections. This democratic form of accountability of governors to citizens ensures that the laws reflect the will of the people. The legal order—a structure of rules which impose constraints and restrictions on what otherwise would be an individual's unbounded freedom of action—is thus justified on the ground that, to all intents and purposes, it is a set of laws which the people have given themselves.

The rights justification similarly starts from the notion of free and equal citizens coming together to establish a system of government. But the argument here is that citizens, being the bearers of natural rights, yield to the collectivity only that portion of those rights which are required to ensure the realization of the proper ends of government. The powers of government are delegated through the consent of citizens to a representative institution. But these powers are not only limited in range, they are also geared to the achievement of certain public objectives. The 'end of law', in Locke's words, 'is not to abolish or restrain but to preserve and enlarge freedom.'[1] The legal order exists mainly to establish and enforce this compact between citizen and government.

In contrast with the approach implied by the democratic model, government under the rights model is not simply the product of *will*, that is, of securing consensus through democratic processes of will-formation. It is essentially a matter of *reason*, of rationally determining the ends of government and then devising the appropriate means for ensuring their effective realization. Although the democratic model recognizes that rules are devised through a deliberative process which acknowledges the essential equality of individuals, restraint on collective action is treated as something to be determined politically, and thus involves *trust*. Under the rights model, constraints over legislative action are formal; they are, in other words, matters of *law*. The concern under the democratic model that majorities in the representative assembly might exploit their power to pass laws which oppress minorities is addressed through custom and convention, hence 'the price of liberty is eternal vigilance'. Under the rights model, this anxiety is dealt with by the imposition of formal, legally binding limitations on the power of legislative bodies. Being contrary to the basic compact between citizen and the state, law which infringes the rights of the citizen is unconstitutional and the judiciary will commonly be authorized to declare such legislation void.

Even in this brief sketch it should be evident that one significant difference between these two philosophies of government concerns the role of law in regulating

---

[1] J. Locke, *Two Treatises of Government*, ii, s. 57.

the conduct of government. The nature of this difference is thrown into relief once we focus on the question of the role of the judiciary and, more specifically, of the constitutional function of judicial review. This task, which operates to protect the basic rights of citizens, is often criticized for being anti-democratic. If the legislature determines that a particular law is conducive to the public good, can it ever be legitimate for an appointed group of judges to strike down that expression of the general will? The modern practice of judicial review, it appears, exposes in an acute form the tension between rights and democracy.

II. The reconciliation of rights and democracy

Although the idea of law as an expression of the democratic will seems to clash with the notion that it exists to guarantee individual rights, it could be argued that this conflict is false, or at least exaggerated. Legislation interfering with the most basic rights of individuals, for example, would seem to deny the principle of equal respect, and this must also rank as a principle underpinning democracy. If, to give an extreme illustration, legislation were passed prohibiting all Muslims from voting, it would surely be argued that such a measure not only infringes a citizen's basic rights but is also profoundly anti-democratic. It might be contended that we are in fact unable properly to understand democracy without having reference to some notion of rights. The idea of democracy cannot adequately be explained without devising rules concerning political participation, and these must inevitably be expressed in the language of rights. This has been a particularly important theme in republican political thought.

Republicanism addresses this tension between rights and democracy by drawing a distinction—which I too propose to adopt—between classical liberalism and civic republicanism. Liberalism is primarily concerned with ensuring that individuals are able to pursue their own interests free from state interference, and it achieves this mainly by drawing a division between the private and public spheres. But the best way of protecting this division varies according to the two schools of government outlined in Section I. One trajectory, that established by Hobbes and (in respect of its democratic credentials) developed by Rousseau, Bentham and J. S. Mill, is to give equal voting rights to citizens, thereby ensuring that government responds to the people's wishes. The other, taken by Kant and Rawls (following Locke's cue), is to protect the individual's fundamental rights, thereby ensuring that government does not exceed the limits of its authority. Following the democratic and rights models respectively, these trajectories come to different answers over the question of which form a constitution ought to take. But both schools suggest that constitutions exist to impose restraints on what government can do and to ensure that governments do not abuse their powers.

It is on this issue of the function of constitutions that republicanism diverges from classical liberalism. Republican thought emphasizes the role which constitutions perform not only in controlling the exercise of public power—the negative function—but also—the positive function—of ensuring that that power is guided towards socially desirable ends. Freedom and democracy are not simple ideas. Being unfree, republicans argue, does not consist in being subject to restraint, but only in being subject to the arbitrary will of another.[2] Thus, although laws that are the product of democratic self-rule impose restraints over the actions of individuals, they do not impose limits on freedom. From this republican perspective, the critical issue becomes one of identifying the conditions required to achieve democratic self-rule. On this point republicans argue that democracy is not essentially concerned with the aggregation of individual preferences through the mechanism of voting.[3] Instead, it is designed to achieve the potential transformation of preferences through the formation of an active public realm which enhances opportunities for discussion and deliberation.[4] Democracy is the expression not just of the will of a majority, but of a will that has been formed after wide-ranging and free discussion.

This divergence of view also permeates the characterization of rights. In classical liberal thought, rights exist to guarantee private autonomy and to protect individual freedom from the potential tyranny of majorities. Within republicanism, rights operate to ensure the realization of the conditions for an authentic deliberative democracy.[5] In this latter conception, rights underpin the institutional structure of constitutional democracy. Basic rights, such as freedom of speech or expression, do not simply provide a zone of protection to the individual but become constitutive of democratic will-formation. Rights provide the basic building blocks of the political structure and give expression to the idea of democracy. Properly understood, rights and democracy do not exist in a relationship of conflict. Rights and democracy are twin sides of the same coin.

III. The foundation of rights claims

Republicanism offers an account of government which reconciles the claims of rights and democracy. It does so, however, by appearing to privilege political rights over civil rights, a leaning which seems to distort the liberal ideal. At its core, liberalism is concerned to vindicate the rights of the individual to life, liberty, and the pursuit of happiness. Rights which guarantee participation in collective decision-making amount only to a small (though not unimportant) part of this concern; liberal rights

---

[2] See P. Pettit, *Republicanism: A Theory of Freedom and Government* (Oxford: Oxford University Press, 1997).

[3] Cf. J.-J. Rousseau, *The Social Contract*, bk. ii, ch. 3.

[4] See J. Elster (ed.), *Deliberative Democracy* (Cambridge: Cambridge University Press, 1998); J. S. Dryzek, *Deliberative Democracy and Beyond: Liberals, Critics and Contestations* (Oxford: Oxford University Press, 2000).

[5] In relation to the complexity of determining authentic preferences, however, see T. Kuran, *Private Truths, Public Lies: The Social Consequences of Preference Formation* (Cambridge, Mass.: Harvard University Press, 1995).

are mainly directed towards the imposition of restrictions on the scope of government and the protection of a zone of individual autonomy.[6] Before proceeding further, then, we should consider the foundation of these claims to individual rights.

In modern times, rights claims have been vindicated mainly by an appeal to the doctrine of natural rights.[7] These natural rights doctrines are most straightforwardly legitimated by appeal to the authority of a divine creator.[8] In a secular age, however, this is unlikely to provide a reliable method of demonstrating their truth. Modern natural rights theorists have therefore engaged in a search for the authority of these rights in some ethical scheme that can be shown to be ingrained in the structure of reason. But this quest, one which stretches from Kant to Rawls, has never been able to produce a compelling account of rights which comes anywhere near satisfying the canons of objectivity. For some, this is beside the point, since natural rights must be taken to rest on their self-evident goodness and respect for them to be essential to the promotion of the 'common good'.[9] Nevertheless, whatever philosophical position one might adopt, it seems clear that, when seeking to make sense of a form of political order, we are left with the contention that such rights are fundamental essentially because they command general support under conditions of (in Rawls's words) 'reasonable pluralism of comprehensive ethical, religious and philosophical views'.[10] The authority accorded basic rights rests on political consensus.

If this is true, rights claims ultimately collapse into some form of a democracy claim: rights must be respected by legislatures because this is what citizens demand.[11] But if rights are rooted in consensus, how can entrenched rights that restrict the power of democratic majorities be defended? If 'we, the people' establish a framework of government, surely the people must similarly be empowered to amend that framework? If they are not, don't appeals to fundamental laws and entrenched rights simply amount to a form of ancestor worship? The work undertaken by the English judiciary in protecting 'sacred' common law rights against statutory incursion has often been accused of amounting to the perpetuation of aristocratic rule in a democratic era, a mechanism for ensuring government of the living

---

[6] See C. Larmore, *Morals of Modernity* (Cambridge: Cambridge University Press, 1996), 182: 'The liberal freedoms set limits to democratic government, and in particular to the form it usually takes, majority rule. Nor is this ranking a mere makeshift. On the contrary, democracy is made subordinate to liberal principles precisely because the value of democratic institutions is held to lie chiefly, if not exclusively, in their being the best *means for guaranteeing* liberal freedoms' (emphasis, original).

[7] See R. Tuck, *Natural Rights Theories: Their Origin and Development* (Cambridge: Cambridge University Press, 1979).

[8] The clearest illustration is provided by the American Declaration of Independence, when Thomas Jefferson maintained: 'We hold these truths to be self-evident . . . that all men are created equal; that they are endowed by their Creator with certain inalienable rights . . .'. See C. Becker, *The Declaration of Independence: A Study in the History of Ideas* (New York: Harcourt, Brace, 1922).

[9] See J. Finnis, *Natural Law and Natural Rights* (Oxford: Clarendon Press, 1980).

[10] J. Rawls, *Political Liberalism* (New York: Columbia University Press, 1996).

[11] See F. I. Michelman, 'Human Rights and the Limits of Constitutional Theory', (2000) 13 Ratio Juris 63.

by the dead.[12] This was also the refrain of Thomas Paine in *Rights of Man*, in which he maintained that, since the only legitimacy acquired by governments came from the consent of the people who elected them, all attempts at entrenchment are fraudulent.[13]

Alongside the republican argument that rights exist to give expression to democracy, the main defence for entrenched rights has fallen under the principle of pre-commitment. We the people, so the argument goes, need to be protected against our own base instincts. Once we have deliberated and reached a reasoned agreement on the nature of the compact between citizen and government, this compact requires protection against the actions of transient majorities who might respond unreflectively to felt necessities or otherwise act solely in accordance with their passions. This amounts to a form of self-binding, like that deployed by Ulysses when he enjoined his crew to ignore his cries for release after being bound to the ship's mast to hear the voice of the Sirens.[14] Many of us use similar devices when we are at our most determined or reflective, and we use them precisely for the purpose of ensuring that at weak moments we do not succumb to our foibles. Such stratagems should not be treated simply as the imposition of restrictions on freedom of action; properly understood, they enable us to take control and assert our autonomy. In short, they reflect the principle of self-government.[15]

Although pre-commitment strategies are often invoked as an explanation of republican notions of self-government, they can also be deployed to justify the protection of a sphere of individual autonomy.[16] This type of argument, though not without its critics,[17] provides some rationale for the action of the Labour government in promoting the Human Rights Act 1998. By authorizing the judiciary to give direct effect to rights enshrined in the European Convention on Human Rights, Parliament made it difficult to claim that this measure, which vests important political decisions on the scope and meaning of these rights to an unelected judiciary, is anti-democratic. And this is especially so given the judiciary's limited power with respect to primary legislation.[18]

---

[12] See e.g. Lord Devlin, 'The Judge as Lawmaker', (1976) 39 *Modern Law Review* 1, 14 (suggesting that when judges moved beyond literal statutory interpretation and 'looked for the philosophy behind the Act' they invariably found 'a Victorian Bill of Rights, favouring (subject to the observance of the accepted standards of morality) the liberty of the individual, the freedom of contract, and the sacredness of property, and which was highly suspicious of taxation').

[13] *Rights of Man, Common Sense and other Political Writings* [1791–2], ed. M. Philp (Oxford: Oxford University Press, 1995), ll 91–2.

[14] See J. Elster, *Ulysses and the Sirens: Studies in Rationality and Irrationality* (Cambridge: Cambridge University Press, 1984). Cf. Elster, *Ulysses Unbound* (Cambridge: Cambridge University Press, 2000), ch. 2.

[15] See S. Holmes, *Passions and Constraint: On the Theory of Liberal Democracy* (Chicago: University of Chicago Press, 1995), ch. 5.

[16] After all, if protections are built in to the deliberative processes of will-formation, there would appear to be less need for the safeguards which entrenched rights provide.

[17] See J. Waldron, 'Precommitment and Disagreement', in L. Alexander (ed.), *Constitutionalism: Philosophical Foundations* (Cambridge: Cambridge University Press, 1998), ch. 7.

[18] Human Rights Act 1998, ss. 3–5.

IV. The foundations of democracy claims

Whether the claim is that rights are constitutive of democratic will-formation or that rights protection is required as part of a bootstrapping operation to protect self-government from the destructive tendencies of the passions, it looks as if rights claims are ultimately justified by some conception of democracy. But critics maintain that, especially at the sharp end of the process where judges are obliged to rule on conflicts between statutes and rights, these types of arguments are unconvincing. They contend that when judges determine these matters, they exercise real policy choice. And whatever justifications are given for 'this arrogation of judicial authority, this disabling of representative institutions', the jurisdiction should not be asserted in the name of democracy.[19] '[T]he fact that there is popular support . . . for an alteration on constitutional procedure', Waldron argues, 'does not show that such alteration therefore makes things more democratic. . . . If people wanted to experiment with dictatorship, principles of democracy might give us a reason to allow them to do so. But it would not follow that dictatorship is democratic.'[20]

At this point, the legitimacy of judicial review appears to hinge on differences in position over what the practice of democracy entails. Three main views about democracy emerge from the discussion. The first, derived from classical liberalism, is that democracy concerns the aggregation of citizen preferences. Democracy involves the participation of the people in institutional processes of political decision-making. According to this view, which might be called the *liberal democratic* position, judicial enforcement of entrenched rights is anti-democratic. Liberal democrats argue that instead of addressing the issue through such abstractions as 'the counter-majoritarian difficulty', we should focus on the practical questions of politics. Should such contentious issues as censorship, discrimination and life and death matters be determined by a majority of judges or by ordinary men and women deciding by a majority? For liberal democrats, as epitomized by Waldron, the proposal to vest responsibility for these decisions in judges 'does not comport with the respect and honour normally accorded to ordinary men and women in the context of a [political] theory of rights'.[21] The only justified restrictions on democratic will-formation are those needed to ensure its maintenance.[22]

The second view, one which accentuates the rights dimension of classical liberalism, has a more jaundiced attitude towards the operation of democratic processes. It is concerned with the possibility of majorities using their political power to oppress minorities. Far from treating democracy as an enabling activity, this conception, which may be called the *bourgeois liberal* position, considers that it is merely

---

[19] J. Waldron, 'A Rights-Based Critique of Constitutional Rights', (1993) 13 *Oxford Journal of Legal Studies* 18, 42.

[20] Ibid. 46.   [21] Ibid. 51.

[22] Cf. the debate on the continuing nature of parliamentary sovereignty: see J. Goldsworthy, *The Sovereignty of Parliament: History and Philosophy* (Oxford: Clarendon Press, 1999), ch. 10.

the least worst option.[23] One means of circumscribing the power of the majority is to create a zone of private autonomy which prevents democratic decision-making authority from invading an individual's fundamental liberties.

These liberal positions can be contrasted with a third conception of democracy, that of civic republicanism. Republicanism maintains that the function of politics is not simply to cumulate and coordinate individual preferences. Republicans argue that the classical liberal view provides us with a kind of economic theory of democracy in which the citizen is treated as consumer. This, they argue, yields an impoverished image of the political process. Republicans replace the market with the forum: democratic processes are designed not merely to record aggregate preferences but to formulate and even transform preferences through debate and deliberation.[24] By highlighting the function of rights in giving institutional expression to this deliberative conception of democracy, republicans stress the importance of the rights to political participation. They thereby bring rights and democracy into harmony. These distinctions are formulated in Table 3.1.

There are, however, also differences within the tradition of republican thought. We can differentiate between the claims of those who prioritize civic virtue, thereby highlighting the importance of the collective processes of democracy, and those who, though recognizing the importance of public duty, contend that that value is compatible with the right to individual autonomy. By drawing this distinction, four rather than three views are to be distinguished. We can first identify a *communitarian* position, one that strongly links democracy with an attachment to the traditions and practices of a distinctive community. This notion of community should not be viewed instrumentally, that is, as a collectivity which exists simply to determine the laws under which all must live (the liberal democratic model). Rather, the community is felt to be constitutive of identity and to provide a powerful source of moral valuation. Communitarians do not dismiss the value of rights. But they do argue against their primacy, contending that 'it would be incoherent to try to assert the rights, while denying the obligation [to belong]'[25] and the duties which follow.

Table 3.1. Liberal and republican notions of democracy and rights

	Classical liberalism	Civic republicanism
Democracy	Will-formation through the aggregation of preferences	Will-formation through deliberation
Rights	Protection of private autonomy	Promotion of political participation

---

[23] For a classic statement of this position see A. de Tocqueville, *Democracy in America*, i, ch. 14.

[24] See J. Elster, 'The Market and the Forum: Three Varieties of Political Theory', in Elster and A. Hylland (eds.), *Foundations of Social Choice Theory* (Cambridge: Cambridge University Press, 1986), 33.

[25] C. Taylor, 'Atomism', in *Philosophy and the Human Sciences: Philosophical Papers*, ii (Cambridge: Cambridge University Press, 1985), 187, 198.

Consequently, communitarians seek to reinterpret the meaning of liberal rights movements; Sandel, for instance, suggests that the American civil rights movement of the 1960s is better understood as according 'the full membership of fellow citizens wrongly excluded from the common life of the nation'.[26] In general, communitarians express grave concerns about the rights regime of liberalism, a system which they contend is 'unbalanced', 'adversarial', 'entrenches fragmentation', and 'makes it harder and harder [for their members] to identify with their political society as a community'.[27]

Others, however, have felt that this contrast between liberals and republicans over the issues of civil rights and civic virtue has been presented in an overly polarized fashion. They argue that the emphasis placed on private autonomy vis-à-vis public responsibility, while inconsistent, is not incompatible and thus can be accommodated. Consequently, a fourth strand of thought on the issue of democracy and rights emerges, one which I will label *liberal republicanism*. Liberal republicanism seeks to reconcile the values of private autonomy, civic virtue, deliberative democracy, and fundamental rights.[28] It argues that, properly understood, rights, including a right to autonomy founded on moral equality, are not only compatible with, but also capable of strengthening social bonds.[29] This type of liberal republicanism thus claims to be able to overcome the objection that liberal rights corrode the sense of belonging that is essential for the maintenance of social order.

Once these republican claims are differentiated, we can identify the polarities of the philosophical debate about rights and democracy. There are two main axes. The first concerns the question of whether values of democracy and rights are in tension and, if so, which takes priority. The second, which so far has only been alluded to but which generally divides liberals and republicans, concerns the question of whether individualism or collectivism provides a more accurate vision of the constitution of social order. From this perspective, the four positions, sketched in Fig. 3.1, can be seen as polarities within the debate. By highlighting the differences in this simplified and stylised form, I hope to be able to tease out the issues when the question of entrenched protection of fundamental rights is placed on the political agenda.

V. From norms to facts

So far, I have dealt mainly with normative theories of rights and democracy. Such theories are useful in so far as they help us to think more clearly about various

---

[26] M. Sandel (ed.), *Liberalism and its Critics* (Oxford: Blackwell, 1984), 6.

[27] C. Taylor, 'Liberal Politics and the Public Sphere', in *Philosophical Arguments* (Cambridge, Mass.: Harvard University Press, 1995), 285. See also M. A. Glendon, *Rights Talk: The Impoverishment of Political Discourse* (New York: Free Press, 1991).

[28] See J. Habermas, *Between Facts and Norms: Contributions to a Discourse Theory of Law and Democracy* (Cambridge: Polity, 1996).

[29] See R. Dagger, *Civic Virtues: Rights, Citizenship, and Republican Liberalism* (New York: Oxford University Press, 1997).

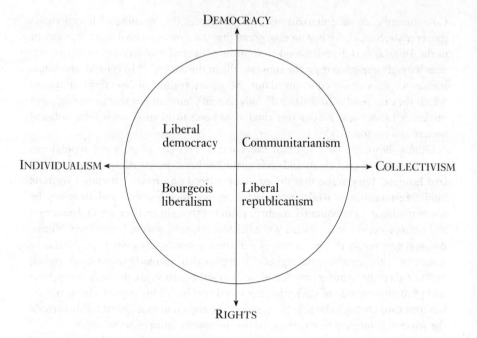

Fig. 3.1 Polarities of liberalism and republicanism

conceptions of rights and democracy and the types of relationship which can be constructed between them. But it must not be assumed that these normative theories provide an explanation of the way in which modern societies are actually constituted. Indeed, given the scale, complexity, and ambiguous character of modern government it would be surprising if government could purchase its legitimacy through such relatively simple claims as those of natural rights or popular sovereignty.

When we turn to consider certain practical questions about the impact of institutionalizing basic rights in legal frameworks, matters become much more complicated. These normative issues now need to be aligned with facts about modern government. The question of the desirability or otherwise of rights protection cannot be properly answered either by an appeal to natural rights or by the assertion that the judiciary lacks the democratic authority to undertake the task. This practical problem can only be evaluated with reference to institutional, political and cultural factors concerning a specific regime at a particular time. Before considering these matters, something must first be said about the general character of modern government.

The political regime of modern Western societies is best understood as that of a 'bourgeois liberal republic', a regime rooted in a belief in limited government based on popular representation and on the acceptance of a free-market economy.[30] Since this is a broad designation which covers all four outlined positions on the issue of democracy and rights, it might not advance matters much. But at least it provides a general context for considering further both the modern institutionalized meaning of democracy and also certain basic issues concerning the relationships between government, constitutions, law, and society.

Within the bourgeois liberal republic, democracy invariably takes a representative form. And representative democracy, it must be emphasized, establishes a form of government far removed from the notion of democracy as collective self-government. Other than for some general, inchoate belief that original political power is located in the people, the modern republic has little in common with the medieval city republics from which the tradition of republican thought derives.[31] Governments of a modern representative democratic character do not in any strict sense express the popular will. Although they elect representatives, the people do not govern, even in the indirect sense of 'choosing individuals who will assemble to put their will into action'.[32] Rather, it would be more accurate to say that the people merely select from amongst the competitors those who will take the political decisions.[33]

During the golden age of parliamentarism, Burke made efforts to link a rather thin conception of representative democracy to notions of deliberation, and thence to the republican ideal.[34] But such notions of parliamentary democracy have been severely eroded as a consequence of the emergence of disciplined political parties. Representative democracy sanctions a mode of government by elites, subject only to an often inadequate form of retrospective accountability. Representative democracy, Manin notes, 'is not a system in which the community governs itself, but a system in which public policies and decisions are made subject to the verdict of the people'.[35] Indeed, it might even be argued that representative democracy has been purposely devised for a modern state which, in Dunn's words, was constructed 'for the express purpose of denying that any given population, any people, had either the capacity or the right to act together for themselves'.[36] The modern state rooted in representative democracy, in short, 'was invented precisely to repudiate the possible coherence of democratic claims to rule'.[37]

---

[30] B. Fontana (ed.), *The Invention of the Modern Republic* (Cambridge: Cambridge University Press, 1994), 2.

[31] See S. E. Finer, *The History of Government*, ii (Oxford: Oxford University Press, 1997), 1019–23. Cf. J. G. A. Pocock, *The Machiavellian Moment* (Princeton, NJ: Princeton University Press, 1975).

[32] J. Schumpeter, *Capitalism, Socialism and Democracy*, 3rd edn. (New York: Harper & Row, 1957), 250.

[33] Ibid.

[34] See E. Burke, 'Speech to the Electors of Bristol, 1774', in *Speeches and Letters on American Affairs* (London: Dent, 1908), 68.

[35] B. Manin, *The Principles of Representative Government* (Cambridge: Cambridge University Press, 1997), 192.

[36] J. Dunn (ed.), *Democracy: The Unfinished Journey 508BC to AD1993* (Oxford: Oxford University Press, 1992), 247–8.

[37] Ibid.

Given the rather limited democratic form which representative government takes, it is difficult to reject a proposal to protect civil and political rights against the action of transient majorities simply on the ground that it is anti-democratic. Vesting responsibility for rights enforcement in an appointed judiciary might be rejected on the ground that the reform would make it more difficult for democrats to realize their political objective of requiring that political decision-making directly reflect the people's will. But given the general character of modern government, this stance requires a detailed, local evaluation of reform proposals, their prospects for implementation, and their likely impact. Without more, the anti-democratic argument against rights entrenchment fails to achieve much leverage.

Before addressing that issue, however, I wish first to turn to another important feature of the bourgeois liberal republic: 'its relatively steady imaginative accept-ance of the economic limits to modern politics, and its continuing readiness to adjust to these limits in the face of disappointing experience'.[38] In other words, modern societies have not mainly been integrated socially (i.e. through values and norms) but systemically through the operation of markets and bureaucracies. This point has, I believe, a particular importance when we address the institutional ques-tion of entrenching rights in law.

Although modern society is often presented as being law-governed, the signific-ance of this claim remains unclear. It is true that government is subject to formal institutional checks, many of which are defined and enforced through law. But much of the imagery of liberal constitutionalism fails to match our knowledge of the way modern government actually functions. Overshadowing the rights-bearing individual is the private corporation exercising extensive economic power. Behind the representative parliament enacting legislation there is an intricate, largely pri-vate network of corporate government through which legislative policy and priori-ties are invariably determined. Running in tandem with public structures of control and responsibility lies the machinery of party discipline through which most of these accountability issues are actually resolved. How these contrasting worlds— those, we might say, of the constitutional lawyer and political scientist respec-tively—interact, and with what consequence, remains puzzling. But our perception of this relationship generally determines the line we take on the nature of the rela-tionship between law and modern government.

In the light of these developments in modern government, it is possible to argue that law has now been displaced from its traditional role of providing a mechanism for social integration. Law, it might be said, can now only be conceived function-ally, as one subsystem amongst several through which modern society operates.[39] If this were the case, it would appear that we can only address the practical questions of rights protection in functional terms. There is a variety of explanations. The introduction of constitutional rights in Britain might be understood, for example,

---

[38] J. Dunn, 'The Identity of the Bourgeois Liberal Republic', in Fontana, n. 30 above, 209.

[39] See W. T. Murphy, *The Oldest Social Science? Configurations of Law and Modernity* (Oxford: Clarendon Press, 1997).

as a product of contemporary electoral politics. Politicians in search of the median voter, having become fixated on their media images, lack the confidence to promote specific measures which protect the rights of unpopular minorities; enacting general principles enables responsibility for such action to pass from legislature to judiciary. More generally, the Human Rights Act might signal a recognition by government of the need for an adjustment to be effected between the political and legal systems, thereby enabling the overloaded political system to alleviate some of those burdens which have threatened its effectiveness. Alternatively (or additionally), such reforms might be seen as an attempt to restructure political expectations into a form which is capable of addressing the economic imperatives of a modern capitalist economy. Again, this initiative, promoted under the banner of political modernization, could be seen as an integral part of the grand European project of harmonizing governmental systems.

Explanations like these, in which law is treated as a device of instrumental rationality, provide a powerful corrective to those accounts—increasingly common in the field of constitutional law—which move effortlessly from normative theory to institutional prescription without considering any of these complex sociological questions. One problem with functionalist accounts, however, is that they seem to leave the field open only to radical critique. Such critical analyses tend to view these institutional reforms either as signalling the (improper) containment of politics by legal means[40] or as marking the demise of a radical political rhetoric of human rights.[41] But the weakness of these liberationist critiques is their utopian, even theological character.[42] They offer insightful analyses of the current situation and an alluring vision of some future state, but provide no programme for moving from one to the other—from fact to norm. For any account that aims to deal with legal-institutionalist concerns, this must count as a debilitating flaw.

I am not offering clear answers to these difficult questions. If we ask whether rights entrenchment is a positive initiative, the claims of normative theory cannot be treated as sociological fact. On the other hand, although 'the vagueness and discontinuity of the interactive boundaries [between theory and practice] are deeply at odds with the fictive clarity and determinacy of the system of public law', law does remain of importance 'as a practical resource for human agents'.[43] Notwithstanding the growing systematization of social life, it might be said that law remains an important but also 'a profoundly ambiguous medium of societal integration'.[44] And on this ambivalent note, I shall now turn to consider the impact of rights entrenchment on the legal order.

---

[40] See E. Christodoulidis, *Law and Reflexive Politics* (Dordrecht: Kluwer, 1998).

[41] See C. Douzinas, *The End of Human Rights: Critical Legal Thought at the Turn of the Century* (Oxford: Hart, 2000).

[42] In the case of Douzinas (ibid.), for example, it is unclear how his appeal to radical natural law as a transcendent standard does not (as in the work of Leo Strauss, whose thought he follows) return us to a form of classical political thought based on a natural order which is intrinsically hierarchical.

[43] Dunn, n. 38 above, 215.   [44] Habermas, n. 28 above, 39–40.

VI. The nature of the legal order

It is necessary first to return to normative analysis. The reforms set in train by the Human Rights Act mark an important stage in Britain's constitutional development. From a juridical perspective, these reforms seem likely to cause a basic shift in the nature of the legal order, one whose nature can be illuminated by those theories of political order we have considered. The shift is from a traditional approach that has taken its conception of law from the liberal democratic model rooted in sovereignty towards a rights-oriented conception of law. Contrary to the position of many advocates of the reform who stress the modest nature of the change, this change seems, potentially, to be foundational.[45] It is capable of marking the transformation of Britain's political constitution into one which is based on law.

In the classical liberal (i.e. Hobbesian) settlement, law is conceived as an instrument of command. Within the framework of representative democracy, the highest expression of law is found in statutes enacted by the sovereign Parliament and which the judiciary faithfully enforce. Law takes shape in texts, and a professional cadre exists to gain knowledge of these texts and apply them to facts. Law is essentially coercive: in Austin's words it is 'the signification of desire' backed by the power 'to inflict an evil or pain'.[46] It is important to stress the fact that this authoritarian image of law is not inimical to liberalism. If law does involve the infliction of pain then there are good reasons both for recognizing the practical limitations on its use and for ensuring that restrictions on individual liberty are imposed only when demonstrably necessary for the public good.

However, it is vital to distinguish between right and law. As Hobbes noted, 'Right consisteth in liberty to do, or to forbeare; whereas Law determineth and bindeth.' Law and Right, he continued, 'differ as much as Obligation and Liberty'.[47] Natural or human rights in this scheme are simply types of political claim; legal rights, by contrast, are a consequence of positive law. Within this scheme, we appeal to a political tradition of civil liberty to defend ourselves against the restrictive impact of the law.

This tradition of liberal democracy, the Whig inheritance, is exemplified by the work of Dicey and his followers. But this liberal democratic conception of law is also one in which many parliamentary socialists have been content to acquiesce. In part this is because this conception of positive law as a coercive, rule-based order yields a realistic account of law and the state. It has the advantage of according due recognition to

---

[45] This is not to say that the shift is realized simply by the enactment of the Human Rights Act. It is the consequence of a more general political project promoted by judges, lawyers, and others over a significant period. See M. Loughlin, 'Rights Discourse and Public Law Thought in the United Kingdom', in G. W. Anderson (ed.), *Rights and Democracy: Essays in UK–Canadian Constitutionalism* (London: Blackstone Press, 1999), ch. 9.

[46] J. Austin, *The Province of Jurisprudence Determined* [1832] (Cambridge: Cambridge University Press, 1995), 21.

[47] Hobbes, *Leviathan*, ch. 14.

the untrammelled political power of parliamentary majorities. And, equally importantly, it does not permit the judiciary to interfere with the work of those executive
bodies which, cloaked with statutory authority and using governmental power, are
empowered to promote progressive social reforms. But acquiescence in this positivist
conception of law should not be taken as agreement on conceptions of democracy and
rights. Most of this group embraced a collectivist social ontology, maintained different (i.e. republican) notions of what freedom entailed, were sceptical about the ability
of 'bourgeois' rights to deliver progressive reforms,[48] and were scathing about the
judiciary's competence to adjudicate on public policy matters.[49] They therefore
placed their faith in parliamentary methods, administrative grievance-handling mechanisms, and the professionalism of public officials.[50] In short, they adopted what I
have called a communitarian position.[51]

However, it was precisely those aspects of the liberal democratic conception of
law which were attractive to those on the left that caused political conservatives so
much concern, especially with the growth of the administrative state in the twentieth century.[52] Conservatives first began to advocate the idea of a rights-based constitutional framework as a solution to these concerns during the 1960s and 1970s.[53]
In the early 1980s, constitutional modernisation became a central policy of the
newly established SDP, and the experience of Thatcherism during the 1980s
caused many on the left to adopt a similar solution, as a constraint on the potentially
absolute power of parliamentary majorities.[54] The Human Rights Act 1998 is a partial realization of the agenda of that unusual coalition. But from a juridical perspective, the work undertaken by the judiciary over the previous twenty years or so
should not be underestimated.[55] Symbolically at least, the 1998 Act marks the shift
from a positivist, liberal democratic model to a rights-based conception of law as a
set of architectonic principles which frames the political order.

With the formal recognition now given to basic constitutional rights, the conditions are in place for effecting a basic shift in our understanding of the character of

---

[48] Cf. K. Marx, 'On the Jewish Question' [1846], in J. Waldron (ed.), *Nonsense on Stilts: Bentham,
Burke and Marx on the Rights of Man* (London: Methuen, 1987), 147: 'None of these so-called rights of
man goes beyond the egoistic man, beyond man as a member of civil society, as man separated from life
in the community and withdrawn into himself, into his private interest and his private arbitrary will.
These rights are far from conceiving man as a species-being.'

[49] See J. A. G. Griffith, *The Politics of the Judiciary*, 5th edn. (London: Fontana, 1997).

[50] On the importance of professionals, see: T. L. Haskell 'Professionalism *versus* Capitalism:
R. H. Tawney, Emile Durkheim, and C. S. Peirce on the Disinterestedness of Professional
Communities', in Haskell (ed.), *The Authority of Experts: Studies in History and Theory* (Bloomington,
Ind.: Indiana University Press, 1984), 180.

[51] I have said enough about their general orientation, I hope, to distinguish what I have labelled the
(British) communitarian position on democracy and rights from some of the political values which are
associated with communitarianism in contemporary American political thought.

[52] See M. Loughlin, *Public Law and Political Theory* (Oxford: Clarendon Press, 1992), ch. 7.

[53] See N. Johnson, 'Constitutional Reform: Some Dilemmas for a Conservative Philosophy' in
Z. Layton-Henry (ed.), *Conservative Party Politics* (London: Macmillan, 1980), ch. 6.

[54] See Loughlin, n. 52 above, ch. 9.

[55] See M. Hunt, *Using Human Rights Law in English Courts* (Oxford: Hart, 1997); Loughlin, n. 45
above.

law. Rather than being viewed as coercive order, law can be seen as a means of main-taining freedom. Rather than being founded on sovereignty and legitimated by the principles of representative democracy, law may be conceived as being based on rights and legitimated by an appeal to moral autonomy. Instead of defining law as a system of subjecting conduct to the governance of rules, it can be understood as an enterprise which subjects governance to the principles of right conduct. Law, it might now be argued, is not fundamentally a matter of will, but an aspect of reason.

One important modification concerns the relationship between law and politics. In the liberal democratic model, law manifests itself as the outcome of a political process (and distinct spheres of the political and legal are drawn); in the rights-based conception, law provides the frame within which politics is conducted. The idea of the constitution thus changes from political bargain to a body of fundamental law. The general implications for juristic thought are profound: principles tend to replace rules as the basic building blocks of the legal order, the positivist separation of law from morals disintegrates (since principles acquire weight by reference to eth-ical considerations), a change from literalistic to teleological canons of interpretation becomes fashionable, and all of these trends impact powerfully on the question of what counts as a good legal argument.

These are important shifts. But, once again, it must be emphasized that these take effect mainly in the (normative) realm of juristic thought. What remains unclear is whether this constitutionalized form of legal discourse is likely to pene-trate the entire legal order (and therefore effect a foundational shift), will function mainly in a relatively discrete public law sphere (and therefore have limited pene-trative influence on the conceptual schemes of private/commercial law), or will exert its influence only within one particular dimension of public law discourse (and thus will influence only those aspects of public law in which government interferes with basic individual rights). What seems most likely is that, even within public law discourse, each of the two modern idioms of liberal political thought—rights and utility—will continue to exert a powerful influence over judicial reasoning processes. This will complicate practice, produce greater uncertainty and con-fusion,[56] and expose more clearly the ideological underpinnings of judicial tech-niques.[57] When one turns from the normative plane of jurisprudence to the actual functioning of the legal system, the issues become even more complex. The adop-tion of a rights discourse will inevitably result in some shift in power between the legislature and the judiciary. But beyond that, many issues remain undetermined.

[56] For illustrations, see M. Loughlin, 'The Underside of the Law: Judicial Review and the Prison Disciplinary System', (1993) 46 *Current Legal Problems* 23, at 44–5; Hunt, n. 55 above`, 298: 'judicial practice long ago left behind the theoretical framework in which courts purport to operate, but the vocabulary of that framework has survived, as the only language the courts consider to be legitimate.'

[57] A good illustration is provided by the recent difficulties experienced by the judiciary in determining whether the statutory frameworks under which public authorities provide various social services impose duties on authorities and, if so, whether the availability of resources is a relevant factor in determining the precise nature of that duty. On which see E. Palmer, 'Resource Allocation, Welfare Rights: Mapping the Boundaries of Judicial Control in Public Administrative Law', (2000) 20 *Oxford Journal of Legal Studies* 63.

VII. Architectonic principles and local politics

The trajectory of change, I have been arguing, is from a liberal democratic model towards a rights-based conception of law. It is a movement that leads to the belief that law establishes the architectonic principles of political order. But it leaves unresolved a host of politico-legal issues. How, for example, should this political order best be characterized: is it one that embraces liberal or republican conceptions of rights and democracy? Will it lead to more enlightened, responsive, and effective government? In order to explore these difficult questions, I want to introduce two general themes concerning the growing interpenetration of law and politics: the constitutionalization of political discourse and the politics of legal discourse.

If in the future law is to be seen as incorporating architectonic principles of political order, then this is likely to lead to a constitutionalization of politics. Politics will increasingly be treated as a practice to be conducted within the frame of legal principles, and this in turn must lead to some modification in our understanding of the character of that practice. At the very least, it will give more political power to lawyers, greater influence to courts in policy processes and much more ideological force to law as a medium for shaping political ideas and action. Is this necessarily a bad thing? Institutionalized rights protection might help protect vulnerable minorities—prisoners, asylum-seekers, homosexual members of the armed forces[58]—against high-handed executive action. Rights discourse is also likely to lead to the emergence of a more rationalized form of political and policy decision-making in which public authorities will be required to specify their general policy objectives and justify the proportionality of the measures taken as means to their realization. But there is also the danger that it will create a degree of stridency in political engagement which, at its most extreme, is anarchic. Douzinas argues that once 'international politics are dominated by the rhetoric of rights, no moral argument can resist the desire of even small groups to acquire autonomy and statehood' and this movement is one which can result in 'greater conflict and misery'.[59] By analogy, and as the communitarian position maintains,[60] a similar argument can be made in respect of domestic politics.

This process of constitutionalization raises an important point about politics. Politics, I believe (revealing my republican tendencies), should not be treated simply as a power struggle between competing interests; it is a deliberative activity which performs the vital task of maintaining a vibrant public space within which

---

[58] See, respectively, *R v. Secretary of State for the Home Dept., ex p. Leech* [1994] QB 198; *R v. Secretary of State for Social Security, ex p. Joint Council for the Welfare of Immigrants* [1997] 1 WLR 275, Asylum and Immigration Act 1996, s. 11(1); *R v. Ministry of Defence, ex p. Smith* [1996] QB 517, *Smith and Grady v. United Kingdom* (2000) 29 EHRR 493, Statement of the Secretary of State for Defence, 342 HC Debs col. 287 ff. (12 Jan. 2000).

[59] Douzinas, n. 41 above, 242. See also M. Koskenniemi, 'The Effect of Rights on Political Culture', in P. Alston (ed.), *The EU and Human Rights* (Oxford: Oxford University Press, 1999), ch. 3.

[60] See e.g. Taylor n. 27 above.

irresolvable social conflicts are managed effectively. But aspects of rights discourse undermine this notion of politics. Rights discourse can lead to the growth of single-issue agendas, a more adversarial form of politics, and a degree of political fragmentation which makes it much more difficult to build coalitions around some conception of the public good. Rights discourse also reorients politics towards the imposition of limitations on the power of government. And at a time when government remains a vitally important agency for dealing with those major challenges—eliminating poverty, handling environmental risks, guaranteeing security against crime, promoting economic success, curbing the potentially abusive powers of major corporations—which continue to require urgent attention, it fosters a style of politics which handicaps governmental effectiveness.

Constitutionalization can thus result in politics assuming the character of legal argumentation. But if politics becomes more legalized, so law becomes more politicized. We see the likely consequences by referring back to the scheme outlined in Fig. 3.1. Quite obviously, a shift is being effected along the democracy–rights axis. But which position on the individual–collective (i.e. liberal-republican) axis best reflects the values on which the British constitution is now founded? Are we moving towards a bourgeois liberal or a civic republican model? The answer to this rather basic question is not, of course, to be found in the Human Rights Act. The text tells us, for example, that 'everyone has the right to liberty and security of the person', and requires that these rights shall not be deprived except in specified ways.[61] It also states that the only legal restrictions that may be placed on the exercise of the rights of freedom of expression, assembly, and association are those which 'are necessary in a democratic society'.[62] But what is meant by 'liberty'?[63] And how can necessity be determined without placing a specific meaning and valuation on 'democracy'?[64] It is evident that in the process of moving from abstract principle to specific judgment, judges will make policy choices. In reaching decisions on such matters, they will be required, however implicitly, to identify, explicate, and rank the basic political values which they believe to underpin governance in Britain.

Notwithstanding some powerful rhetoric about the judiciary's ability to find the 'right answer', this task cannot sensibly be treated as anything other than a major exercise of political judgment. By this I mean that judges will be obliged to deliberate over rival, often incommensurable, values in circumstances in which there is no overarching objective standard by which disputes can be resolved. This is not to say that such political decision-making by judges is therefore unacceptable; that would require a conception of democracy which, as I have indicated, is not reflected in our general arrangements of government. But it is a major task requiring sensitive and dextrous handling. And there is plenty of evidence to indicate that the judiciary is unlikely to be able to respond effectively to the challenge.

---

[61] Human Rights Act 1998, Sched. 1, art. 5.   [62] Ibid. arts. 10, 11.   [63] Cf. Pettit, n. 2 above.
[64] Cf. the discussion in Section IV above.

Given the structure of the 1998 legislation, and especially the arrangement for retaining ultimate parliamentary control over interpretation of the rights regime, the framework clearly is one which seeks a reconciliation between the values of democracy and rights. It therefore appears that the model most closely expressing the values of the contemporary political order is that of liberal republicanism. But the explication of that model would require a major exercise in legal and judicial innovation which, for various reasons, seems unlikely.

For one thing, we have retained in Britain a very traditional adjudicative regime. Consequently, our court systems (and our legal professions) are not well equipped to respond creatively to the new modes of argument, to new types of evidence, or to new managerial responsibilities which will emerge from the growth of constitutional litigation.[65] The prospect of cloistered barristers steeped in the arcane traditions of the common law submitting oral argument on the meaning and significance of constitutional rights in the formal, adversarial setting of our higher courts does little to inspire confidence. It will almost certainly lead to a new era of scholasticism, of the sort which Waldron illustrates in his portrayal of the way in which free speech protection under the First Amendment of the US Constitution is addressed: is pornography speech? Is flag-burning speech? Is topless dancing speech? Is panhandling speech? Is racial abuse speech? This, as Waldron rightly suggests, is not the way to argue about rights.[66]

Alongside these institutional limitations, there are concerns about the competence of the decision-makers. Highly skilled though they may be in forensic techniques, how well equipped are our judges to undertake this sensitive political task? At the beginning of the twentieth century, political experience was virtually a precondition for judicial appointment,[67] and this experience helped the judiciary reach implicit understandings about the appropriate boundary between legal and political matters. For various reasons, such as the growth of the judicial system, the professionalization of politics, and the changing workload of the bar, this has now changed, and the process of judicial appointments has been depoliticized. This may have been a positive development with respect to efficiency and competence in the dispatch of general judicial business, but it has left us with a judiciary with little political experience. It will take more than a quick dip into Isaiah Berlin to get to grips with these responsibilities. And if the vanguard consists of classicists who regard Kant as the pinnacle of political judgment, rights litigation will result in the

---

[65] See e.g. A. Chayes, 'The Role of the Judge in Public Law Litigation', (1976) 89 Harvard Law Rev. 1281.

[66] Waldron, n. 19 above, at 26. On similar lines see also R. A. Posner, *The Problematics of Moral and Legal Theory* (Cambridge, Mass.: Belknap Press, 1999), esp. 144–82.

[67] J. Redlich, *Local Government in England*, ed. F. W. Hirst (London: Macmillan, 1903), ii. 370: 'The competence of the English judge is so vast that serious embarrassments would beset the work of government were it not for the peculiar characteristics and qualifications which convention and training attach to this great office. . . . English judges . . . have not had an official training. They are not drawn from the Civil Service, but from the ranks of practising barristers who have taken some part in public and parliamentary life. Indeed promotion is often—perhaps too often—the reward for political services.'

judiciary embracing a model which I believe to be singularly inappropriate—the model of bourgeois liberalism.

The likelihood of moving towards the bourgeois liberal model has been significantly increased by the decision to integrate constitutional rights into the legal order through ordinary judicial processes. Given the complexity of the judicial challenge, this approach to implementation is guaranteed to ensure that rights will be treated as instruments of negative constitutionalism. But if the challenge is to be taken seriously, it should be recognized as an issue of positive constitutionalization, of treating constitutional arrangements as a means of constructing power and guiding the exercise of that power towards socially desirable ends.[68] To make this happen, however, it would be necessary to establish a specialized constitutional court— one with methods of recruitment and modes of deliberation and decision-making that break radically with our judicial traditions. Only by making a decisive break with the traditions of the common law would it be possible to respond adequately to these new juristic challenges.

This, however, is an uncomfortable conclusion to reach, especially for those who have adopted what I have called a communitarian position on democracy and rights. During the twentieth century, communitarians were content to work with a positivist conception of law derived mainly from a tradition of liberal democracy and to promote social and economic reform through a largely non-juridified welfare state. The dilemma this group faces is especially acute. Do they maintain that, despite the growing influence of rights discourse, positivism retains the power to address all the primary issues of law? Or do they take legal rights seriously and not only engage in a critique of bourgeois rights but also advocate institutional reforms and promote interpretations which advance the republican cause? The latter course of action is risky: not only is the comparative experience discouraging but the strategy of promoting institutional reforms also gives much more authority and legitimacy to judicial processes. Although this requires a difficult judgment, one thing seems certain: the phenomenon of justiciable constitutional rights is not going to go away.

---

[68] Cf. Section II above. See further Holmes, n. 15 above.

4

Legislative Sovereignty and the Rule of Law

JEFFREY GOLDSWORTHY

I. Introduction

Throughout the common law world, it is increasingly assumed that legislative sovereignty—legislative power that is legally unlimited[1]—is incompatible with 'the rule of law'. Those who regard the rule of law as an actual legal principle sometimes argue that it necessarily excludes or overrides any doctrine of legislative sovereignty. Others, who regard the rule of law as a political ideal or aspiration, sometimes argue that it requires any doctrine of legislative sovereignty to be repealed, and legislative power subordinated to constitutionally entrenched rights.

In this chapter I will challenge the assumption, common to both arguments, that legislative sovereignty is incompatible with the rule of law. Strong opinions have been expressed for and against. It has been claimed that '[i]f parliament . . . can change any law at any moment . . . then the rule of law is nothing more than a bad joke'.[2] On the other hand, claims of that kind have been disparaged as 'judicial supremacist rhetoric',[3] and judicial review of legislation as a 'corrupting constitutional innovation—which [only] in vulgar jurisprudence is thought to support the doctrine of the rule of law'.[4] The disagreement is not a new one. Over fifty years ago, F. A. Hayek's argument that bills of rights enhanced the rule of law was severely criticized for confusing 'the Rule of Law' with 'the Rule of Hayek'.[5] The critic, Herman Finer, strongly defended majoritarian democracy, claiming that in Britain '[t]he Rule of Law is not juridical, it is parliamentary'.[6]

II. Legal principle or political ideal?

The rule of law is first and foremost a political principle, an ideal or aspiration that may or may not be guaranteed by law. It can be regarded as a constitutional (but

---

[1] This can be treated as a stipulative definition of 'legislative sovereignty' for the purposes of this chapter. In addition, by 'legal limit' I will mean a judicially enforceable limit.

[2] G. de Q. Walker, *The Rule of Law, Foundation of Constitutional Democracy* (Melbourne: Melbourne University Press, 1988), 159.

[3] M. Elliott, 'Reconciling Constitutional Rights and Constitutional Orthodoxy', [1997] *Cambridge Law Journal* 474, 476.

[4] P. Morton, *An Institutional Theory of Law: Keeping Law in its Place* (Oxford: Clarendon Press, 1998), 371.

[5] *The Road to Reaction* (London: Dennis Dobson, 1945), ch. 4.   [6] Ibid. 38.

non-legal) principle, if a constitutional convention requires compliance with it.[7] If and in so far as it is judicially enforceable, it can also serve as a legal principle.

Most, if not all, common law jurisdictions treat the rule of law as a principle of common law, which unquestionably governs the decisions and actions of the executive and judicial branches of government. In addition, it is sometimes expressly mentioned in written constitutions, or regarded as implicit in them. Whether it is common law, constitutional, or both, the principle is sometimes said to govern the legislature as well as the other branches of government, and to be capable of overriding legislation. Trevor Allan and Sir John Laws, for example, claim that the doctrine of parliamentary sovereignty is incompatible with more fundamental legal principles, including the rule of law, which are supposedly embedded in Britain's largely unwritten constitution.[8] In Canada, the Supreme Court has often stated that the rule of law, expressly mentioned in the Preamble to the Charter of Rights, is also by implication fundamental to the Constitution as a whole.[9] According to one commentator, Supreme Court dicta support the proposition that this constitutional principle binds the legislative as well as the executive branch of government, and could therefore be used to invalidate legislation.[10] In Australia too, the rule of law has frequently been described as a fundamental principle implied by the Constitution, and two members of the High Court have hinted that it might justify the invalidation of certain kinds of unjust legislation.[11]

Notwithstanding the importance and interest of such claims, I will be concerned in this chapter with the rule of law considered as a political rather than as a legal principle. The fundamental issue is the incompatibility of legislative sovereignty with that political principle. It is an important issue in its own right, for both political philosophy and constitutional design. Moreover, the content and scope of the rule of law as a legal principle is ultimately determined by that political principle, subject to limitations and qualifications due to other legal principles. These limitations and qualifications vary from one jurisdiction to another, and raise complex legal questions that are beyond the scope of this chapter.[12] As a political principle,

---

[7] Constitutional conventions are rules or principles governing the exercise of governmental powers, which officials accept as obligatory even though they are not judicially enforceable.

[8] T. R. S. Allan, *Law, Liberty and Justice: The Legal Foundations of British Constitutionalism* (Oxford: Clarendon Press, 1993), 16; Sir J. Laws, 'Law and Democracy' [1995] *Public Law* 72, 85, 88.

[9] *Reference Re Manitoba Language Rights* [1985] SCR 721, 750–1, quoted in P. Monahan, 'Is the Pearson Airport Legislation Unconstitutional? The Rule of Law as a Limit on Contract Repudiation by Government', (1995) 33 *Osgoode Hall LJ* 411, 421–2.

[10] Ibid.

[11] *Kartinyeri v. Commonwealth* (1998) 152 ALR 540, at 569 per Gummow and Hayne JJ. See also the remarks of Justice John Toohey, in 'A Government of Laws, and not of Men?', (1993) 4 *Public Law Review* 158, 160, 174.

[12] I have elsewhere examined and found wanting arguments to the effect that legislative sovereignty is limited by the common law: see J. Goldsworthy, *The Sovereignty of Parliament, History and Philosophy* (Oxford: Clarendon Press, 1999), esp. ch. 10.

the rule of law is a 'supranational concept' of potentially universal significance, rather than a legal principle of a particular jurisdiction.[13]

It is important not to confuse two different questions. The first is whether legislatures are bound by the rule of law considered as a political principle. Few people would deny that they are, just as few would deny that legislatures are also bound by other political principles, such as equality and justice. This is perfectly compatible with legislative sovereignty, which I have defined as legislative power that is legally—not morally or politically—unlimited. In Britain, the doctrine of parliamentary sovereignty co-exists with constitutional conventions requiring Parliament to comply with many principles of political morality, including the rule of law.[14]

I am interested in a different question: whether legislative sovereignty is incompatible with the rule of law—in other words, whether the rule of law requires that legislative power be subject to legal (judicially enforceable) limits.[15] That legislative sovereignty and the rule of law are incompatible has been assumed by critics who have accused A. V. Dicey of inconsistency for simultaneously adhering to both principles.[16] As Martin Loughlin puts it, 'How can an absolutist doctrine of sovereignty rest in harmony with the idea of the rule of law? From the standpoint of mainstream contemporary jurisprudence the issue seems irreconcilable.'[17] Trevor Allan asserts that 'it is ultimately impossible to reconcile . . . the rule of law with the unlimited sovereignty of Parliament . . . An insistence on there being a source of ultimate political authority, which is free of all legal restraint . . . is incompatible with constitutionalism.'[18] More recently, Geoffrey de Q. Walker has proclaimed 'the simple truth that parliamentary omnipotence is an absurdity and that legislative power must be balanced by the rule of law, not just as a set of procedural safeguards, but as a minimum standard for the substantive content of enacted law'.[19]

The increasing popularity of the idea that the rule of law requires even elected legislatures to be subject to judicially enforceable limits is easy to understand. It seems to involve a simple and natural extension of much less controversial requirements that on any view are close to the heart of the rule of law. If the rule of law can be reduced to a single core proposition, it is that laws should limit or control what would otherwise be arbitrary power. It is therefore uncontroversial that

---

[13] See N. Marsh, 'The Rule of Law as a Supra-National Concept', in A. G. Guest (ed.), *Oxford Essays in Jurisprudence*, 1st series (Oxford: Oxford University Press, 1961), 223.

[14] G. Marshall, *Constitutional Conventions* (Oxford: Clarendon Press, 1984), 9, 201.

[15] See n. 1 above.

[16] A. V. Dicey, *An Introduction to the Study of the Law of the Constitution*, 10th edn., ed. E. C. S. Wade (London: Macmillan, 1959).

[17] M. Loughlin, *Public Law and Political Theory* (Oxford: Clarendon Press, 1992), 151.

[18] T. R. S. Allan, n. 8 above, 16. See also Laws, n. 8 above, and F. A. Hayek, *The Constitution of Liberty* (London: Routledge & Kegan Paul, 1960) ch. 12.

[19] Walker, n. 2 above, 359. On the other hand, Walker also says: 'In principle it does not matter whether these restrictions are imposed by way of written constitutional provisions and enforceable by courts, or by the dictates of custom that are enforceable by other means': 26; see also 159. The second option is consistent with legislative sovereignty being subject only to non-legal constitutional conventions, as in Britain today.

administrative officials, even at the highest levels of the executive branch of government, should not enjoy arbitrary power. Their decisions and acts should be governed by judicially enforceable rules or principles. But if so, it might seem that the legislative branch of government should also be denied arbitrary power—that its Acts, too, should be governed by judicially enforceable rules and principles. That is why the American system of limiting legislative power by a bill of rights is sometimes hailed as 'the elevation of the Rule of Law concept to its highest level'.[20]

A full assessment of the force of such arguments requires that two questions be answered. The first is whether legislative sovereignty is inconsistent with the rule of law. The second is whether, even if it is, it is therefore unjustified. Even if it is inconsistent with the rule of law, it might nevertheless be justified on the ground that in this case the rule of law is outweighed by the principle of democracy. In this chapter, I will touch on the second question only in passing. Arguments to the effect that democracy trumps the rule of law have been made by others.[21] I believe it has been too readily conceded that legislative sovereignty is inconsistent with the rule of law. I will therefore concentrate on the first question, and argue that it is not. But the answers to both questions depend partly on the meaning and content of the rule of law as a political principle, to which I now turn.

III. The content of the rule of law

The rule of law is notoriously vague and contested. Sceptics and critics complain that it is 'often used as a mere rhetorical device, a vague ideal by contrast with which legislation, official action, or the assertion of private power is mysteriously measured and found wanting';[22] that it is 'often hazy and unclear, liable to take on any features of law which the writer finds attractive';[23] and so on.

It is generally agreed that the rule of law requires more than 'mere legality', in the sense of compliance with whatever the law of a particular jurisdiction happens to be. The rule of law requires more than the rule of the law: in other words, the law itself might not adequately protect the rule of law.[24] But how much more the rule of law requires is debatable. Proponents of 'thin' or 'formal' conceptions of the rule of law maintain that it requires compliance only with certain procedural and institutional norms: for example, that laws be general, public, prospective, and

---

[20] P. G. Kauper, 'The Supreme Court and the Rule of Law', (1961) 59 *Michigan LR* 531, 532.

[21] e.g. A. Hutchinson and P. Monahan, 'Democracy and the Rule of Law', in Hutchinson and Monahan (eds.), *The Rule of Law: Ideal or Ideology?* (Toronto: Carswell, 1987).

[22] H. W. Arthurs, 'Rethinking Administrative Law: A Slightly Dicey Business', (1979) 17 *Osgoode Hall LJ* 1, 3.

[23] A. Palmer and C. Sampford, 'Retrospective Legislation in Australia: Looking Back at the 1980s', (1994) 22 *Federal LR* 213, 227.

[24] This is true, at least, if the law is conceived of in legal positivist terms. A natural lawyer, who conceives of the law as including transcendent and overriding moral principles, might think that the rule of law requires no more than the rule of the law, which is, ultimately, the rule of those principles.

enforceable by an independent judiciary. Proponents of 'thick' or 'substantive' conceptions maintain that it also includes requirements concerning the substantive content of the law.[25]

Some thick conceptions are criticized for shoehorning every political virtue into the rule of law, which then amounts to the rule of justice or the rule of good law. These conceptions are too broad: while the rule of law is more than the rule of the law, it must be less than the rule of good law. A conception of the rule of law that incorporated every political virtue, properly weighted and balanced, would be useless for practical purposes. Our question, for example, is whether or not the rule of law requires that legislative power be limited by law. If the answer depended on whether judicial review of legislation is desirable all things considered, such as majority rule, minority rights, institutional competence, and so on, then the rule of law would contribute nothing in itself to the enquiry. It would be merely a way of expressing whatever conclusion we reached, without helping us to reach it.

On the other hand, there do seem to be good reasons to go beyond a purely formal conception. Arguably, the rule of law is mainly concerned with limiting or controlling what would otherwise be arbitrary power, whether exercised by public officials or private citizens. For example, chronic lawless violence inflicted by some citizens on others would surely be as antithetical to the rule of law as the lawless tyranny of a king or emperor.[26] The same goes for some kinds of lawful violence. If it would be contrary to the rule of law for a king to possess a legally uncontrolled power of life or death over his subjects, then surely it would equally be contrary to the rule of law for a husband or father to possess the same power over his wife or children. But if so, then every kind of power that one person, group, or organization can exercise over others—such as the power of employers over their employees—would be open to question on rule of law grounds. The rule of law would be concerned with the distribution and extent of all forms of power throughout society, and would be difficult to distinguish from the rule of good law.

Perhaps this would so inflate the rule of law that it would no longer serve a useful function. Fortunately, we are concerned with the exercise of legislative power, not private power. We can therefore bypass the question of the extent to which the rule of law is concerned with the exercise of private as well as public power. For the sake of argument, we will proceed on the basis that in political and legal theory, it requires only 'that the government should be ruled by law and subject to it'.[27]

---

[25] See P. Craig, 'Formal and Substantive Conceptions of the Rule of Law: An Analytical Framework' [1997] *Public Law* 467.

[26] Walker, n. 2 above, 2–3.

[27] J. Raz, 'The Rule of Law and its Virtue', in *The Authority of Law* (Oxford: Clarendon Press, 1981), 210, 212.

IV. 'Thin' conceptions of the rule of law

Thin conceptions of the rule of law have become so popular that a consensus about its content may finally have been reached.[28] Joseph Raz's influential analysis exemplifies these conceptions.[29] He denies that the rule of law means the rule of good law: it must be distinguished from other political ideals such as democracy, justice, equality, and human rights of any kind.[30] The basic goal of the rule of law is to ensure that the law is capable of guiding the behaviour of its subjects.[31] This requires that all laws be prospective, adequately publicized, clear, and relatively stable; that the making of particular legal orders or directives be governed by general laws that satisfy the criteria just listed, and by the principles of natural justice; and that the implementation of all these requirements be subject to review by a readily accessible and independent judiciary.[32]

Raz insists that full compliance with these requirements is neither a necessary nor a sufficient condition for the achievement of justice. It is not a necessary condition because compliance is a matter of degree, and 'maximal possible conformity is on the whole undesirable (some controlled administrative discretion is better than none)'.[33] Since the rule of law is only one of many political ideals, it can occasionally be outweighed by others.[34] It is not a sufficient condition because '[t]he rule of law . . . is compatible with gross violation of human rights';[35] '[m]any forms of arbitrary rule are compatible with the rule of law. A ruler can promote general rules based on whim or self-interest, etc., without offending against the rule of law.'[36]

It is clear that such a thin conception of the rule of law does not require legislative power to be limited by a bill of rights. It is not aimed at eliminating all kinds of arbitrary governmental powers, but only those whose exercise can unfairly upset citizens' expectations about their legal obligations and rights. Extremely unjust or tyrannical laws that are well known to citizens, because they are prospective, adequately publicized, clear, and relatively stable, are not objectionable on rule of law grounds.

It does not follow that on this conception, legislative power can be completely uncontrolled. Raz suggests that judicial review of parliamentary legislation is needed to ensure conformity with the formal requirements of the rule of law, although he adds that this is 'very limited review'.[37] He does not elaborate, but presumably means that the judiciary should be able to invalidate legislation that violates the requirements that legislation be prospective, adequately publicized, clear,

---

[28] T. Endicott suggests that it has, in 'The Impossibility of the Rule of Law', (1999) 19 *Oxford Journal of Legal Studies* 1, 1–2.

[29] Raz, n. 27 above. Other examples are J. Waldron, 'The Rule of Law in Contemporary Liberal Theory', (1989) 2 *Ratio Juris* 79, and R. S. Summers, 'The Principles of the Rule of Law' (1999) 74 *Notre Dame LR* 1691.

[30] Raz, n. 27 above, 211.   [31] Ibid. 214.   [32] Ibid. 214–17.   [33] Ibid. 222.
[34] Ibid. 219, 228–9.   [35] Ibid. 220–1.   [36] Ibid. 219.   [37] Ibid. 217.

and relatively stable, and should not confer excessive discretion on administrators.[38]

But judicial review of legislation on these grounds would be highly impractical. Consider the last four of them. None can possibly be absolute. Legislators cannot be required to ensure that every detail of every new law is brought to the attention of every citizen, that no law include any vague terms, that the law never be changed, or that no administrator ever be granted any discretionary power. Such requirements would be highly undesirable from the point of view of the rule of law itself. For example, the rule of law would suffer if citizens were immune from any law not specifically brought to their attention. In addition, some vagueness in the law is often necessary if the law is not to be irrational and arbitrary.[39] The same is true of legal change, and the granting of discretionary powers to administrators.[40] These requirements raise questions of degree—of more or less—that can be settled only by value judgments. What methods of publicizing new laws give citizens adequate notice of them? When do vagueness in the law, legal change, and administrative discretion cease to be desirable and become excessive? These questions require legislators to balance the competing values at stake, and there is no good reason to think that judges would be better at doing this.

The requirement that seems most conducive to judicial enforcement is that of prospectivity. But not even this should be made absolute. Legislation that changes the law retrospectively can often be justified, sometimes by the rule of law itself. In rare cases even retrospective changes to criminal laws can be justified. The strongest argument against retrospectivity is that it is unfair to upset expectations reasonably based on the state of the law at a particular time. But if expectations are based on mistaken but reasonable beliefs about the state of the law, retrospective legislation may be justified to prevent them from being upset. In addition, some expectations, such as an expectation of legal immunity for grossly immoral conduct, are unworthy of respect, and the threat of subsequent retrospective legislation might help deter such conduct.[41] In other words, it might help to deter the exercise of lawless, arbitrary power. That is why '[t]he trial of the German leaders at Nuremberg by a law made *ex parte*, *ex post facto*, and *ad hoc* has been hailed as a vindication of the rule of law'.[42] Recent legislation retrospectively made it an offence against Australian law for persons in Europe during the Second World War, who may have had no connection with Australia at the time, to have committed 'war crimes'.[43] The legislation was justified, notwithstanding its retrospective operation.

---

[38] If he meant merely that judicial review of 'manner and form' requirements is required, that would not ensure that legislation conformed to the requirements of the rule of law that he lists.

[39] See Endicott, n. 28 above, 4–8.

[40] Ibid. 8–9, on legal change; Raz, n. 27 above, 222, on administrative discretion.

[41] For an excellent and thorough discussion of all these themes, see Palmer and Sampford, n. 23 above.

[42] F. Wormuth, 'Aristotle on Law', in M. R. Konvitz and A. E. Murphy (eds.), *Essays in Political Theory presented to George H. Sabine* (Port Washington, NY: Kennikat Press, 1948), 45.

[43] See *Polyukhovich v. Commonwealth* (1991) 172 CLR 501.

Moreover, even legitimate expectations can be outweighed by considerations of justice. It has been persuasively argued that the British Parliament in 1965 was entirely justified, by considerations of justice and equality, in enacting legislation that not only retrospectively abolished a legal right to compensation but reversed a recent judicial decision awarding compensation to a particular party.[44] For similar reasons, judicial decisions altering the common law may justifiably have retrospective effects, even in criminal cases, which can no longer be concealed by resort to the old 'fairy tale' that judges only declare what the law has always been, and do not really change it.[45] German courts dealing with the prosecution of former East German border guards for shooting people attempting to enter West Berlin have felt justified in adopting novel interpretations of relevant East German laws that in effect amended them retrospectively.[46] The following conclusion to a thorough examination of retrospective legislation in Australia would no doubt be true of most countries:

> Retrospective law-making is neither particularly rare nor necessarily evil. It plays a more sig-
> nificant part in Australian legislation than most would imagine. Much of it can be justified.
> Some of it is very contentious and the justification should be subject to intensive and, hope-
> fully, rigorous debate . . . However, the fact that the proposed statute is 'retrospective' should
> merely be the starting-point of that debate, not its conclusion.[47]

The same goes for another requirement often regarded as central to the rule of law, although not discussed by Raz. This is that legislation should be general in scope rather than aimed at particular persons. Even today, legislation that changes the legal rights or duties of particular legal persons is often regarded as justified—for example, to enable major public works, or unique enterprises such as the staging of an Olympic Games, to proceed expeditiously, by conferring special legal powers and rights on their organizers. Sometimes Acts of indemnity or amnesty, which relieve individuals or groups of liability for breaches of the law, are justified. Usually such breaches have been inadvertent. But as Dicey pointed out, in extra-ordinary situations of internal disorder or war, the executive might have to break the law deliberately 'for the sake of legality itself'—to uphold the rule of law—and then seek an Act of Indemnity.[48]

To sum up, thin conceptions of the rule of law do not require that legislative power be limited by a bill of rights. Moreover, there are powerful reasons for denying that

---

[44] A. L. Goodhart, 'The Burmah Oil Case and the War Damage Act 1965', (1966) 82 *Law Quarterly Review* 97, discussing the War Damage Act 1965, which retrospectively deprived the Burmah Oil Company of a right to compensation that had been upheld by the House of Lords in *Burmah Oil Co Ltd v. Lord Advocate* [1965] AC 75.

[45] A recent example is *R v. R* [1992] AC 599, in which the House of Lords in effect abolished the common law immunity of a husband against being convicted for the rape of his wife, in the course of a case involving a husband charged with that very offence.

[46] See J. Rivers, 'The Interpretation and Invalidity of Unjust Laws', in D. Dyzenhaus (ed.), *Recrafting the Rule of Law: The Limits of Legal Order* (Oxford: Hart, 1999), 40.

[47] Palmer and Sampford, n. 23 above, 277.   [48] Dicey, n. 16 above, 411–13.

even the specific requirements they do impose should be constitutionally guaranteed and made judicially enforceable. They are too vague, and defeasible.[49]

V. 'Thicker' conceptions of the rule of law

To argue that the rule of law requires something like a bill of rights, one must first defend a thicker conception of the principle. Rather than attempt that task myself, I will leave it to those who seek to make such an argument. I will consider whether the argument is plausible even if a thicker conception is acceptable.

It is pertinent to observe that proponents of thicker conceptions do not always maintain that legislative power should be limited by judicially enforceable rights. The International Congress of Jurists that met in New Delhi in 1959 endorsed a thick conception of the rule of law, which Raz criticizes for mentioning 'just about every political ideal which has found support in any part of the globe during the post-war years'.[50] Yet the Congress did not insist that judicial review of legislation was an inherent requirement of the rule of law. Instead, the 'Declaration of Delhi' stated:

In many societies, particularly those which have not yet fully established traditions of demo-cratic legislative behaviour, it is essential that certain limitations on legislative power . . . should be incorporated in a written constitution, and that the safeguards therein contained should be protected by an independent judicial tribunal; in other societies, established stand-ards of legislative behaviour may serve to ensure that the same limitations are observed . . . notwithstanding that their sanction may be of a political nature.[51]

No doubt the desire to achieve consensus among the representatives of many dif-ferent legal systems, some of which included doctrines of legislative sovereignty, was one reason for this conclusion. But there are sound reasons of principle for doubting that the rule of law, even when broadly conceived, requires that legislative power be subject to judicially enforceable limits.

It has frequently been pointed out that the rule of law should not be taken to such extravagant lengths as to condemn all discretionary power. 'No government has ever been a government of laws and not of men in the sense of eliminating all dis-cretionary power. Every government has always been *a government of laws and of men*.'[52] Rules and discretionary power are both essential, and the problem is to find the best combination, given the nature of the task in question and the social and political context in which it must be performed. Among the many powers of government that are necessarily discretionary—which include many judicial as well

---

[49] There may be one or two narrow exceptions—such as a prohibition on acts of attainder—but this does not undermine the general conclusion.

[50] Raz, n. 27 above, 211.

[51] 'The Declaration of Delhi', International Congress of Jurists, New Delhi, India, 5–10 Jan. 1959, (1959) 2 *Journal of the International Committee of Jurists* 7, 8.

[52] K. C. Davis, *Administrative Law: Cases–Text–Problems*, 6th edn. (St Paul, Minn.: West, 1977), 26.

as other powers—is the legislative power. For practical reasons, it is necessarily the most discretionary of all governmental powers; in addition, unlike all others, it is discretionary by definition. Since it is by definition the power to make new laws and repeal old ones, it cannot be completely controlled by pre-existing laws.

Of course, it does not follow that a legislature's powers cannot be limited by special pre-existing laws that it cannot itself amend or repeal. But as to whether doing so would necessarily enhance the rule of law, two possible problems spring to mind.

The first possible problem is that limiting a legislature's powers in this way may achieve little more than to shift the objectionable phenomenon—legally unlimited legislative power—to a higher level. For how could the lawmaking power of whoever imposed those limits be itself limited? There cannot be an infinite regress of lawmakers able to impose limits on the authority of each one in turn.

One possible solution would be to rely on limits to lawmaking power that have not been imposed by any human lawmaker, such as natural law. But on closer inspection, this would not help. According to natural law theories, the most fundamental legal standards are moral standards prescribed by God or built into nature. But as Jeremy Waldron has persuasively argued, even if such a theory could satisfy our worries about the objectivity of moral standards, none has yet been able to provide a methodology that makes moral disagreements any easier to settle.[53] The identity and content of moral standards is often highly controversial and interminably debatable. If they are to perform the legal function envisaged, some official or institution must be accepted as having ultimate authority to decide which of the competing views will have legal force. A decision of that kind is best described as a legislative decision. But that takes us back to our starting point. That decision-maker could not be controlled by any standards other than those it decides it ought to be controlled by.

A related difficulty, or perhaps the same one differently described, is this. One of the core requirements of the rule of law is that decision-making be governed by legal norms whose identity and content can be ascertained without excessive difficulty: they must be relatively clear, adequately publicized, and so on. It would seem difficult for moral standards, whose identity and content are often elusive and controversial, to play that role. If so, decisions that are controlled only by moral standards are not subject to the rule of law—which is no doubt obvious, since that is the complaint about legislative sovereignty that we started with. If legislatures governed by nothing more determinate than moral principles are not subject to the rule of law, why should judges be regarded any differently?

An alternative solution would be to rely on 'reason', as opposed to 'will'. Aristotle's conception of government by law rather than by men is said to have amounted to government by reason.[54] But the bare concept of reason, like Kant's

[53] J. Waldron, 'The Irrelevance of Moral Objectivity', in R. George (ed.), *Natural Law Theory: Contemporary Essays* (Oxford: Clarendon Press, 1992), and in J. Waldron, *Law and Disagreement* (Oxford: Clarendon Press, 1999).

[54] J. Shklar, 'Political Theory and the Rule of Law', in Hutchinson and Monahan, n. 21 above, 1–3.

categorical imperative, lacks substantive content—which it needs if it is to perform the function required of it. And the moment we try to give it content, we run into the same problem that plagues moral argument: the requisite content is inherently controversial and debatable. In practice, pure reason is unavailable to us: we only have access to the variable, fallible, and disputable reason of particular human beings. To say that the rule of law is the rule of reason rather than of will is to beg the question of *whose* reason should rule, and whose should be overridden or discounted on the ground that it is mere 'will'. Should law be based ultimately on the reason of elected legislators, or the reason of judges? It is difficult to see why the rule of law would favour judges rather than legislators.

Another alternative would be to rely on long-standing and immutable customs, rather than deliberately made laws, to limit legislative power. That would be the situation in Britain if the thesis that it has a 'common law constitution', which controls even Parliament, were correct—and if the common law consisted of customs that are 'found but not made' by the judges. But among many difficulties with this idea, it is far too conservative and would cripple the power of elected legislatures. In the modern world of rapid change, legislatures cannot be prohibited from reforming or abolishing customary practices, especially ones that have come to seem oppressive and unjust. Imagine women being told, in the 1970s, that elected legislatures could not validly enact legislation inconsistent with the customary practices that defined their traditional role as wives and mothers! A judicially enforceable 'customary constitution' would be workable only if the judges were able and willing to allow some customs, but not others, to be reformed or abolished. But on what grounds could they do so? Custom itself could not provide them. The judges would have to exercise moral judgment, of exactly the same kind that legislatures currently exercise in deciding when to override established customs.

It seems, then, that at the foundation of any modern legal system there must be a human lawmaker able to make the requisite moral judgments and override even long-standing customs. But this returns us to the problem of how to subject the power of that lawmaker to the rule of law. F. A. Hayek believed that the rule of law would be properly safeguarded only if the power to enact ordinary legislation were limited. But he also believed that the only effective way of doing so was for a superior lawmaker to enact a binding constitution, and that its power to alter that constitution could not itself be limited. Ultimately, therefore, the rule of law could not be 'a rule of the law, but [only] a meta-legal doctrine or a political ideal . . . [that] will be effective only in so far as the legislator feels bound by it. In a democracy this means that it will not prevail unless it forms part of the moral tradition of the community.' [55] On this view, Hobbes was essentially right to claim that at the foundation of any legal system there must be an unlimited and arbitrary power, which cannot itself be bound by law. It is merely a question of whether that power should belong to a monarch, a legislature, a court, 'the people', or some combination of

[55] Hayek, n. 18 above, 206.

them. Ultimately there cannot be a government of laws rather than a government of men, or people (as we should now say). And if there must be a government of people at the foundation of any legal system, there are obvious reasons to prefer a government of 'the people', or their elected representatives, to a government of judges.

But this kind of Hobbesian thinking is now discredited.[56] There is no logical reason that prevents constitutions from including provisions that are unalterable, even by the process of constitutional amendment they themselves prescribe, and some constitutions do so. A prohibition on amendment, like any other element of a rule of recognition, can be effective provided that it is generally accepted as binding.[57] Of course, a constitution prohibiting the amendment of some part of it could be overturned by revolution, but the same is true of any constitution.

On the other hand, although constitutional provisions can be made legally unchangeable, it might be unwise to do so, because it is impossible accurately to foresee what changes may be justified in response to unpredictable future events. Each generation should be equally free to reform its laws—including its constitution—as it deems appropriate. Only very abstract moral principles, such as democracy, justice, and the rule of law, should be regarded as immutable. But they can be embodied in a variety of constitutional arrangements. For example, the rule of law may require that legal disputes be decided by independent judges, but not that any particular judicial structure be preserved for all time. On this view, for practical rather than logical reasons, nothing in a constitution should be made unamendable. If so, we return once again to the problem we started with: the existence of a lawmaking power that is unlimited by law.

However, this may be less of a problem at the level of constitutional amendment than at the level of ordinary legislation. It can plausibly be argued that the rule of law would be enhanced by the imposition of constitutional limits on ordinary legislative power, even if the extra-ordinary power of constitutional amendment cannot be limited, and can be used to release the ordinary legislative power from those limits. This is so provided that the amending power is more difficult to use than the ordinary legislative power, and is therefore less likely to be used (or abused). So the first possible problem with the idea of limiting legislative power by superior laws is not insurmountable.

The second possible problem is less tractable. It is difficult to think of any limits even to ordinary legislative power that should be made absolute, in the sense of being indefeasible come what may. All human rights can justifiably be outweighed or overridden by ordinary legislation in some circumstances. All the rights that are central to modern bills of rights are sometimes outweighed by other important rights and interests. For example, legislatures enact, and courts uphold, laws restricting free speech in order to protect public safety, public decency, national security, confidential information, privacy, reputation, and so on. Even the right to

---

[56] See Goldsworthy, n. 12 above, 236–8.
[57] See H. L. A. Hart, *The Concept of Law* (Oxford: Clarendon Press, 1961), ch. 4.

life itself can be outweighed in unusual situations, such as where self-defence is involved. There is no subject matter over which legislatures should be denied power altogether. All that should be denied them is the unjustified exercise of their power. That is why, in the enforcement of a bill of rights, the crucial question is never simply whether a law intrudes on some protected subject matter such as 'speech', but whether it does so unjustifiably.[58]

This has been known for centuries. It has frequently been pointed out that if rigid limits are imposed on legislative power, and judges appointed to enforce them, the legislature may be disabled from doing good as well as from doing evil, and the disadvantages of the former disability may outweigh the advantages of the latter. The need for some power to alter or override any law whatsoever, if only in an emergency, is a theme that runs through centuries of disquisitions on sovereignty.[59] The seventeenth-century lawyer Bulstrode Whitelocke argued that no subject matter could safely be excluded from the reach of legislative power, because what might be required in order to promote peace and good government could not be predicted in advance.

If it be demanded, what is the subject matter of that good and peace? It will be said: every thing, according as accidents and emergencies, may make application of them, in the wisdom, and judgment, of a public council. And consequently, all matters whatsoever may be accounted legislative affairs, within the authority of parliament.[60]

Constitutional limits to legislative power should therefore not be rigid and absolute. They should allow scope for justifiable qualifications and exceptions. But to decide whether and to what extent a qualification or exception is justified requires judges to make judgments of political morality. They must assess and compare the variable, context-dependent moral weights of all the competing rights or interests that may be affected. The problem with regarding this as a necessary requirement of the rule of law is similar to the problem, mentioned previously, with relying on moral principles as limits to legislative power. The contents of a judicially enforceable bill of rights are principles of political morality whose 'interpretation' is indistinguishable from moral and political philosophy. The fact that they are written is irrelevant. Whether elected legislators, or judges, have ultimate authority to weigh up competing moral principles, and decide which of them ought to prevail, their decisions necessarily depend on controversial judgments of political morality. But why should judges, charged with weighing up and balancing moral principles in concrete cases, be regarded as bound by the rule of law if an elected legislature, responsible for translating the same moral principles into legislation, is not? The

---

[58] In the Canadian Charter of Rights this necessary value judgment is made explicit: s. 1 provides that the Charter 'guarantees the right and freedoms set out in it subject only to such reasonable limits prescribed by law as can be demonstrably justified in a free and democratic society'.

[59] See Goldsworthy, n. 12 above, 'Index of Subjects', 319 ('necessity of power to override law in emergencies').

[60] B. Whitelocke, *Whitelocke's Notes upon the Kings Writt for Choosing Members of Parliament* [etc] (London: C. Morton, 1766), ii. 335; see also ibid. 185.

judges may or may not be better at making moral judgments affecting rights, but that is beside the present point. The rule of judges may be preferable to the rule of legislatures, but we are concerned with the rule of law. If in both cases decisions involve weighing up competing abstract moral principles, why should the judges, but not the legislature, be regarded as 'ruled by law'? The identity of the decision-maker may be different, but the character of the decision itself remains the same. As J. A. G. Griffith put the point,

> For centuries political philosophers have sought that society in which government is by laws and not by men. It is an unattainable ideal. Written constitutions do not achieve it. Nor do bills of rights They merely pass political decisions out of the hands of politicians and into the hands of judges or other persons. To require a supreme court to make certain kinds of polit-ical decisions does not make those decisions any less political.[61]

This point can be taken further. It can be argued, counter-intuitively, that judicially enforceable bills of rights might not only fail to enhance the rule of law, but actu-ally diminish it. Whether or not bills of rights enhance the rule of law must depend on how they affect the exercise of judicial power as well as legislative power. When bills of rights transfer the ultimate review of legislation from legislatures to judges, they make the law that is likely to be applied by the judges less predictable. Instead of being bound to apply legislation, the judges are authorized to reject it for what are essentially reasons of political morality. Judgments of political morality are gen-erally less predictable than judgments about the proper meaning and interpretation of legislation, which depend on the meanings of words and the probable intentions of legislators in enacting them.[62] As Atiyah and Summers argue, content-oriented standards, such as moral principles, generate more uncertainty in the law than do source-oriented (pedigree) standards.[63] In general, legislation that is alleged to vio-late constitutional rights does not obviously do so. It is usually possible to make reasonable arguments on both sides, and courts then decide such cases in the same way that legislatures do: by making finely balanced and controversial judgments of political morality, and settling outstanding disagreements by majority vote. Whether legislation will be subject to constitutional challenge, and whether a chal-lenge is likely to be successful, are often difficult to predict. Legislation that has been widely relied on for some time may unexpectedly be challenged and held invalid, possibly as a result of a perceived or predicted change in judicial philo-sophy.

   All this necessarily produces greater uncertainty about what laws are binding, which should be of some concern to proponents of the rule of law. Indeed, the rule of law has traditionally been concerned much more with the exercise of judicial and

---

[61] 'The Political Constitution', (1979) 42 *Modern Law Review* 1, 16.

[62] Of course, they are not always less predictable. Some issues of political morality are obvious and uncontroversial (such as the immorality of torturing children), and some issues of statutory interpreta-tion are not (words and legislative intentions can both be obscure).

[63] See P. S. Atiyah and R. S. Summers, *Form and Substance in Anglo-American Law* (Oxford: Clarendon Press, 1987), 53.

executive powers than with that of legislative power. As previously observed, legislative power is by definition difficult to limit by pre-existing laws. By contrast, judicial power is by definition ideally suited to it, because in large part it is precisely the power dutifully to apply pre-existing laws. Chief Justice John Marshall expressed this idea in exaggerated terms when he said: 'Judicial power, as contradistinguished from the power of laws, has no existence. Courts are the mere instruments of the law, and can will nothing.'[64] This is exaggerated because judges necessarily exercise powers other than that of applying pre-existing laws. For example, they must sometimes supplement the law, when it is insufficiently determinate to resolve a dispute, or stray from the strict terms of a law in order to do 'equity' in particular cases. Nevertheless, their ability to stray beyond pre-existing law in exercising such powers is supposed to be strictly confined. In his list of the principles of the rule of law, Robert Summers includes this requirement:

[A]ny exceptional power of courts or other tribunals to modify or depart from antecedent law at point of application [should] be a power that, so far as feasible, is itself explicitly specified and duly circumscribed in rules, so that this is a power the exercise of which is itself law-governed.[65]

Of course, Summers is not concerned here with judicial power to invalidate legislation inconsistent with a bill of rights. But his requirement reflects the traditional conception of the judicial function, which does not sit altogether comfortably with the enforcement of bills of rights. In effect, they confer on judges a power to veto legislation retrospectively, on the basis of judgments of political morality.[66] It is a power similar to that exercised by upper houses of review, except that it is exercised after legislation has been enacted.[67] This involves adding to the judicial function a kind of power traditionally associated with the legislative function, except that the unpredictability inherent in its exercise is exacerbated by its retrospective effects. That is why, on balance, it may diminish rather than enhance the rule of law.

This problem cannot be evaded by definition. If 'law' is defined to mean any norm that is enforceable by the courts, then it might seem that to subject legislation to review according to judicially enforceable principles is *by definition* to increase the rule of law. That definition is the subject of debate between so-called 'exclusive' and 'inclusive' legal positivists. The former assert that constitutionally protected rights

---

[64] *Osborn v. Bank of the United States* 22 US 738 (1824), 866.   [65] Summers, n. 29 above, 1694.

[66] In theory the power is not one of changing the law at all, but merely of declaring what the law has always been. But insofar as its exercise is based on unpredictable judgments of political morality, its effect can be indistinguishable from that of retrospective repeal.

[67] It is no accident that judicial review of legislation emerged in the US as an alternative to non-judicial mechanisms for ensuring legislative compliance with constitutional laws. For example, New York State created a Council of Revision, which included the Governor, Chancellor, and Supreme Court Justices, armed with a limited but not final veto over legislation deemed inconsistent 'with the spirit of [the] constitution'. Similar institutions, regarded as political rather than judicial, were proposed in other states. At the Philadelphia Convention, which proposed the new federal Constitution for ratification by the states, James Wilson and James Madison supported judicial review only after a majority rejected their proposal for a Council of Revision. See Goldsworthy, n. 12 above, 212–13.

are principles of political morality, which judges are legally required to enforce, and not principles of law.[68] But even if the inclusive legal positivists are right to argue that such rights are both principles of political morality *and* principles of law, that would not settle the question of the effect of bills of rights on the rule of law. This is because, as previously noted, the rule of law is not the same as the rule of the law. The issue is one of substance, not terminology: it concerns the extent to which governmental acts overall are subject to the rule of the right kinds of law, such as those that enhance predictability. The rule of other kinds of law can diminish, rather than enhance, the rule of law. Requiring judges to enforce abstract, vague, and defeasible principles of political morality arguably have precisely that effect.

The point is not that bills of rights are therefore unjustified. It is merely that they may diminish rather than enhance the rule of law. The point holds even if they do so only to a small extent. But other political principles, such as justice, must also be taken into account. The rule of law is not the rule of justice. It can be argued that judicial enforcement of a bill of rights is likely to enhance substantive justice, to such an extent that substantive justice outweighs the rule of law. Whether or not that is so is beyond the scope of this essay. Either way, it is substantive justice, not the rule of law, which best explains the attractions of bills of rights.

In reply, it might be argued that judicial enforcement of a bill of rights is no more unpredictable in its effects than the exercise of some other judicial powers, such as that of overruling earlier decisions at common law, or applying moral principles enshrined in legislation or case law. But perhaps that merely shows that other judicial powers also tend to diminish rather than enhance the rule of law, whatever their overall merits may be.

It might also be pointed out that judges exercise their powers according to strict procedures that guarantee natural justice: they must reach a decision only after all interested parties have had an opportunity to be heard, they must give reasons for their decisions, and so on. It might then be argued that even if the substance of their power is little different from that of a legislative house of review, their procedures ensure that it is less likely to be exercised in an arbitrary fashion. But it should not be forgotten that legislatures also exercise their power in accordance with mandatory procedures. Legislation in modern democracies does not issue from the mouth of an omnipotent individual. It emerges from the deliberations of a complex, artificial body whose composition, procedures, and forms of legislation are defined and structured by laws and standing orders.[69] The laws that govern these matters of composition, procedure, and form include the entire legal apparatus of representative democracy. Standing orders may be self-imposed and not legally binding, but many judicial procedures are also self-imposed, including the duty of courts to give reasons for their decisions.

---

[68] See W. Waluchow, *Inclusive Legal Positivism* (Oxford: Clarendon Press, 1994).
[69] Dicey relied partly on this: n. 16 above, 402, 405.

This question of procedures is important. It is often too readily assumed that any legislature whose power is not subject to substantive legal limits has 'arbitrary' power that is uncontrolled by law. But laws governing the composition of legislatures, and the procedures and forms by which they must legislate, in themselves exert a powerful kind of legal control.[70] Historically, the requirement that legislation desired by a monarch could not be enacted without the assent of representatives of the community was a major advance for the rule of law, even though this did not involve the imposition of substantive limits on the power to legislate. The same goes for the other constitutional reforms that gave birth to modern representative democracy: the development of bicameralism, electoral reform, the extension of the franchise, and so on. Indeed, British constitutionalism has always relied on representation, together with 'checks and balances' internal to the legislative process, rather than substantive limits to legislative power enforced by an external agency.[71] These methods of controlling legislative power exemplify what Kenneth Culp Davis famously called 'structuring', as opposed to 'confining' and 'checking', the exercise of discretionary power.[72] All three methods of controlling by law the exercise of what would otherwise be arbitrary power can legitimately be regarded as contributing to the rule of law.

The extent to which laws governing these matters of composition, procedure, and form succeed in preventing the arbitrary or tyrannical exercise of legislative power no doubt varies from one country to another. In Britain, deficiencies in the method by which members of the lower house are elected, the length of time between elections, the domination of the lower house by the executive government, and the lack of an adequate upper house of review may explain most of the widespread contemporary disenchantment with parliamentary democracy. These alleged deficiencies of the British system of parliamentary democracy as it currently operates should not be mistaken for deficiencies of representative democracy as such. It follows that the best remedy may not be the enactment of a judicially enforceable bill of rights, but reform of the laws that govern the electoral process, the composition of the legislature, and the procedures and forms by which it must legislate. In other words, if the problem is that the electoral process, and checks and balances internal to the legislature, are now ineffective or non-existent, the best remedy may be to reconstitute or reinvigorate them. It is often argued that such reforms would be preferable to an American-style bill of rights on democratic grounds. Why not improve the system of representative democracy rather than diminish it even further? But less obviously, it can also be argued that such reforms would be preferable on rule of law grounds. They could make more effective review or veto of legislation part of the legislative process itself, taking place

---

[70] See A. L. Goodhart, 'The Rule of Law and Absolute Sovereignty', (1958) 106 *University of Pennsylvania LR* 943, 950–2.

[71] See Goldsworthy, n. 12 above, 7–8, 75, 105–6, 200–1, 234.

[72] K. C. Davis, *Discretionary Justice: A Preliminary Inquiry* (Baton Rouge, La.: Louisiana State University Press, 1969), chs. 3–5.

before legislation is enacted and relied on as law by the community. The alternative of a bill of rights inserts a power of legislative review and veto into subsequent judicial processes, where its exercise on grounds of political morality can have unpredictable, retrospective effects on legislation that has already been enacted, and may have been relied on as law.

VI. Conclusion

My objective has not been to discredit completely the idea of subjecting legislative power to judicially enforceable bills of rights. It has been merely to challenge one increasingly popular argument in favour of doing so: namely, that it is required by the rule of law. I have made the counter-intuitive argument that such a reform might actually detract from the rule of law. I do not claim that this argument is sufficiently powerful to be deployed as a positive argument against bills of rights. But it is useful in a defensive role, to refute the argument that bills of rights are required by the rule of law. Even if they do not detract from the rule of law, they are clearly not required by it. They are certainly not required by 'thin' conceptions of the rule of law, and even if a 'thick' conception is preferable, there are other ways of subjecting the exercise of legislative power to appropriate legal control. Perhaps, in the end, all I have succeeded in doing is to show that the issue is relatively unimportant, both because the rule of law is too indeterminate to provide useful guidance and because in this context other political principles, such as democracy and justice, are much more important. If so, I will be satisfied.

5

Incorporation through Interpretation

TOM CAMPBELL

In the absence of express language or necessary implication to the contrary, the courts therefore presume that even the most general words were intended to be subject to the basic rights
of the individual. In this way the courts of the United Kingdom, though acknowledging the
sovereignty of Parliament, apply principles of constitutionality little different from those
which exist in countries where the power of the legislature is expressly limited by a constitutional document. (Lord Hoffman)[1]

I. Introduction

The Human Rights Act 1998 is widely regarded as a characteristically British compromise, in this case between the giving human rights more weight in the UK polity
and preserving the constitutional primacy of the House of Commons.[2] Thus, the
HRA gives the higher courts the power to declare an Act of Parliament to be incompatible with the European Convention on Human Rights (ECHR), but not to render it invalid.[3] Only Parliament can change its own legislation, an unrestricted
constitutional right that, theoretically at least, remains intact. Similarly, while
courts, along with other 'public authorities' have a duty to conform to the ECHR,
a provision which is likely to prompt more adventurous development of the
common law, they can not override statutory law to achieve such objectives.[4] Nor
are they bound to follow, although they must take into account, the jurisprudence
of the European Court of Human Rights in so doing.[5]

---

[1] *R v. Secretary of State for the Home Department, ex p. Simms* [2000] 2 AC 115, at 131.

[2] Lord Lester of Herne Hill, 'The Art of the Possible: Interpretation of Statutes under the Human
Rights Act', (1998) 3 *European Human Rights Law Review* 665–75 at 668: 'The political compromise represented by an interpretive Bill of Rights of this kind was envisaged by Hersch Lauterpacht in his bril-
liantly original and prophetic study of the need for an "International Bill of Rights" published in 1945.'
See also Lord Irvine of Lairg, 'The Development of Human Rights in Britain under an Incorporated
Convention of Human Rights', [1998] *Public Law* 221, Sir W. Wade, 'Human Rights and the Judiciary',
(1998) 3 *European Human Rights Law Review* 520, and D. Feldman, 'The Human Rights Act 1998 and
Constitutional Principles', (1999) 19 *Legal Studies* 165–206 at 168–9.

[3] S. 4(2): If the court is satisfied that the provision is incompatible with a Convention right, it may
make a declaration of that incompatibility. S. 4(6): A declaration under this section ('a declaration of
incompatibility')—(a) does not affect the validity, continuing operation or enforcement of the provision
in respect of which it is given; and (b) is not binding on the parties of the proceedings in which it is made.

[4] S. 6(1): It is unlawful for a public authority to act in a way which is incompatible with a Convention
right.

[5] S. 2.

Compromise is also apparent in that courts are required to have the ECHR in mind when interpreting Acts of Parliament. This must be done so as to read such Acts, 'so far as it is possible to do so', in a way which renders the Act compatible with the ECHR.[6] This 'interpretation requirement', as I shall call it, encourages courts to read legislation on the presumption that Parliament intends to legislate in accordance with the ECHR, but courts cannot actually ignore or invalidate statutes that are perceived to be clearly incompatible with the Convention. The most that can be done, in such cases, is to issue a 'declaration of incompatibility', which enables the government to use a fast-track parliamentary procedure to amend the offending statute, should it wish to do so.

Despite this complex balancing of powers and the general appearance of moderation and compromise that permeates the text and politics of the HRA, I argue in this chapter that the impact of the HRA will severely diminish the effective authority of elected representatives of the British people. This is concealed by the fact that courts are required to interpret but not to override Acts of Parliament. However, the interpretation requirement, when seen in the context of the theories of interpretation that accompany the judicialisation of human rights, has the capacity to bring about de facto full incorporation of the ECHR to the point where courts are in practice able to overturn legislation that they deem to be in violation of their reading of the ECHR.

The frequently made assertion that the HRA incorporates the ECHR is strictly speaking misleading, since the incorporation involved is largely confined to matters of interpretation. Yet, the interpretive possibilities now available to the judiciary have the potential to bring about full incorporation of the ECHR. The scope and power of the interpretive techniques that are licensed by the HRA will makes judges the determinate body with respect to a wide range of policy issues which have hitherto been fully within the sphere of parliamentary responsibility. The HRA effectively incorporates the ECHR into British law through the interpretive norms that it brings with it. The Lord Chancellor is therefore mistaken in holding that, because the HRA takes an interpretive approach to fundamental rights, it is compatible with the tradition of Parliamentary sovereignty.[7]

Some HRA sceptics argue that the HRA will in practice make very little difference to the law of the UK beyond a small range of matters, such as the tightening of procedural protections for accused persons in criminal process. The conservatism and traditional deference of the British judiciary to elected governments will be enough, it is argued, to ensure that the HRA does nothing more than to reduce the incidence of embarrassing findings against British government by the European Court of Human Rights. While there will be a great deal of new legal activity and

---

[6] S. 3: So far as it is possible to do so, primary legislation and subordinate legislation must be read and given effect in a way which is compatible with Convention rights.

[7] Lord Irvine of Lairg, 'Activism and Restraint: Human Rights and the Interpretive Process', (1999) 10 *King's College Law Journal* 177–97 at 178, n. 3: 'It is this interpretive approach to fundamental rights which facilitates the coexistence of strong rights protection and respect for Parliamentary sovereignty.'

more complexity and expense in the British legal system through the addition of further grounds for legal argument, nothing much will change in relation to the protection and furtherance of human rights. My HRA scepticism is rather different. I argue that it allows an open-ended amount of judicial activism that has the potential to remove control over a broad range of issues from the domain of ordinary, non-legal politics. What actually transpires will depend crucially on the use that the judiciary makes of the central provisions of the HRA, but the constitutional scene is now set for the now legally legitimate but still democratically problematic exercise of greatly enhanced political power by judges in the British political system. Whereas it used to be commonplace to say that the absolute legal sovereignty of Parliament is in effect limited only by political considerations, the new interpretive powers granted to the courts by the HRA are powers that are now subject only to political factors, such as hostile public reaction to court decisions.

II. The scope of the interpretation requirement

Each of the central provisions of the HRA appear quite weak, and even together they may seem to be relatively insubstantial, even innocuous—no more than a quasi- or very partial incorporation of the ECHR. Parliament retains its sovereignty, the courts remain subordinate to the elected government and the ECHR is not directly a part of UK law. However, it may be difficult for governments to ignore declarations of incompatibility or to override through legislation alterations to the common law which have been made by courts with the explicit justification of rendering the common law compatible with the ECHR. At a time when judicially enforced 'human rights' have, in the eyes of the public and the media, greater political legitimacy than the outcome of partisan electoral political processes, governments may not wish to subject themselves to the politically damaging opprobrium which would arise from their ignoring a declaration of incompatibility or legislating to negate a development in the common law that has been presented as necessary to bring existing law into line with the ECHR. Being mindful of the prospect of an appeal to the European Court of Human Rights, and relieved to hand over responsibility for imposing morally controversial laws to the courts, governments are not, it is argued, likely to challenge changes to the common law or interpretations of Acts of Parliament which are said to derive from the provisions of the ECHR.

Nevertheless, these predictions may not unduly trouble the democratically minded citizen, since such effects are postulated on the assumption that governments will seek to avoid the electoral consequences of unpopular decisions, and that accords well enough with basic democratic norms of popular accountability. To be sure, it will mean that the HRA will give more political influence to courts with respect to setting agendas, but the ultimate determinations are made by Parliament, and this in the spotlight of media attention that itself can be regarded as a democratic enhancement. If courts come out with declarations of incompatibility and initiate common law developments that are unpopular, governments will suffer no electoral setbacks by ignoring or overriding them. This may make the anti-majoritarian goals of the ECHR more difficult to achieve, but this is not necessarily a serious concern to majoritarian democrats.

There are, however, more profound worries about the apparently balanced compromise provisions contained in the HRA. Some of these concerns arise from the fear that the interpretation requirement is much more potent than it looks. The instruction to read legislation 'in a way which is compatible with Convention rights' may appear to do little more than legitimate the standard practice of drawing on a number of external sources as aids to the interpretation of formally defective law, that is, law which is unclear, ambiguous, or in need of supplementation if it is to be effective.[8] On this view, it will make the ECHR, when relevant, the preferred 'third umpire' in cases of interpretive doubt, but it does not threaten to upset the standard practices of traditional statutory interpretation as they now operate, allowing the use of external materials and considerations when there is no available evident plain meaning.

The terms of the interpretation requirement suggest something much stronger than this.[9] Certainly, the parliamentary debates indicate a proactive role for judges which displaces the assumption that interpretation is a marginal aspect of adjudication which arises only in penumbral cases.[10] It seems clear that under the HRA legislation must, at the very least, be read from the perspective of the ECHR in something like the way that British courts view statutes as primarily additions to and only sometimes modifications of the common law, in that the presumption is that a statute does not alter the common law unless it explicitly and clearly does so on its face. In practice this means that an effort is made to see if there is a feasible meaning of the text of the statute which does not overturn existing common law and, if there is such a meaning, to adopt it as the 'correct' interpretation. More widely, this is an approach that can be taken to all new law on the grounds that this protects the cohesion and integrity of a legal system. Moreover, the same sort of

---

[8] See Sir A. Hooper, 'The Impact of the Human Rights Act on Judicial Decision-Making', (1998) 3 *European Human Rights Law Review* 676–86 at 686. While Hooper points out that, in some ways, statutory interpretation will be radically altered by the HRA, he argues that 'the higher courts are already very familiar with the Convention and have been reaching decisions which they would have reached post-incorporation'.

[9] The wording of s. 3 of the HRA is certainly stronger than the South African equivalent, which requires 'a reasonable interpretation of the legislation that is consistent with international law over any alternative interpretation that is inconsistent with international law' (Art. 233 of the Constitution of the Republic of South Africa, 1996), and probably stronger than the New Zealand equivalent: 'Wherever an enactment can be given a meaning that is consistent with the rights and freedoms contained in this Bill of Rights, that meaning shall be preferred to any other meaning' (Bill of Rights Act 1990, s. 6). Note also Lord Steyn in *R v. DPP, ex p. Kebeline* [1999] 3 WLR 972: 'Section 3(1) enacts a strong interpretive obligation.'

[10] Thus, the Secretary of State for the Home Department (Mr Jack Straw): 'we want the courts to strive to find an interpretation of legislation that is consistent with Convention rights, so far as the plain words of the legislation allow, and only in the last resort to conclude that the legislation is simply incompatible with them . . .' (HC Deb., 3 June 1998, cols. 421–2).

presumption applies in a stronger form to the displacement of established common law principles in the light of new legislation. Here the rationale goes beyond protecting the integrity of the legal system and is seen as offering some protection for fundamental rights.

In the case of the ECHR the parallel assumption would be that, unless the text indicates clearly to the contrary, there is strong presumption that statutes are read as if they were intended to be in accordance with the ECHR, which is a statement of fundamental rights that is sometimes said to be derived from traditional common law principles. The interpretation requirement will then work in much the same way as current principles of statutory interpretation, whereby statutes are construed so that they do not alter fundamental common law principles or rights unless there is a clear and unequivocal intention apparent in the text of the statute that has such effect.[11] Thus, implied overturning of basic common law is not permitted, although Parliament may alter any part of the common law provided it does so explicitly and clearly. If this approach is adopted with the ECHR, courts will make strenuous efforts to read statutes in ways which are compatible with the ECHR, but where there is an explicit and clear statutory text which is not compatible the ECHR then that text will be applied as law, notwithstanding that incompatibility, although, of course, a declaration of incompatibility may follow. There seems no doubt that a strong presumption of this sort is in accordance with a minimalist reading of the interpretation requirement.[12] Certainly, the view that Parliament will be taken to intend not to legislate contrary to the ECHR is underlined by the provision of the HRA that the government is required to make a 'statement of compatibility' on precisely this matter when introducing legislation.[13]

The rationales for maintaining traditional principles of common law, unless there is a clear parliamentary intention to the contrary that is manifest in the text of a statute, are similar to those for giving the ECHR a similar status, in that both may claim to be loci of fundamental principle. However, in the case of the common law, there is an assumption that there is in existence a relatively cohesive body of rules and principles whose coherence and integrity is to be maintained so that new law is fitted into this framework in a way which does not fragment the existing corpus of law. The same assumption cannot reasonably be made about existing ECHR jurisprudence, although it is to be expected that, in the leeway allowed in the HRA for departures from the body of case law derived from the ECHR, there will be a gradual merging of common law and British ECHR jurisprudence to produce a body of existing judge-made law that is more powerfully resistant to legislative alteration than is existing common law. This scenario fits with the common judicial

---

[11] See *Derbyshire County Council v. Times Newspapers Ltd* [1992] QB 770.
[12] Indeed, it has been put forward as the proper approach for UK courts to take to the ECHR well before the enactment of the HRA. See Lord Browne-Wilkinson, 'The Infiltration of a Bill of Rights', [1992] *Public Law* 397–410.
[13] S. 19(1).

contention that British common law is by and large completely compatible with the ECHR.[14] For this reason the ECHR may come to be seen more and more as closely associated with the common law for purposes of interpretation.

Again, democrats may not be unduly worried by such developments if these interpretive methods are undertaken in good faith, for they should act as a spur to increased clarity, directness, and openness in legislative drafting and enactment. This would make it easier for governments to be held to account for the legislative outcomes, and may generally improve the formal quality of legislation in which crucial issues are frequently fudged as the result of political compromises and poor legislative drafting. Parliaments have a duty to enact clear and unambiguous laws in terms of which they can be judged and held responsible by the electorate. The desirability of explicit and clear law reform is uncontroversial with respect to the idea of the rule of law, even if this ideal is often frustrated by the need to gain political consensus in favour of legislation with carefully constructed ambiguities.

Such a sanguine prognosis of the import of the interpretation requirement of the HRA follows from a belief that fundamental interpretive methods in British courts will be largely unchanged by the introduction of the HRA. Yet it cannot be assumed that traditional principles of interpretation will be followed, and courts will continue to apply statutes in accordance with their evident textual meaning. Currently, the orthodox method is still substantially in place, so that it is only where there is an ambiguity, or obscurity, that courts may look for guidance from external sources, such as Hansard, or the ECHR. Yet it cannot be taken for granted that the ECHR may be admitted to British courts for the purposes of interpretation without bringing with it the interpretive methods which go hand in hand with current rationales for having and deploying Bills of Rights. These methods give far less weight to textually evident meaning, and much more deference to the assumed purposive intentions of legislators with respect to the stated or assumed objectives of the legislation in question. If such purposes are now taken to include conformity with the ECHR, then it follows that the legislation whose compatibility with the ECHR is in question will from the start be read so as to make it compatible with the ECHR. In other words there will be no firm textual basis to serve as the clear and settled meaning of a piece of legislation against which to go on and raise the question of its compatibility with the ECHR. Legislation will already have been 'read down', implications drawn from the intention to comply with the ECHR will already have been 'read into' the text, even before issues of compatibility are addressed.[15]

---

[14] See Lord Browne-Wilkinson, n. 12 above, 465: 'It is now inconceivable that any court in this country would hold that, apart from a statutory provision, the individual freedoms of a private person are any less extensive than the basic human rights protected by the ECHR'. See also, *Attorney-General v. Guardian Newspapers Ltd (No. 2)* [1995] 1 AC 109, at 283. A worrying implication of this assumption is the implication that legislation amending current common law is immediately suspect as being in violation of the ECHR.

[15] See R. A Edwards, 'Reading Down Legislation under the Human Rights Act', (2000) 20 *Legal Studies* 353–71.

It follows that the HRA gives the ECHR a higher status than existing common law. Indeed, the expectation behind the Act as a whole would appear to be that the ECHR should begin to permeate the whole process of lawmaking and law application, to the point that it is not simply a set of side-constraints on law enacted with other objectives in mind but the favoured telos of all legislation and adjudication. Thus it will be expected of any enactment that it is an attempt to instantiate the ECHR and that it is a court's duty to carry this objective forward by reading legislation either narrowly or expansively in the light of the broad purposes of the ECHR itself. This will mean 'interpreting' legislation in a way which sits rather lightly on actual words, particular intentions or the traditional constraints thought to be set in place through deference to the plain and ordinary meanings of the legislation in question. The dynamic picture is not that of the ECHR as existing law to be modified from time to time by explicit legislation, a legitimate process comparable to clear legislative changes being made to the common law. Rather the ECHR is to be seen as directing, limiting, and augmenting legislation in a much more positive way than existing common law, with no assumption that legislation contrary to and overriding and replacing ECHR provisions is to be routine and intentional.[16]

This may seem rather fanciful to those steeped in the ideas of the distinction between legislation and adjudication and the division of powers between courts and legislatures based on that distinction. However, this would to be ignore the steady trend towards more open-ended interpretive methods increasingly deployed in British courts.[17] It is also unmindful of the impetus which will be added to this trend by placing the ECHR more firmly within the purview of ordinary courts. The new interpretive role of the ECHR is not a matter of introducing further legal materials on which existing interpretive methods are brought to bear, but involves the adoption of distinct interpretive methods which have been developed to deal with the particular problems which arise in applying abstract statements of rights to concrete cases. It is not simply that the quantity and range of the materials available for interpretation have been enlarged. Rather, the radical developments in store for British jurisprudence have much more to do with the further development of interpretive norms. Texts of statutes will come to be seen as no more than fallible and defeasible guides to ascertaining an implied legislative 'intent' in the light of the courts reading of the ECHR.

Those who have seen the adoption of more purposive methods of interpretation without apparent damage to the administration of justice may find such talk unnecessarily alarmist. Already it is generally accepted that interpretation must have regard to underlying purpose as well as evident meaning. Indeed, it is generally accepted that often enough the meaning of a legislative text is not evident if we are

---

[16] This is already evident in the substantive tests for administrative review where Convention rights are in point: *R v. Minister of Defence, ex p. Smith* [1998] QB 517 at 554 (concerning what is 'Wednesbury unreasonable'); see also *R v. Chief Constable of North Wales Police & Others* [1997] 4 All ER 691.

[17] A trend that has accelerated once it became acceptable for law officers to acknowledge openly the judicial role in lawmaking. See Lord Reid, 'The Judge as Law Maker', (1972) 12 *Journal of the Society of Public Teachers of Law* 22, and A. Lester, 'English Judges as Lawmakers, [1993] *Public Law* 269.

not aware of the background purpose of an enactment, the reasons why it was introduced, the objectives that its proponents have in mind, and the debates that went
on about its terms. Literal meanings are always to some extent relative to the pur-
poseful context which creates and sustains legislation.

Such purposive interpretation, which is aimed at understanding the meaning of
a text in the light of the context from which it emanates, is not inherently disturbing to democrats if the text that is being interpreted is the enactment of an
elected assembly. Indeed, attention to purposive context may well help to limit the
range of feasible meanings that may be given to a legislative provision in ways
which respect the democratic process. There are, of course, legitimate concerns in
cases where appeal is made to legislative 'purpose' in a way which draws on the
(perhaps suspect) ulterior purposes or motives of legislators. Further, insuperable
problems may arise in determining what exactly is 'the' purpose of any piece of
legislation. But in general the purposive approach has not made an enormous difference to interpretive practice, and where it has been in evidence this has often
been to the enhancement rather than the overruling of 'plain meaning' by bringing into focus the context in which the legislation was brought forward. To know
the problems being addressed, and to grasp the objectives of a piece of legislation,
often clarifies the text of an enactment and renders it more transparent at the point
of application.

The situation is very different when the purposes in question are not those of the
Act that is being interpreted but those which derive from the broad purposes
thought to be enshrined in the HRA itself. And, as we have seen, even in common
law jurisdictions it is accepted that the interpretation of abstract rights must be done
in an open and generous way so as effectively to protect the rights of those who are
vulnerable to the activities of the state. This is in part because of the very abstraction of these statements of rights, but is also affected by the court's view of its role
in providing effective remedies for human rights violations.[18] Interpretation in the
human rights context is an expansive and creative process governed by the assumed
functions of bills of rights, such as protecting the perceived interests of vulnerable
minorities and groups against the majoritarian pretensions, or upholding some
overriding and overarching principles of equality and justice, in a way which turns
legal reasoning, in this context, into a form of legally legitimated moral discourse.
Moreover, the view that constitutional rights have to be seen as enshrining developing moral and political standards negates the power of precedent in such settings.[19] Hence the injunction of the HRA that courts should 'take into account'

---

[18] This is evidenced by developments in Hong Kong that incorporated the International Covenant on
Civil and Political Rights: the Hong Kong Bill of Rights Ordinance 1991. See *Ng Ka Ling v. Director of
Immigration* [1999] 1 HKLR 315, 339–40, which rejects a 'literal, technical, rigid and narrow approach'
in favour of a 'generous interpretation of . . . constitutional guarantees'.

[19] The classic reference here is B. Cardozo, *The Nature of the Judicial Process* (New Haven, Conn.:
Yale University Press, 1921), 98–141. For an adaptation of this approach to the interpretation of the
ECHR, see *Tyrer v. United Kingdom* (1978) 2 EHRR 1.

rather than actually follow the decisions of such bodies as the European Court of Human Rights.[20] For such reasons, while the HRA may seem to confine the use of the ECHR to the interpretive function, it cannot control an expansive view of what counts as interpretation when it comes to reading and bringing to bear a list of fundamental rights and their associated jurisprudence.

Once this sort of textually relaxed and morally purposive approach is adopted with respect to human rights it will not be easily confined to the interpretation of those rights themselves, so that there will be a major impact on legal interpretation in general. Thus, in practice, there will be no clear line between identifying an ambiguity, gap, or other formal deficiency on the one hand and using extraneous material to deal with such problems on the other. The HRA will bring to bear the ECHR on the process of discovering and establishing that there is something resembling an ambiguity in the statutory text. The presence of the ECHR will therefore affect not only the resolution of formal deficiencies of domestic legislation but the creation of these perceived deficiencies. Now that interpretation via the ECHR is in place we will find that such open-ended interpretation comes to pervade the legal process in a quite imperialistic manner. Indeed, it is realistic to assume that the prime long-term impact of the ECHR will derive less from its content than from its displacement of the centrality of plain, literal, or ordinary meaning in favour of a textually unrestrained process of enforcing particular judicial views of the proper goals of a democratic society.

The opening up of the interpretive method which is part and parcel of the HRA is thus a more serious long-term threat to the protection and development of electorally based democracy than the projected deference of Parliament to declarations of incompatibility. The right of Parliament to determine the law of the UK appears better founded that the maintenance of current interpretive methodology, yet the former is vulnerable to the latter. At the extreme, Parliament may pass any legislation it likes in the plainest of terms and have this rendered null by courts that read the legislation in a 'possible' way that reflects a judicial reading of the ECHR. This is all the more likely to happen if, as is predicted, courts will be reluctant to make declarations of incompatibility.[21]

Further, the right of judges to interpret the law is as politically entrenched as the right of Parliament to make law. Interpretation is almost universally seen as the prerogative of the courts because it is part of adjudication, and that is taken to be their exclusive function. It is therefore not only politically difficult but also constitutionally questionable for parliaments to reject a court's particular interpretations or even question a court's interpretive methods. Judicial power that is built on the right to interpret is therefore not vulnerable to democratic pressures, although this could change as the public becomes aware of the nature of human rights interpretation.

[20] S. 2.
[21] As is foreshadowed in recent decisions such as *R v. Secretary of State for the Home Department, ex p. Simms*, n. 1 above.

If the increased judicial powers that are licensed by the HRA become in these ways invasive of legislative authority, this makes the HRA a more impressive instrument for containing elected governments, but it makes for greatly heightened fears as to its democratic credentials. From this perspective, the HRA may turn out to less of a compromise with than a capitulation to the courts. Thus, scepticism as to the feasibility of cabining the ECHR in the role of an interpretive aid follows from the expansive theories of interpretation which come with the global trend to legalize and constitutionalize moral rights. These theories of interpretation enable courts to take to themselves matters previously reserved for democratic decision-making as to how such moral rights ought to be concretized and implemented. This chapter expounds and illustrates this thesis, and suggest ways of heading off such developments before they take on the legitimacy of accepted judicial and constitutional practice.

III. Democratic scepticism

To appreciate the constitutional issues at stake in the way we approach the HRA, it is necessary to be aware of the principal democratic and rule-of-law qualms concerning judicially articulated bills of rights in general.

Central to the main arguments against bills of rights is the uncertain ontological and epistemological status of human or fundamental rights themselves. These difficulties do not concern the idea that some types of positive rights and duties be given a status which enables courts to use them to override other rights and duties, or even the idea that there are rights we might wish to ascribe to and secure for all human beings. Nor do they involve questioning the values embodied in the idea of human rights, such as equal human worth and the relief of suffering and domination. Rather, the difficulties arise when we try to reach agreement as to precisely what these higher-status rights should be and how the values we associate with human rights are to be understood and brought to bear on institutional arrangements and particular decisions. Whatever agreement can be reached at the level of abstract statements, the content, valence, and scope of particular human rights are incurably contestable when it comes down to giving them specific applicable meanings.[22]

This may appear a tendentious way to formulate the issue because it rules out the perspective that the prime task is to find out what these rights actually are, rather than to decide what they should be. From a traditional natural law perspective, for instance, the central task is to find out what our natural rights are and always have been, whether or not they have been recognized or observed in any particular society at any particular time.[23] On this view, we might accept a positivistic analysis of

---

[22] See T. Campbell, 'Human Rights: A Culture of Controversy', (1999) 26 *Journal of Law and Society* 6.

[23] Rooted in the classic natural law theories of Thomas Aquinas but developed in more secular terms throughout the Enlightenment period, the range of philosophers I have in mind include Hobbes, Locke, and Rousseau.

'fundamental rights' as those rights that are, as a matter of fact, given superior or protected status within existing constitutional arrangements, but keep the terminology 'human rights' for pre-existing and historically non-contingent entities called natural or human rights which serve as the grounds or justification for the fundamental rights that we have or ought to have. These human rights are moral entities that have an existence which is independent of human action or belief, and are as much a part of the structure of the universe as the entities whose existence is presupposed and investigated by the physical sciences. However, it is claimed, we do not need a scientific or other specialist training to have acquaintance with and knowledge of human rights, for they are the objects (or perhaps the presuppositions) of the universal human capacity for moral knowledge which is manifest in our foundational insights into or intuitions of moral truth. This means that we can hope to justify the ascription of fundamental rights on the basis that there are human rights that not only in some literal sense already exist but do so in a way which renders them accessible to our cognitive capacities.

Whatever the philosophical attractions of this ontology may be, no agreed method for obtaining knowledge of the specific content of human rights has established itself. Unless we accept that there are authorities with special knowledge of these rights to whom we should all defer, a belief in the existence of human rights is epistemologically and politically insufficient. While it is not possible to disprove the existence of such moral entities and it is possible to make some sense of the claim that there are such things if we adopt certain theological metaphysics which allow us to conceive of a timeless god or gods who have authorized or created such fact/norms, there is no generally accepted method or approach to 'discovering' what these entities are, apart from standard but inconclusive methods of everyday moral reflection and debate. We may simply believe on the basis of religious or some other form of external authority that there are such human rights of which those with the requisite authority have 'knowledge', but this is to reject the possibility of acquiring a philosophical or rational basis for such beliefs.

Of course other, less metaphysical, theories may be deployed to provide grounds for the intelligibility of the idea of ahistorical human rights and their superior moral legitimacy,[24] but these have the same epistemological deficiencies which leave disagreements about the content, form, and valence of human rights unresolved and lack the fallback position of religious or moral authority to make such determinations for us. Again, it is possible to withdraw from the modern imperative to provide objective justifications for moral and political positions and adopt a purely pragmatic posture towards the idea and legitimacy of human rights.[25] This form of postmodernism, which abandons the modernist pursuit of rational and universal justification but seeks to retain the form and rhetoric of such core enlightenment

[24] Recent attempts of this sort are epitomized by J. Rawls, *A Theory of Justice* (Oxford: Oxford University Press, 1971) and R. Nozick, *Anarchy, State and Utopia* (Oxford: Blackwell, 1974).

[25] See e.g. R. Rorty 'Postmodern Bourgeois Liberalism', in R. Hollinger (ed.), *Hermeneutics and Praxis* (Notre Dame, Ind.: University of Notre Dame Press, 1985).

concepts as human rights, is in a particularly weak position to deal with the contested pluralisms of contemporary human rights discourse.

In practice, epistemological disagreement means that we must put aside arguments about the existence or legitimacy of human rights as morally privileged entities or insights and address ourselves to the more tangible issue as to what rights we should adopt as the fundamental positive rights of all human beings and how we should go about making such decisions. This leads to deep and pervasive disagreements, but it does focus us on the sort of issue about which it makes sense to debate and settle between ourselves as best we can. And so we arrive back to the question of how we are going to go about deciding precisely what our positivized fundamental rights should be.

This may still be viewed as a contentious way of putting the matter, since it assumes that we should seek to be precise about fundamental human rights. But is this wise? Is the purpose of human rights discourse not to express broad social and political values on which we can all agree as the basis for legitimate government? Do human rights not represent a broad moral consensus about equality, liberty, fairness, toleration, ownership, justice, and life itself? It is the unhelpful demand to render these abstract concepts into something more precise, it may be argued, that leads to disagreement, division and even scepticism as to status of human rights generally. Should we not be content with statements of general rights that clearly capture our deepest moral commitments to life, liberty, and equality as the consensual basis for a civilized polity?

Certainly, highly abstract statements of rights can serve important social and political functions analogous to grand credal statements that can be affirmed as the condition of membership of a broad church, although even these usually contain historically important specifics and have given rise to sustained disagreements and bloody wars. Indeed, a prime role for human rights discourse, and one which may be lost in the move to positivize human rights, is to express broad value commitments which form a basis and inspiration for establishing more precise political objectives through debate, compromise, and working agreements. Once human rights are identified with a particular set of case law, for instance, there is the danger of diminishing its moral force and utility. Abstract affirmations of equality, liberty, community, the rule of law, and so on can be powerful rhetorical vehicles for engendering moral commitments in ways which help to moralize otherwise coercive and oppressive political systems and generate trust and cooperation that foster a sense of legitimacy.

However, this is not the role for human rights discourse that is envisaged by proponents of the HRA, who see judicial review of legislation as a crucial part of realizing human rights. This judicialization strategy requires courts to pronounce upon the sense and then the validity of legislation as applied to concrete situations, which involves giving sufficiently precise meaning to statements of abstract rights to determine highly specific controversies between particular legal persons. The demand for precision is the result of the move to justiciability that turns human rights from moral principles into rules that bind rather than ideals which inspire. The ambition for precision is laudable in that human rights ideals may make little difference to people's lives unless their particular sufferings can be authoritatively identified as unacceptable and remedies provided. Aspirational human rights lose much of their significance if they do not encourage action to remedy specific evils.

The ECHR does not, however, meet the standards of precision required for transparent judicial application. Statements of human rights such as the ECHR in themselves are far from precise, and the process of specifying their content in suf- ficient detail to begin to know how they apply to specific circumstances is both nec- essary and extremely difficult. We simply do not possess conceptions of individual human rights that are sufficiently clear, precise, and intelligible to guide and con- strain legal judgments by any process of reasoning that can be classified as legal 'interpretation' of a type that can be distinguished from general political and moral debate. Abstract statements of human rights do not make 'good' law because they suffer from the major formal defect vagueness and imprecision.

Again, this may appear contentious. There are respected theorists who canvass the benefits of having few, simple, and abstract laws which can be used by judicia- ries to reach humane, just, and efficient decisions in a flexible way in the light of the particular circumstances of those involved.[26] There is considerable hostility to the provision of specific rules to cover every circumstance on account of the technical 'legalism' involved which gets in the way of commonsense justice. On such a view what matters is impartiality, fairness, wisdom, and experience, qualities which are hindered and constrained by adherence to multiple, complex, and specific systems of law which fail to see the wood (justice) for the trees (the rules).

The contrary arguments for a more positivistic version of the rule of specific laws, according to which the important functions of law, such as the limitation of official power and the establishment of a clear system of interpersonal rules that can be administered and known without recourse to judicial determinations as to countless individual circumstances, are extensive and well known.[27] All that needs to be noted here is that the project of incorporating the ECHR is highly problematic in relation to these considerations. Moreover, this is not simply a matter of human rights com- ing into conflict with other values. The importance of the rule of law, as construed in concrete positive terms, has been central to certain ideas of liberty (the republican ideal of citizen assurance that they can act in the knowledge of what conduct is likely to attract sanctions) and democracy (that governments must act within the confines of existing laws). All these rights are themselves part of the human rights corpus.

Of course, it will be said that these problems will be addressed and solved through the development of a British human rights jurisprudence in which the

---

[26] e.g. J. Shklar, *Legalism* (Cambridge, Mass.: Harvard University Press, 1986) and, from a more pragmatic perspective, R. A. Epstein, *Simple Rules for a Complex Society* (Cambridge, Mass.: Harvard University Press, 1995).

[27] See e.g. F. Schauer, *Playing by the Rules: A Philosophical Examination of Rule-Based Decision- Making* (Oxford: Clarendon Press, 1991).

ECHR will be given justiciable form through incremental case law. This process will have a flying start through having to 'take into account' the human rights jurisprudence of the European Court, the European Commission of Human Rights, and the persuasive force of the prolific case law of jurisdictions throughout the world with similar entrenched rights. What we can expect is a British slant on a well-established and reasonably precise system of legal rules derived from previous legal decisions. Indeed, if this is not forthcoming then history will undermine one of the principal arguments for the HRA: that domesticating the ECHR will reduce adverse findings against the British government in the European Court of Human Rights.

Merely to state this position is to make clear how far the case law model of human rights is removed from the idea of abstract human rights as moral entities. To identify human rights with a historically contingent set of judicial decisions that may or may not accord with the variety of considered views as to what these rights may be is to gain the benefits of positivization to the detriment of using human rights as a basis for external moral critique of existing law. Can the moral force of human rights survive the process of juridification? Such questions turn our attention back on the issue of the 'interpretive' process whereby statements of abstract rights are shaped into a justiciable form that gives birth to a usable set of judicial determinations.

IV. 'Interpretation', human rights style

Just how far proponents of judicial review of legislation on the basis of bills of rights have developed the idea of what counts as legal interpretation can be gleaned from the work of the influential advocate of a bill of rights for Britain, Ronald Dworkin.[28] Any democrat who is comforted by the notion that the ECHR is 'only' an interpretive Act may be considerably discomfited on learning what such enthusiasts for judicially articulated and enforced bills of rights regard as within the legitimate scope of legal interpretation.

A principal attraction of Dworkin's[29] position is that he appears both to incorporate a measure of accommodation to existing law, in that every decision made by a court should 'fit' with the existing corpus of authoritative legal constitutions, enactments, and decisions, and at the same time to advocate a method of interpreting these materials so that they are 'the best that they can be' in terms of the underlying principles of the legal and political system in question. The 'fit' requirement serves to distinguish legal reasoning from other forms of practical reason, which are not

---

[28] R. Dworkin, *A Bill of Rights for Britain* (London: Chatto & Windus, 1990).

[29] There is no one Dworkinian position to be found within his extensive corpus. The brief overview given here is intended to reflect the common and influential understanding of Dworkin's position by those who see his theory of law as providing the basis for a model human rights adjudication. It draws largely on Dworkin, *Law's Empire* (London: Fontana, 1986).

constrained in this way, while the 'best' requirement provides the grounds on which a court can decide which of the many determinations that can reasonably be held to fit existing legal and political sources should be adopted in this particular case, there being no assumption that there is any one correct outcome from applying the criterion of fit alone, even when we apply the test of coherence or consistency to the mass of raw legal data.

The thesis, it should be noted, is not that a court should decide what decision is best overall. That would be too open-ended to count as legal reasoning and could have no precedential value. Rather, the decision has to follow from the best interpretation of the existing legal materials that are relevant to the case in point. The grounding in existing legal materials is what makes it the method 'interpretive', for interpretation, it is asserted, must be of a text.

On the other hand, the interpretation of these texts takes the form of a strenuous intellectual and moral analysis that is required if we are to give any legally useful and politically legitimate meaning to a text. Intellectually, the task is to bring together all relevant rules, principles, statutes, case law, legislative debates, and so on. Morally the task is to mould these into the coherent pattern that can be justified by reference to the underlying moral principles that provide the best justification for these historical materials. That justification of those materials is then applied to give an interpretation of the text in question that maximally furthers the objectives assumed by that justification. This is not a cut and dried process but a complex of moral reflection in which different and competing moral/legal principles are pitted and weighed against each other in an effort to provide a morally coherent outcome which Dworkin calls 'integrity'.[30] Even at the stage of determining the fit between an interpretation of a particular text and the accumulated legal materials, the judge is seeking a moral coherence which requires finding an interpretation that fits the principles that best justify that material. This moral telos becomes even more dominant as the judge comes to a final decision as to which reading of a text is best, once all these relevant facts and the foundational principle of the legal and political system have been taken into account. Relevant factors here include the integrity of the political system, its procedural fairness, and the beliefs of the community it serves. Ultimately, judges' 'interpretations' of legal texts are efforts to achieve a morally coherent decision that fits best into their interpretation of the values of the culture within which they operate.

The outcome may be to override the immediately relevant rules of law,[31] or to give an unexpected reading to a legal text in order to make it exemplify the justificatory principles at work in the law more generally. In Dworkin's examples, most of

---

[30] Ibid. 96: 'It [integrity] argues that rights and responsibilities flow from past decisions and so count as legal, not just when they are explicit in these decisions but also when they follow from the principles of personal and public morality the explicit decisions presuppose by way of justification.'

[31] Dworkin's most cited example of this is *Riggs v. Palmer* 115 NY 506, 22 NE 188 (1889). See *Taking Rights Seriously* (London: Duckworth, 1977), 23. This example is was used by Dworkin to exemplify the role of principles in adjudication. It now requires to be seen in the wider context of the theory of law as integrity.

the work in legal reasoning goes into deciding which interpretation is the best one, remembering that interpretation is not a matter of closer textual examination or of discovering and following the intentions of legislators. It involves bringing to bear on the text principles, such as equality and respect for persons, which are believed to offer the best justification of the existing body of law. Here the term 'justification' relates primarily to moral criteria of political relevance and not to any distinctively legal standards, although the whole idea of developing a morally coherent body of authoritative norms is Dworkin's own interpretation of what law is.

Importantly, there is no assumption involved that the body of legal material which counts as part of the raw material for interpretation is sufficiently consistent to meet any rigorous test of coherence, so that any justification will involve not only giving more weight to some legal data than to other parts of the historical aggregate of constitutional provisions, statutes, and case law but actually disregarding recalcitrant aspects of the tradition in question. 'Fit' does not apply to all the inherited material, but only to that part of it that is in accordance with the basic principles derivable from that system of law in the round. Clearly, there are elements of pick and choose here in that some precedents can be discarded, and countless decisions have to be made about what weight to ascribe to past enactments and decisions. This inevitably involves drawing on the personal preferences of the judges involved to determine which of the principles available within their legal and political culture seem to them to offer the most acceptable justification of the relevant law, although a judge is meant to discount any of his or her moral beliefs which are atypical. So, while the principles used to interpret a particular law are said to be derived from the body of law in question, they also serve to determine what constitutes the acceptable part of that law, a somewhat circular process which gives scope for enormous disagreement and generates considerable doubt about the Dworkinian belief that there is always one 'right answer' to such interpretive exercises.

For our purposes, it is important to note that, when it comes to applying the law, construed as being in accordance with the best justification of the legal data that survive this process of interpretation, it is incumbent on a court to modify the most immediately relevant law to the case in hand if it does not cohere with the interpretation favoured by the judge in question. This means that statute law can be overridden by the principles that have been found to underlie the common law, so interpreted, and even more so by provisions of the constitution as they are perceived in the interpretation in question. In consequence all legal cases are potentially 'hard' cases, for any legal decision may be called into question by the invocation of a moral principle developed in the process of deciding how existing law can be presented as the best that it can be.

While it is not exclusively directed towards constitutional law, Dworkin's account of legal interpretation has to be seen primarily as a model for interpreting and applying constitutional provisions. Here at least Dworkin makes it clear that, whatever judges may say to the contrary, legal reasoning is a form of moral reasoning.[32] Thus, he regards the American bill of rights as an invitation of moral judgment. This has the advantage of making sense of the idea of a 'best' interpretation of vague and inconsistent legal materials. It is also supported by his general criticism of the idea of law consisting entirely of legal rules that can be understood and applied without an element of moral assessment being involved. This is because the terminology involved in expressing legal principles, and indeed the very concept of law itself, are all 'interpretive' in his technical sense that there can be no agreed empirical criteria determining their correct application. It follows that, in this most fundamental area of law at least, moral judgment is the decisive ingredient, and hence, just because such law is fundamental or overriding, all legal judgment has a decisive moral aspect.

This brief account of Dworkin's theory of legal interpretation is presented as an important and influential example of what counts as legal interpretation within the human rights methodology of those who favour court-administered bills of rights. Such theories are vulnerable to the criticism that they extend the conception of 'interpretation' so far that they destroy the distinction between understanding and interpretation on which the tradition of positive law is founded. It can also be argued that there are alternative and better-grounded approaches which confine the role of judicial interpretation through giving much greater weight to the potential of enacting relatively clear and unambiguous rules which have democratic endorsement. Dworkin, it should be noted, contends that such systems are not available to us.[33]

It is not possible to follow through this debate here, but we can note the existence of powerful arguments to the effect that the sort of moral disagreements which Dworkin thinks are best settled in courts are more properly matters for political debate and decision. Accepting the importance of having a system of laws that is at least consistent in regard to what it prohibits and permits, and coherent in its moral goals, does not require us to accept that achieving this cohesion is a judicial duty which requires courts to substitute their moral vision for that of legislatures. The principal argument Dworkin uses to give judges this role is that the law, as a coercive system, must be rendered justifiable to its subjects, which can only be done by a 'community of principle' that does not give the last word to political majorities.[34] This, of course, dismisses alternative accounts of legitimacy in terms of the democratic source of legislation,[35] accounts that have to be put to one side in order to justify the interpretive mechanisms of the HRA. Conversely, Dworkin's theories have been relied upon in many arguments favouring the incorporation of the ECHR into British law. The HRA thus adds legitimacy to the adoption of Dworkinian styles of judicial reasoning in British courts, especially in relation to the ECHR.[36] For most

---

[32] See R. M. Dworkin, *Freedom's Law: The Moral Reading of the American Constitution* (Cambridge, Mass.: Harvard University Press, 1996).

[33] Dworkin, n. 29 above, chs. 4, 9.   [34] Ibid. 190–216.

[35] See e.g. J. Waldron, *Law and Disagreement* (Oxford: Clarendon Press, 1999).

[36] For an example, see F. Bennion 'What Interpretation is "Possible" under Section 3(1) of the Human Rights Act 1998?', [2000] *Public Law* 77.

advocates of judicial review of legislation, applying abstract human rights to concrete circumstances is ultimately a matter of applying general moral principles. Dworkin himself is perfectly open about this, as, increasingly, are his practitioner disciples.[37]

V. Interpretive possibilities

Where does this take our understanding of what it is to interpret an Act of Parliament as compatible with the ECHR 'where possible'?[38] In brief, my argument is that this provision can operate effectively only on the assumption of an approach to statutory interpretation that is in fact rejected by those who seek to juridify rather than democratize human rights. Only if we have an independent way of determining what a legal text means can we address the question of whether or not it is compatible with another text. And if that other text (in this case, the ECHR) is implicated in determining what the original statutory text actually means, this undermines the basis for comparing the two texts. The idea of what is possible or impossible in the interpretation of a statute is itself affected by the Convention with which courts are asked to compare the statute. In other words, at the extreme, in this context anything is 'possible' provided it can be believed to be in accordance with the ECHR.

'Possibility/impossibility' is a multifaceted concept whose meaning can vary from tight logical sense deriving from the notion of self-contradiction, through scientific meanings related to compatibility or incompatibility with established theory or overwhelming empirical evidence, to more everyday meanings of 'unlikely but feasible/not-feasible' or simply 'one of a number of likely or unlikely outcomes'. Thus, in everyday discourse, the injunction to do something 'if possible' can vary from 'do it if you have the capacity and opportunity to do so' to 'do it if it does not interfere with what you would have otherwise have been doing'. In interpretation, as it operates in relation to human rights, most things are 'possible' in the sense of compatible with an available and respected theory of adjudication. At the other extreme, in more interpretive contexts, 'possible' might be taken to require that the statements of law in question, when read according to their plain or natural meaning, should not logically contradict each other.

What limits, then, does 'where possible' place on a court which has to carry through the injunction to interpret a piece of legislation as being in accordance with

---

[37] Dworkin's account of 'integrity' may illuminate the rather obscure 'principle of legality' that has recently been introduced to justify activist interpretive methods. *See R v. Secretary of State for the Home Department, ex p. Simms*, n. 1 above, at 8, per Lord Steyn: 'In these circumstances even in the absence of ambiguity there comes into play a presumption of general application operating as a constitutional principle . . . This is called "the principle of legality"'. See also *R v. Secretary of State for the Home Department, ex p. Pierson* [1998] AC 539, at 573G–575D and 587C–590A.

[38] For an incisive and scathing analyses of this section of the HRA, see G. Marshall, 'Interpreting Interpretation in the Human Rights Bill', [1998] *Public Law* 167, and 'Two Kinds of Compatibility: More about Section 3 of the Human Rights Act 1998', [1999] *Public Law* 377–83.

the ECHR? The most restrictive meaning of 'possible' in this context, in the sense of the meaning with least impact on how statutes are interpreted in the UK, would be that reading a statute according to its plain, natural, or ordinary meaning comes out with a result that does not directly contradict the provisions of the ECHR as understood in the light of the relevant ECHR case law. On one side of the equation 'interpretation' is given a positivist rendering, giving prima facie priority to natural meaning of the statute. On the other side of the equation, no attempt is made to give justiciable meaning to a statement of abstract right, and full weight is given to particular decisions of the European Court of Human Rights as binding precedents. The injunction to make a reading which is compatible amounts in the simplest case to seeing whether the plain meaning of the statute is compatible with existing ECHR case law. On this view it is not possible to read a statute as in accordance with the ECHR if its natural meaning is in conflict with that of a precedential case. It would be 'possible' in the sense of feasible for the courts to abandon respect for natural meaning, or for existing linguistic practices, but this is not held to be 'possible' because it is illegitimate so to do. Unless there is lack of clarity, ambiguity, or evident absurdity, the natural meaning stands as the benchmark on both sides of the equation for establishing compatibility.

However, this strict and clear meaning of 'possible' is clearly not what the government intended in legislating the HRA.[39] Courts are expected to use their new interpretive powers to achieve readings of legislation which effectively protect Convention rights. There are, however, a variety of ways in which the idea of possibility in this context could be made more elastic and the bounds of possibility enlarged to serve the objectives of the Act. The question is whether the degree and form of elasticity that is adopted renders the apparent limits on judicial power ineffectual and takes us down the path of de facto full incorporation.

Thus, on the ECHR side of the equation, more emphasis could be given to the licence which is given to British courts to take account of but nevertheless go beyond the jurisprudence of the ECHR and develop a home-grown body of case law on the basis of independent ideas as to how the ECHR should be read and applied in the British context. There is enormous scope for revisiting and developing the abstract statements of right in the ECHR in accordance with the moral understandings of the judges involved and their view of the limits which can reasonably be placed on Convention rights in a democratic society. There is thus a large speculative aspect as to what it is that legislation is required to be compatible with. Nevertheless, a plain-meaning approach to legislation could provide many clear limitations on the actual application of these case law developments. If human

---

[39] See *Rights Brought Home: The Human Rights Bill* (Cm. 3782, 1997), para. 2.7: 'The Bill provides for legislation—both Acts of Parliament and secondary legislation—to be interpreted so far as possible so as to be compatible with the Convention. This goes far beyond the present rule which enables the courts to take the Convention into account in resolving an ambiguity in legislative provision. The courts will be required to interpret legislation so as to uphold the Convention rights unless the legislation itself is so clearly incompatible with the Convention that it is impossible to do so.'

rights-style interpretation is combined, on the other side of the equation, with a plain-meaning approach to statutory interpretation, then there is the potential for unforeseen and frequent declarations of incompatibility between legislation, traditionally interpreted, and an open-ended content of the ECHR as viewed through the moral lenses of British justices.

However, another and more likely outcome is a dearth of such declarations on account of the requirement that judges interpret statutes so as to make them compatible with whatever they take the ECHR to require.[40] Armed with Dworkinian methods of statutory interpretation in the shadow of fundamental rights, it will not be difficult to imply content into the text on the assumption that Parliament intended to legislate in accordance with the ECHR. The Lord Chancellor allows that apparently 'strained' meanings will be acceptable because they are not simply possible but desirable in terms of the objectives of the HRA. While he does not consider that the HRA will license readings which are 'fanciful' or 'perverse', it is clear that he would not apply these terms to readings which derive from an approved method of interpretation which seeks to make a statute 'the best that it can be'. Indeed, such creativity may be represented as the reverse of perversity and the height of judicial virtue, to be classified as 'imaginative, inventive and sympathetic' rather than fanciful.[41] If, with the Lord Chancellor's blessing, declarations of incompatibility are treated as a 'last resort', it will not be beyond the wit of the British judiciary to adopt highly constructive 'interpretations' of what others may see as texts with a good claim to have the sort of plain meaning which hitherto legislatures were taken to intend. All this could be regarded as in accordance with the 'spirit' of the HRA which carries with it not simply a text but an invocation to change the fundamentals of statutory interpretation.

Moreover, it is important to note the direction in which there is pressure to adapt meanings to obtain 'compatibility'. There is no suggestion that what is needed is a compromise between possible interpretations of statutes on the one side and the ECHR on the other. It is not that readings of the ECHR will be preferred if they are more in accordance with the statute in the same way as readings of the statute will be preferred if they are closer to the interpretation being given to the HRA. Rather, the idea is that it is the legislation rather than the ECHR that should bend to accommodate the goal of compatibility.

[40] Thus, Lord Cooke of Thorndon: 'Traditionally, the search has been for the true meaning; now it will be for a possible meaning that would prevent the making of a declaration of incompatibility' (HL Deb. 3 Nov. 1997, col. 1272). He has since put this into practice in *R v. DPP, ex p. Kebeline* [2000] 2 AC 326, where in his judgment the writings of a distinguished commentator are taken as sufficient evidence that what must be regarded as a 'strained' interpretation is 'distinctly possible': see n. 8 above at 9. For an early example in the context of the application of the ECHR through the Scotland Act 1998, see also *Brown v. Stott*, 2000 JC 328, at 354: 'The Solicitor General accepted that, since the section does not say expressly that the Crown can use the information in a prosecution, it would be possible to read the section restrictively, as simply permitting the police officer to require the keeper to give the information and not as permitting the Crown to use the information to incriminate the keeper at any subsequent trial.'

[41] HL Deb. vol. 583, cols. 535, 840, 306, 280. See Lester, n. 17 above, 271.

Taking this to its logical conclusion, we can see that there is no stable basis on either side of the equation in which statutes are to be compared with the ECHR to see if it is possible to make the two compatible by giving an appropriate 'possible' meaning to the legislation in question. Without a more or less positivist method of approaching legislation there can be no basis for claiming that the text of legislation will provide any sort of restriction on the judicial capacity to make it mean what they deem it good that it should mean. Indeed, the interpretation requirement does not really make sense in a judicial culture that gives no great weight to some conception of plain or contextually evident meaning. Some form of interpretive legal positivism, a theory which is largely incompatible with the philosophy of those in favour of human rights juridification, must be presupposed to give workable content to the injunction to read legislation 'wherever possible' as compatible with the ECHR.

In practice it is likely that the legislative text will be manipulated to make it compatible with judicial interpretations of the ECHR, with an even more interventionist approach to subordinate legislation. The most common tactic will be to read in exceptions to clear rules of law along the lines of 'except in so far as an application of the rule conflicts with the ECHR , as interpreted by the court'. Parliament could only effectively counter this device by an explicit statement that the provision applies 'notwithstanding the ECHR'.[42]

VI. A more democratic interpretation of the HRA

In order to preserve the democratic right of the citizens of the UK to determine the basic principles on which their society is to be governed and to have an equal say in how these principles are to be embodied in binding rules, it will be necessary to hold onto a plain-meaning approach to the interpretation of statutes, and to openly acknowledge that interpreting the ECHR is a matter of moral reasoning in which courts have no special expertise and in connection with which their decisions have no political legitimacy.

From this perspective, it would be best if declarations of incompatibility were to be seen as routine and unproblematic. If moral disagreement over what the provisions of the ECHR should be taken to mean is accepted as commonplace, because of the inherently controversial nature of the issues which call to be determined in making such interpretations, then courts should be regarded as having the right to make only provisional determinations of what it is that human rights asserted in the ECHR require us to do. These determinations may, with perfect propriety, be challenged and overturned by elected governments after public debate.

---

[42] This would be comparable to the Canadian Charter of Rights and Freedoms, s. 33(1): 'Parliament or the legislature of a province may expressly declare in an Act of Parliament or of the legislature, as the case may be, that the Act or a provision thereof shall operate notwithstanding a provision included in section 2 or sections 7 to 15 of this Charter.'

This approach, which preserves the ultimate human right of citizens to determine what their fundamental rights and duties are to be, can be conceptualized as giving them either the right to interpret the ECHR or to override that convention in the light of their understanding of what human rights and whose human rights are to be respected in their polity. The first approach will be preferred by those who equate the ECHR with its subsequent jurisprudence. The second approach will be preferred by those who see the ECHR as an evolving convention attempting to give progressive expression to a certain shared sense that there are moral human rights to which we must constantly seek to approximate. The result will be much the same either way, for both approaches place the democratic political process at the centre of the articulation of the controversial specific content of fundamental rights.

It is of considerable democratic importance that British judges should not see the interpretive opportunities licensed by the HRA as an occasion for regarding themselves as moral authorities, and that the interacting functions of the interpretation requirement and the declaration of incompatibility be accepted as giving legitimate scope for the involving everyone in the determination of fundamental rights. This requires that Parliament and people be able to hold judges to the public meaning of what is enacted as law by the legislature, and that it be accepted as politically as well as legally legitimate for Parliament to exercise its ultimate authority over the question of what nebulously expressed but crucially important fundamental values are to mean in the hard world in which coercion is used to enforce the views and interests of some people over those of others.

It may be objected that this approach will undermine the whole point of the HRA, which is to restrict the capacity of governments to abuse the human rights of vulnerable groups. Surely we do not want to allow even elected representatives to ignore and violate human rights? For all its rhetorical force, this argument simply bypasses the problem of what are to count as human rights and what are to count as violations of them. The unavoidable question is: whose interpretation of 'human rights' should prevail when it comes to the decisions that are enforced as law? There are, of course, good reasons for not giving the authority to determine such questions to anyone, since we may disagree with their opinions on the matter, an argument which applies to granting anyone political power. Indeed, human rights are introduced into political systems precisely because of the fallibility and corruption of elected governments. But the problem of giving final powers of review to another branch of government is that it too may get it wrong, ignore abuses of human rights, and perpetrate injustice in its turn. Judges may appear relatively benign and enlightened, perhaps because they are not subject to the pressure of elections, but when their decisions are widely believed to be unacceptable, perhaps because of the limited moral vision and practical experience of what is in effect an elite corpus of lawyers, they are not accountable or subject to replacement and correction beyond the sphere of their own peers.

These debates take us beyond the analysis of the HRA to the whole question of the benefits and drawbacks of having entrenched bills of rights. That this is where my argument has led amply illustrates the point of this chapter: to demonstrate that all these basic constitutional issues are indeed relevant to the HRA, which, despite its mild and compromising appearance, substantially incorporates the ECHR into British law. In evaluating the HRA we must, therefore, engage in the larger constitutional debate as to the locus of ultimate political power. If we wish to confine the HRA to an interpretive role that does not override legislative authority and to ensure that the development of human rights in the United Kingdom expresses the developing moral convictions of the British people, then we need to focus directly on the right of Parliament and people to have a binding view as to what is to count as a 'possible' legal 'interpretation' in the performance of the judicial role, particularly with respect to the ECHR.

6

The Unbalanced Constitution

K. D. EWING

I. Introduction

In apparently blissful ignorance of the obvious oxymoron, the *Times* Law Report of *County Properties Ltd v. The Scottish Ministers* appeared under the headline 'Company's human rights were abused'.[1] Yet only the naive will be surprised that an attempt has been made by corporate interests so soon to capture the Human Rights Act 1998: its importance for commercial practice was quickly identified by city solicitors representing business clients,[2] the issue has been the subject of a published lecture by N. Bratza QC, the British judge on the European Court of Human Rights,[3] and the Act has already been used by the corporate lobby to dilute legislative attempts to control corruption in the City. Nothing new here. Similar instruments have been used in other jurisdictions by similar interests for similar purposes. In Canada it was a corporation (not workers or consumers) which used the freedom of religion guarantees in the Charter of Rights to strike down Sunday trading legislation; it was a corporation (not consumers or health care professionals) which used the freedom of speech guarantees of the Charter of Rights to strike down restrictions on tobacco advertising; and it was a corporation (not voters or candidates) which used the same guarantees of the Charter of Rights to strike down election spending restrictions previously introduced in the interests of political equality.[4]

So there is a lot to be sceptical about. But we might also be sceptical about the distorted vision of human rights which the Human Rights Act reflects. Modern European democracies which have rebuilt their constitutions in the last fifty years or so have taken a broader view of the discipline, embracing the apothegm in the preamble to the Council of Europe's Revised Social Charter that human rights are indivisible. This in turn is a clear recognition of the unalterable truth of Rousseau's famous aphorism that there is a need for 'a large measure of equality in social rank and fortune, without which equality in rights and authority will not last long'.[5] So

---

[1] *The Times*, 19 Sept. 2000. On a similar point in a not unrelated field, see *R v. Broadcasting Standards Commission, ex p. BBC* [2000] 3 All ER 989. See now *R v. Secretary of State for the Environment, Transport and the Regions* [2001] UKHL 23.

[2] See K. D. Ewing, 'Trade Unions and their Human Rights in Britain', (1998) 48 *Federation News* 1.

[3] N. Bratza, 'The Relevance of the Human Rights Act for Commercial Practice', (2000) 5 *European Human Rights Law Review* 1.

[4] *R v. Big M Drug Mart* (1985) 18 DLR (4th) 321, *RJR-MacDonald Ltd v. Canada* (1995) 127 DLR (4th) 1, and *National Citizens' Coalition Inc. v. Attorney General for Canada* (1985) 11 DLR (4th) 481.

[5] J.-J. Rousseau, *The Social Contract*, bk. iii, ch. 4.

we find in many modern European social democracies a constitutional commitment (variously expressed) to the general welfare of the community: at work and during periods of interruption from work; in housing, health care, and social security; and in retirement. We also find a commitment to social rights and the principle of solidarity by the architects of the new European constitution.[6] But does it matter that there is no such reference in the British constitution or that the incorporation of Convention rights into domestic law is not balanced by the incorporation of social rights? The aim of this essay is to show that it does: by dividing the indivisible there is a danger paradoxically of both undermining and diminishing the human rights of the many, at the expense of the human rights of the few.

II. The common law and legislation

The effect of the Human Rights Act is to create a new hierarchy of rights in British constitutional law. One of the great virtues of the British constitution—and parliamentary sovereignty as one of the two foundation principles—has been its relative neutrality. There is of course no such thing as a truly neutral constitution: all constitutions reflect certain economic structures, and are designed to ensure the political influence of dominant economic interests. But for those wishing to promote social change, the British constitution provided one of the best opportunities for this to be done, particularly after the introduction of universal suffrage and the reform of the House of Lords in 1911 and 1949.[7] True, the 'political supremacy of the working class' has not been the 'inevitable result' of the former (universal suffrage) in Britain any more than elsewhere.[8] British constitutional arrangements nevertheless provided the best means for social reform in the sense that there were no institutional restraints on a legally sovereign legislature and a politically sovereign electorate. And the best means also for social reform in the sense that the hierarchy of rights in the British constitution did not distinguish between rights according to their substance, but only according to their source. So unlike in other constitutional regimes, there was no priority in the British constitution for civil and political rights over social and economic rights. Priority was accorded to legislation at the expense of the common law.

The common law and liberal values

For those seeking to promote a radical social agenda, this is a distinction of great importance, particularly having regard to the nature of the common law which gives

---

[6] Charter of Fundamental Rights of the European Union, 7 Dec. 2000.

[7] Parliament Acts 1911–49.

[8] K. Marx, 'The Chartists', *New York Daily Tribune*, 25 Aug. 1852, repr. in S. K. Padover (ed.), *The Essential Marx: The Non-Economic Writings* (New York: Mentor, 1978), 48. See R. Miliband, *Parliamentary Socialism* (London: Merlin Press, 1961).

rise to several points of concern. The first is the unequivocal commitment to liberty as a fundamental principle: not so much political liberty which has never been a robust principle of the common law,[9] but economic liberty which enables parties to contract as equals, without regard to the relative differences in their position. So far as employment is concerned, parties are free to contract on whatever terms they like, and although there are implied terms which regulate the content of the contract, crucially there is no implied term that workers should be paid a fair wage. So while slavery is not permitted, there is no line drawn at wage slavery. The market would determine the 'wage minimum',[10] but the common law would not determine a 'minimum wage'. It was a question of liberty and a matter of choice. People were free to work for subsistence wages if they chose to do so, and to do so in unhealthy and dangerous conditions if that was also their choice.[11] The parties were also free to contract in a manner which violated what some would regard as human rights: free to discriminate between men and women; and free to discriminate on the grounds of race.[12] Indeed, public authorities were constrained by common law principles—borrowed from equity—to contract on a basis which reflected a total disregard for human rights: discrimination against women was not only permitted by the law but in some circumstances actively required.[13]

The second concern with the common law is the converse of the first: its lack of commitment to equality as a constitutional principle, except as a rhetorical figleaf.[14] This is reflected in a number of ways: most obviously in the freedom of individuals to contract with whom they like, and on what terms they like; but secondly and more subtly in its unwillingness to accommodate social institutions which would ameliorate social inequalities. Perhaps the greatest equalizing force in liberal society is the trade union.[15] But so far as the common law is concerned, trade unions are illegal, as being in restraint of trade. It might well be protested that such comments are ridiculous: the authority for that proposition is a case in 1867;[16] the common law

---

[9] See K. D. Ewing and C. A. Gearty, *The Struggle for Civil Liberties: Political Freedom and the Rule of Law in Britain, 1914–1945* (Oxford: Oxford University Press, 2000), ch. 1.

[10] K. Marx, *Wage Labour and Capital*, repr. in K. Marx and F. Engels, *Selected Works* (Moscow: Progress Publishers, 1968), 72.

[11] But see *Smith v. Charles Baker & Sons* [1981] AC 325.

[12] For a good account of the common law, see A. Lester and G. Bindman, *Race and the Law* (Harmondsworth: Penguin, 1970), ch. 1.

[13] *Roberts v. Hopwood* [1925] AC 578. See J. A. G. Griffith, *Judicial Politics since 1920* (Oxford: Blackwell, 1993), ch. 1.

[14] Cf. J. Jowell, 'Is Equality a Constitutional Principle?', (1994) 47 *Current Legal Problems* 1, and B. Hepple, 'Social Values in European Law', (1995) 48 *Current Legal Problems* 39.

[15] Recent evidence in the UK and the USA suggests that workers in unionized enterprises are likely to have higher income levels than their counterparts elsewhere. It is also the case that the equality gap is narrower in Europe (excluding the UK) than elsewhere, with European countries having extraordinarily high levels of collective bargaining coverage. On this last point, see ILO, *World Labour Report 1999* (Geneva: ILO, 2000), 248.

[16] *Hornby v. Close* (1867) LR 2 QB 153. For an account of the implications of the case, see H. Pelling, *A History of British Trade Unions*, 2nd edn. (Harmondsworth: Penguin, 1971), 64–5.

has moved on. But the protest would be in vain: in 1994 the Court of Appeal reminded us forcefully that so far as the common law is concerned, trade unions are in restraint of trade, a reminder all the more significant for the fact that it was delivered by a person who is now a Lord of Appeal in Ordinary.[17] But of course it is not only the existence of trade unions which the common law was unable to accommodate: the same is true of their activities. In the memorable words of Sir William Erle, 'Every person has a right under the law as between himself and his fellow subjects to full freedom in disposing of his own labour or his own capital according to his will.'[18] Again it is true of course that these are old authorities, and that the courts have now recognized that the right to strike is a basic human right.[19] Yet it is a human right for which there is no space in the common law: it remains a breach of contract to take part in a strike,[20] and tortious to induce a breach of that contract.[21]

Legislation and social values

Although the common law thus betrays a commitment to economic liberty at the expense of other principles, it has been possible through legislation to find space for these other principles. It is through legislation that political liberty has been established as a constitutional principle, often in the face of common law restraints. This is true above all of the right to vote, the right to form a political party to represent particular interests,[22] and the right to stand for election on equal terms with others. But it is not only liberty which has been expanded by legislation. So too has equality, both in terms of political equality and social equality (the latter being a precondition to the former).[23] So far as political equality is concerned, we can point to the abolition of plural voting, the spending limits on candidates and parties in an election, and the broadly equal size of parliamentary constituencies.[24] So far as social equality is concerned, it is through legislation that social institutions (such as trade unions) have been released (though now only to a limited extent) from the thrall of the common law; and that fundamental social values have been established to modify the principles of liberty to be found in the common law: a minimum wage,

---

[17] See *Boddington v. Lawton* [1994] ICR 478 (Nicholls LJ).

[18] Quoted by Lord Brampton in *Quinn v. Leathem* [1901] AC 495.

[19] *London Underground Ltd v. RMT* [1995] IRLR 636, at 641.

[20] *Miles v. Wakefield MDC* [1987] 1 All ER 1089, at 1097 (per Lord Templeman).

[21] For a full account, see J. Hendy QC, 'Industrial Action and International Standards', in K. D. Ewing (ed.), *Employment Rights at Work: Reviewing the Employment Relations Act 1999* (London: Institute of Employment Rights, 2001), ch. 4.

[22] See e.g. the Trade Union Act 1913, reversing (with qualifications) *Amalgamated Society of Railway Servants v. Osborne* [1910] AC 87.

[23] Equality is not the only principle jostling for attention, and indeed recognized in different ways in our constitutional order. It has been suggested in Canada that fraternity is a constitutional principle, albeit from a part of Canada with a rich tradition in continental Europe. See Mr Justice C. D. Gonthier, 'Liberty, Equality, Fraternity: The Forgotten Leg of the Trinity, or Fraternity: The Unspoken Third Pillar of Democracy', (2000) 45 *McGill LJ* 567, a treat for those of us weaned on the thin gruel of English extrajudicial writings.

[24] For full details, see R. Blackburn, *The Electoral System in Britain* (Basingstoke: Macmillan, 1995).

fair(er) working conditions, rent control and social housing, universal health care, social security, and retirement pensions.

Few would make claims about the adequacy of any of these measures, and in all cases there is room for significant improvement and the raising of standards. Yet none of these gains would have been made by the common law, and they were often made to overcome common law restraints. Their importance for our purposes, however, is that neither the establishment of social measures by legislation nor their improvement or enhancement had to be justified by reference to a higher law: they had no subordinate status as a matter of constitutional law. But they did have to be construed and applied by the courts. And here we encounter a further difficulty, in terms of the enduring impact of the influence of the common law. For here we find that the values by which the common law is informed are also the values brought to bear in the construction of social legislation: such legislation is seen by the courts as a threat to the principles which they have developed by the medium of their own legislative powers (the common law is a legislative process). Who can forget Lord Diplock's comments about legislation complying with international human rights standards which allowed trade unions to take secondary action in support of workers involved in a dispute with their employer? It is not only that the legislation 'tended to stick in judicial gorges', but also that the immunity from tort (as if the common law had some divine quality or unalterable truth) 'was intrinsically repugnant to anyone who has spent his life in the practice of the law or the administration of justice'.[25] But although particularly memorable to a particular generation, resistance of this kind (rarely expressed with such reckless abandon) is by no means isolated.[26]

III. The Human Rights Act 1998: a new hierarchy of rights

So there is no such thing as a neutral constitution. Every legal system will have a constitutional structure and a framework of legal principles which will benefit the interests of some members of the community more than others. This is true of the United Kingdom as of other communities, though with an important difference. The principle of parliamentary sovereignty provided an opportunity in theory for political sovereignty to be asserted by the majority and for that sovereignty to be

---

[25] See respectively *Express Newspapers Ltd v. McShane* [1980] ICR 42, at 57, and *Duport Steels Ltd v. Sirs* [1980] ICR 161, at 177.

[26] Recently we had *Associated Newspapers plc v. Wilson* [1995] 2 All ER 100, in which the House of Lords reversed two decisions of the Court of Appeal to hold that an employer could discriminate against a trade unionist on matters relating to pay where he refused to enter into a personal contract. Lord Browne-Wilkinson reached this conclusion (on a point on which two members of the court dissented, though they also found for the employer) in the knowledge that 'it leaves an undesirable lacuna in the legislation protecting employees from discrimination' (112). The decision led to findings against the UK by the ILO supervisory bodies as violating ILO Convention 98, and by the Council of Europe's Committee of Independent Experts operating under the Social Charter. Both treaties were cited by counsel, but neither was referred to in any of the speeches delivered by the court. See generally K. D. Ewing, 'Dancing with the Daffodils', (2000) 50 *Federation News* 1.

used to displace the common law.[27] But that relationship has been disturbed by the Human Rights Act, which, although it does not formally empower the courts to strike down legislation, does nevertheless give them power over both primary and secondary legislation of a hitherto unprecedented nature. What is worrying about this is the perception on the part of (at least some of) the judges that there is no difference between Convention rights and values on the one hand and common law rights and values on the other.[28] Indeed 'much of the Convention reflects the common law'.[29] The obvious problem which this creates is that it reinforces the liberal values of the common law, at the expense of other political values and constitutional principles. In particular it thereby gives a formal legal priority to liberty at the expense of equality. Although it is true that other constitutions have similarly entrenched (or in our case semi-entrenched) rights, in modern constitutions this is balanced by what Spanish lawyers refer to as provisions designed to secure substantive equality.[30]

Liberal rights reinforced

So what we now have is a situation in which social and other rights designed to promote substantive equality or the institutions of substantive equality are to be tested in accordance with the renewed and reinvigorated values of the common law which they are designed to displace. Although it would have been possible to have given an equal constitutional status to both of the Council of Europe's principal human rights treaties, we have chosen deliberately to confound what the preamble to the Revised Social Charter of 1996 refers to as the indivisibility of human rights. In the process we have chosen deliberately to create a new hierarchy of rights which is based as much on the substance of the rights as on their source. Civil and political rights have a new priority over all others. Convention rights will trump all other considerations, and with them the individually oriented focus which they bring. In some cases, it is true, it will be possible to defend any laws or practices which violate Convention rights if it can be shown that they are 'necessary in a democratic society' on a number of prescribed grounds which vary from article to article. But just as the rights themselves are vague and open-ended (a remarkable power of veto and restraint in itself), so there is no guidance in the Act or in the Convention about what is meant by 'a democratic society'. These are matters which we have handed

---

[27] For a valuable reassessment of the principle of parliamentary sovereignty, see A. W. Bradley, 'The Sovereignty of Parliament', in J. Jowell and D. Oliver (eds.), *The Changing Constitution*, 4th edn. (Oxford: Oxford University Press, 2000), ch. 2.

[28] H. Woolf, 'Judicial Review: The Tensions between the Executive and the Judiciary', (1998) 114 *Law Quarterly Review* 579.

[29] *R v. Home Secretary, ex p. Simms* [1999] 3 All ER 400, at 412, per Lord Hoffmann. See also his 'Human Rights and the House of Lords', (1999) 62 *Modern Law Review* 159.

[30] M. Alonso Olea and F. Rodriguez-Sanudi, 'Spain', in R. Blanpain (ed.), *International Encyclopaedia for Labour Law and Industrial Relations*, xii (Deventer: Kluwer, 1996), para. 9.1.

to the judges to decide, to impose their own view not only on the content of the rights but on when in the interests of democracy they may be restrained.[31]

This curious retreat for progressive forces begs many questions, including the following, though there are doubtless others:

- Why should the outcome of the democratic process (legislation) be subject to scrutiny by those (judges) who are in general not part of the process of democratic election and accountability?
- Why should the outcome of the democratic process (legislation) be determined on the basis of standards of democracy determined by those (judges) who are not accountable for the values they develop and impose on the rest of the community?
- Why should the people be denied the opportunity to determine the nature of the democracy in which they wish to live, particularly as modern Europe presents us with competing visions, both in terms of principles and procedures?

These concerns about process and procedure barely mask the related concerns about the substantive values which will be imposed by those to whom the responsibility for determining the nature of a democratic society has been shifted. Why should we expect the judicial vision of democracy to be very different from the values of the common law (with its emphasis on liberty further reinforced by the Convention) which the judges shape and mould? And why should we do anything but assume that those who have 'spent their life in the practice of the law or the administration of justice' will consider the values of the common law to contain the fundamental building blocks of a democratic society?

Liberal visions of democracy

So restraints on liberal rights will now have to be justified as being necessary in a democratic society. But neither the ECHR nor the Human Rights Act 1998 guide us as to the meaning of democracy for this purpose: the issue is at large and we are all at sea. It might be thought that the matter is one on which the ECHR would by now have a developed view. But there is precious little guidance in the jurisprudence of the Court.[32] Indeed, the matter has hardly advanced since the *Sunday Times* case in 1974, when it was said that the tolerance, pluralism, and broad-mindedness were hallmarks of a democratic society. But this is what they are: hallmarks; no more, no less. The Strasbourg court's vision of democracy to date is one which is dominated

---

[31] For one view, see J. Laws, 'The Constitution: Morals and Rights', [1996] *Public Law* 622. For another, see S. Sedley, 'The Sound of Silence: Constitutional Law without a Constitution', (1994) 110 *Law Quarterly Review* 270, 'Human Rights: A Twenty-First Century Agenda', [1995] *Public Law* 386, and *Freedom, Law and Justice* (London: Stevens, 1999). For a critique, see J. A. G. Griffith, 'The Brave New World of Sir John Laws', (2000) 63 *Modern Law Review* 159, and 'The Common Law and the Political Constitution', (2001) 117 *Law Quarterly Review* 42.

[32] For two valuable accounts, see A. Mowbray, 'The Role of the European Court of Human Rights in the Promotion of Democracy', [1999] *Public Law* 703, and C. A. Gearty, 'Democracy and Human Rights in the European Court of Human Rights: A Critical Appraisal', (2000) 51 *Northern Ireland Legal Quarterly* 381.

by a concern that political parties should be permitted to operate freely, on the ground that they 'represent their electorate, draw attention to their preoccupations and defend their interests',[33] and because of the 'essential role' of political parties 'in ensuring pluralism and the proper functioning of democracy'.[34] It is a vision which is dominated also by a concern that government in particular should be exposed to scrutiny and criticism,[35] and that public officials should be politically neutral.[36] There is a strong commitment further to press freedom, the press being seen to perform a 'vital role of "public watchdog" in imparting information of serious public concern'.[37]

These are clearly important developments. But there are also other fundamental issues at stake: questions about underlying principles, and questions about institutional design. So far as the former are concerned, there are deep questions about the nature and content of these principles, to say nothing of the weight they are to bear in any particular case. But what are the underlying principles of democracy from which judgments can be made about whether a restriction on a Convention right can be justified? For example, is equality a principle of democracy for the purposes of the ECHR? If so, what does it mean? Does it mean legal equality in the sense of a formal equality before the law? Does it mean political equality, in the sense of an equal opportunity to take part in the political process, and to influence political outcomes? Does it mean social equality, in the sense of a minimum standard of social and economic power relative to others in the community, and the protection and promotion of institutional forms which will maintain and protect that power? There are no answers to these questions in the jurisprudence. The best we have is an acknowledgement of 'the principle of equality of treatment of all citizens in the exercise of their right to vote and their right to stand for election', heavily compromised by a statement that this does not mean that 'all votes must necessarily have equal weight as regards the outcome of the election or that all candidates must have equal chances of victory'.[38]

Liberal democracy and social rights

So we are faced with a formal re-allocation of priority in terms of the substance of constitutional rules: liberty at the expense of equality; or what T. H. Marshall

[33] *Incal v. Turkey* (1998) 29 EHRR 449, 480.
[34] *United Communist Party of Turkey v. Turkey* (1998) 26 EHRR 121, 147.
[35] *Ceylan v. Turkey* (1999) 30 EHRR 73.   [36] *Ahmed v. United Kingdom* (1998) 29 EHRR 1.
[37] *Bladet Tromsø. Norway* (1999) 29 EHRR 125, 167.
[38] *Mathieu-Mohin v. Belgium* (1987) 10 EHRR 1, 17. The Court also stresses that 'the choice of electoral system by which the free expression of the opinion of the people in the choice of legislature is ensured—whether it be based on proportional representation, the first past the post system or some other arrangement—is a matter in which the State enjoys a wide margin of appreciation' (*Matthews v. United Kingdom* (1999) 28 EHRR 361, 403). See also *Bowman v. United Kingdom* (1998) 26 EHRR 1: the Court is not prepared to allow the need to maintain a strict financial equality between parliamentary candidates (to stop corruption and the buying of elected office) to trump all other considerations.

referred to as civil and political rights at the expense of social and economic rights.[39] In this sense what we see is a historic retreat from the path which Marshall identified:[40] it is becoming overgrown and obstructed.[41] It is true of course that there is no *absolute* priority for so-called civil and political rights in the sense that they can be restrained to promote some pressing need. But, as we have seen, there is so far no recognition in the jurisprudence that social equality is a fundamental principle of democracy; and in any event the onus is on the party imposing the restriction to make out that it is necessary in a democratic society for a purpose set out in the Convention. This in a sense reinforces further the priority of liberal principles: if we want to introduce limits on how much money corporations can spend in a referendum in the interests of political equality,[42] or if we want to restrict private property rights by giving trade unions access to an employer's premises in the interests of social equality,[43] the onus is on the person imposing the limit on liberty, not on those who wish to maintain limits on equality. State initiatives to promote social equality must now overcome an additional hurdle.

It is also true, however, that the ECHR and the Human Rights Act have the capacity to enhance social rights in limited respects. A good example recently is *R v. North and East Devon Health Authority, ex p. Coughlin*,[44] where Article 8 was invoked in judicial review proceedings to assist an elderly woman whose publicly run home was being closed. What cases such as *Coughlin* reveal is that the state as provider of public services may be regulated by the Human Rights Act in the allocation of these services. Yet it is still not the case that the state is under a duty to provide public services, such as housing. By focusing on the state as provider, we may be tempted to deflect our attention from the central point about social rights, which is that they are designed not only to impose duties on the state on behalf of the community as a whole but also to regulate the exercise of private power: the power of the employer, the landlord, and the supplier of goods and services. The purpose of social rights is to regulate these relationships in private law by legislation, and the danger created by the Human Rights Act is that regulation of this kind will be undermined rather than facilitated by a device which seeks to restore the values of liberty on which these relationships in private law are based, and which are the object of regulatory schemes. In other words, there is a danger that the Human Rights Act will provide a shield for the bearers of private power who are the targets of social regulation.

[39] T. H. Marshall, *Citizenship and Social Class* (Cambridge: Cambridge University Press, 1950).

[40] On which see K. D. Ewing, 'Democratic Socialism and Labour Law', (1995) 24 *Industrial Law Journal* 103.

[41] See A. Giddens, *Beyond Left and Right* (Cambridge: Polity Press, 1994), ch. 2; and *The Third Way* (Cambridge: Polity Press, 1998), 70–2. But for an interesting reassessment of Marshall's work, see R. Lister, 'Citizenship, Exclusion and the "Third Way", in Social Reform', (2000) 7 *J. of Soc. Sec. Law* 70.

[42] See Political Parties, Elections and Referendums Act 2000, s. 118. Cf. *Libman v. Quebec* (1997) 151 DLR (4th) 385. See C. Feasby, '*Libman v. Quebec (AG)* and the Administration of the Process of Democracy under the Charter: The Emerging Egalitarian Model', (1999) 44 *McGill LJ* 5.

[43] See DTI, Code of Practice on Access to Workers During Recognition and Derogation Ballots (2000), paras. 26–40. Cf. *Lechmere, Inc. v. NLRB* 502 US 526 (1992).

[44] [2000] 3 All ER 850.

IV. Redressing the balance

We have thus reinforced the liberal constitution, and created another obstacle to social democratic progress. The simple point is that the way in which we entrench rights and the rights to which we accord a higher status says a lot about the values of our society and the nature of the democracy which we wish to build. This may explain why constitutions differ: why the liberal constitution of the US is not the social democratic constitution of Italy and other continental European systems. It is also revealed in the attempts at constitution-building in the EC: the EU Charter of Fundamental Rights adopted at Nice in December 2000 is based on a European social model, in which provision is made for both civil and political rights on the one hand and social and economic rights on the other. But of course it is not only constitutional texts which matter: equally important are the values of those charged with the responsibility of determining what the texts mean. A liberal constitution could be made to serve social democratic ends if social democratic values were dominant and pervasive. Equally, a social democratic constitution could be rendered useless by the narrow reading by those educated and trained in a different tradition. Nevertheless the Human Rights Act has created a constitutional imbalance, and the need for additional reform to ensure that social values are also constitutional values to be taken into account in constitutional law. How could this be done?

The interpretation of the Human Rights Act

One way by which social values can be introduced to the Human Rights Act is through the medium of section 2, and in particular the duty of the courts to have regard to (though not be bound by) the jurisprudence of the Strasbourg Court and Commission. An important development here is the willingness on the part of the Court and the Commission to have regard to other international treaties in the interpretation of the ECHR, and in particular treaties dealing with fundamental social rights. Both the Court and the Commission have referred to not only ILO Convention 87 but also the Council of Europe's Social Charter of 1961 to help construe the Convention. It is true that in the early cases before the Court, the Social Charter was used paradoxically to read down the scope of Convention rights.[45] But the position has changed in more recent decisions. Particularly important is *Cheall v. United Kingdom*,[46] where the Commission held that in the construction of Article 11 of the ECHR it is necessary to have regard to ILO Convention 87. Similarly, in *Sigurjonsson v. Iceland*[47] the Court held that it was appropriate to have regard to the Social Charter, in this case overcoming concerns expressed in the earlier cases that

---

[45] *National Union of Belgian Police v. Belgium* (1975) 1 EHRR 578; *Swedish Engine Drivers' Union v. Sweden* (1975) 1 EHRR 617; and *Schmidt and Dahlström v. Sweden* (1975) 1 EHRR 632.
[46] (1986) 8 EHRR 74.   [47] (1993) 16 EHRR 462.

not all parties to the Convention had ratified the Charter, and concerns that those who had ratified the Charter had not accepted all of its obligations.[48]

If followed, this jurisprudence would allow international treaties to have a greater role in the British legal systems. In the first place it would help to expand the scope of Convention rights which overlap with social and economic rights. The obvious example here is Article 11, which could be greatly enriched if construed in accordance with international labour standards, and the conclusions of the Social Rights Committee of the Council of Europe. Secondly, it would help to reinforce the view that social values have a role to play in determining what is a democratic society for the purposes of Convention rights. Measures which compromise liberty are more likely to be accepted if they can be shown to have been taken in implementation of fundamental social rights in other international treaties, such as ILO Conventions and the Council of Europe's Social Charter of 1961. If the courts were seriously to engage with other international treaties in this way (and particularly those such as ILO Conventions and the Council of Europe's Social Charter dealing with social and economic rights), they would go a long way towards addressing some of the scepticism and concerns about the substantive values which adjudication under the Human Rights Act will introduce and reinforce. But it would be a triumph of faith over experience to believe that this is likely to happen.[49]

The scrutiny of legislation

A second way of introducing a social dimension to the rights scene is by some form of parliamentary scrutiny. One of the potentially most important consequences of the Human Rights Act (and perhaps a highly beneficial consequence) is its possible impact on the relationship between Parliament and the executive. With our increasingly court-oriented constitutional culture (leading to a significant increase in the Government Legal Service),[50] this is a dimension which has been greatly ignored, as has the role which will be played in the legislative process by the legal members of the House of Lords (not the Law Lords), some of whom have great expertise in the ways of Convention rights. But it is not only the relationship between the government and Parliament which will be affected: particularly affected will be the role

[48] In this case the Court confirmed that the right to freedom of association in Art. 11 includes a freedom not to associate, thereby finishing a job which had been started in *Young, James and Webster v. United Kingdom* (1982) 4 EHRR 38. The Social Charter was used in the building of this argument. Perhaps not an auspicious example, and it remains to be seen whether the same tools will be used in building arguments where workers or trade unions claim that the positive dimension to the freedom has been violated (as in the cases referred to in n. 45 above).

[49] Although in recent years the courts have been willing to engage with the ECHR (even before the Human Rights Act), there does not appear to be a single case in which the courts have referred to the Social Charter, while ILO Conventions have been mentioned and dismissed in the same breath. Both the Social Charter and ILO Conventions were cited by counsel in *Associated Newspapers plc v. Wilson*, n. 26 above, but not referred to by any members of the court. The House of Lords preferred to dance on the head of a grammatical pin rather than meet international obligations.

[50] *Independent*, 26 Feb. 2001.

and status of the House of Lords in the uncertain times which we now inhabit following the House of Lords Act 1999. It has been proposed for some time that a new Joint Committee on Human Rights should be established,[51] and on 1 February 2001 it was announced that the two Houses of Parliament had appointed such a Committee.[52] Under its terms of reference, the Committee may consider and report on matters relating to human rights in the United Kingdom (excluding consideration of individual cases), as well as proposals for remedial orders under the Human Rights Act 1998, s. 10 and Schedule 2.

There is no restriction confining human rights to Convention rights, and indeed it appears to be accepted that the jurisdiction of the Committee will extend to social and economic rights. So the Committee could in principle assume a wide monitoring role in relation to human rights treaties other than the ECHR, including in particular ILO Conventions and the Council of Europe's Social Charter of 1961.[53] It could draw to the attention of both Houses any Bill which violated these treaties, as well as any failure to comply with the standards which they embrace. But of course, persuading the Committee to exercise its jurisdiction in these areas is another matter altogether: there is a danger that social and economic rights will be subordinated by issues relating to the ECHR, with criminal justice and trial by jury likely to consume litres of hot air. It is also the case that a device of this kind would be effective only to stop legislation in violation of international standards, something which is not to be underestimated. Yet even if the Committee were effective in this respect, the real weakness is that it can offer no protection for social legislation which is the subject of judicial review under the Human Rights Act. No matter how bullish the Committee might be in raising concerns about the violation of international standards protecting social rights, it will have no voice in legal proceedings in which these rights are under attack.

The Human Rights Act as a template

So a parliamentary committee may be a useful device; but it would be less effective in the case of social rights than it would in the case of Convention rights. It would not be in a position to compel, though it could delay and encourage either House to restrain. This suggests a need for a third way, in which human rights treaties dealing with social rights are used not just as an aid to the construction of the Human Rights Act and/or as an instrument of parliamentary scrutiny, but in which human rights treaties dealing with social rights are incorporated into domestic law and given an equal constitutional status with the ECHR. This gives rise to a number of

[51] HC Debs, 14 Dec. 1998, col. 604.

[52] Joint Committee on Human Rights, Session 2000/2001, Press Notice No. 1.

[53] For a review of the current state of British non-compliance with ratified ILO freedom of association conventions, see S. Mills, 'The International Labour Organisation and Freedom of Association: An Annual Cycle of Condemnation', (1997) 2 *European Human Rights Law Review* 35. For the position under the Social Charter, see K. D. Ewing, 'Social Rights and Human Rights: Britain and the Social Charter—The Conservative Legacy', (2000) 5 *European Human Rights Law Review* 91.

practical considerations, and in particular whether such rights could be made justiciable. It is one thing to say that it is common practice for the constitutions of Europe to include provision for social rights. But it does not follow that they are justiciable in the same way. Even those democracies which embrace the European social model by means of constitutional law sometimes distinguish between social rights and political rights by giving the latter an enhanced constitutional status. A number of arguments are sometimes to be heard about why social rights cannot be made justiciable in the same way as civil and political rights. But at the heart of it lies what is sometimes seen as the fundamental difference between the two: one category is designed to restrain the state from a certain course of action; the other requires the state to act in a particular way.

But it is not clear why this difference is conclusive. It is possible to adopt a maximalist and a minimalist position on the constitutional entrenchment of social rights, while noting in passing that it is not quite true to say that civil and political rights restrain rather than require action (think, for example, of the right to a speedy trial and the obligations relating thereto imposed by the Human Rights Act itself). The maximalist position would respect fully the indivisibility of human rights and give them the same formal legal and constitutional status as civil and political rights.[54] This would mean incorporating the Council of Europe's Social Charter on the same basis as the ECHR. Legislation would have to be construed by the courts where possible to ensure that it complied with Charter rights, and where this is not possible the courts would be empowered to declare it incompatible with the Charter. It would be open to individuals to assert Charter rights directly against appropriate public authorities, who have to be financed to meet the claims of those whose Charter rights were denied. And it would bite on the common law if, following the example of the Human Rights Act, the courts were bound to follow Charter principles in disputes between private parties.[55] Indeed, it is on the common law that the impact of the Charter would be greater, providing an irreducible minimum below which private parties could not contract, for example in the employment field.[56]

---

[54] There are variations of a minimalist position. One option would be to follow the Quebec example of social rights which are not justiciable but which could be taken into account in litigation under the Human Rights Act to help define what is meant by a democratic society (though the Quebec Charter prohibits discrimination on grounds of social condition, a useful measure which has been used by disadvantaged workers and welfare claimants denied access to rented housing). On Quebec, see P. Bosset, 'Les droits économiques et sociaux, parents pauvres de la Charte Québécoise?' (Montreal: Commission des droits de la personne et des droits de la jeunesse, 1996). Another would be to provide that social rights of a procedural nature are justiciable but those of a substantive nature are not. On this distinction, see K. D. Ewing, 'Social Rights and Constitutional Law', [1999] *Public Law* 104.

[55] This is developed more fully ibid., and in K. D. Ewing, 'The Charter and Labour', in G. Anderson (ed.), *Rights and Democracy: Essays in UK–Canadian Constitutionalism* (London: Blackstone Press, 1999).

[56] The minimum wage would be based on the European decency threshold of 60% of the national average male wage. See Council of Europe, Committee of Experts, *Conclusions XIV-2* (1998), 50–2.

V. Conclusion

The essence of the argument in this essay is that the British constitution has been built on the principle of liberty, but mainly economic liberty. There was little recognition of equality as a constitutional principle, save only in the most formal manner of equality before the law in terms of the right of access to the courts. But even that principle bore no relationship to legal reality. So no political equality and no social equality. Both of these principles had to be established by Parliament in the face of common-law presumptions to the contrary, and both were undermined by a truculent judicial branch. Through legislation it has been possible gradually to overcome some of the obstacles to equality which the common law has created, legislation being the greatest form of expression of the will of the people in a democracy (however imperfectly the system may operate). The effect of the Human Rights Act is to disturb this process by reasserting the liberal principles of the constitution, and by putting on a constitutional pedestal the principle of liberty which is given a new legal priority. It is true that the priority is not absolute, but there is inadequate guidance of the circumstances in which liberal principles and liberty itself may be constrained, or of the overriding values which such constraints may promote. We are left to the benevolence of the judges who wax lyrical about individual rather than popular sovereignty and who are now empowered to reassert these claims against the other branches of government.[57]

Paradoxically for those sceptical about Bills of Rights on grounds of democratic principle, the Human Rights Act has thus created a democratic imperative for even more entrenched rights. This is particularly the case if we wish to underpin the principle of equality (an essential precondition of both liberal and social democracy), and legislation as well as administrative practices designed to enhance it. By taking such a step we would follow the practice of other European democracies which balance a constitutional protection for civil and political rights with a guarantee and protection for social and economic rights. This takes different forms in different systems, but the case for constitutional balance could best be met by the incorporation of the Council of Europe's Social Charter on the same basis as the ECHR. But any talk about extending the domestic human rights agenda confronts the problem of the courts. This is particularly true of promoting social rights, which would run against the grain of the common law and which could expect to encounter resistance as a result. For we should not lose sight of the fact that what is contemplated by the constitutional incorporation of social rights is nothing less than the *socialization of the common law*, by displacing liberty as the only principle and introducing accompanying principles of substantive equality and solidarity.

But there is in fact a more urgent reason why the position of the judges needs to be addressed. We now have a constitutional system in which the output of the

---

[57] See esp. Laws, n. 31 above. On popular sovereignty, see the splendid piece by H. J. Laski, 'The Theory of Popular Sovereignty', (1919) 7 *Michigan Law Review*, esp. 213–15.

democratic process can avoid successful challenge and possible censure only if it can pass a test of democracy developed by a group of public officials who have escaped all forms of democratic scrutiny and accountability. (It is true, of course, that the courts are not empowered to strike down an act of Parliament because it is in breach of the Convention: but just how realistic is it to suppose that an act of Parliament will be able to survive a declaration of incompatibility?)[58] Those who would presume to sit in judgment of democracy and indeed determine its content and values must themselves be exposed to some form of democratic scrutiny. This is one of the other great issues raised by the Human Rights Act, though it has always been a problem of the constitution, given the role of the courts as legislators in the making and the application of the common law on the one hand, and in determining and giving effect to the will of Parliament on the other. The challenge now is to find a process of recruitment to the courts which helps to produce a representative bench,[59] and the development of procedures which help to ensure that the judges as political actors are more fully accountable to the people over whom they govern, in a manner which enhances rather than undermines their independence.[60] It is a tall order.

[58] Yet according to a report of a press briefing, the Lord Chancellor maintains that there may be circumstances where this may happen, even though it could lead to an application to Strasbourg and an obligation under international law to change domestic law. See *Guardian*, 21 Sept. 2000.

[59] Not just on grounds of race or gender, though that would be a good start. Why is it that the House of Lords is the last bastion of white male exclusivity? Are we really to conclude that there is no woman in the UK who is good enough to sit on our highest court, and that there never has been a woman in the UK who is good enough to sit on our highest court? For a full account, see Lord Chancellor's Department, *Judicial Appointments Annual Report 1999–2000* (Cm. 4783, 2001).

[60] For a full discussion, see K. D. Ewing, 'A Theory of Democratic Adjudication: Towards a Representative, Accountable and Independent Judiciary', (2000) 38 *Alberta Law Review* 708.

7

Human Rights in a Postnational Order: Reconciling Political and Constitutional Pluralism

NEIL WALKER

I. Two debates over rights

The domestic enactment and implementation of the Human Rights Act 1998 has coincided with a sharp upturn in the profile of human rights within the European Union. In a recent chapter of the European Union's 'semi-permanent Treaty revision process',[1] the Cologne European Council of June 1999, in parallel with its decision to convene a new post-Amsterdam Inter-governmental Conference, gave the green light to the drafting of a Charter of Fundamental Rights of the European Union. A Convention including members of national and European parliaments, national governments, and the European Commission (and thus, more broadly inclusive than the formal Treaty amendment process itself) was duly appointed to prepare a Charter. Over the following months there was considerable debate in and beyond the Convention not only as to the content of the Charter but also as to its appropriate legal status and force and its scope of application.

When a final version of the Charter was presented for consideration by the European Council in Biarritz in October 2000, it bore all the hallmarks of a grand compromise.[2] On the one hand, it is remarkably wide-ranging, its six substantive heads covering dignity, justice, and citizenship rights and the wider catalogue of classical 'first generation' freedoms, together with 'second generation' rights organized under the rubric of equality and solidarity. On the other hand, the Convention drew back from a number of more expansive formulae that had been tabled, choosing to restrict the application of the Charter to the 'institutions and the bodies of the Union' and, significantly, to ' the Member States only when they are implementing Union law'.[3] Neither could the Charter 'establish any new power for the

---

[1] B. De Witte, 'The Closest Thing to a Constitutional Conversation in Europe: The Semi-Permanent Treaty Revision Process', in P. Beaumont, C. Lyons and N. Walker (eds.), *Convergence and Divergence in European Public Law* (Oxford: Hart, 2001).

[2] See e.g. G. de Búrca, 'The Drafting of the EU Charter of Fundamental Rights,' (2001) 26 *European Law Review* 126; B. De Witte, 'The Legal Status of the Charter: Vital Question or Non-Issue?', (2001) 8 *Maastricht Journal of European and Comparative Law* 81; K. Lenaerts and E. de Smijter, 'A "Bill of Rights" for the European Union', (2001) 38 *Common Market Law Review* 273.

[3] Art. 51(1). Amongst the proposed formulas for extension to member states in earlier drafts was the reasonably expansive 'to the Member States exclusively within the scope of Union law', CHARTRE

Community or the Union'.[4] Furthermore, when exercising its authority to decide the Charter's legal status in Nice in December 2000, the European Council confirmed what for long had seemed a fait accompli, namely that it should be a merely declaratory document. Yet for all that its edge has been somewhat blunted during the diplomatic endgame, the Charter process retains significant momentum. The public and political debate which its relatively open procedures helped engender continues apace. More concretely, the new Treaty, also concluded as projected at Nice, sets out a broad constitutional agenda for the next Inter-governmental Conference to be convened in 2004, including further consideration of the status of the Charter;[5] and in the meantime, on past experience of the reception of human rights discourse by the European judiciary, we can expect its capacious terms to begin to insinuate themselves into the jurisprudence of the European Court of Justice.[6]

The Charter episode represents a significant, though hardly discontinuous, moment in the saga of EU treatment of fundamental rights. The EU and its predecessors have a long record of ambivalence towards fundamental rights, but the past decade has witnessed a significant 'hardening' of approval in terms of Treaty recognition, building upon the much earlier, if limited, endorsement of the European Court of Justice[7] and subsequent 'soft' support of other Community institutions in the form of non-binding political initiatives.[8] Extending the Treaty of Maastricht's commitment to respect the fundamental rights guaranteed by the ECHR and by national constitutional traditions,[9] the Treaty of Amsterdam

4360/00 of 14 June 2000. The formula finally adopted is not only significantly more restrictive than this earlier draft, it is also more restrictive than the current jurisprudence of the ECJ, which has at various points sought to extend its jurisdiction to national institutions wherever 'they act in the context of European law' (see e.g. Case 5/88, *Wachauf* [1989] ECR 2609; Case 292/97, *Kjell Karlsson*, judgment of 13 Apr. 2000—a very vague and open-ended permission; see further de Búrca, n. 2 above. Regardless of textual limitations, however, it would be naive to contemplate the Charter as in any way reducing the existing jurisdiction of the ECJ, and indeed Art. 53 of the Charter explicitly rules out any restriction in levels of protection. More generally, even in the absence of textual amendment, we should not rule out a continuing gradual expansion in scope of application. Both the generally shifting boundaries of EU law and the increase in instances of 'reverse discrimination'—where national citizens suffer in comparison to non-nationals who take advantage of the EU's anti-discrimination rules—will create significant pressure for the extension of rights protection further into the body of national law (see N. Nic Shuibhne, 'The European Union and Fundamental Rights: Well in Spirit but Considerably Rumpled in Body?', in Beaumont et al., n. 1 above). More broadly, the ECJ now has so many human rights sources to choose from—or to be inspired by—that it would be ingenuous to believe that its principles of selection will be guided by a restrictive rather than an expansionary sensibility.

[4] Art. 51(2).

[5] *Declaration on the Future of the Union to be included in the Final Act of the Conference*, Annexe IV of the Treaty of Nice, SN 533/00, para. 5.

[6] See the Commission's Communication 'on the legal nature of the Charter of Fundamental Rights of the European Union', COM(2000)644, 11 Oct. 2000, esp. 5. See also De Witte, n. 2 above.

[7] After initial resistance, the turning point in the ECJ's jurisprudence came in Case 29/69, *Stauder v. City of Ulm* [1969] ECR 419.

[8] The language of 'hard' and 'soft' approval is taken from P. Craig and G. de Búrca, *EU Law: Text, Cases and Materials*, 2nd edn. (Oxford: Oxford University Press, 1998), 331–3.

[9] Contained in the original Art. F(2), TEU.

declared the Union to be 'founded on' the principles of liberty, democracy and respect for human rights and fundamental freedoms, which principles are for the first time directly justiciable before the ECJ.[10] Against that backdrop, and bearing in mind also the contemporaneous decision of the ECJ that the Community lacked competence to accede to the parallel framework of the ECHR[11]—and thus to have the measures of its own institutions directly bound to conformity with the ECHR's standards—the political momentum behind the dedicated Charter initiative starts to become explicable. In short, prior to the Charter there was already observable an emergent treatment of human rights discourse within the Treaty framework as a species of higher law for the Union, albeit indirect in status, limited in content, and restricted in scope. With the proclamation of the Charter there is introduced a constitutional dynamic which, in the long run at least, promises to consolidate the elevated status of human rights through an approach which is more direct, more expansive in content, and which carries the potential to be more expansive in its scope of application also.[12]

The point of the present contribution, however, is not to chart and explain the emergence of a human rights discourse within the EU in detail, nor even to catalogue the expanding range of measures presently in place.[13] Neither is it my purpose to comment on the strange relation—or 'irrelation'—between the two highly topical spheres of fundamental rights debate, domestic and EU. To be sure, some academic commentators, including contributors to the present volume,[14] have tracked the busy intersections between domestic law, Convention law, and EU law in areas such as discrimination law and labour law. Yet it remains the case, even more emphatically at the level of political discourse than at the level of academic discourse,[15] that the overall significance of human rights developments in the EU domain for the 1998 Act has been given little attention. Brief speculation might suggest as prominent amongst a lengthy list of possible candidates to explain this disconnection: first, a resilient domestic ignorance of the EU's human rights

[10] New Art. 6, TEU. The companion Art. 7, which will be amended and strengthened by the Treaty of Nice, allows the Council to suspend some of the rights of a member state under the TEU in the event of its being found responsible for a serious and persistent breach of these fundamental principles on which the Union is founded. On the bluntness of this sanction in the light of the Haider controversy in Austria, see de Búrca, 'Convergence and Divergence in European Public Law: The Case of Human Rights', in Beaumont et al., n. 1 above. See also the report on Austria's human rights commitment mandated by the 14 other member states through the President of the European Court of Human Rights by Ahtisaari, Frowein, and Oreja (Paris, 8 Sept. 2000). The broad anti-discrimination principle now provided in Art. 13, EC Treaty represents a further, arguably even more significant, extension of the Union's human rights capacity under the Treaty of Amsterdam.

[11] Opinion 2/94, *Accession by the Community to the Convention for the Protection of Rights and Fundamental Freedoms* [1996] ECR I-1759.

[12] See n. 3 above.

[13] Long neglected, these are now the subject of a burgeoning literature. See esp. Craig and de Búrca, n. 8 above, ch. 7, and the contributions collected in P. Alston (ed.), *The EU and Human Rights* (Oxford: Oxford University Press, 1999).

[14] See esp. chapters by Fredman, McColgan, and Malik.

[15] One outstanding exception to the catalogue of academic neglect is M. Hunt, *Using Human Rights in English Courts* (Oxford: Hart, 1997).

agenda; secondly, scepticism about the seriousness of the EU's intentions in this field, or, more charitably, the feasibility of its aspirations; thirdly, an extension to all international or supranational organizations of the influential strain within domestic political attitudes,[16] echoed and reinforced in the courts,[17] that the technical reception of international norms involved in the 1998 Act is the cue for the assertion, indeed the recovery, of a robust indigenous rights tradition which, paradoxically, should now become *less* rather than *more* influenced by 'external' sources.

Whatever the reasons, I would argue that those who retain a healthy scepticism (rather than cynicism) about the beneficial consequences of the implementation of the 1998 Act, and the possible hardening of its strong principle of favourable interpretation towards the ECHR catalogue, its judicial declaratory power of incompatibility, and its monitoring of executive and parliamentary prior compliance into a de facto system of domestic entrenchment, cannot afford to disregard the EU dimension. Scepticism about rights' constitutionalism has many sources, but its deepest and least easily dislodged foundation has always been one of democratic principle. As we shall see, however, the development of the EU as a higher tier of government, with its own (however imperfect) claims to democratic legitimacy, disturbs some of the empirical premises of this key aspect of the sceptic's argument; so much so, indeed, that the incipient development of rights' constitutionalism within the EU offers a new challenge, arguably unprecedented in its vigour, to the sceptical position. The precise nature of this challenge, whether and to what extent it may be answered, and with what implications for the optimal development of a rights framework at the European level, is the subject of the discussion that follows.

II. The democratic critique of rights' constitutionalism

Perhaps the most eloquent and most formidable recent defence of the sceptical position, and one with which, *considered as a thesis about the treatment of rights within a discrete state polity*, I have a great deal of sympathy, is that mounted by Jeremy Waldron.[18] It is impossible to do justice to the force and subtlety of his arguments in an essay with a rather different agenda, but the gist of his case is as follows. For Waldron, the attitude which is struck by those who would constitutionally entrench rights against the wishes of democratic majorities is a combination of 'self-assurance and mistrust'.[19] Both attitudes are viewed as problematical. Self-assurance is

---

[16] New Labour's pre-legislative White Paper, *Rights Brought Home: The Human Rights Bill* (Cm. 3782, 1997) is a typical example.

[17] See e.g. *Barrett v. Enfield Borough Council* [1999] 3 All ER 193(HL); Lord Hoffman, 'Human Rights and the House of Lords', (1999) 62 *Modern Law Review* 159; see also the general discussion by Hunt, n. 15 above, ch. 7) of the emergence of an indigenous common law constitutionalism within academia and amongst the higher judiciary.

[18] See esp. J. Waldron, *Law and Disagreement* (Oxford: Clarendon Press, 1999) chs. 10–13; *The Dignity of Legislation* (Cambridge: Cambridge University Press, 1999); 'A Right-Based Critique of Constitutional Rights', (1993) 13 *Oxford Journal of Legal Studies* 118.

[19] *Law and Disagreement*, 221.

expressed through a commitment to privilege one's own conception of what truly is a matter of fundamental right over other possible candidates in the strong sense of placing one's own conception beyond the contradiction of democratic opinion. Mistrust is expressed through the lack of conviction that one's fellow citizens will share one's convictions, or even if they do, a lack of conviction that they, or indeed their successors, will in the longer term remain sufficiently steadfast in these convictions. As Waldron asserts, these attitudes sit uneasily with 'the aura of respect for the autonomy and responsibility [of individuals] that is conveyed by the substance of the rights which are being entrenched in this way'.[20] That is to say, as a theory of rights itself requires to be underpinned by a particular conception of the good, the best candidates for which conception tend to identify the importance of individual dignity, integrity, and self-realization within a broad conception of moral agency, the constitutional entrenchment of rights tends to disregard, contradict and undermine the very values the entrenchers profess to hold dear.

Rights constitutionalists find themselves in this bind, according to Waldron, because they do not take seriously the need for a theory of authority in politics to complement their substantive theory of the good.[21] Their epistemological self-confidence—arrogance even—blinds them to the inevitability of sustained disagreement over deep questions such as justice, policy, and the content, meaning, and priority of rights in circumstances of political pluralism,[22] and so to the indispensability of a decision procedure to resolve such disagreements. For Waldron, it is at this prior stage, in response to the question: 'who shall decide what rights we have?', that a democratic commitment becomes axiomatic, as evident in his answer: 'the people whose rights are in question have the right to participate on equal terms in that decision.'[23]

As implied above, the strength of Waldron's argument lies in the fact that it takes on the rights constitutionalists on their own terms. He is critical of the lazy assumption that a political theory which includes a strong commitment to rights necessarily implies a constitutional design which accords special protection to rights, in particular special protection in the form of entrenchment of rights and judicial review of the compatibility of legislation with these entrenched rights. He wants to argue not only that no such inference is justified but, more strongly, that a position which takes rights seriously in political theory, as his own position seeks to do, is best supported by a constitutional design which does *not* entrench rights. In other words, his is a 'rights-based'[24] critique of constitutional rights. If a strong commitment to rights flows from a belief in the ordinary individual as the proper focus for moral and political concern, and from faith in and respect for the autonomous individual as a competent arbiter of questions arising from that fundamental concern

---

[20] Ibid. 222. [21] Ibid. esp. 243–54.

[22] See e.g. R. Bellamy, *Liberalism and Pluralism: Towards a Politics of Compromise* (London: Routledge, 1999); N. Walker, ' Beyond the Unitary Conception of the United Kingdom Constitution?', [2000] *Public Law* 383.

[23] *Law and Disagreement*, n. 18 above, 244. [24] Ibid. 252.

(central amongst which are self-regarding and other-regarding questions of individual entitlement—or right), then a theory of authority which demands equal participation in decisions over rights is appropriate inasmuch as 'it calls upon the very capacities that rights *as such* connote, and it evinces a form of respect in the resolution of political agreement which is continuous with the respect that rights as such evoke'.[25]

But even if one is convinced, with Waldron, that the right to equal participation should be privileged as a conception of political authority from a perspective which is itself rights-based, there is still much work to be done in nailing down precisely what is meant by the right to equal participation. At this stage of Waldron's argument,[26] he must defend a second wave of attack from rights constitutionalists. This attack comes from two different angles but, arguably at least, from the same ultimate source. That source is the proposition that in elaborating our conception of an optimal democratic framework—in specifying precisely what we mean by the right to equal participation in political decision-making—we are bound to conclude that certain entitlements are prerequisite to the effective realization of democratic participation and thus must themselves not depend on that same democratic process for their protection. The two types of right in question, providing the two angles of the rights' constitutionalist counter-attack, are, on the one hand, those procedural rights that are directly constitutive of the democratic process[27] and, on the other, those rights which embody more general conditions necessary for the legitimacy of democracy.[28] The procedural rights concern matter such as the basis of suffrage, campaign finance and organization, and the voting system. The other category of democracy-legitimating right is more open-ended, embracing not only rights at the (controversial) margins between process and substance—such as freedom of speech and of association—but also, perhaps, rights associated with freedom of conscience and religion, and even substantive social and economic rights without which individuals might be said to lack the wherewithal necessary to participate effectively in the democratic process.[29]

---

[25] *Law and Disagreement*, 252. [26] Ibid. ch. 13.

[27] The best-known exposition of this argument is by J. H. Ely, *Democracy and Distrust* (Cambridge, Mass.: Harvard University Press, 1980).

[28] The best-known exposition of this argument is by Ronald Dworkin, especially in his more recent writings; see esp. *Freedom's Law: The Moral Reading of the American Constitution* (Cambridge, Mass.: Harvard University Press, 1996). Waldron (*Law and Disagreement*, n. 18 above, 285) agrees with Dworkin—correctly in my view—that Ely is wrong to draw a sharp distinction between the force and import of the argument concerning democracy-constitutive rights and the force and import of the argument concerning rights more generally constitutive of a democratic culture. Both sets of arguments issue the same type of challenge to the constitutional rights sceptic, and both types of argument, as we shall see, are open to the same type of criticism. To be sure, the *scope* of the second type of 'rights associated with democracy' (Waldron, 284) is more controversial, but this does not affect the existence in principle of the second type of right, or the basic form of the argument which would found such a right.

[29] Indeed, it is possible to draw this second category of rights associated with democracy from an even broader justificatory framework, embracing not only rights which are—directly or indirectly—instrumental to an effective democratic framework but also other collateral rights which flow in a separate stream from the same moral theory of respect for individual agency as feeds the case for democracy (ibid. 285).

Waldron's riposte to this type of argument, which is complex yet less fully developed than other parts of his thesis,[30] revisits the circumstances of deep political disagreement upon which his theory of democratic authority is initially constructed. For him, a decision about the constitutional content and status of rights associated with democracy can be made either on procedural grounds or on results-based grounds. That is to say, one can either appeal to the procedure which best encapsulates the democratic culture and otherwise displays the strongest democratic credentials or to the procedure which is likely to produce the best results, again measured in terms of compatibility with what are ultimately *democratic* criteria. The results-based approach is ruled out by Waldron[31] on the ground that, just as we are fated to disagree about the content, meaning, and priority of fundamental rights in general, so too we are fated to disagree about which particular configuration of rights is most supportive of and conducive to the realization of a properly democratic culture. Precisely because our different senses of democracy are so 'thick', so closely tied both to our different substantive aspirations (e.g. libertarian versus social democrat versions of democracy) and to our different conceptions of human agency and of the dynamics of collective engagement and thus of the likely consequences for democratic practice of the choice of particular procedural pathways, we cannot 'bracket off' these decisions *in advance of* democratic deliberation. To do so would again be to seek to avoid the need for a theory of authority by definitional fiat, through invoking the falsely conclusive authority of rights—in this case *democratic* rights.

Of course, as Waldron is well aware, the argument for rejecting a rights-instrumentalist or results-based solution to the problem of elaborating the optimal terms of political participation also calls into question the legitimacy of his own purportedly non-results-based solution.[32] If questions of democratic institutional design *cannot* be separated from inherently and *irresolvably* controversial questions of political theory, then it is no more a comprehensive solution to the problem of legitimating the form of democracy to proceed in ostrich-like fashion as if these questions *can* be separated than it is (as the rights-instrumentalists attempt) to proceed as if the inherently controversial questions of political theory to which questions of the optimal meaning of democracy are inextricably connected can in fact *be resolved*. Waldron's answer to this appears to be twofold. Accepting that the depth and interconnectedness of our disagreements on large questions of political theory is such that the legitimacy of *any* conception of political authority, even one as healthily sceptical of our capacity to resolve deep disagreements on any other level

---

[30] Perhaps because it is in large part presented as an argument in negative terms, *against* Dworkin's attempt to posit a strong connection between rights' constitutionalism and democracy in *Law's Freedom*, rather than as one which emphasizes their incompatibility. For a critique of Waldron which dwells on this part of his argument, see C. Fabre, 'The Dignity of Rights', (2000) 20 *Oxford Journal of Legal Studies* 271.

[31] Here Waldron includes amongst his targets not only Dworkin and Ely but also Rawls's approach to constitutional design in *A Theory of Justice* (Cambridge, Mass.: Harvard University Press, 1971). See Waldron, *Law and Disagreement*, n. 18 above, 294 and ch. 7 generally.

[32] See esp. ibid. 295 and 298–301.

as his own, can be thrown into doubt,[33] he nevertheless favours his own solution on both relative and pragmatic grounds.

In relative terms, a procedure which continues to stress the importance of equal participation in decision-making by ordinary people over decision-making by a supposedly expert minority—such as judges engaged in review of legislation—is on balance to be preferred. To be sure, either procedure might produce results which may be more or less offensive to democratic sensibilities and frustrating of democratic aspirations, but since such results-based judgments are precisely what remain deeply contested, there is no independent basis on which we can measure their relative merit in those terms. All else being equal (or equally indecisive), then, we are left with a bare comparison of the 'thin' democratic credentials of one approach over another. And if there is no authority *necessarily* equipped to resolve questions of rights within a particular constituency any better than that constituency itself, then on these thin democratic grounds, the more inclusive majority decision-making procedure of the popular constituency will always be more attractive than the less inclusive majority decision-making procedure of appellate judges.

Secondly, on pragmatic grounds, simply in order to sustain a constitutional design and a political culture committed to democracy and rights, we need *some* ongoing authoritative decision-making procedure, as a political vacuum serves no conceivable conception of democracy or rights protection. To decide among procedural alternatives A and B, say, on questions concerning the terms and limits of legitimate electoral finance—alternatives which necessarily invoke different conceptions of how rights to freedom of expression and information are optimally articulated with and within democracy—we always/already '*need a procedure*',[34] even if that procedure itself necessarily assumes or is at least more amenable to a particular and controversial conception or class of conceptions of the appropriate mutually constitutive relationship of democracy and rights. The only, or default, candidate on this pragmatic basis is the democratic procedure, however imperfect, that we already have.

But the default solution need not be defended as a mere expedient of continuity of governance, and here it is possible to provide additional ballast to support Waldron's own arguments. We might argue, in more positive vein, that since the procedure in place is also, at least presumptively, a procedure that has commanded effective support until now, it remains reasonably likely to command continuing authority in the contemporary context. More tellingly, the fact of its being the procedure in place within a political culture that is basically (however imperfectly from the standpoint of certain perspectives and interests) committed to democracy lends its authority a measure of legitimacy. Its legitimacy flows from the fact that, in positive terms, it is the product of, and, in negative terms, it has survived the scrutiny of, a polity whose ongoing constitutional culture and procedures are geared not only instrumentally to the pursuit of democracy but also reflexively to the ongoing

---

[33] *Law and Disagreement*, 300.   [34] Ibid. 301.

contemplation and argument about what is meant by democracy, and in a context where there are no strong pre-commitment rules to prevent any resulting modifications in the preferred meaning of democracy being acted upon. Of course, some would argue, and not without foundation, that actually existing democratic procedures within a political culture committed to, but in disagreement over, the best articulation of democracy can systematically favour particular interests and in so doing allow such interests an unduly influential say in the retention of such procedures. That may be true, but is an unavoidable danger. As we have seen, no democratic procedure exists which, on a results-based analysis, can be conclusively argued not to favour unfairly certain interests and conceptions of justice over others, and no democratic procedure *other* than the one presently in place has the strong presumptive legitimacy derived from being the extant outcome of a continuing constitutionally grounded democratic culture.

III. The limits of a state-centred approach

Thus Waldron seems to have developed a position which, although it may not convince rights' constitutionalists,[35] provides a solid intellectual fortress for the location of authority within a polity such as the UK within ordinary democratic processes, unqualified by any special system of judicial protection of particular entitlements. One basic assumption, however, which remains unexamined by Waldron and by most of those with whom he engages is that the object of analysis, and the framework of legitimate authority associated with that object of analysis, is best conceived of in one-dimensional terms. His discourse, and that of his interlocutors, tends to be conducted within the frame of a Westphalian conception of a world order of states. That is to say, it presuppose a configuration of global authority where states and states alone are democratically constituted and are politically authoritative in the last instance, and so provide the sole or main object of all inquiries concerning the adequacy of their democracy and the legitimacy of their political authority.

This does not mean that the state-centred perspective cannot have anything to say about the legitimacy of the authority claims made in or on behalf of polities other than states, that it must pass over such entities in silence. However, what is or might be said[36] from a statist perspective, which remains sometimes an explicitly defended thesis but more often a working assumption for many writers across a whole range of intellectual sub-disciplines,[37] tends to underscore the derivative

---

[35] See Fabre, n. 30 above. See also M. Darrow and P. Alston, 'Bills of Rights in Comparative Perspective', in P. Alston (ed.), *Protecting Human Rights through Bills of Rights* (Oxford: Oxford University Press, 1999).

[36] A collection which is typical in this respect is D. Held, *Political Theory Today* (Cambridge: Polity, 1991).

[37] Not just political theory, but also in (cross-cutting) sub-disciplines such as international relations, international law, European legal studies, and European political studies. For a useful overview and critique, see J. Shaw and A.Wiener, *The Paradox of the European Polity*, Harvard Jean Monnet Working Paper 10/99 (1999).

status of the non-state polity and to assess its authority against the backdrop of its legitimation-in-the-last-instance by the Westphalian state.

For example, much domestic discussion of the ECHR—more emphatically so in the years before its limited domestic reception in the 1998 Act, but also an undercurrent in the new indigenous rights' constitutionalism which, as we have seen,[38] has accompanied the emergence of the new Act—has operated on the premise that the legitimation of the Strasbourg system within our resiliently dualist[39] domestic understanding of international law depends upon the approval and democratic authority of the UK government as our internally constitutionally endorsed representative in the domain of international law. In other words, it is a matter of the exercise of external state sovereignty, which is linked back in a direct chain of authority to the fact and locus of internal sovereignty, and in turn to the legitimation of such sovereignty in terms of an ethic of representative democracy. And on this assumption of the superiority and foundational status of the domestic authority system, it was for a long time common for arguments to be mounted, for instance, about the illegitimacy of the findings of 'foreign' judges in Strasbourg: about the legitimate trumping of a Convention right or its particular application in a Strasbourg judgment by domestic executive diktat or legislative pronouncement, however formulated; about the need for a strong 'margin of appreciation' to be permitted by Strasbourg in deference to domestic political sensibilities; about the legitimacy of a robust national approach to reservations and derogations; and even about the highly conditional character of continuing UK subscription to the Convention as a whole.

Whatever one thinks of the normative credentials of this state 'sovereigntist'[40] mindset at various stages in the postwar debate about the nature of the UK's international human rights commitments, it is strongly arguable that the empirical ground has now shifted, and so in turn have the normative arguments which might reasonably be sustained on that ground. It is no longer adequate, if it ever was, to conceive of non-state political structures and the authoritative implications of the type of rights or other juridical claims they make in terms which are merely derivative of and parasitic upon the authority claims made on behalf of state polities, or, indeed—to acknowledge another paradigm of thought which gave implicit comfort to the statist perspective—to conceive of them in purely self-contained terms, dissociated from and so unchallenging to the hegemony of state polities. For in the second half of the twentieth century, the gradual globalization of economic

---

[38] See Section I and nn. 15–17 above.

[39] Although I would argue that the same state-derivative mindset can to a greater or lesser degree be found in the dogmatic legal cultures of those other signatories to the ECHR which are monist rather than dualist, and which therefore accord status to international law independent of any specific act of domestic recognition. For in the final analysis, a monist theory of international law, like a dualist theory, *is a position within and authorized by a domestic legal system.* The ultimate authority of the domestic system therefore remains axiomatic, even if the prospects of the assertion of such domestic authority and the conditions under which it might be asserted may be very different.

[40] See Hunt, n. 15 above; see also N. Walker, 'Setting English Judges to Rights', (1999) 19 *Oxford Journal of Legal Studies* 133.

organization, communications media, and cultural forms[41] has become interwoven with the generation of authority systems below,[42] above, and beyond the state in a dynamic and ongoing process. And even if this new multi-dimensional configuration of authority can be *historically* derived from the Westphalian one-dimensional system of states and the decisions taken in constitutional law and in international law by these states, it does not follow that it is any longer accurate to characterize the authority of non-state polities as *normatively* derivative of the authority of the state polity.

As I have argued elsewhere,[43] this distinction between lineage and pedigree on the one hand and contemporary normative claims and credentials on the other can be developed conceptually by invoking the idea of 'metaconstitutional' authority to make sense of a range of emerging non-state-based authority systems. Such systems, of which the European Union is undoubtedly the most highly developed example, have a 'meta' quality—a *secondary* discursive character, in the double sense that they are derivative of and dependent upon (historically speaking) a primary state-based authority system, but also claim discursive authority over or independence from (normatively speaking) that state-based system. Yet the point is not to privilege the claims of these non-state or 'postnational'[44] sites of 'constitutional' authority and legitimacy over state sites by endorsing a reversal of the previous hierarchy. Rather, we must begin to think beyond a unitarian framework—statist or otherwise—and embrace the possibility of a plurality of territorially determined and delimited state constitutional orders and of functionally determined and delimited non-state constitutional orders, in which there is ongoing interaction, sometimes competitive and sometimes cooperative, between these different authority systems with their mutually influential jurisdictions. From such a perspective, there is no 'master discourse' situated outwith the various authority sites which asserts the necessary superiority of one type of authority site—state or non-state— over others. Rather, there is a provisional and changeable set of relations—putatively authoritative, strategic, and dialogical—between those various coexisting and overlapping authority sites. Sovereignty, if it continues to be a meaningful concept within this changing configuration, no longer refers to a claim to ultimate or original authority which can only be effective within the territorial space to which it refers if it is the *exclusive* plausible claim made over that space, as was the case in the

---

[41] See D. Held, A. McGrew, D. Goldblatt, and J. Perraton, *Global Transformations* (Cambridge: Polity, 1999).

[42] See the chapters by Himsworth, Rawlings, and Harvey in this volume, on Scotland, Wales, and Northern Ireland respectively. Many of the points about the articulation of and competition between democratic authority systems and how this alters the sceptic's perception on the status and legitimacy of forms of constitutional rights protection apply *mutatis mutandis* to the Scottish, Welsh, and Northern Irish examples, and are well brought out by the authors.

[43] See e.g. Walker, 'Flexibility within a Metaconstitutional Frame: Reflections on the Future of Legal Authority in Europe', in de Búrca and Scott, *Constitutional Change in the EU: Between Uniformity and Flexibility?* (Oxford: Hart, 2000); n. 22 above.

[44] See e.g. Shaw and Wiener, n. 37 above; J. Tully, *Strange Multiplicity: Constitutionalism in an Age of Diversity* (Cambridge: Cambridge University Press, 1995).

one-dimensional, mutually exclusive system of states. Instead, the sovereign claim need be and can only plausibly be a claim to an *autonomous* competence within that space, one which overlaps with other plausible claims to jurisdiction within that territory which are themselves autonomously grounded, with neither deferring to the other.

If we return to the immediate question of the EU and its growing human rights claims, this emerging constitutional pluralism poses a particularly acute challenge to state-centred authority claims, and in particular the democratically grounded, state-centred authority claim of the rights sceptic. In the first place, it causes us to look anew at the empirical content and context of the two basic and interrelated premises upon which the rights sceptic has built an argument to resist the trumping claims of rights. These premises concern in turn (1) the possible sites of democratically self-determined community and (2) the ways in which the democratic self-determination of such a community may be limited.

As regards the first of these ideas, the possibility of the democratically self-determined community, like the notion of political authority itself, has traditionally been conceived of in one-dimensional statist terms. In other words, there could only be one democratically self-determined community in any territorial space, for all such communities were arranged in the mutually exclusive territorial parcels called states. The development of the EU alters this context. More so than most post-national sites, although in many ways imperfectly, the EU has its own democratic credentials, and its own institutional structure through which its claim to autonomous and fundamental legal authority is democratically endorsed. To be sure, these claims continue to be challenged from a one-dimensional state-centred perspective, but this merely underlines the plural and competitive nature of the new configuration of legal authority, rather than providing conclusive grounds to sustain the authority-in-the-last-instance of the state-based perspective. In Waldron's terms, we can no longer look to the constitutionally endorsed democratic procedural protocols of the state as the basic and exclusive reference point for claims about how to legitimate democratic culture. For democratic culture is now multi-layered between the state and the supra-state level of the EU (and also to a certain extent the sub-state level, although, in the UK context at least, this level remains at the present juncture[45] subordinate to the state level and cannot claim the same effective autonomy as a polity as the supra-state level). There is, in other words, no longer a single demos in whose exclusive terms and by whose exclusive reference we can build and defend a conception of political authority, but multiple and overlapping demoi, each with their own political authority systems and their own default rules about legitimate democratic process and the relationship between democracy and rights.

If the empirical ground of the idea of democratic self-determination has now shifted from a one-dimensional towards a multi-dimensional configuration, this

---

[45] However, the present juncture is by no means a stable state of affairs; see Walker, n. 14 above. See also n. 42 above.

shift also alters our understanding of the available forms and manners of limitation of democratic self-determination, whether by rights or by any other type of claim or constraint. Leaving aside external coercion by another state or association of states, whose democratic illegitimacy is clear in principle, within a statist framework the idea of the limitation of democratic self-determination is bound up with the idea of *self-limitation* over time, and thus with the notion of pre-commitment.[46] That is to say, if a legally constituted sovereign polity within a one-dimensional configuration of states is unable to make legislative acts or take executive action in accordance with its normal democratic rules and procedures where such laws or actions would be at variance with a norm within a particular catalogue of rights, it is because a prior decision (which itself may possess stronger or weaker democratic credentials) made by that same sovereign polity has bound it to such an attitude of self-limitation.

It is well known, of course, that the internal constitutional order of the United Kingdom, and in particular its 'top rule'[47] of parliamentary sovereignty, precludes such self-limitation. Under a plural configuration, on the other hand, the curtailment of the comprehensive authority of a particular polity can be *exogenous* as well as *endogenous*. The placing of limitations on the democratic self-determination of a particular community in the name of rights, or indeed any other type of norm, need not be a self-denying ordnance but can also be as a result of the encroachment of other jurisdictions upon the previously exclusive and comprehensive territorial jurisdiction of the state. Significantly, too, it is clear that this exogenous limitation does not in principle depend upon the norms in question being ascribed the status of higher law and being entrenched against ordinary law and protected from repeal in the manner of ordinary law within the encroaching jurisdiction. From the point of view of statist democracy, and pushing its basic premise to its logical conclusion, *any* external encroachment, regardless of its status within the other jurisdiction, is sufficient to qualify the notion of comprehensive democratic self-determination. Nonetheless, where in addition, as with the developing catalogue of EU human rights, these norms do acquire the status of higher law in the encroaching jurisdiction, the challenge to statist democratic self-determination is clearly all the greater. In such circumstances, the exogenous limitation becomes, as it were, double-layered.

To be sure, against my distinction between endogenous and exogenous restrictions, it could be argued that in the context of the UK's relationship to the EU even external encroachment remains in one sense a form of self-limitation, and indeed a reversible form of self-limitation. As we noted above, the new constitutional pluralism has a statist pedigree. The post-state authority of the EU which now effectively circumscribes the authority of the state in the name of its new legal order, including a progressive order of rights, would not exist and would not be in a position to challenge

---

[46] Waldron, *Law and Disagreement*, n. 18 above, ch. 12.
[47] H. W. R. Wade, 'The Basis of Legal Sovereignty', [1955] *Cambridge Law Journal* 172, at 187–9.

the comprehensive authority of the state but for the prior consent of the state; furthermore, the statist legacy remains sufficiently strong that the top rule of parliamentary sovereignty continues to look outwards as well as inwards, and so, from its perspective, the option of withdrawal from and thus effective repeal of the normative order of the EU remains.[48] Yet the relevance of such an obdurately unitarian perspective for a radically altered pluralist configuration of authority is clearly tenuous. The exogenous limitations imposed by the normative order of the EU are real and far-reaching and, given the economic, political, and cultural imperatives towards deep regional integration within the new global configuration, the supposedly decisive option of withdrawal is in fact no option at all. Or, to put the same point in a vividly comparative context, the likelihood of the United Kingdom reconstituting its legal order and reclaiming its comprehensive territorial jurisdiction outside the framework of the EU, and thus removing the exogenous limitations to democratic self-determination, is probably no less remote than that of the people of the United States reconstituting themselves through a legal revolution as an unqualified parliamentary democracy, and thus removing their endogenous constitutional limitations to democratic self-determination. The American limitations may have been around for much longer and take a very different form, but it is arguable that the British limitations are today just as firmly entrenched.

IV. Reconciliation

If the exogenous limitations imposed by the EU, with its developing human rights jurisprudence and agenda, appear to be here to stay, how do rights sceptics reconcile themselves to this altered state? The fact that their position is outdated—has been overtaken by events—does not for that reason alone make it irrelevant or wrong. If the *comprehensive* democratic self-determination of particular political communities through law is no longer possible, and instead these communities find their collective will constrained by internal or, in the case of the UK, external normative commitments including rights commitments, then rights sceptics must seek to find in this new situation some basis for reconciliation with their standing democratic commitments. Otherwise, their options are stark: either to adopt a kind of structural fatalism, an acceptance that the new political configuration within which they live is illegitimate yet irresistible, or to join the flat-earthers who obdurately hold to the feasibility and desirability of withdrawal from the European Union.

---

[48] Although the legal incidents of membership are such, in particular the doctrines of the supremacy and direct effect of EU law in its own sphere and the operation of the preliminary reference procedure under Art. 234 of the EC Treaty, that even from the perspective of national sovereignty any intermediate form of challenge to the normative order of the EU short of complete withdrawal appears no longer possible. See e.g. Sir W. Wade, 'Sovereignty—Revolution or Evolution?', (1996) 112 *Law Quarterly Review* 568; see also T. R. S. Allen, 'Parliamentary Sovereignty: Law, Politics and Revolution', (1997) 113 *Law Quarterly Review* 443; N. MacCormick, *Questioning Sovereignty* (Oxford: Oxford University Press, 1999), ch. 6.

If, as surely all rights sceptics who are not also unalloyed Eurosceptics would, we dismiss these unpalatable alternatives and consider the affirmative option, we can identify four distinct but connected bases on which reconciliation may be sought— democratic, prudential, compensatory, and structural. None is entirely satisfactory in itself, being either of limited force or merit or, as befits the shifting and indistinct patterns of the emerging plural landscape, highly tentative and speculative. In combination, however, they may provide a reasonable basis for squaring a continuing commitment to democratic pluralism with the new constraints and commitments of constitutional pluralism.

First, then, there is a direct democratic response to the demise of the comprehensive democratic self-determining community. This argument has both a processual and a substantive aspect, and provides the basis, implicitly at least, on which most rights sceptics would reject the extreme alternative of withdrawal from the European Union. In terms of process, it is arguable that the formation of the new Europe has valid and, indeed, very familiar democratic credentials. Just as we have contended that there is a direct historical link between state and post-state—member state and EU—political authority systems, Richard Bellamy has shown in an insightful recent essay how this direct line of descent might also extend to the respective democratic credentials of these polities.[49] For Bellamy, it is typically the case that 'struggles for citizenship and between citizens . . . entail redefinitions of the *subjects, spheres, scope and styles of politics* that lead to a continuous reconstitution of the polity and hence of the rights of its citizens' (emphasis added).

These struggles are as old as politics itself, and were for long in the modern age largely contained within the capsule of the state system. But the process of struggle and the renegotiation and re-imagining of political community which accompany it, amongst their many and diverse affects, have lately led to a reconstitution of the spheres of politics of an order which goes beyond mere internal negotiation and structuring of polities along federal lines, or in terms of other less orderly patterns of internal division (as in the asymmetrical devolution produced by the contemporary constitutional politics of the UK), and, indeed, even beyond the construction of international treaty organizations of which the concluding state parties, as a matter of traditional international law, remain the undoubted masters. The continuous, organic renegotiation of the spheres of politics in the British context has led, in addition—through the initial legislative act of joining in 1972, the 1975 referendum, and, thereafter, periodical ratifications of IGC negotiations—to the emergence and sustenance of a new and autonomously authoritative democratic polity, the European Union, whose coexistence with the traditional state polities provides, as we have seen, the paradigmatic instance of the emerging multi-dimensional configuration of authority.

---

[49] 'The "Right to Have Rights": Citizenship Practice and the Political Constitution of the European Union', in R. Bellamy and A. Warleigh (eds.), *Citizenship Practice and the Political Constitution of the European Union* (London: Pinter/Continuum, 2001).

One might object, as does Waldron in his discussion of the democratic legitimacy of precommitment, that grand acts or 'constitutional moments'[50] of popular sovereignty do not grant or guarantee the continuing democratic status of the entity or entities shaped by the act of popular sovereignty.[51] Process cannot always legitimate outcome, and certainly cannot do so indefinitely. This is of course a valid objection, since if process were unimpeachable then any manner or form of democratic abuse could be justified in the name of popular pre-commitment. Yet it is a less telling objection to the type and trajectory of process that we are concerned with here. For where the limiting act and expression of sovereignty involves not *time* but *space*—not pre-commitment of one and the same territorial polity but instead its dispersal of jurisdiction to other polities and sites of authority—then the democratic legitimacy of the process may be continued and endorsed through the substantive democratic credentials of the other polity or polities to whom authority is dispersed.

But, to turn to the question of democratic substance, despite its directly elected Parliament and indirectly representative Council of Ministers, the democratic deficiencies of the Union are notoriously stubborn. In particular, the empowerment of the European Parliament, especially in legislative matters, has been slow, grudging, and incomplete, the resulting variability in the institution's capacities and procedures imposing further costs in terms of public understanding and transparency; and, its formal powers aside, the Parliament's remoteness, its lack of political cohesion, its low media visibility, and its perennially low voter turnout and consequentially weakened mandate further diminish its capacity to support a vibrant European democracy. Of course, this catalogue of complaints invites the obvious counter-objection that all democracies, state democracies included, show the same symptoms of malaise, if not necessarily in such an extreme form: that European democracy should not be expected to carry the can for the failings of democracy *in general*, and so should not for that reason have the legitimacy of its authority impugned, including its authority to generate norms, such as human rights norms which constrain national democratic communities.

But that would be too easy a retort, for what it neglects is that at least some of the failings of European democracy, however familiar they sound, are directly linked to its structural position within a multi-dimensional political configuration, and to that extent vindicate the concerns of those who fear the dispersal of authority away from the democratic community of the state. In the first place, the sheer size and complexity of the European Union as a supra-state polity leads to 'a diminution in the specific gravity, in the political weight, in the level of control of each individual within the redrawn political boundaries'.[52] Secondly, and more profoundly, there is the famous 'no demos' critique[53] which holds that outside the relatively culturally

---

[50] B. Ackerman, *We the People: Foundations* (Chicago: Chicago University Press, 1991).

[51] Waldron, *Law and Disagreement*, n. 18 above, 255.

[52] Weiler, *The Constitution of Europe* (Cambridge: Cambridge University Press, 1999), 264.

[53] Most closely associated with the judgment of the German Constitution Court in *Brunner* [1994] 1 CMLR 57.

homogeneous political community of the state, democracy in terms of a genuine expression and monitoring of the collective will is simply not viable, and so is destined to be a hollow affair. While this position is surely overstated, and rests on too complacently (and, in its extreme 'ethnic' manifestations, dangerously) essentialist a view of national community and too cynical an appraisal of more cosmopolitan forms and levels of belonging and mutual recognition, it nevertheless raises some real concerns. The problem of securing a plurality of forms and foci of engagement, attention, understanding, and commitment from the multi-level citizenry of a plural constitutional order is genuine if by no means insuperable, and the low salience of democracy at the European level is surely not unconnected to this genuine concern.[54]

In sum, the democratic response to the democratic critique of the development of a supranational normative order goes some but not all of the way to answer the latter's concerns. EU democratic practice alone cannot assuage the concerns of those who would question the fact or extent of development of the legal normative order of the EU. Moreover, while EU democracy does help substantially in legitimating in democratic terms ordinary EU legislation, it cannot address in a satisfactory manner the second layer of objections—the additional legitimacy concerns associated with higher, entrenched norms, such as the emerging human rights catalogue—any more than can the healthy incidence of democracy at the national level justify precommitment to higher law norms in that context.

This leads us directly to the second basis for justifying such a discourse. If the democratic argument rests on the legitimacy and effectiveness of the democratic culture of the European Union, the prudential argument, by contrast, concedes the limitations in this democratic culture, and argues for the protection of rights precisely as a way of enhancing or reinforcing the benefits of democratic scrutiny and control. The gist of this approach is captured in the idea of 'complex accountability'—'that multiple forms of accountability of powerful government actors can compensate for the imperfections of single lines of accountability'.[55]

Of course, this approach raises again the difficult problems addressed by Waldron about the ways in which and the extent to which certain rights may be said to be constitutive of democracy. On what authority is it possible to impose supposedly democracy-enhancing rights on a polity other than through the democratic mandate of that polity itself? Again, the problems associated with the justification of rights entrenchment threaten to replicate themselves at the supranational level. Yet the relatively impoverished state of the democratic culture within the European Union does provide a tentative answer. Arguably, at least as regard these rights whose *core* content is uncontroversially linked to a healthy democratic culture, in particular expression, association, and information—in at least some of which areas

[54] See Weiler, n. 52 above, ch. 8.
[55] M. Saward, 'A Critique of Held', in B. Holden (ed.), *Global Democracy: Key Debates* (London: Routledge, 2000) 30, 41–2.

the malaise of European democracy has been particularly manifest[56]—the struc-turally rooted deficiencies of European democracy argue some way in favour of a greater, and so perhaps entrenched, guarantee of judicial protection.

The third argument in favour of reconciliation between democracy and rights constitutionalism in the European context also applies a compensatory logic, but one which is much broader in scope. This line of analysis focuses on the particular historical emphasis and restricted trajectory of development of the European polity. It concentrates on the development of the EU as a functionally limited polity, con-cerned primarily with the development of a common market amongst its member states. Although there were from the outset powerful voices arguing for a broader human rights agenda,[57] the only rights which were clearly recognized in the origin-al framework were those specifically concerned with economic integration—the four fundamental freedoms of movement of persons, goods, services, and capital, together with the property rights and economic freedoms necessary to make these commerce-predicated mobility rights fully effective.

Yet this initial limitation did not hold, and was never likely to do so. There are two reasons for this. In the first place, certain human rights, in particular those first-generation rights concerned with ensuring that individual liberty is not interfered with or compromised by other actors, in particular powerful government actors, do not easily fit with a functional or sectoral logic. That is to say, to revert to the lan-guage of the Charter, rights of due process and other justice rights, rights of good administration and other citizen's rights, dignity rights of life and physical integrity, and other general freedoms such as those associated with expression, association, and privacy, have a relevance across all sectors of government activity, and cannot be conceived of as a functionally separate policy sphere. Yet since a purely functional logic is blind to their significance, there is a strong case for their instead being implied within the general framework of the functionally limited polity.

Secondly, as is well known, the functionally limited polity is never in a steady state. Functionally limited polities create their own expansionary dynamic—their own 'spillover' effect[58]—as policy initiatives in particular areas create strong argu-ments for compensatory adjustment in others. Famously, the completion of the

---

[56] In particular, the right to obtain information about the decision-making processes of the political institutions of the Union, including the Council, the Commission, and the 'comitology' Committees, where there has been a spate of recent cases before the ECJ and the Court of First Instance. See Case T-194/94, *Carvel* [1995] ECR II-2767; Case T-174/95, *Union of Swedish Journalists* [1998] ECR II-2289; Case T-14/98, *Hautala v. Council of the EU*, ruling of 19 July 1999 171; Case T-188/97, *Rothmans*, judgment of 19 July 1999; Case C-58/94, *Netherlands v. Council* [1994] ECR I-2169. See generally D. Curtin, 'Citizens' Fundamental Right of Access to EU Information: An Evolving Digital *Passepartout?*', (2000) 37 *Common Market Law Review* 7.

[57] For example, the plans for the European Political Community in 1952–53, one of the abortive pre-decessors of the Treaty of Rome, included as a primary aim the protection of human rights and proposed incorporation of the ECHR.

[58] See e.g. L. N. Lindberg, *The Political Dynamics of European Integration* (Stanford, Calif.: Stanford University Press, 1963).

1992 Single Market Programme and the unrestricted circulation of goods and persons that this promised was deemed by the political authorities of the Community to require compensatory measures in the area of security policy, leading to the development at Maastricht of the new Third Pillar competence in justice and home affairs, and thereafter, at Amsterdam, to the redefinition of the Union as an 'area of freedom, security and justice'. More relevant to our immediate purpose, the unavoidable impingement of the project of economic integration upon the European labour market and the European consumer market in services provoked claims, gradually and unevenly answered, for worker-centred and consumer-centred rights of equality of employment conditions and access to services, and, yielding a yet slower and more faltering response, for solidarity rights associated with workplace democracy and the provision of social welfare guarantees.[59]

How compelling are these compensatory arguments for rights?[60] The short answer is that in the particular social and historical context of the development of the Union they are very compelling. The relevance of classical rights as a cross-sectoral balancing theme is persuasive, although there is still no reason of democratic principle why such cross-sectoral rights should be given entrenched status. Yet contextually, this could be justified by the fact that the fundamental economic freedoms were built into the original Treaty framework, and in order not to be trumped by these foundational premises, the non-sectoral rights had to be accorded the same status. The functional spillover argument is less immediately persuasive, since, despite the suggestion of some of its proponents, there is nothing inexorable about functional extension. What counts as an appropriate compensatory measure is always a matter of choice and priority. Of course, provided that choice is exercised democratically, as has been the case to a significant extent with the introduction of 'second-generation' rights into the European Union's normative framework,[61] then for that reason it becomes unobjectionable as a matter of democratic principle. However, the prospect of the further elevation of these rights to the status of general principles of higher law through the mechanism of the Charter reintroduces the democratic objection, which again can only be answered pragmatically and contextually as a way of ensuring that these rights are not trumped and marginalized by the other rights.

[59] For a similar argument from a UK-centred perspective, see Ewing's chapter in this volume.

[60] There, is of course, no definitive line that can be drawn between non-sectoral rights and compensatory 'spillover' rights. In so far as activities require active intervention rather than forbearance from governments—positive rather than negative integration in the language of European law, they may be better viewed as spillover rights rather than as non-sectoral rights. However, as regards 'equality' rights in particular, the key term is so wide-ranging that it overlaps both categories. Some of the relevant questions in this area are addressed in the ongoing debate within the ECJ and elsewhere about the ways in which and extent to which equality can be viewed as a self-standing right. See, e.g. C. Barnard, 'Gender Equality in the EU: A Balance Sheet', in Alston, n. 13 above, 215.

[61] See e.g., pursuant upon the introduction of the general anti-discrimination clause in Art. 13 EC Treaty, Directive 2000/78 EC on a general framework for equal treatment in employment and occupation; and Directive 2000/43 EC implementing the principle of equal treatment between persons irrespective of racial or ethnic origin.

In other words, what we observe in the history of the European Union is a jurisprudential 'ratchet effect'—an equalization upwards of rights. Given its original status as a functionally limited entity which inevitably gave priority to particular objectives and to the entitlements associated with these objectives in its 'higher law' formative Treaty framework, it is difficult to see how it could have been otherwise without conceding the indefinite and unqualified hegemony of these narrowly conceived initial priorities across the broader sweep of an ever-expanding polity. But this confronts the rights sceptic with something of a paradox. The historical justification may well be compelling, but the result is a framework which, if and when the Charter duly consolidates its higher law status either in formal terms or informally through the jurisprudence of the ECJ, may privilege the broadest range of rights claims over the democratic choices made in ordinary EU legislation. The rights sceptic might claim that in an ideal world he or she would not start from that position. Yet in the only world we now have, the one of functionally delimited non-state polities operating in a context of constitutional pluralism, there is simply no other place to start from.

If this places the rights sceptic in something of a bind, the final basis upon which a principled reconciliation might be possible suggests a method of escape within the deep normative structure of the new post-Westphalian order. It is one thing to reconstruct this new order historically; it is quite another to attempt to do so normatively. That is to say, we might assess the new constitutional pluralism not (or not just) in terms of its actual dynamics of emergence, but also in terms of how its development might best be interpreted and its future role best imagined. Earlier I suggested that rights sceptics need not and should not trim their values merely to accommodate the new context of constitutional pluralism. But is it not possible that the new context might directly challenge these values? In other words, even if one accepts that democratic self-determination is the *Eigenwert* of the one-dimensional system of states, it does not necessarily have the same status with regard to the various parts—or indeed the whole—of the multi-dimensional order of constitutional pluralism. Is there, then, something about the new configuration, and in particular the structural relationship of the EU to its member states within that new configuration, which would persuade the rights sceptic to re-evaluate the EU in terms which do not place the concept of democracy in a position of moral primacy over other values, in particular those other values which the thesis of rights constitutionalism might independently foster?

This is patently a large question, and one whose surface we can only scratch here. One suggestive line of inquiry, however, has been opened up by Joseph Weiler in a well-known series of recent works.[62] In looking beyond the legal mandate and jurisdiction of the Union, and beyond the pattern and thrust of narrow

---

[62] Many of which are collected in Weiler, n. 52 above. For other imaginative attempts to rethink the place of democracy within a plural configuration, see MacCormick, n. 48 above, ch. 7; M. P. Maduro, 'Europe and the Constitution: What if This is as Good as it Gets?', in J. H. H. Weiler and M. Wind (eds.), *Rethinking European Constitutionalism* (Cambridge: Cambridge University Press, 2001).

political and economic interests and priorities which would account for its developments in instrumental terms, Weiler contends that the Union can also be characterized in terms of ideals—in terms of the animating framework of ideas which
have provided (at least) a rhetorical accompaniment to its progress. He names
three ideals: peace, prosperity, and supranationality. We will look here only at the
third, not only because Weiler, with some reason, is pessimistic about the continuing mobilizing potential of the first two ideals fifty years on from the raw experience of postwar austerity,[63] but also, and more significantly, because the third
ideal, unlike the other two, has a structural rather than a substantive quality. That
is to say, supranationality, unlike the other two ideals, is not concerned with the
general and discrete external purposes of the polity. Instead, it is concerned, self-
referentially, with its own structural characteristics and distinctive identity as a
polity—including its internal institutional shape and design, and, crucially in a
multi-dimensional order, its relation with other polities.

This notion of a structural ideal—of the polity's defining identity *qua* polity—
is, in my view, one which requires particularly urgent attention under circumstances of constitutional pluralism generally and in the context of the EU
particularly. Under the one-dimensional state system, the structural ideal underpinning sovereign states was simple if profoundly important. It was nothing less
than the provision of a framework for a *comprehensive* political community, one
which was competent to deal with all the political affairs and aspirations of its citizens, and one which could therefore give substance to the idea of comprehensive
democratic self-determination. In the post-Westphalian world—especially in
respect of the EU, towards whose very status as a polity many remain opposed or
undecided—we need in response to invest the very idea of a *limited* polity, a new
and strange animal, with a similarly compelling meaning and rationale.

For Weiler, the idea of supranationality, stripped of many of its academic
glosses, supplies this rationale.[64] The supranational polity is something juridically
situated between international society and the state and is conceived of in explicitly
relational terms, with reference to how it helps us redefine the old idea of the state,
and also of the nation which is contained within the state capsule. On this view, the
idea of the nation state, sustained by notions of popular sovereignty and democratic
community, has generated indivisible benefits and costs. It has been a prime vehicle for the key human values of belongingness and originality, but the legal, geo-
graphic, and cognitive boundaries mobilized to achieve this have also carried the
potential for abuse: for internal discrimination and external aggression, for cultural
insularity and imperialism. For Weiler, the supranational ideal exists precisely 'to
tame the national interests with a new discipline'.[65] Led by the flagship idea of
post-national citizenship,[66] itself a necessarily more robust animal than the anaemic

---

[63] Ibid. 256–7.   [64] Ibid. 246–52, 258.   [65] Ibid. 251.

[66] Ibid. ch. 10; see also J. Shaw, *Citizenship of the Union: Towards Post-National Membership?* Harvard
Jean Monnet Working Paper Series 6/97 (1997); N. Walker, 'All Dressed Up', (2001) 21 *Oxford Journal
of Legal Studies* 563.

creature of Maastricht and Amsterdam,[67] supranationalism has the potential to achieve this purpose. The larger political identity that supranationalism creates guards against the dangers of communitarianism and exclusive belonging at the level of national citizenship, encouraging the Self to respect and for some purposes embrace the Other, yet never to sublimate the Other.

In institutional terms, this line of reasoning may provide a more compelling justification for entrenched rights protection at EU level, as part of the very definition of supranationalism as a structural ideal, than the previous three candidates. For under this analysis rights protection does not become a means of second-guessing or qualifying the discrete democratic will of the European people, and in so doing also curbing the freedom of action of the primary nation-state demos, in the name of some other substantive non-democratic values. Rather, it involves a recognition that, in circumstances such as those of the EU, where the interpenetration and mutual engagement of primary democratic communities through thick commercial ties, population flow, redistribution of allocative resource and regulatory costs, and the like, becomes so dense as to justify the need for a new democratic community alongside and over these primary communities, we have to look afresh at the institutional articulation of the animating ideals of constitutionalism. In particular, we have to concede the possibility that the sense of equal respect for the autonomy and dignity of the individual which Waldron convincingly claims is at the root of all of all attempts to take both democracy and rights seriously, and which is also at the heart of Weiler's formulations about recognizing and respecting the Other, may not be best served by merely re-aggregating, and therefore ignoring, the specificity and collective identity of these primary democratic communities at the broader level. Rather, the new and larger democratic community, in order to demonstrate respect for each and all of these prior identities—and, indeed, openness towards new transnational identities—sufficient to gain public confidence and encourage public engagement in its operation as a coherent umbrella form of governance in a multi-level context, has to be qualified by the commitment to mutual tolerance and altruism which only a guaranteed rights framework may bring.

V. Conclusion

We must of course remind ourselves that Weiler's thesis, and in particular my development of it, does not and cannot pretend to be a compelling analysis of and set of inferences from the actually existing state of emergent constitutional pluralism, but rather amounts to no more than a series of tentative projections of how the EU–state interface might be re-thought in ways which make the case for fundamental rights protection more compelling from a democratic perspective. But whether or not my speculative conclusions are accepted, what is clear from this

---

[67] EC Treaty, Arts. 17–22.

analysis is that in the EU we are faced not only with the specific legitimacy challenge of justifying rights constitutionalism but also with a more general legitimacy challenge concerning the very shape and structure of the new multi-dimensional polity—a broader challenge, moreover, the rights sceptic must concede, which democratic theory, with its strong one-dimensional statist legacy, cannot meet unaided. In these circumstances an attractive option, and one which is at least plausible, is to resolve these two legitimacy challenges together by presenting EU rights constitutionalism as an essential building block in justifying the overall relational structure between EU and state, and thus also in justifying the very status of the EU as a polity.

More specifically, the tenacious difficulties posed to the sceptic by rights constitutionalism in Europe, and equally, posed to the rights constitutionalist by the sceptic, yield at least one more definite, if modest, institutional conclusion. The four arguments from democratic practice, prudence, compensatory requirements, and structural innovation rehearsed above may struggle, singly or in combination, to provide a definitive basis for reconciling the rights sceptic's insistence upon strong democracy as a response to the fact of political pluralism with the emerging profile of right-entrenching constitutional pluralism. Yet in each case the justification for entrenchment would be strengthened by looking beyond grand constitutional designs to the adoption of a more robust human rights *policy* for the EU polity. Recently the subject of influential advocacy, such a policy would seek to complement and to match the EU's existing high human rights profile in external relations with a clear commitment to the internal development of rights awareness and development at all political and bureaucratic levels, including a dedicated Directorate-General within the Commission, enhanced standing before the ECJ of individuals and public interest groups alleging human rights violations, a European Human Rights Monitoring Agency, and a central policy-making and supervisory role for the Parliament.[68] Given the undeniably close links between rights and democracy, such an approach would undoubtedly enrich the democratic culture which must underpin constitutional commitment to rights. Improved monitoring and court access would sharpen the prudential argument for strong judicial protection and, together with a more active policy debate, would provide a more sensitive and deliberative context for assessing the force and deciding the practical import of the various compensatory arguments within the extended chain of rights. Finally, deeper awareness of rights questions and commitment to rights discourse would improve the prospects of a meaningful debate about the claim of human rights to a central place within the very *raison d'être* of the world's first post-state polity.

---

[68] See esp. P. Alston and J. H. H. Weiler 'An "Ever Closer Union" in Need of a Human Rights Policy: The European Union and Human Rights' in Alston, n. 13 above, 3–68. This analysis was adapted from a report prepared for the *Comité des Sages* which was responsible for 'Leading by Example: A Human Rights Agenda for the European Union for the Year 2000', reproduced as annexe 1 of the above volume. See also J. H. H. Weiler, 'Editorial: Does the European Union Truly Need a Charter of Rights?', (2000) 6 *European Law Journal* 95–7.

Part II

The Impact and Implications of the Human Rights Act

8

Rights versus Devolution

CHRIS HIMSWORTH

I. Introduction

The title of this chapter is prompted by that of a book by Alan Cairns, *Charter versus Federalism*, published in 1992.[1] In that book Cairns develops an inquiry into the impact of the Charter of Rights on Canadian federalism. He writes of the Charter producing a transformation of constitutional discourse. It has generated a dialogue on citizen–state relations that is an alternative to the federal–provincial discourse.[2] Although, in a formal sense, the Charter constrains both orders of government impartially, its actual impact on central and provincial governments is different. When the Charter nullifies a provincial executive or legislative action, 'it limits provincial variations in policy and administrative behaviour by invoking Canadian values. In a competition between a Charter-sustained Canadian value and a provincial value, the latter will lose.'[3] Elsewhere Cairns has written:

The relation of the Charter to federalism is straightforward. In general, it was a device to limit the creation of provincial diversities by the exercise of provincial jurisdictional power— a consequence that has already appeared in several areas, such as Sunday closing and provincial film censorship, where Canada-wide standards are emerging from court decisions in areas where provincial variety formerly flourished. The Charter was to induce citizens to evaluate the conduct of provincial governments through the lens of a rights-oriented Canadianism.[4]

The purpose of this paper is not to provide a critique of Cairns's ideas in so far as they relate to his own jurisdiction but rather to use them as a basis for testing similar propositions in relation to the devolutionary settlement established by the Scotland Act 1998. If the effect of the Charter of Rights in Canada is to suppress Canadian provincial diversity, then the effect of the United Kingdom's great human rights project may be to suppress the diversity, the opportunity for difference, that the creation of the Scottish Parliament was intended to create. The parallel between the two cases can, of course, be traced only at quite a general level because there are many obvious differences. In Canada, the Charter arrived more than a century after federalism had been established whilst in Scotland, the

---

[1] A. C. Cairns, *Charter versus Federalism: The Dilemmas of Constitutional Reform* (Montreal: McGill-Queen's University Press, 1992).

[2] Ibid. 74.   [3] Ibid. 76–7.

[4] A. C. Cairns, 'The Past and Future of the Canadian Administrative State', (1990) 40 *University of Toronto LJ* 319 at 334 (footnotes omitted).

Scotland Act and the Human Rights Act are of the same date and are to be seen as two parts of the same broad project of constitutional reform. We should also be cautious about any attempts to construct superficial comparisons between constitutional arrangements—federalism and devolution—which are so manifestly different, formally at least. The status of the Charter is also plainly different from that of the ECHR, as incorporated by the Human Rights Act. And, perhaps above all, it may be argued that the parallel breaks down because, whereas in Canada the Charter may be viewed as a Canadian restraint nationally imposed, the ECHR is not a UK instrument. It is a multinational regime to which Scotland, along with the rest of the United Kingdom, has been subject for nearly fifty years. To this last point it may, however, be responded that, whilst the general regime is European, the specific mode of 'incorporation' of the ECHR is peculiarly British and may be seen as a national UK restraint imposed with a high degree of uniformity. It is UK legislation which directly subordinates the Scottish Parliament to the Convention and imposes the particular model of judicial enforcement of rights.

There may be an objection at this point that it is quite inappropriate to seek out ways to criticize the reforms introduced by the Human Rights Act as in any way antagonistic to the spirit of devolution which underpins the Scotland Act. Supporters of the New Labour constitutional project will see one as entirely supportive of the other. Human rights are an additional benefit to devolved government, not some sort of constraint upon it. Devolutionary democracy is enhanced by the addition of the human rights dimension. It is, however, the role of the sceptic to subject such propositions to critical scrutiny and, whilst the specific consequences of the interaction of the two Acts of Parliament will be considered below, one of the starting points of this paper is the assumption that, in line with Cairns's critique of Canada, there may indeed be an element of tempering of the devolution project by the human rights project. It may be going a little far to claim that the Human Rights Act was a deliberate 'device to limit diversity', but there is at least scope for considering how far that has been, or will be, the effect.

It may be interesting to recall the last period in which UK governments adopted the judicial protection of human rights into their constitutional programmes. In the post-Second World War era of constitution-making for former colonies, UK governments inserted entrenched bills of rights into independence constitutions. This took a bit of explaining. As Stanley de Smith pointed out, 'Anglo-Saxon attitudes' towards constitutional bills of rights had been almost uniformly unfavourable.[5] Suddenly, however, the old attitudes were discarded and new attitudes assumed; but why?[6] De Smith goes on to explore this puzzle and answers it largely in terms of the emergence of ideas of rights in the old Commonwealth, the creation of the ECHR, and particular concerns about minority protection from majoritarian oppression. These had not, however, been arguments sufficient to persuade UK

---

[5] S. A. de Smith, *The New Commonwealth and its Constitutions* (London: Stevens, 1964), 162.
[6] Ibid. 163.

governments in relation to the home jurisdictions—nor in relation to the colonies until they were poised for liberation and new governments of their own election. Protection from those governments suddenly became important in a way that it had not been under British administration. Imperial government had been conducted without the need for the niceties of rights.[7]

Once again, however, we should be cautious about drawing crude parallels. Devolution of power to Scotland by the Act of 1998 bears little direct resemblance to the enactment of independence constitutions in the 1960s. A reasonable comparison may, nevertheless, be drawn between the two processes in that each involves the transfer of political power and the imposition of constraints on the exercise of that power, albeit in the pursuit of different purposes. There is, after all, nothing surprising about an analysis of devolution which sets up a balance sheet with the gross amount of legislative and executive power on the one side and the countervailing forces of central control on the other. If power devolved may indeed be power retained,[8] we are as much concerned to examine the areas of reserved legislative power, the powers of financial constraint, the other powers of UK governmental control (even if under the framework of the Memorandum of Understanding[9] and concordats), as the actual devolved powers themselves. We are interested in the impact of proportional representation—gifted so far to the devolved regimes but not to the UK Parliament; and the other constraints imposed on the devolved institutions including, very importantly, the impact of EC law upon the devolution settlement as a whole. Power which is devolved in the sense of not being explicitly reserved to the UK Parliament but which has, for practical purposes, become an EC competence over which the UK government retains a much more direct control at Brussels than the Scottish institutions can ever achieve is, once again, a form of power retained.

In this context, it is not at all odd to view the imposition of a particular regime for the judicial enforcement of human rights, as in the Human Rights Act 1998 and the Scotland Act 1998, as another mechanism in the overall process of the restraint of devolved power. Whether the restraint is to be seen as generally desirable in the pursuit of some higher constitutional interest, is another issue, but its presence is undeniable. Its effect, if not its constitutional origins and purpose, may be quite closely related to the restraint imposed by EC law. It may also be linked to the financial restrictions on devolution. To the extent that rights cost money and other resources,[10] the imposition on the devolved government of Scotland of the obligation to sustain the new rights regime was bound to impose financial and other burdens. Some are already becoming apparent.

---

[7] See e.g. Y. P. Ghai and J. P. W. B. McAuslan, *Public Law and Political Change in Kenya* (Oxford: Oxford University Press, 1970), ch. 11.

[8] Enoch Powell's widely quoted aphorism, cited e.g. at A. Marr, *The Battle for Scotland* (Harmondsworth: Penguin 1992), 122.

[9] Cm. 4444, 1999; SE/99/36.

[10] See S. Holmes and C. R. Sunstein, *The Cost of Rights* (New York: Norton, 2000).

A closely related way of looking at the addition of human rights protection to the devolution settlement is to consider what is the constitutionally appropriate level of government at which decisions about specific human rights regimes should be made. Assuming that the overarching status of the ECHR is to be unaffected, at what level should the manner of its incorporation be made? Is it self-evident that the state, because it is the member of the Council of Europe and party to the Convention, should decide? Or should the application of the principle of subsidiarity force this question down to a 'lower' level? Should the debate about whether to incorporate and, if so, on what model be conducted at the national (UK) or the national (Scotland) level? If a debate between enthusiasts of judicial protection and those of more sceptical disposition should take place, at what level should it be—or have been—conducted? There is certainly no general argument which points inevitably to a decision at the higher level. There is no general argument that rights protection cannot vary within federal states. The position in Quebec illustrates that. The UK has, in the past, sought a more differentiated pattern and continues to do so. Human rights regimes in Northern Ireland have been, and continue to be, different.[11] Nor is there anything in the argument that it has to be the prerogative of the UK authorities to determine the character of enforcement regimes simply because the UK is itself accountable to the Convention authorities for the supervision of implementation of the Convention. If that were the case, the UK would be compelled to adopt a much more interventionist line in respect of the Isle of Man and the Channel Islands.[12]

Nor can a 'centralist' argument be sustained on the basis that the central contribution is merely to provide a floor of rights, upon which devolved governments and parliaments may, with freedom, build further rights without ceiling. There will always be dangers in the use of the metaphor of a one-dimensional building of rights from a common floor since the definition and implementation of rights (perhaps excluding those providing absolute protection from torture and the like) will always be the result of trading off different claims and interests rather than of the inexorable progress to higher and higher levels of protection in an open sky.[13]

Whatever the general answer, if there is one, in the application of the principle of subsidiarity to the level at which the specific characteristics of human rights regimes should be decided, it may be thought that the Scottish case produces an especially nice irony. If the *point* of judicial protection was to address the failure of democratic protection by the Westminster Parliament, it was also the point of the devolution of political power to Scotland to produce there a better quality of democratic decision-making. Before the new Scottish Parliament had got down to demonstrating its new

[11] The Northern Ireland Human Rights Commission launched a consultation on a Northern Ireland Bill of Rights on 1 Mar. 2000.

[12] For comparisons drawn between Scotland, the Isle of Man and the Channel Islands in the course of debate on the Human Rights Bill, see HL Deb. 584, cols. 1303–9.

[13] For discussion, see e.g. C. M. G. Himsworth 'Things Fall Apart: The Harmonisation of Community Judicial Procedural Protection Revisited', (1997) 22 *European LR* 291. See also R. Bellamy in the present volume, chapter 2.

democratic strengths, it was saddled with judicial protection procedures designed to bear down more heavily upon it than those imposed on the Westminster Parliament itself.

These are issues to which this paper returns in Section IV below. Before that, however, Section II provides an overview of the relevant provisions of the Human Rights Act 1998, the Scotland Act 1998, and the relationship between the two. Section III provides a brief account of Scottish human rights litigation in 1999–2000 and other developments.

II. The Human Rights Act 1998 and the Scotland Act 1998[14]

The general provisions of the Human Rights Act are becoming well known, and do not have to be restated here. Very important for present purposes, however, is the distinction drawn in the Act between the treatment to be afforded, on the one hand, to 'primary legislation' held to be incompatible with a Convention right and, on the other, to subordinate legislation and other acts of public authorities. It is a distinction which has important consequences for the treatment of the legislation of the Scottish Parliament. Because the Human Rights Act does not, in a strong sense, incorporate[15] the Convention and make it part of UK law, it leaves earlier Acts of the Westminster Parliament unaffected by any implied repeal by the Convention's terms, and instead makes provisions of both earlier and later Acts subject to the procedure in section 4 of the Act, according to which their compatibility with the Convention rights may be adjudicated upon and, if appropriate, a superior court may make a declaration of incompatibility. Remedial action may be taken under section 10 and Schedule 2. Under the scheme adopted by the Human Rights Act, however, all legislation which is not defined by the Act as 'primary legislation' is treated as 'subordinate legislation' which may, like other acts of a public authority, be held by a court to be unlawful if incompatible with a Convention right and subject to the procedures laid down in sections 6–9 of the Act.

The Human Rights Act apart, an issue on which reasonable people can disagree is whether Acts of the Scottish Parliament are correctly styled primary legislation or secondary (or subordinate) legislation. Plainly they are not 'primary' in the same way that UK Acts are 'primary', as they are themselves made under the authority of such a primary Act. On the other hand, some distinction needs to be drawn between the lawmaking powers of the Scottish Parliament (or the Northern Ireland Assembly) and those of the Welsh National Assembly. Equally a distinction is

---

[14] This section draws upon C. Himsworth, 'The Homebringing: Devolving Rights Seriously', in A. Loux et al. (eds.), *Human Rights and Scots Law* (Oxford: Hart, forthcoming, 2002).

[15] For the argument that the Act did not 'incorporate' the Convention, see e.g., the Lord Chancellor at HL Deb. 585, col. 422 (5 Feb. 1998).

usefully drawn between the powers of the Scottish Parliament and those of the Scottish ministers. In both cases, these distinctions point to the need to dub Acts of the Scottish Parliament 'primary'.

Be that as it may, it is, on the face of it, clear that Acts of the Scottish Parliament are not to be treated as 'primary legislation' under the Human Rights Act and are, therefore, vulnerable not to the incompatibility and remedial procedures of sections 4 and 10 and Schedule 2 but to the more immediate procedures under sections 6 to 9. That this was an accurate reading of the position and that it was quite right in principle that Acts of the Scottish Parliament should be treated as 'subordinate legislation' was reaffirmed in debate on the Bill.[16]

This is not, however, a position which went entirely uncontested. It may be argued that, although it is possible to draw a sharp line between Acts of the Westminster Parliament and all other types of legislation, whether local authority by-laws or Acts of the Scottish Parliament, that is a categorization which produces too little differentiation on the 'subordinate' side of the line. On this view, a distinction could and *should* be drawn between the legislative product of a local authority or a minister and the legislative product of a Parliament.[17] The Scottish Parliament should be treated in a manner similar to that adopted for the Westminster Parliament.

Such arguments have, however, been rejected in the general scheme of the Human Rights Act and, as we shall see, the Scotland Act. Acts of the Scottish Parliament do not join Measures of the Church Assembly, Orders in Council under the Royal Prerogative, or commencement orders in respect of UK Acts (provided they are made by UK ministers and not members of the Scottish Executive[18]) as primary legislation, but instead join rules, regulations, and by-laws as subordinate legislation. On the other hand, it seems possible that the primary/subordinate classification may yet be a cause of difficulty and discrimination in the operation of the Human Rights Act's own provisions. An existing Westminster Act may be amended by a later Act of Parliament and, also, in relation to Scotland and if within its legislative competence, by an Act of the Scottish Parliament. Such amendments could be made in identical terms and could, therefore, raise identical questions of compatibility with Convention rights. They

---

[16] See e.g. the Lord Chancellor at HL Deb. 583, col. 539 (18 Nov. 1997); Lord Lester, ibid. col. 543. See also A. Bradley, 'Constitutional Reform, the Sovereignty of Parliament and Devolution', in *Constitutional Reform in the United Kingdom: Practice and Principles* (Oxford: Hart, 1998), 35.

[17] See R. Reed QC (now Lord Reed), 'Devolution and the Judiciary', ibid. 28. See also Lord Henley at HL Deb. 582, col. 1304 (3 Nov. 1997).

[18] Thus, for instance, the Welfare Reform and Pensions Act 1999 (Scotland) (Commencement No. 8) Order 2000, SSI 2000 No. 238, is subordinate legislation, whilst the commencement orders made by the Secretary of State are primary legislation. Similarly, the Environment Act 1995 (Commencement No. 17 and Savings Provision) (Scotland) Order 2000, SSI 2000 No. 180, which provides for the commencement of most of s. 57 of the Environment Act 1995, is subordinate, whilst the Environment Act 1995 (Commencement No. 18) (Scotland) Order 2000, SI 2000 No. 1986 (which applies to the remainder of s. 57), is primary.

would, however, produce different consequences for their resolution under the Human Rights Act.[19]

Turning to the Scotland Act itself, we find the human rights restrictions on the Scottish Parliament and Executive represented in a different way. They appear as limitations on the legislative competence of the Parliament and then, by extension, on the competence of the Executive. The Parliament may make laws to be known as Acts of the Scottish Parliament.[20] However, an Act is not law 'so far as any provision of the Act is outside the legislative competence of the Parliament'.[21] In turn, a provision is outside that competence so far as any of a list of conditions apply. Of greatest importance to the general devolutionary scheme is the stipulation that a provision will be outside the competence of the Parliament if it relates to 'reserved matters' as defined by Schedule 5 to the Act. A provision will also, however, be outside the competence if 'it is incompatible with any of the Convention rights', as defined in the Human Rights Act 1998,[22] or if it is incompatible with Community law.

Of most direct relevance to this account is clearly the restriction on legislative competence which derives from incompatibility with Convention rights, but it is important first to take note of the restrictions contained in the 'reserved matters'. There is no general reservation of matters relating to human rights. Part I of Schedule 5 reserves some aspects of 'the Constitution'[23] but these have no direct bearing on human rights. Also reserved by Part I of the Schedule, however, are international relations, but that reservation is expressly stated not to include observing and implementing international obligations, obligations under the Human Rights Convention (or under Community law), or assisting ministers of the Crown in matters of international relations.[24] It would not be within the competence of the Scottish Parliament or Executive to negotiate a new international convention. Observing and implementing existing obligations is, however, competent provided that they do not concern reserved matters. Probably the only other reservation which has direct consequences for human rights is that contained in Section L2 of Part II of Schedule 5. This reserves 'equal opportunities' by reference to the subject-matter of the four anti-discrimination Acts[25] and represents a significant restriction on the Parliament's competence.[26] It was a restriction strongly opposed in debate on the Bill.[27]

---

[19] This takes at face value the Act's categorization of the Acts of the Scottish Parliament as being always 'subordinate legislation' in s. 21(1). Presumably this means that they themselves could never be another 'instrument' which amends primary legislation and thus primary legislation? The definition of 'primary legislation', which seems not to correlate precisely to that of subordinate legislation, includes instruments amending primary legislation with the specific exception of instruments made by a member of the Scottish Executive, but not, in so many words, Acts of the Scottish Parliament.

[20] S. 28(1).   [21] S. 29(1).   [22] S. 126(1).   [23] Schedule 5, para. 1.

[24] Ibid. para. 7.

[25] The Equal Pay Act 1970, the Sex Discrimination Act 1975, the Race Relations Act 1976, and the Disability Discrimination Act 1995.

[26] A restriction which has subsequently been given recognition by s. 5(3) of the Standards in Scotland's Schools etc. Act 2000 (asp 6).

[27] See e.g. HC Deb. 309, cols. 1114–32 (31 Mar. 1998).

As far as members of the Scottish Executive are concerned, they derive their general powers from sections 52 and 53 of the Scotland Act and their 'devolved competence' is defined by reference to the Parliament's legislative competence including, therefore, compatibility with Convention rights. It is, in addition, provided that '[a] member of the Scottish Executive has no power to make any subordinate legislation, or to do any other act, so far as the legislation or act is incompatible with any of the Convention rights or with Community law'.[28]

As well as imposing these restrictions on the competence of the Scottish Parliament and Executive, the Scotland Act contains special procedural provisions for securing compliance and for the resolution of disputes. As a precautionary device similar to that required by section 19 of the Human Rights Act, a member of the Scottish Executive in charge of a Bill must make a statement that, in his or her view, the provisions of the Bill would be within the legislative competence of the Parliament, a formula which embraces compatibility with Convention rights.[29] Under section 33 a Bill which has been passed by the Scottish Parliament may be referred to the Judicial Committee of the Privy Council by the Advocate-General, the Lord Advocate, or the Attorney-General for consideration of whether the Bill (or any provision in it) would be within the Parliament's legislative competence. Any such reference must be made within four weeks of the passing of the Bill, and submission of the Bill for Royal Assent has to be deferred for the purpose.[30] A Bill which is held to be outwith competence cannot be submitted for Assent in its unamended form. In addition to this pre-Assent challenge by a law officer, there is scope for post-enactment challenge to the competence of an Act of the Scottish Parliament (or something done by member of the Scottish Executive) in ordinary proceedings thereafter, including judicial review. This is, however supplemented by Schedule 6 to the Scotland Act, which defines and makes special provision for the handling of 'devolution issues'. Thus a question whether an Act of the Scottish Parliament or any provision of an Act of the Scottish Parliament is within the legislative competence of the Parliament is a devolution issue, and this is joined by questions of whether the exercise (or proposed exercise) of functions by members of the Scottish Executive is within devolved competence, or incompatible with any of the Convention rights. A question whether a *failure* to act by a member of the Scottish Executive is similarly incompatible can also be a devolution issue.[31] The procedures laid down for the handling of devolution issues (arising in England and Wales and Northern Ireland as well as in Scotland) include special provision for the involvement of law officers and the reference of devolution issues, whether directly or on appeal, to the Judicial Committee of the Privy Council.[32]

---

[28] S. 57(2). For interesting discussion of the impact of this provision, see I. Jamieson, 'Relationship between the Scotland Act and the Human Rights Act', 2001 SLT (News) 43.

[29] Scotland Act, s. 29. There is not, of course, the option of making a statement of non-compliance, as is permitted by s. 19 of the Human Rights Act.

[30] S. 32.   [31] Schedule 6, pt. i. See Jamieson, n. 28 above.   [32] Ibid. pts. ii–v.

The provision made by the Scotland Act for the imposition of human rights limitations on legislative and executive competence and then for their classification as devolution issues raises certain boundary questions. One concerns the line drawn between, on the one hand, the bodies whose activities may raise human rights questions and which may on that account give rise to devolution issues and, on the other hand, those which are incapable of giving rise to devolution issues as defined. Thus, the Scottish Parliament apart, only the legislative and other activities of the Scottish Executive can give rise to devolution issues and not, for instance, the activities of bodies beyond the Executive itself. Local authorities, health bodies, and quangos are not included, and, although the practical consequences of the distinction may turn out to be not very great, it is, at the very least, a curiosity that whilst the low-level act of a civil servant in a Scottish Executive department may give rise to a devolution issue (perhaps being referred for its resolution to the Judicial Committee), a decision by a health authority or by the Scottish Environment Protection Agency will not. If Scottish Homes were to remain a quango, its activities would not raise devolution issues. When it is relocated as a (next steps) agency within the Scottish Administration,[33] they may do so.

There must be added to this account of the two Acts some further consideration of the ways in which they can operate in combination:

1. There is first the transitional point that, in its earliest months of operation, the Scotland Act stood alone. That Act was almost entirely in force by 1 July 1999,[34] but the Human Rights Act was not generally in force until 2 October 2000. This was an eventuality anticipated in the Scotland Act itself.[35]

2. An additional comment is, however, required on the impact of the Scotland Act on the remedial procedures in section 10 and Schedule 2 of the Human Rights Act.[36] Section 5(2) of the Human Rights Act itself already anticipates the involvement of the Scottish Ministers by enabling a member of the Scottish Executive to become a party to any proceedings in which a court is considering whether to make a declaration of incompatibility in relation to a provision of an Act of Parliament. This is because, in areas where competence is devolved, the Scottish Ministers may have an interest in the outcome and it will fall to a member of the Scottish Executive to take any remedial action under section 10. The general provisions of the Scotland Act ensure that, within areas of 'devolved competence', executive authority is transferred from Ministers of the Crown to the Scottish Ministers[37] and that procedures in relation to subordinate legislation in the Westminster Parliament are translated into procedures in the Scottish Parliament.[38] Within the devolved field, incompatibilities are to be remediated by the Scottish Ministers, with recourse to the Scottish

---

[33] See Housing (Scotland) Act 2001, Pt 4.
[34] Scotland Act 1998 (Commencement) Order 1998, SI 1998 No. 3178.   [35] See s. 129(2).
[36] Sched. 2 has been amended to clarify the adaptation of Westminster parliamentary procedures to apply to Holyrood by the Scotland Act 1998 (Consequential Modifications), Order 2000, SI 2000 No. 2040, art. 2 and sched. para. 21.
[37] Ss. 53, 54 and 117.   [38] S. 118.

Parliament. In contrast with a remedial amendment made at Westminster, however, but in line with the general distinction between primary and subordinate legislation already mentioned, any remedial order made by a member of the Scottish Executive is, in terms of section 21 of the Human Rights Act, subordinate rather than primary legislation.

3. The shared reliance of both Acts upon the concept of 'the Convention rights' has already been mentioned. Interlinkage between the Acts assumes a common interpretation of those rights, but whilst this is not the place to develop general questions about the difficulties that this process of interpretation may pose for courts in general, two specific points should be mentioned. One is that, in so far as Convention rights questions are taken as 'devolution issues', they may be finally resolved by the Judicial Committee, whereas the same question, whether from Scotland or elsewhere but not taken as a devolution issue, will (in civil matters) be determined by the House of Lords. The other is that a Convention rights issue taken as a matter of the competence of the Scottish Parliament, or in relation to sub-ordinate legislation (but not the other acts) of a member of the Scottish Executive, will be interpreted with reference to section 101 of the Scotland Act. That section requires that, if a provision *could* be read in such a way as to be outside competence, it shall be read 'as narrowly as is required for it to be within competence, if such a reading is possible, and is to have effect accordingly'. The meaning to be attributed to this section may not be wholly clear, but the point has been taken that its interpretation may produce a result which is different from that which might be produced when section 3(1) of the Human Rights Act is applied.[39] That subsection provides simply: 'So far as it is possible to do so, primary legislation and subordinate legislation must be read and given effect in a way which is compatible with the Convention rights.'[40] Whether these features will, in practice, produce different results is not easy to predict, but the use of a different court and reference to a different interpretative aid may quite reasonably result in different outcomes.[41]

4. Some further steps were, however, quite deliberately taken to try to assure a parallel application of the law by specific provision in the Scotland Act. Section 100(1) restricts general access to courts on Convention grounds to 'victims', in line with section 7 of the Human Rights Act. That restriction is expressly not applied to law officers and would not, therefore, curb their right of pre-assent challenge to a Bill in the Scottish Parliament. Section 100(3) restricts the award of damages for

[39] See Lord Mackay of Drumadoon at HL Deb. 593, cols. 1954–6 (28 Oct. 1998).

[40] That the application of this interpretive aid may not always produce a result favourable to a 'generous' application of the Convention has already been commented on. See G. Marshall, 'Interpreting Interpretation in the Human Rights Bill', [1998] *Public Law* 167 at 170. See also *McLean v. HMA* (JCPC, unreported, 24 May 2001), para. 70.

[41] For further speculation about the possible consequences of setting up the two different procedural routes, see Lord Hope of Craighead, 'Devolution and Human Rights', (1998) 3 *European Human Rights Law Review* 367, and A. O'Neill, 'The Scotland Act and the Government of Judges', 1999 SLT (News) 61. Mr O'Neill refers to the particular difference that might emerge from the availability to courts of s. 102 of the Scotland Act under which the effects of retrospective decisions on matters of legislative competence may be varied.

breach of a Convention right, in line with section 8(3) and (4) of the Human Rights Act. By section 57(3), a similar protection is extended to the Lord Advocate, in relation to criminal prosecutions and investigation of deaths, as is given by section 6(2) of the Human Rights Act to authorities required to enforce provisions which are themselves incompatible with a Convention Right.[42]

5. One question which the initial version of the Scotland Bill left unclear was whether the Human Rights Act would be amendable or indeed subject to repeal by the Scottish Parliament.[43] The obligation not to legislate in a manner incompatible with the Convention did not seem to protect the actual terms of the Human Rights Act. There was no reason why its subject matter should be treated as a reserved matter as part of 'The Constitution'. If, however, this was a loop hole in the original scheme, it was one which was closed at report stage in the Commons.[44] The structure of legislative competence was redesigned, with a new role given to Schedule 4 to the Act. It serves to 'entrench' certain statutory provisions against amendment by the Scottish Parliament. Among these 'constitutional Acts'[45] is the Human Rights Act.[46] That Act may not be modified by amendment or repeal. The same applies to the provisions of the Scotland Act mentioned in paragraph 4 above.

An interesting position has, therefore, been created in which 'human rights' are not, as such, a reserved matter, although some aspects of human rights—notably equal opportunities—*are* reserved. On the other hand, the Human Rights Act itself cannot be modified by the Scottish Parliament. The full consequences of this conjunction of rules on legislative competence will no doubt be worked out in practice. Whether difficulties arise will depend as much as anything on the enthusiasm of the Scottish Parliament for legislating in this area. Issues may be raised if, for instance, the Parliament chooses to enact legislation which is parallel to but different from the Human Rights Act itself. Such legislation must not expressly amend the Human Rights Act or the Scotland Act, but presumably (for instance) legislation to establish a human rights commission in Scotland would cause no difficulty?[47]

What would be the result, however, if the Scottish Parliament, without reference to the Human Rights Act, enacted a comprehensive new code of rights protection— perhaps more 'generous', perhaps more restrictive than the ECHR, perhaps some

---

[42] On the differences of practice between Scotland and England in the review of prosecutorial decisions, see Lord Hope, ibid 377, and see also HL Deb. 583, col. 805 (24 Nov. 1997). The court rejected arguments based on s. 57(3) in *Starrs v. Ruxton*, 2000 JC 208 at 230 and 255; (2000) SLT 42 at 58 and 73.

[43] See C. M. G. Himsworth, 'Devolving Rights', (1998) 3 *Scotland Forum* 3.

[44] HC Deb. 312, col. 261 (12 May 1998).

[45] Others include Articles 4 and 6 of the Acts of Union so far as they relate to freedom of trade, and s. 1 and some other provisions of the European Communities Act 1972.

[46] The 'reservation' of the Human Rights Act 1998 does not prevent the exercise of executive authority under it by the Scottish Ministers. See Scotland Act 1998, sched. 4, paras. 12–13. The remedial powers have been mentioned. See also rule-making in the Human Rights Act 1998 (Jurisdiction) (Scotland) Rules 2000, SSI 2000 No. 301; and the Acts of Sederunt and Adjournal, SSIs 2000, Nos. 314, 315, 316.

[47] The Scottish Executive are currently consulting on the creation of a commission: 'Protecting our Rights: A Human Rights Commission for Scotland' (Mar. 2001).

of each, but at all events different? Would a court be empowered to strike down as legislatively incompetent something which appeared to be an implied amendment of the Human Rights Act? Would any additional problem be caused if the new code purported to provide access wider than that offered to Convention 'victims' or to provide a wider range of remedies than is currently permitted?

III. Developments in the Long Year 20 May 1999 to 1 October 2000

On 20 May 1999, the Lord Advocate and the Solicitor-General for Scotland ceased to be law officers in the UK Government and assumed responsibilities instead as members of the Scottish Executive.[48] From that date, therefore, they became subject to the human rights regime imposed by the Scotland Act 1998 and were joined on 1 July 1999 by the remaining members of the Scottish Executive and the Scottish Parliament. Between 20 May 1999 and 1 October 2000, Convention rights were justiciable in Scotland in a way not experienced in England[49] until 2 October 2000, and the events of that year are plainly relevant to this account. In many ways, however, it was bound to be an atypical period. Not only was it the first year, but it was a year in which Convention rights were of only partial application even in Scotland, since most public authorities were excluded.[50]

Sceptics will, in any event, be very wary of the risks of jumping too quickly to conclusions based on the early months of a new experiment. They will want to look beyond the first test case or the first high-profile confrontation between individual and state. They will be looking for signs well beyond the courts themselves,[51] and they will be looking to the longer term and the impact over time. Of course, some comment would be required if several Acts of the Scottish Parliament had already been struck down on human rights grounds. That has not, however, been the case. The Parliament passed only one Act in 1999 and there were only another thirteen in 2000. On the other hand, the one Act that *was* passed in 1999 has indeed been subject to the only challenge to an Act so far. The Mental Health (Public Safety and Appeals) (Scotland) Act 1999 was passed as an emergency measure in the Parliament's first weeks to provide new rules on the detention of mental health patients. In *Anderson v. Scottish Ministers*[52] a challenge to the Act based on Article 5 of the ECHR was rejected. Detention for the purposes not of treatment but of protecting the public was legitimate.

---

[48] Scotland Act 1998 s. 44, and the Scotland Act 1998 (Commencement) Order 1998, SI 1998 No. 3178.

[49] The lack of 'executive' involvement in prosecutions has produced a different situation in Wales.

[50] It was, for instance, important in *Varey v. Scottish Ministers*, 2001 SC 162, 2000 SLT 1432, to distinguish acts of the Scottish Parole Board from those of the Scottish Ministers.

[51] One other phenomenon is precautionary legislation. In parallel with UK measures, there have been the Bail, Judicial Appointments etc. (Scotland) Act 2000 and the Regulation of Investigatory Powers (Scotland) Act 2000. See also the Convention Rights (Compliance) (Scotland) Bill.

[52] Reported as *A (A Mental Patient) v. Scottish Ministers*, 2000 SLT 873.

Anderson has been the only case raised against an Act of the Parliament in which a devolution issue of any sort has been argued, and it may be of some significance that it had a basis in Convention rights rather than, for instance, requiring adjudication upon reserved matters. The same is true of the devolution issues taken against the Executive. There have been over 900 devolution issues raised, and it appears that *all* have been based on Convention rights arguments and virtually all have been raised in respect of procurators fiscal[53] in relation to alleged breaches of the Convention in criminal proceedings. Even the landmark case of *Starrs v. Ruxton*,[54] which outlawed the use of temporary sheriffs, was based on the failure of the procurator fiscal to prosecute before an independent and impartial tribunal. Perhaps even more artificially, the challenge in *Clancy v. Caird*,[55] in which the use of temporary Court of Session judges was upheld, had to be entertained on the basis that it would be a failure of the Scottish Ministers to ensure the provision of an impartial tribunal in civil cases. The only case in which the Scottish Ministers have been challenged directly has been the landmark case of *County Properties Ltd v. Scottish Ministers*,[56] in which the independence and impartiality of planning 'call-in' procedures (including the use of reporters) were successfully attacked.[57]

This is not the place to argue the merits of decisions so far made. Nor is it possible to make an early judgment on their impact. Many issues are subject to appeal,[58] and it therefore remains unclear what the final outcome will be, for instance, on the requirement of keepers of vehicles to identify drivers under section 172(2)(a) of the Road Traffic Act 1988[59] or planning procedures, in both cases with consequences for England and Wales[60] as well as for Scotland.

It is simply too early to judge how the reasoning of the courts in human rights cases is developing, although there may already be signs of some judicial irritation with the diversity of authority cited before them. This may be especially evident in *Clancy v. Caird* and *Clark v. Kelly*[61] as compared with *Starrs v. Ruxton*, but *Clancy v. Caird* did also raise issues which were very sensitive for Court of Session judges. It was not surprising that the Court showed a reluctance to disqualify their own temporary brethren, especially if it came close to implying that any judge

---

[53] The concession that the acts of procurators fiscal were, for the purposes of the Scotland Act, the acts of the Lord Advocate was made in *Starrs* below.

[54] 2000 JC 208; 2000 SLT 42. See also *Clark v. Kelly*, 2000 SLT 1038, in which the role of clerks to district courts came under scrutiny.

[55] 2000 SC 441; 2000 SLT 546.

[56] 2000 SLT 965. See also *Lafarge Redland Aggregates Ltd v. Scottish Ministers*, 2000 SLT 1361, which was decided after 2 Oct. 2000.

[57] Distinguishing *Bryan v. United Kingdom*, (1996) 21 EHRR 342.

[58] The first devolution issue to reach the JCPC was heard by the court in July 2000 (*Montgomery v. HMA*, 2001 PC 1). By May 2001, three further cases had been decided.

[59] *Brown v. Stott*, 2000 JC 328; 2000 SCCR 314. This decision was reversed by the JCPC—2001 PC 43.

[60] See on planning: *R (on the application of Alconbury Developments Ltd) v. Secretary of State for E,T,R* [2001] 2 All ER 429.

[61] 2001 JC 16.

nominated by the Lord Advocate might be vulnerable.[62] In the case of temporary sheriffs, the consequences of disqualification were more distant, and it was perhaps less troubling to issue a decision based on the implicit assumption that, at the level of the sheriff court, there had been a long-standing failure to ensure that justice be seen to be done.[63]

Two other phenomena may be mentioned in the early experience of human rights litigation in Scotland. Sceptics will be alert to the possibility of signs of capture of the process by commercial interests. This seems to be barely tenable so far, although *County Properties* may be a sign of a move in that direction. The motivation and the enthusiasm of legal firms for some types of human rights litigation may, however, bear examination in due course. The case of *Starrs* may have brought about the demise of the temporary sheriff. The two panels, Messrs Starrs and Chalmers, were ordered to appear for trial before a permanent sheriff.[64]

Secondly, there are clear indications of the forced preoccupation of the law officers and the Scottish Executive at large not only with the defence of the challenges raised against them but, more importantly, with picking up the pieces afterwards. In circumstances where no one at all claimed that there was a risk in *Starrs* that an injustice would actually be done, and there was no evidence at all that an injustice has ever been done through the lack of independence or impartiality of a temporary sheriff, was it rational for a consequence of the decision to be the immediate suspension of all holders of the office? Great strain was immediately placed on Scotland's system of criminal justice, with negative consequences for the conduct both of criminal trials[65] and, apparently, of fatal accident inquiries.[66] Is it rational that the normal processes of public decision-making can be trumped and trampled on in this way?

IV. In the longer term

Despite this flurry of activity just described in the first eighteen months or so of Convention rights litigation in the Scottish courts, any thoughts about the longer-term impact of the human rights project on the devolution project must be highly provisional and speculative. It may, however, be appropriate to draw those thoughts together under three different heads. In the first place, there is devolved Scotland as constitutional pilot or test tube. Then there is devolved Scotland as a relatively small and perhaps insecure political system. Finally, in a more direct return to the

[62] See also *Gibbs v. Ruxton*, 2000 JC 258.

[63] See also acknowledgements in *HMA v. H*, 2000 JC 552 (and *HMA v. Little*, 1999 SCCR 625) that there was no general rule against delay in Scottish criminal proceedings.

[64] Successive delays in the Linlithgow sheriff court eventually led to the abandonment of the prosecutions (*Scotsman*, 14 May 2001).

[65] For a debate in the Scottish Parliament on the ECHR but with much emphasis on the impact on the criminal justice system, see SPOR, 2 Mar. 2000, col. 301. See also *Millar v. Dickson* (unreported, PC, 24 July 2001).

[66] *Scotsman*, 25 Aug. 2000.

ideas floated in Section I, there is scope for a little further discussion of the different status accorded by the Human Rights Act and the Scotland Act to Acts of the Scottish Parliament. It will be useful, at that point, to reflect on the different status of the legislation of the two Parliaments in the light of ideas of 'dialogue' between courts and legislatures which have been generated in other jurisdictions. Such dialogue is itself, of course, a concept to be subjected to sceptical scrutiny, but it may assist analysis.

Devolved Scotland as constitutional experiment

It would be outrageous to draw anything but the most distant parallel between the year (1999–2000) during which Convention rights became enforceable in Scottish courts with the year (1989–90) when the poll tax was introduced in Scotland, a year ahead of its implementation in England and Wales. It does seem entirely likely, however, that it must have occurred to ministers and officials in the Scottish Executive and the Crown Office that, whether this was directly intended or not, they were being pushed over the top into not only the sniper fire (as might have been predicted) but also into the heavy guns of the rights protagonists. Watching the skirmishing of the Scottish regiments, the Lord Chancellor and the Home Secretary lay in their bunkers for another year, refining their plans and training their troops.[67] Whatever else, the human rights element of the devolution settlement made life more interesting than it might have wished for the Scottish Executive. Engineering governmental change of the dimensions required by the Scotland Act was always going to be a challenge. In addition, however, there have been the hundreds of challenges to the criminal justice system; the Executive was blamed for not anticipating that a large proportion of the judiciary would have to be fired; they were the first to confront the possibility that a linchpin in the fight against speeding on the roads would have to be abandoned; they had to face serious challenge to the fifty-year-old system of development control; and the very first Act of the Scottish Parliament (itself an emergency measure) came under heavy attack.

Scotland as a small political system

Some of this fire may now be directed to other parts of the United Kingdom, and the first year of the human rights experiment in Scotland may turn out to have been uniquely dramatic. In some respects, for instance, issues such as road traffic prosecutions and development control have acquired a more obviously UK aspect as cases move up towards the Judicial Committee of the Privy Council or the House of Lords, and responses, despite devolution, may be generated in a coordinated way

---

[67] An illustration of the concern within the Lord Chancellor's Department about the level of litigation in Scotland and the probable consequences for England appeared at HC Deb. 10 Apr. 2000, col. 21(WA).

by the different UK administrations acting collaboratively. This, of course, has consequences for devolved decision-making to which we shall return.

On the other hand, some first-year activity may provide clues as to the future impact of those human rights issues which arise solely or very largely in relation to Scotland alone. Experience so far has been short and obviously bound up with the transitional and start-up problems of a new political system. One feature which may endure, however, is that of the turbulence of a relatively small political system and, in particular, the vulnerability of such a system to pressure-group activity of potentially disabling dimensions. Such vulnerability does not necessarily attach to the particular form of devolved government now operating. It might apply equally to an independent Scotland. Vulnerability to pressure is, in any event, perhaps an intended feature of a system of government designed to be more responsive to popular concerns, less dominated by party machines, and enjoying the benefits of such novelties as proportional representation. If, however, the 'section 28' controversy and the role of Mr Brian Souter and his campaign for a private referendum contain any lessons for the future, these may concern the higher risk of derailment of governments in small political systems. Any other considerations apart, it must be easier and cheaper to organize a postal referendum across Scotland than across England or the whole of the United Kingdom. To this the response might well be that Mr Souter's success was very limited—'section 28' was repealed[68]—and that, in the neighbouring and much larger political system, the government has been derailed by the House of Lords. It may also be argued that the very point of human rights incorporation is to rescue a small political system from some of the turbulence just described. The courts will protect citizens from pressure group politics.

The sceptic, however, will remain unconvinced by this. He or she will be aware of the risk of the capture of human rights issues by the rich and powerful, and will suspect that this tendency may be more exaggerated in smaller systems. Sceptics will also have noted with concern the campaign already launched in the courts against the Protection of Wild Mammals (Scotland) Bill[69] and the declared intention of that campaign to move on to the use of Convention rights arguments.[70]

Rights versus devolution: nonsense in a kilt?

Even if the problems of smallness are not as great as supposed or if they turn out to be transitory, there will remain the question of whether the contribution of the human rights element in the devolution package will tend to be supportive or destructive of that package as a whole. This chapter is premised on the assumption that devolution itself is an honourable objective and that the commitment to Scotland-based power and accountability must be sustained. It is also premised on

---

[68] Ethical Standards in Public Life etc. (Scotland) Act 2000 s. 34. But the obligation to have regard to the value of stable family life was imposed on councils by s. 35. See also s. 56 of the Standards in Scotland's Schools etc. Act 2000.

[69] See *Whalley v. Lord Watson*, 2000 SC 340.   [70] See e.g. *Scotsman*, 11 Aug. 2000.

the assumption that the rights of citizens must be respected and that there is nothing objectionable in principle about their source in a European treaty. The chapter is not at all to be associated with the blanket antipathy to both devolution and European human rights reflected in some of the Scottish political debate.[71] It insists simply that the centralizing tendency of a rights regime is at least problematic when superimposed on a constitutional system committed to the decentralization of power through devolution. If there is a generally centralizing tendency of human rights regimes,[72] how far is it likely to be realized in the specific conditions established for the operation of Scottish government under the Scotland Act 1998 and then for human rights protection by that Act and the Human Rights Act 1998? There are, I think, a couple of pointers—one based on indications in the cases decided so far and the other which derives from the formal status given to the Scottish Parliament and which was discussed in Section II.

Practically all the litigation so far initiated has focused on challenges based on executive rather than legislative activity, and this may continue to be the case. Where such challenges are successful, however, a legislative response may be required; and, as suggested earlier, it seems inevitable that, in jurisdictions which force rights issues up to the same (or similarly constituted) supreme courts, there will be a similarity of outcome and, almost as inevitably, a similarity of response by the different administrations and legislatures.[73] The common characteristics of human rights cases may produce a centralizing tendency across swathes of Scottish administration and, perhaps even more significantly, of areas of Scots private law previously untouched by UK or English decision-making. Human rights issues have the potential to reach deep into the Scottish legal system, and English court decisions on human rights may come to have a significant new effect on Scots law. With legal professional practice increasingly merging in the commercial areas, human rights practice may follow with even greater energy. If these sorts of development do occur, it may be that ultimate outcomes will not depend greatly on the formal status of the Scottish Parliament and its legislation discussed in Section II. A centralizing conformity may be achieved, even though few Acts of the Scottish Parliament are directly challenged and even fewer struck down.[74] At least symbolically, however, the distinction between the status of ASPs and UK Acts remains. UK Acts are vulnerable only to a declaration of incompatibility by a superior court (whether that incompatibility is to be resolved by the UK Parliament or by the Scottish Parliament) whilst ASPs may be challenged directly in a court at any level.

---

[71] One additional feature of 1999 was the consequence for Lord McCluskey of his particular brand of scepticism. See *Hoekstra v. HM Advocate (No. 1)*; *(No. 2)*, (2000) JC 387, 391. See also, in the JCPC, *Hoekstra v. HM Advocate (No. 3)*, 2001 PC 37.

[72] See Mark Tushnet in this volume, chapter 19.

[73] See also the similarity of 'precautionary' legislation at n. 51 above.

[74] A very interesting new interaction between the English and Scottish courts, with potentially 'centralizing' consequences, may be observed in *Alconbury*, where the House of Lords commented on an Outer House decision in the Court of Session. See *Alconbury*, n. 60 above, at paras. 131, 162, 171, 180. The *County Properties* decision was subsequently reversed by the Inner House

I would conclude with two brief points. In the first place, the argument can still be sustained that the Scottish Parliament (and the Northern Ireland Assembly) should, in principle, have been treated not like a parish council, quango, or minister but in a manner much more closely resembling that granted by the UK Parliament to itself. The incompatibility principle and procedure have been conceived narrowly as a protection for parliamentary sovereignty and, therefore, applicable only to UK Acts. More positively, they may be seen as readily and appropriately extendable to any parliament and any form of parliamentary legislation. The reason why the Scottish Parliament should be protected from the summary nullification of its Acts is not because of any claim to sovereignty but because there should be an opportunity for any parliament to reflect, to consider options, without the pressure of immediate chaos and to produce a viable solution. These are conditions reasonably claimed by a parliament, whether devolved or not.

Secondly, if this point is located within the 'dialogue' debate which has flourished in the area of human rights, that conclusion may be reinforced. The suggestion has been made that in the long run legislatures always win against courts in carrying forward their proposals into law. They may be thwarted by courts, but only temporarily.[75] The concept of dialogue between courts and legislature on which that suggestion is based has the capacity to offer what is perhaps the strongest challenge to rights scepticism. In its generality, however, it is not an idea to be pursued here, and it is in any event an idea which is not readily applied directly to the Human Rights Act regime. The overriding role of Strasbourg complicates matters. If, however, the notion of dialogue does have attractions and if, by building the incompatibility principle into the UK system, some explicit acknowledgement is given to the strength of that notion, this must give added force to the claim of the Scottish Parliament to be accorded equal esteem. If the pressure placed on planning procedures were to develop (*pace Alconbury*) into a successful challenge not of a single call-in but of the validity of the Planning Acts themselves, there will be an opportunity for the remediation procedures to operate both at Westminster and Holyrood because the Planning Acts are, at present, 'primary legislation'. If, in due course, there were a successful challenge to the content of the Bail Acts just passed, the procedures would, because of the secondary nature of the Scottish Act, diverge for reasons which are difficult to sustain. The devolved jurisdiction is twice subordinated—once at the point the legislation is passed, and then at the point when its validity is contested.

[75] See esp. P. W. Hogg and A. A. Bushell, 'The *Charter* Dialogue between Courts and Legislatures', (1997) 35 *Osgoode Hall LJ* 75.

9

Contested Constitutionalism:
Human Rights and Deliberative Democracy
in Northern Ireland

COLIN J. HARVEY

I. Introduction

The Good Friday (or Belfast) Agreement concluded in 1998 contains an impressive commitment to the protection of human rights.[1] The document, which followed many years of public and private negotiation, is evidence that political processes can be made to yield impressive practical results, even in Northern Ireland. The language of rights flows through the Agreement, and rights-talk has framed the ongoing debate on implementation in many areas of legal and political life. This is unsurprising given the Northern Irish context, but it marks a radical departure from the piecemeal approaches of the past. Human rights abuse was a consistent feature of a conflict in which over three thousand people lost their lives. It is often argued that better forms of legal protection would have reduced, but not necessarily eradicated, the problems of Northern Ireland.[2] What is now evident is that abuses of human rights fuelled the conflict, and that the Agreement is an attempt to bring these to an end within the context of a complex constitutional order.[3]

The debate which has emerged in Northern Ireland reflects many of the pressing issues in modern legal scholarship, in particular the relationship between processes of transition, human rights protection, and political democracy. A core aspect of the current political process, which marks it out from the past, is its focus on the principle of inclusivity. The right to participate underpins many aspects of the Agreement, the Northern Ireland Act 1998, and what has followed. The institutional design of the new arrangements provides legal authority for continuing political dialogue between the two main political communities and others, on an inclusive basis. It is consociational in significant respects with confederal elements, and it essentially recognizes the fact that Northern Ireland is both Irish and British.[4]

---

[1] Cm. 3883.

[2] B. Dickson, 'The Protection of Human Rights—Lessons from Northern Ireland', (2000) 5 *European Human Rights Law Review* 213.

[3] See generally B. O'Leary, 'The Nature of the Agreement', (1999) 22 *Fordham International Law Journal* 1628.

[4] J. McGarry and B. O'Leary, *Policing Northern Ireland: Proposals for a New Start* (Belfast: Blackstaff Press, 1999), 1.

The structure includes the expressed desire to mainstream human rights norms in the governance of Northern Ireland. The image is one of a human rights culture which rests on changing the way that public power is exercised.

This chapter explores the context of the rights debate in Northern Ireland and the new structures which have been created in the wake of the Agreement, and looks at the role of the Northern Ireland Human Rights Commission. One of the tasks of this Commission is to advise the Secretary of State on a Bill of Rights for Northern Ireland. This process has brought scholarly arguments over rights discourse firmly into the public sphere. Rights discourse forms one part of the reconstruction of Northern Ireland. It is one aspect of the complex picture which, it is argued, is part of the attempt to nurture a form of contested constitutionalism, where the only legitimate struggles of the future are purely political ones. In other words, Northern Ireland, as a constitutional entity, remains 'up for grabs'. So, rather than concentrate on a particular rights issue, such as the regulation of parades or the use of emergency powers, this chapter examines the structures which have been erected to make the right to participate meaningful in the constitutional context of Northern Ireland. The argument is that human rights discourse functions as an important tool in the struggle to achieve the goals of deliberative democracy. In Northern Ireland it has assisted in promoting dialogue in the public sphere on issues that might otherwise be ignored and which go beyond borders.

II. The context

Northern Ireland was scarred from birth by coercion and violence. It has never functioned as a 'normal' constitutional entity and has existed in an almost permanent state of emergency.[5] Some of the worst human rights abuses have occurred in the area of emergency law, and the reliance on this body of law has been questioned. The ghosts of coercion have haunted Northern Ireland since its inception, and it has struggled to secure recognition as a legitimate constitutional project. On reflection, the partition of Ireland in the 1920s was an exercise in avoidance. The solution to contestation on the island was division and a crude process of boundary-drawing. The nationalist/republican community in Northern Ireland found itself locked into a jurisdiction which regarded it as the 'enemy within'. The new 'state' also perceived itself as under threat from the south of Ireland. The result was a process of exclusion which relegated members of the nationalist/republican community to a marginalized position. One direct response to this process of exclusion was the emergence in the 1960s of a movement in support of civil rights.[6] The aim of this movement was at first to seek equality within the existing structures, and

---

[5] See F. Ni Aolain, *The Politics of Force: Conflict Management and State Violence in Northern Ireland* (Belfast: Blackstaff Press, 2000); C. Campbell, *Emergency Law in Ireland 1918–1925* (Oxford: Clarendon Press, 1994).

[6] R. F. Foster, *Modern Ireland 1600–1972* (London: Penguin Books, 1989), 587–90.

reflected growing self-confidence in the nationalist/republican community. This gained political expression in 1970 with the formation of the Social Democratic and Labour Party (SDLP). The focus was on securing an improvement in the material conditions of the nationalist/republican community as well as formal recognition. Here a tension was present, and it remains a challenge in relation to the continuing politics of Northern Ireland. Calls for equality were within the context of the UK legal and political order, and participation in the structures of governance could be presented as recognition of the legitimacy of Northern Ireland as a constitutional project. For nationalists and republicans this was problematic, and has consistently made discussion of participation a contentious issue. The use of human rights discourse in Northern Ireland must therefore be located against this backdrop of continuing constitutional contestation. The Agreement manages but does not resolve this contestation: it primarily seeks to alter the means of engagement by 'institutionalizing' the conflict within formal political structures.

The difficulty for those seeking to deploy human rights discourse was to find a mode of expression which was not merely immanent to the UK legal order. As was later discovered, one useful way to avoid excessive reliance on arguments internal to the UK legal order was to appeal to international human rights standards. The resort to international standards proved a useful device to avoid the difficulties of engaging purely with the existing legal order in its own terms.[7] The difficulty for those who continue to contest the legitimacy of Northern Ireland is that the debate remains tied to the UK legal order. If the Agreement really is binational in nature, then stronger recognition will need to be given to the Irish dimension. The concern is that without this the debate in Northern Ireland will be captured as part of a sophisticated project of constitutional renewal in the UK. These are only some of the issues which must form part of any contextual assessment of rights discourse in Northern Ireland.

III. An agreed future?

Since the imposition of direct rule in 1972, several attempts have been made to encourage a constitutional settlement. These took place in the context of widespread political violence and the existence of extensive emergency powers. The history has tended to be one of failure to secure agreement. Human rights abuse was a persistent feature of life, with violations coming from both state and non-state actors. While the discourse of human rights could be, and was, actively deployed against the British state, there was much debate about how the activities of non-state actors were to be addressed. During the conflict an individual's right to life was

---

[7] There have been a number of Northern Irish cases before the European Court of Human Rights; see e.g. *Jordan v. UK*, judgment of 4 May 2001; *McKerr v. UK*, judgment of 4 May 2001; *Kelly and others v. UK*, judgment of 4 May 2001; *Shanaghan v. UK*, judgment of 4 May 2001: *Brogan and others v. United Kingdom* [1991] 13 EHRR 439; *Brannigan and McBride v. United Kingdom* [1994] 17 EHRR 359.

more at risk in practice from non-state than from state actors. This is not to under-play state abuse (quite the reverse), but there are interesting questions raised by the challenge which this presents to the human rights movement. Other issues lent a slightly unreal air to discussion of Northern Ireland. The imagery of British constitutionalism proved highly inappropriate in the context of a serious internal conflict. As is now well known, paradigmatic understandings dictate what is seen in the world. The framework of British constitutionalism provided a poor basis upon which to understand Northern Ireland and on which to base suitable responses. Until the Agreement there had been a failure to adapt legal and political responses to the particular circumstances of Northern Ireland. This was already evident from the failures of fifty years of devolution.[8] Little or no thought was given to the severe problems of the local context and the potential dangers of placing the grid of Westminster-style government on Northern Ireland. The flaws were accepted and acted upon in the 1970s, when thought turned from majoritarian to consociational democracy.

The current political process has complex origins. However, it is safe to say that the Anglo-Irish Agreement 1985 marked a break with previous constitutional efforts by recognizing that there would be an Irish dimension in any future settle-ment.[9] The Agreement provoked an outcry from the unionist community, yet the British–Irish element is now clearly established and accepted by most. The decision of the leader of the SDLP, John Hume, to begin a political dialogue with the President of Sinn Fein, Gerry Adams, was a major factor in persuading the Provisional Irish Republican Army (PIRA) to declare a ceasefire in 1994. While John Hume was severely criticized for taking this step, it helped to create the clim-ate which made eventual compromise possible. Thinking within the republican movement evolved to the extent that armed struggle was eventually abandoned in favour of more sophisticated ways of achieving political objectives.[10] The challenge then became the formulation of a right to self-determination which would reflect the particular circumstances of Northern Ireland.[11] The Downing Street Declaration 1993 was another significant development, followed closely by the PIRA and Combined Loyalist Military Command (CLMC) ceasefires in 1994. The Framework Document 1995 reflected further evolution in thinking, but it was not until 1997 that the parties entered serious political negotiations. The eventual result of this political process, in April 1998, was the Agreement. The Agreement was not the first document to contain extensive references to human rights. The history of the political process is full of a variety of attempts to give voice to the importance of human rights protection. Both the Downing Street Declaration and the Framework

---

[8] For analysis see B. Hadfield, *The Constitution of Northern Ireland* (Belfast: SLS, 1989).

[9] J. J. Lee, *Ireland 1912–1985* (Cambridge: Cambridge University Press, 1989), 456.

[10] On the use of law by the republican movement, see K. McEvoy 'Law, Struggle, and Political Transformation in Northern Ireland', (2000) 27 *Journal of Law and Society* 542.

[11] See C. Harvey and S. Livingstone, 'Human Rights and the Northern Ireland Peace Process', (1999) 4 *European Human Rights Law Review* 162.

Document contained rights language. In fact the language of human rights was part of official and unofficial documentation since the 1970s. While there was suspicion in government circles about the deployment of the discourse, there has been considerable consensus among the political parties in Northern Ireland on the importance of, for example, a Bill of Rights. There would appear to be consensus on the notion that rights are a 'good idea'. Less agreement exists on the precise meaning of these rights. The participants in the process have accepted that there should be self-imposed limits to democratic government. However, disagreement remains over the extent of these limitations.

IV. Complex conversations

The Agreement contains extensive references to human rights. As one would expect, its language is not fully replicated in the Northern Ireland Act 1998, but it is generally agreed that the legislation reflects the human rights commitments contained in the Agreement. The purpose of the 1998 Act is to implement the Agreement and therefore it can be regarded as a constitutive moment in the development of Northern Ireland.[12] The Agreement has a specific section entitled 'Rights, Safeguards and Equality of Opportunity', but the language of rights is to be found in other sections also. The Declaration of Support commits the participants to the 'protection and vindication of the human rights of all'.[13] It also contains recognition of continuing disagreement:

We acknowledge the substantial differences between our continuing, and equally legitimate, political aspirations. However, we will endeavour to strive in every practical way towards reconciliation and rapprochement within the framework of democratic and agreed arrangements.[14]

The right of self-determination is addressed in a formulation which was intended to be persuasive for republicans. This effectively resulted in the acceptance of what is termed the 'consent principle'. The idea is that the status of Northern Ireland ultimately rests on the consent of a majority of its population, and that for now the preference is for continuing membership of the UK. It is here that the idea of 'double protection' is brought in. The theory is that whatever choice is eventually made by the people of Northern Ireland, the power of the government with jurisdiction there

shall be exercised with rigorous impartiality on behalf of all people in the diversity of their identities and traditions and shall be founded on the principles of full respect for, and equality of, civil, political, social and cultural rights, of freedom from discrimination for all citizens, and parity of esteem and of just and equal treatment for the identity, ethos, and aspirations of both communities.[15]

---

[12] See generally C. J. Harvey (ed.), *Human Rights, Equality and Democratic Renewal in Northern Ireland* (Oxford: Hart, 2001).

[13] Para. 2. [14] Para. 5. [15] Constitutional Issues para. 1(v).

This flexibility on jurisdictional issues is also reflected in the stress on the inter-dependent nature of all the institutions. The settlement is not an internal Northern Ireland one; rather, the focus is on interlocking processes of constitutional develop-ment. It gives expression to the possibility of a new set of dynamic relations between these islands.

The notion of rights (but not only rights) as safeguards figures prominently in the Agreement. This is in the section on 'Democratic Institutions in Northern Ireland', or Strand One. The idea underpinning this part of the Agreement was to create insti-tutions in Northern Ireland which would be inclusive and subject to safeguards of the rights and interests of all sides of the community. The safeguards are there to secure a deliberative purpose. They exist to guarantee that all sections of the com-munity can participate.[16] Rights form one part of this list of safeguards, which includes: the European Convention on Human Rights (ECHR); any Bill of Rights adopted for Northern Ireland; and the Human Rights and Equality Commissions. Other safeguards relate to the proportionate allocation of committee chairs, min-isters, and committee membership, special voting rules, human rights proofing, the pledge of office for ministers as well as a code of conduct. Taken together these constitute an impressive array of protections, with the aim of securing full partic-ipation. There is a democratic basis to this stress on participation in the sense that con-tested constitutionalism in Northern Ireland must be based exclusively on argumentation rather than the use of force. One of the weaknesses is the lack of imagination in relation to the role of the courts: the Agreement baldly states that dis-putes over legislative competence are to be dealt with by the courts.[17] These com-mitments in the Agreement can be found in the 1998 Act, which provides more detail on the precise role of the courts on matters of legislative competence. Those who drafted the Agreement realized the merit in institutionalizing civil society. Reflecting this, provision is made for a Civic Forum.[18] This body has sixty members and is now operational. It acts as a consultative mechanisms on social, economic, and cultural issues. As with the other institutions, it is an innovative institution intended to build further participation and reflection into the process of governance.

The absence of any reference to rights protection in Strand Two (North/South Ministerial Council) is compensated for in later sections of the Agreement, where reference is made to the rights of everyone living on the island of Ireland.[19] Strand Three deals with British–Irish relations and the 'totality of relationships among the peoples of these islands'.[20] Here reference is made to a new British–Irish Council and a new British–Irish Intergovernmental Conference. Reference to rights is rather limited, with some mention in the issues to be addressed by the Conference.[21] Provision for these new institutions can be found in the 1998 Act and in bilateral agreements between the British and Irish governments.

---

[16] Democratic Institutions in Northern Ireland para. 5.   [17] Ibid. para. 28.   [18] Ibid. para. 34.
[19] On problems that have arisen in relation to Strand Two, see *In re Bairbre De Brun and Martin McGuinness* (unreported, 2001).
[20] British–Irish Council para. 1.   [21] British–Irish Inter-governmental Conference para. 6.

Human rights are fully addressed in the section of the Agreement entitled 'Rights, Safeguards and Equality of Opportunity'. Here the parties affirm rights to the following: free political thought; freedom of expression and religion; pursuit of democratically national and political aspirations; the search for constitutional change by peaceful and legitimate means; choice of place of residence; equal opportunity in all social and economic activity, regardless of class, creed, disability, gender or ethnicity; freedom from sectarian harassment; and the right of women to full and equal political participation.[22] The rest of the section is concerned with the commitments of the British and Irish governments. The British government committed itself to complete incorporation of the ECHR. It is arguable that this task remains incomplete, as the Human Rights Act 1998 does not include the whole of the ECHR. The government made commitments on a statutory equality duty which would 'create a statutory obligation on public authorities in Northern Ireland to carry out all their functions with due regard to the need to promote equality of opportunity in relation to religion and political opinion; gender; race; disability; age; marital status; dependants; and sexual orientation'.[23] The equality provisions of the 1998 Act are one of its more innovative features, and merit close attention from those interested in securing participation in public decision-making.[24]

The Agreement provides for the establishment of a new Northern Ireland Human Rights Commission[25] which would be invited to consult and advise on a Bill of Rights for Northern Ireland.[26] The Commission began its work on 1 March 1999, and the Bill of Rights process began one year later on 1 March 2000. This is discussed in more detail below. Provision is also made for a new, unified Equality Commission for Northern Ireland.[27] This Commission started work on 1 October 2000.

The attempt to embed human rights principles in Northern Ireland goes beyond these institutions. Human rights discourse has, for example, framed the debates on policing[28] and criminal justice.[29] What is distinct about current developments in Northern Ireland is that they go beyond the piecemeal enunciation of principles. The intention is to mainstream human rights norms in the governance of Northern Ireland. The human rights culture which is explicit is one which is tied to deliberative democracy and founded on the need to alter institutional contexts to reflect normative commitments.

---

[22] Rights, Safeguards and Equality of Opportunity para. 1.   [23] Ibid. para. 3.

[24] C. McCrudden, 'Mainstreaming Equality in the Governance of Northern Ireland', (1999) 22 *Fordham International Law Journal* 1696.

[25] Rights, Safeguards and Equality of Opportunity para. 5   [26] Ibid. para. 4.

[27] Ibid. para. 6.

[28] See Independent Commission on Policing for Northern Ireland, *A New Beginning: Policing in Northern Ireland* (Sept. 1999). For comment see B. Dickson, 'Policing and Human Rights after the Conflict', in M. Cox, A. Guelke and F. Stephen (eds.), *A Farewell to Arms?* (Manchester: Manchester University Press, 2000), 104. The Police (Northern Ireland) Act 2000 received Royal Assent on 23 Nov. 2000.

[29] Criminal Justice Review Group, *Review of the Criminal Justice System in Northern Ireland* (Mar. 2000).

The Irish government has also undertaken human rights commitments through the Agreement, in particular to 'take steps to further strengthen the protection of human rights in its jurisdiction'.[30] Taking account of the work of the All-Party Oireachtas Committee on the Constitution and the Report of the Constitution Review Group, the Irish government agreed to advance proposals to strengthen and underpin the constitutional protection of human rights.[31] The Agreement states that these proposals will draw upon the ECHR 'and other international legal instruments in the field of human rights', and that the issue of incorporation of the ECHR will be further examined. The overriding purpose is to ensure 'at least an equivalent level of protection of human rights as will pertain in Northern Ireland'.[32] This commitment to equivalence can be traced directly to the constitutional basis of the Agreement. The basic idea is that whichever state exercises jurisdiction over Northern Ireland there should be no difference in the levels of human rights protection. This sensible approach has substantial practical implications for Britain and Ireland, if it is to be taken seriously by all. The Irish government also agreed that it would: establish a Human Rights Commission; ratify the Council of Europe Framework Convention on National Minorities as quickly as possible; implement enhanced employment equality legislation; introduce equal status legislation; and 'continue to take further active steps to demonstrate its respect for the different traditions on the island of Ireland'.[33] It has acted on a number of these issues, with the enactment of the Equal Status Act 2000 and the Employment Equality Act 1998. The establishment of the Irish Human Rights Commission took some time and the process of appointments caused considerable controversy. The Agreement does not envisage the two Human Rights Commissions working in isolation from each other: a Joint Committee of both Commissions will operate as a 'forum for consideration of human rights issues in the island of Ireland'.[34] One of the matters for consideration is a charter which would reflect and endorse agreed measures for the protection 'of the fundamental rights of everyone living in the island of Ireland'.[35]

This is a modest sketch only of some of the more important aspects of the Agreement and the 1998 Act. Human rights discourse is deployed to secure a deliberative purpose and goes beyond Northern Ireland to include the protection of the rights of everyone on the island of Ireland. The result is a continuing dialogue about the governance of Ireland, north and south, and the relations between these islands.

V. A human rights commission in a political democracy

There has, in recent times, been a steady increase in the number of national institutions for the protection of human rights. These are intended to give an added boost to human rights protection at the national level. As noted, the Agreement

---

[30] Rights, Safeguards and Equality of Opportunity para. 9.   [31] Ibid.   [32] Ibid.
[33] Ibid.   [34] Ibid. para. 10.   [35] Ibid.

provides for the establishment of two Commissions, one for the north and the other for the south of Ireland. While the northern one is not strictly speaking a national human rights Commission, it follows broadly international trends. The Northern Ireland Human Rights Commission is not the first such body. The Northern Ireland Constitution Act 1973 provided for the establishment of the Standing Advisory Commission on Human Rights (SACHR). SACHR suffered from a number of weaknesses and is generally regarded as not having had a major impact in practice. The intention was to replace it with a body which would have, according to the Agreement, 'an extended and enhanced role beyond that . . . exercised by [SACHR]'.[36] The new Commission was intended to reflect the community balance in Northern Ireland and to be independent of government.[37] The functions and powers of the Commission are set out in the 1998 Act, but reference should also be made to the Agreement. The relevant paragraph merits full citation:

A new Northern Ireland Human Rights Commission, with membership from Northern Ireland reflecting the community balance, will be established by Westminster legislation, independent of the Government, with an extended and enhanced role beyond that currently exercised by the Standing Advisory Commission on Human Rights, to include keeping under review the adequacy and effectiveness of laws and practices, making recommendations to Government as necessary; providing information and promoting awareness of human rights; considering draft legislation referred to them by the new Assembly; and, in appropriate cases, bringing court proceedings or providing assistance to individuals.[38]

The Commission consists of a full-time Chief Commissioner[39] and nine part-time Commissioners. In appointing Commissioners the Secretary of State is under a duty to ensure as far as practicable that they are representative of the community in Northern Ireland.[40] The Commission's functions include: keeping under review the adequacy and effectiveness in Northern Ireland of law and practice relating to the protection of human rights;[41] the provision of advice to the Secretary of State and the Executive Committee of the Assembly on measures to be taken to protect human rights;[42] and advice to the Assembly on whether a Bill is compatible with human rights.[43] The Commission may provide assistance to individuals and bring

---

[36] Ibid. para. 5.

[37] Ibid. The Commission has adopted a Mission Statement: 'The Northern Ireland Human Rights Commission will work vigorously and independently to ensure that the human rights of everyone in Northern Ireland are fully and firmly protected in law, policy and practice. To that end the Commission will measure law, policy and practice in Northern Ireland against internationally accepted rules and principles for the protection of human rights and will exercise to the full the functions conferred upon it to ensure that those rules and principles are promoted, adopted and applied throughout Northern Ireland. In carrying out its functions the Northern Ireland Human Rights Commission will be independent, fair, open, accessible and accountable, while maintaining the confidentiality of information conveyed to it in private if permitted by the law. The Commission is committed to equality of opportunity for all and to the participation of others in its work. It will perform its functions in a manner which is efficient, informative and in the interests of all the people of Northern Ireland.'

[38] Rights, Safeguards and Equality of Opportunity para. 10.   [39] Prof. Brice Dickson.

[40] Northern Ireland Act 1998 s. 68(3).   [41] Ibid. s. 69(1).   [42] Ibid. s. 69(3).

[43] Ibid. s. 69(4).

proceedings on law and practice relating to human rights protection.[44] In addition, the Commission has an educational function in promoting understanding and awareness of the importance of human rights issues in Northern Ireland. In fulfilling this function it may undertake research and educational activities.[45] It has the power of investigation, but it is a rather limited one.[46] The reference to human rights in the relevant provision of the 1998 Act is not confined to the Human Rights Act 1998, thus permitting the Commission to draw upon the full range of international standards.[47]

The Commission has been involved in a wide range of activities. It has established a number of committees, including an Equality Committee, a Legislation and Policy Committee, and a Bill of Rights Committee. It has been extensively involved in education and training around the Bill of Rights process. A number of submissions have been made on legislation and other measures, and the Commission has been involved in several third party interventions. The Commission has also conducted a critical evaluation of human rights training provided to the Royal Ulster Constabulary (RUC).[48]

The potential problems of further judicial involvement were evident in the case *In re Northern Ireland Human Rights Commission*.[49] The case arose following the attempt of the Commission to make a submission to the HM Coroner for Fermanagh and Tyrone during the inquest into the Omagh bombing. The Coroner concluded that the Commission did not have the power to make such submissions, and this decision was upheld by Carswell LCJ in judicial review proceedings. This judgment was severely criticized by the Commission, and runs counter to the relevant provisions of the legislation and parliamentary intent.[50] It does, however, display a particular judicial attitude to human rights. The judgment of Carswell LCJ was upheld by the Northern Ireland Court of Appeal. The Human Rights Commission has sought leave to appeal to the House of Lords.

It is too early to make any definitive judgement about the Northern Ireland Human Rights Commission. Overall it is, however, making an important contribution to promoting human rights protection in Northern Ireland by encouraging an inclusive dialogue on this issue.

---

[44] Northern Ireland Act 1998, s. 69(5)(a), (b) and s. 70.　　　　[45] Ibid. s. 69(6).

[46] Ibid. s. 69(8). The Commission has decided that it will select matters for investigation in two instances: (a) where a pattern of alleged abuse has been identified; or (b) where a serious human rights abuse has allegedly occurred: see Northern Ireland Human Rights Commission, *First Annual Report 1999–2000*, HC 715.

[47] Northern Ireland Act 1998 s. 69(11)(b).

[48] Northern Ireland Human Rights Commission, *Report on the RUC's Training on the Human Rights Act 1998* (Oct. 2000).

[49] Unreported, 2000.

[50] 'Human Rights Commission Shocked at Court's Decision on its Powers', press release, 8 Dec. 2000.

VI. A Northern Irish bill of rights

Northern Ireland is locked into the logic of the UK legal and political order. This legal order has traditionally been hostile to formal declarations of human rights, and has been based on a pragmatic and conservative mindset.[51] The Agreement is a practical attempt to make a fresh start and break the hold of orthodox UK constitutionalism on Northern Ireland. Its explicit basis in normative principle marks it as a significant departure. While this might be presented as another part of the Labour government's project of constitutional reform, it goes far beyond mere tinkering with the constitution. The Agreement gained the overwhelming consent of the people of Ireland and thus has a constitutional legitimacy which should command widespread respect. The difficulty is that even after securing an imaginative settlement the novelty of the arrangements are in practice filtered through British constitutionalism with problematic results.

The idea that Northern Ireland requires a Bill of Rights has been around for some time. There appears to have been a broad political consensus that it was a worthwhile venture. However, it is only with the adoption of the Agreement that the aspiration has become a real possibility. It is arguable that a Bill of Rights which was operational during the conflict might have stemmed some of the more blatant human rights abuses. The primary focus of the participants and the British and Irish governments was on securing a political settlement. This political settlement provides the legitimacy for the Bill of Rights exercise. The Agreement states:

The new Northern Ireland Human Rights Commission . . . will be invited to consult and to advise on the scope for defining, in Westminster legislation, rights supplementary to those in the European Convention on Human Rights, to reflect the particular circumstances of Northern Ireland, drawing as appropriate on international instruments and experience. These additional rights to reflect the principles of mutual respect for the identity and ethos of both communities and parity of esteem, and—taken together with the ECHR—to constitute a Bill of Rights for Northern Ireland. Among the issues for consideration by the Commission will be:

the formulation of a general obligation on government and public bodies fully to respect, on the basis of equality of treatment, the identity and ethos of both communities in Northern Ireland; and

a clear formulation of the rights not to be discriminated against and to equality of opportunity in both the public and private sectors.[52]

The 1998 Act places a duty on the Secretary of State to request the advice referred to in this paragraph.[53] The consultation process was launched on 1 March

---

[51] See C. McCrudden, 'Northern Ireland and the British Constitution' in J. Jowell and D. Oliver (eds.), *The Changing Constitution*, 3rd edn. (Oxford: Oxford University Press, 1994), 323; N. Walker, 'Beyond the Unitary Conception of the United Kingdom Constitution?', [2000] *Public Law* 384.

[52] *Rights Safeguards and Equality of Opportunity* para. 4.   [53] Northern Ireland Act 1998 s. 69(7).

2000. The Commission has stressed the inclusive nature of the process and its desire for innovation and creativity. The timescale has been subject to amendment, and it would appear that the final advice will not be submitted to the Secretary of State until 2002. After identifying a number of areas in which supplementary protection might be needed the Commission created working groups on: equality; education; children and young people; language; culture and identity; social and economic rights; victims; criminal justice; and implementation. The working groups were intended to be one part only of the broader process of consultation, and included experts in the identified areas. The groups reported in January 2001.

There are several difficult issues to resolve in this process, some of which are directly related to the concerns of this chapter. The implementation and enforcement of the Bill of Rights presents particular challenges.[54] Some have argued for the establishment of a new Human Rights Court which would operate as a guardian of the Bill of Rights. The reasoning here is that there is a mistrust of the current judiciary among the nationalist/republican community, and that a new judicial body might address these concerns. In addition, the Agreement is full of the language of new beginnings, and a Human Rights Court might be a signal that this is taken seriously. One argument against this is that it might detract from attempts to mainstream human rights by encouraging the development of a specialized court. While this argument might make sense in other contexts, it has perhaps less weight in relation to Northern Ireland. There is a more profound argument against the establishment of a new court, which relates to the nature of the Agreement. The Agreement, and the political process in Northern Ireland generally, is based on the principle of inclusivity. The stress is consistently on participation and deliberation. It may seem odd in this context to seek to establish a new judicial body with substantial powers, which might effectively remove important issues from discussion in the public sphere. There are ways to counter this argument by, for example, designing the Bill of Rights in such a way that participation is central to any new court's self-understanding. This would require an innovative approach to institutional design, and there is a strong argument that the particular circumstances of Northern Ireland merit this. In addition, if a new Human Rights Court is established the process of appointments will have to be carefully regulated. No one should, if the focus on participation remains central, be appointed to such a body without a transparent process.

The other major issue is which rights to include. The Agreement states that the rights should be supplementary to the ECHR. It is worth noting that the Human Rights Act 1998 does not give effect to all aspects of the ECHR and there is reason to believe that it is inadequate in the particular circumstances of Northern Ireland. But this still leaves the question of which rights. By establishing the working groups the Commission demonstrated its views on the areas which might be covered.

---

[54] See *Bill of Rights: Implementation Issues Working Group Report* (Jan. 2001).

There will be considerable debate around social and economic rights.[55] This is an area where the ECHR is weak and where familiar debates have emerged around the precise status of the rights. This may be the time for the European Social Charter (Revised) 1996 to make its mark on the human rights debate. The Commission will have to resolve the competing perspectives on this and other issues and ensure that a Bill of Rights for Northern Ireland is tied closely to the Agreement while also reflecting best international practice. If, as has been suggested, the Agreement is based around the principle of inclusivity any Bill of Rights adopted for Northern Ireland must take its place as part of the process of revitalizing the public sphere.[56]

VII. Conclusion

The Agreement contains a rich vision of human rights protection in these islands. The language of rights flows through the document, and there has been a marked increase in the deployment of rights discourse in Northern Ireland since its adoption. Interests which in the past would have been constructed in different terms are now being reinvented in the language of rights. In practice, rights discourse need not have progressive implications: it is a malleable tool. The focus in Northern Ireland must remain, as elsewhere, on careful and critical analysis of the precise impact of rights discourse. There must also be a willingness to acknowledge the role and importance of other political values. Human rights discourse should complement other political and legal values rather than displace them entirely. The contest over the precise meaning of human rights in specific contexts will not resolve some of Northern Ireland's deeply embedded problems. However, by encouraging political and legal engagement it will arguably promote more reflective approaches which map onto postnational forms of association. Human rights discourse is particularly suited to this task, as it functions as a local and global mechanism for disrupting institutional inertia. This will be important for the future governance of Northern Ireland. The suggestion in this chapter is that rights discourse is only one part of the story in the continuing development of Northern Ireland. There are other important legal and political values upon which the new arrangements are based. The overall aim of all of this is to make the commitment to participation meaningful in practice. If it is to be taken seriously human rights discourse must be judged against its ability to assist in the task of revitalizing the public sphere in Northern Ireland. The contestation of discourses in the public sphere should be encouraged, as it is essential to the creation of a progressive democratic polity.

[55] See *Bill of Rights: Social and Economic Rights Working Group Report* (Jan. 2001); Committee on the Administration of Justice, *Fundamental Social Rights in Northern Ireland: Building upon the Agreement and the European Social Charter* (Oct. 1999).

[56] For a persuasive argument in support of the fundamental importance of continuing contestation in the public sphere see J. S. Dryzek, *Deliberative Democracy and Beyond: Liberals, Critics, Contestations* (Oxford: Oxford University Press, 2000).

10

Taking Wales Seriously

RICHARD RAWLINGS

For the legal anthropologist or sociologist, Wales is currently one of the most interesting of places. How could it be otherwise in conditions, on the one hand, of a form of national devolution or emergence of a distinctive Welsh polity and, on the other, of a differential and overarching legal architecture, in the guise of the essential unity of the English and Welsh legal system? At the heart of the development is the vexed question of the legal protection of human rights, Wales now having its own distinctive regime of entrenched provisions as well as being subject to the general law of the United Kingdom in the form of the Human Rights Act 1998.

This chapter introduces a bottom-up perspective, one that looks to legal and constitutional development inside the newly delineated territorial entity, and which is part of the intellectual effort of devolution. In contrast that is to the powerful anglo-centric and metropolitan tradition of public law scholarship in the United Kingdom, which—shades of Dicey and the (English) doctrine of parliamentary sovereignty—has reflected and reinforced an idea of the unitary state, with its stress on (territorial) uniformity in policy and practice.[1] Special emphasis will here be laid on the idea of the devolution legislation—the Government of Wales Act 1998 (GWA)—as a written constitution as well as a statute subject to revision at Westminster.[2] That is, from the Welsh or territorial viewpoint, an overarching and entrenched constitutional instrument, which establishes, refines, and constrains the National Assembly for Wales.

I. Duality and ambiguity

An essential feature is the duality of the Welsh devolutionary development. Seen in comparative perspective, it is a weak form of devolution, which is justified on grounds of limited consensus for change and a history of exceptionally close integration with England.[3] Yet it also transformational, precisely because of the limited

I am grateful to Stephen Grosz for comments on a draft of the chapter. The usual disclaimer applies.

[1] See N. Walker, 'Beyond the Unitary Conception of the United Kingdom Constitution?', [2000] *Public Law* 384.

[2] See R. Rawlings, *Delineating Wales: Legal and Constitutional Aspects of National Devolution* (Cardiff: University of Wales Press/Board of Celtic Studies, forthcoming); also K. Patchett, 'The New Welsh Constitution: The Government of Wales Act 1998', in J. Barry Jones and D. Balsom (eds.), *The Road to the National Assembly for Wales* (Cardiff: University of Wales Press, 2000).

[3] See, for elaboration, R. Rawlings, 'The New Model Wales', (1998) 25 *Journal of Law and Society* 461.

prior development of a distinctive Welsh polity (and legal institutions). It is then both a small step and a giant leap, as was famously said on another excursion into the unknown.

The Welsh devolutionary development may further be read as distinctive or peculiar, and as a microcosm of broad trends in comparative constitutional development. On the one hand, attention is drawn to the strange internal architecture of the Assembly, it being a corporate body with no formal or statutory separation between the executive and legislative branches.[4] And not only is this a scheme of executive devolution, as predicated on the horizontal division of lawmaking functions with (the primary legislative process at) Westminster, but also one that is highly specified and thus very complex and technical in terms of the allocation of devolved competencies.[5] On the other hand, reference may be made to the rise of so-called meso-government, that is the intermediate level between central and local government, which in terms of comparative public law and administration in Europe is one of the most significant phenomena of the last half-century.[6] In turn, the increased force of models of multi-layered governance, the relocation of decision-making powers from the central state to supranational institutions and to territories and localities, has generally been recognised.[7] A comparative latecomer in one sense, the United Kingdom now boasts some very advanced examples in the light of devolution. Including in the case of Wales, where the special role of considerations of economic development in promoting basic constitutional change, and in particular the idea of the territory as a player in the competitive struggle that is constituted in the EU Single Market, has been strongly articulated by government.[8]

It has been said that 'globalisation, which in one sense erodes territorial distinctiveness, in other ways enhances the importance of territory and gives impetus to the construction of territorial societies'.[9] Once again the emergence in Wales of a distinctive polity and administration represents something of an ideal type, not least in terms of the interaction between forces of universality and locality, or of the parallel processes of (EU) integration and fragmentation.[10] Sub-state restructuring, together with enhanced supranational ordering and permeability of the nation-state, is of the essence here, including in the world of the law.

---

[4] See GWA, s. 1. What is variously known as the 'devolved administration' or 'Welsh Government' is thus dependent on a complex system of internal delegation of powers by the Assembly: see esp. GWA, ss. 62–3.

[5] As demonstrated (voluminously) by the original transfer of functions order, SI No. 672, 1999. And see further below.

[6] See e.g. L. Sharpe (ed.), The *Rise of Meso Government in Europe* (London: Sage, 1992); also R. Leonardi, *Convergence, Cohesion and Integration in the European Union* (London: Macmillan, 1995).

[7] e.g. G. Marks, 'An Actor-Centred Approach to Multi-Level Governance', (1996) 6 *Regional and Federal Studies* 20.

[8] *A Voice for Wales*, Cm. 3718 (1997), esp. ch. 2.

[9] M. Keating and H. Elcock, 'Introduction: Devolution and the UK State', (1998) 8 *Regional and Federal Studies* 1, 5.

[10] See, for elaboration in terms of the contested concept that is globalization, R. Rawlings, 'Law, Territory and Integration: A View from the Atlantic Shore', (2001) *Journal of the International Institute of Administrative Sciences* (forthcoming).

Such are the general considerations that underlie this chapter, where the con-tribution of the HRA in terms of the devolutionary development in Wales is seen as a profoundly ambiguous one. The discussion thus involves a range of cross-grained factors. Most obvious perhaps is the general flattening effect of the HRA: less administrative diversity and legal pluralism (which might be thought to be the logic of devolution), more pressure for uniformity in policy-making and implementation (in the United Kingdom). All the more so, it may be said, in the case of an infant or inexperienced body confronted by some thirty years of Strasbourg jurisprudence. Together, that is, with the not inconsiderable burden of risk assessment in the exer-cise of legislative initiative, which is itself underscored by the official interpretation of the European Convention as a living instrument,[11] or the strong dynamic char-acter of the jurisprudence.

Another key element is introduced: the way in which judicial supervision or oversight of the activities of the new institutions is made an integral part of the UK devolutionary design.[12] At one and the same time, government is brought closer to the people by an injection of democratic procedures and practices in the form of meso-government, and the constitutional role of the (non-elected) judiciary is enhanced by reason of a package of fundamental reforms that includes the HRA. From the standpoint of a constitutional lawyer from a federal tradition, this may seem unremarkable. In Britain, however, it involves a fundamental shift in the clas-sical functions of the judiciary, a striking reversal of the traditional subsidiary roles of law, lawyers, and judges in British government.

Human rights law raises important questions of legal and political responsibility in the new modalities of multi-layered governance. In the case of Wales, particular strains or tensions arise from use of the model of executive devolution, which is very dependent on administrative and political goodwill in central government for legit-imacy and effective operations.[13] The constitutional dimension will thus be high-lighted in this chapter, in terms of applying the HRA, by reference to the vexed issue of the style of Westminster delegation of powers to make secondary legisla-tion.

Then again, human rights law is the essence of the idea of a newly textured demo-cratic culture, which has gained much currency in the context of the UK devolu-tionary development.[14] Seen in comparative perspective, the case of Wales is also interesting in this regard. Moving beyond the standard UK government line of the HRA and devolution as twin strands in a project of modernization and citizen empowerment, there is significant scope for interplay with, or role for, an autochthonous constitutional development. A special emphasis that has been laid at territorial level on the value of transparency, what I call the Welsh model of gov-ernment in the sunshine, will be seen to be important here. Different but related, a potential for synergies with the requirements of the devolution statute will be

---

[11] See the classic authority of *Marckx v. Belgium* (1979) 2 EHRR 330.
[12] In the guise most obviously of so-called devolution issues: see below.
[13] See further Rawlings, 'The New Model Wales'.   [14] Ibid.

demonstrated, which notably involves a use of law to stimulate political and administrative action in the broad sphere of human rights.

In light of the history of Wales, constitutive and energizing effects in terms of the local legal profession and institutions is a special feature. In conjunction, that is, with what may be called the serious legal business of devolution. To explicate, there is a basic problem of fit in the Welsh constitutional development, comprising a model of government that is second to none in terms of dependency on legal tools and techniques and the legacy of a local vacuum or stunted tradition of public law inside the territory. In turn, human rights law is one strand in what I have identified elsewhere as the rise of Legal Wales.[15] This is a broad phenomenon that encompasses such developments as novel (Welsh) forms of professional networks, the rapid expansion of the Office of the Counsel General (the new legal branch of the Assembly),[16] and a process of decentralization or administrative devolution to Wales inside the formal court system. Let us look more closely.

II. Historical legacy and the condition of Wales

England's first colony: beyond legal assimilation

Wales occupies a very special position in the historical development of the so-called common law globe. As England's first colony, nowhere has the process of legal (and political and administrative) assimilation been deeper or more thoroughgoing. That Wales, unlike Scotland and (Northern) Ireland, did not retain a separate system of courts but shares one with England may be considered a feature of first-class constitutional importance. In this context the use of the title 'Lord Chief Justice of England', which was only changed to 'Lord Chief Justice of England and Wales' in the wake of devolution, says much.

It is not fanciful to see the Statute of Rhuddlan (1284)—'a dictated peace *par excellence*'[17]—as the original model for the centuries-long process of common law expansion on the back of military conquest and commercial endeavour, culminating with Dicey and the Victorian splendour of the British ('outer') Empire. With the completion of the Plantagenet conquest of Wales under Edward I, the Statute provided for the importation of the English criminal law (and extension of the shire system). In contradistinction, that is, to the famous Welsh codification which was an outstanding legal achievement on the European scale: the tenth-century Law of Hywel.[18] In the words of the historian, as the indigenous Welsh law 'became increasingly moribund, an element which had been central to Welsh identity was lost'.[19]

---

[15] R. Rawlings, 'Living with the Lawyers', (1999) *Journal of the Institute of Welsh Affairs* 32. See also T. Watkin (ed.), *Legal Wales: From Past to Future* (Cardiff: Welsh Legal History Society, 2001).

[16] Most obviously the Wales Public Law and Human Rights Association, founded in 1999.

[17] N. Davies, *The Isles* (London: Macmillan, 1999), 371.

[18] See, for a classic account, D. Jenkins, *The Law of Hywel Dda* (Llantysul: Gomer, 1986)

[19] J. Davies, *A History of Wales*, (London: Allen Lane, 1993), 168.

In the words of the so-called Act of Union of 1536: 'his Highness therefore, of a singular zeal, love and favour that he beareth his subjects of . . . Wales . . . established that this said country . . . shall be . . . incorporated, united and annexed to and with this realm of England . . .' Such was the Tudor policy of an integrated Wales, that which, splendidly envisioned, was once called 'the experiment of killing "Welshery" by trusting Welshmen'.[20] Implementation meant sweeping away the remnants of Welsh law, or, in the words of the statute, the 'sinister usages and customs' regulating life in Wales.

A general trend of administrative centralization in the 'English' legal system is also relevant.[21] After 1830 Wales was joined in the circuit system that had operated in England, but especially with the establishment of the Commercial Court in 1895, specialist legal work was increasingly done in London. For present purposes special reference must be made to the institutional development in terms of public law. On the one hand, it will be seen that this is the sphere in which the new National Assembly has its various competencies. On the other hand, within the 'English' legal system, nothing has been more centralized than the special machinery for dealing with issues of constitutional and administrative law. By which is meant formerly, the Prerogative Orders and exercise of jurisdiction by the Divisional Court (of Queen's Bench) and, more recently, the Application for Judicial Review and assignment of cases on the so-called Crown Office List. [22]

In the years following the failure of Welsh devolution in 1978,[23] this feature of the legal system was greatly accentuated by reason of two related developments. One is the significant increase in the scale and intensity of judicial review of public authorities familiarly associated with this period. The other is the famous case of *O'Reilly v. Mackman*,[24] where a rigid public/private law divide was asserted with a view to expanding the procedural ambit of the judicial review machinery, and thus involved the further channelling of cases to the Royal Courts of Justice in London. In terms of the development of Legal Wales, this public law monopoly has been a pernicious one, operating to denude the territory of relevant legal specialization. It was the standard practice of central government in Wales, in the form of the territorial department that was the Welsh Office, to look to the Inns of Court in London for expert sources of advice. Nor is it surprising to learn, in view of the lack of local visibility, that Wales was producing very little by way of judicial review.[25] In sum, conditions have conspired against a firm local legal grounding for the public law

---

[20] W. Llewelyn Williams, *The Making of Modern Wales* (London: Macmillan, 1919), 16.

[21] See J. Thomas, 'Legal Wales: Its Modern Origins and its Role after Devolution: National Identity, the Welsh Language and Parochialism', in Watkin, *Legal Wales*.

[22] See C. Harlow and R. Rawlings, *Law and Administration*, 2nd edn. (London: Butterworths, 1997), ch. 16.

[23] Reference is here being made to the ill-fated Wales Act 1978, effectively aborted by popular referendum.

[24] [1983] 2 AC 237.

[25] Only 30 or so cases a year involving the Welsh Office, many concerning planning matters: see J. Thomas, 'The Legal Implications of Welsh Devolution', in D. Miers (ed.), *Devolution in Wales* (Cardiff: Wales Public Law and Human Rights Association, 1999).

project that is Welsh devolution. A spill-over effect in terms of the practice of human rights law is demonstrated later in this chapter.

As indicated, however, things are also changing in this respect. Important is the way in which an administrative decentralization of judicial review proceedings has effectively been piggybacked on the requirement to elaborate the special juridical regime of the GWA (and other devolution statutes). Coverage thus extends to 'an issue concerning the Welsh Assembly, the Welsh executive, or any Welsh public body (including a Welsh local authority) whether or not it involves a devolution issue'.[26] Such cases may now be handled at local centres by the recently established Administrative Court in Wales.[27]

In the words of the Counsel General, 'an inevitable consequence of devolution is that Wales will develop its own body of public law. It stands to reason that this should evolve through the courts in Cardiff rather than in London.'[28] Human rights law, it may be added, is no exception. Indeed, there are the makings of a competitive struggle between the local legal profession and the powerful London elite operating in this sphere.

How then to characterize what is inevitably a complex situation? It would be absurd to speak of a flowering of Welsh legal culture, as defined in terms of the complex webs of beliefs, values, understandings, and practices of lawyers and judges. Such a thing is far away, and may never happen. However, it would be equally absurd to ignore the seeds of indigenous legal development that have now been planted in the context of the GWA; and, further, the process of nurturing that is already under way.[29] At one and the same time, consideration of the rise of Legal Wales points up the powerful constraints associated with the strong centralized character of the English common law and the greater sense of legal pluralism that is a natural product of the devolutionary process. The phenomenon is also an essential feature in understanding the role and impact of human rights law in the newly delineated territorial polity.

The condition of Wales

Let us expand the theme. Analysis of the role and impact of the novel form of litigation demands consideration of the social and economic condition of the country concerned. A critical or sceptical view of the HRA based solely on the jurisprudence or precedents hardly suffices! It is appropriate here to mention two key aspects of the Welsh condition.

---

[26] Practice Direction, 'Judicial Review' (Aug. 2000), para. 3.1.

[27] A territorial offshoot of the new Administrative Court that (in the context of the HRA) has replaced the Crown Office List: see C. Blake, 'Procedural Changes to Judicial Review', (Oct. 2000) Legal Action 26.

[28] Winston Roddick QC, quoted in Rawlings, *Delineating Wales*.

[29] The case for going further and establishing distinctive judicial offices and institutions for Wales is discussed ibid.

First, Wales is consistently found at or near the bottom of the UK regional league tables of income and competitiveness. In so-called First World terms we are not dealing here with an especially prosperous entity. Furthermore, the general figures obscure significant intra-territorial variations, with high levels of socio-economic deprivation being concentrated among the two-thirds of the population and geographical area that make up west Wales and the old coal valleys. That this area now has the status of a lagging region[30] under the European Regional Development Fund says much: most of Wales has a GDP of less than 75 per cent of the European Union average.

Both in the short term, given the high pound (sterling) and uncertainties over the EU single currency, and in the long term, in the context of EU enlargement and undermining of the historical position of Wales as a low-wage economy inside the Single Market, the auguries are not good. The strict contours of the devolutionary development are also relevant in this context. By which is meant the lack of a tax-raising power in the Assembly, and the fact that the new body is operating under the dictates of the so-called Barnett formula for the calculation of territorial finance, which (unlike in Scotland) has in the past been less than generous to Wales.[31]

In this respect the conditions are ripe for some sharp forms of legal conflict under the rubric of human rights, and of economic and social rights in particular. Limited resources and uneven service delivery, demands for prioritization; such factors take on fresh prominence in the light of the construction and development of the new territorial polity.

Second, there is that great survivor, the Welsh language. Emblematic of a strong cultural content in the expression of Welsh national feeling, historically it was the treatment of the language which excited most controversy concerning the situation of Wales in the 'English' legal system.[32] English the only medium of the courts: such was the blunt message of the so-called language clause of the Act of Union. Only gradually and in the face of considerable resistance was the position ameliorated, culminating pre-devolution in the Welsh Language Act 1993. This recognised a cultural right, establishing the general principle of equal treatment of the English and Welsh mediums in the conduct of public business and administration of justice.[33] The GWA will be seen to underscore the development in the political and legislative sphere. As regards human rights cases, enough has been

---

[30] So-called 'Objective 1 status', which has attracted ERDF funding of some £1.2 billion for the period 2000–6. See further Rawlings, 'Law, Territory and Integration', and L. McAllister, 'Devolution and the New Context for Public Policy-Making: Lessons from the EU Structural Funds in Wales', (2000) 15 *Public Policy and Administration* 38.

[31] Recent financial provision for Wales (under the auspices of the Comprehensive Spending Review) perhaps signals a new attitude in the wake of devolution. See J. Osmond (ed.), *Devolution Looks Ahead* (Cardiff: Institute of Welsh Affairs, 2000).

[32] See R. Lewis, *Cyfiawnder Dwyeithog (Bilingual Justice)* (Llantysul: Gomer, 1998); and M. Ellis Jones, '"The Confusion of Babel?": The Welsh Language, Law Courts and Legislation in the Nineteenth Century', in G. Jenkins (ed.), *The Welsh Language and its Social Domains 1801–1911* (Cardiff: University of Wales Press, 2000).

[33] i.e. within the borders of Wales: see *Williams v. Cowell, The Times*, 12 Aug. 1999.

said to indicate another significant source or potential for litigation, one that (in a striking historical reversal) will surely include monolingual English speakers.

III. Welsh devolution: four characteristics

Now let us consider some of the chief features of the Welsh devolutionary scheme that bear on the issue of the protection of human rights. The great swathes of legal uniformity in terms of the United Kingdom in general, and with England in particular, must, however, always be kept in mind. What I call 'taking Wales seriously' involves looking to the interplay of the elements, on the one hand, of continuity and change and, on the other, of symmetry and asymmetry in the UK constitutional development.[34]

National devolution

The idea that Wales is or might be a nation[35] is at the heart of the devolutionary scheme, as is demonstrated by the full title of the Assembly. In the context of a new brand of constitutional litigation, it would be absurd to overlook the political and cultural sensitivities here. All the more so when one is confronted by the fact of judicial decision-making in an essentially undifferentiated English and Welsh court architecture.

This dimension is given a very practical edge by the rise of what we may call distinctive Welsh 'state' machinery. The devolution statute, for example, created the offices of an Auditor-General for Wales and the Welsh Administration Ombudsman, notably basic machinery for securing accountability in the realm of public law (including in the latter case in the sphere of human rights). Special reference must be made to the Children's Commissioner for Wales, established under the Care Standards Act 2000,[36] a novel instrument for human rights protection in the UK. In summary, the relevant administrative terrain is increasingly different in Wales, and also involves particular grievance-remedial initiatives that overlap with litigation techniques. The potential here for creative combinations of public and private advocacy will be readily appreciated.

---

[34] R. Rawlings, 'The Shock of the New: Devolution in the United Kingdom', in E. Riedl (ed.), *Aufgabenverteilung und Finanzregimes im Verhältnis zwischen dem Zentralstaat und seinen Untereinheiten* (Baden-Baden: Nomos, 2001); idem, 'Quasi-Legislative Devolution: Powers and Principles', (2001) 52 *Northern Ireland Legal Quarterly* 54.

[35] See G. Williams, *When Was Wales?* (Harmondsworty: Penguin, 1985). See also, in the context of the devolutionary development, B. Taylor and K. Thompson (eds.), *Scotland and Wales: Nations Again?* (Cardiff: University of Wales Press, 1999).

[36] See also the current Children's Commissioner for Wales Act 2001 (strengthening of the powers of the Commissioner).

Executive devolution and legalization

The method of empowering the Assembly has already been mentioned. Whereas the Scottish Parliament is afforded general legislative competence subject to reservations, the Assembly is assigned specific powers in more limited fields: statute by statute, section by section, subsection by subsection. To this effect, it currently has legal and constitutional responsibility of an uneven width and depth in some eighteen fields of public law. The situation is the more complicated because the initial allocation of powers was essentially based on those functions that in typically piecemeal and ad hoc fashion had come to be exercised by the Welsh Office (see Table 10.1).[37]

This form of devolution is also by its very nature a moving target. The method thus implies an ongoing allocation of powers as new statutes come on stream. The Assembly has in this way been a recipient of functions virtually from the moment of its birth. The chapter then comes with a serious health warning: the picture presented could well look very different in a few years' time, depending on the style and substance of the delegation of powers in relevant primary legislation. It suffices to add that pressures are already growing in Wales for a more generous approach to the devolution of secondary lawmaking powers, for example by the recourse to so-called framework legislation; perhaps leading on (as I venture to predict will happen) to a form of legislative devolution. The statement by Ron Davies,[38] the ministerial architect of the scheme, that 'devolution is a process not an event' strikes a particular chord in Wales.

Speaking more generally, the Welsh model of executive devolution epitomizes a process of legalization, by which I mean the infusion of legal considerations and

Table 10.1. Initial fields of devolved competencies

Economic development	Industry
Agriculture, forestry, fisheries and food	Transport
Highways	Town and country planning
Education and Training	Health and health services
Social Services	Housing
Local government	The environment
Water and flood defence	Tourism
Culture (including museums, galleries and libraries)	The Welsh language
Sport and recreation	Ancient monuments and historic buildings

[37] See D. Lambert, 'The Government of Wales Act: An Act to be Ministered in Wales in Like Form as It Is in This Realm?', (1999) 30 *Cambrian Law Review* 60.

[38] R. Davies, *Devolution: A Process Not an Event* (Cardiff: Institute of Welsh Affairs, 1999). See also D. Elis Thomas, *National Assembly: A Year in Power?* (Cardiff: Institute of Welsh Politics, 2000); and G. Prys Davies, *The National Assembly: A Year of Laying the Foundations* (Cardiff: Law Society in Wales, 2000).

techniques in the conduct of government, which is commonly associated with the UK government's programme of constitutional reform in general, and the HRA in particular. On the one hand, the British tradition of informality in public administration was nowhere more pronounced than in the small village that was the Welsh Office.[39] On the other hand, civil servants in Wales must now learn to navigate a fragmented system of devolved powers, as well as engage with the intricacies of secondary lawmaking (of which there was very little experience in the Welsh Office).

Constitutional culture and legal precept

A third main characteristic is introduced: the quest for, and heavy use of legal precept in the service of, a newly textured democratic culture. Building on the idea of the GWA as a written constitution, there is now a raft of hard and soft law instruments, including entrenched standing orders and guidance to Assembly Members, giving practical expression in the new polity to the constitutional values of transparency and integrity, participation, and inclusiveness. In turn, the groundwork is clearly laid for some innovative approaches in the field of constitutional litigation including human rights—in particular, free from the stifling effects of the traditional British approach to official secrecy. As indicated, the Welsh way is now very much a model of open government, to the extent for example of publication of the minutes of Assembly Cabinet meetings.[40]

The concept of inclusiveness needs special emphasis in this context (notwithstanding a general drift in the Assembly towards more oppositional or Westminster-style forms of proceeding).[41] In the words of the minister responsible, the National Assembly was so titled in order 'to stress that it will be for everyone in Wales'.[42] An element of proportional representation is one aspect, so also the careful provision that is made for the Welsh Language, notably in former times a very divisive political issue inside the territory. At one and the same time, devolution is grounded in territoriality but must contend with the contemporary sense of a more cosmopolitan society, whose people have multiple identities. Gender issues, for example, have rightly been seen in Wales as a touchstone for a new kind of politics—the Assembly is one of the most gender-balanced representative institutions in Western Europe.[43] Again, inclusiveness has been invoked as a counterpoint or important balance to the sense of

---

[39] See, for an insider's view, W. Roberts, *Fifteen Years at the Welsh Office* (Aberystwyth: National Library of Wales, 1995).

[40] Available (with much else) on the Assembly web site: www.assembly.wales.gov.uk

[41] Especially in the context of a governing coalition (Labour and the Liberal Democrats), which in Oct. 2000 replaced a minority (Labour) administration; see also J. Osmond, 'A Constitutional Convention by Other Means: The First Year of the National Assembly for Wales', in R. Hazell (ed.), *The State and the Nations* (London: Imprint Academic, 2000).

[42] R. Davies, quoted in J. Osmond, *New Politics in Wales* (London: Charter 88, 1998), p. 12. And see, for a healthy dose of scepticism, G. Day, D. Dunkerley, and A. Thompson, 'Evaluating the New Politics: Civil Society and the National Assembly for Wales', (2000) 15 *Public Policy and Administration* 25.

[43] At the time of writing, 25 of the 60 Assembly Members are women.

national identity that Welsh devolution projects.[44] Reference may here be made to the concept of a civic (and not ethnic) nationalism, residency in Wales being seen as the necessary and sufficient condition for involvement in the new body politic.

Special juridical regime

As is well known, the establishment of a special juridical regime for handling 'devolution issues' is a common feature of the devolutionary schemes in Scotland, Wales, and Northern Ireland, and one which includes provision for adjudication on 'Convention rights'.[45] A complex set of reference procedures (from the ordinary or general processes of litigation) has thus been introduced, with at the apex of the system that symbol of the old outer empire, the Judicial Committee of the Privy Council. However, the fact that the judicial architecture of devolution presents a formal symmetry should not be allowed to obscure a real substantive asymmetry that derives from the differing nature and extent of the constitutional allocation of functions to the devolved territories.

The question is raised: why the special juridical regime for Wales and matters of subordinate legislation? A choice of the House of Lords and ordinary procedure would have better fitted the longstanding unity of the English and Welsh legal system.[46] Effectively, however, the matter was predetermined. Not only was there an example to hand, the earlier use of the Judicial Committee in the case of Northern Ireland. There were also Scottish sensitivities, centred on historical resistance to a role for the House of Lords in Scots criminal appeals, as well as the constitutional objection to part of the UK Parliament adjudicating on the division of legislative competence.[47] Together, that is, with the natural pull of symmetry, or desire of government to establish a standard form of jurisdiction in devolution issues. In short, in paradoxical fashion, a choice of judicial machinery which further differentiates Wales from England[48] also serves to illustrate the junior status of Wales among the territories of the Union, and in particular in the UK devolutionary development.

IV. Wales and human rights: three sources of law

In preparing this chapter I naturally enquired into the state of the veritable cottage industry that is constituted by books concerning the HRA. After all, in Wales as in

---

[44] Davies, *Devolution*, 7.

[45] See GWA s. 109 and Schedule 8; and P. Craig and M. Walters, 'The Courts, Devolution and Judicial Review', [1999] *Public Law* 274.

[46] See D. Williams, 'Devolution: the Welsh Perspective', in J. Beatson, C. Forsyth, and I. Hare (eds.), *Constitutional Reform in the United Kingdom: Practice and Principles* (Cambridge: Cambridge Centre for Public Law, 1998).

[47] C. Boyd, 'Parliament and Courts: Powers in Disputes Resolution', in T. St J. Bates (ed.), *Devolution to Scotland: The Legal Aspects* (Edinburgh: W. Green, 1997).

[48] The tension here is brilliantly illustrated by the statutory formulas for (Welsh) devolution issues of proceedings in 'England and Wales', and in 'Scotland' and 'Northern Ireland' (GWA, Schedule 8, Parts II–IV).

Scotland (and Northern Ireland) so-called 'Convention rights' have bound the new devolved administration from the very beginning.[49] The findings were sobering, especially given the place of devolution and human rights in the New Labour Government's general or overarching programme of constitutional reform. Of the eight works consulted, five made no mention of devolution, Welsh or otherwise. A sixth volume managed one page on the three Celtic lands. The remaining two books contained useful but minimalist accounts of the Welsh situation, with notably no discussion of the texture or quality of the new democratic structures and processes established under the GWA.[50] Anglocentricity, it may be observed, dies hard in the Union State.

It is worth referring to some recent observations by Lord Justice Sedley, one of the UK's leading authorities in the field of human rights: 'An important aspect of the reorientation of the United Kingdom's constitution towards a culture of human rights is that it draws upon not one but two new sources of law. One is the pervasive Human Rights Act 1998; the other is the overarching European Convention on Human Rights. The two will be largely but by no means entirely co-extensive.'[51] In the case of Wales, however, we must also look to a third new source: the devolution statute. And specifically to a series of general principles or legal precepts in this written constitution that serve to guide or constrain the discretion of the Assembly in matters of policy development, establishment, and implementation. It is one reason why the treatment of Wales in the flurry of books on human rights in the UK is so disappointing. It is worth adding that this feature is not replicated in Scotland, where the Parliament is left more to its own devices.

To explicate, the new body of Welsh public law incorporates special provisions on the cultural heritage of language, sustainable development, and equality of opportunity. A bilingual approach, for example, is made an article of faith in this Celtic land.[52] The Assembly must treat the English and Welsh languages equally in the conduct of business, so far as is appropriate and reasonably practicable (GWA, s. 47), and the bilingual texts of Assembly instruments are afforded equal legal status (GWA, s. 122). Such provision is familiar in other jurisdictions, but it marks a new departure in the legal and constitutional history of the United Kingdom. Welsh as a language of the law is quite literally being reinvented. The development is also highly symbolic in view of the historic wrong perpetrated against a minority population in the Union, or what would now be regarded as a flagrant breach of human rights.

In what is a constitutional development unique in Europe, the Assembly is required to make a statutory scheme setting out how it proposes, in the exercise of

---

[49] GWA, ss. 107, 153(2).

[50] S. Grosz, J. Beatson, and P. Duffy, *Human Rights: The 1998 Act and the European Convention* (London: Sweet & Maxwell 2000); and A. Lester and D. Pannick (eds.), *Human Rights Law and Practice* (London: Butterworths, 2000).

[51] S. Sedley, 'Foreword', in Grosz et al., *Human Rights*.

[52] See C. Williams, 'Operating Through Two Languages', in J. Osmond (ed.), *The National Assembly Agenda* (Cardiff: Institute of Welsh Affairs, 1998).

its functions, to promote sustainable development (GWA, s. 121).[53] In the event, a broad approach has been taken, one that encompasses the environmental, economic, and social aspects, and the process has also been characterized by an exceptionally thorough and open process of consultation.[54] Potentially there are major implications in terms of legal challenges to the Assembly in such matters as planning decisions. Nonetheless, the provision powerfully demonstrates an alternative approach to constitutional protection based on a justiciable bill of rights, one which both establishes and reserves to the political and administrative process the primary responsibility in a complex and controversial field. It is a subtle use of legal technique.

As regards non-discrimination, GWA s. 120(1) provides:[55]

The Assembly shall make appropriate arrangements with a view to securing that its functions are exercised with due regard to the principle that there should be equality of opportunity for all people.

The formulation is borrowed from s. 71 of the Race Relations Act 1971 involving local authorities, where it was held in the leading case of *Wheeler v. Leicester City Council*[56] to establish a specific obligation in respect of all relevant functions. Although not user-friendly for the individual litigant—what the obligation entails has never been seriously tested—the provision should not be lightly dismissed. In terms of the proactive effect designed to be induced, it has in fact been taken very seriously, both by the Assembly's Equal Opportunities Committee and by the relevant division, appropriately called PEP (Public Administration, Equality and Public Appointments), of the Welsh government. By way of example, equal opportunity policy has been one of the defining strands of the Assembly's strategic plan, *Better Wales*.[57]

The Welsh provision on non-discrimination is the more noteworthy for being all-embracing.[58] It reflects and reinforces the special premium placed on inclusiveness, and recognizes the primary need to balance the interests of different sections of Welsh society in the representative institution that is the Assembly. What could be more fitting in the quest for a newly textured democratic culture?

Tensions will no doubt arise here in view of the broad trajectory of the European Convention, or what the Lord Chancellor, Lord Irvine, has called 'a real opportunity for Wales to give a lead in the enforcement of rights in favour of the individual

---

[53] See K. Bishop and A. Flynn, 'The National Assembly for Wales and the Promotion of Sustainable Development: Implications for Collaborative Government and Governance', (1999) 14 *Public Policy and Administration* 62.

[54] See National Assembly, A *Sustainable Wales: Learning to Live Differently* (2000); and *Official Record of Proceedings*, 16 Nov. 2000.

[55] GWA s. 48 further requires the Assembly to have due regard to equal opportunities in the conduct of its business.

[56] [1985] AC 1054. See also *R v. Lewisham LBC ex p, Shell UK Ltd* [1988] 1 All ER 938.

[57] Available on the Assembly web site.

[58] In this respect the approach fits with the (EU) Charter of Fundamental Rights, agreed at Nice in Dec. 2000 (Article 21, non-discrimination).

and of business'.[59] But enough has also been said to indicate the general scope for synergies in the case of Welsh devolution and human rights. It would be foolish to expect the special legal precepts in the GWA somehow to be pigeon-holed, and so not to lock up together with developments under general human rights law relating, for example, to environmental protection, as well as to discrimination (European Convention, Article 14). Such is the logic of three sources of law: European, Union, and Welsh.

This is not to overlook the interesting question of the extent to which the courts in general, and the Privy Council in particular, will allow different approaches to human rights questions within the devolved administrations and how far they will seek to impose uniformity.[60] Speaking more generally, the role of the courts in determining the extent to which devolution gives an opportunity to Wales to elaborate a distinct legal (and political) identity could prove an important one. Let us hope that a proper measure of judicial deference is accorded to the national representative institution that is the Assembly.[61]

V. The Assembly and the HRA: form and substance

In terms of the need for compliance with the human rights obligations now 'brought home' or incorporated in UK domestic law, the Assembly would appear to be bound in two ways. First, there is the rule in the devolution statute that Assembly acts or orders incompatible with a Convention right are *ultra vires* (GWA, s. 107). Second, there is the general law: 'It is unlawful for a public authority to act in a way which is incompatible with a Convention right' (HRA, s. 6(1)). And the victim may so 'rely on the Convention right or rights concerned in any legal proceedings' (HRA, s. 7(1)(b)).[62]

As indicated, there are some particular twists in the case of Wales by reason of the form or substance of the scheme of executive devolution. One of the difficult situations with which the HRA must deal is where a public authority is required to act by statute in a certain way but doing so is incompatible with a Convention right. Both the GWA (s. 107(4)) and the HRA (ss. 3, 4, 6) allow for a form of justification. A public authority in this position will not be said to be acting unlawfully, and in particular the validity, operation, and enforcement of any subordinate legislation so made is not affected, which in turn opens up the possibility of a declaration of incompatibility for the governing statute. The special relevance for Wales of this legislative exception will be readily appreciated. Effectively the provision would be sidestepped if central government were to accede to the wishes of the Assembly and

---

[59] Lord Irvine, 'Foreword', in Miers, *Devolution in Wales*.
[60] An issue already directly raised in the context of Scotland; see esp. Ch. 8 in this volume.
[61] The argument is pursued in Rawlings, 'Living with the Lawyers'.
[62] The vexed question of procedural exclusivity between the devolution statutes and the HRA lies beyond the scope of this chapter.

move to broad-framework legislation as a means of empowering the devolved administration. Should the pendulum swing the other way, however, as perhaps it might under a future Conservative government, then the issue of the scope of the protection for the Assembly by reason of this form of justification could move to centre stage.

There is also the small matter of Assembly competencies, and their match or fit with the Articles of the European Convention now incorporated in domestic law. Some of the rights in question may appear to have little to do with the functions of the Assembly; the relevance of others is more immediately apparent. But such is the expansive interpretation over thirty years and, further, the cross-cutting or horizontal character of certain of the rights that it is hard to overstate the potential scale of their application. The devolved function that in large measure is education is an excellent illustration. The starting point is Article 2 of the First Protocol to the Convention, since this deals directly with the right to education, including in terms of teaching in conformity with the religious and philosophical convictions of parents. Other general provisions, however, may also be relevant, such as Article 3 (freedom from inhuman or degrading treatment), historically important in relation to corporal punishment, and Article 8 (right to respect for private and family life), hugely potent[63] and bearing, for example, on the language of education. Then there is Article 6 (right to a fair trial), the most frequently invoked provision of the Convention, relevant, for example, to school exclusions. To this catalogue might be added Article 9 (freedom of thought, conscience, and religion), Article 10 (freedom of expression), and Article 14 (prohibition of discrimination).

It is worth adding that many of the Articles of prime concern to the Assembly involve qualified rights, which raise the difficult issue of proportionality or test of equivalence of official means and ends. A good example is Article 1 of the First Protocol (right to the peaceful enjoyment of property), which is important in relation to planning powers especially of compulsory purchase. Given the exceptionally low base of legal and administrative development in terms of Wales pre-devolution, it is hard to exaggerate the scale of the learning curve for the new institution in such matters.

Looking forwards, some key areas of human rights challenge can be identified. As indicated, Wales will no doubt make a major contribution in terms of linguistic issues, for example in relation to the delivery of services or provision of resources, where the Convention jurisprudence is notably weak.[64] As a comparative source, Canada looms large, there already being in Welsh legal circles the clear expectation of comparative borrowings and influences, especially from the leading common law jurisdictions, courtesy of the Internet. The way in which a territory like Wales is subject to, and made part of, processes associated with the rise of supranational ordering or so-called globalization of law, is liable to be brilliantly illustrated.

[63] See, for an instructive example, *Johansen v. Norway* (1996) 23 EHRR 33.
[64] *Belgian Linguistic Case* (1968) 1 EHRR 252. National Assembly, *Bilingual Lawmaking and Justice*, 2001.

As well as education, one would also anticipate significant contests in health provision (including under Article 2 (right to life)); and especially in relation to the treatment of vulnerable people (perhaps Article 3 or 8, together with Article 14). Not least, it may be said, in view of the concentrations of socio-economic deprivation in much of Wales. A leading human rights practitioner has already added to the list 'residential care home and nursing registrations, access to public records, Gypsy eviction proceedings, agricultural development issues (particularly if these are environmentally damaging), road developments, public finance issues, etc'.[65]

Turning to the intricate modalities of multi-layered governance, the great bulk of Assembly spending is indirect, channelled through local government, Assembly Sponsored Public Bodies, and so on. On the one hand, it is only with the general application of the HRA to such service providers, as distinct from Convention Rights constraining the Assembly under the rubric of the GWA, that the full force of the HRA has begun to be felt inside the territory. On the other hand, intriguing and wholly novel questions are raised concerning the legal and political responsibility of (a form of meso-government like) the Assembly for securing the compliance with Convention rights of those bodies that it funds and in respect of which it commonly has a regulatory function.[66]

A new frontier of constitutional and human rights litigation is identified here, and one which is underscored by the incentive for interest groups etc. engaging in campaigning litigation[67] to try to draw the Assembly into relevant disputes. By this is meant especially the unrivalled opportunities for creative mixes of legal and political leverage in the new Welsh polity, already mentioned. The general sense of the Assembly as a national or strategic body is important in this context.

Mainstreaming

However sceptical one cares to be, no analysis of the role and impact of the HRA can be complete without reference to its reception inside government. Behind the scenes, valiant efforts have been made to draw human rights considerations into the mainstream of the new Welsh administrative process, from policy-making to decision-taking, and on into service delivery. The approach fits both with the positive obligations that public authorities now have to ensure respect for human rights, and with the declared aim of the (UK) government that 'an awareness of the Convention rights permeates our government and legal systems at all levels'.[68]

[65] L. Clements, 'Devolution in Wales and the Human Rights Implications', (July 1999) *Legal Action*, 20; idem, 'The Government of Wales Act 1998 and Human Rights', in Miers, *Devolution in Wales.*

[66] The transfer of functions from the Secretary of State for Wales (Welsh Office) has armed the Assembly with a myriad powers of direction and guidance in such areas as social services and education provision.

[67] See, on the rich heritage of campaigning litigation in Britain, another important historical determinant of the role and impact of the HRA, C. Harlow and R. Rawlings, *Pressure through Law* (London: Routledge, 1992).

[68] Human Rights Task Force, *A New Era of Rights and Responsibilities* (London: Home Office, 2000), 4.

The key instrument has been an Assembly Action Plan (similar to those devised for central government departments). It has typically involved legal as well as pro-motional, networking, and educational functions:[69]

- To ensure that Assembly legislation, practices and procedures are consistent with the Convention rights and not likely to lead to legal challenge on human rights grounds.
- To ensure that all staff are aware of the implications of the Convention Rights for their work—particularly where this involves establishing policies or mak-ing decisions that affect individuals.
- To ensure that public authorities which the Assembly funds or sponsors are aware of the implications of the HRA for their work and the action they need to take to ensure compliance with the Act.
- To ensure that private and voluntary bodies are aware of the HRA and its implications for them when they are carrying out public functions.
- To contribute within Wales to UK wide efforts to promote public awareness of the significance of incorporating the European Convention into domestic law, especially among young people.

Several features are directly relevant to this discussion. There is the fact of very close collaboration at official level with the Home Office and its Human Rights Task Force in London. That is, a prototypical example of intergovernmental cooperation and coordination in the new devolutionary age. There is a clear incentive here, not least in terms of the continuing vulnerability of the UK government to legal chal-lenge in Strasbourg. To this effect, I have elsewhere drawn attention to increased interdependence across hierarchical state structures as a key ingredient of the simultaneous processes of (European) integration and fragmentation.[70]

Then there is the difficulty of achieving cultural change of this magnitude across the complex set of structures and processes of the kind that now comprises the Welsh Government. Officially, according to the Welsh chief minister, Rhodri Morgan, it has been 'easier for us' because the Assembly 'has no tradition'. In con-trast, according to a senior official involved, 'a mind set of human rights' has been 'difficult to deliver' especially because of 'the scale of civil service change' in Wales associated with devolution.[71]

At the same time, there is practical illustration of the synergies between the var-ious sources of law now operative in Wales. The connections are not seamless, but, for example, in the words of an official dealing with school exclusions and human rights, 'because of the blending into equal opportunities we have given [the issue] greater emphasis'. And again, with reference to the idea of a newly textured demo-cratic culture, 'we don't want to get stuck just on the legal side. Human Rights is one element together with complaints [procedures], equality of opportunity etc.,

---

[69] National Assembly, *Human Rights Act Implementation: Action Plan* (Jan. 2000).
[70] Rawlings, 'Law, Territory and Integration'.   [71] Quoted in Rawlings, *Delineating Wales*.

and cross cuts into issues like social exclusion. It's about developing a wider perspective . . .'[72]

The theme is worth pursuing. The Assembly Members themselves have been slow to engage with the implications of human rights law and practice. More recently, however, there have been signs of a growing awareness of the opportunities as well as the demands for Assembly policies and actions in this sphere.[73] Looking forwards, one could envisage a firm political focus developing inside the Assembly, perhaps in the form of a committee on human rights together with equal opportunities. Speaking more generally, the demand has arisen[74] for a statutory Human Rights Commission to promote and protect human rights inside the territory, perhaps constructed (in line with national devolution) on a Welsh basis or (in accordance with the prevailing court (and penal) structure) in terms of England and Wales.

Chalk and cheese

The long year between the beginning of devolution and full implementation of the HRA in the United Kingdom was marked in Scotland by a crop of human rights litigation, much of it of the dustbin variety, but also with some interesting and controversial cases.[75] Yet there was not a single challenge to the National Assembly for Wales on the basis of Convention Rights in this period, or indeed any significant challenge under the rubric of devolution issues, for example according to the ordinary domestic law principles of judicial review.[76] It is then a case of chalk and cheese, for which there are several layers of explanation.

Most obviously, there is the basic asymmetry in terms of competencies as between the devolutionary schemes in Wales and Scotland. Strictly speaking, this is not so much a function of executive devolution, as characterized by the horizontal division of labour in terms of primary and secondary lawmaking powers, but rather a product of the differential ranges of fields in which powers are given. Where to date the Scottish cases are concentrated, general criminal law and process,[77] is the very same area where the Assembly lacks jurisdiction.

Reference has already been made in this context to the Assembly model of indirect administration. It is also the case, in part a reflection of the initial phase of minority administration,[78] in part because of the steep learning curve confronting the actors, that thus far the Assembly has not been particularly assertive in the exercise of its

---

[72] Quoted in Rawlings, *Delineating Wales*.

[73] As illustrated by Welsh Government statements on the HRA, *Official Record of Proceedings*, 21 Nov. 2000 and 14 Dec. 2000.

[74] Echoing developments elsewhere in the 'Atlantic Isles'. See L. Clements and S. Spencer, *A Human Rights Commission in Wales?* (London: Institute of Public Policy Research, 2001).

[75] See Ch. 8 in this volume.   [76] The position remains the same at the time of writing (June 2001).

[77] As in the emergent devolution jurisprudence of the Privy Council: see e.g. *Montgomery v. Her Majesty's Advocate and the Advocate General for Scotland* (Oct. 2000) and *Brown v. Stott* (Dec. 2000).

[78] See n. 40 above.

various lawmaking and regulatory powers. Welsh subordinate legislation has essentially been driven from elsewhere, via requirements to act in new primary legislation and EU Directives.[79] Substantial legal challenge, it could be said, will be a mark of the constitutional and political maturation of the new democratic institution.

In assessing the significance of an absence of litigation, one can scarcely ignore the role of internal checks, and in particular here the role of the lawyers in the Office of the Counsel General.[80] Nowhere in the United Kingdom is the *vires* of subordinate legislation checked more thoroughly than in Wales: a natural product of the model of executive devolution. It is worth noting the way in which the traditional formulation for legislative scrutiny[81] of statutory instruments on the ground of *vires*—'if there appears to be a doubt'—takes on new meaning in this context, precisely because of the strong dynamic quality of the jurisprudence under the European Convention. A rather different margin of appreciation, emblematic of a cautious legal and administrative approach to such matters in the Assembly, is made evident here.[82]

There is also the historical legacy, the limited tradition of public law in Wales. Once again the contrast with Scotland, where a confident and established local legal profession was in place prior to devolution, is very great. Matters have been compounded not only by the complex character of the Welsh scheme, so hard to get to grips with, but also by the lack in Wales of an open constitutional debate prior to the devolution legislation, which would surely have helped to promote a general legal interest.[83] Looking forwards, one would anticipate on this front gradual change—but obviously much quicker if Wales moved to a form of legislative devolution. The HRA will have an important role of catalyst, for example in spreading in areas such as family and criminal law a greater awareness of public law techniques.

VI. Conclusion

This chapter has ranged broadly. Some might say *force majeure*, there being no cases to report at the time of writing. But I would rather stress the formidable intellectual challenge presented by the topic of devolution and human rights. By this is meant not only a stress on such matters as the socio-economic dimension or close integration of historical and political perspectives, but also the pursuit of a bottom-up

---

[79] See further R. Rawlings, 'Scrutiny and Reform', in J. Barry Jones and J. Osmond (eds.), *Inclusive Government and Party Management* (Institute of Welsh Affairs, 2000).

[80] See, on the further role played by inter-institutional agreements or 'concordats' in damping down litigation, R. Rawlings, 'Concordats of the Constitution', (2000) 116 *Law Quarterly Review* 257.

[81] In the sense of so-called 'adverse reporting' by the Joint Committee on Statutory Instruments at Westminster, and now by the Legislation Committee of the National Assembly.

[82] See, for practical illustration, Rawlings, 'Scrutiny and Reform'.

[83] Reference may here be made to the important animating role of the unofficial Scottish Constitutional Convention: see esp. *Scotland's Parliament. Scotland's Right* (1995).

approach which pays due regard, on the one hand, to the local legal and administrative culture and, on the other, to the legal and political diversity that is the logic of devolution. Expressed slightly differently, such endeavour must be informed by close consideration of the interaction of the forces of universality and locality, which today finds tangible expression in the rise of supranational ordering and domestic or internal subsidiarity. A culture of human rights, derived from more than a couple of sources, is emblematic of the contemporary dynamics of constitutional change.

The case of Wales, I have argued, highlights many of the general themes. As regards Wales *qua* Wales, a distinctive polity is in the course of construction, which, however ill-formed, further involves flanking developments in the structures and processes of public administration. Specifically rendered in terms of integration, the English and Welsh legal system can hardly be immune from pressures for change in such conditions. Again, it is a mistake to see the devolutionary development simply in terms of the dictionary definition, 'the process of transferring power from central government to a lower or regional level'.[84] Such usage effectively drains the devolutionary process of social, cultural, and economic meaning, an aspect brilliantly illustrated in the case of national devolution to Wales.

To expand the point, consideration of the role and impact of the HRA in terms of 'British' constitutional culture or democratic tradition is necessary but insufficient. Now more than ever, the unwritten or anglocentric assumption of a unitary state, in the broad sense of monolithic structures and processes of government and administration, will not wash. It is, after all, issues concerning the degree of rebalancing in favour of a more pluralist approach, or of the competing comparative concept of the union state, which underpin so much of the intellectual fascination with the UK devolutionary process. So in this chapter emphasis has been laid on the role of the HRA in terms of an emergent Welsh constitutional tradition, one which in its own ways both draws on Westminster and Whitehall practice and procedure and involves a quest for a newly textured democratic culture. That at one and the same time the HRA confines the scope of, and operates in aid of establishing, a vibrant tradition of public law in Wales is a good illustration of the scope for variation in the devolved territories on a general theme of constitutional and legal reordering.

These are early days. The picture is the more complex by reason not only of the strong sense of contingency in the contemporary UK constitutional development but also of the distinctive nature of Welsh executive devolution, and in particular the strong perception of continuing evolutionary change in the constitutional situation of Wales. In the terms of this volume the inventive use of legal precept or technique to promote political and administrative engagement with such concepts as sustainable development or equality of opportunity has a special resonance. Indeed, in this respect, the written constitution that is the GWA may now be looked to for a lead in the comparative sense. A thousand years on from the great codification of Welsh law, it is time once again in the law to take Wales seriously.

---

[84] D. Robertson, *Dictionary of Politics*, 2nd edn. (Harmondsworth: Penguin, 1993), 135.

11

Scepticism under Scrutiny:
Labour Law and Human Rights

SANDRA FREDMAN

Labour lawyers in Britain have been understandably sceptical of the role of the judiciary in the field of labour law. A century of bruising encounters with judges determined to manipulate the common law and legislation to extinguish rights of workers has left its mark. The case for scepticism scarcely needs further elaboration. In this chapter, I nevertheless want to be sceptical about scepticism. Given that we are now firmly in an era of human rights and statutory protections, is there a way in which rights can be constructed so as to further rather than undermine the aims of social democracy? This seems to me to be an urgent matter. If social democratic labour lawyers are determined to swim against the tide and allow scepticism to prevail, the current of history may well leave us behind. Is it possible instead to use existing tools to shape a rights-based labour law which can further the aims of social democracy rather than defeat them? There is generally unequivocal support among social democratic and left-wing labour lawyers for the International Labour Organization and its set of guaranteed rights. Moreover, few would now argue that it is possible or even desirable to insulate industrial relations entirely from the courts, as was advocated by the ideology of collective laissez-faire.

In this chapter, my scepticism about scepticism does not entail support for a liberal, individualist and property-oriented notion of human rights. Instead, I hope to use the insights of the sceptical approach to move through scepticism towards a possible reconstruction of human rights in a social democratic context. In particular, I examine whether there is the potential to create a set of human rights which can enhance rather than detract from participatory democracy, which can restrain rather than expand the powers of the courts, and which can in addition support collective, socialist, and egalitarian values.

In order to do this, I begin by examining the foundations of the scepticism of the role of human rights in the labour law context. Does it relate to the judges themselves, to the method of adjudication, to the content of the rights or to the underlying values? It is striking that even the most sceptical of social democratic labour lawyers believe strongly in the value of the ILO. I then build on these insights in order to discover whether it is possible to construct an alternative view of human rights.[1]

---

[1] This chapter draws on and expands my arguments in 'Judging Democracy: The Role of the Judiciary under the HRA 1998', (2000) 53 *Current Legal Problems* 99–129.

I. Human rights and democracy: the arguments against

There are two arguments from democracy against a system of human rights. The first begins with the premise that rights are fundamentally contested.[2] Rational and genuine arguments can be mounted leading to a variety of different conclusions, all of which are plausible, but no one of which is uncontroversially correct. Thus the key issue is not which decision should be made, but who should make it. A democratic response to this question points inexorably to the legislature. As Waldron argues, if we believe that individuals are worthy rights bearers, then we must believe they are worthy of the responsibility of making decisions as to what rights individuals have.[3] Indeed, he argues, the right to participate in decision-making is itself the 'right of rights';[4] and there is no reason to exclude decisions about democracy from this right. It is thus deeply contradictory to assert that, on issues of fundamental disagreement, the responsibility should be given to a handful of unelected, unaccountable judges.

According to the second argument, judges given power by a bill of rights will inevitably obstruct the development of social democracy.[5] On this view, judges inevitably have a specific value system, based on an individualistic, liberal, and property-oriented view. The state is envisaged in judicial eyes as a potential threat to individual liberty, and the role of human rights as protecting individuals from such a threat. Social democratic policies, in which the state is not an adversary but has positive obligations to further the welfare of the individual by securing rights to work, housing, education, etc. will, on this view, inevitably be construed by the courts as a form of interference with individual liberty and be struck down. Formulated in this way, it can be seen that this approach, while sharing the scepticism of the judiciary found in the previous approach, differs in that it does not begin with the premise that all rights are controversial. Instead, it takes a substantive view, requiring rights to support the values of social democracy.

Labour law is a particularly appropriate arena for conducting this debate. Labour rights are among the most contested of rights, and therefore arguably only legitimately determined by the legislature. In fact, the shape and content of labour law is almost invariably a reflection of political decision-making. Labour law also provides positive proof of the unsuitability of the judiciary for determining the content of rights, thereby supporting the shared premise of both the value-neutral and the substantive schools of democratic opponents of human rights. The history of labour law in the UK is replete with examples of a judicial hostility to labour rights. Where the legislature repealed criminal prohibitions on trade union organization and

---

[2] See Lord Hoffman 'Human Rights and the House of Lords', (1999) 62 *Modern Law Review* 159 at 160, 165; J. Waldron, *Law and Disagreement* (Oxford: Clarendon Press, 1999).
[3] Ibid. 223, 250.   [4] Ibid. ch. 11, n. 3.
[5] K. Ewing, 'Human Rights, Social Democracy and Constitutional Reform', in C. Gearty and A. Tomkins (eds.), *Understanding Human Rights* (London: Pinter, 1999), 40–59.

strikes, the courts refashioned the common law to create civil liabilities. The legislature responded with statutory immunities against these civil liabilities, only to find that them outflanked by new judicially created torts.[6] Fresh evidence of continued judicial hostility to collective rights of trade unions was available as recently as 1995, when a highly restrictive interpretation was given to the already limited statutory protections for freedom of association. Thus in the well-known cases of *Wilson* and *Palmer*,[7] the court in effect held that freedom of association did not extend to a right to representation by the union, but entailed bare membership of the trade union only. Still more recently, rights to unfair dismissal have been diluted by construing the reasonableness criteria widely to reflect the employers' norms rather than the rights of the employee. Attempts by an adventurous Employment Appeal Tribunal to recast the definition were stonewalled by the Court of Appeal[8] as recently as 2000.

II. Scepticism under scrutiny

The sceptical argument is, on the face of it, very convincing. However, there are two aspects which require critical scrutiny. The first is the assumption that the legislature as it is presently structured can indeed be trusted either to function as the sole avenue for participatory democracy or to deliver substantive social democratic policies. I suggest that participatory democracy can be enhanced by properly constructed human rights litigation. The second is the view that a bill of rights will give the judiciary more power than it already has. I argue instead that it is the very absence of a codified bill of rights which gives the courts too much power. In other words, far from enhancing the power of the judiciary, a bill of rights can in fact constrain that power, provided the legislature retains proper control over the content and interpretation of the rights. Each of these points will be elaborated in turn.

The weakness of Parliament

As will be recalled, the first, or value-neutral, type of democratic argument against human rights is based on the view that the content of rights is fundamentally contested and therefore can be determined only by the majority of the people through the legislature. On the face of it, this position was well represented by Britain prior to the Human Rights Act 1998. A strong principle of parliamentary sovereignty and a corresponding subordination of the judiciary established a constitutional framework within which decisions about rights take place entirely through the political process. Democratic power appeared to coalesce within Parliament, and not in the hands of an unelected judiciary.

---

[6] See e.g. *D. C. Thomson & Co. Ltd v. Deakin* [1952] Ch 646; *Merkur Island v. Laughton* [1983] ICR 490 (HL); *Falconer v. ASLEF* [1986] IRLR 331.

[7] *Associated Newspapers v. Wilson; Associated British Ports v. Palmer* [1995] IRLR 258 (HL).

[8] *Midland Bank v. Madden* [2000] IRLR 827 (CA).

This argument depends on real participation by the electorate in the determination of the content of rights. Yet a vote at a general election is scarcely an opportunity to participate in decisions about human rights. A combination of the 'first past the post' electoral system and strong party discipline means that in effect policy decisions are made by a small group of politicians backed up by an influential but anonymous civil service. The executive therefore exercises substantial power over primary legislation. Moreover, there is a growing trend for Parliament to enact skeletal primary legislation, devolving wide powers to the executive to put flesh on the bones of the law through delegated legislation. This was particularly clear in the field of labour law with the enactment of the Employment Relations Act 1999. Much of this Act is in the form of delegated powers, with the substance of the legislation being provided by executive action, with only cursory parliamentary scrutiny. In addition, 'Henry VIII' clauses, which permit primary legislation to be amended by secondary legislation, are not uncommon,[9] and primary legislation often gives wide discretionary powers to the executive. Equally important is the extensive use of non-legislative means to implement policy, through contracting powers and other types of wealth deployment.[10]

Of course, the weakness of Parliament does not mean that democracy would be improved by giving greater power to the judiciary. There are alternative and much more democratic means of dealing with these weaknesses. This is particularly true in the field of labour law. The traditional response to judicial activism was not to create positive rights for workers, which would themselves be hostage to judicial hostility, but to insulate collective action from the courts by creating a set of of legislative immunities from specific torts when the action was taken in contemplation or furtherance of a trade dispute. This legal abstentionism, or preference for self-regulation, was trumpeted as a positive virtue of labour law in Britain, particularly by the foremost modern theorist of labour law, Otto Kahn Freund.[11] The role of collective bargaining in regulating basic terms and conditions could be seen par excellence as a form of participatory democracy. At EU level, the response to the democratic deficit has been through the Social Dialogue, leaving it to the social partners to negotiate the content of employment rights.

In practice, however, it has become clear that neither of these alternatives can function alone, without substantive underpinning in the form of legal rights. Collective bargaining in the absence of statutory rights was dependent on a favourable economic climate, with full employment and a sympathetic state. Even then, it failed to provide protection for weaker groups of employers, specifically in the area of sex and race discrimination. Self-regulation in areas such as unfair dismissal became too unstable from an industrial relations point of view, and collective

---

    [9] See e.g. HRA 1998, s. 10(2).
    [10] T. Daintith, 'The Executive Power Today: Bargaining and Economic Control', in J. Jowell and D. Oliver (eds.), *The Changing Constitution* (Oxford: Clarendon Press, 1989), 193–4.
    [11] P. L. Davies and M. R. Freedland (eds.), *Kahn-Freund's Labour and the Law* (London: Stevens, 1983), ch. 1.

bargaining did not necessarily provide protection on issues which did not affect the majority of members. As a result, the 1970s saw a significant modification of the view that labour law functioned best without juridification of rights. This led to the enactment of a framework of rights to compensation for redundancy and unfair dismissal, in part at least to channel disputes into tribunals and thereby make it unnecessary to take strike action in cases of dismissal.[12] Similarly, anti-discrimination laws were necessary to fill a significant gap in the coverage of collective bargaining.[13]

The more recent experience of the Social Dialogue can be analysed along similar lines. The participation of the social partners in the formulation of social legislation significantly enhances participative democracy. But the fact that it is based entirely on interest bargaining without any underpinning by substantive rights has meant that the result is a direct reflection of the balance of power, normally favouring employers and the dominant interests in trade unions.

Nor can the second, substantive school of sceptical democrats consistently rest its faith in Parliament as the only legitimate vehicle for the delivery of rights of any kind. As will be recalled, this school takes the view that judges cannot be trusted to interpret rights in line with a social democratic legislature; to the contrary, they will inevitably subvert it. Yet can we trust the legislature to enact legislation which embodies these values? Certainly the degree and extent of repressive labour laws which emanated from the Conservative government in power from 1979 to 1997 demonstrates otherwise. It is striking that these laws were quite rightly criticized, not just on the basis of political disagreement, but on the grounds that Parliament was itself in breach of fundamental rights such as the right of freedom of association in the ILO Conventions.[14] For example, critics normally sceptical of human rights were quick to draw on the 1998 report of the Council of Europe's Committee of Experts, to the effect that the combined effect of the various regulations governing the right to strike in the UK constituted an unjustifiable restriction on the right to strike in Article 6(4) of the European Social Charter. This at least suggests that there is a role for human rights in constraining legislative action, although the form of enforcement of those rights may need to be carefully considered.

The power of the judiciary

The chief common premise of democratic arguments against human rights is that a bill of rights would give too much power to the judges. However, a closer look at the current system of rights protection demonstrates that, paradoxically, there are many crucial areas in which the judiciary already holds too much power. This is not only because there is no entrenched bill of rights; there is a conspicuous absence of any codified set of rights at all. Instead we have that familiar but mythical creature, the 'negative right'. Although in principle an individual is free to do anything

---

[12] See generally the Employment Protection (Consolidation) Act 1978.
[13] Sex Discrimination Act 1975; Race Relations Act 1976.
[14] K. Ewing *Britain and the ILO*, 2nd edn. (London: Institute of Employment Rights, 1994).

provided it is not prohibited by law, legal prohibitions are substantial. The right to freedom of assembly is found in the interstices of public order law, the law of trespass, and the law regulating use of the highway. Freedom of speech lurks somewhere between laws against obscenity, contempt of court, and defamation; theatre and cinema licensing regulations; and Parliamentary privilege. Freedom of association and the right to belong to a trade union are protected obliquely by bundles of provisions including the right not to be dismissed[15] or be subject to detrimental treatment for being a member of or participating in the activities of a trade union.[16] There is also protection for refusal to employ on grounds of trade union membership, but not activities,[17] and the right to time off for trade union activities.[18]

For Dicey, this means of protecting rights was a great strength,[19] a view enthusiastically endorsed by Lord Goff as recently as 1990, when he declared in the *Spycatcher* case:

We may pride ourselves on the fact that freedom of speech has existed in this country perhaps as long as, if not longer than, it has existed in any other country in the world. The only difference is that, whereas [the European Convention on Human Rights] . . . proceeds to state a fundamental right and then to qualify it, we in this country (where everyone is free to do anything, subject only to the provisions of the law) proceed rather upon an assumption of freedom of speech and turn to our law to discover the established exceptions to it.[20]

It is clear from this statement that substantial power is left to the judges. In the absence of a constitutional document setting out the fundamental principles, it is left to the judges to decide the scope of the right, the nature of permissible restrictions on the right, and the relative weight to be given to the right and the asserted justification for its restriction. But because there is no explicit framework of positive rights, judicial reasoning is rarely focused on the content of a human right or the legitimacy of a derogation. There is little scope for parties to present arguments about the substantive rights themselves, and no need for judges to ground their decisions in express human rights considerations. The sophisticated debate on questions of principle and interpretation that characterizes similar cases in other jurisdictions is conspicuously lacking.

The absence of proper rights-based constraints on the judiciary is particularly evident in the labour law field. The notion that basic rights are protected by the common law[21] is simply untrue. As we have seen, strikes have almost inevitably been held to be a breach of the individual contract of employment. Similarly, the common law has been shaped and extended to yield a range of torts, such as conspiracy, intimidation, and inducing breach of contract, giving rise to liability on behalf of organizers of strikes.[22] It is notable that even the statutory employment protection rights introduced by the legislature have been built on the shifting sands

---

[15] Trade Union Labour Relations Consolidation Act 1992, s. 152.   [16] Ibid. s. 146.
[17] Ibid. s. 137.   [18] Ibid. ss. 168, 170.
[19] A. V. Dicey, *The Law of the Constitution* 10th edn. (London: Macmillan, 1960), 197–9.
[20] [1990] 1 AC 109 at 283. See also *Derbyshire CC v. Times Newspapers Ltd* [1992] 3 WLR 28.
[21] See Dicey, n. 19 above.   [22] See e.g. cases cited in n. 6 above.

of the common law. The contract of employment remains at the core of labour law; and unfair dismissal rights were based on a reasonableness criterion inviting extensive judicial discretion.

It is arguable that had a set of positive rights been established at this stage, there would have been less scope for encroachment either from the judiciary or from the legislature. If a positive right to strike had been introduced rather than a set of narrow immunities, the judges would have had less latitude to outflank the liabilities. If the right to unfair dismissal had not been based on a reasonableness criterion, there would have been less scope for its subversion into an employer-oriented measure. If freedom of association were protected by a positive right, there would have been less opportunity for the judges to undermine it, as they did in the case of *Wilson*. Similarly, a rights-based system might have been more resilient in the face of legislative incursion during the Thatcher and Major era. The absence of an established set of rights for trade unions was exploited to the full on an ideological level by a government intent on undermining the role of trade unions in industrial relations. Thus 'immunities' were quickly translated into 'privileges', and privileges could easily be portrayed as setting unions above the law and therefore apparently justifiably removed or restricted. Equally effective was the hijacking of the vocabulary of rights and democracy in order to justify highly restrictive policies on trade unions and workers.[23] Thus, instead of granting workers rights as against their employer, they were granted rights as against their unions. The right to work was transmuted into a right to defy a strike order, even if endorsed by a majority. Similarly, the appeal of democracy was used to justify the imposition of detailed and technical rules on balloting, breach of which led not to enhanced power of the workers, but instead to the right of employers to harness the injunctive powers of the courts to prevent strike action. By contrast, there was notably less encroachment on those areas of labour law which had already been regulated by positive statutory rights. Although rights not to be unfairly dismissed were narrowed, they were not removed; and discrimination law, buttressed by the powerful influence of EC law, was one of the few areas in which workers' rights were relatively robust.

III. A democratic bill of rights?

Can we therefore construct a bill of rights which enhances participatory democracy and has a good chance of embodying substantive social democratic values? I would argue that this is possible if three principles are followed. First, there must be real legislative control of the judiciary. Second, the process of litigation must be recast as a channel of participation, albeit one which is unique and different from that of the legislature. Finally, there must be fundamental changes in the composition of

---

[23] For further elaboration of this point, see S. Fredman, 'The New Rights: Labour Law and Ideology in the Thatcher Years', (1992) 12 *Oxford Journal of Legal Studies* 24–44.

the judiciary. I shall argue in the final section that the HRA 1998 goes some way towards achieving this, but ultimately stops well short of the democratic ideal.

Legislative control of the process of judicial decision-making

So far as primary legislation is concerned, the democratic argument is largely met by ensuring that Parliament has the final say. It is a salient feature of the HRA 1998 that the courts cannot invalidate legislation, but only declare it to be incompatible with Convention rights. It could be objected, as Lord Hoffman has argued, that the distinction between the power to invalidate a decision and the declaration of incompatibility is merely a technical one, because the political pressure to bring the law into line with a judicial declaration will be hard to resist.[24] However, the crucial difference is that a declaration of incompatibility generates political pressure rather than legally binding obligations. It is as part of the political debate that the judicial role is both democratic and meaningful.

But ensuring that Parliament has the final say over primary legislation is not sufficient. In addition, there should be detailed input from the legislature into the human rights principles to be applied. Much of the democratic criticism of judicial decision-making arises because judges have had to interpret very broad statements of principle in controversial situations. Thus the Equal Protection Clause of the Fourteenth Amendment in the US gives a right to equal treatment without specifying when differential treatment is legitimate and when it is not. It was left to the courts to formulate a set of constitutional principles to address race and sex discrimination. Similarly, the legitimacy of abortion or capital punishment has had to be fashioned from very general constitutional guarantees. Judicial power will be subject to far more democratic constraints if there is a codification of rights in which controversial issues have been given close legislative attention.

This is particularly true in respect of secondary legislation and the exercise of executive discretion. In these areas, the courts do have the power to invalidate, although express legislative intervention can overturn their decisions. As we have seen, the line between primary legislation and these forms of decision-making is often thin. In this respect, it is particularly important for Parliament to give appropriate democratic guidance to the courts, both by specifying the content and scope of human rights and by setting out the basic values and precepts of the society it serves. In the absence of such guidance, judges are left to formulate human rights for themselves, as well as applying them to the facts in the case, subject only to retrospective rebuttal by Parliament. This is not to say that judicial value judgments can or should be avoided altogether. But in the absence of a codified set of rights and a general statement of values, such value judgments become inappropriately influential. In this sense, far from increasing the power of the judges, the enactment of a properly codified bill of rights functions as an appropriate democratic constraint on the courts.

---

[24] Lord Hoffman, n. 2 above, 160.

Of course it is arguable that the nature of the judiciary is such as to inevitably corrode even positive rights. Certainly the right to freedom of association has not prevented the ECtHR from taking a determinedly narrow view of that right. This points towards the need not only for a clear set of rights to be promulgated by the legislature, but also a set of underlying values. Many bills of rights are prefaced by a set of values which guide the judiciary in the application of the rights to controversial situations. Indeed, a look at other jurisdictions indicates that in the hands of the right sort of judiciary, and underpinned by a clear statement of values, it is possible to fashion strong collective labour rights. The Israeli labour court, for example, has fashioned a strong right to freedom of association and to strike from the general constitutional guarantee of human dignity and freedom in the Israeli Basic Law passed in 1992. This has been openly defended by the President of the Israeli Labour Court on the grounds that courts have a responsibility to protect social rights, including workers' freedom of association. In the absence of specific written constitutional social law, he argues, general constitutional principles should be used to further social rights. In an important recent case, the Court relied on these principles to reach the opposite conclusion from the UK court in *Wilson*: to subject workers to specific detriment on grounds of their trade union membership was held to violate their freedom of association. This and two other decisions furthering workers' rights were expressly held to be based on three considerations. First, in light of the current weakness of trade unions, it was necessary to give preference to collective values and the right to strike over individual rights and management's property rights. Second, freedom of association for workers, including the right to organize and strike, would be meaningless if there were no strong unions to join. Third, equality in the workplace included equality for the union worker as compared to the non-union worker.

Litigation as a channel of democratic participation

The second way of constructing a democratic bill of rights is to view the process of litigation itself as an avenue of participative democracy augmenting the role of Parliament. The idea here is to regard judicial decision-making as one input into the parliamentary process of decision-making, and litigants as a crucial input into judicial decision-making. Care must, however, be taken to avoid the opposite danger, namely the attempt to transform litigation into an inappropriate replica of the political process. The judicial contribution can be appropriate only if it is based on a reasoning process which is quite different from that of the legislature. It is here that the importance of codification of human rights is again highlighted. If judicial input entails the application of a democratically agreed principle to a particular dispute, based on detailed arguments and supported by articulated reasons, then judicial decisions can function as a meaningful part of the process of ultimate determination of rights without collapsing into political bargaining. Judges should not be asked to decide wide questions of policy on the basis purely of balancing of interests or responsivity to an electorate. Instead, they should apply a clearly formulated set of principles to a particular dispute. It is this which makes judicial reasoning uniquely legal. As Sir John Laws has argued, the best way of rebutting the argument that a bill of rights would give judges the licence to decide wide questions of policy which legitimately belong to the elected Parliament is to ensure that courts deal with human rights as questions of law rather than morality.[25]

However, to view litigation in this way requires an adaptation of the traditional private law model of litigation, with a bipolar, adversarial system. An adversarial action assumes that the dispute is between two parties only, with the court a passive arbiter, dependent on the information supplied by the two parties. Yet human rights issues are not simply disputes between a particular individual and the state concerning that person's interests; nor, as we have seen, is there a single right answer. Therefore, the process of decision-making in itself needs to be enriched by opening up for consideration the variety of perspectives and possibilities which affect the decision. Many jurisdictions have achieved this by wide rules of standing, the encouragement of interest group participation, class actions, and specialist interventions.

This approach to the litigation process is capable of augmenting the rights of ordinary citizens to participate in important decisions. A vote for a political party once in five years in an election cannot be a vote for a particular interpretation of a human right. Individual voices and voices of public interest groups may make a valuable contribution through the litigation process which is denied during the ordinary political process. However, again care must be taken to avoid collapsing the litigation process into a purely political one. A more accessible litigation process does not tell us what part should be played in the decision by the arguments presented in court. The answer to this is related to the earlier characterization of judicial decision-making as a process of deliberation rather than political bargaining. Within this process, the role of litigants and interveners should not be seen as one of representing particular interest groups. Instead, the purpose is to enrich the process of deliberation by bringing to the notice of the judiciary expert information, perspectives, and arguments which a bipolar process could not bring to light.

However, this approach also has its dangers. Why should some individuals have double the voting power, once in elections and once in court? Even more problematic is the risk of usurpation of the litigation process by the powerful corporations and bodies which have a disproportionate influence on both the political and litigation process. Ewing and Sedley both rightly point to the dangers of the 'big battalions getting an unfair share of [human] rights adjudication'.[26] The expense and inaccessibility of the courts in the current system makes this a very real danger. A serious commitment to participative democracy would require radical changes to the process of litigation to ensure equality of access regardless of resources. It would

---

[25] Sir J. Laws, 'The Limitations of Human Rights', [1998] *Public Law* 254 at 257.

[26] S. Sedley, 'Human Rights: A Twenty-First Agenda', [1995] *Public Law* 386 at 393; Ewing, n. 5 above.

also need a clear articulation of a notion of substantive equality, so that judges are sensitive to their role in facilitating greater equality among litigants and potential litigants.

The composition of the judiciary in human rights litigation

The final mechanism for enhancing participation is concerned with the process of appointment of those judges involved in human rights adjudication. Critics of the judicial role in human rights adjudication routinely point to the fact that judges are unelected and unaccountable. It is of course inappropriate to submit judges to the same system of elections as Members of Parliament, and accountability should not prejudice independence. Nevertheless, participative democracy in the selection of judges for human rights adjudication can be enhanced by the establishment of clear criteria for selection, and a transparency in the process of applying those criteria. Several jurisdictions have striven to achieve appropriate democratic input into the selection of those judges involved in human rights adjudication.

It could be argued, however, that this begs many questions. An open selection process for the judiciary does not itself tell us what criteria of selection should be used. The narrow social base of the current judiciary is often criticized, but little attention is paid to why the judiciary, particularly in their constitutional roles, should reflect more closely the diversity of the society which it serves. Clearly, if human rights adjudication were no more than a highly skilled process of working out the legal answer to a puzzling human rights question, only judicial expertise, and not judicial backgrounds, would be relevant. But given the fundamental disagreement about rights, this is not a sufficient answer. At the same time, judges are not strictly representatives of the people; and they are not expected to be accountable to particular interests. The real reason for the need for diversity, I would suggest, is based in the recognition that, since there is no abstract, impartial answer to human rights questions, the particular life experience of the decision-maker is reflected in his or her view. Since class, gender, and race remain such strong determinants of a person's life experience, the overwhelming predominance of one class, gender, or race in decision-making make it unlikely that the experience and perspectives of the excluded group will be articulated.[27] Greater diversity on the bench functions to open up new perspectives on decision-making, to cast light on assumptions that the dominant group perceives as universal, and to enhance the store of 'social knowledge'. This also means that it is unnecessary to insist on exact proportionality of representation. The contribution of particular perspectives is valuable regardless of how many individuals make that contribution.

It is notable that in the field of labour law, these notions have to some extent been put into practice, in the form of the employment tribunal. The two lay members, drawn from representatives of employers and employees respectively, are not

---

[27] A. Phillips, *The Politics of Presence* (Oxford: Oxford University Press, 1995), 4, 52.

expected to function as representatives of a particular set of constituents. Instead, their experience is believed to cast a valuable perspective on the industrial relations issues at hand. The belief in the usefulness of particular perspectives has been extended in practice, so that a woman is usually expected to be one of the panel in sex discrimination cases, and a member of an ethnic minority is ideally on the panel in a race discrimination case. The influence of the lay members has been significant. But the fact that their decisions on questions of law are subject to appeal in the ordinary courts has inevitably kept them within the constraints of traditional judicial perspectives. Indeed, it is largely the appeal courts which have insisted on a contractual analysis of employment law, and which have imposed an employer-oriented formula on the reasonableness criterion in unfair dismissal cases. In addition, collective disputes are still adjudicated in the ordinary courts.

IV. The influence of the HRA

I have argued thus far that the contested nature of human rights calls for a democratic decision-making process. However, under the current system, the right of citizens to participate in decisions about rights is so attenuated as to be almost fictional, largely because of the weakness of Parliament relative to an all-powerful executive. Moreover, the lack of codification of human rights paradoxically gives too much power to the judiciary in supervising rights protection. Both these problems could be rectified by a Human Rights Act. In principle, codification of rights could provide substantive constraints both on executive and on judicial power. At the same time, a Human Rights Act could enhance the rights of citizens to participate in decisions about human rights, both through legislative action in formulating rights and through litigation in representing a wide range of perspectives. Judicial accountability could be enhanced by greater attention to methods of selection of the judiciary, and by ultimate subordination of their decisions to that of the legislature.

To what extent, then, does the HRA fulfil these requirements? It is argued here that this Act will go some way towards enhancing participatory democracy. However, by simply transplanting an unmodified ECHR into unaltered judicial procedures, a valuable opportunity has been missed genuinely to enhance the right of citizens to participate meaningfully in decisions about rights. The result is that a wide arena of unrestrained judicial power remains.

The HRA has two central strengths. First, rights are codified. Thus the Act makes it unlawful for any public authority to act in a way which is incompatible with a Convention right,[28] and public authority for these purposes includes the courts.[29] This means that both executive power and judicial scrutiny of that power are guided by a codified set of principles. The fiction of deemed parliamentary intent is replaced by an open mandate to the courts to read and give effect to primary and subordinate legislation in a way which is compatible with Convention rights.[30] The

---

[28] HRA 1998, s. 6(1).   [29] Ibid. s. 6(3).   [30] Ibid. s. 3.

courts are no longer confined to cases of ambiguity: they should interpret legislation to uphold Convention Rights 'unless the legislation itself is so clearly incompatible with the Convention that it is impossible to do so'.[31] At legislative level, codification creates the impulse for debate and scrutiny, albeit in a non-binding sense. Thus, where any bill is introduced in either House, the minister responsible for the bill is required to make a statement that he or she believes the bill is compatible with Convention rights, or alternately that the government wishes the House to proceed despite incompatibility.[32]

The second main strength of the HRA is the fact that while the judiciary is given a role in human rights adjudication, the last word remains with the legislature. The court cannot strike down legislation; its powers extend only to declaring that legislation is incompatible with a Convention right.[33] It is then up to Parliament to decide whether or not to amend the provision, and if so, how. Thus a dialogue of sorts is set up between the courts and Parliament, with the court's contribution playing an important but not decisive role in the process. In this way, some of the central arguments against a Human Rights Act are defused: it is not an entrenched Bill of Rights, so it does not give power to the judiciary to override the elected representatives of the people. At the same time, the legislation allows the judges to make a distinctive contribution to the debate. The Act therefore contains the potential for enriching participative democracy in some of the ways described above. Judges are neither given final determinative power nor required to imitate the legislative process.

Thus far, then, the HRA appears both to trammel the power of the judiciary through codification and to enhance the rights of citizens to participate in decision-making. However, there are at least three ways in which it falls short of the democratic ideal. First, there has been minimal democratic discussion of the content of the rights in issue. Instead, the European Convention has simply been transplanted unadapted. This means that a crucial opportunity has been lost to reach a consensus on the points of disagreement that will inevitably arise. It is well known that a Bill of Rights incorporating a right to life might raise challenges to the legality of abortion. A right to free speech will raise questions about the legality of prohibitions on racist speech, or provisions capping election spending. A right to freedom of association raises the controversial question of the closed shop, or union security agreements. The debates in Parliament are resounding in their silence about these issues. Only two issues were opened up for discussion, and then only at the last minute and under pressure from powerful interest groups representing the Church and the press.[34]

By failing to open up more issues of this sort for discussion and resolution, legislators have abdicated responsibility for ensuring the democratic content of the

---

[31] Lord Irvine, 'The Development of Human Rights in Britain', [1998] *Public Law* 221 at 228; for a commentary on the complexities of this provision, see G. Marshall, 'Two Kinds of Compatibility', [1999] *Public Law* 377.

[32] HRA 1998, s. 19.   [33] Ibid. s. 4.   [34] Ibid. ss. 12 and 13.

rights document itself. The ECHR was drafted in the immediate aftermath of the Second World War, and its content expresses the concerns of its period.[35] The rights are broad and open-textured, and there is no preamble or other statement setting out the basic values which should guide judicial interpretation.[36] Moreover, the courts are required to perform the complex balancing act between rights and derogations. Wide-ranging derogations are permitted in the Convention in respect of core rights such as the right to respect for privacy and family life, the right to freedom of thought, conscience, and religion, the right to freedom of expression, and the right to freedom of association and peaceful assembly.[37] The court is required to decide whether a limitation can be justified as furthering one of a list of specified aims, including public safety, public order, public health or morals, national security, and the prevention of crime or disorder. The only guidance in the Convention itself as to the balance to be struck is contained in the words 'prescribed by law and necessary in a democratic society'. Given the width and flexibility of the acceptable aims, it is not difficult for a state to bring its action within one of the stated exceptions.[38] Thus the weight of decision falls almost entirely on the concept of 'necessary in a democratic society'. Yet this thrusts the court onto the horns of the core dilemma. When should the 'public interest' or the 'interests of society as a whole' override the interests of the individual?[39] Arguably, the democratic answer to this dilemma is that the determination of the public interest should lie with the legislature, and not the courts at all. And yet, the *raison d'être* of a bill of rights may well be thought to be the protection of individual rights against unnecessary incursions in the name of the public interest.

At an even more basic level, it is possible for a bill of rights to be relatively specific as to which conception of democracy is to be preferred. This would counter the argument that human rights protection is necessarily a reflection of a conception of democracy based on liberal individualism, in which the function of human rights is to protect the individual against an over-intrusive state. Ewing, for example, argues that it is inevitable that a bill of rights will obstruct the development of social democracy, in which the state is not an adversary, but has positive obligations to further the welfare of the individual by securing rights to work, housing, education, etc.[40] However, it is possible for the constitution itself to formulate a conception of democracy which includes social values. Both the Canadian and South African constitutions include an express reference to substantive equality.[41] Such explicit reference

---

[35] See also Lord Steyn's address to *Liberty* on International Human Rights Day, 10 Dec. 1999.

[36] The preamble simply states: 'Reaffirming their profound belief in those fundamental freedoms which are the foundation of justice and peace in the world and are best maintained on the one hand by an effective political democracy and on the other by a common understanding and observance of the human rights upon which they depend.'

[37] Arts. 8–11 ECHR.

[38] See F. Jacobs and R. White, *The European Convention on Human Rights*, 2nd edn. (Oxford: Oxford University Press, 1996), 304.

[39] See the very useful discussion in A. McHarg, 'Reconciling Human Rights and the Public Interest', (1999) 61 *Modern Law Review* 671.

[40] Ewing, n. 5 above.   [41] See SA Constitution ss. 1, 7(1), 9(2); Canadian Charter s. 15(2).

to fundamental values could resolve some of the issues which have been the subject of most criticism, including the use of freedom-of-speech rights to strike down restrictions on election spending.[42] It is the absence of a notion of substantive equality and an abstract, formal view of freedom of speech which has led to decisions such as these. In addition, an explicit reference to substantive equality could assist judges to ensure that human rights adjudication is not used to 'permit money and economic power disproportionate access to the decision-making process'.[43]

The second reason why the HRA has fallen short of the democratic ideal relates to the composition of the judiciary. No changes to the composition of the judiciary are included in the human rights package. There will be no specialist court dealing with human rights issues. Instead, the declaration of incompatibility may be made by the ordinary High Court and any of its superior courts;[44] and the new Act specifically places an obligation on all courts, from tribunals and magistrates' courts to the House of Lords in its judicial capacity, to act consistently with the enumerated rights.[45] This is characterized by Lord Irvine as a positive virtue: 'We have not considered it right to create some special human rights court alongside the ordinary system: the Convention rights must pervade all law and all court systems.'[46]

Yet, as the Law Society has recently emphasized, the present system of judicial appointments is 'fundamentally flawed and needs radical reform'. Most problematic has been the lack of transparency surrounding the appointment of British judges, a system based on 'secret soundings' which has been criticized by the Law Society as 'having all the elements of an old boy's network'.[47] It is not surprising that the social background, gender, and ethnic membership of the UK judiciary is quite so uniform, with the benches largely populated by relatively elderly, white, middle-class Christian men.[48] Some helpful suggestions were made in the recent report by Sir Leonard Peach on the judicial appointments system.[49] But this report stops short of recommending a fully independent and open judicial appointments commission responsible for selecting judges, preferring instead a commissioner whose role is limited to monitoring the present system and dealing with grievances. The system of secret soundings will be required to use slightly better criteria for selection, but will otherwise remain intact.[50] There is no suggestion that different criteria should be appropriate for judges sitting on a constitutional or human rights court. The result is that, unlike the case in other countries, there will be little or no public debate or political scrutiny of the judges who will be entrusted with the interpretation and development of the newly incorporated Convention. Yet, as Lord

---

[42] *Buckley v. Valeo* 424 US 1 (1976).   [43] Ewing, n. 5 above, 47.   [44] HRA 1998, s. 4(5).

[45] Ibid. s. 6(3).   [46] [1998] *Public Law* at 232.

[47] Quoted in *New Law Journal*, 1 Oct. 1999, 1430.

[48] There have been independent moves by the Lord Chancellor to make the process slightly less opaque, including the advertisement of judicial posts, and a specific commitment to increasing the numbers of women judges.

[49] *Appointment Process of Judges and Queen's Counsel in England and Wales*, available at www.open. gov.uk/lcd

[50] *New Law Journal*, 10 Dec. 1999, 1851.

Steyn suggested forcefully in an address to the Bar Council in October 1999, the case for a judicial appointments committee is even further enhanced by the new human rights jurisdiction, given that it is inevitable that the political content of judicial review will be greater.[51]

Thirdly, no attempt has been made to adapt the traditional adversarial bipolar litigation to one more suited to human rights litigation. Apart from a provision requiring that the Crown be notified that a court is considering whether to make a declaration of incompatibility and giving a minister of the Crown the right to be joined as a party to the proceedings,[52] the presumption is that human rights cases will proceed in the usual adversarial mode. This can be contrasted with adaptations in other countries, which have relaxed the bipolar structure by widening standing rules, permitting class actions, and permitting interventions from institutional and public interest litigators. Thus the 'victim' is no longer the sole spokesperson; the procedure permits the court to take more cognizance of the wider effects on other parties. Limitations in the ability to assess social facts have been addressed by permitting expert interventions such as Brandeis briefs. Remedies have been adapted in order to replace retrospective and individualized compensatory remedies, with more prospective orders, making it possible to balance different interests.

None of these adaptations has been considered in the Human Rights Act. No Human Rights Commission is to be established. Most seriously, standing at least in cases of review of executive discretion and subordinate legislation is limited to the 'victim' of an alleged human rights abuse.[53] This encapsulates a particular view of the judicial function, namely to do no more than protect individuals who can point to personal detriment as a result of an alleged breach of a human right. In all other situations in which legislation or executive action appears to conflict with human rights, the only redress is through the political process. It is noteworthy that UK administrative law has already moved beyond this paradigm, with judicially developed rules of standing gradually widening towards acceptance, in some situations, that a 'public-spirited citizen' should have standing.[54] By contrast with the 'victim' standard, this assumes that the function of judicial review is to prevent unlawful action by public authorities, even when no individual harm can be identified. It is noteworthy that there is no specific provision on standing in relation to a claim for a declaration of incompatibility of primary legislation.[55] It may well be that this approach will be, where possible, transposed into the human rights context. Indeed, the *Pinochet* cases[56] appeared to suggest a growing willingness on the part of the

---

[51] See *Guardian*, 11 Oct. 1999. Of course, judicial tenure is vulnerable to challenge under the HRA itself: see *Smith v. Secretary of State* [2000] IRLR 6, challenging the independence of lay members of an employment tribunal.

[52] HRA 1998, s. 5.   [53] Ibid. s. 7(1).

[54] *R v. Secretary of State for Foreign Affairs ex p. World Development Movement* [1995] 1 All ER 611.

[55] HRA 1998, s. 4.

[56] *R v. Bow Street Magistrate ex p. Pinochet Ugarte (No. 1)* [1998] 3 WLR 1456; *R v. Bow Street Magistrate ex p .Pinochet Ugarte (No. 2)* [1999] 2 WLR 272; *R v. Bow Street Magistrate ex p. Pinochet Ugarte (No. 3)* [1999] 2 WLR 827.

courts themselves to adapt procedure to allow third-party interventions by interested non-governmental organizations. However, judicial development is inevitably on a case-by-case basis, making it difficult to predict the response in particular situations. Indeed, in the last and most recent of the Pinochet decisions, *In re Pinochet Ugarte (2000)*,[57] the Divisional Court refused to give Human Rights Watch leave to intervene, stating that in criminal proceedings there would need to be overwhelming reasons why participation by bodies representing the interests of victims and defendants should be permitted at the level of Court of Appeal and Divisional Court.

V. Conclusion

The Human Rights Act has gone a short distance down the path towards creating a democratic system of human rights adjudication. Most importantly, it has begun to construct a framework for constraining the judiciary, both in respect of codification of rights and by giving Parliament the prime responsibility for protecting human rights, both in the original process of legislation and in having the final word on the matter. However, the fears of democratic sceptics are only partially met, largely because the legislature chose not to articulate and resolve so many of the issues which could have both guided and constrained the judiciary. The questions of judicial appointment and tenure, the process of litigation, and most importantly, the substantive values underlying the document have not been subjected to any open discussion or revision. It is this which paradoxically hands the judiciary too much power. Nevertheless, litigators still have the opportunity to use the process of litigation to advance social democratic arguments. We have recent examples of such arguments eventually being absorbed into the legal system: take the development of the concept of equality in relation to pregnancy, and in particular the eventual acceptance of the fact that pregnancy is unique and should not be characterized as an illness. Individual litigators like Defrenne and Marshall have made an important impact on the substance of European law, as have Smith and Grady on the substance of the law of the ECHR. Such principles have also filtered back into the legislative process: take, for an example, the pregnant workers directive. Even if these arguments are rejected by judges, they have been articulated in an important arena, entered the public domain, and exercised some influence, however oblique. The very rejection of Lisa Grant's claim in the *Grant* case[58] may well have created important pressure on legislators at EU level to fill a glaring gap in legislation. There is still plenty of scope to use the insights of democratic sceptics to refashion human rights to serve social democratic aims.

---

[57] *Times Law Reports*, 16 Feb. 2000.
[58] Case C-249/96, *Grant v. South West Trains Ltd* [1998] ECR I-621.

12

Discrimination Law and the Human Rights Act 1998

AILEEN MCCOLGAN

I. Introduction

The Human Rights Act 1998 incorporates into British law Article 14 of the European Convention on Human Rights (ECHR), which provides that:

The enjoyment of the rights and freedoms set forth in this Convention shall be secured without discrimination on any ground such as sex, race, colour, language, religion, political or other opinion, national or social origin, association with a national minority, property, birth or other status.

Article 14 has been widely, and rightly, criticized for its parasitic nature, the ECHR containing no free-standing prohibition on discrimination.[1] But the grounds upon which it regulates discrimination are broad and non-exhaustive.[2] And the 'rights and freedoms set forth in th[e] Convention' and the protocols thereto and incorporated, together with Article 14, by the 1998 Act include rights to life; to freedom from inhuman or degrading treatment; to a fair trial; to respect for private and family life; to freedom of thought, conscience, and religion, expression, peaceful assembly and association; to marry and to found a family; to education and to the peaceful enjoyment of possessions. The purpose of this chapter is to consider the implications of incorporation for domestic discrimination law.

Currently, statute regulates discrimination on grounds of sex (including gender reassignment);[3] race;[4] disability;[5] and (in Northern Ireland alone) religion and political opinion.[6] In addition, specific statutory prohibitions are imposed in relation to some forms of work-related discrimination on grounds of trade union membership, enforcement of employment rights, etc. The statutes regulating sex, race, and disability discrimination are of more general application and, although not

My thanks to Conor Gearty for helping to clarify my thoughts on the subject matter of this chapter. Any muddled thinking is mine alone.

[1] Though the 12th Protocol, discussed below, would go some way towards this if adopted.

[2] *Rasmussen v. Denmark* [1984] A 87, 7 EHRR 371, *James v. UK* [1986] A 98, 8 EHRR 123, *Salgueiro da Silva Mouta v. Portugal* (Application No. 00033290/96, decided 21 Dec. 1999 and available (in French) at www.dhcour.coe.int/Eng/Judgments.htm). This issue is further discussed below.

[3] The Equal Pay Act 1970 and the Sex Discrimination Act 1975, as amended by the Sex Discrimination (Gender Reassignment) Regulations 1999, SI 1999, No. 1102.

[4] The Race Relations Act 1976.   [5] The Disability Discrimination Act 1995.

[6] Most recently the Fair Employment and Treatment Order 1998.

applying to all fields of activity, extend beyond the employment and employment-related fields to cover discrimination in, *inter alia*, housing, education, and the provisions of goods and services.

It is clear from the preceding paragraphs that many heads of discrimination are not regulated by statute. Article 14 refers to discrimination '*on any ground such* as with 'sex, race, colour, language, religion, political or other opinion, national or social origin, association with a national minority, property, birth or other status' (my emphasis). While discrimination on grounds of sex, race, colour, and national origin, together with some instances of discrimination on grounds of language, religion, and association with a national minority,[7] are covered by the Sex Discrimination and Race Relations Acts, religious discrimination is prohibited only in cases where it is closely associated with ethnicity,[8] otherwise only in Northern Ireland by the Fair Employment and Treatment Order, which also proscribes discrimination on grounds of political opinion. Discrimination on grounds of political or other opinion, social origin, property, birth, or other status (which has been read to include, *inter alia*, sexual orientation and age)[9] is not generally prohibited.

Even where statute does regulate particular grounds of discrimination, lacunae remain. Constraints of space forbid any detailed discussion of the various statutory regimes, but among the problems are the definitions of discrimination adopted by the sex and race legislation and the exclusion from the reach of all the legislation many instances of discrimination.[10]

Both the Sex Discrimination and the Race Relations Acts define direct discrimination as less favourable treatment 'on grounds of' sex or race and indirect discrimination as the unjustifiable application of a 'requirement or condition' with which a 'considerably smaller proportion' of the applicant's relevant group than of others can comply and which is to the applicant's detriment because she or he cannot comply with it. The interpretation of direct discrimination under the Acts has become ensnared with difficulties relating to appropriate comparators, a fate spared the Disability Discrimination Act because of its definition of discrimination as less favourable treatment 'connected with' disability.[11] And the technicalities of indirect discrimination under the Race Relations Act and the Sex Discrimination Act

---

[7] See *Weathersfield v. Sargent* [1999] IRLR 94.   [8] This is further discussed below.
[9] Also illegitimacy—*Markx v. Belgium* [1979] A 31, 2 EHRR 330, *Inze v. Austria* [1987] A 126, 10 EHRR 394.
[10] For discussion of these and other shortcomings see A. McColgan, *Discrimination Law: Text, Cases and Materials* (Oxford: Hart, 2000), esp. chs. 2 and 4.
[11] Compare the pregnancy-as-sex-discrimination saga played out over the 12 years between the decision of EAT in *Turley v. Allders Department Stores Ltd* [1980] IRLR 4, and that of the House of Lords in *Webb v. EMO Air Cargo (UK) Ltd (No. 2)* [1994] QB 718, with the decision of the Court of Appeal in the disability discrimination case of *Clark v. TDG Ltd (t/a Novacold)* [1999] IRLR 318. The pregnancy question has been largely settled (though see McColgan, n. 10 above, 368–74). But problems remain with the selection of appropriate comparators in sexualorientation-related cases—see Case C-249/96, *Grant v. South-West Trains Ltd* [1998] ECR I-621; *Bavin v. NHS Trust Pensions Agency & Anor* [1999] ICR 1192. The Court of Appeal's decision to refer the case to the ECJ is, as yet, unreported.

have been multiplied by their judicial interpretation (the Court of Appeal demanding in *Perera v. Civil Service Commission*, for example, that a 'requirement or condition' amount to an 'absolute bar' in order to found a claim[12]).

The sex, race, and disability legislation apply only to discrimination in particular contexts (including employment, housing, and the provision of facilities, goods, and services).[13] Even within these contexts, not all discrimination is prohibited. In *Adekeye v. Post Office (No. 2)*, for example, the Court of Appeal ruled that discrimination in a post-dismissal appeal fell outwith the scope of the Race Relations Act.[14] And while discrimination by qualifying bodies is prohibited by the sex and race legislation (but not, as yet, by the Disability Discrimination Act), the prohibition does not extend to discrimination by health insurance companies in selection onto panels of approved surgeons, to discrimination by a housing executive in the selection onto panels of approved solicitors, or to discrimination by the Attorney-General in the selection of lay magistrates.[15] Further, the anti-discrimination legislation affords protection only to individual applicants.[16]

One of the most significant restrictions on the scope of the statutory provisions was confirmed by the House of Lords in *Amin v. Entry Clearance Officer, Bombay*. There, by a majority, their Lordships limited the application to the Crown of the 'goods and services' provisions of the Sex Discrimination Act to 'acts which are at least similar to acts that could be done by private persons'.[17] The decision, which concerned a challenge to discriminatory immigration rules, operated so as to shield much administrative decision-making from the reach of the discrimination legislation.[18]

---

[12] [1983] ICR 428 though, cf. *Falkirk Council v. Whyte* [1997] IRLR 560 on the interpretation of the SDA. Council Directive 97/80, which defines indirect discrimination in terms of 'an apparently neutral provision, criterion or practice', must be implemented in the UK by July 2001; the similar definitions in Council Directive 2000/43/EC (in relation to race) and Council Directive 2000/78/EC (religion or belief, disability, age, and sexual orientation, applying the concept of 'indirect' discrimination to all but disability discrimination) by Dec. 2003 in the case of religion, belief, and sexual orientation, Dec. 2006 in the case of age.

[13] The SDA and RRA apply also in relation to education, the application of the DDA in this context being, as yet, more limited.

[14] [1997] ICR 110. Cf. *Coote v. Granada Hospitality Ltd (No. 2)* [1999] IRLR 452 on the SDA, applying the decision of the ECJ in Case C-185/97, *Coote v. Granada Hospitality Ltd* [1998] ECR I-5199.

[15] Respectively, *Tattari v. PPP Ltd* [1998] ICR 106; *Loughran & Kelly v. Northern Ireland Housing Executive* [1998] IRLR 70 and *Arthur v. Attorney-General & Ors* (unreported, cited by EAT in *Sawyer v. Ahsan*, [1999] IRLR 609).

[16] See *Kelly & Loughran v. Northern Ireland Housing Executive* [1999] 1 AC 428 on the application of the analogous Fair Employment Act 1989 (which pre-dated the FETO).

[17] [1983] 2 AC 818 *per* Lord Fraser, with whom Lords Brightman and Keith agreed, Lords Scarman and Brandon dissenting on this issue. The Court of Appeal had taken a similar approach in *Kassam v. Immigration Appeal Tribunal* [1980] 1 WLR 1037.

[18] Lord Fraser, for the majority, approving of the decision of the Divisional Court in *Home Office v. Commission for Racial Equality* [1982] QB 385, which adopted the same approach to s. 20 RRA. Note also s. 41 RRA, which exempts from the prohibition on discrimination acts done under statutory authority (for the application of this section see *Hampson v. Department of Education and Science* [1991] 1 AC 171). The equivalent provision of the SDA (s. 51) was narrowed in 1989 as a result of a reasoned opinion by the European Commission that the section as originally passed was too broad.

The Race Relations (Amendment) Act 2000 has partially reversed the effect of *Amin* in the field of race discrimination, new s. 19B of the Race Relations Act providing that '(1) It is unlawful for a public authority in carrying out any functions of the authority to do any act which constitutes discrimination'. But many forms of discrimination remain excluded from the Act as amended, among them much discrimination on grounds of ethnic origins (as distinct from nationality) in immigration; race discrimination in decisions not to institute or to continue criminal proceedings; and discrimination in connection with secondary legislation.[19] No action has yet been taken to reverse the impact of *Amin* in the sex discrimination context, although the UK government has indicated that the Sex Discrimination Act will be amended in line with the Race Relations Act when legislative time permits.

II. Discrimination and the common law

To the extent that discrimination falls outside the statutory provisions, a question arises concerning its status at common law. In *Amin*, Lord Fraser accepted that the immigration rule at issue discriminated on grounds of sex but, having ruled that immigration fell outwith the Sex Discrimination Act, went on to state: 'not all sex discrimination is unlawful . . . Discrimination is only unlawful if it occurs in one of the fields in which it is prohibited by . . . the Act.'[20] But in *Kruse v. Johnson* Lord Russell CJ, for the majority of the specially constituted (seven-strong) Divisional Court, stated that there could be cases

in which it would be the duty of the Court to condemn by-laws, made under such authority as these were made, as invalid because unreasonable . . . If, for instance, they were found to be partial and unequal in their operation as between different classes; if they were manifestly unjust; if they disclosed bad faith; if they involved such oppressive or gratuitous interference with the rights of those subject to them as could find no justification in the minds of reasonable men, the Court might well say, 'Parliament never intended to give authority to make such rules; they are unreasonable and ultra vires.'[21]

This declaration was accompanied by the statement that considerable deference should be accorded to democratically enacted subordinate legislation. *Kruse* was followed by *Short v. Poole Corporation*, in which Warrington LJ uttered the oft-cited statement that 'if the defendants were to dismiss a teacher because she had red hair, or for some equally frivolous and foolish reason, the Court would declare the attempted dismissal to be void' as *ultra vires* their statutory power.[22] Lord Greene MR relied on this dictum in *Associated Provincial Picture Houses Ltd v. Wednesbury*

---

[19] See new sections 19B–F Race Relations Act, read with s. 41 of the same Act.
[20] Lords Scarman and Brandon, who dissented on the first issue, concurring with the majority on the second.
[21] [1898] 2 QB 91.   [22] [1926] Ch 66.

Corporation, in which the Court of Appeal set out the grounds upon which the legality of administrative action could be challenged.[23] Having stated that executive discretion 'must be exercised reasonably', the Master of the Rolls stated for the Court that:

a person entrusted with a discretion must, so to speak, direct himself properly in law. He must call his own attention to the matters which he is bound to consider. He must exclude from his consideration matters which are irrelevant to what he has to consider . . . Similarly, there may be something so absurd that no sensible person could ever dream that it lay within the powers of the authority. [Having cited the red-haired teacher example, he continued] . . . That is unreasonable in one sense. In another sense it is taking into consideration extraneous matters. It is so unreasonable that it might almost be described as being done in bad faith; and, in fact, all these things run into one another . . .[24]

The question to which we now turn concerns the extent to which *Kruse v. Johnson,* as subsequently applied, regulates discrimination in the exercise of public power. We saw, above, the view taken by the House of Lords in *Amin* that the Sex Discrimination Act represented the beginning and the end of any domestic legal prohibition on sex discrimination. In *R v. Immigration Appeal Tribunal ex p. Manshoora Begum,* Mr Justice Simon Brown (as he then was) applied *Kruse* to declare an immigration rule invalid on the ground that it was 'partial and unequal' in its operation between different classes—there the categories of dependents living in more and less affluent countries.[25] But in *Kwapong v. Secretary of State for the Home Department* the Court of Appeal refused to apply *Kruse* so as to declare unlawful an immigration rule which discriminated on grounds of sex.[26] Having considered the application of that principle in *ex p. Begum,* Gibson LJ went on to stress the dictum of Russell LCJ in *Kruse* to the effect that the courts should accord a generous degree of deference to (in that case) democratically enacted by-laws before concluding: 'where there is a set of statutory provisions stating the limits of rules of sex discrimination, and it is the case that Parliament had not seen fit to apply them to the Immigration Rules, it is impossible to argue that [discrimination by a rule on grounds of sex] could enable this Court to condemn that Rule as irrational.'[27]

---

[23] [1948] 1 KB 223.

[24] In *CCSU v. Minister for the Civil Service* [1985] AC 374, Lord Diplock reclassified the grounds for judicial review as relating to illegality, irrationality, and procedural impropriety. *Wednesbury* unreasonableness is generally understood as constituting the second of these categories, the principle established in *Kruse v. Johnson* as an aspect of *Wednesbury* unreasonableness (see e.g. the decision of Jowitt J in the Divisional Court's decision in *R v. Secretary of State for Foreign and Commonwealth Affairs, ex p. Manelfi* (25 Oct. 1996, unreported)).

[25] [1986] Imm. AR 385, those in the latter class being less likely to be able to comply with the rule that their standard of living was significantly below the norm for their country of residence. See also *R v. London Borough of Barnet ex p. Johnson and another* (1989) 88 LGR 73.

[26] [1994] Imm. AR 207.

[27] In *ex p. Begum,* Simon Brown J had accepted that a greater degree of deference was appropriate in a case in which, as there, 'the relevant power is given . . . to a Minister responsible to Parliament . . . [and] the rules in question were laid before Parliament and subject to a process akin to negative resolution' (citing *Nottinghamshire CC v. Secretary of State for the Environment* [1986] 1 All ER 199). This dictum was

Jeffrey Jowell has argued that equality is a 'constitutional principle' in English common law. Equality in its Diceyean sense is an aspect of the Rule of Law which requires that 'laws are applied or enforced equally, that is, evenhandedly, free of bias and without irrational distinction'.[28] As Jowell points out, the Rule of Law 'does not prohibit unequal laws. It constrains, say, racially-biased enforcement of laws, but does not inhibit apartheid-style laws from being enacted.' Certainly, Dicey himself was resolutely opposed to female suffrage. But Jowell argues that this 'derided but . . . important', 'instrumental' equality is supplemented by a 'conception of equality that requires government not to treat people unequally without justification'. This conception of equality, he argues:

> derives from the nature of democracy itself. Basic to democracy is the requirement that every citizen has an equal vote, and therefore an equal opportunity to influence the composition of the government. The notion of equal worth is thus a fundamental precept of our constitution [citing Dworkin] . . . It is constitutive of democracy . . . This conception of equality . . . prevents distinctions that are not properly justified . . . equality may be expressly violated if Parliament so requires. Like the Rule of Law, however, its apparent violation will provoke strong questioning and require rational justification.[29]

Citing cases including *Edwards v. Sogat*,[30] *Nagle v. Fielden*,[31] *Prescott v. Birmingham Corporation*,[32] *R v. Port Talbot BC, ex p. Jones*[33] and the notorious *Bromley LBC v. GLC*,[34] as well as *Kruse* and *ex p. Begum*, Jowell declares: 'There is no doubt that equality is used as a test of official action in our law' and: 'Our constitution rests upon an assumption that government should not impose upon any citizen any burden that depends upon an argument that ultimately forces the citizen to relinquish her or his sense of equal worth. This principle is deeply embedded in our law, although it is rarely made explicit.'

Equality may be 'used as *a* test of official action in our law' (my emphasis). But 'equality', whatever the term may mean, is not a free-standing entitlement in English law. In the *GLC* and *Birmingham* cases, judges defended private property interests against redistributive decisions taken by local government. The *Port Talbot* case did involve a challenge to preferential access to council housing accorded to a councillor, but the impugned decision had been illegally reached (not having been taken by the person in whom authority rested), and the preferential treatment given to the councillor so evidently turned on the consideration of factors irrelevant to the proper allocation of council housing that it was foursquare within *Wednesbury*. *Edwards* turned on the 'right to work' and the restraint of trade doctrine, the Court of Appeal declaring *ultra vires* a trade union rule permitting arbitrary and capricious withdrawal of temporary membership in a closed

---

applied by Hidden J in *R v. Secretary of State for the Home Department ex p. Islam Bibi & Anor* [1995] Imm. AR 157. See also *R v. Secretary of State for Health ex p. Richardson* (5 May 1994, referred to the ECJ as Case C-137/94 and reported at [1995] ECR I-3407); *ex p. Manelfi*, n. 24 above.

[28] 'Is Equality a Constitutional Principle?', (1994) 47 *Current Legal Problems* 1, 4.
[29] Ibid. 7.   [30] [1970] 3 WLR 713.   [31] [1966] 2 QB 633.
[32] [1955] Ch 210.   [33] [1988] 2 All ER 207.   [34] [1983] 1 AC 768.

shop context. *Nagle v. Fielden* similarly rested on the restraint of trade doctrine, the Court of Appeal there ruling that a challenge to the Jockey Club's refusal of training licences to women, in circumstances in which the Club exercised a monopoly over horse-racing, should not have been struck out as showing no cause of action.

According to Dankwerts LJ in *Nagle*, the appeal could have been allowed simply because, striking out being appropriate only in the most 'plain and obvious cases, when the action is one which cannot succeed or is in some way an abuse of the process of the court', it was inappropriate on the facts. But he went on, as did Lord Denning MR and Salmon LJ, to suggest that a complete refusal by a monopoly body such as the Jockey Club to license women would be in breach of the doctrine against restraint of trade as the 'arbitrary', 'capricious', or 'unreasonable' denial of the right to work. He further suggested that, although the exclusion of women from this particular job 'may have appeared a natural attitude in Victorian times or earlier . . . in present day conditions it seems to me to be restrictive and nonsensical'. Salmon LJ declared that 'It would be as capricious to [refuse Ms Nagle a licence solely on the ground that she is a woman] as to refuse a man a licence solely because of the colour of his hair. No doubt there are occupations, such as boxing, which may reasonably be regarded as inherently unsuitable for women; but evidently training racehorses is not one of them.'[35]

A number of cases can be found in which discrimination has been regarded as founding at least an arguable claim in the absence of any statutory provisions. With the exception of the decision in *Nagle*, however, these have involved the control of executive action by the courts in their exercise of their powers of judicial review.[36] Lester and Bindman protested, in 1972, that:

the courts have been prepared to refuse to give effect to English contracts which offend against public policy, whether because the objects of the contract are plainly illegal, or because they are harmful to good government, or because they are improper interferences with the workings of the machinery of justice, or because they are injurious to family life. But apart from their disapproval of slavery, English judges have never declared that acts of racial discrimination committed in this country are against public policy.[37]

---

[35] Cf. the successful claim by Jane Couch against the British Boxing Board of Control over that body's refusal to grant her a boxing licence, *The Times*, 28 Apr. 1998.

[36] *Nagle* was described by A. Lester and G. Bindman (*Race and Law*, Harmondsworth: Penguin, 1972, 52) as 'an important exception' to the English cases dealing with discrimination: 'a rare example of the creative development of the Common Law by the courts in response to changing social values'. But, as they go on to point out, '*Nagle*'s case applies only to monopoly situations'. In *R v. Jockey Club, ex p. Aga Khan* [1993] 1 WLR 916, Hoffman LJ suggested that the remedy in *Nagle* had 'an improvisatory air', and stated that an injunction would probably no longer be available in the circumstances.

[37] Ibid. 25 (emphasis omitted). The authors note that, in *Santos v. Illidge* (1859) 6 CB (NS) 841, (1860) 8 CB (NS) 861, the English courts refused to invalidate a contract made by a British subject for the sale of slaves in Brazil, in which country slavery was lawful. At 34: 'Despite the enactment of [English] anti-slavery legislation, the judges still would not accept that slavery was against public policy.'

The only category of cases in which the courts have consistently regulated discrimination has been that concerning innkeepers and common carriers.[38] As Lester and Bindman conclude: 'the innkeeper's duty is of theoretical interest as a rare example of a Common Law obligation to give equal treatment [but] its practical value is limited.'[39] Had the common law taken a more active interest in combating discrimination, there would not have been the overwhelming need for legislation which, eventually, resulted in the passage of the Equal Pay Act, the Sex Discrimination Act, and the Race Relations Act.

In *Clayton v. Ramsden* the House of Lords declared void for uncertainty a testamentary condition to the effect that the estate would be forfeited if the beneficiary should marry a person 'not of Jewish parentage and of the Jewish faith'.[40] All five Law Lords took the view that the condition as to parentage was uncertain, the required degree of 'racial purity' being incapable of ascertainment. All but Lord Wright took a similar approach to the condition as to religion. According to Lord Romer, with whom Lords Atkin and Thankerton agreed: 'The testator has . . . failed to give any indication what degree of faith in the daughter's husband will avoid, and what degree will bring about, a forfeiture of her interest in his estate.'[41] But in *In re Lysaght* the High Court upheld the validity of a legacy to fund training of British-born non-Jews and non-Roman Catholics.[42] According to that court the stipulation, though 'undesirable . . . [was] not . . . contrary to the public policy'. And in *Blathwayt v. Baron Cawley* the House of Lords upheld a testamentary condition excluding those who were or became Roman Catholic.[43] According to their Lordships, the forfeiture clause was invalidated neither by uncertainty nor by public policy.

Lord Wilberforce, who spoke for the House on this issue, declared himself neither obliged nor entitled to extend 'the conclusion . . . reached [by the majority in *Clayton*], as to uncertainty, to other clauses relating to other religions or branches of religions . . . the decision . . . was a particular [one] on a condition expressed in a particular way about one kind of religious belief or profession'. Nor was the condition regarded as offending public policy:

---

[38] See e.g. *Constantine v. Imperial Hotels Ltd* [1944] 1 KB 693, discussed by Lester and Bindman, n. 36 above, 63. The limitations of the innkeeper's duty are evident from *Rothfield v. Northern British Railways Company* [1920] SC 805, discussed at 63–4.

[39] Ibid. 64–5.   [40] [1943] AC 320.

[41] Lord Russell declaring that it was unnecessary, in view of his conclusions as to the first limb of the condition, to decide this issue but stating nevertheless that he would have had 'difficulty in holding that their meaning was clear or certain'.

[42] Respectively, [1942] IR 19, [1958] 3 All ER 220, and [1966] 1 Ch. 191.

[43] [1976] AC 419. See also *Horne v. Poland* [1922] 2 KB 364, in which the High Court accepted that race discrimination in the provision of insurance was potentially reasonable, and *Cumings v. Birkenhead Corporation* [1972] Ch 12, in which the Court of Appeal upheld the *vires* of an education authority rule that children who had attended Roman Catholic primary school would be considered only for Roman Catholic secondary schools. In *Cumings* Lord Denning insisted that a rule allocating places in according to hair 'or, for that matter', skin colour 'would be so unreasonable, so capricious, so irrelevant to any proper system of education that it would be *ultra vires* altogether, and this court would strike it down at once'.

I do not doubt that conceptions of public policy should move with the times and that widely accepted treaties and statutes[44] may point the direction in which such conceptions, as applied by the courts, ought to move. It may well be that conditions such as this are, or at least are becoming, inconsistent with standards now widely accepted. But acceptance of this does not persuade me that we are justified, particularly in relation to a will which came into effect as long ago as 1936 and which has twice been the subject of judicial consideration, in introducing for the first time a rule of law which would go far beyond the mere avoidance of discrimination on religious grounds. To do so would bring about a substantial reduction of another freedom, firmly rooted in our law, namely that of testamentary disposition.[45]

Lester and Bindman refer to the 'ethical aimlessness' of the common law.[46] But Conor Gearty[47] cites *In re Lysaght*, together with *Schlegel v. Corcoran* and *Scala Ballroom (Wolverhampton) Ltd v. Ratcliffe*, as illustrative of 'a system of laws which prioritized . . . interests in property and contract to the exclusion of other public interests'. In *Schlegel* an Irish court upheld the reasonableness of a refusal to transfer rooms to a Jewish dentist on the grounds that the practice 'may, under Mr Gross, develop a Jewish complexion . . . such an anticipation is not groundless in a locality with a number of Jewish residents'. In *Scala* the English Court of Appeal upheld the legality of a bar on non-white entrants to the ballroom as 'a course which [the company was] entitled to adopt in [its] own business interests'. Understood as concerned with 'interests in property and contract', a number of the cases considered by Jowell, above, may be reconciled with those discussed by Gearty.

Returning to questions of public law, the limitations (pre-Human Rights Act) on judicial review as a tool for challenging discrimination are evident from *Amin* and *Kwapong*, above (in the case of discrimination on grounds in respect of which statutory provisions apply). It is clear from the dicta in *Kruse*, *Wednesbury*, and the *Port Talbot* case that some grounds of discrimination will render decisions irrational or illegal (as founded on irrelevant considerations). But this seems capable of capturing only the most bizarre (*Short v. Poole*, *Wednesbury*) or obviously unfair (*Port Talbot*) grounds of discrimination. It is not difficult to appreciate that denying a job on the grounds of hair colour and preferring a councillor in the allocation of council housing are, respectively, irrational to the point of lunacy and manifestly wrong. But the real problem with many grounds of discrimination is precisely that they are not generally regarded as problematic.

Lord Justice Warrington's oft-cited dictum in *Short v. Poole* formed part of a decision upholding the right of an education authority to dismiss married women teachers on the grounds (as put forward by the authority itself) that

---

[44] Referring to the ECHR and the RRA.

[45] *Per* Lord Wilberforce, with whom Lords Simon, Cross, Edmund-Davies, and Fraser concurred.

[46] N. 36 above, 70.

[47] 'The Internal and External "Other" in the Union Legal Order: Racism, Religious Intolerance and Xenophobia in Europe', in P. Alston, M. Bustelo, and J. Heenan (eds.), *The EU and Human Rights* (Oxford: Oxford University Press, 1999), 327 at 341.

(1) the duty of the married woman was primarily to look after her domestic concerns, and they regarded it as impossible for her to do so and to act effectively and satisfactorily as a teacher at the same time; and (2) it was unfair to the large number of unmarried teachers who were at present seeking situations that the positions should be occupied by married women who presumably had husbands capable of maintaining them.

Romer J had ruled that the decision to dismiss was *ultra vires* the authority's powers, which had to be exercised 'for the purpose and with the object of giving effect to the statutory duties imposed upon it [*viz*] . . . of maintaining efficiency in the schools'. That the decision to dismiss was not taken on these grounds was established to the judge's satisfaction by the evidence that no complaints had been made about Ms Short's discharge of her teaching duties, that she was childless and in the position of having ample domestic assistance, and that the authority was prepared to employ married women whose husbands were not capable of supporting them financially, apparently without concern as to any alleged shortfall in their efficiency. The Court of Appeal, declarations about 'irrational' discrimination notwithstanding, overturned Romer J's decision on the grounds that the council was entitled to make a general inference as to efficiency from female marital status and to make exceptions in respect of financially needy married women teachers.

   Short v. Poole is not an isolated example, as is evident from the discussions of *Blathwayt*, *Schegel*, and *Scala*.[48] One might question whether the references to discrimination on the grounds of hair colour in *Nagle*, *Wednesbury*, and *Short v. Poole* were made on the grounds that discrimination on grounds of skin colour would not have been regarded as so patently unreasonable.[49] We shall see below, in the discussion of *ex p. Smith*, that a ban on gays in the military was upheld by the Court of Appeal in 1996 on the grounds that it could not be regarded as irrational. Leaving aside cases in which the alleged pursuit of 'equality' has operated so as to protect property from the attempts of democratically elected authorities to redistribute it in accordance with their electoral mandate,[50] any judicial commitment to non-discrimination appears to have been honoured significantly in the breach.

III. Domestic legal protection of 'fundamental rights'

In *Nagle* the Court of Appeal was prepared to give effect to the prohibition on restraint of trade even in the absence of any contract between the applicant and the Jockey Club, and in *Edwards v. Sogat* to overlook the express provisions of the contract between the union and its members. More recently, in the public law context, the Court of Appeal and the House of Lords, in *R v. Secretary of State for the Home Department, ex p. Leech* and *R v. Secretary of State for the Home Department ex p. Simms* respectively, appeared to accord a high degree of protection to what they

---

[48] See also *Horne v. Poland* and *Cumings*, n. 43 above.   [49] Though cf. *Cumings*, n. 43 above.
[50] *Prescott v. Birmingham*, n. 32 above; *Bromley v. GLC*, n. 34 above.

accepted were 'vested common law rights'. In *Leech* the Court of Appeal ruled that the Secretary of State had exceeded his powers in providing, under the Prison Rules, that prison governors could interfere with correspondence between a prisoner and his or her legal adviser.[51] Citing the decision of the House of Lords in *Raymond v. Honey*[52] to the effect that 'every citizen has a right of unimpeded access to a court', Steyn LJ ruled that the rule at issue was not expressly authorized by the primary legislation and continued:

There is a presumption against statutory interference with vested common law rights. That must entail a presumption against a statute authorising interference with vested common law rights by subordinate legislation . . . It is a principle of our law that every citizen has a right of unimpeded access to a court . . . Even in our unwritten constitution it must rank as a constitutional right . . . such rights can as a matter of legal principle be taken away by necessary implication . . . It is not without significance that counsel could not refer us to a single instance where subordinate legislation was employed, let alone successfully employed, to abolish a common law privilege where the enabling legislation failed to authorise the abolition expressly . . . It will be a rare case in which it could be held that such a fundamental right was by necessary implication abolished or limited by statute. It will, we suggest, be an even rarer case in which it could be held that a statute authorised by necessary implication the abolition or limitation of so fundamental a right by subordinate legislation.[53]

In *R v. Secretary of State for the Home Department ex p. Simms* the House of Lords interpreted the right recognized in *Raymond v. Honey* to require that access be permitted to prisoners by journalists, without signature of any agreement not to publish the resulting interviews, in cases in which those interviews were sought in connection with alleged miscarriages of justice.[54] Lord Steyn, with whom Lords Browne-Wilkinson, Millett, and Hoffmann agreed,[55] declared that 'only a pressing social need can defeat freedom of expression' and (citing *ex p. Smith*, below) that 'the more substantial the interference with fundamental rights the more the court will require by way of justification before it can be satisfied that the interference is reasonable in a public law sense'. Lord Steyn interpreted the prison rules so as to render unlawful the challenged policy. Lord Hoffmann, who agreed with Lord Steyn, added:

Parliamentary sovereignty means that Parliament can, if it chooses, legislate contrary to fundamental principles of human rights . . . But the principle of legality means that Parliament must squarely confront what it is doing and accept the political cost. Fundamental rights cannot be overridden by general or ambiguous words. This is because there is too great a risk that the full implications of their unqualified meaning may have passed unnoticed in the democratic process. In the absence of express language or necessary implication to the contrary, the courts therefore presume that even the most general words were intended to be subject to the basic rights of the individual.

---

[51] [1994] QB 198.   [52] [1983] 1 AC 1.

[53] See *R v. Lord Chancellor ex p. Witham* [1998] QB 575, in which Laws J (as he then was) found 'great difficulty in conceiving a form of words capable of making it plain beyond doubt to the statute's reader' its intention to remove the fundamental right there considered—access to court.

[54] [2000] 2 AC 115.   [55] Lord Hobhouse, with whom Lord Millett also agreed, concurred.

The robust approach taken by the Court of Appeal in *Leech* and the House of Lords in *Simms* to the judicial protection of individual rights[56] must be contrasted with that which had been adopted in *Brind v. Secretary of State for the Home Department*.[57] Counsel for the applicants had argued there that executive discretion had to be exercised within the limits established by the European Convention. According to Lord Donaldson MR, in the Court of Appeal, this involved 'imputing to Parliament an intention to import the Convention into domestic law by the back door, when it has quite clearly refrained from doing so by the front door'. Lord Bridge declared that 'where Parliament has conferred on the executive an administrative discretion without indicating the precise limits within which it must be exercised, to presume that it must be exercised within Convention limits would be . . . a judicial usurpation of the legislative function'. And in *Kwapong* the Court of Appeal rejected the argument that the Secretary of State's power to make the immigration rules ought to be understood subject to the qualification that the rules had to be compatible with the provisions of the European Convention (discussed further below), Ralph Gibson LJ, for the court, relying on the decision of the House of Lords in *Brind*.

The relationship between *Brind* and *Kwapong* on the one hand and *Leech* and *Simms* on the other was clarified by the decision of the Divisional Court in *R v Worcester County Council and another, ex p. SW*.[58] There the Court considered a challenge by a teacher to the inclusion of his name on the 'Consultancy Service Index', a list of persons considered unsuitable for work with children maintained by the Department of Health. Allegations of sexual assault had been made against him. Relying on the decision of the Court of Appeal in *R v. Secretary of State for Health ex p. C* that the Secretary of State had a common law right to maintain the index,[59] the Court rejected the applicant's argument that this power was constrained by the need to protect his fundamental rights (here his right to privacy under Article 8 of the European Convention). Counsel for the applicant argued that the principle of legality recognized by the House of Lords in *Simms* should be taken to limit the exercise of the Secretary of State's power in this area. The Divisional Court (Newman J) rejected this argument:

Mr Drabble [for the applicant] cannot assert a common law right to private life . . . [In *Simms*] Lord Steyn states: 'The starting point is the right of freedom of expression.' He was identifying a right at common law, whereas Mr Drabble is unable to identify a common law right to private life, and thus has no 'starting point'.[60]

It was the existence of the fundamental right which operated, according to constitutional principle, upon the breadth of language of [the relevant rules], so as to restrict their application. In my judgment Mr Sales [for the respondent] is correct to characterise the principle of legality as a rule of construction.

---

[56] See also *R v. Secretary of State for the Home Department, ex p. Saleem* [2000] 4 All ER 814.
[57] [1991] 1 AC 696.   [58] [2000] 3 FCR 174.   [59] [2000] 1 FCR 471
[60] Cf. post incorporation, the decision of the Court of Appeal in *Douglas v. Hello Ltd* [2001] IP&T 391 discussed below.

Newman J claimed, in *ex p. SW*, that the *Simms* approach applied only vis-à-vis intervention alleged to be authorized by statute rather than the common law, but this view appears untenable in light of *Derbyshire County Council v. Times*, in which the House of Lords ruled that the law of defamation must be interpreted in compliance with what their Lordships there recognized as the common law principle of freedom of expression.[61] It seems rather that, prior to the implementation of the Human Rights Act 1998, the strong protection afforded by *Leech* and *Simms* applied only in respect of rights recognized as fundamental by the common law, as distinct from the Convention.[62] It has been argued, above, that the right to be free from discrimination cannot be regarded as a fundamental tenet of the common law.

This is not to say that discrimination cannot offend the common law. It is clear from *Kruse*, *Wednesbury*, and *ex p. Begum* that discrimination may be 'irrational' and may therefore render administrative action unlawful. But the limits of this are evident from *Kwapong*, above, the failure of the relevant Act to prohibit a particular type of discrimination appearing to render such discrimination legal.[63] And even where the ground is not already occupied by statutory provisions, the *Wednesbury* irrationality test provides a high threshold for review.

In *R v. Ministry of Defence, ex p. Smith and Ors* (the 'no gays in the military' challenge)[64] the Court of Appeal accepted the argument, put forward by David Pannick QC for the dismissed servicemen and woman, that the appropriate standard of review in cases in which fundamental rights were at issue could be stated as follows:

> The court may not interfere with the exercise of an administrative discretion on substantive grounds save where the court is satisfied that the decision is unreasonable in the sense that it is beyond the range of responses open to a reasonable decision-maker. But in judging whether the decision-maker has exceeded this margin of appreciation the human rights context is important. The more substantial the interference with human rights, the more the court will require by way of justification before it is satisfied that the decision is reasonable in the sense outlined above.

This test, the Court accepted, was the distillation of the House of Lords' decisions in *Bugdaycay v. Secretary of State for the Home Department* and in *Brind*.[65] But the Court of Appeal rejected the appellants' argument that the ban on gays in the military was irrational. According to Lord Bingham MR, the ban 'cannot . . . be stigmatised as irrational at the time when these appellants were discharged . . . The threshold of irrationality is a high one. It was not crossed in this case'.

---

[61] [1993] AC 534. The Court of Appeal had reached the same conclusion on the basis of Art. 10. The House of Lords, *per* Lord Keith, adopted the dicta of Lord Goff in *Attorney-General v. Guardian Newspapers Ltd (No. 2)* [1990] 1 AC 109, that 'there was no difference in principle between English law on the subject and article 10'.

[62] The argument in *Brind* was concerned with freedom of expression under Art. 10, it being assumed that the common law right was compatible with the restrictions challenged.

[63] Cf. the comments by Dinah Rose, who appeared for the applicant in *ex p. Richardson*, n. 27 above.

[64] [1996] QB 517.   [65] Respectively, [1987] AC 514 and n. 57 above.

IV. Discrimination and the Human Rights Act

It is clear from the above that the protection which domestic law affords against discrimination is far from complete. Many grounds of discrimination are regulated only tangentially in the sense that they might, in a suitable case, provide the basis of a decision that executive action was irrational, or private action unlawfully in restraint of trade. Even in respect of discrimination regulated by statute, many gaps remain. Here we turn to consider the extent to which the implementation of the Human Rights Act is likely to alter this position. It will be presumed, for reasons of space, that the reader is familiar with sections 3–7 of the Act, and that the incorporated Articles will have horizontal effect along the lines suggested by Murray Hunt.[66]

Section 2 of the Act provides that 'A court or tribunal determining a question which has arisen in connection with a Convention right must take into account' any relevant jurisprudence which has arisen in the application of the Convention. The question how the Convention organs have interpreted Article 14 and those other Convention provisions relevant to discrimination is therefore of considerable significance in assessing the possible implications of incorporation on discrimination law. No attempt will be made here to deal with this other than in outline.

Article 14: an introduction

The first point which must be made concerns the 'parasitic' nature of Article 14[67] which comes into play only in conjunction with the other Convention rights. It does not require a breach of another such right in order itself to be violated, but the discrimination in respect of which it is argued must 'fall within the ambit of'[68] or 'relate to'[69] Convention rights. In *Abdulaziz*, for example, the European Court of Human Rights (ECtHR) found a breach of Article 14 as a result of sexually discriminatory immigration rules which, although preventing the applicants from being joined in the UK by their fiancés, were held not to violate Article 8's prohibitions on interference with family life (said families being free to live as families elsewhere).[70] And in *Karlheinz Schmidt v. Germany*, the Court found that the imposition of an obligation to pay a financial contribution in lieu of service as a firefighter was compatible with Article 4 but, applying only to men, nevertheless breached that provision read with Article 14.[71]

---

[66] 'The "Horizontal" Effect of the Human Rights Act', [1998] *Public Law* 423. See, in support of this, Sedley LJ in *Douglas*, n. 60 above.

[67] D. J. Harris, M. O'Boyle, and C. Warbrick, *Law of the European Convention on Human Rights* (London: Butterworths, 1995), 463.

[68] *Rasmussen v. Denmark*, n. 2 above; *Inze v. Austria*, n. 9 above.

[69] *Belgian Linguistic* case [1968] A 6, 1 EHRR 252.

[70] *Abdulaziz, Cebales & Balkandali v. UK* [1985] A 94, 7 EHRR 471. Cf. *Family K & W v. Netherlands* [1985] 43 DR 216.

[71] [1994] A 291-B, 18 EHRR 513. See also *Markx v. Belgium* and *Inze v. Austria*, n. 9 above.

Protocol No. 12 to the Convention provides that '[t]he enjoyment of any right set forth by law shall be secured without discrimination', and that '[n]o one shall be discriminated against by any public authority' 'on any ground such sex, race, colour, language, religion, political or other opinion, national or social origin, association with a national minority, property, birth or other status'. The Protocol was opened for signature in November 2000, but the UK has made no plans as yet to ratify it, much less to incorporate it into domestic law. Until such ratification occurs, Article 14 may be relied on only to the extent that it can be read with another incorporated provision. In some cases this is relatively straightforward. If, for example, the Human Rights Act were used to challenge religious discrimination, Article 14 could be read with Article 9, which provides that 'everyone has the right to freedom of thought, conscience and religion'. Article 9(2) permits restrictions on freedom of religion, but if a restriction discriminates as between religions, or (though on its face neutral) is applied in a discriminatory fashion, Article 14 might be breached even if Article 9 is not.

Article 8 can be relied upon (whether in isolation or in conjunction with Article 14) to challenge sexual orientation discrimination. In the British gays in the military cases the ECtHR accepted that discrimination on grounds of sexual orientation (there in the discharge of service personnel in pursuance of the ban on gays in the military) breached the right to privacy protected by Article 8 of the Convention.[72] This is not to say that every case of sexual orientation discrimination will breach Article 8, interference with the rights protected thereby being capable of justification where it is 'in accordance with the law' and 'necessary in a democratic society' in pursuit of one or more of the legitimate aims contemplated by the second limb of that Article. In the gays in the military cases the Court decided that the nature of the interference with the applicants' private and family lives (the dismissals, with their impact on the future employment prospects of the applicants) was disproportionate to what it accepted as the legitimate aim of the authorities: the 'maintenance of the morale of service personnel and, consequently, of the fighting power and the operational effectiveness of the armed forces'. It is possible that lesser interference (a refusal to appoint, for example) might not be regarded as disproportionate to the pursuit of this or some other 'legitimate aim'. On the other hand, it is possible that Article 14 might bolster a claim in these circumstances.

The ECtHR declined to consider, in *Lustig-Prean & Beckett* and in *Smith & Grady*, whether the discrimination at issue also breached Article 14, such consideration being unnecessary in view of its findings under Article 8.[73] But, in a case in which non-discriminatory interference with private life might otherwise be compatible with

---

[72] *Lustig-Prean & Beckett v. UK* (2000) 29 EHRR 548, and *Smith & Grady v. UK* (2000) 29 EHRR 493. The cases were not the first in which the ECtHR had applied Art. 8 to sexual orientation discrimination—see *Dudgeon v. UK* [1982] A 45, 4 EHRR 149, *Norris* [1988] A 142, 13 EHRR 186. But they were the first in which discrimination other than by way of criminal sanction had been found to breach that Article.

[73] See also *Dudgeon*, n. 72 above.

Article 8, the discriminatory nature of an interference might tip the balance if Article 14 were taken into account.[74] In *Salgueiro da Silva Mouta v. Portugal*, for example, Article 8 was read in conjunction with Article 14 to declare that the denial of custody to a homosexual parent on the grounds of his sexual orientation breached the ECHR.[75]

'Age' amounts to 'other status' within Article 14.[76] But, whereas religion is protected by Article 9 and sexual orientation to some extent by Article 8, the legality of age-related discrimination will depend entirely on the context in which that discrimination takes place. Such discrimination might certainly breach Articles 2 and 14 if, for example, medical treatment was withheld on age-related grounds; Articles 3 and 14 if elderly people were subject to grossly inadequate standards of care in residential homes; and Articles 8 and 14 if elderly and infirm couples were separated from each other in residential care. But it is difficult to see what Convention provisions might be breached by, for example, age-related employment discrimination.

Similar problems arise in relation to those grounds of discrimination currently regulated by domestic legislation. Although sex and race (the latter including 'colour, language, national origin and association with a national minority') are enumerated within Article 14 and disability can be regarded as 'other status' within that provision, discrimination on these and other grounds is prohibited by the Convention only insofar as it relates to the 'enjoyment of the rights and freedoms set forth in th[e] Convention'. Article 8, as we saw above, will give some protection where the challenged discrimination can be regarded as interfering with an applicant's 'private and family life'; Article 3 in respect of 'degrading treatment'; and Article 10 in connection with freedom of expression. Article 6 can be relied upon where the discriminatory treatment relates to 'the determination of [an applicant's] civil rights and obligations' and Article 11 where it is connected with freedom of association. But in every case where the Convention is relied upon to challenge a lacuna in domestic law, Article 14 must be read together with another provision of the Convention if it is to provide an applicant with recourse under the ECHR.

Employment and Convention rights

The other points which should be made about the Convention rights concern their application by the Convention organs whose jurisprudence must be taken into account by (although it is not binding upon) the domestic courts. Leaving aside, for the moment, the particular problems relating to discrimination, significant concerns include the willingness of the Convention organs to conclude, particularly in the context of employment, that no interference with Convention rights has been established and, where such interference is found, to regard it as justified. In both

---

[74] See also *Markx*, n. 9 above, but cf. *X, Y and Z v. UK* (1997) 24 EHRR 143.
[75] N. 2 above.   [76] See e.g. *Bouamar v. Belgium* [1988] A 129, 11 EHRR 1.

Glasenapp v. Germany and *Kosiek v. Germany*, for example, the ECtHR ruled that no interference had occurred with the freedom of expression of teachers (one a Communist and the other a member of the Nazi party) who had been refused permanent positions (both had, in fact, been employed for significant periods).[77] Attributing their 'non-appointments' to their failure to meet the 'personal qualifications' for appointment to the 'civil service' (such qualifications including, in Germany, commitment to 'the principles of the free democratic constitutional system' of West Germany and the non-membership of any organization 'actively opposed to those principles'), the ECtHR ruled that they had suffered no interference with their freedom of expression.

In *Ahmad v. UK* and in *Stedman v. UK*, too, the European Commission dismissed challenges to workplace rules which prevented employees from complying with their religious obligations, in both cases on the grounds that there had been no interference with the applicants' Article 9 rights.[78] The Commission took the view that the employees had voluntarily 'contracted-out' of protection by undertaking the employment in question. Mr Ahmad, a Muslim teacher, was free to resign in order to fulfil his religious obligation to attend prayers on a Friday afternoon. Ms Stedman, who was sacked for refusing to agree to a contractual variation requiring Sunday working, had been dismissed for 'failing to agree to work certain hours rather than her religious belief as such and was free to resign and did in effect resign from her employment'.[79]

Even in cases in which employment-related interferences with Convention rights have been found by the Commission, employers' justifications have been readily accepted. Claims dismissed as 'manifestly unfounded' on this basis have included Article 10 claims brought by employees dismissed or subjected to disciplinary action for speaking out about safety fears at Aldermaston defence installation (*B v. UK*); for accusing employers of discrimination on grounds of sexual orientation (*Morissens v. Belgium*); and (in the case of a doctor employed at a Catholic hospital) for expressing a measure of support for the availability of abortion (*Rommelfanger v. Germany*).[80]

---

[77] Respectively [1986] A 104, 9 EHRR 25 and [1986] A 105, 9 EHRR 328, though cf. *Vogt v. Germany* [1995] A 323, 21 EHRR 205 and *Thlimmenos v. Greece*, (2000) Appl. No. 34369/97, available at www.dhcour.coe.int/Eng/Judgments.htm

[78] Respectively (1982) 4 EHRR 126 and (1997) 23 EHRR CD.

[79] A similar decision was reached by the Commission in *Karaduman v. Turkey* [1993] 74 DR 93, which involved the prohibition of headscarves by a Turkish university in pursuit of secularism in education

[80] Respectively [1985] 45 DR 41; [1988] 56 DR 127; [1989] 62 DR 151. See also *Ahmed v. UK* (2000) 29 EHRR 1. These cases are discussed by J. Bowers and J. Lewis, 'Whistleblowing: Freedom of Expression in the Workplace', (1996) 1 *European Human Rights Law Review* 637 and by A. McColgan, 'Article 10 and the Right to Freedom of Expression: Workers Ungagged?', in K. D. Ewing (ed.), *Human Rights at Work* (London: Institute of Employment Rights, 2000), 51–84.

The approach to 'discrimination' under Article 14[81]

Particularly problematic, as far as the Article 14 jurisprudence is concerned, is the approach taken by the Convention organs to establishing a difference of treatment such that justification is called for. The question which has to be addressed by the Court is whether there has been different treatment of persons in 'similar situations'.[82] In a number of cases the European Court has addressed this question in such a way as to avoid demanding justification for treatment which, on one view at least, discriminates on Article 14 grounds in respect of one or more Convention rights.[83]

In *Moustaquim v. Belgium*, for example, the Court asserted that a Moroccan national resident in Belgium from the age of two who was deported because of his persistent offending 'cannot be compared to Belgian juvenile delinquents [who] . . . have a right of abode in their own country and cannot be expelled from it'.[84] In *Van der Muselle v. Belgium*, in which a Belgian advocate challenged the requirement placed on this profession alone to engage in *pro bono* work, the Court declared that 'between the Bar and the various professions cited by the applicant ['medical practitioners, veterinary surgeons, pharmacists and dentists'], including even the judicial and parajudicial professions, there exist fundamental differences . . . as to legal status, conditions for entry into the profession, the nature of the functions involved, the manner of exercise of those functions, etc.'[85] And in *S v. UK*, the Commission ruled that a stable lesbian relationship was not analogous to 'family life' for the purposes of Article 8.[86]

In none of these cases did the Convention organs attempt to weigh the differential treatment complained of in the light of the differences accepted as placing the applicants in a different position from those with whom they wished to compare their treatment. The same was true in *Dudgeon*, in which the Court skipped to considering the justifiability of protecting those under 21 from the perils of homosexual sex without comparing the rules for heterosexual (or lesbian) sex and failed, therefore, to consider whether such arguments justified the *differential* treatment of homosexuals, as distinct from the restriction of intercourse with young persons generally.[87]

---

[81] See generally S. Livingstone, 'Article 14 and the Prevention of Discrimination in the European Convention on Human Rights', (1997) 2 *European Human Rights Law Review* 25.

[82] *Van der Mussele* [1983] A 70, 6 EHRR 163; *Sunday Times v. UK* [1991] A 217, 14 EHRR 229; *Observer v. UK* [1991] A 216, 14 EHRR 153.

[83] For a discussion of this issue see P. van Dijk and G. van Hoof, *Theory and Practice of the European Convention on Human Rights*, 3rd edn. (The Hague: Kluwer, 1998) 724–7.

[84] [1991] A 193, 13 EHRR 802. The Court did, however, find that his expulsion was in breach of Art. 8 as disproportionate to Belgium's legitimate aims.

[85] N. 82 above. See also *Stubbings v. UK* (1996) 23 EHRR 213.

[86] [1986] 47 DR 274. The burden to establish similarity is on the applicant—*Fredin v. Sweden* [1991] A 192, 13 EHRR 784.

[87] [1981] A 45, 4 EHRR 149. See also *Grandrath*, (1967) Yearbook X 626

Even in those cases in which a difference in treatment is found, discrimination may be more readily justified under the Convention than is the case, for example, under European Community law. This is, in one sense, inevitable because of the very broad grounds (enumerated and unenumerated) covered by Article 14. Not until the amendment of the EC Treaty by the Treaty of Amsterdam did the Community have jurisdiction to legislate save in respect of sex and nationality discrimination.[88] Direct discrimination on these grounds would only rarely be accepted as justified, a similar position applying under the domestic sex and race discrimination legislation, both of which permit the justification of direct discrimination only on specific grounds. Indirect discrimination is subject to a general justification defence. But the ECJ has adopted a fairly robust approach to this matter, demanding in *Bilka-Kaufhaus* that the disparately impacting practice challenged 'correspond[s] to a real need on the part of the undertaking, [is] appropriate with a view to achieving the objective in question and [is] necessary to that end'.[89] The extent to which this approach has been embraced by the domestic courts is arguable, and it does not in any event bind them in relation to race discrimination, which is for the most part, at present, outside the EC jurisdiction. And the specific grounds upon which direct sex and race discrimination are permitted by the relevant Acts have been criticized as unduly wide.[90] But, however flawed the current domestic approach is, the general justification of direct sex and race discrimination is not possible and the justification of indirect discrimination on these grounds is subject to an objective assessment which requires a balance to be struck 'between the discriminatory effect of the condition and the reasonable needs of the party who applies the condition'.[91]

Given the breadth of grounds covered by Article 14, its prohibition of 'discrimination' (direct or indirect) must necessarily be interpreted to mean 'unjustified', 'arbitrary', or 'unfair' discrimination. In the *Belgian Linguistics Case*, the ECtHR ruled that Article 14 is violated by discrimination having 'no objective and reasonable justification'.[92] Discrimination in pursuit of a 'legitimate aim' would be justified unless it was 'clearly established that there is no reasonable relationship of proportionality between the means employed and the aim sought to be realized'. The contrast between this and the approach taken by the ECJ in *Bilka-Kaufhaus* is pronounced. And in the *Belgian Police* and *Swedish Engine Drivers* cases the Court took an even more restricted approach to Article 14, asking only whether the treatment at issue had a justified aim in view or whether the authorities pursued 'other and ill-intentioned designs'.[93]

---

[88] For the current position see n. 12 above. The directives were adopted under new Art. 13, inserted into the Treaty Establishing the European Community by the Amsterdam Treaty.

[89] Case 170/84, *Bilka-Kaufhaus GmbH v. Weber von Hartz* [1986] ECR 1607.

[90] D. Pannick, *Sex Discrimination Law* (Oxford: Oxford University Press, 1985), 255 ff.

[91] Balcombe LJ in *Hampson v. Department of Education and Science* [1990] 2 All ER 25. The *Hampson* approach applies also to the justification of indirect discrimination under the SDA and the Equal Pay Act—see the decision of the House of Lords in *Rainey v. Greater Glasgow Health Board* [1987] 1 AC 224.

[92] [1968] A 6, 1 EHRR 252.

[93] Respectively, [1975] A 9, 1 EHRR 578 and [1975] A 20, 1 EHRR 617.

It is true that, where sex discrimination is considered, the ECtHR tends to take a more robust approach to the justification issue, declaring frequently that 'very weighty reasons would have to be put forward before a difference of treatment on the sole ground of sex could be regarded as compatible with the Convention'.[94] A similar stance has been taken in relation to discrimination based solely upon religion, nationality, and illegitimacy.[95] But even in cases where distinctions drawn on such fundamental grounds are challenged, the Convention organs fall short of requiring states to eradicate all such discrimination. So, for example, in *Petrovic v. Austria*, the Court rejected an Article 8 and 14 challenge to Austrian legislation granting mothers, but not fathers, a parental leave allowance after the expiry of maternity leave allowance.[96] According to the Court, 'the Contracting States enjoy a certain margin of appreciation in assessing whether and to what extent differences in otherwise similar situations justify a different treatment in law'. Taking note of the fact that Austria had, between the date of the discrimination at issue and that of the hearing, extended to men the right to take parental leave, the Court continued:

at the material time . . . the majority of the Contracting states did not provide for parental leave allowances to be paid to fathers . . . Only gradually, as society has moved towards a more equal sharing between men and women of responsibilities for the bringing up of their children, have the Contracting States introduced measures extending to fathers, like entitlement to parental leave. In this respect Austrian law has evolved in the same way . . . It therefore appears difficult to criticise the Austrian legislature for having introduced in a gradual manner, reflecting the evolution of society in that sphere, legislation which is, all things considered, very progressive in Europe.

Judges Bernhardt and Spielman dissented on the grounds that

It is in reality the traditional distribution of family responsibilities between mothers and fathers that gave rise to the Austrian legislation . . . The discrimination against fathers perpetuates this traditional distribution of roles and can also have negative consequences for the mother; if she continues her professional activity and agrees that the father stay at home, the family loses the parental leave allowance to which it would be entitled if she stayed at home.[97]

In theory Article 14 regulates indirect as well as direct discrimination, the ECtHR in the *Belgian Linguistics* case having referred to the 'aims *and effects*' (my emphasis) of the impugned legislation. But the case law in this area is extremely underdeveloped, and the same conflation of differential treatment and justification tends to occur as in cases concerned with direct discrimination. In *Abdulaziz*, for

---

[94] See e.g. *Abdulaziz*, n. 70 above; *Schuler-Zgraggen v. Switzerland* [1993] A 263, 16 EHRR 405; *Burghartz v. Switzerland* [1994] A 280-B, 18 EHRR 10; *Karlheinz Schmidt v. Germany*, n. 71 above; *Van Raalte v. Netherlands* (1997) 24 EHRR 501.

[95] *Hoffman v. Austria* [1993] A 255-C, 17 EHRR 293; *Gaygusuz v. Austria* (1996) 23 EHRR 365; *Markx*, n. 9 above; and *Vermeire* [1991] A 214-C, 15 EHRR 488.

[96] 27 March 1998, Appl. No. 00020458/92, available at http://www.dhcour.coe.fr/Eng/Judgments.htm

[97] See *Rasmussen*, n. 2 above, for an example of justified sex discrimination, and *H v. United Kingdom* (Appl. No. 14818/89, 4 Dec. 1989, unpublished) for an example of the incremental approach to the elimination of race discrimination.

example, the ECtHR upheld an immigration rule which required that fiancés had previously met. The rule disproportionately disadvantaged those from the Indian subcontinent, where arranged marriages were particularly common.[98] According to the Court 'such a requirement cannot be taken as an indication of racial discrimination: its main purpose was to prevent evasion of the rules by means of bogus marriages or engagements. . . The Court accordingly holds that the applicants have not been victims of discrimination on the ground of race.' The ECtHR did not expressly consider whether the disparate impact of the rule was justified by its purpose.

The shortcomings of the approach taken under the ECHR to indirect discrimination are also evident from the decisions in *Ahmad* and in *Stedman*, discussed above, in which the Commission refused to impose upon employers any duty to accommodate the religious obligations of their staff. The recent decision of the ECtHR in *Thlimmenos v. Greece*,[99] however, may indicate the development of a more robust approach by the Court. There, the ECtHR ruled that 'The Right not to be discriminated against in the enjoyment of the rights guaranteed under the Convention . . . is violated when States without an objective and reasonable justification fail to treat differently persons whose situations are significantly different' as well as where they 'treat differently persons in analogous situations without providing an objective and reasonable justification'. This clarified the application of Article 14 to indirect as well as direct discrimination, though it remains to be seen how robust will be the approach taken by the ECtHR to the justification of such discrimination.

Using the Human Rights Act to challenge discrimination

What, then, is the potential of incorporation for domestic discrimination law? A distinction must be drawn between discrimination by 'public authorities' and by others. Section 6 provides that breaches of the Convention rights by 'public authorities' (including judges) will be unlawful unless required by primary legislation or 'in the case of one or more provisions of, or made under, primary legislation which cannot be read or given effect in a way which is compatible with the Convention rights, the authority was acting so as to give effect to or enforce those provisions'.[100] Where a court decides that a provision of primary legislation is compatible with a Convention right, it 'may make a declaration of that incompatibility' which will not, however, affect the enforcement of the provision.

Action may be taken against public authorities either directly under section 7 of the Human Rights Act or, in suitable cases and subject to the same restrictions on standing as are imposed in relation to section 7 actions, by way of judicial review. In

---

[98] N. 70 above. See see Harris, n. 67 above, 477–8. Harris also discusses *X v. Ireland* [1978] A 25, 2 EHRR 25, in which the Court did not examine why no Loyalists were interned beyond the government's statement that their activities were directly differently.

[99] N. 77 above.   [100] S. 6(2)(a) and (b) HRA.

addition, judicial obligations in respect of interpretation of statute will apply whether the alleged discriminator is a public authority or not. The same is true in relation to judicial obligations regarding the application and development of the common law.

In some cases the interpretive obligations imposed in respect of existing legislation will suffice to protect Convention rights. Taking first of all discrimination on grounds which are already caught within the domestic legislative provisions, the Human Rights Act may provide an instrument whereby the inadequacies of that legislation might be challenged. To the extent that a breach of the Convention rights is found, the courts will be obliged to interpret the legislation 'so far as is possible' to give effect to the right. If, for example, a sex-specific dress code was found to breach Articles 10 and 14 (this being highly unlikely for the reasons discussed above),[101] the Sex Discrimination Act could easily be interpreted to give effect to this in domestic law.[102] If the claim was brought by a person denied access to services because of a HIV diagnosis (again, assuming a breach of one or more incorporated provisions is found),[103] the courts might strain to bring the claim within the Disability Discrimination Act.[104] If the discrimination at issue consisted of a dismissal from employment they might, alternatively, regard themselves as bound to declare it unfair.

Similar judicial 'fixing' may be possible in relation to some grounds of discrimination which currently fall outside the legislative framework. The obligations imposed upon the judiciary by sections 3 and 6 might be sufficient to force the inclusion within the Race Relations and Sex Discrimination Acts respectively of discrimination on grounds of religion and sexual orientation (this regardless of the public or private status of the litigating parties). Discrimination connected with religion is currently caught by the Race Relations Act only in the case of certain major faiths,[105] the most notable exceptions being Muslims and Rastafarians.[106] It is possible that the obligation to give effect to Article 9, read with Article 14, will suffice to extend the remit of the Act to discrimination on these grounds, although not all religious discrimination can be forced into the constraints of a prohibition on 'race' discrimination, however broadly defined. As far as sexual orientation discrimination is concerned, the Scottish EAT has already read the Sex Discrimination Act so as to prohibit sexual orientation discrimination in

---

[101] See text to nn. 78–100 above. See also *Kara v. UK*, Appl. No. 36528/97 (available at www.echr. coe.int/Eng/Judgments.htm), in which the Commission rejected a challenge to a dress code brought under Arts. 8, 10, and 14.

[102] For the current approach of the courts to sex specific dress codes see McColgan, n. 10 above, 397–402.

[103] Article 8 alone or in conjunction with Article 14.

[104] For the current position see McColgan, n. 10 above, 454–71.

[105] The area is regulated by the decision of the House of Lords in *Mandla v. Dowell Lee* [1983] 2 AC 548 (which left intact the decision in *Seide v. Gillette* [1980] IRLR 427 to the effect that Jews constituted a 'racial group' for the purposes of the Act).

[106] See *Commission for Racial Equality v. Dutton* [1989] QB 783, and McColgan, n. 10 above, ch. 7. See also McColgan, n. 80 above.

MacDonald v. Ministry of Defence,[107] albeit prior to the implementation of the Human Rights Act and on the mistaken view that *Salgueiro da Silva* interpreted sexual orientation as an aspect of 'sex' within Article 14 (rather than as an 'other status' on the grounds of which discrimination was prohibited).[108] The EAT's reasoning is likely to be contradicted on appeal, but the higher courts may find themselves obliged by sections 3 and 6 to interpret the Sex Discrimination Act so as to prohibit discrimination on grounds of sexual orientation regardless.[109]

Assuming that a breach of one or more Articles of the Convention is found in circumstances where the discrimination at issue cannot be brought within the provisions of one of the anti-discrimination statutes however broadly interpreted, the course of action open to the court depends on the details. In the employment context section 3 of the Human Rights Act might require the interpretation of the Employment Rights Act's unfair dismissal provisions to prohibit dismissals in breach of the Convention.[110] The recent decision of the House of Lords in *Fitzpatrick v. Sterling Housing Association*[111] illustrates the scope for similar approaches outside the sphere of employment. There their Lordships, by a majority, interpreted the term 'family' in the Rent Act 1977 to include a homosexual partner for the purposes of affording him the right to succeed to his lover's tenancy. This decision was reached prior to the implementation of the Human Rights Act, and the Convention provisions were cited as much by the dissenters as by the majority judges. It serves, nevertheless, to illustrate how statutes not on their face concerned with discrimination may nevertheless be interpreted so as to give effect to Convention rights in domestic law. In the case of statutes themselves requiring discrimination, a declaration of incompatibility will be the only option.

To the extent that discrimination which breaches the Convention cannot be remedied through statutory interpretation, *Douglas v. Hello Ltd* illustrates the possibility of incremental change to the common law. It is possible, for example, that the duty relating to mutual trust and confidence which is implied into contracts of employment might be regarded, post-incorporation, as prohibiting discrimination which breaches the Convention rights. The development of this implied term into one which is all but capable of overruling express contractual terms has been

---

107 [2000] IRLR 748.

108 This permitting EAT to find 'sex' within the SDA sufficiently 'ambiguous' as to whether it included sexual orientation to have regard, according to the interpretive convention (see *Garland v. British Rail* [1983] 2 AC 751 at 771, *per* Lord Diplock) to have regard to the ECHR as an international obligation to which Parliament would be taken to have intended, in the event of ambiguity, to give effect in the relevant statute.

109 On the strength of the interpretive obligation see Lord Lester of Herne Hill, 'Opinion: The Art of the Possible—Interpreting Statutes under the Human Rights Act', (1998) 3 *European Human Rights Law Review* 665, 669–72.

110 This would also render unfair any constructive dismissal which might result from discrimination short of dismissal—again, it might be possible to regard breach of a Convention right as a fundamental breach of contract of employment, perhaps through the mechanism of the implied term relating to trust and confidence.

111 [1999] 3 WLR 1113.

remarkable.[112] In *Douglas*, Sedley LJ declared that, if domestic law did not already include a right to privacy, and

if the step from confidentiality to privacy is not simply a modern restatement of the scope of a known protection but a legal innovation, then I would accept . . . that this is precisely the kind of incremental change for which the Act is designed: one which without undermining the measure of certainty which is necessary to all law gives substance and effect to s. 6.[113]

Applying this to the implied term relating to trust and confidence, its further evolution to prohibit discrimination may be 'precisely the kind of incremental change for which the Act is designed'. As against this, however, the traditional concern of the common law with freedom of contract may well restrict this development, if it occurs at all, to the area of employment.

Turning to the potential of incorporation specifically in the field of public law, discrimination which is in breach of the Convention is, as a result of the Human Rights Act, directly challengeable in domestic courts for the first time on that ground alone. If the applicant chooses to proceed by way of judicial review, breach of a Convention right will found a claim of illegality. The proviso, and it is a significant one, is that the applicant will win his or her case under the Human Rights Act or by way of judicial review only if the domestic courts accept that there has been a breach of the Convention, an issue to which we return below. But the potential impact can be seen by considering *R v. Ministry of Defence, ex p. Smith and Ors* as a post-incorporation case. The question posed by the Court of Appeal in 1995 was whether the ban on gays in the military was irrational, the assessment taking into account the 'human rights context' and the fact, in particular, that 'the more substantial the interference with human rights, the more [it] . . . will require by way of justification'. Post-incorporation the question would simply be whether the ban breached the applicants' human rights. We know from the decision of the ECtHR in the *Smith & Grady* and *Lustig-Prean* cases that it did. We know, further, that in this context the pre–Human Rights Act irrationality test, however modified in the human rights context, was inadequate to protect the applicants' Article 8 rights as required under the Convention.[114]

V. Conclusion

It is clear from the above that the incorporation of the ECHR provisions will have some effect on domestic anti-discrimination law. But what cannot be over-

---

[112] See e.g. the judgments of Browne-Wilkinson VC and Stuart Smith LJ in *Johnstone v. Bloomsbury Health Authority* [1991] IRLR 118, and the recent decisions in *Adin v. Sedco Forex International Resources Ltd* [1997] IRLR 280, *Bainbridge v. Circuit Foil UK Ltd* [1997] IRLR 305, *Brompton v. AOC International Ltd* [1997] IRLR 639, and *Villella v. MFI Furniture Centres Ltd* [1999] IRLR 468.

[113] Citing Hunt, n. 66 above.

[114] See McColgan, n. 10 above, ch. 1. In *Smith & Grady*, n. 72 above, the ECtHR rejected the UK's argument that the *Wednesbury* test, adapted to human rights cases, satisfied the requirement that remedies be available for breach of Convention rights.

emphasized are the limitations of the approach taken by the Convention organs both to the meaning of 'discrimination' and to the application of the Convention provisions in the employment sphere. The domestic courts are, of course, free to interpret the incorporated provisions more generously than the Convention organs have (s. 2 requiring only that they 'take into account' any relevant jurisprudence, rather than follow it). But, given that many shortcomings of the existing discrimination legislation arise from its interpretation by the judges, rather than from the bare letter of the legislation (the meaning of indirect discrimination, for example; the scope of 'race' and 'sex' discrimination; the non-application of the discrimination legislation to actions of public authorities not akin to those carried out by private actors),[115] this scarcely appears likely.

The other point which must be addressed concerns the positive dangers posed by incorporation. We have seen that among the cases cited by Jowell in support of his alleged 'constitutional principle of equality' have been those such as *Prescott* and the *GLC* case in which the courts have struck down redistributive action by local government, such action being within the express powers granted them by statute.[116] Article 14 has been held to regulate discrimination between landlords having long and short leaseholds;[117] between lawyers and other professionals;[118] between military personnel having different rank;[119] between small and large landowners;[120] and between private and public sector tenants.[121] We have seen, above, that discrimination falling within Article 14 is not itself contrary to the Convention. But Article 1 of the First Protocol to the Convention, which has also been incorporated into domestic law by the Human Rights Act, provides that '[e]very natural or legal person is entitled to the peaceful enjoyment of his possessions'.[122] This provision is applied subject to a generous margin of appreciation by the European Court.[123] But, read with Article 14, it may provide the domestic judiciary with heavy artillery with which to challenge all manner of redistributive measures. Fired with the common law's concern for property rights, the domestic courts may be less ready than

---

[115] See generally McColgan, n. 10 above, chs. 2 and 4.

[116] Its illegality thus turning on judicial reading-down of the powers to accord with their vision of 'equality'—see also *Roberts v. Hopwood* [1925] AC 578 on judicial approaches to 'equality'.

[117] *James v. UK*, n. 2 above. The challenge to legislation affording tenants with long leases of houses a right to buy the freehold reversion was brought on behalf of the Duke of Westminister.

[118] *Van der Mussele*, n. 82 above. The case concerned a challenge to a requirement that Belgian advocates engage in some *pro bono* work.

[119] *Engel v. Netherlands* [1976] A 22, 1 EHRR 706.

[120] *Chassagnou v. France* (2000) 29 EHRR 615.

[121] *Larkos v. Cyprus*, 18 February 1999, Appl. No. 00029515/95, available at http://www.dhcour.coe.fr/Eng/Judgments.htm

[122] 'No one shall be deprived of his possessions except in the public interest and subject to the conditions provided for by law and by the general principles of international law. (2) The preceding provisions shall not, however, in any way impair the right of a State to enforce such laws as it deems necessary to control the use of property in accordance with the general interest or to secure the payment of taxes or other contributions or penalties.'

[123] See e.g. *James v. UK*, n. 2 above; *Lithgow v. UK* [1986] A 102, 8 EHRR 329; *Mellacher v. Austria* [1989] A 169, 12 EHRR 391; *Pine Valley Developments Ltd v. Ireland* [1991] A 222, 14 EHRR 319.

the Convention organs to find that such discrimination is justified. This in turn has implications for the lawfulness of positive measures taken in order to ameliorate the disadvantage experienced by particular groups.

The measure successfully challenged in *Prescott* was the provision to the elderly of free public transport between the hours of 10 a.m. and 4 p.m. Sunday to Friday. The Court of Appeal accepted that 'in the absence of an equality clause, or some necessary implication to the like effect, a person or body, having statutory power to charge tolls or rates, or, for that matter, fares, is entitled to discriminate in the charges made to different people'. But Jenkins LJ, for the Court, went on to declare that local authorities, although

not, of course, trustees for their ratepayers . . . do, we think, owe an analogous fiduciary duty to their ratepayers in relation to the application of funds contributed by the latter. Thus local authorities . . . are not, in our view, entitled to use their discriminatory power as proprietors of the transport undertaking in order to confer out of rates a special benefit on some particular class of inhabitants whom they, as the local authority for the town or district in question, may think deserving of such assistance. In the absence of clear statutory authority for such a proceeding (which to our mind a mere general power to charge differential fares certainly is not) we would, for our part, regard it as illegal.[124]

The Court of Appeal in *Prescott* found 'some support' in the House of Lords' decision in *Roberts v. Hopwood* for their conclusion that the concessionary travel scheme was not a proper exercise of any discretion conferred on it 'with respect to the differential treatment of passengers in the matter of fares'. That decision involved the upholding of a surcharge imposed upon councillors in respect of their 'overpayment' (i.e. equal payment) of the women workers. Their Lordships took the view that the councillors had breached their duty to administer their funds 'with a due and alert regard to the interests' of ratepayers. Jowell defends the decision in *Hopwood* on the grounds that its 'ratio . . . was based upon a . . . sober consideration of the lack of "rational proportion" between the rates paid to the women and the going market rate'. But the reason for this lack of proportion lay, precisely, in the market undervaluation of women's work relative to that of men.

Neither *Roberts* nor *Prescott* is of recent vintage. But the majority speeches in *Fitzpatrick v. Sterling* notwithstanding, few domestic judges have demonstrated any significant commitment to the pursuit of equality. Judicial attitudes towards the discrimination legislation have at times been little short of obstructive, particular hostility being reserved for legislative attempts to eradicate race discrimination.[125] There

---

[124] N. 32 above, 235.

[125] See e.g. the decisions in *Science Research Council v. Nasse* [1979] QB 144, *Hillingdon London Borough Council v. Commission for Racial Equality* [1982] AC 779, *R v. CRE ex p. Prestige Group PLC* [1984] ICR 472, and *R v. CRE ex p. Amari Plastics* [1982] 2 All ER 499, discussed in McColgan, n. 10 above, 293–313. See also the extrajudicial utterances of Lord Hailsham at 373 HL Debs. (20 July 1976), col. 745, and, more recently, of Sir John Laws in 'Law and Democracy', [1995] *Public Law* 72, criticized by J. A. G. Griffith, 'The Brave New World of Sir John Laws', (2000) 63 *Modern Law Review* 159, 163–4.

have been many judicial utterances as to the importance of non-discrimination,[126] but the common law has afforded scant protection to it. The constitutional affirmation of the principle of non-discrimination which is to be found in the Human Rights Act 1998 is weak, sharing as it does the flaws inherent in Article 14 itself. But it is to be hoped (perhaps against hope) that the Act proves to encourage judges to give flesh to the current rhetorical commitment to equality.[127]

---

[126] For a recent example see *Matadeen v. Pointu, Minister of Education and Science* [1999] 1 AC 98.

[127] Though for disappointing early indications see *R (on the application of Montana) v. Secretary of State for the Home Department*, Court of Appeal (23 Nov. 2000, unreported).

13

Tort Law and the Human Rights Act

CONOR GEARTY

I. Introduction

It is clear that in the United Kingdom the judges have long been engaged in the discharge of functions of a legislative as well as of a judicial character.[1] Indeed the responsibility of the English judges for the formulation and development of the common law pre-dates both the establishment of Britain in its present form and the entrenchment of a democratic form of government within the nation's borders.[2] In the twentieth century, the 'evolution' of the tort of negligence alone saw a great expansion in the liability of property owners, public officials, and others for actions and/or omissions that could be retrospectively characterized as negligent by the courts.[3] Never has the legislative character of the common law been clearer than at the turn of the last century, with a series of major cases in the House of Lords imposing liability on local educational authorities,[4] on officials with child care responsibilities,[5] and (in a marked volte-face on an earlier line of authority) on barristers and other legal practitioners involved in court advocacy.[6]

It is only the common lawyer's familiarity with this system of lawmaking that blinds him or her to its peculiarity in a country that considers itself to be a representative democracy. The legislative character of the common law has never been explicitly acknowledged, however, with the system being said to be capable not of formulating new rules but of evolving fresh versions of old ones. In *SW and CR v. United Kingdom*[7] the demands of the European Convention on Human Rights almost forced the whole subterfuge to the surface, thereby destroying it. The two applicants were men convicted of serious sexual offences against their wives; in the first case rape, in the second attempted rape. In Strasbourg, both pointed to the fact that the common law had long held men not to be legally liable for the rape of their wives, on the ground that the consent of the wife to all such sexual contact was inherent in the marriage contract. In an important domestic ruling involving one of the applicants, the House of Lords had held that the husband's immunity in fact no

[1] See K. D. Ewing, 'The Unbalanced Constitution', above.
[2] See generally on the common law J. H. Baker, *An Introduction to English Legal History*, 3rd edn. (London: Butterworths, 1990).
[3] M. Lunney and K. Oliphant, *Tort Law: Text and Materials* (Oxford: Oxford University Press, 2000) is a good, up-to-date survey.
[4] *Phelps v. Hillingdon Borough Council* [2000] 3 WLR 776.
[5] *Barrett v. Enfield London Borough Council* [1999] 3 All ER 193.
[6] *Arthur Hall & Co v. Simons* [2000] 3 WLR 543.
[7] *SW v. United Kingdom; CR v. United Kingdom* (1995) 21 EHRR 363.

longer formed part of the common law.[8] This decision meant not only that this man's guilt was confirmed but also that any challenge by the second applicant to his own conviction was bound to fail. Were the men's convictions in breach of their Article 7 right not to be 'held guilty of any criminal offence on account of any act or omission which did not constitute a criminal offence under national or international law at the time when it was committed'?

Only at a most artificial level could the expansion in the ambit of the law of rape achieved here by the House of Lords be characterized as other than a legislative act. The conduct of the two men had not been criminal when it occurred but had been designated as having been such by subsequent decision of the nation's supreme court. It was only with great difficulty that this could be described as an example of a non-legislative 'evolving' of an old law in a new direction. In reality, the judges had engaged in a legislative act that had neither been processed through a legislative assembly, nor made the subject of democratic debate, nor promulgated in any public kind of way. Article 7 is the clearest expression of a principle of legality that permeates the European Convention, with the limited departures from some of the rights set out in that instrument being required to be 'prescribed by' or 'in accordance with' law. Is the common law 'law' for Convention purposes when it engages retrospectively in the kind of radical 'evolution' that persons unschooled in its subtleties might mistake for something akin to legislation?

In *SW and CR v. United Kingdom*, four members of the European Commission took the view that Article 7(1) had been infringed. '[T]he removal of the immunity resulted in the application of the criminal law to conduct which had never previously constituted an offence. This step would have not been reasonably foreseeable to the applicant even with the assistance of legal advice.'[9] Instead '[s]uch change could have been effected through legislation'.[10] The majority of the Commission, and the Court by unanimous vote, took a different view. 'In a common law system, not only written statutes but also rules of common or other customary law may provide sufficient legal basis for the criminal convictions envisaged in Article 7 of the Convention.'[11] In such a legal system, 'the courts may exercise their customary role of developing the law through cases but in doing so may not exceed the bounds of reasonably foreseeable change'.[12] All that had happened in these cases was that a 'purported immunity based on a presumption as to one ingredient of the offence— consent—. . . was definitively removed'.[13] This development would have been 'reasonably foreseeable to an applicant with appropriate legal advice'.[14]

    [8] *R v. R* [1992] 1 AC 599.
    [9] *SW v. UK*, n. 7 above, dissenting opinion of Mr L. Loucaides, joined by MM S. Trechsel, M. A. Nowicki, and I. Cabral Barreto, at 381. Mr Loucaides went on to explain why he considered that the saving in Art. 7(2) for conduct generally recognised as criminal did not apply. In *CR v. UK*, n. 7 above, Mr Loucaides was joined only by Mr Nowicki, with Mr I. Békés filing a separate dissenting opinion.
    [10] *CR v. UK*, dissenting opinion of Mr Loucaides, 396.
    [11] *SW v. UK*, Opinion of the Commission, para. 46; *CR v. UK*, para. 47.
    [12] *SW v. UK*, para. 49; *CR v. UK*, para. 50.   [13] *SW v. UK*, para. 54; *CR v. UK*, para, 55.
    [14] *SW v. UK*, para. 59; *CR v. UK*, para. 60.

The idea of a would-be rapist calmly seeking legal advice in advance of his planned assault would no doubt seem a trifle unreal to those working in rape crisis centres and to other professionals involved in front-line work on behalf of the female victims of sexual and other assaults from men. The same is surely true of potential tortfeasors as well. Since the rule-making nature of the common law could not be gainsaid, the Strasbourg court was forced to replace the traditional sub-terfuge—that the common law never changes—with another, rooted in the concept of the 'reasonable forseeability' of such changes. This intellectual contrivance pro-tects the common law from wholesale subversion at the hands of a document that insists that those who are adversely affected by a law should know in advance of its existence. Though sounding entirely reasonable, this was never a right that the common law could ever deliver, or could deliver only at a cost to its own dynamism and vitality. Thus, when at the end of 2000 Michael Douglas and Catherine Zeta Jones became involved in proceedings against a magazine for the publication of unauthorized photographs of their wedding, alleging that their right to privacy had been infringed, no point appears to have been made that the 'recognition' of this right for the first time in these proceedings was arguably a breach of the defendant company's own entitlement not to have the common law transform itself to its own, retrospective detriment.[15]

The common law in general, and (for present purposes) the judge-made law of tort in particular, may therefore be reasonably safe from obliteration by the Human Rights Act 1998. But the impact of the Act on both the statute-based and common law of tort is bound to be immense. The expansion of the law of negligence men-tioned above as having occurred at the end of the twentieth century is in large part a reaction (sometimes explicitly, more often implicitly) to Strasbourg decisions on the European Convention and the imminence of their applicability within this juris-diction.[16] Likewise the Douglas/Zeta Jones litigation draws strength from, and might not even have been initiated without, the potential for the development of a law of privacy inherent in the incorporation of Article 8 of the European Convention into domestic law.[17] In this chapter we outline first the provisions of the Human Rights Act and of the European Convention which, when viewed together with the Strasbourg case law, demonstrate why it is likely that the Act will have such a large impact on tort law. We then consider what sort of effect this is likely to be by having regard to the ideological structure that underpins the 1998 Act and the Convention to which it gives further effect. We consider finally some obstacles that lie in the way of a coherent reception of the Human Rights Act into UK law.

---

[15] *Douglas v. Hello! Limited* [2001] 2 WLR 1038.

[16] See *Osman v. United Kingdom* (1998) 29 EHRR 245. But see now *Z v. United Kingdom*, European Court of Human Rights, 10 May 2001; *TP and KM v. United Kingdom*, European Court of Human Rights, 10 May 2001.

[17] *Douglas v. Hello! Limited*, n. 15 above.

II. The Human Rights Act 1998 and the law of tort

The English law of tort is composed both of statute and common law. As far as the first of these is concerned, the relevant section of the Human Rights Act is section 3. In particular, section 3(1) requires that '[s]o far as it is possible to do so, primary legislation and subordinate legislation must be read and given effect in a way which is compatible with the Convention rights'. Though not permitting the courts to trump primary legislation or secondary legislation necessitated by such Acts,[18] this is a very wide, indeed novel, principle of interpretation. It permits the judges to revisit all past legislation in order to review its meaning for Convention compatibility. It allows, indeed mandates, a transformation in the meaning of settled provisions where this is deemed necessary and possible to protect the provision from incompatibility with the Convention.[19] Section 3(1) also asserts a power to reach into the future and to mould not yet enacted provisions of Acts of Parliament to its own wishes, requiring these too to be given meanings which might be at odds with their intent if this can be said to be required to avoid incompatibility, and if it can be said also to be 'possible' given the words that this hypothetical Parliament of the future has used. It remains to be seen whether this effort by the 1998 Parliament to speak from the grave will be entirely successful. But clearly its potential effect on the many statutes that now help to make up our modern tort law is great, a point to which we return when we consider the substance of the Convention rights.

Turning now to the common law, one of the more difficult strands of development in the law of tort in recent years has related to the liability in negligence of public authorities.[20] Section 6(1) of the Human Rights Act has thrown an important new element into this already complex equation. It states: 'It is unlawful for a public authority to act in a way which is incompatible with a Convention right.' Though there are savings for conduct made inevitable by the requirements of an incompatible primary provision,[21] this is a new statutory duty on public authorities of potentially a very wide reach. 'A person who claims that a public authority has acted (or proposes to act) in a way which is made unlawful by section 6(1) may—(a) bring proceedings against the authority under this Act in the appropriate court or tribunal, or (b) rely on the Convention right or rights concerned in any legal proceedings' as long as he or she can be characterized as a 'victim' of such an act, a

---

[18] See s. 3(2).

[19] The consequence of which finding, given that Acts of Parliament cannot be struck down, can be a (non-enforceable) declaration of incompatibility which places both the executive and legislative branches under some political and (to a lesser extent) legal pressure to act to remedy the breach: see ss. 4 and 10 and sched. 2; and, for two early examples, *R(H) v. Mental Health Review Tribunal, North and East London Region and Another*, Court of Appeal, 28 Mar. 2001, [2001] EWCA Civ. 415; *Winsor v. First County Trust Ltd*, Court of Appeal, 2 May 2001, [2001] EWCA Civ. 633.

[20] See M. Andenas and D. Fairgrieve, 'Sufficiently Serious? Judicial Restraint in Tortious Liability of Public Authorities and the European Influence', in M. Andenas (ed.), *English Public Law and the Common Law of Europe* (London: Key Haven 1998), ch. 14. A good recent survey is M. Amos, 'Extending the Liability of the State in Damages', (2001) 21 *Legal Studies* 1.   [21] See s. 6(2).

term which carries its own jurisprudential baggage from Strasbourg to which regard must be had.[22] Faced with such a case, the courts may 'grant such relief or remedy, or make such order, within its powers as it considers just and appropriate'.[23]

No award of damages may, however, be made unless, 'taking account of all the circumstances of the case, including—(a) any other relief or remedy granted, or order made, in relation to the act or question (by that or any other court), and (b) the consequences of any decision (of that or any other court) in respect of that act, the court is satisfied that the award is necessary to afford just satisfaction to the person in whose favour it is made'. The concept of 'just satisfaction' explicitly invokes the jurisdiction of the European Court of Human Rights, whose case law on the award of damages is specifically required to be referred to by the domestic judges.[24] Clearly an effort is being made here to restrict the award of damages against public bodies. The spectre of *Factortame*[25] probably hung over Treasury input into the measure when it was at its earliest planning stages. It remains to be seen whether the effort will be wholly successful, particularly bearing in mind section 11 of the Act, which expressly safeguards 'any other right or freedom' which a person might enjoy under existing UK law.[26]

An important provision relating to the potential reach of the Human Rights Act into the common law is section 6(3)(a), in which the term 'public authority' is expressly stated to include 'a court or tribunal'. Quite what this subclause was intended to achieve was the subject of a very lively debate in the period between publication of the Bill and its full implementation in October 2000; a whole spectrum of academic opinion was to be found, ranging from the view that its impact on private inter partes disputes was likely to be minimal or nonexistent[27] to the opinion that its effect was indirectly to introduce a cause of action as between private parties for breach of their Convention rights.[28] Somewhere in the middle was the view of Murray Hunt, to the effect that a limited 'horizontality' had been achieved by the Act, and it has been this position that has gathered ground as the debate has deepened.[29] It now seems to be the case that the common law will be required to

---

[22] S. 7(7).   [23] S. 8(1).

[24] S. 8(4). See Law Commission, Scottish Law Commission, *Damages under the Human Rights Act 1998* Cm. 4853 (2000), and Sir R. Carnwath, 'ECHR Remedies from a Common Law Perspective', (2000) 49 *International and Comparative Law Quarterly* 517. See on exemplary damages *Kuddus v. Chief Constable of Leicestershire*, House of Lords, 7 June 2001, [2001] UKHL 29.

[25] *R v. Secretary of State for Transport, ex p. Factortame Ltd (No. 2)* [1991] 1 AC 603, and esp. *R v. Secretary of State for Transport, ex p. Factortame (No. 5)* [2000] 1 AC 524.

[26] And see further Law Commission, *Damages under the Human Rights Act 1998*, n. 24 above.

[27] The Rt. Hon. Sir R. Buxton, 'The Human Rights Act and Private Law', (2000) 116 *Law Quarterly Review* 48.

[28] Sir W. Wade, 'Horizons of Horizontality', (2000) 116 *Law Quarterly Review* 217.

[29] M. Hunt, 'The "Horizontal Effect" of the Human Rights Act', (1998) *Public Law* 423; G. Phillipson, 'The Human Rights Act, "Horizontal Effect" and the Common Law: A Bang or a Whimper', (1999) 62 *Modern Law Review* 824. See also N. Bamforth, 'The True "Horizontal Effect" of the Human Rights Act 1998', (2001) 117 *Law Quarterly Review* 34. The early case law favours such an approach: see *Douglas v. Hello! Limited*, n. 15 above; *Venables and Thompson v. News Group Newspapers Limited, Associated Newspapers Ltd and MGM Limited*, Queen's Bench Division, 8 Jan. 2001.

develop in a Convention-compatible way but will not be permitted spontaneously to create new forms of action in the absence of a tort upon which to piggyback the Convention arguments.

Quite how far-reaching all these legislative provisions are likely to be for the law of tort needs now to be further explained by examining the range and potential reach of the Convention rights which are introduced into UK law in section 1 of the 1998 Act and set out in schedule 1 to the Act. An important provision in this regard is section 2, under which courts and tribunals are required to have regard to (but not necessarily to 'follow' in the common law sense) the case law of both the Court of Human Rights and the (now superseded) European Commission of Human Rights.[30] What follows is a brief survey of these Convention rights and of their likely impact on domestic tort law, but readers are directed to more detailed treatment of all of these points in the standard works on tort law, which are slowly gearing themselves to absorb the Strasbourg jurisprudence.[31]

Article 2 of the Convention declares that 'Everyone's right to life shall be protected by law'. In the Strasbourg case law, this has been extended to include both a positive duty on public authorities to protect life[32] and a negative duty on such bodies not to act in such a negligent manner as to cause the death of a person.[33] Clearly, both aspects of Article 2 have the potential greatly to expand the liability of public authorities such as the police, the local authorities, the National Health Service, and the prison service, and it has implications too for the openness of the legal process.[34] Bodies which are exercising public functions will not be able to point to their technically private status as a means of avoiding such liability,[35] and this makes it likely that 'human rights' lawsuits will be launched where persons have died as a result of what is alleged to be the negligence of a service provider such as British Gas or (possibly) British Airways. Indeed, it is not entirely unlikely that Railtrack's extraordinary reaction to the Hatfield rail accident in autumn 2000, closing down so much track for instant maintenance that the system effectively collapsed, was a decision taken with Article 2—and the possibly catastrophic financial consequences of a further crash—firmly in mind.[36]

Article 3 of the Convention declares simply, 'No one shall be subjected to torture or to inhuman or degrading treatment or punishment.' This provision has been expan-

---

[30] S. 2(1). The requirement to have regard to data from the Committee of Ministers is not likely to lead to a wholesale reliance on the decisions of that body.

[31] Such as Lunney and Oliphant, n. 3 above, ch. 1.III.   [32] *Osman v. United Kingdom*, n. 16 above.

[33] *McCann and others v. United Kingdom* (1996) 21 EHRR 97; *Keenan v. United Kingdom*, European Court of Human Rights, 3 Apr. 2001; *Jordan and others v. United Kingdom*, European Court of Human Rights, 4 May 2001.

[34] *R v. Lord Saville of Newdigate, ex p. A* [2000] 1 WLR 1855. A good recent study is F. Ní Aolain, 'The Evolving Jurisprudence of the European Convention Concerning the Right to Life', (2001) 19 *Netherlands Quarterly of Human Rights* 21.

[35] HRA 1998, s. 6(3)(b).

[36] Note that the restriction on damages attempted by the HRA may not affect actions for damages rooted in pre-existing causes of action, and there is also the additional possibility of exemplary damages: see n. 24 above.

sively interpreted in Strasbourg, so as to bring certain forms of parental chastisement within its reach.[37] There may as a result be a lack of fit between pre-existing UK law on this subject and what the Convention authorities would seem to require. One of the early tests of the reception of the Convention case law will be the extent to which it has achieved a dilution of the old common law line on the appropriateness of parental beatings.[38] It is Article 3 that has also caused schools, National Health Trusts, and other public bodies to be concerned about their possible liability for the bullying of persons—pupils, hospital staff, and so on—for whom they are responsible.[39] A third area of possible importance is the very interesting line of Strasbourg authorities which deploys Article 3 as a means of reversing the burden of proof in cases where a person detained by the authorities has been injured while in custody.[40] The traditional common law position, of course, is that the claimant must prove his or her case. It will be interesting to see whether, as a result of Article 3, the police and prison authorities will find themselves with the primary burden of establishing innocence of maltreatment in cases where what would now be merely an evidential burden has been successfully negotiated by claimants. If this were to happen, the effect on police and prison officer practice might in the medium to long term be extensive.

Articles 4 and 5 concern the prohibition of slavery and the right to liberty respectively, and their implications for tort law need not be extensively rehearsed here, though clearly there will be some interface with the torts of assault, battery, and false imprisonment.[41] Article 6(1) is, however, of very great importance. Insofar as is material, it provides that '[i]n the determination of his civil rights and obligations . . . everyone is entitled to a fair and public hearing within a reasonable time by an independent and impartial tribunal established by law'. Clearly, the common law in the main delivers the safeguards that are to be found set out here, so it would not seem at first glance as though the provision should have much application in UK law. This was indeed the case in the early days, when its main impact was in the sphere of administrative law, which the European Court was able to encompass within Article 6(1) by adopting an expansive approach to the phrase 'determination of civil rights'. In a way that is too complex to be elaborated here, this case law over time produced the concept of an implied right of access to a court, which right only became available, however, where an applicant could show that he or she had an

[37] *A v. United Kingdom* (1998) 27 EHRR 611.

[38] For the way the facts in A were dealt with in domestic law, see ibid. 613–14. The applicant's step-father was found not guilty of assault occasioning actual bodily harm. See now *R v. H*, Court of Appeal Criminal Division, 25 Apr. 2001, [2001] EWCA Cri. 1024 (summing up by judge in prosecution for assault seems to take account of *A v. United Kingdom* when reliance is being placed on defence of reasonable chastisement).

[39] And see *Z v. United Kingdom*, n. 16 above, which imposes a strong duty on public authorities to avoid breaching the Art. 3 rights of those for whom they are responsible.

[40] *Ribitsch v. Austria* (1995) 21 EHRR 573. See further *Satik v. Turkey*, Appl. No. 31866/96 European Court of Human Rights, 10 Oct. 2000.

[41] See J. L. Murdoch, 'Article 5 of the European Convention on Human Rights: The Protection of Liberty and Security of the Person' (H(92)13, Council of Europe, Strasbourg, 1992).

arguable case (at the domestic level) that his or her civil rights had been wrongly interfered with.[42] That these two streams of authority potentially were in contradiction with each other became apparent when they collided in a UK case involving not administrative law in the strict sense but rather the law of tort, or at least that branch of the law dealing with the liability in negligence of public authorities.

In *Osman v. United Kingdom*[43] the main issue related to the liability of the police for the allegedly negligently way that they had failed to protect the applicants' family from attack by a mentally unstable person of whom the authorities were aware. This was an Article 2 point and it was unsuccessful in Strasbourg. It had also failed in the UK courts, where the negligence action had been struck out as disclosing no reasonable cause of action on the authority of *Hill v. Chief Constable of West Yorkshire*.[44] In Strasbourg, however, the European Court went on to hold (unanimously) that the strike-out decision had itself infringed Article 6(1), since it had denied the applicants a proper hearing of their case. On the one hand Article 6(1) was engaged because 'the rule [in *Hill*] does not automatically doom to failure such a civil action [as that initiated by the Osmans] from the outset but in principle allows a domestic court to make a considered assessment on the basis of the arguments before it as to whether a particular case is or is not suitable for the application of the rule'.[45] On the other hand the application of the *Hill* exclusionary rule in this case was too inflexible, and therefore amounted to a breach of Article 6(1) as involving 'a disproportionate restriction on the applicants' right of access to a court'.[46]

The *Osman* decision appears to have wide implications for the strike-out procedure as currently deployed in UK law. The case has been controversial, having received probably more critical comment from a wider range of sources than any other Strasbourg judgment.[47] The underlying rationale of *Osman* is rooted in a reluctance to deny to any litigant the chance to have his or her day in court. This does not, however, mean that limitation periods and other procedural controls on civil litigation need to be struck down; on the contrary, such devices have been routinely upheld in Strasbourg.[48] It seems to have been the particularly decisive nature of the preliminary strike-out on grounds of policy rather than the merits of the case that provoked such a negative reaction from the Strasbourg bench in the *Osman* decision.[49]

The remaining articles of the Convention are likely to be less surprising in their impact on domestic law. Article 8(1)'s guarantee to everyone of 'the right to respect for his private and family life, his home and his correspondence' is subject to vari-

---

[42] See generally C. A. Gearty, 'Unravelling Osman', (2001) 64 *Modern Law Review* 159.
[43] N. 16 above.
[44] [1989] AC 53. The Court of Appeal judgment is reported at *Osman v. Ferguson* [1993] 4 All ER 344.
[45] *Osman*, n. 16 above, para. 138.   [46] Ibid. para. 154.
[47] The literature is reviewed in Gearty, n. 42 above. *Osman* has been sharply modified by the recent decisions of *Z v. United Kingdom*, n. 16 above, and *TP and KM v. United Kingdom*, n. 16 above.
[48] The leading case is *Stubbings v. United Kingdom*, (1996) 23 EHRR 213. See generally Guy Mansfield QC, 'Costs, Conditional Fees and Legal Aid', in R. English and P. Havers QC (eds.), *An Introduction to Human Rights and the Common Law* (Oxford: Hart, 2000), ch. 3.
[49] Cf. *Bromiley v. United Kingdom*, Appl. No. 33747/96, 23 Nov. 1999, (1999) 29 EHRR CD 111; *Powell v. United Kingdom*, Appl. No. 45305/99, 4 May 2000.

ous limitations rooted in what is 'in accordance with the law and is necessary in a democratic society', but despite this the provision is widely expected to have a large effect on the law of tort. Particular attention has been drawn to the tort of nuisance and to the likelihood that that tort will be 'developed' so as to permit actions to be taken by persons who do not have the (currently required) interest in land.[50] As indicated above, it has also been widely anticipated that Article 8 will provide the final push for the common law in its slow march towards a tort of privacy, encompassing actions not only against the state but also as between private individuals.[51] The Douglas/Zeta Jones litigation may well provide the appropriate platform for the emergence of this right to be confirmed.[52] If it does, then the newspapers may well have cause to regret their unanimous and strong support for a bill of rights in the period prior to publication of the Human Rights Bill, their enthusiasm possibly having been based on a high awareness of the value to them of Article 10 without a similar degree of knowledge about the rest of the Convention.

It is certainly the case that Article 10 will be of great assistance to the press and the electronic media in that it unequivocally declares that 'Everyone has the right to freedom of expression' and this is a right that is said explicitly to 'include [the] freedom to hold opinions and to receive and impart information and ideas without interference by public authority and regardless of frontiers'. Though the provision is of course restricted in various ways,[53] in the hands of the European Court of Human Rights it has been moulded into a strong guarantor of press freedom, particularly in the field of political debate and discussion.[54] In the Human Rights Act it is further supplemented by section 12, which sets out various safeguards against the issuance of *ex parte* relief where such a remedy 'might affect the exercise of the Convention right to freedom of expression'.[55] In particular, '[n]o such relief is to be granted so as to restrain publication before trial unless the court is satisfied that the applicant is likely to establish that publication should not be allowed'.[56]

Supplementing Article 10 is the freedom of assembly and association to be found in Article 11. In recent years, a number of cases challenging various aspects of the law on freedom of assembly have reached Strasbourg from the United Kingdom, with the Court having tended to regard these as primarily Article 10 rather than Article 11 cases. However a guarantee of freedom of assembly may have implications for the law on trespass and nuisance; indeed, the spectre of its implementation may already have affected the common law, a point that we consider below.[57] The

---

[50] *Hunter v. Canary Wharf Limited* [1997] AC 655. Cf. *Pemberton v. Southwark London Borough Council* [2000] 3 All ER 924, esp. at 933 and 935.

[51] For a recent survey, see G. Phillipson and H. Fenwick, 'Breach of Confidence as a Privacy Remedy in the Human Rights Era', (2000) 63 *Modern Law Review* 660. For a good exposition of Art. 8's European jurisprudence, see J. Liddy, 'Article 8: The Pace of Change', (2000) 51 *Northen Ireland Legal Quarterly* 397.

[52] N. 15 above.   [53] See Art. 10(2).

[54] The leading case is *Lingens v. Austria*, (1986) 8 EHRR 407.

[55] S. 12(1). See *Imutran Ltd v. Uncaged Campaigns Ltd*, Chancery Division, 11 Jan. 2001.

[56] S. 12(3).

[57] *DPP v. Jones* [1999] 2 AC 240. See however H. Fenwick and G. Phillipson, 'Public Protest, the Human Rights Act and Judicial Responses to Political Expression', [2000] *Public Law* 627.

impact of the right to property which is set out in the First Protocol to the Convention (Article 1) and which has been included in the Human Rights Act may, however, be less dramatic than is hoped by those seeking to protect their possessions and property from what they see as inappropriate governmental intrusion. The safeguard is heavily qualified, and has in any event been conservatively applied by the European Court.[58] Its best hope of success may come in being applied in tandem with Article 14, under which '[t]he enjoyment of the rights and freedoms set forth in this Convention shall be secured without discrimination on any ground such as sex, race, colour, language, religion, political or other opinion, national or social origin, association with a national minority, property, birth or other status'. It will be noted immediately that this is not a free-standing right to equal treatment but is rather parasitic on the other rights set forth in the Convention, a position that will change radically if a new protocol on equality is accepted by the UK government and introduced into domestic law.[59]

III. The ideological structure of the Human Rights Act and the European Convention: three principles[60]

So much for the potential impact of the Convention on domestic law. The large number of articles and textbooks[61] that have poured from the legal presses in the months between enactment of the 1998 Act and its full implementation have sought to capture the essence of the case law from Strasbourg so as to equip readers with a clear understanding of the breadth and range of this all-encompassing new area of law. This has, however, proved a difficult task. The volume of material to be absorbed is enormous: thousands of decisions from the European Commission of Human Rights before its demise following the 1998 reforms to the Convention's structure[62] together with a huge and ever-increasing volume of decisions from the Strasbourg court itself. By the end of 1999 there were 12,635 cases before the Court, but by September 2000 this figure had risen to 15,107. Applications per month are now averaging 855, so despite the Court's effort to dispose of 600 cases a month— its target last year and a huge increase in productivity over recent years—the backlog is certain to grow.[63] To add to these cases must now be included the array of decisions on the 1998 Act that have already begun to pour from domestic courts, a

---

[58] The leading authorities from the UK are *James v. United Kingdom* (1986) 8 EHRR 123; *Lithgow v. United Kingdom* (1986) 8 EHRR 329. Cf. *Parochial Church Council of Aston Cantlow and Wilncote with Billesley, Warwickshire v. Wallbank and Another*, Court of Appeal, 17 May 2001, [2001] EWCA Civ. 713.

[59] Protocol No. 12. Note also that the EU has been active in this area: see Lord Lester of Herne Hill at [2000] *Public Law* 562.

[60] Cf. D. Feldman, 'The Human Rights Act 1998 and Constitutional Principles', (1999) 19 *Legal Studies* 165.

[61] For a review of some of them, see C. A. Gearty (2000) 11 *King's College Law Journal* 291.

[62] See Protocol No. 11, ETS No. 55.

[63] See the comments of the Irish judge on the Strasbourg Court, Judge John Hedigan, speaking at a conference on human rights organized by the Law Society of Ireland: *Irish Times*, 16 Oct. 2000.

stream of authorities that is unlikely to abate in the short to medium term. How is the common lawyer to cope with this explosion of data?

It would seem clear that the old habits of legal research will have to change. The sheer volume of the Strasbourg material, together with the kind of arguments to be found in that case law, make quite inappropriate an approach to the law which involves solely the ferreting out of old cases and their triumphant application to an analogous contemporary situation. The way the Human Rights Act is constructed, with its unusually broad language and its emphasis on Convention case law, confirms this assessment. A deeper understanding of the 1998 Act, and of the Convention that lies behind it, will be needed if the case law is to be fully understood, good legal advice given, and future decisions accurately predicted. At this rather practical level, it is perfectly correct to say that the Human Rights Act will inevitably, sooner or later, change the legal culture in the UK.[64] In particular, it will require a new approach rooted in principle if the Act and the Convention are to be fully understood. It will also require a fresh way of looking at the problems that lie in the way of an effective application of those principles to the facts of the disputes that come before the courts. What follows in the rest of this chapter is a short, inevitably inadequate attempt to make a start on such a project. In this section, I begin by outlining three principles that can be said to underpin the Act. In the next part I sketch out three aspirations with which these principles will need to combine if the Human Rights Act is indeed to realize its promise and the hopes that are entertained for it by its drafters as well as by its many supporters and enthusiasts.

Turning first to principle, it can be said with some confidence that there are three basic ideas which underpin the quasi-constitutional settlement set out in the 1998 Act: the principles of respect for civil liberties, human dignity, and legality. As far as the first of these is concerned, the primary civil liberty, viewed from a theoretical perspective, is the right to vote, and the Convention includes a guarantee 'to hold free elections at reasonable intervals by secret ballot, under conditions which will ensure the free expression of the opinion of the people in the choice of the legislature'.[65] More importantly from the point of view of the case law and the law of tort the Convention's affirmation of the secondary civil liberties of expression, association, and assembly[66] has been interpreted by the European Court of Human Rights in a way which has explicitly prioritized the importance of political speech to the proper functioning of a representative democracy.[67] This has in turn led the Court to set out in a number of important decisions a set of principles emphasizing the importance of press freedom.[68] The effect of Article 10 on the law of defamation has been the subject of the attentions of the Strasbourg court,[69] and the

---

[64] See M. Hunt, 'The Human Rights Act and Legal Culture: The Judiciary and the Legal Profession', (1999) 26 *Journal of Law and Society* 86.

[65] Art. 3 of the First Protocol, included in the 1998 Act, sched. 1.   [66] See Arts. 10 and 11.

[67] *Lingens v. Austria*, n. 54 above.

[68] Notably *Jersild v. Denmark* (1994) 19 EHRR 1; *Fressoz and Roise v. France* (1999) 31 EHRR 28..

[69] See *Tolstoy Miloslavsky v. United Kingdom* (1995) 20 EHRR 442.

Convention's potential for diluting the property-based torts, such as trespass and nuisance, so as to permit peaceful political protest has already had an indirect influence on domestic law.[70] Of course there are grey areas in the application of this principle of respect for civil liberties,[71] but its existence can hardly be gainsaid, and it has been powerfully affirmed in the Human Rights Act, where (as we have seen) the decisions of the representative legislature cannot themselves be overridden by judicial fiat, and where the practical actions needed to make those decisions real on the ground are likewise immunized from challenge.[72] Could there be a more thorough vindication of the primacy of the right to vote (and therefore the principle of civil liberties) than this continuing commitment to the supremacy of the dictates of our representative assembly? At the same time, the lateral application of the Convention to disputes between private parties may infuse the common law of tort with a much wider ethical base than is currently available to it, and in particular allow arguments rooted in civil liberties principles that would previously have been brushed aside.

The second principle to permeate the Human Rights Act and the European Convention is that of respect for human dignity. Here the law of tort will be engaged at many levels. The origins of the European Convention in the post-Second World War period make clear that a recovery of respect for human dignity was perhaps its primary goal. Hence the prominence given at the very start of the Convention's section on rights and freedoms to the right to life, the prohibition of torture, the prohibition of slavery and forced labour, and the right to liberty and security of the person. The freedoms of thought, conscience, and religion[73] and the right to marry[74] also fit easily within this strand, as does Article 8's guarantee of respect for privacy, which has been interpreted by the European Court of Human Rights in a way which has had large implications for the dignity of persons who have been able to argue successfully that domestic law prohibitions on the expression of their sexual orientation have been in breach of this guarantee.[75]

As with the principle of respect for civil liberties, the application of this principle of human dignity has sometimes been controversial, with the Court for example having resolutely refused in recent decisions to extend the protective remit of the Convention to consensual sado-masochistic sexual activity[76] and (less resolutely) to male-to-female transsexuals.[77] The dignity is of the 'possessive individual' as well as of the person as such, so property is protected, and where appropriate even the

---

[70] *Jones v. DPP*, n. 57 above; *Redmond-Bate v. DPP*, Queen's Bench Division, 23 July 1999.

[71] See *Bowman v. United Kingdom* (1998) 26 EHRR 1, criticized in C. A. Gearty, 'Democracy and Human Rights in the European Court of Human Rights: A Critical Appraisal', (2000) 51 *Northern Ireland Legal Quarterly* 381, esp. 392–5.

[72] See HRA 1998, ss. 3(2)(b) and 6(2).   [73] Art. 9.   [74] Art. 12.

[75] *Norris v. Ireland* (1988) 13 EHRR 186; *Dudgeon v. United Kingdom* (1981) 4 EHRR 149. See D. Feldman, 'Privacy-Related Rights and their Social Value', in P. Birks (ed.), *Privacy and Loyalty* (Oxford: Clarendon Press, 1997), 15–50.

[76] *Laskey, Jaggard and Brown v. United Kingdom* (1997) 24 EHRR 39.

[77] *Sheffield and Horsham v. United Kingdom* (1998) 27 EHRR 163.

'dignity'-based provisions of the Convention can be relied upon by corporate and other artificial entities.[78] Once again we note the breadth of the ethical base that underpins the Human Rights Act as opposed to traditional tort law's narrower pre-occupation with interests such as the right to property and freedom of contract.

The third of the principles that I am tentatively suggesting underpins the Convention and the Human Rights Act is the principle of legality. Its power has already been evident in the *SW* and *CR* cases, discussed above. The principle exists at a number of levels of abstraction. At its most basic, some might even say platitudinous, the Convention stands for the idea of the rule of law as opposed to the rule of men, for the notion that the 'common heritage of political traditions, ideals, freedom and the rule of law' should be reflected in a document designed 'to take the first steps for the collective enforcement of certain of the rights stated in the Universal Declaration [of Human Rights]'.[79] This commitment is reflected in the prohibition on punishment without law (Article 7) and in the broadly based guarantee of the right to fair trial set out in Article 6. The pre-eminence of the rule of law is further evident in the degree to which all the qualifications and exceptions that are permitted to the Convention rights are required to be 'prescribed by law', 'in accordance with a procedure prescribed by law' or 'in accordance with the law'. Even where no such qualification appears on the face of the Convention right (such as is the case with Article 6(1)), the judges of the Strasbourg Court have been robust in their assertion of the rule of law over general rules in member states where the effect of these has been, in the Court's judgment, to deprive individuals of the right to have their legal claims adjudicated before their domestic courts. It is into this groove that the line of authorities epitomized by the *Osman* decision fits, with the principle of legality coming close in such a case to being an assertion of judicial primacy in the sphere of public decision-making.[80] It is too early to tell how great an impact on tort law this line of cases is likely to have.

IV. The Human Rights Act: three aspirations

A confident understanding of these three principles should enable the judges in the United Kingdom to find their way through the juristic maze thrown around them by the Human Rights Act. We turn now to three aspirations that need rigorously to be adhered to if the journey through that maze is not to be foiled by diversion into a variety of dead ends. A first aspiration of particular relevance to tort law and civil law generally is what could with semi-irony be called the goal of proportionate intrusion. As we have seen, the Human Rights Act is unique in its potential reach into all areas of law. It is this unprecedented capacity that ministers have had in

---

[78] e.g. *Air Canada v. United Kingdom* (1995) 20 EHRR 150.

[79] See the preamble to the Convention.

[80] See *in re H (A Child) (Adoption: Disclosure)*; *in re G (A Child) (Adoption: Disclosure)* Fam. Div., 30 Nov. 2000, *The Times*, 5 Jan. 2001.

mind when they have called for lawyers operating the Act to display some self-restraint in their deployment of the arguments that it makes possible. Quite whether it is the job of an advocate to engage in this kind of self-censorship is a question that has not yet been fully explored. Much will depend on how the courts respond to arguments that are put before them. Novelty should not be enough in itself to warrant rejection; after all, as Lord Hope has reminded us in *Kebilene*, the entire body of law is in need of fundamental review, with the only question being as to the necessity of such reform (by the judiciary of course) in particular circumstances.[81]

Here a presumption of proportionate interference might be helpful. Is the area of law under scrutiny in such bad shape in terms of any or all of the aforementioned human rights principles that the upheaval which would flow from application of the Human Rights Act is justified, despite the short-term inconvenience? Can the extent of the intrusion of the Human Rights Act be linked to the depth of the mischief at which the Act is aimed? In crude terms, is the mess of the disturbance, in terms of new transaction costs (for e.g. fresh litigation) and the uncertainty of the outcome worth it? A legal justification for such an approach can be contrived by working an old presumption of statutory interpretation (that Parliament acts compatibly with its international law obligations) into a new, slightly grander presumption of compatibility with human rights, which would apply both to past and to future statutes. Countries with written constitutions are familiar with this idea, and it is both inevitable and right that it should develop within the United Kingdom as well.[82]

The second of our guiding aspirations could be thought of as an adjunct of our first, and it also flows out of a realization that with the Human Rights Act it is possible to do everything, so that new criteria apart from mere legal justification become necessary. To phrase the aspiration in the form of a question, is what the court is being asked to do within its institutional competence? To answer the question in any given case, some underlying understanding of the role of the courts in a representative democracy is required.[83] Of course the Human Rights Act has already transferred an extensive legislative power to the judges. But Parliament has not explicitly given away its general policy or resource allocation powers, and it would be quite wrong (though often possible in the narrow legal sense) for the courts to use the Human Rights Act in order to seize the initiative in such areas. Does the country spend enough on health care? on facilities for the disabled? on education? Such questions could be answered in the negative by the courts and different priorities imposed through the deployment of Articles 2, 3, 8, the right to

---

[81] *R v. DPP, ex p. Kebilene* [2000] 2 AC 326 at 374–5.

[82] See e.g. *East Donegal Co-Op Ltd v. Attorney General* [1970] IR 317.

[83] See P. A. McDermott, 'The Separation of Powers and the Doctrine of Non-Justiciability', (2000) 35 *Irish Jurist* (n.s.) 280. See *R v. Camden and Islington Health Authority, ex p. K*, Court of Appeal, 21 Feb. 2001, [2001] EWCA Civ. 240. A remarkable recent decision from Ireland which is at the very boundaries of the judicial function and possibly well beyond them is *Sinnott v. Ireland and the Minister for Education, Irish Times*, 13 Nov. 2000.

education in the first protocol, and the notion of positive state duties. But if this were to happen, what would there be left for the legislature to do? A future as the executive arm of the judicial branch would be a demeaning one for any government, particularly one that has a self-image of having been elected by the people for some more ambitious purpose. Of course there will always be grey areas, where the judiciary has long had a policy input and an indirect financial engagement (the criminal law, the prison system, asylum law) and a continuation of judicial activism can for historical and institutional reasons be expected in these areas. But well-meaning though so many human rights practitioners are, the Human Rights Act neither is nor should become a substitute for politics, and the presentation of a case as one rooted in an action for damages for breach of statutory duty should not be allowed to obscure this fact.

It is likely that the courts will try to meet this aspiration of institutional competence. The new torture/inhuman/degrading treatment cause of action under Article 3 is unlikely to transform the NHS.[84] The positive duty to prevent bullying in schools will not (deliberately at least) be so interpreted as to require the addition of new, anti-bullying staff in schools whose budgets are currently consumed by a desperate search for trained teaching staff. The Article 2 duty to protect life alone cannot and should not be the only engine driving massive reinvestment in the railways, and so on. There may be more problems sticking to our third aspiration for the Act, which is the goal of consistent analytical coherence. That the task ahead is a challenging one is evident from the *Osman* decision.[85] Few claim with any confidence to understand the decision, either in relation to its outcome (are all strike outs an infringement of the Convention?) or its underlying reasoning (how can a case that is domestically arguable one minute be one which has not a chance of success in the next?). The language deployed by the European Court of Human Rights in the course of its judgment makes no concessions whatsoever to any reader who might be unimmersed in the technicalities and complexities of the Court's Article 6(1) jurisprudence as it has developed over many years.

The result of this form of reasoning is a mystifying array of apparently disconnected paragraphs which culminate in a decision that appears to reveal little appreciation of the way in which the strike-out procedure actually works in the tort of negligence.[86] Similar (though less severe) difficulties are encountered when trying to understand other parts of Article 6(1), such as what is meant by a 'civil right' and what is required by the guarantee of a 'fair and public hearing'. The British judges have the double challenge of retaining analytical coherence while at the same time seeking both to understand the Strasbourg case law and to apply it within the

---

[84] See *R v. North West Lancashire Health Authority, ex p. A, D, G* [2000] 1 WLR 977; *Powell v. United Kingdom*, n. 49 above.

[85] N. 16 above.

[86] For an excellent critique from a tort law perspective, see M. Lunney, 'A Tort Lawyer's View of *Osman v. United Kingdom*', (1999) 10 *King's College Law Journal* 238. See now *Z v. United Kingdom*, n. 16 above, and *TP and KM v. United Kingdom*, n. 16 above.

jurisdiction. Fortunately, section 2 of the Human Rights Act gives them some freedom of manoeuvre in that (as we have seen) it does not require such decisions to be followed, merely taken into account.

As if the difficulties posed by the Convention jurisprudence were not enough, a further series of analytical booby traps are to be found scattered across the body of the Human Rights Act itself. Universally acclaimed as a magnificent piece of drafting, the Act's cleverness may return to haunt it.[87] What is the relationship between the Convention rights and the safeguard for existing rights (section 11), the freedom of expression guarantee (section 12) and the protection for the freedom of thought, conscience and religion (section 13), all also to be found in the 1998 Act? If only a 'victim' can take a Human Rights Act case, may only a victim make human rights arguments in court?[88] How will the attempt to restrict damages in section 8 fit with the guarantee that a reliance on a Convention right does not restrict a person's 'right to make any claim or bring any proceedings which he [or she] could make or bring apart from sections 7 to 9' (section 11(b))?

At an even more technical level, which bodies are 'public authorities' or can be said to be exercising 'functions of a public nature' so as to be liable for breach of statutory duty under section 6(1) whenever they infringe Convention rights? If a person is the latter rather than the former, does this mean that (unlike the former) it may be as reckless as it desires in Convention terms in its own private time while rigidly adhering to the Human Rights Act in its public business? Will not this distinction produce an avalanche of procedural litigation beside which the *O'Reilly v. Mackman*-inspired[89] mistakes of long ago will appear insignificant? And does it matter anyway, in light of the inclusion of the courts and tribunals as public authorities: does this mean that such bodies are bound in their rulings to adhere to the Convention even where there is no public authority in the case before them, since for Convention purposes they are a sufficient public authority in themselves for the section 6(1) duty to bite?[90] It would be disastrous if the Human Rights Act were to become primarily a part of UK procedural rather than substantive law, but careful management will be required for this fate to be comprehensively avoided once the Act begins to bite in the civil as opposed to the criminal sphere (where its remit has so far been relatively uncontroversial).

V. Conclusion

From the ivory tower, it is easy to see (or to believe that one can see) the right path ahead for the Human Rights Act. It is a bridge into a new legal environment, with

---

[87] A very perceptive critique is that of D. Morris, 'The Human Rights Act: Too Many Loose Ends?', (2000) 21 *Statute Law Review* 104.

[88] Cf. *R v. Weir* [2001] 1 WLR 421 (HL).   [89] *O'Reilly v. Mackman* [1983] 2 AC 237.

[90] See s. 6(3)(a). The literature and case law on the application of the HRA to private disputes is likely to be vast; for a selection see the articles cited at n. 29 above. See now *Douglas v. Hello! Limited*, n. 15 above.

an array of prizes beckoning if the legislation can be properly deployed. For the law of tort the trophy is a branch of law newly energized by principle and with a broader and more ethical base than has ever existed in the past. Were section 6(3)(a) to lead to the infusion of Convention rights into the common law, superseding the old bias towards property with a new, broader ethical base, then not only would pre-existing torts be renewed but fresh causes of action reflecting this new moral order would also over time be fashioned. The same result would be achieved by a section 3(1) reworking of the statute-based law of tort. The principles outlined above, of respect for civil liberties, dignity, and legality, would discipline the flood of litigation, determining which cases would succeed and which would not, and the interaction between these principles and the aspirations of proportionate intrusion, institutional competence, and analytical coherence (also discussed above) would ensure that the right balance was maintained between the various branches of government in our representative democracy.

It is a tempting scenario, but will it happen? It is not what Parliament meant, nor the words that it used, but litigation that will be the driving force behind the Human Rights Act. The politicians, having had their say, will drop from the scene, handing over responsibility to the judiciary. And there is no greater enemy of strategic thinking than adversarial litigation. Judges might have an intuitive feel of where they want the Act to go, they might even have read Dworkin and think of themselves as Herculean in their potential to do principled good.[91] But they are stuck with the litigants that force themselves to their attention, with the priorities set by the legal advisers to such litigants, and with the still essential truth that, quasi-legislature though they now are, their principal responsibility remains not the explicit promulgation of general rules (after rational analysis as to their long term utility) but rather the discharge of their ancient function of deciding as between two competing parties on which side the law should come down. We may have hugely empowered the judiciary by giving them the Human Rights Act, but we have chosen resolutely to persist in our pretence that all they still do is decide what the law is in cases involving two parties in dispute. This lack of fit between appearance (adjudicating disputes) and reality (generating through such adjudications general rules) means that the Human Rights Act is not likely to follow any rational course, of the type outlined above, or indeed of any other type. Instead it will be buffeted on the waves of litigation, thrown back and forth between various litigants, sometimes doing good, sometimes doing bad, occasionally being washed up on useless analytical islands where it will be stuck for years on end until a rescue by some tidal wave of fresh thinking, only to be buffeted endlessly in some new direction. The only thing of which we can be sure is that in ten years' time human rights law will be unrecognizable to us today. And so, almost certainly, will the law of tort.

---

[91] R. Dworkin, *Taking Rights Seriously* (London: Duckworth, 1977), esp. 105–30.

14

Criminal Justice, Judicial Interpretation, Legal Right: On Being Sceptical about the Human Rights Act 1998

ALAN NORRIE

The passing of the Human Rights Act 1998 into effective law is upon us, requiring a response from academic lawyers as from practitioners. My initial response is complex. While not a protagonist of human rights law, nor am I a legal nihilist. I find the rhetoric around the Human Rights Act unconvincing, but I think the Act will have practical, though not far-reaching, effects, and some of these may be positive. Andrew Ashworth has written that one might take a cynical or a constructive view of the Act,[1] and that one might be either a minimalist or a maximalist,[2] or, most recently, a 'non-minimalist'.[3] This range of possibilities misses out that which covers my own position, which is that of the sceptic, and in this chapter, I explore what that means.

I focus on the Human Rights Act vis-à-vis criminal justice. This is one area where it is likely to be potentially of great relevance because of questions concerning the relationship between the individual and the state raised by the criminal process. Whether the Act will have much impact is another question. Article 6(1) of the European Convention on Human Rights (ECHR) states that in 'the determination . . . of any criminal charge against him, everyone is entitled to a fair and public hearing'. Article 6(2) states that 'Everyone charged with a criminal offence shall be presumed innocent until proved guilty according to law'. Article 6(3) spells out certain minimum rights which derive from these positions. These are broad statements of principle which one might think could have a substantial impact on the system. According to one influential view, English criminal justice, with its emphasis on 'case construction' by the police and courts, operates with a system of presumptive guilt rather than innocence. Andrew Sanders writes that criminal justice serves broad functions of social integration and exclusion in which 'the system prioritises authority and control over the less powerful above justice, the Rule of Law, and the

Thanks to Elaine Player and Andrew Sanders for their comments on a draft of this chapter.

[1] *Principles of Criminal Law*, 3rd edn. (Oxford: Oxford University Press, 1999), 66.
[2] 'The European Convention and Criminal Law', in Centre for Public Law, University of Cambridge, *The Human Rights Act and the Criminal Justice and Regulatory Process* (Oxford: Hart, 1999).
[3] 'The Human Rights Act and the Substantive Criminal Law: A Non-Minimalist View', [2000] *Criminal Law Review* 564.

interests of victims'.[4] In practice this means that 'Even in court the presumption of innocence is compromised by the erosion of the right of silence, the guilty plea system, and bail systems whereby most decisions are made on the basis of police information'.[5]

This kind of view is based on the systematic accumulation of sophisticated empirical evidence over many years.[6] If it is accepted, the whole idea of what is meant by a fair trial is thrown into doubt by any serious investigation of the English system based on human rights principles. That the ECHR could indeed have a radical impact on the criminal justice system is supported by John Spencer's detailed comparison of English and continental systems of justice concerning the practice of sentencing discount for a guilty plea. This is a structural or systemic feature of English criminal justice. It has been the focus of empirical and normative inquiry and criticism over many years. It leads continental jurists to ask how 'routinely giving heavier sentences to [those who] exercise their right to make the State prove them guilty . . . is compatible with the 'fair trial' requirement of Article 6(1)'.[7] How is it possible under such a system to 'avoid innocent persons being pressured to admit crimes they did not commit by the threat of heavier punishment if they continue to assert their innocence'? Spencer concludes that while the desirability of this practice 'seems to be the one single issue on which judges, barristers and Home Office officials habitually agree',[8] English practice may well be fundamentally at odds with Article 6.

I will return to the question of the sentencing discount below, but for the moment let me simply contrast this radical view of the disparity between ECHR principle and English practice with that of David Thomas. He suggests that 'Conformity to the Convention will not demand a complete restructuring of the sentencing system'.[9] Rather, it will lead to the crystallization of a small number of issues which may need to be resolved in its light. Certainly, the attitude of the judges, such as Lord Bingham, has been to follow the Thomas rather than the Spencer line:

While I do not intend to downplay the importance of the Convention or to disparage its significance, I do think it important that we keep our feet on the ground. Our procedures for

---

[4] 'From Suspect to Trial', in M. Maguire, R. Morgan, and R. Reiner, *The Oxford Handbook of Criminology*, 2nd edn. (Oxford: Oxford University Press, 1997), 1085.

[5] Ibid. 1084.

[6] See e.g. M. McConville, A. Sanders, and R. Leng, *The Case for the Prosecution* (London: Routledge, 1991), M. McConville, J. Hodgson, L. Bridges, and A. Pavlovic, *Standing Accused* (Oxford: Oxford University Press, 1994); S. Choongh, *Policing as Social Discipline* (Oxford: Oxford University Press, 1997). A. Sanders and R. Young, *Criminal Justice*, 2nd edn. (London: Butterworths, 2000) is an excellent compilation and analysis of the research.

[7] J. Spencer, 'The European Convention and the Rules of Criminal Procedure and Evidence in England', in Centre for Public Law, n. 2 above, 59.

[8] Ibid. 60. For further discussion, see R. Henham, 'Bargain Justice or Justice Denied? Sentence Discounts and the Criminal Process' (1999) 62 *Modern Law Review* 515.

[9] D. Thomas, 'Incorporating the European Convention on Human Rights; Its Impact on Sentencing', in Centre for Public Law, n. 2 above, 81.

arresting, charging, interrogating and identifying suspects and trying those accused of crime have been the subject of constant review over the last two or three decades, and have been the subject of comprehensive consideration by two Royal Commissions. We have not, doubtless, achieved a perfect answer . . . [but] I think we have every reason to believe that in most respects we comply with Convention standards. . . . We should not be too ready to find breaches of Articles 5 and 6, which are after all based on principles we have all been brought up to respect.[10]

The question is, which of these two views, the radical or the cautious, will win out? My answer is that it will be the latter on the basis of consideration of the legal and political contexts in which the Act has been introduced, and also of the form of right it recognizes. The essay pursues two related directions. On one hand, I consider reactions to the Human Rights Act and how it is likely to be interpreted. On the other, I am concerned at a deeper level with how the Act might or might not be used to interrogate the underlying structural and systemic features of the criminal justice system. These two directions are linked in that how judges interpret the Act vis-à-vis criminal justice will depend on how they perceive the operation of the criminal justice system and vice versa. More fundamentally, there is a question about the nature of the Act itself and how its form might legitimate a defence of the status quo rather than promote significant change. My scepticism about the Act stems from the view that both the *context of legal interpretation* and the *form of legal right* are conducive to its being a disappointment.

I. The context of legal interpretation

The legal context

I begin with a brief examination of the progress of human rights jurisprudence in the European Court and as it is emerging in the House of Lords. These are early days and all due caution must be exercised, but a likely approach is seen in the House of Lords case of *R v. DPP ex p. Kebeline*.[11] This was a case of judicial review of a decision of the Director of Public Prosecutions to prosecute three Algerian nationals under section 16A of the Prevention of Terrorism (Temporary Provisions) Act 1989. Under this provision, there is a reversal of the burden of proof in relation to findings of articles which might be used for terrorist purposes. Where such articles are found on private premises occupied by a person, this gives rise to a rebuttable presumption that they were in the possession of that person. Such a provision, it was argued, runs counter to Article 6(2) of the European Convention, which holds that 'Everyone charged with a criminal offence shall be presumed innocent until proved guilty according to law'.

The House of Lords' judgment in *Kebeline* was given in October 1999, a year before the coming into force of the Human Rights Act. That did not stop some of

---

[10] Lord Bingham CJ, 'Keynote Speech', ibid. xii.   [11] [1999] 3 WLR 972.

the judges from considering the likely effect of the Act on the issues raised, and it is interesting to see the differing views that were taken. In partial support of a reading of the 1989 Act as incompatible with Article 6(2), Lord Cooke noted that Article 6(2) was a 'straightforward provision'. To 'introduce concepts of reasonable limits, balance or flexibility, as to none of which Article 6(2) says anything, may be seen as undermining or marginalising [its] philosophy'.[12] While the Article might be 'highly inconvenient', it was 'at best . . . doubtful whether Article 6(2) can be watered down to an extent that would leave section 16A unscathed'. Having said this, however, Lord Cooke suggested two avenues whereby his own conclusion might be evaded. It was not possible, first, to exclude the possibility that the European Court might 'treat terrorism as a special subject or perhaps to found a reading down on "according to law" '.[13] Second, it might be possible to save the section by interpreting it as establishing an evidential but not a persuasive burden of proof on the defendant.

Lord Cooke's hedged view must be read alongside the more developed position of Lord Hope, which begins with the seemingly liberal observation that 'a generous and purposive construction is to be given to that part of a constitution which protects and entrenches fundamental rights and freedoms'.[14] What such a construction might entail is developed in a section of his speech headed 'The Discretionary Area of Judgment'. There, his Lordship first incorporates the concept of a 'margin of appreciation' into the interpretation of domestic law. While such a concept is not directly relevant to domestic law, it is nonetheless indicative of a general need to recognize that the ECHR is a 'living system [which] does not need to be applied uniformly by all states but may vary . . . according to local needs and conditions'.[15] Such a view translates into the recognition by the national courts that the ECHR is 'an expression of fundamental principles rather than . . . a set of mere rules' and that this 'will involve questions of balance between competing interests and issues of proportionality'.[16] This will give rise to 'an area of judgment within which the judiciary will defer, on democratic grounds, to the considered opinion of the elected body or person whose act or decision is said to be incompatible'.[17] Note then that the generosity of construction supposedly required for a provision protecting fundamental rights and freedoms turns into a way of interpreting such rights and freedoms *against* that which is labelled fundamental in favour of balance, proportionality and deference to elected bodies.

On this basis, Lord Hope doubts whether section 16A is necessarily incompatible with Article 6(2), and adduces 'the question of balance, as to the interests of the individual as against those of society'.[18] He cites European authority in favour of his standpoint that 'account may legitimately be taken, in striking the right balance, of the problems which the legislation was designed to address'. Such jurisprudence suggests that even where an article, such as 6(2), is expressed in absolute terms, it is

---

[12] [1999] 3 WLR 986.   [13] Ibid. 987.   [14] Ibid. 988.   [15] Ibid. 993.
[16] Ibid. 994.   [17] Ibid.   [18] Ibid. 997.

not necessarily regarded as 'imposing an absolute prohibition on reverse onus clauses'.[19]

Three points emerge from this early essay in interpretation of the Human Rights Act 1998. The first is that both Lords foresee the possibility of a 'balancing' or tempering of what Ashworth terms 'strong' Convention rights[20] against the needs of the situation. In this regard, they are replicating the standing conflict in English criminal jurisprudence between 'principle' and 'policy' so that there is no difference in judicial reasoning despite the fact that the Act establishes a seemingly principled basis for judgment. It makes no real difference as to how the judges interpret their task: with a swift rhetorical flourish, the new instrument is brought under the old regime of interpretation.

Or perhaps it does make a difference, but in the opposite direction from that imagined by supporters of the Act. Consider what the effect of human rights jurisprudence might be on judicial interpretation of the substantive criminal law. Over the past thirty years, it has been customary in this area for the judges to feel themselves constrained by considerations of principle and, where they reject these, to be slightly embarrassed to admit that alternative purposes—'policy' or 'commonsense'—should prevail. The need for an individualist, 'principled', common law has been to the fore in their thinking even though such principles are not formally articulated rules of law. What is interesting about the Human Rights Act is that it affirms the importance of principle as a part of the law, but in so broad a way that it invites accommodation to those contingencies of the situation which are caught under the rubric of 'policy' in the conventional view. The paradox is that this new 'principled' approach invites the judges more openly to articulate the 'policy' considerations than had previously been the case. The result of this may be a general opening of the door to policy arguments against those based on principle. As the judges get their heads around the kinds of argument already articulated by Lord Hope, it could be that the human rights jurisprudence works *against* the importance of principled argument. An *open-textured* principled approach may do as much damage as good to questions of individual liberty and justice.

The second point concerns the influence of the European jurisprudence on the British approach. While Lord Cooke appears more inclined to uphold principle against policy, he wonders if the European Court might not be inclined to see terrorism as involving a 'special case'. Similarly, Lord Hope cites European authority for just the kind of flexible interpretation he adopts. Of reverse presumptions, the European Court has held in *Salabiaku v. France*[21] that countries must 'remain within certain limits', explaining these as 'reasonable limits which take into account the importance of what is at stake and maintain the rights of the defence'. An observation so 'Delphic'[22] as this plainly leaves plenty room for manoeuvre.

---

[19] Ibid.   [20] N. 1 above, 65.   [21] (1988) 13 EHRR 379.
[22] Sir R. Buxton, 'The Human Rights Act and the Substantive Criminal Law', [2000] *Criminal Law Review* 331, 339.

The general point is that, as Ashworth notes, the European case law does not always 'shine as [a] beacon of enlightenment'.[23] Even where a step forward is taken in terms of protecting human rights it seems to be accompanied by one back. While *McCann v. UK*[24] held that the UK had violated the right to life of three suspected IRA members shot dead in Gibraltar, *Andronicou and Constantinou v. Cyprus*[25] held that wild shooting by the forces of the state did not contravene Article 2. In other high-profile European cases involving English law, the European Court has not upheld seemingly strong complaints. The criminalization of consensual sado-masochistic activity (*R v. Brown*,[26] appealed in *Laskey, Jaggard and Brown*[27] under Article 8) and the judicial declaration that forcible sex within marriage was rape (*R v. R*,[28] appealed in *SW v. UK; CR v. UK*[29] under Article 7) were not held to be in contravention of the Convention.

None of this is to say that the European Court's position will give the English courts *carte blanche* to ignore challenges to English practice or authority, but it is to suggest that there will generally be sufficient leeway for the kind of flexible approach adopted in *Kebilene*. It is true that some practices will come under scrutiny, such as the use of the *contra bonos mores* test for binding over (*Hashman and Harrup v. UK*).[30] But even here, as Sir Richard Buxton points out,[31] the English approach had already been attacked by the Law Commission, so might have been thought a sitting duck for Strasbourg.

This leads to a third point about enactment of the human rights legislation. It is that the coming into force of the Human Rights Act 1998 may make the decisions of the English judges *less* susceptible to criticism from Europe. As Lord Justice Laws has observed of the 'margin of appreciation' doctrine, this 'may be *greater* than has up to the present time been accorded by Strasbourg to our domestic governmental decision-makers, since . . . our judges will for the first time be adjudicating directly on Convention rights. . . .'[32] The European Court may be more reluctant to criticize English law where it has been scrutinized for human rights issues by the English legal system.

Putting together the British attitude to interpretation of the 1998 Act and the character of Convention jurisprudence before the European Court, we are left with a pretty convincing picture that the 1998 Act is unlikely to disturb conventional UK attitudes to adjudication, or what the issues to be adjudicated are. The forms of the debate may change as a new language comes into place, and much expensive legal activity is to be expected, but the overall result is likely to be pretty much business as usual. This is already the declared attitude of Lord Bingham, as we have seen. Confirmation is provided by Lord Justice Laws, who depicts the incorporation of the Convention as no more than a continuation of what the common law has always done. It is not 'an alien add-on . . . because the principles of freedom and fairness

---

[23] N. 3 above, 565.   [24] (1996) 21 EHRR 97.   [25] (1998) 25 EHRR 491.
[26] [1994] 1 AC 212.   [27] (1997) 24 EHRR 39.   [28] [1992] 1 AC 599.
[29] (1995) 21 EHRR 363.   [30] [2000] *Criminal Law Review* 185.   [31] N. 22 above, 333.
[32] Lord Justice Laws, 'An Overview', in Centre for Public Law, n. 2 above, p. xiii.

which the Convention enshrines are the very principles respected by the common law'.[33] Little change, then, is to be expected.

The sociopolitical context

Is this unduly pessimistic? What would stop a radical interpretation of Convention rights? For A. T. H. Smith, there is a degree of unpredictability as to how the judiciary will respond, and he cites the New Zealand Bill of Rights as an example where there was a perception in advance of implementation that it would be toothless. Yet this was a case where 'it did not take the judiciary long to shake the media, the legal profession, politicians and the public out of its apathy'.[34] Enactment of the New Zealand Bill of Rights 'coincided with a spring-tide of judicial enthusiasm for the enforcement of fundamental rights and control of government power'.[35] Why should the same not occur here?

The answer to this question relates to the differing social and political contexts facing the New Zealand judiciary in the 1980s prior to the enactment of the Bill of Rights and the British judiciary in the first decade of the twenty-first century. The former context was one that was comparable to the early experience of Thatcherism in the United Kingdom. In 1984 a new Labour government was elected in New Zealand which sought to undo the protectionist and welfarist approach of previous governments to the economy in favour of an aggressive, privatizing, neo-liberal strategy. According to Jane Kelsey, implementation of the new economic strategy by reformers did not allow

any room for dissent, or even discussion, over their basic assumption that the pursuit of an internationally competitive market economy and the retrenchment of the welfare state would ultimately benefit all New Zealanders. . . . [They] required the paring of state bureaucracy and services to the bone. Paradoxically, they also required a strong central state to drive through their programmes, thus minimising the risk of scrutiny by democratic processes, the vagaries of political decision-making and the influence of electoral interests and sector-group politics. In these terms, healthy participatory democracy was a threat to the success of the reform programme, and indeed to the national interest itself.[36]

In a context of increasing conflict, in which the forces of a 'strong state' threatened consensual legitimizing mechanisms of accountability, inclusiveness, and welfare, judges like Sir Robin Cooke (now Lord Cooke in the House of Lords) became increasingly vociferous in favour of concepts of legal right and fairness. To defend fairness, he drew on the concept of a common law which was 'of its very nature . . . an instrument of principled justice capable of fresh life and vigour'.[37] The aim was

---

[33] Ibid.

[34] Taggart, *Constitutional Reform* (1988), quoted in A. T. H. Smith, 'The Human Rights Act 1998: The Constitutional Context', in Centre for Public Law, n. 2 above, 9.

[35] P. Rishworth, quoted in Lord Irvine of Lairg, LC, 'Activism and Restraint: Human Rights and the Interpretive Process', in Centre for Public Law, n. 2 above, 21.

[36] J. Kelsey, *Rolling Back the State* (Wellington: Bridget Williams, 1993), 28.

[37] Quoted ibid. 196.

to restore fairness within a 'more or less common set of values and that this value [i.e. fairness] be high among them'.[38] While New Zealand was 'in many respects a vocal and divided society', Cooke believed that 'the ideal of fairness and a sense of what it requires in particular cases is quite strongly evident'.[39] In other words, Cooke deployed the rhetoric and resources of the common law on behalf of a consensual conception of fairness against the prevailing political programmes of a divisive and 'unfair' state in a period of polarization and conflict. It was such an attitude which animated, albeit briefly, the more vigorous uses of the Bill of Rights when it came into force.

Compare this historical backdrop to judicial activism around human rights with the state of the British polity in the year 2001. The Human Rights Act 1998 is a product of the present 'New Labour' government, and is part of the raft of constitutional provisions which constitute its main programme. These include devolution and reform of the House of Lords. What kind of programme is this? In comparison to the aggressive neo-liberalism that accompanied human rights legislation and judicial activism in New Zealand, New Labour's programme lacks anything very much in the way of radicalism, left or right, at any level. Indeed, following in the wake of the slow demise of Thatcherism, it is marked by a conscious lack of desire to do anything other than maintain a steady, middle-of-the-road course. Economically, New Labour has reaped the 'benefits' of the period of neo-liberal global expansion, and its main *raison d'être* is to maintain these. However, to gain office, it needed politically to provide the appearance of a radical programme that could be dressed up as a project for government over a five- to ten-year period. One way of achieving this was a process of constitutional reform to address some perceived needs (such as devolution or reform of the House of Lords) without doing anything that rocked the economic boat. Constitutional reform became a symbolic 'modernizing' substitute for a programme of real social and economic change, a way of doing as little as possible to the status quo while appearing to offer a significant 'third way' agenda.

In Tom Nairn's description, New Labour's policy was dictated by 'over-adaptation to the economics of Thatcherism and deregulated liberalism, extreme canniness over all matters fiscal and financial, and a convert-like disavowal of Socialist money-throwing antics', and these 'became the surprising preconditions of renewal and change'.[40] But this foundation of New Labour policy would generate a sterile conservatism unless it was accompanied by 'an ostentatious, perfectly sincere and fireproof form of "radicalism" ' to balance that tendency. Labour had to 'offset their mummified economics with an ostentatious display of verbosely political radicalism'[41] in which the radical was a half-hearted project of state modernization. Oddly, Nairn mentions a number of manifestations of this, such as reform of the House of Lords, a 'half-Freedom of Information Act', reform of the monarchy, joining Europe

---

[38] J. Kelsey, *Rolling Back the State* (Wellington: Bridget Williams, 1993). 196.   [39] Ibid.
[40] T. Nairn, 'Ukania under Blair', (2001) 1 *New Left Review* 73.   [41] Ibid.

(eventually), but he misses one of the most noteworthy developments: the Human Rights Act. Surely this is an archetypal piece of New Labour legislation. It has been propagandized by Cherie Booth, a human rights lawyer and New Labour supporter, as 'modernising Britain to make it a strong and confident democracy in the 21st century'. It is to create 'a new culture in which people respect each other's human rights and where rights are balanced against responsibilities', and to represent (unsurprisingly) 'the third way: a vision of human rights enjoyed by individuals on an equal basis and in a strong community'.[42]

Precisely what this means is unclear; like much New Labour rhetoric, it occupies a woolly place where words are all things to all people. In that, it is no different from most political slogans, but the point is that these are New Labour slogans, and the Human Rights Act is a New Labour piece of legislation. It therefore fits into the general framework of a 'government whose pretensions were to virtual radicalism alone. Or (more precisely) to virtuality fused with profound caution and a mounting sense of stately duty.'[43]

But what of the judges? It is one thing to assert that a government's purposes extend only to the appearances of radicalism, but it is another to consider the judges' likely response to the material they are asked to work with. Why should the judiciary still not take a radical approach to the legislation, despite the wishes of the government? The answer to this is that, in the abstract, there is no reason why it should not, but in context, the prevailing climate is one that does not provoke radicalism either of the left or of the right. Unlike the New Zealand context of a polarized and conflictual political situation, the UK context is that of the middle of the road. Judges are encouraged by the present Home Secretary to fulfil the comforting, consensual function of applying a 'purposive approach' to 'create a fair and decent society, not to let criminals off the hook'.[44] This seems a role that British judges would be happy to play, one that reflects their own 'common law attitude' to the achievement of balance and consensus. It is only in a situation where the political system is out of kilter with these values that a New Zealand-style judicial radicalism (which proved only to be temporary) has much chance of getting off the ground.

II. The form of legal right

The above comments might be thought to give rise to only a limited scepticism. Granted that the judges may be conservative and cautious and that the political climate may encourage this, these are not criticisms of the Human Rights Act per se, but of its interpretation. My scepticism so far tells us little about the Act itself. At this point I want to introduce some considerations concerning the formal structure

---

[42] C. Booth and R. Singh, *Daily Telegraph*, 7 Aug. 2000.   [43] Nairn, n. 40 above, 88.
[44] J. Straw, *Guardian*, Aug. 2000.

of those human rights which the Act introduces, and to suggest that there is reason to be sceptical about the very idea of individual human rights, certainly insofar as these are introduced by the Act. The basic objection concerns the limits of the legal individualism which lies at its core. I begin with some observations about legal individualism, and then consider how these might be translated into an analysis of the criminal process. From there, I return to the issue of the sentencing discount raised in my introductory comments and consider how the Act might address it.

Expressive and repressive characteristics of the legal subject

In previous work on the theory of punishment and the substantive criminal law,[45] I have examined the nature of criminal justice as it is constructed around the form of the abstract legal subject, an individual attributed with certain general powers of personhood such as reasoning, intentionality, and agency. Such an individual is central to the liberal theory of criminal justice. It operates as a generic subject producing a conception of individual responsibility which can legitimate punishment. The legal subject expresses important liberal norms concerning the irreducible value of, and therefore respect for, the individual within the criminal process. It is an attractive Kantian model affirming the freedom and rights of the responsible individual. Let us characterize what it does under this description as its *expressive* function.

At the same time, however, the abstract legal individual has a darker side. It can be seen as a limited ideological figure, a homunculus that excludes and represses important moral and political features of human life. Focusing on generic characteristics of the person, it ignores issues of the social context in which persons operate and thereby excludes questions of structural or social responsibility for individual acts. By regarding the individual as the source of responsibility, society is able to ignore the broader nature of crime and criminality and its links with injustice and inequality. Abstract legal responsibility becomes a convenient way of 'blaming the victim'. Let us call this its *repressive* function. Thus the legal individual in one and the same moment expresses and represses certain moral truths about individuals. On the one hand human beings are responsible and intentional persons worthy of respect; on the other, their human powers only operate within social relations which condition, contextualize, and are *sine qua non* for what they do. Through this double play of expression and repression, the legal individual 'stands up for' the human being granted legal personality, but in the same moment isolates and condemns him as the hypostasized subject of blame and punishment. This is the Janus-faced character of the legal subject.[46]

Could one apply this model, developed out of interrogation of the legal subject in the theory of punishment and the substantive criminal law, to the criminal process more generally? A good place to start would be Herbert Packer's famous treatment

---

[45] A. Norrie, *Crime, Reason and History*, 2nd edn. (London: Butterworths, 2001).
[46] Ibid. 221–5.

of the criminal justice system as reflecting opposing ideals of due process and crime control.[47] I suggest that the expressive role of liberal legal subjectivity is observed in his due process model. To the 'administrative, almost . . . managerial, model'[48] of crime control reflected in the practice of criminal process practitioners, Packer opposes a legal due process model imposing juridical limits on administrative discretion. Such a model asserts 'the primacy of the individual' and 'limitation on official power' and 'fosters personal privacy and . . . the dignity of the individual'.[49] In short, it controls 'encroachment on the area of human freedom'[50] by affirming the liberal subject. Andrew Sanders and Richard Young describe the workings of Packer's two models in the following (simplified) way:

> Crime control values prioritise the conviction of the guilty, even at the risk of the conviction of some (fewer) innocents, and with the cost of infringing the liberties of the suspects to achieve its goals; while due process values prioritise the acquittal of the innocent, even if risking the frequent acquittal of the guilty, and giving high priority *to the protection of civil liberties as an end in itself.*[51]

Thus it seems that the due process model endorses an expressive view of the liberal subject as the *persona* that stands up for the human person. But if due process affirms the civil liberties of the subject, can it also be said to have a repressive quality?

Repression and the guilty plea

Mike McConville has recently argued that what he calls the 'juridification' of the defendant is an important feature of the English criminal justice system.[52] By this, he refers to the way in which the system relies upon a series of 'responsible', 'knowing' decisions 'freely' undertaken by the defendant *qua* legal subject as the basis for its smooth operation. Yet the defendant's decisions are taken in circumstances where she may have scant control and where her practical experience is of dependency, ignorance, and being without choice. Citing the empirical case of 'Janet Smith', McConville shows how in a series of interactions with her defence lawyer, the defendant's experience of her action as innocent became translated into a guilty plea, for which she carried full responsibility:

> The lived experience . . . contrasted markedly with the juridical characterisation of her encounter with the law. For the law, Janet Smith was the super-competent, all-powerful actor, the animating force behind the entry of the guilty plea . . . freely entered into, voluntary, and for which she took . . . full responsibility. The facts needed to establish guilt were before the court, accepted by her, and urged upon the court by her own lawyer carrying out her instructions.[53]

---

[47] H. Packer, *The Limits of the Criminal Sanction* (Stanford. Calif.: Stanford University Press, 1968).
[48] Ibid. 159.   [49] Ibid. 165.   [50] Ibid. 179.
[51] Sanders and Young, n. 6 above, 25–6 (emphasis added).
[52] M. McConville, 'Plea Bargaining: Ethics and Politics', (1998) 25 *Journal of Law and Society* 562.
[53] Ibid. 576.

Janet Smith, the formally free legal subject, entered into a guilty plea where her (not unreasonable, as McConville shows) understanding of what happened indicated that she was not guilty. The example shows how the concept of the free legal subject becomes not the expressive subject who 'speaks up for' the defendant, but rather an auto-repressive subject who condemns herself 'out of her own mouth'. It is legal subjectivity, extolled by the expressive, due process model of criminal justice, that also represses the human being both graced and hidden by its form.[54] For McConville, actors in the criminal process are accorded characteristics as 'autonomous and rational individuals making free . . . and voluntary choices' not to defend themselves but to legitimate the guilty pleas they make, often against their will or instinct. Legal empowerment does not compensate for social disempowerment, it perfects it. Defendants ' "initiate" plea discussions and "instruct" counsel to act on their behalf', taking 'sole responsibility for the guilty plea'. In so doing, 'the classic fictions of freedom of contract are perpetuated [in] the criminal justice process'[55] by the abstract legal subject.

McConville's argument concerns juridification as a recent phenomenon related to the increasing pressure placed on the criminal process to produce results with diminished resources through the 'commodification' of cases. Yet he acknowledges that juridification has always been part of the process. In the context of sentence bargaining and discount, consider *R v. Turner*,[56] for thirty years the leading authority on the question of what indication it is acceptable for a judge to give defence counsel as to the sentence he will impose. The starting point in *Turner* is that counsel 'must be free to . . . give the accused the best advice he can and, if need be, in strong terms'. This includes advice that a guilty plea 'might enable the court to give a lesser sentence'. In addition, there must be 'freedom of access between counsel and judge' to discuss *inter alia* 'whether it would be proper, in a particular case, for the prosecution to accept a plea to a lesser offence'. However, the judge should 'never indicate the sentence . . . he is minded to impose', for this could be 'taken to be undue pressure on the accused, thus depriving him of that complete freedom of choice which is essential'.[57] What the judge can do is indicate whether a particular sentence will be imposed regardless of whether or not the defendant pleads guilty or not.

Despite the limited character of the discussion that should take place under *Turner*, it appears, according to Sanders and Young, that sentence bargaining 'is an endemic and entrenched phenomenon' which the Appeal Court has deplored but

---

[54] This is one way to explain Doreen McBarnet's otherwise seemingly overstated claim that 'crime control is *for* due process' (*Conviction* (London: Macmillan, 1983)). The original claim was that what were seemingly due process forms were actually formulated to enable crime control to occur. The point of my argument is to suggest that legal subjectivity has two dialectical aspects (the expressive and the repressive), so that the form of the abstract legal subject performs the crime control function *through* the idea of legal freedom.

[55] McConville, n. 6 above, 583.   [56] [1970] 2 WLR 1093.

[57] Ibid. 1097–8. The sentence discount is now placed on a statutory basis by the Criminal Justice and Public Order Act 1994, s. 48.

been unable to stop. 'Lawyers and judges in the Crown Court', they say, 'habitually follow their own working assumptions rather than adhering to the legal rules' even if the senior judiciary 'have signalled their determination to stamp out sentence bargaining'.[58] Yet it could be said that *Turner*, the Court of Appeal authority, is itself the problem. It encourages defence counsel to give advice 'in strong terms' to their clients about a guilty plea and it permits counsel to meet with judges. One can imagine how the limited guidance a judge can give could become the basis for further informal indication or guesswork concerning the judge's view. *Turner* opens a door, which it seeks to dissuade counsel and judges from walking through. As Sanders and Young state, it is 'artificial and unrealistic for the law to encourage guilty pleas through the sentence discount whilst simultaneously denying defendants the opportunity to discover exactly what is on offer in the case at hand'.[59]

What, however, underlies such artificiality is the formulation in *Turner* of a test as to when the defendant is and is not a juridically free subject, able to decide her plea with or without 'undue pressure' from the judge or the system. I suggest that 'juridification' is at play here, and my question is: what is the relationship between the model of individual legal freedom under *Turner* and the Human Rights Act?

Sentence bargaining and the Human Rights Act

As we saw at the beginning of this essay, the process of sentence bargaining is one that could easily be criticized as a denial of justice.[60] According to Ashworth, there are no fewer than four possible objections to it under Articles 6(1) and (2),[61] and also Article 14.[62] However, some of these objections relate to the question whether the defendant entering into a sentence bargain voluntarily waived his right to trial,[63] and here, one must ask precisely what it means to do something 'voluntarily' in law.

Consider narrower and broader conceptions of 'voluntariness' that might be available to the law. For the Victorian judge Stephen, an extreme view was that action was voluntary even when it was compelled directly by circumstance. A 'criminal walking to execution is under compulsion if any man can be said to be so, but his motions are just as much voluntary actions as if he were to leave his place of confinement and regain his liberty'.[64] Stephen's point was that where there was physical freedom, there was voluntary action. In contrast to this very broad view of

---

[58] Sanders and Young, n. 6 above, 425.   [59] Ibid. 423.   [60] Above, 262.

[61] The right to a fair and public hearing under Art. 6(1), to be presumed innocent until found guilty under Art. 6(2), and to be privileged against self-incrimination under 6(2). See A. Ashworth, *The Criminal Process*, 2nd edn. (Oxford: Oxford University Press, 1998), 286–92.

[62] The right to be treated without discrimination: the sentencing discount could constitute a form of indirect discrimination against Afro-Caribbeans (ibid. 291). See also Sanders and Young, n. 6 above, 431–2.

[63] 'There is no objection to an informed waiver of the right to be tried, but one can argue that the voluntariness of the waiver should be ascertained by the court' (Ashworth, n. 61 above, 287).

[64] J. F. Stephen, *History of the Criminal Law*, ii (London: Macmillan, 1883), 102. The issues discussed here are pursued in a different context in Norrie, n. 45 above, 112–14.

voluntariness, H. L. A. Hart has suggested a narrower one which takes into account the moral circumstances of choice and insists upon both a 'capacity for choice' and 'fair opportunity'. The latter involves a 'conception of a human agent as being most free when he is placed in circumstances which give him a fair opportunity to exercise normal mental and physical powers . . . *without pressure from others*'.[65]

These narrower and broader conceptions of voluntary choice are available to the law, but which approach is a court likely to take in deciding whether a waiver of trial was voluntary? While not the same, Stephen's broader conception of voluntary action is closer to the way in which the law on sentence bargaining has worked until now. In *Turner*, Lord Parker was clear that the accused must not be placed under pressure by hearing directly from the judge (i.e. as reported by counsel) what the precise terms of the sentence bargain might be. That would be 'undue pressure on the accused, thus depriving him of that complete freedom of choice which is essential'.[66] 'Complete freedom of choice' is incompatible with a clear judicial statement of the terms of the sentence bargain. It is nonetheless compatible with the existence of sentence bargaining, strong pressure from counsel to make a bargain, and the possibility of some discussion between counsel and judge as to its terms. Thus the required ('complete') freedom of choice is incompatible with *direct or formal* judicial pressure, but not with *indirect or informal*, systemic pressure involving the judge. Even though the latter has, and is meant to have, the same effect as the former, it—apparently—preserves the fiction of 'complete' freedom of choice, removed from undue pressure.

It is true that Lord Parker does not go so far as Stephen, in that he sees that a choice made under compulsion is an involuntary one. He does not see, however, that there are indirect as well as direct forms of compulsion and that the latter may be just as effective as the former. Here Hart's emphasis on 'fair opportunity . . . without pressure from others' might generate a different result, but it is not the result on which the Court of Appeal has based its approach for thirty years. Nor, as we saw with McConville's work, is it the approach that takes place in the criminal courts. There, legal practice can serve to repress the accused's understanding of her situation precisely *by turning her into* an 'autonomous and rational [individual] making free . . . and voluntary choices'.[67] The law's choices in both Appeal Court jurisprudence and daily practice gain their legitimating value precisely because, and insofar as, they ignore the pressure brought to bear on the individual by treating her as an abstract legal subject. There is no strong reason to think that judges dealing with this same issue under the Human Rights Act would arrive at a different conclusion.

It is this ability of abstract legal individualism to construct a decontextualized notion of free or voluntary choice that leads me to my deeper scepticism about the value of the Human Rights Act. The Act is capable of entrenching just this kind of

[65] H. L. A. Hart and A. Honoré, *Causation and the Law* (Oxford: Oxford University Press, 1985), 138 (emphasis added).

[66] [1970] 2 WLR 1093, at 1098.   [67] McConville, n. 52 above, 583.

expressive/repressive legal subject who can rationalize a systematically unfair legal practice like the sentence discount, as one founded on subjective free choice. There is no a priori reason why judges interpreting Article 6 should choose a narrow conception of involuntary action over the broader one outlined by Hart. However, the Court of Appeal's test of involuntariness has operated for thirty years with an approach that is closer to the former in its ability to overlook undue pressure on the defendant (where it does not directly implicate the judge). Critical sociolegal work such as that of McConville only reveals that the *Turner* conception of freedom is replicated in daily practice. My scepticism is therefore that there is no need for unjust legal practices like the sentence bargain to fear for the Human Rights Act. The Act can instantiate a repressive legal subjectivity through the kind of conception of voluntary waiver of trial which already permits sentence bargaining to take place. Scepticism about the Act is thus related not just to the contexts in which it is interpreted but also to the form in which it is expressed. Naturally, the two feed off each other, so that a cautious and conservative judicial approach is just the one most likely to exploit the 'juridifying' potential of the Act.

III. Conclusion

I conclude by consolidating my scepticism and entering a note of qualification. From the pronouncements of leading figures in the law and politics, it is clear that the Human Rights Act is intended, so far as it relates to criminal justice, to tidy up problems at the margin rather than to form the cutting edge of a substantial critique of the system. There are also deeper questions about the potential of the language of the Act to deliver such a critique, or whether that language would not in any case dovetail with a minimalist approach to systemic problems. The issue here relates to the nature of the liberal legal subject as an abstract persona with both expressive and repressive aspects. The rightful subject of Article 6 is as capable of covering up the deficiencies of the system as it is of exposing them. So doing, it could play an important legitimating role, for now it will be possible to argue that the system is not just good because 'we say so' but because it has undergone a rigorous human rights audit, and, barring problems at the edge, been pronounced fair. This will be possible even though no substantial changes have been made to the system as a whole such as might be required by the sentence discount.

At this point, I enter a note of caution. My scepticism is just that: a set of doubts about the effects and value of the Human Rights Act, rather than a wholesale rejection. Why so? Recall that my basic analysis of the legal form of individual right is that it possesses both expressive and repressive aspects. Liberal theories of criminal justice focus on the former and tend to ignore the latter, whereas I, writing in a sceptical mode, have 'bent the stick' in the opposite direction. Legal concepts of free subjectivity should not be rejected out of hand; rather they should be recognized for their strengths and weaknesses, in terms of their *limits*.[68] When the Human Rights Act is used to a progressive end, as it may be, we should applaud. My argument has been, however, that I do not think there will be many occasions for applause for the reasons of context and form given above.

To return to my main theme, I began with a quote from Andrew Sanders, and now end with one. He describes briefly the following bleak view of the criminal process, where

Patterns of bias on the street particularly concerning class and race are reproduced throughout the system, so that in the prisons black and working class people in particular are grossly over-represented.[69]

In such a system, 'Cynicism about criminal justice abounds'. If the Human Rights Act does not address the systemic problems Sanders and others identify, it too may fall prey to cynicism. Insofar as we are considering criminal justice, my scepticism indicates why the Act's social and historical fate may be in this direction, rather than that it will help forge a 'strong and confident democracy' or 'strong community',[70] whatever these are.

---

[68] A. Norrie, 'The Limits of Justice: Finding Fault in the Criminal Law', (1996) 59 *Modern Law Review* 540.

[69] N. 4 above, 1085.

[70] See above, n. 42.

15

Minority Protection and Human Rights

MALEIHA MALIK

Adopting a sceptical approach to human rights from the perspective of protection of minorities seems to be a daunting task. Many contemporary national, regional and international human rights documents were adopted as a response to the horrors of the Holocaust in Europe which required a response. Moreover, as a postwar human rights document which was introduced as a reaction to the atrocities of the Second World War, minority protection can be seen to be the *raison d'être* of the European Convention on Human Rights. More recently, the calls for incorporation of the ECHR have explicitly cited its role in protecting minorities as one of its main virtues.[1] Not surprisingly, it is a common and stubborn assumption that judicially enforced human rights should be the main focus for minority protection, and that the ECHR provides a blueprint for such a strategy.

The assumption, however, fails to capture the more complex relationship between minority protection and judicially enforced human rights. This essay questions whether judicially enforced human rights should be seen as the alpha and the omega for minority protection. It is argued that reasons for scepticism become clear once the theoretical assumptions underlying human rights documents such as the ECHR are analysed, and moreover, that there are substantial advantages in dealing with minority issues via representative institutions. Of course, the practical obstacles faced by minorities who seek to advance their aims via political processes often make the judicial route the only viable way of getting a result. However, this speaks to the need for reform of representative institutions to make them a viable route for minority protection rather than abandoning them in favour of a judicial solution.

I. The HRA and procedural liberalism

A search for any one theoretical perspective which underlies the ECHR would be reductionist. Even within the generic term 'liberalism' which is associated with the ECHR, there is a vast difference between the neutrality-based arguments of anti-perfectionists and the appeal to 'wellbeing and the good' which underlies the work

I would like to thank the editor of the *Modern Law Review* for permission to draw on work previously published as M. Malik, 'Governing after the Human Rights Act', (2000) 63 *Modern Law Review* 281.

[1] See F. Klug, *Values for a Godless Age: The Story of the United Kingdom's New Bill of Rights* (London: Penguin, 2000).

of perfectionist liberal writers.[2] Despite this increased choice in liberal theory, Ronald Dworkin's defence of liberalism is an obvious starting point to make explicit the normative foundations of convention rights, not least because of its influence on those who have supported a British bill of rights.[3] In his summary of liberalism, Dworkin distinguishes between two kinds of moral commitment: on the one hand there are concepts about what constitutes the good life; on the other there are ideas about what it is to treat others fairly, justly, and in a way so as to respect their dignity as human agents.[4] Dworkin argues that it is a distinguishing characteristic of a liberal theory of justice that it takes no position about the ends of a good life but it remains strongly committed to safeguarding the principle of treating people with equal respect. Neutrality as to the substantive goals of individuals is essential for showing a person equal respect and respecting their dignity as agents. Given the diversity of goods that individuals can choose, a failure to remain neutral in relation to substantive principles would be tantamount to saying to those whose conception of the good is not preferred that their views are not as worthy as those of other citizens. It would be a failure to accord them individual liberty and dignity.

Despite modification to his arguments since *A Theory of Justice*,[5] John Rawls also adopts this idea as a key feature of his liberalism in *Political Liberalism*.[6] In these contexts neutrality operates as a political principle. The requirement is not that all individuals should be neutral in relation to the good in their private lives. Rather, public decision-making should remain neutral between substantive principles, allowing an individual to choose and revise their own concept of the good.[7] Nor is it the case that the appeal to neutrality is necessarily an appeal to scepticism or relativism. According to Dworkin, neutrality is required 'not because there is no right or wrong of the matter, but because that is what is right'.[8] This support for neutrality takes claims about individuals as the initial starting point (as the input) for a theory of justice. For example, Dworkin's analysis is based on the right of each individual to 'equal respect and concern', whilst Rawls is committed to the idea that all citizens are 'free, moral and equal'. In addition, rights are the end product (the output) of this approach to politics. For Dworkin these are the fundamental

---

[2] For a perfectionist defence of constitutional judicial review, see J. Raz, *Ethics in the Public Domain* (Oxford: Oxford University Press, 1994), 55–8.

[3] See M. Loughlin, *Public Law and Political Theory* (Oxford: Oxford University Press, 1992): 'The main handle for promoting reforms based on this liberal normativist analysis has been the European Convention of Human Rights' (207) and 'The jurisprudential foundations of this programme have been laid mainly by Ronald Dworkin who, during the last 20 years, has developed a normative theory of law based on liberal, rationalist premises' (207). For examples of liberal normativist support for a Bill of Rights, see A. Lester: 'The Constitution: Decline and Renewal', in J. Jowell and D. Oliver (eds.), *The Changing Constitution* (Oxford: Oxford University Press, 1985), ch. 12; A. Lester et al., *A British Bill of Rights* (London: Institute of Public Policy Research, Consultation Paper No. 1, 1990). See also R. Dworkin, *A Bill of Rights for Britain* (London: Chatto and Windus, 1990).

[4] R. Dworkin, *A Matter of Principle* (Oxford: Oxford University Press, 1985), ch. 8.

[5] (Oxford: Oxford University Press, 1972).

[6] (New York: Columbia University Press, 1993), lecture 5.

[7] See e.g. Rawls's discussion of 'The Political Conception of the Person', ibid. 29

[8] N. 5 above, 191 and 203.

principles of individual freedom which act as a 'trump' over collective goals and policies.[9] In Rawlsian terms, his theory of justice includes the first principle of justice: equal right to basic liberties such as integrity of the person and freedom of expression.[10] This has lexical priority over other political principles.

The substance and form of this version of liberalism, often labelled procedural,[11] are immediately familiar. Interests of the individual in liberty (i.e. freedom of speech, association, personal integrity, and the values of the rule of law) are safeguarded. The form for protecting these interests is typically through the judicial review of the acts of the state. Despite some limited variation, this model provides the preferred structure for a range of constitutional documents in Western democracies as well as international and regional human rights documents. Its central ideas are also reflected in the ECHR, which is overwhelmingly concerned with guaranteeing individual rights to be secured through judicial review of state action. These rights ensure integrity of the person through a right to life, rights against torture and servitude (Arts. 2–4), and the values of the rule of law (Arts. 4–7 deal with the right to liberty, a fair trial, and against retrospectivity in the application of the criminal law). Family life (Art. 8), the right to marry and found a family (Art. 12), and freedom of conscience and religion (Art. 9) are safeguarded. The ECHR also protects individual choice and action through the right to free speech (Art. 10) and association (Art. 11). Finally, Article 14 ensures that the rights and freedoms set out in the ECHR are enjoyed without discrimination on any grounds (sex, race, colour, language, and religion are, *inter alia*, specified grounds). Not all rights are absolute, and limits based on the requirements of what is 'necessary in a democratic society' and state derogation from the ECHR are permitted in some circumstances.[12] The HRA incorporates Articles 2–12 and Article 14 of the ECHR, as well as provisions from the First Protocol (the right to the peaceful enjoyment of possessions) and Sixth Protocol (abolition of the death penalty).

Although it is sometimes argued that the principles underlying convention rights can be understood as an aspect of the common good and as substantive values, this approach 'leaves the requirements of the public good and the scope and content of the rights and duties which citizens should possess largely as matters for independent debate and analysis'.[13] These individual rights create an overarching framework

---

[9] See Dworkin's defence of this position in 'Is There a Right to Pornography?', (1981) 1 *Oxford Journal of Legal Studies* 1.

[10] See Rawls, n. 7 above, lecture 8.

[11] This term is used and discussed in the context of the liberal–communitarian debate by C Taylor, 'Cross Purposes: The Liberal–Communitarian Debate', in *Philosophical Arguments* (Cambridge, Mass.: Harvard University Press), 186.

[12] For a more detailed discussion of the rights and structure of the ECHR, see P. Van Dijk and G. J. H. van Hoof, *Theory and Practice of the European Convention on Human Rights* (London: Kluwer, 1998).

[13] See T. R. S. Allan, 'The Rule of Law as the Rule of Reason: Consent and Constitutionalism', (1999) 115 *Law Quaterly Review* 224. Allan comments that the liberal ideal of the rule of law can be given a more substantive role: it can be understood as a doctrine which promotes equality and impartiality and ensures that the exercise of power by the state against an individual must be justified by reference to some aspect of the common good. For a discussion of the values of the rule of law as an aspect of the common good, see J. Finnis, *Natural Law and Natural Rights* (Oxford: Clarendon Press, 1980), ch. 10.

within which individuals can pursue their own conception of the good without interference either by the state or by other individuals.[14] Convention rights fit comfortably into the tradition of liberalism made popular by Dworkin and Rawls which gives central importance to the 'priority of the right over the good'.[15]

The debate which preceded the Human Rights Act, between the rival constitutional discourses of 'new constitutionalism' and the 'sovereigntists', rarely addressed theoretical issues.[16] Moreover, critical surveys of the ECHR have tended to focus on its narrow range of interests, noting that neither socioeconomic rights[17] nor collective rights[18] have been given precedence in this way, and arguing for an extension of the range of rights which are entrenched. More specifically, those concerned with minority protection also pointed to the weak protection given to anti-discrimination, arguing that this rendered the ECHR an inappropriate basis for the protection of minorities. These concerns do not, however, fully capture the force of the main objections from the perspective of minorities. The deadlock in the debate between 'new constitutionalism' and the 'sovereigntists' has obscured these more fundamental concerns. This debate gives priority to the question of who exercises power in a liberal state. However, the issue of whether those making decisions are judges employing a human rights discourse through common law constitutionalism or decision-makers in representative institutions becomes less important when considered from the point of view of minorities, because from this perspective criticism about the unelected and unrepresentative nature of the judiciary has to be balanced against the reality that minorities also face significant obstacles in advancing their claims through political processes and representative institutions. The 'politics/undemocratic nature of the judiciary' critique of judicially enforced human rights needs to be reformulated in the context of minority protection. In this context, the shift of power from one institution (Parliament) to another (the judiciary), remains significant. Like the majority, minorities should be concerned about the consequences of the resulting allocation of power to an unelected body of decision-makers. However, this shift also raises a critical question about the relationship between public institutions, private identity, and the nature of participatory democracy. I want to explore this relationship in the next section in the specific context of minorities. In particular I examine whether an emphasis on judicially enforced human rights rather than decision-making through representative institutions may have a detrimental impact on participatory democracy.

[14] See D. Miller, *Market, State and Community* (Oxford: Clarendon Press, 1989), 254. For a recent discussion of this issue, see Sir J. Laws, 'The Constitution: Morals and Rights', [1996] *Public Law* 622, who develops this idea by distinguishing between negative and positive rights. He states in relation to positive rights: 'The decision in any such case, and the formulation of policy, are for Parliament. But in its duty to the people, which is based on every individual's autonomy, Parliament will abide by a framework which gives pride of place to negative fundamental rights' (634).

[15] See Rawls, n. 7 above.

[16] This is the contrast developed by N. Walker, 'Setting English Judges to Rights', (1999) 19 *Oxford Journal of Legal Studies* 133.

[17] K. D. Ewing, ' Social Rights and Constitutional Law', [1999] *Public Law* 104.

[18] See M. Malik, 'Communal Goods as Human Rights', in C. Gearty and A. Tomkins (eds.) *Understanding Human Rights* (London: Mansell, 1996), 147–51.

II. The HRA and participatory democracy

How could the incorporation of a human rights instrument such as the ECHR act as a barrier to participatory democracy for minorities? Popular calls for greater 'participation' seldom concentrate on what is meant by the term. One way of giving this rallying cry more substance is to notice that a key aspect of a successful participatory model in politics is a strong identification with the fate of the political community.[19] This in turn requires *institutional identification* (the identification of minorities with key legal and political institutions) and *national identification* (whereby minorities feel included within definitions of the national political community). These two issues, institutional and national identification, come together in the context of minority protection in a particularly urgent way. Under conditions of pluralism and diversity which characterize the political reality in most Western democratic states, the sense of belonging to a political community which is provided by identifying with political and legal institutions also becomes the only viable egalitarian mechanism on which to base a national identity.

Once the issue is approached from the perspective of participatory democracy, the objection to judicially enforced human rights is not just that they vest power in the hands of unelected judges or that the range of interests which they protect is narrow and individualistic. This objection leaves unchallenged procedural liberalism's use of neutrality and the public/private dichotomy as its main structuring device.[20] It also fails to reveal that one of the main objections to the ECHR must be that its neo-liberal insistence on grounding issues of individual freedom and toleration in the 'neutrality' of the public sphere, as well as scepticism about opaque issues of 'private identity', prevent all citizens, but especially minorities, from achieving meaningful identification with political decisions. This in turn acts as a barrier to developing more participatory forms of politics which are a critical strategy in any long-term goal of minority protection in the UK. This objection challenges the normative foundations on which the ECHR is based.

The neo-liberal claim of neutrality, and the strict separation of the private sphere (where individuals form and revise their conception of the good) and the public sphere (which preserves neutrality between individuals), have been the subject of well rehearsed criticism. The relevant point for our analysis is that public institutions are not, and should not be viewed as, neutral agents. Rather, they have a wide range of functions which influence private identity, as well as political and civil society. This in turn challenges the strict separation of the private and the public sphere. It also raises questions about national identification which are discussed below. The increasing importance of 'recognition' as a political demand which

---

[19] See C. Taylor, *Reconciling the Solitudes*, ed. Guy La Forest (Montreal: McGill-Queen's University Press, 1993), 97.
[20] See also C. Pateman, 'Feminist Critiques of the Public/Private Dichotomy', in A. Phillips (ed.), *Feminism and Equality* (Oxford: Blackwell, 1987).

characterizes recent political struggles illustrates one consequence of the link between private identity and the public sphere.[21] Moreover, there are certain types of institution which perform a critical function as a locus for private identity. They are like magnets attracting political conflict because the definitions and actions of these institutions are not just objective facts which individuals record and observe. Instead, they are matters which implicate the self-definition of citizens at a deeper level. Identification with these institutions means that individuals regard their own private identity and wellbeing as linked with the success of the institution, and their concerns as expressed and represented within it.[22]

This vision of institutions also gives them a role which goes beyond their importance to individuals. Public institutions allow individuals to participate in shared social practices, and they are a source for creating the common meanings which are a basis for community.[23] Recent Anglo-American legal theory, especially the work of Ronald Dworkin, has revived the importance of community which was a key feature of common law theory. However, the argument that certain political, legal, and civic institutions are constituted by, and draw on, common meanings develops the idea of community in a much stronger form. It suggests that there are certain institutions which rely on and sustain inter-subjective meanings. These can be understood by all participants, and they contribute towards the development of a common language and vocabulary.

Common meanings and beliefs are embedded in and constitutive of the community, i.e. the social and political culture and its institutions. These features cannot be understood by merely noting either their impact on or their importance for individual agents. They are not merely the shared beliefs and attitudes of an aggregate of all the individuals in a society. Rather, they form the basis for a common understanding of those social practices and institutions which cannot be understood as anything but communal. The common meanings which are associated with political, legal, and civic institutions, and which they in turn sustain, are the basis for community. People have to share and participate in a language and understanding of norms which allows them to talk about these institutions and practices.[24] If there is a stronger constitutive relationship between these institutions and private identity, then it follows that these institutions have an important function to play in creating and sustaining a political community.

Those who emphasize these constitutive features attribute an important function to institutions which goes beyond that of public decision-making. They are also a source for constructing private behaviour and giving it meaning through the self-interpretation of participants. This complex social function assigns to these types of

---

[21] See Taylor, n. 19 above, 225   [22] A. Mason, 'Political Community' (1999) 109 *Ethics* 261 at 272.

[23] See C. Taylor, 'Interpretation and the Sciences of Man', in *Philosophy and the Human Sciences* (Cambridge: Cambridge University Press), 32–4. For a discussion of how legal institutions make a contribution to these goals see G. Postema, *Bentham and the Common Law Tradition* (Oxford: Clarendon Press, 1996), 73.

[24] Ibid.

institutions an important role as a bank of collective wisdom and a source for 'public rituals'. Postema has made this point most forcefully in his work on the common law:

One might say that the processes and practices of Common Law, on this view, define a kind of secular public ritual. . . . The Common Law, then, not only defines a framework for social interaction, a set of rules and arrangements facilitating the orderly pursuit of private aims and purposes, but it also publicly articulates the social context within which the pursuit of such aims takes on meaning. It is the reservoir of traditional ways and common experience, and it provides the arena in which the shared structures of experience publicly unfold.[25]

'Institutions which identify' can be contrasted with institutions which merely 'provide a service' (e.g. a commercial organization providing goods) and which are of purely instrumental value in the lives of citizens.[26] This is a distinction which Charles Taylor has used in his discussion of the relationship between public institutions, personal identity, and national life. He argues that there is a critical connection between these concepts which has been consistently marginalized by traditional liberal theory. Taylor concludes: 'Most institutions can move along the spectrum between these extremes. Their significance may reside more or less in their function of identification; or, conversely they may slide in the direction of pure service structures.'

Once this criterion of participatory democracy, with its twin features of institutional and national identification, is adopted, the main objection to the new constitutionalism is not that it is an undemocratic form of governance.[27] This line of attack underestimates the extent to which both the new constitutionalism and the sovereigntist discourse draw on contrasting visions of citizen power, control and participation.[28] Both models can be justified as a legitimate basis for organizing democratic institutions: they are able to deliver preference satisfaction and serve an 'instrumental role'; in addition they can meet the need for the 'intrinsic desirability of democracy as a means of participating in the public life of one's community'.[29] A form of governance which gives priority to judicial review of state action on the basis of convention rights, and based on ideas of neutrality as to the good associated with the work of writers such as Rawls and Dworkin, draws on 'sceptical and semi-sceptical arguments' which 'are thought to buttress, among other things, the conclusion that, while we may guide our own lives by our beliefs about the nature of the good life, we should refrain from relying on these beliefs when we act politically'.[30]

---

[25] Ibid. 73.   [26] See Taylor, n. 19 above, 123.

[27] See e.g. M. Mandel, 'A Brief History of the New Constitutionalism, Or "How We Changed Everything So That Everything Would Remain the Same"' (1998) 32 *Israel LR* at 252.

[28] For discussions of the idea of democracy which underlies the new constitutionalism, see Laws, n. 14 above, 17.

[29] See Raz, n. 2 above, 109–17.

[30] Ibid. Raz distinguishes between the anti-perfectionist 'neutrality in relation to the allocation of the good to others' of writers such as Rawls, Nozick, and Ackerman on the one hand and Dworkin on the other (109). However, for our purposes the important point is that these writers can be associated with the view that 'external preferences (i.e preferences "for the assignment of goods and opportunities to

This model has been challenged by perfectionist liberals, who argue that justification for democratic institutions is more appropriately grounded in concepts of the good and the wellbeing of individuals. However, this form of politics is not 'undemocratic' per se. Rather, it is consistent with an understanding of citizen power as the ability to influence decision-making and 'trumping' either the decision of others with whom they disagree or collective action which threatens to interfere with individual rights. This model does not exclude citizen participation or control altogether but rather defines it in a specific way. Citizen participation in the legal and political processes which affect their lives is ensured because of their ability to retrieve and rely upon the individual rights which are entrenched in the founding document.[31]

A very different vision of citizen participation informs the sovereigntist discourse, with its greater focus on representative institutions. Within this model, citizen freedom and dignity does not lie in the ability to 'veto' collective decision-making by reference to a set of individual rights or principles. Rather, participation in the political process is secured through coming together with others to form a consensus on substantive and controversial values.[32] One aspect of these contested values will be that they concern the provision of goods which cannot be secured individually and which require collective and coordinated action.[33] Debating ideas, building majorities, participating in elections, and seeking to ensure that the ruling party reflects decisions relating to the common good becomes the focus of political activity. Within this more 'republican' model, citizen power and freedom do not lie in blocking the decision of the community. Nor is it the case that there is no room at all for dissent or opposition. Rather, 'Full participation in self-rule means at least part of the time, to have some part in forming a ruling consensus, with which one can identify along with others. To rule and be ruled in turn means that at least some of the time the governors can be "us", not always "them"'.[34]

It has been argued that these two models are mutually compatible and can be comfortably accommodated within a single system. This 'complimentary thesis'

others") . . . should not be given weight in political decisions. Constitutional rights, according to Dworkin, are justified if they manage to exclude from the democratic process decisions which people are likely to take because of their external rather than internal preferences' (see Raz's critique of this argument at 109–13). Raz provides an instrumental justification for democracy which grounds it in notions of the wellbeing of individuals rather than neutrality as to external preferences. He defines democracy in the following terms: 'Democracy is best understood as a political system allowing individuals opportunities for informed participation in the political process whose purpose is the promotion of sound decisions. Democracy is justified inasmuch as it is necessary to serve the well being of people' (117).

[31] See e.g. the comments of the Home Secretary, Jack Straw, who introduced the Human Rights Bill in the House of Commons with the following comment: ' It will strengthen representative and democratic government. It does so by *enabling citizens to challenge more easily actions of the state if they fail to match the standards set by the European convention*' (emphasis added). HC Debs. 306 (16 Feb. 1998), 769.

[32] For a discussion of this vision of constitutional reform in the context of social democracy, see K. D. Ewing, 'Human Rights, Social Democracy and Constitutional Reform', in Gearty and Tomkins, n. 18 above.

[33] For a definition and discussions of the common good, see Finnis, n. 14 above. ch. 6.

[34] See Taylor, n. 11 above, 200.

suggests that judicial review on the basis of fundamental rights and decision-making through representative institutions both have a distinct role in a fully functioning constitutional democracy.[35] However, once the assumption of the neutrality of the public sphere is weakened, and the causal relationship between private identity, public institutions, and forms of governance is recognized, then this 'complimentary thesis' is rendered problematic. The new constitutionalism and the sovereigntist models have embedded within them *contrasting* visions of citizen power and control. Giving priority to the new constitutionalism and making it the focus of political life is likely to encourage citizens to view themselves, their relationship towards each other, and political institutions according to the ideas embedded in this constitutional tradition. A preference for this model is therefore likely to discourage the development of private identity along more 'republican lines' which encourages citizens to view their own role, their relationships to others, and their political institutions as a coming together within political processes to create and sustain a common good. This in turn leads to the conclusion that these two contrasting forms of governance give effect to incommensurable visions of democracy: as individual control over decisions on the one hand, and as participation in a vision of the common good on the other.[36]

The 'British model' of incorporation has ensured that both forms of governance have a role. The debate on the balance and proper relationship between them will be heated and controversial. From the narrower perspective of institutional identification, however, there are clear disadvantages in tilting the balance in favour of the new constitutionalism. As discussed, judicial review on the basis of entrenched convention rights discourages the explicit discussion of substantive principles and the common good in the public sphere. It is therefore unsuited to generate a vision of politics as an activity where citizens come together to create, revise, or articulate a vision of the common good or the substantive principles which will govern their collective action. This affects the issue of institutional identification, because where an institution opens up a dialogue about the terms of the common good, and is seen to be a focus for its provision, it also implicates the private identity of the citizen: the well-being and flourishing of the individual are linked with the success of the institution.

[35] For a recent discussion of this issue, see Sir J. Laws, 'The Constitution: Morals and Rights', [1996] *Public Law* 622, who develops this idea by distinguishing between negative and positive rights. He states in relation to positive rights: 'The decision in any such case, and the formulation of policy, are for Parliament. But in its duty to the people, which is based on every individual's autonomy, Parliament will abide by a framework which gives pride of place to negative fundamental rights' (634) and ' The good constitution has to recognise and entrench a bedrock of rights, based on the principle of minimal interference. Good government of any political colour must pursue its own vision of the morality of aspiration, which is itself a function of power held on trust. Where its vision cuts across the rule of minimal interference the courts have to say so . . . And for reasons I have sought to give; the rule of minimal interference and the morality of aspiration share the same roots in man's nature; the function of courts and government are therefore complementary, and any tension between them should be creative, not destructive' (635).

[36] See M. Sandel, 'The Procedural Republic and the Unencumbered Self', (1984) 12 *Political Theory* 81. See also Taylor, n. 11 above, 201: 'These two kinds of capacity are incommensurable. We can't say simply which is greater. For people of an atomist bent, there is no doubt that model A will seem preferable, and for republicans model B will seem the only genuine one.'

Substantive discussions concerning the common good also contribute towards creating a common language of beliefs, and enable collective action, which are in turn the basis for sustaining community.[37] Individuals recognize that they cannot obtain this type of collective public good in their lives through individual action, but at the same time they are able to recognize their value. The resulting dialogue is an important source for creating 'common meanings' within a community.[38] These common meanings cannot be understood by merely noting their impact on, or importance for, individual agents. They are not an aggregation of the shared beliefs and attitudes of all individuals in a society. Rather, they form the basis for an understanding of social practices and institutions which cannot be understood as anything but communal. A strategy which avoids a debate around substantive issues of the common good carries with it the risk that citizens will find it more difficult to identify with political institutions and decision-making. Consequently, they are more likely to view political institutions as an 'instrumental' rather than a 'constitutive' part of their lives.[39]

III. Minorities and participatory democracy

Participatory democracy (defined as institutional and national identification) is important for the majority as well as the minority. However, it takes on special significance in the context of minority protection. Most obviously, minority groups whose members and viewpoints are not represented within major political and legal institutions will find it difficult to identify with them. These difficulties become even more significant when we consider the second aspect necessary for successful participatory politics: identification with the fate of a political community.

The traditional liberal approach constitutes the British public as members of a political community based on rational, liberal values. Citizenship identifies an unmediated relationship between individual and state; any involvement by citizens with voluntary, private or civil organizations must be uncoerced and consensual. This draws upon the idea of a neutral public sphere as its essential structuring device, and relegates issues of personal identity to the private sphere. The ECHR recreates this liberal 'cultural contract' by adopting a dual approach to minority protection. Its predominant concern is with the toleration of minorities, often cited as one of the main advantages of the domestic incorporation of the ECHR. Citizens are free to express their particular identity in the private sphere, either individually or in association with others, without state interference. Recent strategy for the protection of minorities has

---

[37] See ibid. 36–9. See also C. Sunstein, *The Partial Constitution* (Cambridge, Mass.: Harvard University Press, 1993), and esp. ch. 6 for Sunstein's argument in support of deliberative democracy.

[38] See Taylor, n. 11 above, 32–41.

[39] M. Sandel develops this contrast between instrumental and constitutive community in a critique of Rawlsian liberalism in *Liberalism and the Limits of Justice* (Cambridge: Cambridge University Press, 1982), ch. 4.

supplemented toleration with a second strategy guaranteeing an individual right to non-discrimination. Although most versions of this right permit a limited measure of discrimination in the private sphere, non-discrimination ensures that minorities have access to politics, the economy, and key sectors such as public services and education. This clearly affects the way in which the majority will conduct not only their private but also some of their public affairs.[40] The non-discrimination clause in Article 14 of the ECHR is limited in its application to the rights and freedoms covered by the Convention.[41] However, it has been ensured a wide application through decisions of the European Commission and European Court which confirm that there is no need to establish the violation of another article of the ECHR before Article 14 applies.[42] Moreover, the *Belgium Linguistics Case (No. 2)* has affirmed that Article 14 provides some scope for positive steps to accommodate minorities: differential treatment of groups is permissible and 'equality of treatment is violated if the distinction has no objective and reasonable justification'.[43] This is in line with the European Court's recognition that democracy requires not only tolerating but also positively responding to the needs of minorities.[44] Recent proposals to strengthen the ECHR's role in the protection of minorities have led to the adoption of an additional protocol which broadens the field of Article 14 to include a free-standing prohibition on discrimination,[45] although this has not yet been signed by the UK.[46]

One alternative to a traditional liberal definition of political community is 'conservative nationalism', which remains a popular mechanism for defining national identity. This strategy defines the terms of belonging to a political community according to criteria such as race, common memories, a dominant culture, or a majority religion.[47] In this context national identity becomes something which is

[40] For justifications of the anti-discrimination principle, see C. McCrudden, *Anti-Discrimination Law* (Aldershot: Dartmouth, 1991).

[41] Art. 14 states: 'The enjoyment of the rights and freedoms set forth in this Convention shall be secured without discrimination on any ground such as sex, race, colour, language, religion, political or other opinion, national or social origin, association with a national minority, property, birth or other status.'

[42] *Grandrath v. Federal Republic of Germany* [1967] 10 YBECHR 626 at 678; *Belgium Linguistics Case (No. 2)* (1968) 1 EHRR 252.

[43] Ibid. 284. Even this wider interpretation of Art. 14 is a limited model to ensure the accommodation minority cultures. In the *Belgium Linguistics Case (No. 2)* case the Court found that there was no general right for parents who wanted children to be educated in the language of their choice

[44] *Young, James and Webster v. UK* (1981) 4 EHRR 38 at 57. See S. Poulter, *Ethnicity, Law and Human Rights* (Oxford: Oxford University Press, 1998), 86.

[45] Protocol No. 12 to the Convention for the Protection of Human Rights and Fundamental Freedoms, ETS No. 177 states: 'Article 1—General prohibition of discrimination: (1) The enjoyment of any right set forth by law shall be secured without discrimination on any ground such as sex, race, colour, language, religion, political or other opinion, national or social origin, association with a national minority, property, birth or other status. (2) No one shall be discriminated against by any public authority on any ground such as those mentioned in paragraph 1.' At a ceremony on 3–4 Nov. the representatives of the member states of the Council of Europe met at the Campidoglio in central Rome to open for signature Protocol No. 12 (non-discrimination) to the ECHR.

[46] A full list of signing states can be found at http://conventions.coe.int. Once 10 member states have ratified it, the Protocol will come into force, but only for ratifying states.

[47] For a discussion of the intellectual roots of conservative nationalism, see D. Miller, *On Nationalism* (Oxford: Oxford University Press, 1995), 124–31.

given historically rather than a matter of choice or negotiation. In most Western democracies, the presence of large numbers of racially and culturally diverse groups is a permanent barrier to forging a shared national identity along the lines advocated by conservative nationalists. The fear in contemporary plural states is that the inflexible use of these criteria will necessarily exclude, or coercively assimilate, large numbers of citizens. These fears explain liberal constitutionalism's suspicion of the idea of national identity. Despite these justified reservations, anti-nationalists are coming under increasing pressure to recognize that a wide range of benefits follow from a shared national identity. It has been persuasively argued that a shared national identity minimizes the risk of alienation from political institutions; it allows compromise in the face of conflicting interests; and it is a prerequisite for a politics of the common good and policies of social reform.[48]

It is against this background that a national identity as 'a sense of belonging to a political community' is advocated. This preferred concept relies on citizens identifying with the common legal and political structures in the state.[49] Even those who argue that a shared national identity is not essential accept that this 'sense of belonging to the polity' is vital for stable democratic institutions.[50] Its attraction is that it avoids the dangers of conservative nationalism whilst at the same time recognizing (unlike the traditional liberal approach) that national identification performs an important function for participative democracy. Diversity (of culture, ethnicity, and belief) will continue to be a problem in this context. Minorities faced with political institutions in which neither their members nor their values are adequately represented will find it difficult to view them as structures of identification. Doubts about the capacity of 'neutral' forms of governance to generate institutional identification inevitably take on a greater urgency in this context.

These doubts are exacerbated by the fact that traditional neo-liberal approaches to the protection of minorities (with their focus on toleration and non-discrimination) are increasingly seen as a necessary but insufficient policy response to the most pressing contemporary challenges to safeguarding the interests of minorities. The approach of the ECHR to minority protection reflects the main terms of the liberal cultural contract by sustaining a neutral public sphere which avoids references to private identity such as culture, race, religion, or language. The challenge posed to this equilibrium by the politics of multiculturalism which raged on in the 1980s and 1990s was both empirical and theoretical. These political conflicts are provoked when citizens insist on 'recognition' of their private identity (formulated on the

---

[48] See Mason, n. 22, above and Miller, n. 14 above, 237. For a detailed discussion of liberal nationalism, see also Y. Tamir, *Liberal Nationalism* (Princeton, NJ: Princeton University Press, 1993).

[49] See Mason, n. 22 above, and J. Habermas, 'Citizenship and National Identity: Some Reflections on the Future of Europe', in *Theorising Citizenship*, ed. R. Beiner (Albany, NY: SUNY Press, 1995).

[50] See Mason, n. 22 above, 261: 'it is important nevertheless for these states to forge and sustain a shared national identity, for they believe that in the absence of such an identity the realization of liberal values is jeopardised. In effect liberal-nationalists of this kind believe that national community is a precondition for the viability of political community as liberals conceive it.'

basis of sexuality, religion, or culture) in the public sphere.[51] The liberal cultural contract which relegates issues of private identity to the private sphere is not a suitable basis for responding to these demands. Theorists have increasingly questioned the adequacy of traditional liberalism's focus on universal individual rights as a sufficient guarantee for minority protection. Under conditions of ethnic or cultural diversity it is increasingly argued that concentrating exclusively on tolerance and an individual right to non-discrimination may operate as a form of 'benign neglect' of minority groups and that multiculturalism can provide a solution.[52]

Multiculturalism, as a normative rather than descriptive term, requires policies which go beyond non-discrimination in important respects. Its concern is not limited to the protection of individuals against specific instances of discrimination. It also extends to ensuring the flourishing and survival of diverse groups (as a collective entity) within one political community.[53] Although convention rights (and the extended reading of Article 14 which permits a limited form of differential treatment) provide some scope for taking these positive steps to accommodate minorities, they stop short of requiring states to 'promote the conditions necessary for persons belonging to . . . minorities to maintain and develop their culture and preserve the essential elements of their identity'.[54] Some forms of multiculturalism seek to address this problem by giving overwhelming priority to mechanisms of belonging which draw on the many sources of private identity (both individual and group) such as race, ethnicity, or sexuality.[55] The argument is not only that these sources

[51] See C. Taylor, *Multiculturalism and 'The Politics of Recognition'* (Princeton, NJ: Princeton University Press, 1990). See also I. M. Young, *Justice and the Politics of Difference* (Princeton, NJ: Princeton University Press, 1990), 163–73.

[52] For a summary of the theoretical arguments, see the introduction in W. Kymlicka, *The Rights of Minority Cultures* (Oxford: Oxford University Press, 1995). In Britain these issues have recently been considered in the report of the Commission on the Future of Multi-Ethnic Britain, which was chaired by Professor Lord Parekh: see *The Future of Multi-Ethnic Britain: The Parekh Report* (London: Profile Books, 2000). The Commission was set up in Jan. 1998 by the Runnymede Trust, an independent think tank concerned with issues of racial justice. See http://www.runnymedetrust.org/meb/TheReport.htm for a summary of the report (accessed on 10 Feb. 2001).

[53] For a discussion of forms of multiculturalism, see Miller, n. 14 above, 130–41. For a liberal defence and definition of multiculturalism, see Raz, n. 2 above, 170.

[54] Art. 4(2) of the draft Framework Convention for the Protection of National Minorities, for example, stated: 'The Parties undertake to adopt, where necessary, adequate measures in order to promote, in all areas of economic, social, political and cultural life, full and effective equality between persons belonging to a national minority and those belonging to the majority. In this respect, they shall take due account of the specific conditions of the persons belonging to national minorities.' As Sebastian Poulter notes, this would have provided a basis for introducing policies of multiculturalism within the ECHR structure. However, at a summit meeting held in Vienna in 1993 this draft of the protocol was not adopted. At the Vienna Meeting in 1993, the Council of Europe commissioned work on drafting a protocol in the cultural field which guaranteed individual rights of persons, especially those of national minorities. Poulter notes: 'this represented a marked shift of emphasis towards a universalist rather than a particularist approach to the issue, stressing the need to recognize the cultural rights of all rather than exclusively those of minorities.' See Poulter, n. 44 above, 90. For a discussion of the Council of Europe's Framework Convention for the Protection of National Minorities, see P. Keller, 'Re-thinking Ethnic and Cultural Rights in Europe', (1998) 18 *Oxford Journal of Legal Studies* 29.

[55] See e.g. I. M. Young, n. 51 above, 167. D. Miller has described these as 'radical multiculturalism': see n. 14 above, 135.

of identity should be tolerated in the private sphere but that they should in fact be positively 'recognized' in the public sphere. Where there is a conflict between the established public or national identity and these various sources of private identity, the latter should always be given preference. This form of multiculturalism can compensate for the obvious defects of the liberal 'cultural contract' which relegates issues of personal identity to the private sphere. It also avoids the exclusionary consequences of 'conservative nationalism' which defines national identity according to historically given criteria.[56] However, seeking a solution in such an uncompromising version of multiculturalism is not free of difficulties. If participatory politics requires national identification by the minority, then this is equally true for the majority. An 'exclusive' version of multiculturalism which ignores the needs of the majority also fails to meet the criteria for an inclusive form of participatory politics.[57]

The liberal cultural contract assumes that the public sphere is a neutral space which makes no reference to issues of private identity or culture and therefore allows all groups to function without disadvantage. An exclusive version of multiculturalism on the other hand gives overwhelming priority to the accommodation of private identities of minorities within the public sphere. Both ignore the possibility that a common public sphere can emerge which is neither neutral between cultures nor a perfect mirror for personal identity.[58] This common culture will be influenced by a process of renegotiation between the diverse cultural groups within a political community. Developing 'a sense of belonging' which remains attentive to both the majority and the minority, and generating a common public culture within which different groups coexist, requires compromise and adjustment by the parties.[59] For the minority, this means that their private identity cannot automatically be reflected in the public sphere without some limited assimilation to the shared values which are the agreed basis for a common public life.[60] For the majority, this renegotiation carries with it significant costs. These costs will be an inevitable outcome of attempts to transform the public sphere and institutions: from exclusively reflecting the dominant culture, towards a common culture which also seeks to accommodate some of the most urgent needs of minorities.[61]

[56] D. Miller has criticized the priority which such 'radical' forms of multiculturalism give to affirming group difference at the expense of commonality. See ibid. 135–40.

[57] Ibid. 132–41.

[58] Raz states that there are a number of catalysts for generating a common culture, e.g common education concerning a range of cultural groups within a society; the fact that members of all communities will interact in the same economic environment; and the fact that all cultural groups belong to the same political society. See Raz, n. 2 above, 188.

[59] See Poulter, n. 44 above, 24–6.

[60] See Mason's justification for moderate assimilation, n. 22 above, 265–71. See also Poulter's argument, n. 44 above, that there needs to be some consensus around shared democratic values (22). He also concludes that ' a culturally diverse population also requires strong elements of social cohesion around a set of shared core values, which impose certain uniform standards in the wider public interest. There are limits beyond which a tolerant attitude is inappropriate. Although such limits are hard to define with precision, they are best seen as arising from the formal, institutional values reflected in the key political and legal concepts employed in a modern liberal democracy' (36).

[61] See ibid. 34.

This brings the discussion back to the critical importance of institutional identification as part of a minority protection strategy. It is because citizens are more likely to identify with the decisions of representative institutions that they are an ideal forum for policies which go beyond the toleration of minorities, e.g. non-discrimination policies which impact on the majority and multiculturalism. In this context, is the model of democratic politics introduced by the Human Rights Act appropriate? The idea of participation as the ability to 'trump' the majority which underlies the 'new constitutionalism' discourse has appeal in relation to a strategy of toleration, where the aim is to safeguard certain basic rights which will provide the minimum guarantee of minority protection. It can also provide a solution to the most obvious forms of discrimination. The individualistic and even adversarial nature of this way of seeing participation (as control over decisionmaking) is not inappropriate in this context. However, this model of governance becomes less appropriate once we move beyond these techniques. There are also other strategies for minority protection which are more likely to involve wider social redistribution of resources or greater compromise and renegotiations between the majority and the minority. These are recurring issues in the context of certain types of indirect discrimination,[62] positive (affirmative) action or multiculturalism. In these contexts, the ability of representative institutions to secure identification with their decisions by both the majority and the minority becomes a significant advantage. It could be argued that constitutional common law can successfully involve citizens in this project. A more expansive reading of the constitutional principle of equality and an individual right to non-discrimination have been successfully adopted to ensure that public institutions are restructured in order to accommodate minority interests.[63] Landmark constitutional decisions such as *Brown v. Board of Education* are usually cited as a paradigm example, confirming the ability of constitutional courts to mobilize public opinion and promote discussion on controversial issues of minority protection.[64] In this way, asserting minority interests in litigation can be a focal point for involving both the relevant minority and the majority as well as acting as a catalyst for a wider political movement.

However, and ironically, a landmark decision such as *Brown v. Board of Education* can also provide support for the opposite point of view, and especially where minorities are making demands which require social reform. In his analysis of the decision, Cass Sunstein notes that in the decade which immediately followed *Brown* there was no dramatic change in the numbers of black children attending

---

[62] See also *Eldridge v. British Columbia (AG)* [1997] 3 SCR 624, in which the Supreme Court of Canada confirmed that the failure to take positive steps to ensure that members of a disadvantaged group benefit equally from services offered to the general public (in this case the need to allocate funds to provide sign language interpreters for disabled groups) was in breach of s. 15 of the Canadian Charter of Rights and Freedoms. The court also affirmed that this right is subject to the principle of reasonable accommodation.

[63] As stated above, there is some scope for developing Art. 14 of the ECHR thereby enabling differential treatment which accommodates minority interests.

[64] See e.g. *Brown v. Board of Education* 347 US 483 (1954), or *Roe v. Wade* 410 US 113 (1973).

desegregated schools,[65] and that it was not until the involvement of Congress and the executive after 1964 that significant change occurred. Sunstein's analysis of *Brown*, and other major US Supreme Court decisions, provides an invaluable lesson in this area. He argues that where political decisions also entail social reform (and costs for citizens) there are inherent limits to the judicial model.[66] These will be familiar arguments to those who have examined the power of the courts in the US to engineer social change. In that context, it has often been argued that framing issues in legally sound ways also robs them of political and purposive appeal, and that the 'legal rights approach to expanding democracy has significantly narrowed their conception of political action itself' and 'legal tactics not only absorb scarce resources that could be used for popular mobilization [but also] make it difficult to develop broadly based, multitissue grassroots associations of sustained citizen allegiance'.[67] In his study of US case law, Rosenberg has concluded that constitutional courts are 'constrained' when faced with litigants seeking significant social reform. He argues that these are

powerful constraints. First, they must convince the courts (or legislators) that the rights they are asserting are required by the constitutional or statutory language. Given the limited nature of constitutional rights, the constraints of legal culture, and the general caution of the judiciary this is no easy task. Second, courts are wary of stepping too far out of the political mainstream. Deferential to the federal government and potentially limited by congressional action, courts may be unwilling to take the heat generated by politically unpopular rulings. Third, if these two constraints are overcome and cases are decided favorably, litigants are faced with the task of implementing the decisions. Lacking powerful tools to force implementation, court decisions are often rendered useless given strong opposition. Even if litigators seeking significant social reform win major victories in court, when implemented they often turn out to be worth very little. Borrowing the words of Justice Jackson from another context, the Constrained Court view holds that court litigation to produce significant social reform may amount to little more than 'a teasing illusion like a munificent bequest in a pauper's will'. (*Edwards v. California* 1941, 186).[68]

IV. Concluding comments

The fact that citizens are more likely to identify with the decisions of representative institutions makes the latter an ideal forum where minority protection policies require significant social change, re-allocation of power or resources and multiculturalism.

[65] C. Sunstein, *The Partial Constitution* (Cambridge, Mass.: Harvard University Press, 1993), 146–9.

[66] Ibid. Sunstein sets out three specific disadvantages of a judicial forum in these contexts: reliance on the courts may impair democratic channels for seeking change by diverting energy and resources from politics and foreclosing a political outcome; judicial decisions are ineffective at bringing about social change; and the focus of adjudication is narrow.

[67] M. McCann, *Taking Reform Seriously: Perspectives on Public Interest Liberalism* (Ithaca, NY: Cornell University Press, 1986).

[68] G. N. Rosenberg, *The Hollow Hope: Can Courts Bring about Social Change?* (Chicago: University of Chicago Press, 1991), 21.

Affirming the potential contribution of representative institutions to minority protection generally, and multiculturalism in particular, is not synonymous with displacing the well-earned and pivotal role of judicially protected individual rights for minorities. However, it is a much-needed antidote to the cherished assumption that a judicial remedy should be the sole focus of attention. Minority groups can lobby representatives to take their interests into account before formulating policies. The impact of minority protection issues on other social programmes can be considered. Policy-makers can be encouraged to take into account the interests not only of minorities but also of other interested parties who will be affected by the decision.[69]

This is not to say that representative institutions are a panacea. Minorities face obvious difficulties in advancing their interests through political processes in the absence of real political power and adequate representation of their interests. Simplistic appeals to political equality leave all the most intractable difficulties unanswered in this context. 'Each citizen shall count for one' fails to account for those situations where certain individuals are a permanent minority and whose concerns are not adequately represented within the political process. However, this speaks to the need for reform rather than abandoning the role of representative institutions altogether. It requires a focus on transforming elected assemblies, whether at a local, regional, or national level. The assumption that a judicial solution is always the first and natural option acts as a barrier to developing imaginative use of political processes by minorities to advance their interests.[70]

This issue has not been explicitly or adequately addressed in the government's constitutional reform programme.[71] The omission is in sharp contrast to the redistribution of power to regional assemblies, ensuring that national minorities have greater control over, and are able to identify with, the political decisions which affect their daily lives.[72] The gap in the present constitutional reform agenda is also

---

[69] Poulter, n. 44 above, provides a detailed case study to show how this process can work effectively. His discussion of the events surrounding the enactment of the Construction (Head Protection) Regulations 1989 illustrate this point. Following a large numbers of representations from members of the Sikh community demanding an exemption (to accommodate their need to wear turbans), the government introduced a special exemption. Poulter's analysis of the debates in the House of Commons and the House of Lords suggested that the decision was made after a detailed debate and after considering all the empirical evidence relating to the number of Sikh construction workers who would be affected (313–22).

[70] For a discussion of policy options, see Mason, n. 22 above, and Kymlicka, n. 52 above, pt. 5 ('Minority Cultures and Democratic Theory').

[71] The Labour Party manifesto did not specifically address the issue of minority representation in its programme for reform of the House of Commons and the House of Lords: see *New Labour: Because Britain Deserves Better* (London: Labour Party, 1997). Under a section on 'Real Rights for Citizens' (35) it refers to the incorporation of the ECHR as a source of statutory human rights, and states: 'We will seek to end unjustifiable discrimination wherever it exists. For example, we support comprehensive enforceable civil rights for disabled people against discrimination in society or at work, developed with all interested parties.' The main reference to multiculturalism is in the context of a new offence of racially motivated violence to protect ethnic minorities which resulted in the creation of racially aggravated offences in the Crime and Disorder Act 1998, see M. Malik ' Racist Crime: Racially Aggravated Offences in the Crime and Disorder Act 1998, Part II', (1999) 62 *Modern Law Review* 409.

[72] For a discussion of the government's redistribution of power and the new constitutional changes, see R. Brazier, 'The Constitution of the United Kingdom', [1999] *Cambridge Law Journal* 96.

lamentable because representative institutions perform an invaluable function in minority protection. They are an ideal forum for involving all citizens and generating a debate about the appropriate balance between the needs of minorities and the wider public interest.

The argument which I have developed in this essay is that institutional identification is more likely where substantive issues concerning the common good are discussed. This in turn makes a unique contribution towards developing common meanings and a sense of community. In the context of complex plural states, I have argued that the only viable and inclusive way of defining national identification is to ensure that all citizens can identify with key political and legal institutions. This argument makes it essential that minority issues are raised in forums and at 'the point where people engage with the full range of political alternatives and the full spectrum of policy concerns'.[73] The likelihood that both the majority and the minority will treat representative institutions as structures of identification becomes significant for minority protection generally. It is of critical importance where the non-discrimination principle requires significant social reform, the reallocation of resources from one group to another, or strategies of multiculturalism.

---

[73] A. Phillips, *The Politics of Presence* (Oxford: Oxford University Press, 1995), 182.

Part III

The Experience of Elsewhere:
Reasons to be Sceptical

16

The South African Experience of Judicial Rights Discourse: A Critical Appraisal

SARAS JAGWANTH

I. Introduction

It is difficult to be sceptical of the South African experience of entrenching a justiciable Bill of Rights and this chapter does not claim to be an exception. It aims rather to critically assess the extent to which the transformative goals in the South African Constitution have been capable of being meaningfully realized through enforcement by the judiciary since the shift from parliamentary sovereignty to constitutional supremacy, together with the establishment of the Constitutional Court,[1] in 1994. There can be no doubt that the Constitutional Court has played an important role in certain respects, particularly in relation to testing the constitutionality of legislation passed by the old Parliament. But despite the fact that the South African experience is often cited as support for the proposition that a Constitution with an entrenched and justiciable Bill of Rights can play a major role in egalitarian social transformation, there are many limitations to the extent to which this can be realized through judicial rights discourse. In attempting to illustrate this, the cases used are unavoidably selective.

Why are there few, if any, sceptics in South Africa? Progressive sceptics, including those in this volume, share a concern about the tension between entrenched and justiciable rights and democracy. The South African Bill of Rights, by contrast, *embodies* democracy. It expressly declares itself to be the 'cornerstone of democracy' and affirms the democratic ideals to which the post-apartheid society is committed. Thus, the South African Constitution '[v]iewed in context, textually and historically'

I am grateful to Fred Soltau for his insightful comments on an earlier draft of this chapter.

[1] The Constitutional Court was established under the interim Constitution to be the highest court for the protection and enforcement of the provisions of the Constitution. Under South Africa's hybrid system, the Constitutional Court and the Supreme Court of Appeal share jurisdiction as the highest courts in the land in South Africa. The Constitutional Court is the highest court in constitutional matters and is limited to deciding constitutional matters and issues connected with constitutional matters. It also has the power to decide what is a constitutional matter. While the Supreme Court of Appeal and the High Courts do have substantial constitutional jurisdiction, including the power to declare an Act of Parliament invalid, any declaration of invalidity of an Act of Parliament or provincial legislation must be confirmed by the Constitutional Court before it has any force. The Constitutional Court has exclusive jurisdiction in certain areas, mainly relating to disputes between organs of state and spheres of government. The Constitutional Court acts largely as an appellate court, and apart from disputes between organs of state and levels of government, direct access to the court, or engaging it as a court of first instance, by ordinary litigants is allowed in exceptional circumstances only.

has a 'depth of meaning not echoed in any other national Constitution'.[2] It has been described as 'different' from any other constitution:[3] it

represents a decisive break from, and a ringing rejection of, that part of the past which is disgracefully racist, authoritarian, insular, and repressive and a vigorous identification of a commitment to a democratic, universalistic, caring and aspirationally egalitarian ethos, expressly articulated in the Constitution. The contrast between the past which it repudiates and the future to which it seeks to commit is stark and dramatic.

The South African Constitution is 'different' and enjoys widespread legitimacy both for the inclusive and consultative process by which it was adopted as well as for its content. The Constitution was negotiated as part of a two-phase process involving most existing political parties, an intensive public participation campaign, and the Constitutional Court which had the task of certifying that it complied with certain principles agreed to by political stakeholders.[4] In relation to content, the South African Constitution is manifestly transformative. The preamble specifically recognizes the injustices of South Africa's history, honours those who worked for freedom, and aims to heal the divisions of the past. The Constitution itself embodies social rights and a substantive conception of equality, affirmative state duties, horizontality, participatory governance, multiculturalism, and historical self-consciousness.[5] The imperative for transformation, for the establishment of 'a society based on democratic values, social justice and fundamental human rights',[6] in a country with a history such as South Africa need hardly be repeated. Institutional oppression and grotesque human rights abuses were so endemic in the apartheid era that South Africans welcomed the new constitutional dispensation which gave expression to our country's new ethos and to opening 'a new chapter in the history of our country'.[7] As expressed by a judge of the Constitutional Court, the ushering in of a new constitutional era in South Africa 'represented more than merely entrenching and extending existing common law rights, such as might happen if Britain adopted a bill of rights'.[8]

In this regard the relevance of the South African experience for the UK, or for that matter most other countries, may be limited by the vastly different context in which constitutionalism and the Bill of Rights was introduced in South Africa, and the explicit transformation goals contained in its Constitution. Under the British

[2] Kriegler J in *Du Plessis v. De Klerk*, 1996 (5) BCLR 658 (CC) at para. 126.

[3] Mohamed J (as he then was) in *S v. Makwanyane*, 1995 (6) BCLR 665 (CC) at para. 262.

[4] See generally H. Ebrahim, *The Soul of a Nation: Constitution Making in South Africa* (Cape Town: Oxford University Press, 1998). See also *In re Certification of the Constitution of the Republic of South Africa, 1996*, 1996 (10) BCLR 1253 (CC), and *Certification of the Amended Text of the Constitution of the Republic of South Africa, 1996*, 1997 (1) BCLR 1 (CC).

[5] Karl Klare uses these concepts to describe the main features of the South African Constitution in 'Legal Culture and Transformative Constitutionalism', (1998) 14 *South African Journal on Human Rights* 146.

[6] See the preamble to the Constitution of the Republic of South Africa Act 108 of 1996 (hereafter referred to as 'the Constitution').

[7] See the preamble to the Constitution of the Republic of South Africa Act 200 of 1993 (hereafter referred to as 'the interim Constitution').

[8] Sachs J in *S v. Mhlungu*, 1995 (7) BCLR 793 (CC) at para. 111.

Human Rights Act a court may issue a declaration of incompatibility but may not declare legislation invalid. South African judges have the power to grant 'appropriate relief' to a litigant whose rights have been violated, which includes the power to strike down legislation in conflict with the Constitution, and make any order that is considered 'just and equitable' including putting the legislature on terms to cure the defect in the law.[9] Because of its explicit transformation objectives, it is primarily in the context of the role that the Constitution in general and the Bill of Rights in particular has played in achieving a transformative social justice in South Africa that the South African experience is most usefully analysed. In particular, this chapter attempts to ascertain the extent to which the judiciary (and in particular the Constitutional Court), now the avowed guardian of the Constitution, has contributed to the meaningful change that democracy in South Africa has promised.

II. Principles of constitutional interpretation

Given the force of the normative principles expressly articulated in the constitutional text, it is not surprising that the Constitutional Court pronounced on the importance of observing its dictates in the process of constitutional interpretation in its very first judgment. In *S v. Zuma*[10] Kentridge AJ for a unanimous court noted:

While we must always be conscious of the values underlying the Constitution, it is nonetheless our task to interpret a written instrument. I am well aware of the fallacy of supposing that general language must have a single 'objective' meaning. Nor is it easy to avoid the influence of one's personal intellectual and moral preconceptions. But it cannot be too strongly stressed that the Constitution does not mean whatever we might wish it to mean.

Encapsulated in this statement is the court's concern about its role in a democracy. Despite the explicit recognition of the indeterminacy of the language of the text and the influence of the interpreter's personal moral convictions, legal constraint and interpretive fidelity must be the foundation for constitutional interpretation lest the court stray beyond its proper adjudicative role. In spite of this apparent commitment to the words of the text, however, the interpretive process has been fundamentally altered by the introduction of the Constitution and the Bill of Rights. While the textual differences between the South African Constitution and the HRA are relevant, it is likely that the introduction of the ECHR in the interpretive process in the UK will also fundamentally change the way in which the interpretive function is carried out by British judges.[11] Nowhere is this clearer than from the decision of the Constitutional Court in *S v. Mhlungu*.[12] Here the Constitutional Court was faced with the question of the

---

[9] S. 172(1) of the Constitution. [10] 1995 (7) BCLR 401 (CC).
[11] See esp. the contribution by Tom Campbell in this volume. [12] N. 8 above.

proper interpretation of s 241(8) of the interim Constitution, which provided as follows:

All proceedings which immediately before the commencement of this Constitution were pending before any court of law, including any tribunal or reviewing authority established by or under law, exercising jurisdiction in accordance with the law then in force, shall be dealt with as if this Constitution had not been passed: Provided that if an appeal in such proceedings is noted or review proceedings with regard thereto are instituted after such commencement such proceedings shall be brought before the Court having jurisdiction under this Constitution.

The ordinary meaning of the words in section 241(8) are clear: pending proceedings are to be dealt with 'as if the Constitution had not been passed'. Mahomed J, delivering the majority judgment of the court, however, rejected the literal interpretation and held that the only purpose of section 241(8) was to confer authority on a court or tribunal to continue dealing with proceedings which were pending before the commencement of the interim Constitution. The minority view delivered by Kentridge AJ was that one of the effects of section 241(8) was to exclude the applicability of the interim Constitution in proceedings which were pending before 27 April 1994, the date of its commencement. Mahomed J reasoned that the literal approach to section 241(8) would deny to large groups of people protection of fundamental rights simply on the basis that proceedings in their cases had begun before the commencement of the interim Constitution. This was problematic, because the interim Constitution promised the equal protection of the laws and an end to discrimination and arbitrary governmental and executive action. A literal approach would thus invade the objectives of the interim Constitution because it would arbitrarily exclude one category of persons from its protection. This is the 'generous and purposive' approach to constitutional interpretation: the interpretation of section 241(8) must be based not only on the literal meaning of the words seen in isolation, but on the context of the provision, including the 'larger context of the Constitution regarded as a holistic and integrated document with critical and important objectives'.[13]

In his dissenting judgment, Kentridge AJ found that the reluctance of some judges to give literal effect to section 241(8) was 'understandable'. He acknowledged the importance of taking into account the spirit and tenor of the interim Constitution when interpreting section 241(8). He found, however, that there were some provisions where the 'language used, read in its context, is too clear to be capable of sensible qualification'. He concluded that the values which underlie an open and democratic society based on freedom and equality would not be promoted 'by doing violence to the language of the Constitution in order to remedy what may seem to be hard cases'.[14] Sachs J, who came to the same conclusion as the majority but for different reasons, accepted that a purposive approach to interpretation would involve a degree of strain on the language used. He endorsed the view that judges should 'function in an unapologetically purposive fashion and not be afraid

---

[13] Para. 15.   [14] Para. 84.

to acknowledge that they can and do "rectify" the text when the words used in a particular formulation defeat or go against the general purpose of the statute'.[15]

The *Mhlungu* judgment has been described as involving 'a minority which sought to discover the meaning of the words and a majority which strove to find words for a predetermined meaning'.[16] However, it has also been argued that a literal approach to interpretation would render the new constitutional enterprise in South Africa nugatory, and the majority judgment has been described as an 'honest attempt to challenge the restrictive shibboleths of a conservative jurisprudence'.[17] The force of this observation is derived from and may be justified by the transformative goals of the South African Constitution itself. In the wider context, however, there are obvious dangers in endorsing this degree of judicial carte blanche in the process of constitutional interpretation which remains inherently subjective, unclear, and incoherent. Indeed, as will be seen below, the Constitutional Court itself has since been inconsistent and often unpredictable in its interpretation and use of the transformative provisions of the Constitution in many areas, including the right to equality and its application to the common law governing private relations.

Related to the question of interpretive fidelity is the court's characterization of its work as a legal and not a political exercise. It is ironic that when the court is engaged in one of its typical political questions, it disavows all politics and reverts to strict legalism. In striking down the death penalty as unconstitutional, the court noted that its function was to interpret the text of the interim Constitution as it stood. Thus whatever the judges' personal views on the subject of capital punishment, the court's response must be a legal one.[18] Indeed, many of the justices stressed the essentially legal nature of their endeavour and the differences between a political decision made by a legislative organ and a decision made by the judiciary.[19] The former takes into account the political preferences of the electorate, while the latter requires a 'judicious interpretation and assessment' of a range of factors to determine what the *Constitution* permits and what it prohibits.[20] These factors include not only the text of the constitutional provisions and the interplay between them, but also[21]

legal precedent relevant to the resolution of the problem both in South Africa and abroad; the domestic common law and public international law impacting on its possible solution; factual and historical considerations bearing on the problem; the significance and meaning of the language used in the relevant provisions; the content and sweep of the ethos expressed in the structure of the Constitution; [and] the balance to be struck between different and sometimes potentially conflicting considerations reflected in its text.

---

[15] Para. 124.   [16] E. Fagan, 'The Longest Erratum Note in History', (1996) 12 *South African Journal on Human Rights* 79 at 89.

[17] D. Davis, 'The Twist of Language and the Two Fagans: Please Sir May I Have More Literalism', (1996) 12 *South African Journal on Human Rights* 504 at 512.

[18] Sachs J in *S v. Makwanyane*, n. 3 above, para. 207.

[19] This was the approach adopted by Chaskalson P, Mohamed, Mokgoro, Madala, and Sachs JJ.

[20] Mohamed J in *S v. Makwanyane*, n. 3 above, para. 266.   [21] Ibid. para. 273.

This approach is not out of line with a growing international trend in human rights adjudication towards a 'purposive' approach to interpretation, to seek the meaning of provisions of bills of rights from a number of sources that may not be evident from the textual meanings of the provisions themselves. But even a cursory analysis of these factors reveals that they are inherently and unavoidably subjective and open to a number of different outcomes depending on the personal and moral convictions of the interpreter. It is now commonly accepted that the meaning of statements of abstract rights is imprecise, uncertain, and incoherent. Thus, in seeking to find the meaning of the words of the Constitution, it is necessary to go beyond the words of the text and to engage in a form of political and moral reasoning.[22] Indeed, the Constitution in section 39(1) enjoins a court to promote the values that underlie an open and democratic society based on human dignity, equality, and freedom. Thus, particularly in South Africa, the content of the text 'will be contested by competing visions of how [it seeks] to re-constitute our society'. The inherently political nature of the process is thus clear and, for some, unapologetic: 'our Constitution will be contested and refashioned and in this context our politics will be fought.'[23] But the court's claim to be engaging in a strictly legal exercise attempts to conceal the fundamentally political and moral exercise in which it engages which many would argue properly belongs on the agenda of the legislature. It is a thinly veiled attempt which is difficult to reconcile with the court's earlier statements about the process of constitutional interpretation discovering and revealing the 'critical and important objectives' of the Constitution.[24] The fact is that judges do politics. The question is therefore not only the extent to which they are suited to this role, but what sort of politics they do and the extent to which they assist the project of social democracy and redistributive justice. The rest of this chapter attempts to address these questions.

III. The Constitutional Court and equality

In this part of the paper I focus on the equality guarantee and its application by the Constitutional Court in some detail. This is because the right to equality occupies a primary place in South Africa's new constitutional order.[25] Given the history of

---

[22] Anton Fagan has argued that the source of constitutional rules must be the constitutional text and the latter must be given its ordinary meaning. Written constitutional rules constitute a more reliable and legitimate guide to interpretation than the moral convictions of the judges. See 'In Defence of the Obvious: Ordinary Language and the Identification of Constitutional Rules', (1995) 11 *South African Journal on Human Rights* 545.

[23] D. Davis, 'Democracy and Integrity: Making Sense of the Constitution', (1998) 14 *South African Journal on Human Rights* 127 at 145.

[24] See the text to n. 13 above.

[25] The centrality of the right to equality has been recognized by the Constitutional Court in many of its judgments. See e.g. *Fraser v. Children's Court, Pretoria North and Others*, 1997 (2) BCLR 153 (CC) *per* Mohamed J: 'There can be no doubt that the guarantee of equality lies at the very heart of the Constitution. It permeates and defines the very ethos upon which the Constitution is premised' (para. 20). See also *President of the Republic of South Africa v. Hugo*, 1997 (6) BCLR 708 (CC) *per* Kriegler J: '[I]n the light of our own particular history, and our vision for the future, a Constitution was written with equality at its centre' (para. 74).

apartheid, this is no surprise. The centrality of equality in the vision of democracy embodied by the Constitution is apparent throughout the Constitution. In particular, in chapter 2 of the Constitution, the Bill of Rights, equality is listed as the first substantive right and, unlike most of the other provisions in the Bill of Rights, it explicitly applies horizontally and binds private persons.[26] Given the importance and pre-eminence of the right to equality, and the fact that its substantive realization is a precondition for transformative change in South Africa, how has the Constitutional Court interpreted and given meaning to it?

The full test for equality, and the circumstances under which different treatment may constitute unfair discrimination was articulated by the Constitutional Court in *Harksen v. Lane*.[27] Differentiation will amount to discrimination if it is based on one of the sixteen specified grounds in section 9(3) of the Constitution, or if it is objectively based on a ground which has the 'potential to impair the fundamental human dignity of persons as human beings or to affect them adversely in a comparably serious manner'.[28] Unfairness is presumed if the discrimination is based on one or more of the listed or specified grounds in section 9(3).[29] The effect of this is that if the differentiation is on a listed ground, it not only immediately establishes discrimination but also gives rise to a presumption of unfairness. In *Harksen* it was held that in order to determine whether discriminatory treatment is unfair, various factors must be considered, including the position of the complainants in society and whether they have suffered from past patterns of discrimination; the nature of the provision or power and the purpose sought to be achieved by it; and any other relevant factors, including the extent to which the discrimination has affected the rights or interests of the complainants and whether it has led to an impairment of their fundamental human dignity.[30]

The test for unfairness is said to be at the heart of the equality analysis.[31] It is this part of the test that is intended to be contextual, because it is here that factors such as whether past patterns of disadvantage are being exacerbated are considered. Thus understood, the unfairness test is intended to show that discrimination may have

---

[26] See s. 9 of the Constitution.   [27] 1997 (11) BCLR 1489 (CC).   [28] Ibid. para. 46.

[29] The presumption of unfairness is triggered by s. 9(5).

[30] The test for equality, and particularly the inclusion of the dignity component in both the discrimination and unfairness stages of the analysis, has been severely criticized. See C. Albertyn and B. Goldblatt, 'Facing the Challenges of Transformation: Difficulties in the Development of an Indigenous Jurisprudence of Equality', (1998) 14 *South African Journal on Human Rights* 248, and D. Davis, 'The Majesty of Legoland Jurisprudence', (1999) 116 *South African Law Journal* 398. The argument is that considering both group-based systemic disadvantage and individual dignity as equal factors to be taken into account mutes the substantive nature of the equality test. Equality, it is argued, is concerned with issues related to material, economic and social interests, and its primary purpose should be to address group-based disadvantage, not individual personality issues. Thus the intention of the equality clause must be 'to advance equality, not dignity, and that the dignity provisions in the Bill of Rights should take care of protecting dignity' (*National Coalition for Gay and Lesbian Equality v. Minister of Justice*, 1998 (12) BCLR 1517 at para. 20).

[31] See W. Freedman, 'Understanding the Right to Equality', in (1998) 115 *South African Law Journal* 243. See also J. Kentridge, 'Equality', in M. Chaskalson et al. (eds.), *Constitutional Law of South Africa* (Cape Town: Juta, 1998), 14–18.

different impacts in different contexts. It sorts permissible from constitutionally impermissible discrimination. The effect of this is that 'even though the prohibition on unfair discrimination . . . seeks not only to avoid discrimination against people who are members of disadvantaged groups'[32] the more vulnerable the group against whom the discrimination is directed, the more likely the discrimination will be found to be unfair.[33]

The Constitutional Court has been at pains to highlight the substantive nature of its approach to equality. In particular, it has held that the right to equality must be understood in the context of South Africa's own history:[34]

Particularly in a country such as South Africa, persons belonging to certain categories have suffered considerable unfair discrimination in the past. It is insufficient for our Constitution to merely ensure that, through its Bill of Rights, that statutory provisions which have caused such unfair discrimination in the past are eliminated. Past unfair discrimination has ongoing negative consequences, the continuation of which is not halted immediately when the initial causes thereof are eliminated, and unless remedied, may continue for a substantial time and even indefinitely.

Such a conception of equality sees the primary purpose of the provision being that of eradicating past patterns of disadvantage, and interpreting discrimination within the context of past and existing social, political, and economic disparities. Such an approach also highlights the importance of the need for remedial or restitutionary equality, to ensure that addressing past patterns of discrimination is the most important function of the equality guarantee.

However, the case law reveals that it has not been the most historically disadvantaged groups who have thus far invoked, often successfully, the protection of the equality provision. Three gender equality cases have been heard by the Constitutional Court: *Brink v. Kitshoff*,[35] *Fraser v. Children's Court, Pretoria North*,[36] and *President of the Republic of South Africa v. Hugo*.[37] In these three cases, two of the applicants (Fraser and Hugo) claiming the protection of the sex equality guarantee were men. In *Fraser* the applicant, an unmarried father, successfully challenged the provisions of the Child Care Act 74 of 1983 which allowed the adoption of children born out of wedlock without the consent of the father. In *Hugo* the applicant, a convicted prisoner, challenged the Presidential Act of 1994 which granted a remission of sentence to certain women prisoners with children under the age of twelve, while not extending the same benefits to fathers. Even in *Brink* the applicant was a woman who clearly fell on the more privileged side of the spectrum, who sought to challenge the validity of section 44 of the Insolvency Act 24 of 1936 which would have deprived her of a life insurance policy valued at approximately R2 million ceded to her by her deceased husband.

This pattern of relatively privileged groups seeking the protection of the equality guarantee is not only evident in the sex equality cases. In *Harksen*[38] the applicant,

---

[32] *Hugo*, n. 25 above, para. 41.   [33] Ibid. para. 112.
[34] *National Coalition for Gay and Lesbian Equality v. Minister of Justice*, n. 30 above, para. 60.
[35] 1996 (6) BCLR 752 (CC).   [36] N. 25 above.   [37] Ibid.   [38] N. 27 above.

owner of property worth over R6 million, challenged the validity of section 21 of the Insolvency Act which placed an onus on the solvent spouse to prove that his or her property should not be dealt with as part of the insolvent estate. The appellant in *Prinsloo v. Van Der Linde*[39] was a farm-owner who contended that the presumption of negligence in section 84 of the Forest Act 122 of 1984 discriminated against defendants in veld fire cases. This trend has only occasionally been broken, with two cases having been successfully brought on the basis of the right against discrimination on the basis of sexual orientation[40] and one on the basis of HIV discrimination.[41] The first sexual orientation case involved a challenge to legislation which prevented sodomy and sexual intercourse between men, and the second to the provisions of the Aliens Control Act which afforded certain benefits to spouses of permanent South African residents but did not afford the same benefits to gays and lesbians in same-sex life partnerships. It is noteworthy, however, that the application in the both sexual orientation cases was brought by the National Coalition of Gay and Lesbian Equality, a voluntary association of gay people in South Africa and sixty-nine organisations and associations representing such people. It is clear that an important part of the reason for the success achieved in these cases by this group relates not only to its size but also to the fact that it is a highly organised and politically active lobbying and pressure group in South Africa.

The pattern of the equality provision being used by those relatively advantaged is due in no small measure to the institutional obstacles and access to resources beyond the control of the court, but the question to be asked is to what extent the application of our equality jurisprudence remedies or prevents unfair discrimination against groups suffering social, political and legal disadvantagement in our society. A few selected cases will be used to illustrate the difficulties and contradictions in the judicial implementation of the concept of substantive equality in South Africa.

City Council of Pretoria v. Walker[42]

The background to the matter in *Walker* was the consolidation of a number of previously black townships, including Atteridgeville and Mamelodi, into the formerly white municipality of Pretoria in 1994. Charges for services rendered in these areas were, largely for historical reasons, levied on a different basis. Residents in the formerly white areas (referred to in the judgment as 'old Pretoria') were charged on the basis of their actual consumption measured by meters installed on their properties. Residents of Atteridgeville and Mamelodi were charged a uniform or 'flat' rate for services, as no meters had been installed to measure individual consumption in these areas. The flat rate was calculated on the basis of an average cost of the bulk

---

[39] 1997 (6) BCLR 759 (CC).

[40] *National Coalition of Gay and Lesbian Equality v. Minister of Justice*, n. 30 above, and *National Coalition of Gay and Lesbian Equality v. Minister of Home Affairs*, 2000 (1) BCLR 39 (CC).

[41] *Hoffman v. South African Airways*, 2000 (11) BCLR 1211 (CC).   [42] 1998 (3) BCLR 257 (CC).

supply of services measured over a period of time and dividing the cost amongst the number of houses in the townships.

The applicant, the City Council of Pretoria, sued the respondent for arrear charges for services rendered during a nine-month period. The respondent, a white resident of old Pretoria, contended that he was entitled to withhold payment as it was unfair discrimination under section 8(2) of the interim Constitution for the Pretoria City Council to levy a flat rate in Atteridgeville and Mamelodi which was lower than the metered rate in old Pretoria, and to take legal action to recover arrears only against residents of old Pretoria while following a policy of non-enforcement of debts in Atteridgeville and Mamelodi.

Walker was an example of the application of the principle of indirect discrimination. Even though the differentiation was on the basis of geographical locations, Langa DP for the majority found that there was indirect discrimination on the basis of race as '[t]he effect of apartheid laws was that race and geography were inextricably linked and the application of a geographical standard, although seemingly neutral, may in fact be racially discriminatory'.[43] As the discrimination was based on one of the listed grounds, the city council had the burden of rebutting the presumption that the discrimination was unfair. The council was not able to rebut the presumption that the selective enforcement of debt recovery was unfair discrimination.

Some of the flaws inherent in the application of the equality test are clear from this case. The choice by the majority in Walker to categorize the differentiation on the basis of the listed ground of race rather than the unlisted ground of geographical location (as was done by the dissenting judgment) was central to the court's finding that there had been unfair discrimination because the council was eventually unable to rebut the presumption of unfairness triggered by section 9(5) of the Constitution. If complainants base their claims on a listed ground there is an automatic presumption of discrimination and unfairness. The presumptions are triggered because, as Goldstone J observed in *Harksen*, the specified grounds have in the past been used 'to categorize, marginalise and often oppress persons who have had, or who have been associated with, these attributes and characteristics'.[44] However, the presumption applies notwithstanding the nature and consequences of the differentiation. The grounds listed in section 9(3), such as race and sex, are couched in neutral terms, and the presumption operates notwithstanding *how* the complainant has been affected in the past by being a group member of one of the listed grounds. A more contextual approach should recognize that discrimination on a listed ground is a matter of constitutional concern where it occurs against a backdrop of past or existing disadvantage and prejudice.

The consequences of not following this approach are clear from the outcome of the case in *Walker*, where the court concluded that white people belonged to a racial minority that could be regarded in a political sense as vulnerable and who 'in a very

---

[43] At para. 32.   [44] N. 27 above, para. 49.

special sense' need the protection of the Bill of Rights. If the group identified in *Walker*—white middle-class suburban dwellers having benefited rather than been adversely affected by apartheid in the past—can be classified as a vulnerable group deserving of special protection, one would be at great pains to find a group that would *not* be so classed. Sachs J, the dissenting judge, held that the discrimination was not on race but geographical location, and also recognized that an automatic presumption of both discrimination and unfairness 'becomes particularly incongruous' in a case where the complainant belonged to a racial group which 'benefited directly in the past from programmes that were systematically law-enforced and overtly racist'.[45] He held that in order for a differentiation to be discriminatory it must impose some identifiable disadvantage on the complainant or threaten to touch on or reinforce patterns of disadvantage. The majority judgment has raised questions about whether the Constitution's commitment to equality, in terms of addressing systemic and pervasive group-based inequality, is being upheld. Indeed, the requirement of past patterns of disadvantage inherent in the unfairness test to ensure that the equality clause would not become muted by claims of more privileged groups seems to assume lesser importance.

Harksen v. Lane[46]

In *Harksen* the validity of section 21 of the Insolvency Act, which placed an onus on a solvent spouse to prove that his or her property should not be dealt with as part of the insolvent estate, was challenged on the basis that it violated the right to equality. The differentiation in this case was on an unlisted ground, viz. between solvent spouses and all other persons who had dealings with the insolvent. The court found that the differentiation amounted to discrimination as it was based on characteristics and attributes which had the potential to undermine the fundamental dignity of human beings, viz the close and intimate relationship between spouses. As it was based on an unspecified ground, the applicant bore the onus of showing it was unfair. Applying the unfairness test, Goldstone J for the majority held that the discrimination was not unfair. This was because solvent spouses were not a vulnerable group adversely affected by discrimination, and the section had the legitimate purpose of protecting the interests of creditors. While the impugned section might cause some inconvenience to the solvent spouse it did not impair his or her dignity, as it was of the same kind as that experienced by any person when litigating.

In her dissenting judgment O'Regan J held that the discrimination was unfair. She observed that in the past there had been discrimination against married people, particularly against those who were married according to religions or customs not recognized by the law, and against married women in particular. She found that the impact of the impugned provision on the spouses of insolvents was substantial. All the property of the solvent spouse, even those not linked to the business affairs of

---

[45] At para. 113.   [46] N. 27 above.

the insolvent spouse and even if it is of an intrinsically personal nature, is auto-matically vested in the Master of the High Court[47] and then the trustee. This may happen suddenly without notice to the solvent spouse, and in a way which dispro-portionately favoured the interests of the creditors while being overly burdensome on the solvent spouse. The discrimination was consequently unfair.

Like *Walker*,[48] the majority decision in this case does not appear to examine fully the historical and social context of the complainant in question. This tendency has been described as a 'somewhat worrying disjuncture between stated principle and its actual application'.[49] In theory the unfairness test requires the court to examine the history, impact, and context of the discrimination on the affected group, an exercise not apparently engaged in by the majority. The judgment shows scant consideration for the position of married people and the historical and present factors which have affected them. Instead, the majority judgment focuses almost exclusively on the financial impact on the creditors at the expense of a consideration of the impact on the solvent spouse and has been noted for its 'clinical commercialism.'[50]

President of the Republic of South Africa v. Hugo[51]

Hugo involved a challenge to the action of the State President who, acting under his powers to pardon and reprieve offenders under section 82 of the interim Constitution, granted a remission of sentence to all mothers in prison on 10 May 1994 with children under the age of twelve years old. Hugo, a male prisoner with a twelve-year-old child, challenged the constitutionality of the President's decision on the ground that it discriminated against him on the basis of sex, a listed ground under section 8(2) of the interim Constitution.

The majority agreed that by releasing only mothers and not fathers there was dis-crimination on the basis of sex. The discrimination, being on a listed ground, was presumptively unfair, and the President bore the onus of rebutting this presump-tion. The court accepted that by releasing mothers only, the President had relied on a generalization that women were primarily responsible for child care in our soci-ety. The court also accepted that '[t]he result of being responsible for children makes it more difficult for women to compete in the labour market and is one of the causes of the deep inequalities experienced by women in employment. The gener-alization on which the President relied is therefore a fact which is one of the root causes of women's inequality in our society.'[52]

Despite this observation, the majority found that the discrimination was not unfair. This was because fathers were not a vulnerable group adversely affected by discrimination, that given South Africa's high crime rate it would have been diffi-cult if not impossible to release both mothers and fathers, and in any event the

---

[47] The Master of the High Court is an administrative official based in the superior courts whose main functions are to keep records of, and administer and control, estates.

[48] N. 42 above.   [49] Albertyn and Goldblatt, n. 30 above, 262.   [50] Ibid.

[51] N. 25 above.   [52] At para. 38.

release of male prisoners would not have contributed to the President's goals since fathers, as a general rule, do not play a major role in child care. As to the last leg of the unfairness analysis, the court held that it was not the President's decision which impacted on rights and obligations of fathers, but rather their convictions for having committed crimes.

In a strongly worded dissenting judgment, Kriegler J held that he could not find that although the President relied on the very stereotype which results in women's inequality, it was nonetheless constitutionally permissible. He held that limited benefit in this case (to the 440 mothers released from prison) is outweighed by the detriment to all South African women. He held:[53]

The limited benefit in this case cannot justify the reinforcement of a view that is a root cause of women's inequality in our society. In truth there is no advantage to women qua women in the President's conduct, merely a favour to perceived child minders. On the other hand there are decided disadvantages to womankind in general in perpetuating perceptions foundational to paternalistic attitudes that limit the access of women to the workplace and other sources of opportunity. There is also more diffuse disadvantage when society imposes roles on men and women, not by virtue of their individual characteristics, qualities or choices, but on the basis of predetermined, albeit time-honoured, gender scripts. I cannot agree that because a few hundred women had the advantage of being released from prison early, the Constitution permits continuation of these major societal disadvantages.

O'Regan J in a separate concurring judgment held that women's primary responsibility for child-rearing was a social reality. She pointed out that while an egalitarian society required men and women to share the responsibilities for child-rearing, the fact of the matter is that they do not. She held that the disadvantage to women lay not in the President's statement, but in the social fact of the role played by mothers in child-rearing, and more particularly, in the inequality which resulted from it.

This case illustrates the very real tension which exists between a matter of important principle and the concrete lives of people in the litigation of equality issues.[54] In the application of the equality test, the majority judgment does show an understanding of the social context of women, and particularly the position of mothers with young children in a society in which child-rearing carries no economic value. They do this at the expense of the principle articulated by Kriegler J. They appear to be saying that concrete gain for women under these circumstances is more important than the resolute defence of principle, particularly where this would lead to no substantive transformation at all. However, it is has been pointed out that the major flaw in the case is that it does not 'locate the complainant, as a single father, within his social context'.[55] However, as in *Walker*,[56] the indeterminacy and complex nature of selecting a group in which to locate the complainant for the purposes of the equality analysis is clear. Hugo as a father and a primary caregiver is both simultaneously privileged and

---

[53] At para. 83.
[54] See Justice A. Sachs, 'Equality Jurisprudence: The Origin of the Doctrine in the Constitutional Court', (1999) 5 *Review of Constitutional Studies* 76 at 89.
[55] Albertyn and Goldblatt, n. 30 above, 264.   [56] N. 42 above.

disadvantaged. This is the case too in *Harksen*.[57] The cases cited above show that the task of courts to judge whether a group is vulnerable and deserving of protection under the equality guarantee is an extremely complex one, with political and ideological dimensions for which they are often not suited. The cases also show that the courts, when faced with such a task, engage in a value-laden, subjective, and indeterminate exercise which does not always result in the achievement of substantive equality. They show, too, that those who would benefit most from the protection of the equality provision—indeed, those whom the provision was specifically designed to protect—have limited access to its application.

IV. The socio-economic rights

It has been argued that the inclusion of socio-economic rights in a bill of rights serves to ensure that democratic constitutionalism is promoted. This is because without those basic resources citizens would not be able to participate effectively in the democratic process.[58] By protecting rights that are important to the majority of South Africans, socio-economic rights also have an instrumental value in that they provide legitimacy to the Constitution.[59] Again, the South African Constitution has been hailed for its progressive and relatively novel protection of a range of socio-economic rights.[60] The Constitution provides that the state is required, within its available resources, to take reasonable legislative and other measures to achieve the progressive realization of these rights. Despite much academic debate on the matter, the justiciability of socio-economic rights was confirmed early in the Constitutional Court's jurisprudence. In the judgment in which the court was required to certify the new constitutional text for its compliance with the constitutional principles embodies in the interim Constitution,[61] it was held:

It is true that the inclusion of socio-economic rights may result in the court making orders which have implications for budgetary matters. However, even when a court enforces civil and political rights such as equality, freedom of speech or the right to a fair trial, the order it makes will often have such implications. A court may require the provision of legal aid, or the extension of state benefits to a class of people who were formerly not beneficiaries of such benefits. In our view it cannot be said that by including socio-economic rights within a Bill of Rights, a task is conferred upon the courts so different from that ordinarily conferred upon them that it results in a breach of the separation of powers. . . . We are of the view that these rights are to some extent justiciable. . . . At the very minimum, socio-economic rights can be negatively protected from improper invasion.

---

[57] N. 27 above.

[58] See N. Haysom, 'Constitutionalism, Majoritarian Democracy and Socio-economic Rights', (1992) 2 *South African Journal on Human Rights* 451.

[59] See E. Mureinik, 'Beyond a Charter of Luxuries: Economic Rights in the Constitution', (1992) 2 *South African Journal on Human Rights* 464.

[60] See esp. ss. 26–9 of the Constitution.

[61] *In re Certification of the Constitution of the Republic of South Africa 1996*, n. 4 above.

The judicial enforcement of socio-economic rights in the Constitutional Court has had mixed success. In the first case in which the court was required to apply the socio-economic rights, *Soobramoney v. Minister of Health, Kwazulu-Natal*,[62] the appellant, an unemployed man in the final stages of chronic renal failure, challenged the policy of a provincial hospital to refuse to provide him with ongoing dialysis treatment. The policy was necessitated by a shortage of resources. In dismissing the appeal, the court held that that the obligation on the state extended only to its available resources. The decisions which the government makes with respect to its allocation of resources involved difficult policy choices and a court will be 'slow to interfere' with them. The court noted that '[t]he hard and unpalatable fact is that if the appellant were a wealthy man he would be able to procure such treatment from private sources; he is not and has to look to the state to provide him with such treatment. But the state's resources are limited and the appellant does not meet the criteria for admission to the renal dialysis programme.'[63]

However, in the recent decision of *Government of the Republic of South Africa v. Grootboom*[64] the Constitutional Court found that the failure of the government's nationwide housing programme to provide relief for those in desperate need fell short of the obligation imposed upon it by section 26 of the Constitution.[65] The respondents in this case were evicted from the informal settlement they occupied on private land set aside for formal low-cost housing. Many of the respondents had been on a waiting list for subsidized low-cost housing from the municipality for many years, and they lived in abject poverty in the squatter settlement they had previously occupied. The conditions under which they lived prompted them to occupy the vacant land from which they had been evicted. The court examined the measures taken by the government in its national housing programme and found that, despite its laudable medium- and long-term objectives in securing housing, its failure to take steps immediately to ameliorate the circumstances of those in crisis did not meet the requirement of reasonableness contained in section 26. In doing so, the court highlighted the interconnectedness of civil and political rights and socio-economic rights, and amongst the socio-economic rights themselves. It held that the foundational values of the Constitution, those of human dignity, freedom, and equality, are denied to those who have no food, clothing, or shelter. In particular, the reasonableness of state action in respect of housing had to be determined with regard to the foundational value of human dignity. The housing programme did not meet this requirement. In the result the court made a declaratory order requiring the state 'to devise and implement within its available resources a comprehensive and coordinated programme progressively to realise the right of access to adequate housing'.[66] The programme must include measures to provide relief to those with no access to land or shelter, and those living in intolerable or crisis situations. The

---

[62] 1997 (12) BCLR 1696 (CC).   [63] At para. 30.   [64] 2000 (11) BCLR 1169 (CC).
[65] S. 26 provides that the state must take reasonable measures within its available resources to ensure the progressive realization of the right to access to adequate housing.
[66] At para. 99.

Human Rights Commission, as part of its constitutional duty to oversee the implementation of the rights in the Bill of Rights, was given the responsibility of monitoring and reporting on the efforts made by the state in this regard.

The *Grootboom* judgment has been acclaimed for its contribution towards the achievement of the transformative goals of the Constitution. In relation to the HRA, it signals the importance of the presence of socio-economic rights in a bill of rights, since it is precisely these rights which must be realized if the Constitution is to play a role in social transformation. In addition, the existence of these rights can be used to infuse the content of all other rights with a substantive socio-economic dimension. The court in *Grootboom* made an important move in this direction by recognizing the interrelationship between all the rights in the Bill of Rights. Despite this, the impact of the *Grootboom* decision should not be overestimated. The court came to its conclusion on the basis that the housing plan failed to meet the test of reasonableness in that it did not cater for those in desperate need. The order eventually made required the state to devise a plan for the realization of the right to access to adequate housing within its available resources, taking into account the needs of those living in crisis situations. However, as *Soobramoney* shows, the court will still adopt a narrow and deferential approach to the interpretation of the term 'available resources', and will be slow to interfere with the policy choices made in respect of their allocation. In addition, the court in *Grootboom* could itself provide no immediate relief to the successful litigants, leaving it up to the state and the Human Rights Commission[67] to implement and monitor a more inclusive housing plan with little or no guidance, terms, or conditions. It must, however, be noted that the overall lesson from *Grootboom* is that the presence of socio-economic rights in a bill of rights can fundamentally alter the ways in which judicial rights discourse has been traditionally articulated, in relation both to the interpretation and understanding of these rights themselves and to the ways in which they influence the interpretation and content of other rights. In short, if an entrenched rights document is chosen or inevitable, then the inclusion of socio-economic rights in the document is crucial.

V. Horizontality and the development of the common law

It has been suggested that because the HRA requires courts to have regard to the ECHR, more robust development of the common law in the light of the fundamental rights will take place. In short, this has not been the South African experience, despite explicit constitutional provisions requiring the courts to develop the common law in the light of the Bill of Rights.[68] This has been so despite the generous

---

[67] The Constitution itself makes provision for the Human Rights Commission to monitor the realization of socio-economic rights and report to Parliament. In terms of s. 184(3), relevant organs of state are required to report annually to the Commission in this regard. This is an important constitutional recognition that strategies other than litigation are necessary to give effect to the socio-economic rights.

[68] S. 39(2) of the Constitution.

and purposive approach to interpretation adopted by the Court described above. In Du *Plessis v. De Klerk*[69] the court found that the interim Constitution did not apply directly to the common law as it governs relations between individuals. It found, however, that the common law could and should be developed in the light of the interim Constitution. Kentridge AJ for the majority reached this conclusion on the grounds both of the text of the interim Constitution and of the traditional function of bills of rights being to protect the individual against the abuse of state power. As has been pointed out by Davis, the powerful dissenting judgment of Kriegler J shows that the majority judgment was a product of judicial choice[70]—again indicative of the subjective and value-laden alternatives available in the process of constitutional interpretation. Kriegler J premised his judgment on the recognition that inequality and oppression are not limited to state and individual relationships in South Africa, but continue to exist in the realm of relationships between individuals. With only few exceptions,[71] subsequent cases before the Supreme Court of Appeal, now the main guardian of the development of the common law, have sometimes developed or altered the common law without even a mention of the influence of the Constitution[72] or have neglected to subject it to the provisions of the Constitution at all, even in cases of obvious constitutional conflict.[73]

There are a number of difficulties with the approach of the majority in *Du Plessis*. It has been argued that it is arbitrary and irrational to exclude one body of the common law (that which governs private relations) from direct constitutional scrutiny, and ignore the prevalence of private power which remains the major source of inequality in South African society. In the light of the more robust approach the court takes to the constitutionality of acts and legislation passed by the democratically elected legislature, it is difficult to understand why the judge-made common law remains sacrosanct, only to be developed on a case-by-case basis and along 'incremental lines'.[74] One of the consequences of this approach is to posit the state as the main threat to the exercise of democratic rights. Yet it is ironic that the private sphere—the primary area of social inequalities and injustice in society— remains insulated from constitutional scrutiny, while the democratic arm of government best able to address those causes is subject to restraint.[75] The position may well have changed in the light of the text of the final Constitution,[76] but the

---

[69] N. 2 above.   [70] D. Davis, *Democracy and Deliberation* (Cape Town: Juta, 1999), 105.

[71] See e.g. *National Media Limited v. Bogoshi*, 1991 (1) BCLR 1 (SCA).

[72] See e.g. *S v. Jackson*, 1998 (1) SACR 470 (SCA).

[73] See e.g. *Mthembu v. Letsela*, 2000 (3) SA 867 (SCA).

[74] Kentridge AJ in *Du Plessis*, n. 2 above, para. 58.

[75] See however C. Sprigman and M. Osborne, '*Du Plessis* is Not Dead: South Africa's 1996 Constitution and the Application of the Bill of Rights to Private Disputes', (1999) 15 *South African Journal on Human Rights* 25, who argue that it is also counter-majoritarian for the Bill of Rights to apply directly to the common law as it places restraints on the ability of parliament to codify the law on the terms that it wishes.

[76] See esp. s. 8. See also S. Jagwanth and P. J. Schwikkard, 'An Unconstitutional Cautionary Rule', (1998) 11 *South African Journal of Criminal Justice* 87; and H. Cheadle and D. Davis, 'The Application of the 1996 Constitution in the Private Sphere', (1997) 13 *South African Journal on Human Rights* 44.

majority judgment in *Du Plessis* remains reflective of the inconsistent and incoherent approach the court has adopted in this area, including the development of the common law to eradicate the disparities in private power in South Africa.[77]

VI. Conclusion

This chapter has intended to show that the process of judicial constitutional adjudication is an inevitably unpredictable, subjective, and inherently political exercise which has often resulted in only sporadic achievements in the quest for social transformation in South Africa. This points to the importance of an understanding that the constitutional rights and values are not within the main realm of enforcement by the judiciary. A more promising sign regarding the application of the provisions of the South African Constitution is to be found in spheres outside judicial enforcement, including policy and legislative initiatives. This includes legislation dealing with unfair discrimination and the promotion of equality, as well as legislation introduced in the employment sector to address historical disadvantage and power imbalances in South African society. There has also been recent legislation promoting access to information and administrative justice, as well as legislation designed to address issues affecting women, including domestic violence, choice on termination of pregnancy, and maintenance. Many of these pieces of legislation were mandated by the Constitution itself and are intended to give effect to some of the rights in the Bill of Rights. It highlights the fact that the drafters also intended the legislature to flesh out the constitutional rights and determine their realization. In the final analysis, whether the judiciary is institutionally ill-suited, unwilling, or inaccessible, protection and implementation of rights must become part of public consciousness and thus of the democratic process in order to be meaningful.

---

[77] Recently the Constitutional Court has taken a more robust approach to the common law as it regulates the exercise of *public* power. See *Pharmaceutical Manufacturers; in re ex p. Application of the President of RSA*, 2000 (3) BCLR 241 (CC). The decision in *Du Plessis* is rendered even more incoherent as a result of this judgment.

17

Rights–Based Constitutional Review in Central and Eastern Europe

WOJCIECH SADURSKI

I. Introduction

In his excellent book on American constitutionalism, Stephen M. Griffin observes:

Deciding to place the protection of basic rights in the hands of the judiciary is also a decision to remove such issues from the agenda of the elected branches. This restricts the basic right of citizens to participate in important political decisions respecting the content of such rights. While this consideration is by no means decisive, it provides a salutary reminder that the decision to adopt judicial review involves restricting some basic rights in order to promote others. This immediately raises the question of whether the rights to be promoted are of greater importance than the political rights that are restricted.[1]

This insight, identifying as it does a fundamental reason to take a sceptical approach to constitutionalizing rights, is strangely absent from the dominant discourse about constitutional rights in the post-communist states of Central and Eastern Europe. Those countries have embraced, almost without reservation, the power of constitutional courts to strike down legislation under constitutional charters of rights. While there have been occasional public expressions of dissatisfaction with this or that major decision, the legitimacy of the constitutional tribunals to replace the legislators' understanding of constitutional rights with its own has gone virtually unquestioned. More fundamental challenges, in the constitutional and political theory of these countries, to the supremacy of courts' visions of human rights over that of the legislators' have been very few and far between.

What are the reasons for this uncritical acceptance—among constitutional scholars, but also more generally within the political and intellectual elites—of robust, activist, rights-based judicial review in the countries undergoing transition from communist to democratic rule? Two explanations seem most plausible. First, the general acceptance tracks the comparatively high social prestige of constitutional courts in these societies as a whole. As an example, one might cite a study which showed that in 1995, the most activist constitutional court in the region—the Hungarian one—enjoyed support of 58 per cent of the population, with the government having 35 per cent and the Parliament a mere 26 per cent.[2] This may be

---

[1] *American Constitutionalism* (Princeton, NJ: Princeton University Press, 1996), 123.

[2] See G. Halmai and K. Lane Scheppele, 'Living Well is the Best Revenge: The Hungarian Approach to Judging the Past', in A. J. McAdams (ed.), *Transitional Justice and the Rule of Law in New Democracies* (Notre Dame, Ind.: University of Notre Dame Press, 1997), 181, fig. 1.

seen as a consequence of the general disenchantment with political branches of the government. Not unlike the case of Germany after the fall of the Third Reich, the practice of politics was largely discredited after the fall of communism, and there has been a widespread cynical conviction that politics is a dirty business. As new institutions with a post-communist pedigree (with the exceptions of Poland and Yugoslavia),[3] constitutional courts did not share the opprobrium of the institutions tainted by their former complicity in non-democratic practices.

The second reason has less to do with general public opinion than with the participants in constitutional discourse (constitutional scholars and judges) themselves. Self-congratulatory rhetoric supports both the position of the constitutional judiciary and law professors because these groups live in a state of symbiosis. The strong position of constitutional review strengthens the academic position of constitutional lawyers within law faculties, while the supportive doctrines produced by constitutional lawyers elevate the position of constitutional judges vis-à-vis political branches. Both these phenomena are mutually reinforcing. But there is, no doubt, more to it than simple self-interest. Many constitutional lawyers in the countries of Central and Eastern Europe sincerely believe that the only means of guaranteeing constitutional rights, especially against the background of the previous regimes which had contempt for both constitutions and rights, is to entrust a quasi-judicial, unelected body with this task.

Be that as it may, the constitutional systems of post-communist countries of Central and Eastern Europe have 'imported' a novel institutional form without at the same time importing the set of doctrinal and philosophical critiques which have accompanied that institution for many years. Constitutional courts of West European countries—in particular of Germany, but to a lesser degree also of France, Spain, Italy, etc.—provided a model for constitutional review after the fall of communism, but the doctrinal controversies surrounding the rights-based review in countries such as Germany and France have not affected constitutional discourse in Central and Eastern Europe.

This chapter provides an account of rights-based constitutional review in Central and Eastern Europe. Part II outlines the institutional model of constitutional courts in the region, serving as a background to the two main parts of the article—a discussion of the 'activism' of constitutional courts under the rights provisions (Part III) and an attempt to establish the record of the constitutional courts in the region (Part IV). Of particular import is the question of whether, on balance, the existence and the practices of constitutional courts have been beneficial from the point of view of respect for, and protection of, fundamental values expressed in the form of constitutional rights.

Two caveats are in order. First, 'Central and Eastern Europe' is a description of a large region, and the constitutional courts in the region do not fit one single

---

[3] In the former Yugoslavia, the Constitutional Court (and the corresponding courts at the level of particular republics) was introduced in 1963. In Poland, the Constitutional Tribunal was set up in 1985.

account. It is very hard to draw a composite picture of twenty or so courts, each with a different institutional design, degree of independence, and track record. I will therefore focus on some of the most activist, robust, and independent constitutional courts. They are the most significant institutions from our point of view, and the trend suggests that with the consolidation of democracy in other countries, they will follow the lead given by activist courts. Second, constitutional courts under discussion here are all comparatively new institutions. They have just embarked upon a path of maturing, and generalizations must be treated with a degree of circumspection. They are very much work-in-progress institutions, and so is the account of their activities.

II. The model of constitutional review in post-communist states

All post-communist constitutions in Central and Eastern Europe contain provisions on constitutional courts. While there are certain local variations, one may attempt a description of the common model of a constitutional tribunal in the region. The model adopted is that of a 'concentrated' or 'centralized' constitutional review, composed of judges appointed for limited tenure by political branches of government, exercising abstract, ex-post, and final review of constitutionality of statutes and other infra-constitutional acts. Each of these features is unpacked below.

Centralized and concentrated review is understood as an arrangement by which only one institution in each of these countries has the right authoritatively to scrutinize laws for their constitutionality. No ordinary judge has such a right. The most they can do if they have doubts about constitutionality of a legal rule which they are called on to apply is to suspend the proceedings and refer the question to the constitutional court (so-called 'concrete review'). The rule against the ordinary judiciary's power to strike down infra-constitutional law is very strict, based as it is on fear of a possible threat to the unity of the legal system should individual judges have such power. But it is also based on more contingent factors. The regular judiciary in these countries, following a continental model, enjoys a relatively low status and cannot be trusted (in the views of constitution-makers) with making such momentous judgments as those concerning the compatibility of a statutory provision with the Constitution.

Hence, this task is conferred upon a special body, established outside the regular judicial system, and often regulated by constitutional provisions separate from the chapters on the judiciary.[4] The only, and minor, exception is Estonia, where a constitutional court is known as the 'Chamber of Constitutional Review' and is

---

[4] For example, the provisions regarding constitutional courts are separate from the chapters on the judiciary in the constitutions of Romania, Hungary, Lithuania, Bulgaria, and Ukraine. In the constitutions of Slovakia, the Czech Republic, Russia, and Poland constitutional courts are governed by constitutional regulations alongside the judicial bodies.

structurally a part of the National Court (the equivalent of the Supreme Court). This, however, does not importantly affect its position in the overall constitutional system, and for all practical purposes the Estonian Chamber can be viewed as a constitutional court, like any other in the region.

Judges of constitutional courts are appointed for limited tenure, usually for nine years.[5] With very few exceptions, constitutional justices tend to be either legal scholars (with a marked preponderance of constitutional law professors) or senior members of the 'regular' judiciary. The appointment process is thoroughly political, although 'high legal qualifications' (or an equivalent description) is usually listed as one of the criteria of eligibility. In most Central and Eastern European countries, constitutional judges are appointed in a process which requires the participation of both the legislative and executive branches (Romania, Albania, Czech Republic, Slovakia, Russia, etc.). In some countries, the highest bodies representing the judiciary are also involved (Bulgaria, Lithuania, and Ukraine). Two of the most active constitutional courts of the region constitute an exception. In both Hungary and Poland, constitutional justices are appointed exclusively by the parliaments. This has been criticized by an eminent Polish legal scholar (who is also currently a constitutional court judge) as creating a 'risk of excessive politicization' of the appointment process.[6]

The most important power of constitutional courts, for present purposes, is their exercise of abstract judicial review. This means that the statutory rule is considered not in the actual context of a specific case but *in abstracto*. It is the textual dimension of the rule, rather than its life in the application to real people and real legal controversies, which is assessed by judges in comparison with their understanding of the text of a relevant constitutional rule. Most of these courts also exercise a power of *concrete* review, initiated by other courts,[7] and some of them (Hungary, Poland, Slovenia, etc.) will also hear citizens' constitutional complaints, brought by those individuals who believe that their constitutional rights have been violated by a judicial and/or administrative decision issued on the basis of the infra-constitutional law, the constitutionality of which is questionable. However, it is the 'abstract' review initiated by other bodies (the President, the government) or by a group of MPs (usually, members of the minority outvoted on a law which they subsequently challenge before the Court) which raises the gravest legitimacy problems. It is on such occasions that the clash of different views about what an open-textured constitutional norm 'really' means is most marked, and the question 'who should have the last word?' seems most apposite.

Abstract review is problematic for a number of reasons. From the perspective of the division of authority between the legislature and the constitutional court, abstract review is troubling for the reason that it is often initiated by those political

---

[5] Although other limits can apply: 6 years in Moldova, 8 in Croatia, 10 in the Czech Republic.

[6] L. Garlicki, 'Trybunał Konstytucyjny w projekcie Komisji Konstytucyjnej Zgromadzenia Narodowego', (1996) 51 *Państwo i Prawo* 6.

[7] Although not in Ukraine, where only abstract review is envisaged.

actors dissatisfied with a majoritarian decision of the parliament—that is, they lost the debate. It also makes no necessary allowance for those principles which reduce the clash between the legislature and the judiciary where the review of constitutionality is dependent upon consideration of a specific case. Consider the doctrines elaborated by the US Supreme Court that the court will avoid deciding 'political questions', or cases which are not 'ripe' enough, or which are 'moot', all of which constrain judges from deciding questions of constitutionality. But no such doctrines are relevant to the system of 'abstract' review. A challenge to recently passed legislation, depending on its substance, may be very much a 'political question', is 'ripe' automatically when the law is passed, and will not cease being 'moot' as long as the law is on the books.

The dominant model in Central and Eastern Europe is of an ex post review, that is, review of the laws already enacted, although there are some exceptions. In Romania, abstract review can apply only to statutes adopted by the Parliament but before the promulgation (while there is also a path open for a concrete review, initiated by courts, which by its very nature can be only ex post). This resembles the position of French *Conseil constitutionnel*, which also can review parliamentary acts only before promulgation. Further, some other constitutional courts in the region (in Poland, Hungary, and Estonia), in addition to their more routine, ex post review, can be asked by the respective Presidents to conduct an ex ante review of the act just passed by the Parliament, and one court (in Hungary) can even be asked to issue an advisory opinion about a bill not yet voted on by the Parliament. There is, however, a marked tendency to view the prospective review and advisory opinions as an exception rather than the rule.

With the exception of Romania, decisions about unconstitutionality of statutes in all Central and Eastern European countries are final, and there is no way of reversing the verdict other than by a constitutional amendment. This is, of course, a difficult and politically costly process. Hungary provides the only example of such a step—not surprisingly, a system where constitutional amendments are relatively easy—where the parliament explicitly reversed a constitutional court decision of 1990 and denied in the Constitution itself to Hungarians living abroad the right to participate in general elections. The court had earlier decided that the absence of such an opportunity constituted a constitutional violation. In Romania, verdicts of the constitutional court resulting from an abstract review, conducted prior to promulgation, can be overridden by a two-thirds majority of both chambers. In Poland, a similar possibility existed until the Constitution of 1997 introduced the finality of all constitutional court decisions.

Finally, it should be mentioned that constitutional courts in the region—consistently with their Western European prototypes—perform a number of other functions, such as deciding in the cases of conflicts regarding the powers of other constitutional bodies, about the status of political parties, about constitutionality of international treaties, and about elections or referendums. These matters, however, lie beyond the scope of this chapter.

III. 'Activism' of rights-based review

How 'activist' are the most dynamic constitutional courts under the rights provisions of their respective constitutions? Is the judicial activity of these courts significantly altering the preferences of the parliamentary majorities, and—more importantly—departing from the views of the constitution makers? Elsewhere (especially in the United States) a reliance on the 'original intent' in the area of constitutional interpretation is largely—and deservedly—in disrepute, but when the constitution is brand new and the constitution makers are still very much around, the hostility to the very idea of the original intent is less understandable. After all, it is the Constitution which provides the basis for legitimacy of the constitutional courts' decision-making. It is difficult to establish what the criteria of 'judicial activism' should be, and the concept itself is suspect to many legal scholars, but we do not need to get embroiled in the controversy about the term. What is important is that the phenomenon which it is supposed to denote here is important and raises understandable concerns, namely, a substitution of the parliamentary majority's view by the court's majority view about the proper articulation of the meaning of a constitutional right when these two views collide. As a working test, I suggest that an inquiry into 'judicial activism' of constitutional courts involves two criteria: the importance of the laws invalidated under the rights provisions and the nature of the reasoning leading to such invalidation.

As far as the first criterion is concerned, the relative importance of a norm is admittedly in the eyes of beholder, and whether a rule which has been struck down is relatively significant or relatively trivial is a matter which cannot be ascertained in a non-controversial fashion. When, for example, the Estonian Chamber of Constitutional Review struck down Tallin city regulations concerning removal of illegally parked vehicles,[8] some will probably say that this is a relatively trivial matter, in a broader scheme of things. Others will look at the decision more closely and, having ascertained that the conclusion has been reached under an interpretation of the right to private property, will conclude that it posits a fundamental and potentially far-reaching principle of demarcating individual autonomy and the state's police power.

At the end of the day, what matters for the characterization of the courts as 'activist' is not so much a proportion of relatively 'trivial' matters decided by these courts but rather the very fact that, even if very rarely, some truly fundamental political choices on central public issues have been reversed by the courts—rather as an author of a single masterpiece will remain a genius even if all her other works are trite. And there is little reasonable disagreement that some of the Central European constitutional courts have, at least occasionally, displaced the parliament's will on fundamental matters.

---

[8] See (1996) 3 *East European Case Reporter of Constitutional Law* 5.

What follows is a rather random list of examples. The laws invalidated (or partly invalidated, but with significant effects on the original laws) included rights to abortion (Poland, Hungary), the death penalty (Hungary, Lithuania, Albania, Ukraine—in all these countries abolition of the death penalty was a product of constitutional courts' decisions), economic austerity measures of the government (Hungary), important aspects of taxation laws and tax provisions of the annual budgets (Poland), requirements for naturalization (Slovenia), privatization of public land (Slovenia), and restrictions of certain rights of same-sex couples (Hungary). This is an admittedly random list, and it will be supplemented by examples of some of the most important judicial decisions in the next part of this paper. But I believe that this list suffices to convince a reader that at least in some of the Central European countries, constitutional courts have on occasion displaced the preferences of parliamentary majorities on fundamental matters.

The importance of the laws overturned is only one part of a test for 'activism' of the constitutional courts in the domain of constitutional rights. Another, equally essential factor is the nature of the reasoning which led to invalidation decisions. After all, if the courts *are* constitutionally mandated to check the statutes for unconstitutionality, they may have no choice but to overturn the laws which, on their face, clash with constitutional provisions. But then, the consistency or otherwise of two legal provisions (one of which is constitutional) is always a matter of interpretation, and people may disagree in good faith about an interpretation of any two provisions: the one which is subject to a constitutional challenge, and the one which is the basis for a possible invalidation decision.

Rather than getting embroiled in a theoretical discussion about what renders a judicial reasoning 'activist' (and whether such a characterization makes sense at all), I will give some examples of characteristic patterns of reasoning of constitutional courts of the region discussed here, and appeal to certain intuitive, common-sense, and relatively uncontroversial views about how these patterns are symptomatic of judicial restraint or judicial activism of the courts in question. I will, further, discuss in some detail two important decisions on the death penalty and on abortion, from Hungary and Poland respectively, to give the reader an insight into the judicial reasoning of the constitutional courts in these countries.

In all fairness, one should note that the rhetoric of judicial *restraint* is certainly present in the case law of constitutional courts—and often the rhetoric is adhered to in the actual structure of argument. The courts, when engaging in judicial review, often emphasize the presumption of constitutionality of statutes. For example, the Polish Constitutional Tribunal, in a 1997 decision on collective agreements in the workplace, stated:

The burden of argument is on whoever challenges the constitutionality of a law and unless he or she produces concrete and convincing legal argument to prove his or her thesis, the Constitutional Tribunal will recognise the laws under challenge as constitutional.[9]

---

[9] Decision K. 19/96 of 24 Feb. 1997, in *Orzecznictwo Trybunału Konstytucyjnego, Rok 1997* [*Case Law of the Constitutional Tribunal, 1997*] (Warsaw: C. H. Beck, 1998), 72.

In a similar fashion, the courts often acknowledge the wide scope of the legislator's legitimate discretion. The Hungarian constitutional court in its 1991 decision on abortion stated: 'Where the law should draw the line between the unconstitutional extremes of total prohibition and unrestricted availability of abortions is for the legislature to decide.'[10] The courts also like to declare that, within the domain of legislative discretion, it is a political rather than constitutional responsibility which controls the legislator.[11] They also characterize their own role as, at best, a 'negative legislator', rather than a positive one, repeating a well-known Kelsenian formula for a constitutional court.[12] Most of all, they never tire of reminding their audience that the grounds of their decisions are not 'political' but 'strictly constitutional', implying that the judges' political or moral preferences do not enter into the process of review.[13]

But there have been also some important decisions of the constitutional courts which are unmistakably 'activist'—in the sense that the court *had* an option of upholding the statute, within recognized conventions of judicial reasoning, and yet decided to overturn it. If a set of recognized conventions of judicial reasoning makes it possible for the court to uphold the law, but also makes it possible to overturn it, a tendency to choose the latter path may be seen as an indicator of 'activism'. This happens when, for example, a court grounds its decision in very abstract, general, and vague constitutional notions, about the specific articulation of which reasonable people may disagree, even though it had an option of founding its decision on narrower and less ambiguous notions. 'Human dignity' used as a sufficient basis for overturning specific statutes is a good example. The Hungarian court appealed to this notion in different contexts. For example, in a 1990 decision the court proscribed trade unions from representing employees without their consent; the court relied on 'human dignity' and established the following general principle: 'When none of the . . . named fundamental rights are applicable for a given state of affairs' then the 'general personal right [to dignity] . . . may be relied upon any time by the Constitutional Court'.[14] This is all the more remarkable since, as one (friendly) commentator of the court noted, rather than relying upon the right to dignity, the court could have easily held that the constitutional clauses which specifically relate to the rights of unions 'to safeguard and represent the interest of employees' only authorize representation with consent.[15]

---

[10] Decision no. 64/1991 (XII 17) AB of 17 Dec. 1991, (1994) 1 *East European Case Reporter of Constitutional Law* 27.

[11] e.g. Decision of Polish Constitutional Tribunal no. K 22/95 in *Orzecznictwo Trybunału Konstytucyjnego, Rok 1996* [*Case Law of the Constitutional Tribunal, 1996*], vol. i (Warsaw: C. H. Beck, 1996), 120.

[12] See Decision of Polish Constitutional Tribunal no. K 13/95 of 24 Sept. 1996, in *Orzecznictwo Trybunału Konstytucyjnego, Rok 1996* [*Case Law of the Constitutional Tribunal, 1996*], vol. ii (Warsaw: C. H. Beck, 1996), 104.

[13] e.g. Decision of Polish Constitutional Tribunal no. K 19/96 of 24 Feb. 1997, n. 9 above, 72–3.

[14] Quoted by G. Halmai, 'Comment: The Constitutional Court of the Republic of Hungary', (1994) 1 *East European Case Reporter of Constitutional Law* 116.

[15] Ibid.

Arguably, the most telling example of use of vague and ambiguous notions in the service of overturning a clear legislative and constitutional intention is provided by the same court's decision invalidating the death penalty.[16] To reach this—laudable, from the point of view of this author—result, the court had to face the problem that the Constitution, on the basis of which it allegedly acted, contained a stipulation that 'no one may be arbitrarily deprived of life and human dignity' (Art. 54(1)). While silent about the specific issue of death penalty, this provision clearly implied that a 'non-arbitrary' deprivation of life was constitutionally permissible. A judge faced with this textual implication who is intent on striking down the death penalty as unconstitutional can theoretically reach this result in one of two ways, neither of which is quite satisfactory. She may either (a) claim that death penalty is necessarily arbitrary and thus prohibited under Article 54(1) or (b) find another constitutional provision which would constitute a basis for invalidating death penalty, and give precedence to that other provision over Article 54(1). In the opinion for the majority, the latter path is taken. The court relies on Article 8(2), which proclaims that 'rules on fundamental rights and obligations shall be determined by laws which, however, shall not impose any limitations on the essential contents of fundamental rights', in connection with the right to life and dignity. The court said that the death penalty necessarily intrudes upon the 'essential content' of the right to life, and so—to the extent that Article 54(1) may be read as permitting a non-arbitrary deprivation of life—it is superseded by Article 8(2). But, of course, whether a non-arbitrary enforcement of death penalty violates an 'essential' aspect of human right and dignity is a moral proposition about which reasonable people may—and do—disagree. The court opted therefore for a controversial moral judgment over a more precise and narrow constitutional permission.

Interestingly, in his concurring opinion, Chief Justice Làszló Sólyom used *both* strategies, and it is no wonder that applying both of them creates a clear impression of an overkill. As to strategy (a), he argues that capital punishment necessarily intrudes upon an 'essential' area of life and dignity because they are 'an absolute value' and form an 'indivisible and unrestrainable right'. But if this were true, then any law affecting adversely life and dignity, even if marginally, would have to be invalidated. As to strategy (b), he argues that capital punishment is necessarily 'arbitrary', not in any empirical, sociological sense (e.g. because it fails to achieve its purported aims) but rather 'conceptually'. Apparently, 'capital punishment is arbitrary not because it limits the essential content of the right to life but because the right to life and dignity—due to their characteristics—is from the outset unlimitable'.[17] This is a strange statement, and can hardly be read in any other way than as an expression of strong moral disapproval for death penalty. Such moral disapproval is plausible and resonates with many people's feelings—but as it happened,

---

[16] Decision 23/1990 of 31 Oct. 1990, repr. in L. Sólyom and G. Brunner, *Constitutional Judiciary in a New Democracy: The Hungarian Constitutional Court* (Ann Arbor: University of Michigan Press, 2000), 118–38.

[17] Ibid. 133 (Sólyom, P., concurring).

not with those of the majority of Hungarians, nor with the majority of the Hungarian MPs acting both in its law-making and in its constitution-making mode. Why *their* moral judgments, as expressed in legal practices, should be replaced by that of the court is *the* true issue which should have been addressed in this decision, but was not.

As another example, consider a momentous 1997 decision of the Polish Constitutional Tribunal on abortion law.[18] The Tribunal struck down as unconstitutional some liberal aspects of the then Polish abortion law, basically finding any abortion other than justified on strictly defined medical grounds (because of threat to mother's health, or the genetic defects of the foetus) or resulting from rape, as contrary to the Constitution. The decision was all the more remarkable since it ran contrary not only to the then majority opinion of the legislators (the Parliament was dominated by the centre–left coalition at the time) but also to the clear implications of the constitutional text. At the time the decision was handed down, a so-called Little Constitution (an interim constitutional document, virtually free of constitutional rights) was in force, and it contained no reference to the 'right to life', much less a right to life from the moment of conception. More importantly, a new, fully-fledged Constitution had been already adopted, including being passed in a national referendum, and was about to enter into force as from October 1997.[19] While formally speaking, the new Constitution was not binding on the judges of the constitutional court, it provided a good insight into the views of the constitution-makers. The new Constitution *did* make a reference to a right to life yet importantly, demands to include the proviso 'from the moment of conception' had been considered and explicitly rejected by the drafters. At the very least, constitutional judges knew that the constitution-maker had chosen not to prohibit abortion.

Faced with these textual constraints, the court nevertheless proceeded to argue that the availability of abortion on grounds other than those of (1) the danger to the life or health of a pregnant woman, (2) genetic defects of the foetus, or (3) pregnancy being a consequence of rape are contrary to the Little Constitution. In the absence of any reference to right to life in that interim document, the Court decided to base its conclusion, somewhat improbably, on the interpretation of the concept of the democratic 'state based on law', or *Rechtsstaat*, proclaimed in the first article of the Constitution. The centrepiece of the reasoning of the majority (and one should add that the decision was accompanied by three strongly worded dissenting opinions) was that the *Rechtsstaat* presupposes a community of people, and that the essential attribute of individuals is their life, which has to be constitutionally protected 'at each stage of its development'.[20] While the 'value' of life is not subject to gradation

[18] Decision no. K 26/96 of 28 May 1997, in *Orzecznictwo Trybunału Konstytucyjnego, Rok 1997* [*Case Law of the Constitutional Tribunal, 1996*], (Warsaw: C. H. Beck, 1998), 173–246; repr. in (1999) 6 *East European Case Reporter of Constitutional Law* 38–129.

[19] The new Constitution was adopted by the National Assembly on 2 Apr. 1997, subjected to the constitutional referendum on 25 May 1997, promulgated by the President on 16 July 1997, and entered into force on 17 Oct. 1997.

[20] N. 18 above, 181.

as a function of different stages of its development, the intensity of the protection can be varied, depending on the conflict of this value with other constitutional values and interests, the Tribunal announced.

A connection between this principle and the line drawn between some kinds of abortion (such as abortions necessitated by the health of a pregnant woman, which are permissible) and other kinds (abortions because of 'hard life conditions or difficult personal situation' of a pregnant woman) rests on a value judgment which cannot be inferred from the Constitution itself. The court decided to ignore the 'authentic interpretation' of the meaning of the Constitution, provided by the very recent process of drafting of a new Constitution, and established as law its own judgment on a very controversial matter. Many observers suggested that the decision was a response to the pressures by the Catholic Church, which was, at the time strongly agitating to deliberalize the abortion regime in Poland, and that the decision might have been related to the impending visit to Poland of Pope John Paul II.

Another symptom of activism of some of the Central European Constitutional Courts is their predilection for a 'balancing jurisprudence', especially of the least deferential kind, namely, of assessing whether the legislative measures are necessary to attain approved legislative purpose. As is known, the use of balancing 'is transforming constitutional discourse into a general discussion of the reasonableness of governmental conduct', and is therefore the kind of reasoning which situates the court in a characteristically legislative mode.[21] A 1997 decision of the Slovenian Constitutional Court provides a good example. It concerned the proposed referendum on amendments to the law on reprivatization of real property, mainly, agricultural lands and forests.[22] The referendum, proposed by three parties which obtained the support of over 50,000 voters, was meant to water down the reprivatization law of 1991 by (among other things) introducing a limit on the size of the lands returned to the former owners, and also by banning the return of the land 'of feudal origins'. The Court, exercising its power of review of referendum questions, largely disarmed the referendum proponents. It struck down the central question, aimed at introducing the limit of 100 hectares of land or forests, by refuting—on allegedly empirical grounds—the rationale provided by the proponents of the referendum, namely, that the return of very large areas was not within the capacities of the state, and would hinder the return of smaller pieces of land. This is clearly a sort of judgment on the cost/benefit calculus which is characteristically a domain of the political branches, not the court. As to the prohibition of a return of the lands 'of feudal origins', the court inserted its own proviso that this prohibition must not apply to the land owned by churches and other religious institutions. Contrary to the intentions of the authors of the referendum, the constitutional court argued that 'it would not be constitutionally permissible to equate the nationalised property of the church and religious communities *in view of their role as institutions of general*

---

[21] See T. A. Aleinikoff, 'Constitutional Law in the Age of Balancing', (1987) 96 *Yale Law Journal* 943.
[22] Resolution U-I-121/97 of 23 May 1997, repr. in (1997) 4 *East European Case Reporter of Constitutional Law* 279–303.

benefit and their position in the Slovenian legal system, with the estates of feudal origin'.[23] In other words, a preferential exemption for the churches has been carved out by the constitutional court on the grounds of a positive assessment of the social role of the church. This assessment by the court pre-empted a judgment by the general public whether the prohibition of return of feudal property should apply also to religious institutions. This judgment was made by the court within the pattern of strict scrutiny (not a concept used explicitly by the Court), namely, on the basis that the

proposed measures must be unavoidable in a democratic society, dictated by urgent public need [and that] the . . . measures . . . must, in compliance with the principle of proportionality, be appropriate and unavoidable in order to reach the legislator's objectives. . . .[24]

If the standard of scrutiny of a statutory regulation is whether the measures adopted by legislators (or, as the last case illustrates, the measures contemplated by referendum questions) are 'unavoidable' and 'necessary' to attain the approved goals, the pattern of reasoning of the judges becomes virtually the same as that of legislators. It also expresses a high degree of distrust of the legislature's judgment, and reduces the likelihood of affirming the regulation. It is almost always possible to establish an availability of a *different* measure from the one adopted by the legislature, and if such a demonstration is sufficient to defeat the legislation, no trace of deference to the legislative judgment can be found in the court's approach.

IV. The record of constitutional courts in the field of rights

What is the record of the constitutional courts in the field of protection of rights in Central and Eastern Europe? The evaluation is hard to make for the following three reasons. First, treating the region as a single entity leads to a distorted and misleading judgment: a 'correct' decision in, say, Albania, does not redress an 'incorrect' decision in, say, Slovakia. Each country would need to have a careful balance of 'correct' and 'incorrect' decisions made separately, and such an exercise obviously cannot even be attempted in the framework of this chapter. Second, what are the criteria of 'correct' decisions regarding the articulation of human rights provisions? These provisions yield moral judgments which are eminently controversial and, whether or not a court should have invalidated a statute under *its* interpretation of a constitutional right, hinges upon *our* view about whether this interpretation gives effect to *our* value judgments. The value judgments of this writer do not have to be (and are likely not to be) the same as those of the reader. Should the criminal penalty for desecration of national symbols be upheld or invalidated under constitutional right to free expression? This, and dozens of other controversial issues, do not lend themselves to easy answers by a simple appeal to 'liberal democratic' values, or a

---

[23] Ibid. 288 (emphasis added).   [24] Ibid. 286.

similar ideological platform. Liberal democrats may sincerely disagree about the 'correct' contours of a right to freedom of expression, etc.

Third, even if the difficulties raised by the first two remarks were somehow put to one side, the 'record card' would not simply call for a comparison of a number of 'correct' decisions (invalidations which are conducive to the implementation of a constitutional value which we endorse) with 'incorrect' ones (invalidations which are detrimental to a realization of a constitutional value which we endorse). The calculation would have to be more subtle and more complex. On the side of 'incorrect' decisions we would have to put *both* the invalidations which are not conducive to a value which we share *and* those cases of upholding a statute when the court *should* have (from the point of view of a constitutional value which we share) and *could* have (from the point of view of the legal resources available to it) invalidated the provision and yet failed to do so. The latter category may at first blush seem inappropriate as a factor weighing on the negative side of the score card. After all, one may claim that the erroneous upholdings do not detract from the protection of a system of rights in a given country because, in the absence of a constitutional court, the legislature would have enacted a given provision anyway. The existence of a court (the argument goes) does not affect the picture as far as the erroneous laws upheld by the court are concerned. But this is not so. The existence of a constitutional court to some extent 'releases' the political branches from a special degree of care in bringing about legislation which may implicate constitutional rights. This is because the very fact that there will be a likely review of a statute by a court may encourage the other branches to be more cavalier with lawmaking—after all, the bad laws are likely to be struck down, so the stakes are not that high. Legislators may try to test a particular provision whilst knowing full well that constitutional court scrutiny is likely—in a way which they would not have risked in the absence of such a scrutiny. Legislating in the shadow of constitutional review affects the motivations and the risk calculation of legislators, and therefore an erroneous upholding of a rights-implicating provision is a negative, rather than neutral, factor in the calculation of costs and benefits of constitutional review.

It is clear that such a calculation is extremely difficult to conduct. But I would venture a hypothesis that, if one ignores these three difficulties, the final judgment about the impact of constitutional courts on protection of human rights in Central and Eastern Europe must be positive. More often than not, the decisions of the constitutional courts in the region strengthened rather than weakened statutory protection of individual rights and freedoms. A short review of some of the main types of right which received enhanced protection by those courts will aim to support this thesis.

The most important contributions by the constitutional courts in the region have been in the area of freedom of expression. In Hungary, the court struck down provisions of the criminal code penalizing the offence of the denigration of the Hungarian nation (in 1992), those which criminalized defamation of public officials (in 1994), and quite recently, those which punished the deliberate spreading of panic (in 2000). The Czech constitutional court also found unconstitutional the criminal prohibitions of defamation of the parliament, government, and the constitutional court itself, though it maintained intact the penalty for the 'defamation of the Republic' (in 1994). The Lithuanian constitutional court in 1998 struck down the provisions of the Law on Officials which effectively prohibited public servants from public expression of disagreement with official policy.

Freedom of the press and other media also, occasionally, received a helping hand from the constitutional courts. In 1997, the Bulgarian court struck down the provisions for selecting a media council on the basis that they tended to perpetuate partisan interference with national media. The Hungarian court invalidated, in 1992, a provision of the decree on Hungarian radio and TV which subjected public broadcasters to the supervision of the Council of Ministers.

In the area of access to information and privacy, the Hungarian constitutional court has made some positive contributions. In 1992, it struck down certain provisions of the Act on Local Government which restricted public access to the local councils meetings and their minutes, and two years later it held that statutory restriction of access to government archives unduly restricted the constitutional 'freedom of science'. Regarding personal privacy, the same court twice struck down the laws introducing personal ID numbers (in 1991 and 1995), and also the governmental regulations compelling citizens to declare their assets (in 1993).

As examples of Court protection of the right to association one might mention the decisions by the Russian constitutional court and the Estonian chamber of constitutional review. The former struck down in 1993 a presidential decree which banned the activities of some 'extremist organizations' (such as the Front of National Liberation), on the basis of violation of the constitutional right to associate. The latter, struck down in 1996 the provisions of the Act on Non-Profit Associations which implicitly prevented minors from joining the associations, and which also created the possibility of administrative bodies interfering with the activities of non-profit associations.

A number of courts in the region improved importantly the integrity of the judicial process and the protection of rights of criminal defendants. The court of the Czech Republic invalidated, in 1995, the provisions of the criminal code which allowed for the anonymity of witnesses. In one way, however, the results of this change were disastrous, as hundreds of witnesses apparently withdrew their testimonies for fear of reprisals. The Albanian court struck down in 1999 provisions of the Law on the Organization of Judicial Power, as a result of which the stringency of tests for professional verification of judges would have been significantly lowered. In 1999 the Hungarian court found unconstitutional the amended provisions of the code of criminal procedure regarding drug-related offences, on the basis that they violated the principle of non-retroactivity of criminal law.

Now these and other decisions of the courts which corrected statutory provisions in the direction of stronger protection of individual rights have to be weighed against decisions going in the opposite direction, that is, those which replaced more liberal statutory rules with more restrictive choices represented by the courts. The abortion decisions of the constitutional courts in Hungary and in Poland constitute perhaps the most striking examples of such choices. The Hungarian court considered the matter of abortion twice, and in each case its decisions were slightly more restrictive—but only just—than the choices of the political branches. As Kim Lane Scheppele remarked, 'Hungary's adoption of a restrictive abortion law was not initiated in Parliament'[25] but rather originated from a constitutional court decision in 1991 which restricted the legislature's discretion over fashioning the abortion law. The court struck down the existing, relatively liberal abortion regime, on the grounds that it should have been controlled by parliamentary statutes rather than— as was the case at the time—by regulations promulgated by the health ministry. The court also used this occasion, however, to establish some substantive guidelines as a result of which the parliament enacted in 1992 a law which added certain additional rigours to the pre-existing situation (such as the woman's statement that she was in crisis, a mandatory cooling-off period, and mandatory counselling about the risks of abortion). The court revisited the issue of abortion in November 1998. While it found that the termination of a pregnancy based on an 'emergency situation' was not unconstitutional per se, it objected to the constitutional validity of a regulation concerning the pregnant woman's statement about the 'emergency situation'. It declared these provisions of the 1992 law to be impermissibly vague, and instructed the parliament to specify more clearly the criteria as to what constitute 'emergency circumstances'. Legal commentators agreed that this decision would lead to a moderate restriction of the previously liberal practices in this regard.[26]

A much more striking reversal of a relatively liberal into a highly restrictive abortion regime occurred in Poland, as a result of the 1997 decision of the constitutional tribunal which was discussed in some detail earlier in this chapter. As a result, the abortion regime which had allowed reasonably easy access by women to a safe and dignity-respecting termination of pregnancy was converted into one of the most restrictive systems of abortion rights in Europe.

A separate category is constituted by those cases when constitutional courts failed to remove non-liberal statutory provisions though they were legally capable of doing so. Consider some of the statutes with clear (and negative) implications for freedom of speech, which nevertheless passed the muster of judicial scrutiny. In Poland, in 1992, the constitutional court upheld a media law which required public radio and TV to respect 'Christian values' in their broadcasts. In the event, the requirement has proved rather toothless, but the warning by Helsinki Watch at the time that the upheld law could 'chill legitimate speech as broadcasters are forced to censor themselves to fit within the undefined boundaries of the law'[27] cannot be

---

[25] K. L. Scheppele, 'Women's Rights in Eastern Europe', (1995) 4(1) *East European Constitutional Review* 68.

[26] See 'Constitution Watch', (1998) 7(4) *East European Constitutional Review* 17.

[27] Quoted in M. F. Brzezinski, 'Constitutionalism and Post-Communist Polish Politics', (1998) 20 *Loyola of Los Angeles International and Comparative LJ* 445, n. 38.

easily dismissed. More controversially—because the issues of hate speech and offensive 'symbolic speech' are very contentious, even for the liberals themselves— some of the more activist constitutional courts in the region upheld laws restricting the speech of extremist organizations (Czech Republic, 1992) and laws prohibiting the display of 'authoritarian symbols' (including a swastika and a red star!) as well as a desecration of the national symbols (Hungary, 2000). In Moldova, the consti- tutional court recently upheld a law providing for severe civil sanctions against journalists for harm to honour and dignity—and the compensation awarded by the court may be quite hefty—up to 200 times average salary (if the compensation is to be paid by the newspaper) or up to 100 times average salary (if awarded against an individual journalist).

Constitutional courts in the region made some moderately positive contributions to rectify laws on the basis of the principle of non-discrimination, although some of the central aspects of gender inequality remained intact.[28] The Hungarian court struck down in 1995 a ban on same-sex concubinate and compelled the parliament to allow succession of property within homosexual couples. The Bulgarian court tackled, in a positive way, a sensitive issue of discrimination based on national and ethnic origin. It saved, in a decision of April 1992, a largely Turkish-based political party, the Movement for Rights and Freedoms (MRF), from proscription proposed on the basis of a constitutional prohibition of political parties based on 'ethnic, national or religious principles'. Applying a rather ingenious interpretation of this principle to the MRF, the court stated that the party was not to be outlawed because it did not *exclude* any people from its membership on the basis of national or ethnic origin.

The constitutional courts in Central and Eastern Europe have been active in other areas of constitutional rights, and only the most cursory list must suffice here, for reasons of space. On the basis of a constitutional right to private property, courts in the Czech Republic, Slovakia, and Romania removed certain restrictions upon restitution of property to former owners and privatization. With a similar effect, the Slovenian constitutional court judged unconstitutional certain questions in a pro- posed referendum which attempted to restrict the reach of the reprivatization law— as mentioned above, in Part III of this chapter.

Some of the most activist courts of the region—notably in Poland and Hungary— devoted much of their attention to socio-economic rights. Post-communist consti- tutions contain quite 'generous' lists of social and economic rights, and in some cases—such as Hungary—no formal distinction is drawn between these rights and more classical, civil and political rights. The rights spelled out by the Hungarian constitution include the right to work, the right to compensation that corresponds to the amount and quality of work performed, the right to the highest possible level of physical and mental health, and the right to social security. The Hungarian court sensibly refused to consider these rights to be equally justiciable as more traditional

[28] See Scheppele, n. 25 above.

rights, and drew its own distinctions between these two categories of rights, adopting a principle that socio-economic rights have a 'programmatic' character and are not directly justiciable. Nevertheless, it has at times quite actively interfered with governmental programmes which enjoyed parliamentary support at the time. The most spectacular case was a series of decisions in 1995 striking down the governmental package of austerity measures including changes to maternity and family support, reduction of household allowances, of state-subsidized sick leave, and raising of the interest rate on state loans to home-builders. Similarly, the Polish constitutional tribunal invalidated several budgetary and taxation measures, including a 1991 law reducing old age pensions and banning from further employment those pensioners who had to retire because their employers had closed down. Both Polish and Hungarian constitutional courts acted in these areas usually on the basis of the constitutional notion of *Rechtsstaat* (and the consequent idea of vested rights, legitimate expectations, trust, etc.) or social justice, rather than on the basis of specific constitutional provisions on social and economic rights.

Finally, special mention should be made of courts' dealings with various forms of so-called 'lustration' and/or decommunization laws—the laws aimed either at screening the public officials suspected of collaboration with former communist secret services ('lustration') or at excluding certain categories of ex-functionaries of the communist apparatus from the opportunity to occupy certain public functions ('decommunization'). Perhaps the most dramatic clash of the desire to settle accounts with the requirements of formal legality occurred on the occasions that legislatures attempted to lift the statutes of limitations for politically motivated crimes committed during the communist regimes. In Hungary, the constitutional court considered such laws twice. In 1992 it rejected the law as unconstitutional due to the violation of the principle of non-retroactivity. In 1993 it upheld much of the better-drafted law (in so far as it directly referred to crimes against humanity or war crimes, as those to which statutes of limitations did not apply on the grounds of international agreements ratified by Hungary), and struck down only those provisions which made no such references to international law.

In contrast, the Czech constitutional court turned out to be more lenient towards the suspension of statutes of limitations than its Hungarian counterpart. In December 1993 it upheld an Act of Parliament declaring the communist regime to be 'illegal and illegitimate' and lifting the statutes of limitation for criminal offences committed in the years 1948–89 for political reasons. The contrast between the Hungarian and Czech courts' approaches is revealing not just of different public sentiments in these two countries to the functionaries of the *ancien régime* but also of the different natures of the last decades of communist rule in these countries. As a result, the Hungarian judges preferred to deal with the communist past within the framework of formal legality while the Czechs resisted such an approach. It is symptomatic of the Czech approach that the court defended its decision to disregard the statute of limitations established by the law of the communist era on the basis that, in that period, 'the infringement of legality in the entire sphere of legal life became a component of the politically as well as governmentally protected regime of illegality'.[29]

V. Conclusions

The record of constitutional courts in Central and Eastern Europe, as undertaken cursorily above, is on balance positive. While there have been some important decisions in which these courts reversed liberal legislative choices and substituted their own, more restrictive articulations of constitutional rights, and there have also been many cases of missed opportunities to rectify non-liberal legal provisions, on the whole the correctives introduced by the courts must be viewed as positive, from the point of view of human rights. More often than not, the change made by the courts in specific areas should be applauded by observers concerned with a robust protection of civil and political rights. This is, at least, the case of the most activist and independent courts of the region: in Hungary, Poland, Slovenia, Czech Republic, and—to a lesser degree—in the Baltic states, Romania, and Bulgaria.

But this is not the end of the calculus. As the quotation from Stephen Griffin with which this chapter opened suggests, every rights-based exercise of judicial review can be seen as a choice to promote some rights and—in the process—to restrict others. Those *other* rights are those of political participation, and—in a representative democracy—of having one's elected representatives decide about the policies and the laws, within constitutional limits. As those limits, when expressed in the form of constitutional rights, are subject to diverse interpretations, and those diverse interpretations give effect to conflicting value judgments, the power of a constitutional court to have the last word on the validity of statutes which implicate constitutional rights necessarily limits the political rights of citizens in a system of representative democracy.[30]

This consequence has been hardly considered as really serious, both in general public discourse and in the constitutional scholarship of post-communist societies of Central and Eastern Europe. This is notwithstanding the fact that, as I suggested in Part III above, at least some of these courts have been, at least on some occasions, fairly 'activist'. The fact that they could get away with this without any fundamental challenge to their position in the system can be partly explained by two factors which I mentioned in the Introduction: a broad public disenchantment with the political branches of government (and, against this background, the relatively high social standing of constitutional judges) and an effective provision of the legitimating rationale for constitutional review by constitutional scholarship in these countries. But these are only partial explanations.

---

[29] Cited in P. Holländer, 'The Role of the Czech Constitutional Court: Application of the Constitution in Case Decisions of Ordinary Courts', (1997) 4 *Parker School Journal of East European Law* 452.

[30] See J. Waldron, 'A Right-Based Critique of Constitutional Rights', (1993) 13 *Oxford Journal of Legal Studies* 18.

The discourse of the legitimacy of constitutional review—not just in post-communist systems, but universally—can be perhaps seen as a conflict of two narratives. The first is an argument about the possibility of reasonable disagreement about rights. True, constitutional rights do and should limit the scope of legislative discretion, the argument goes, but those limits lend themselves eminently to reasonable disagreement about their meaning and implications for specific constitutional dilemmas. Should a constitutional right to free speech prohibit the legislators from setting limits on political advertising or, to the contrary, mandate the legislators to establish such limits? This and innumerable other controversies show that there are no absolute answers about constitutionality of statutes to be drawn from constitutional bills of rights. The question is, therefore, who should have the last word about the articulation of the 'true' meaning of these rights. And once the main question is framed in this way, the proponents of this argument have little difficulty in suggesting that such power should rest with the elected representatives of the voters.

The second narrative pulls in the opposite direction. It is the 'parade of horribles' story. Legislators, when left without any supervision, can get out of control and disregard constitutional limits altogether. Drawing the lines between those constitutional provisions about the articulation of which an external watchdog should decide (say, on the matters of procedure and separation of powers) and those where the legislators can have the last word (say, on constitutional rights) is not feasible, and leads to a cavalier attitude to the constitution as a whole by the lawmakers. What if the parliamentary majority enacts limits on freedom of speech, discriminates against an embattled ethnic minority, or imposes burdens upon the exercise of an unpopular religion? The 'parade of horribles' has no limits. The only limit is the imagination of the worriers.

If this 'parade of horribles' narrative has greater purchase on the collective imagination in Central and Eastern Europe than the narrative about reasonable disagreement about rights, it is because people know that the horribles in their part of the world *do* happen. The idea that lawmakers can be selfish, arrogant, unwise, self-serving, or plain corrupt is not a mere theoretical possibility for citizens of Poland, the Czech Republic, or Hungary, not to mention Russia, Ukraine, or Belarus. Memories of the pliable 'parliaments' subjected to the communist apparatus in the bad old days, combined with the often unwholesome conduct of the new political class, makes this scenario painfully realistic. It will take time before the new democracies of the region become more stable and—in the perceptions of the general population—irreversibly so. Only then will the arguments of sceptics about the rights-based judicial review of statutes be likely to gain in weight and influence. At this stage, most people in those new democracies believe—rightly or wrongly—that the rights likely to be *enhanced* by the intervention of constitutional courts are of higher value than the political rights of participation, which are affected adversely by the role of the constitutional court as a guardian of the behaviour of the political branches.

18

The Canadian Charter of Rights: Recognition, Redistribution, and the Imperialism of the Courts

JUDY FUDGE

The entrenchment of the Canadian Charter of Rights and Freedoms[1] in 1982 was but one instalment in the worldwide trend towards constitutional bills of rights that has now reached the UK.[2] In Canada, the Charter triggered what has become an increasingly polarized debate about the relationship between judicially enforced rights and democracy. In 1982 Charter critics were in a distinct minority, confined mostly to the left in law schools. Since then dissatisfaction with its impact upon Canadian political practices and constitutional arrangements has spread outside of academic journals and across the political spectrum. Over the two decades that judges have given concrete meaning to abstract rights, celebration of constitutional rights has turned to scepticism and the institutional legitimacy of the courts has been questioned.[3]

This chapter assesses the impact of the Canadian Charter of Rights on respect for human rights, democratic practices and political discourses in Canada to see what broader lessons, if any, can be distilled for the UK. Inevitably, this task involves a selective reading of both the Charter jurisprudence and how rights discourse has influenced political claims and practices. The chapter begins by placing the rights debate within the Canadian context, paying particular attention to how its terms shifted. Section II provides a heuristic to make sense of the different types of rights claim that are being asserted by progressive social movements, and examines what the Supreme Court has done with such claims and the political response to these decisions. It is also attentive to how Charter claims have influenced the demands of the social movements. The next section moves beyond 'progressive' rights claims to explore the meaning that the Supreme Court has attributed to the freedom of expression. By concentrating on a specific right in a range of contexts, Section III attempts to identify the salient features of the dominant rights discourse articulated

---

[1] Pt I of the Constitution Act,1982, being Sched. B to the Canada Act 1982 (UK), 1982, c. 11.

[2] See T. Vallinder, 'The Judicialization of Politics: A Worldwide Phenomenon', (1994) 15 *International Political Science Review* 91; and M. Mandel, 'A Brief History of the New Constitutionalism, or How We Changed Everything so that Everything Could Remain the Same', (1998) 32 *Israel LR* 250.

[3] See A. Lajoie, E. Gelineau, and R. Janda, 'When Silence is no Longer Acquiescence: Gays and Lesbians under Canadian Law', (1999) 14 *Canadian Journal of Law and Society* 101; and T. Morton and R. Knopff, *The Charter Revolution and the Court Party* (Peterborough: Broadview Press, 2000).

by Canadian courts. The chapter concludes by considering whether there are other mechanisms that may have better success in enhancing human rights and fostering democracy than a justiciable bill of rights.

[I]t seems that hardly a day goes by without some comment or criticism to the effect that under the Charter courts are wrongfully usurping the role of the legislatures. (Mr Justice Frank Iacobucci, Supreme Court of Canada, *Vriend v. Alberta*[4])

I. The rights debate in Canada

In Canada, the debate over the value of judicially enforced bills of rights in a demo-cracy has changed dramatically in the two decades since the Charter was entrenched. The initial currents are still visible, but they have been joined by a number of different streams, which together have shifted the direction of the over-all debate. The ranks of Charter critics have swelled. And although a 1999 national survey indicated that 82 per cent of those polled thought that the Charter was a 'good thing,' it also showed that they were divided evenly on the proposition that 'the right of the Supreme Court to decide certain controversial issues should be reduced'.[5] To a certain extent, this is an inevitable outcome of the process of elaborating rights through adjudication. At the level of a specific case, rights are more likely to conflict, and it is the job of the courts to resolve many of the contradictions. This pulls the judiciary and the law directly into political debate.

In Canada, an entrenched bill of rights was sold as part of a 'people's package', in which power would be transferred from the political elites to the people and demo-cracy would be enhanced. However, the political impetus behind it was the federal government, which saw an entrenched bill of rights as a device for centralizing political power in the face of accelerating regionalism, especially from Quebec.[6] It was also a response to the growing dissatisfaction with traditional parliamentary politics and part of a worldwide trend to institutionalize respect for fundamental human rights. In this context, it is not surprising that supporters far outweighed detractors. Political dissatisfaction with the Charter was largely confined to aborig-inal groups and the political elites within Quebec, who were unhappy not only with the content of the Charter but with its role in a larger political package from which they were excluded.[7] Scholarly opinion was predominantly favourable; the vast

---

[4] [1998] 1 SCR 493 [hereinafter *Vriend*].   [5] Morton and Knopff, n. 3 above, 5.

[6] See Y. de Montigny, 'The Impact (Real or Apprehended) of the Canadian Charter of Rights and Freedoms on the Legislative Authority of Quebec', in D. Schneiderman and K. Sutherland (eds.), *Charting the Consequences: The Impact of Charter Rights in Canadian Law and Politics* (Toronto: University of Toronto Press, 1997), 3; and M. Mandel, *The Charter of Rights and the Legalization of Politics in Canada*, 2nd edn. (Toronto: Thompson Educational Press, 1994).

[7] See M. Boldt and J. A. Long, 'Tribal Philosophies and the Canadian Charter of Rights and Freedoms', in Boldt and Long (eds.), *The Quest for Justice: Aboriginal Peoples and Aboriginal Rights* (Toronto: University of Toronto Press, 1985); Mandel, n. 6 above.

majority of legal scholarship on the Charter offered arguments for how the court ought to interpret it, and political scientists emphasized its democratic potential.[8] Discontent was confined to the Critical Legal or socialist scholars in Canadian law schools,[9] who emphasized the indeterminacy of the abstract language of rights and the institutional history and jurisprudential legacy of the courts.[10]

By the early 1990s the terms of the rights debate had begun to shift when the Charter lost some of its early lustre as actual decisions began to tarnish it. The most ardent rights supporters were disappointed by what they considered to be the courts' overly narrow treatment of equality issues.[11] However, their quarrel was not with the Charter, which they endorsed, but rather with the courts' interpretation of it; the law is willing but the judges are weak.[12] The remedy proposed is to bolster judicial independence and the quality of judicial reasoning by reforming the judicial appointment procedure.[13]

At the same time, critics of justiciable bills of rights, especially those who emphasized limitations in the legal form, were admonished to be more attentive to nature of the right's claim being made and the context in which it was asserted.[14] Progressive groups won Charter cases, suggesting that general denunciations of justiciable rights did not fit with a political reality that was more complex. Victories, especially relating to the recognition of rights of historically dispossessed groups such as refugees and gay men and lesbians, provided sustenance for equality-seeking groups. However, these cases provided a focus for the backlash against judicially enforced rights.[15]

---

[8] A. Dobrowolsky, 'The Charter and Mainstream Political Science: Waves of Practical Contestation and Changing Theoretical Currents', in Schneiderman and Sutherland, n. 6 above, 322; and R. Sigurdson, 'Left and Right Wing Charter Phobia in Canada: A Critique of the Critics', (1993) 7 *International Journal of Canadian Studies* 89.

[9] J. Hiebert, 'Debating Policy: The Effect of Rights Talk', in L. Seidle (ed.), *Equity and Community: The Charter, Interest Advocacy and Representation* (Montreal: Institute for Research on Public Policy, 1993), 31.

[10] See J. Bakan, *Just Words: Constitutional Rights and Social Wrongs* (Toronto: University of Toronto Press, 1997); J. Fudge and H. Glasbeek, 'The Politics of Rights: A Politics with Little Class' (1992) 1 *Social and Legal Studies* 45; A. Hutchinson, *Waiting for CORAF: A Critique of Law and Rights* (Toronto: University of Toronto Press, 1995); and Mandel, n. 6 above.

[11] See D. Beatty, *Talking Heads and the Supremes: The Canadian Production of Constitutional Review* (Toronto: Carswell, 1990); D. Beatty, 'A Conservative Court: The Politics of Law', (1991) 41 *U. of Toronto LJ* 147; G. Brodsky and S. Day, *Canadian Charter Equality Rights for Women: One Step Forward or Two Steps Back?* (Ottawa: Advisory Council on the Status of Women, 1989); and S. Day and G. Brodsky, *Women and the Equality Deficit: The Impact of Restructuring Canada's Social Programs* (Ottawa: Status of Women Canada, 1998).

[12] D. Beatty, 'The Canadian Charter of Rights: Lessons and Laments', in G. Anderson (ed.), *Rights and Democracy* (London: Blackstone Press, 1999) 26–7.

[13] See Beatty, *Talking Heads*, n. 11 above.

[14] See D. Herman, 'The Good, the Bad, and the Smugly: Sexual Ordination and Perspectives on the Charter', in Schneiderman and Sutherland, n. 8 above, 200; and J. Bakan and M. Smith, 'Rights, Nationalism and Social Movements in Canadian Constitutional Politics', in Schneiderman and Sutherland, n. 8 above, 218.

[15] C. Clark, 'Supreme Court must be reined in, McGill Professor says', *National Post*, 24 Nov. 1999; 'Judicial activism is not a figment of the imagination', *Globe and Mail*, 26 Oct. 1999; Herman, n. 14 above, 201; and K. Mahoney, 'Charter Equality: Has it Delivered?', in Anderson, n. 12 above, 121.

This backlash, which has been dominated by academics and politicians of the right, is a new phenomenon in Canada[16] and has obtained a great deal of media attention.[17] Its targets are judicial supremacy and the Court party,[18] two forces which are identified as undermining parliamentary supremacy, the rule of law, and social values in Canada. Populists criticize the Charter for shifting power to unaccountable judges who have been hijacked or hoodwinked by the arguments of special interests such as feminists.[19] Decisions that touch on values, norms, or institutions that are central to the positions of social conservatives, especially those relating to the family or sexuality, have precipitated a great deal of public criticism of the courts. Some provincial governments, moreover, have publicized their reluctance to follow the courts' lead in extending equality rights to gays and lesbians, for example.[20]

Stung by complaints that it has overstepped its institutional boundaries and trampled on democracy, the Supreme Court of Canada has responded to criticisms of its institutional competence and legitimacy. In speeches, articles, and decisions, it has begun to speak of the partnership in governance in which it is engaged, downplaying the adversarial dimension of its relationship with the legislature and emphasizing its supportive or corrective function.[21] Although different metaphors have been used to express the appropriate relationship between the courts and government, today dialogue is the dominant, although not unanimous, contender.[22] But, the problem of the courts' institutional legitimacy is enduring.

Concern about the lack of democratic accountability in Canadian institutions is not directed exclusively at the courts; it is much more pervasive. A number of forces

---

[16] G. Hein, *Interest Group Litigation and Canadian Democracy* (Quebec: IRPP, 2000), 4; Herman, n. 14 above, 207; and Morton and Knopff, n. 3 above, 17.

[17] See Clark, n. 15 above; *Globe and Mail*, n. 5 above; 'High court reopens battle between judges, politicians', *National Post*, 21 May 1999; and A. Pellatt, 'Equality Rights Litigation and Social Transformation: A Consideration of the Women's Legal Education and Action Fund's Intervention in *Vriend v. R*', (2000) 12 *Canadian Journal of Women and the Law* 17.

[18] Court party is a term coined by R. Knopff and F. L. Morton in *Charter Politics* (Scarborough, Ont.: Nelson, 1992) to characterize the special interests who have rallied around the Charter.

[19] See A. A. Peacock (ed.), *Rethinking the Constitution: Perspectives on Canadian Constitutional Reform, Interpretation and Theory* (Toronto: Oxford University Press, 1996), p. ix; R. Knopff, 'Populism and the Politics of Rights: The Dual Attack on Representative Democracy', (1998) 31 *Canadian Journal of Political Science* 883; Knopff and Morton, n. 18 above; and Morton and Knopff, n. 3 above.

[20] Both the Alberta and Ontario governments made much of their unhappiness with the Supreme Court of Canada's decisions to invalidate provincial legislation on the ground that it discriminates against gay men and lesbians. See S. Boyd, 'Family, Law and Sexuality: Feminist Engagements' (1999) 8 *Social and Legal Studies* 369; Ontario Ministry of the Attorney-General, 'Ontario protects traditional definition of spouse in legislation necessary because of the Supreme Court of Canada decision in *M v. H*' (Government of Ontario, press release, Oct. 1999), Http://www.newswire.ca/government; Clark, n. 15 above; and S. Patten, 'Citizenship, the New Right and Social Justice: Examining the Reform Party's Discourse on Citizenship', (1999) 57–8 *Socialist Studies Bulletin* 25.

[21] See L. Chwialkowska, 'Rein in lobby groups, senior judges suggest', *National Post*, 6 Apr 2000; B. McLachlan, 'Charter Myths', (1999) 33 *University of British Columbia Law Review* 23; and *Vriend*.

[22] See Chwialkowska, n. 21 above; P. Hogg and A. A. Bushnell, 'The Charter Dialogue between the Courts and the Legislature (or Perhaps the Charter of Rights isn't such a Bad Thing after all)', (1997) 35 *Osgoode Hall LJ* 73; and C. Manfredi and J. Kelly, 'Six Degrees of Dialogue: A Response to Hogg and Bushnell', (1999) 37 *Osgoode Hall LJ* 513.

are regarded as putting democracy in peril. They include the proliferation of supra-national agreements that constrain the policies of those holding national elected office, the financial dependency of political parties on corporate finance, and the consolidation of power within the executive.[23] The Charter is a symptom rather than a cause of changes in Canadian politics. However, it has a tendency to reinforce particular kind of politics and political claim.

II. Recognition versus redistribution: the politics of Charter rights

The debate about the legitimacy of the courts' role in applying the Charter has been influenced by perceptions of the Charter's impact. But the question of how to meas-ure this impact is itself controversial. Legal scholars tend to be court-focused in their evaluation, looking primarily at the courts' Charter jurisprudence,[24] although some, especially when engaging in discussions with political scientists,[25] have stud-ied the broader picture of the courts' relation with the legislature by compiling and examining statistics of what the courts have done.[26] Doctrinal and empirical analy-ses provide important evidence of the impact of the Charter; however, some polit-ical scientists caution against conflating the effect of law on litigation strategies with its effect on social movement politics.[27] They argue that it is important to broaden the focus beyond the law and the courts to how the Charter influences the political discourse and practices of the groups that invoke it.

The experience of social movements with the Charter is a good illustration of the impact of entrenching a bill of rights on political discourses and practices. On account of their strong support of justiciable rights they have been called the Court party,[28] charter advocacy groups,[29] or Charter Canadians.[30] These groups, among

[23] See K. Ewing, *Money, Politics and the Law* (Oxford: Oxford University Press, 1992); J. Fudge and H. Glasbeek, 'A Challenge to the Inevitability of Globalization: The Logic of Repositioning the State as Part of the Terrain of Contest', in J. Drydyk and P. Penz (eds.), *Global Justice, Global Democracy: Twelve Socialist Studies* (Halifax: Fernwood, 1997), 219; and D. Savoie, 'The Rise of Court Government in Canada', (1999) 32 *Canadian Journal of Political Science* 635.

[24] See Beatty, *Talking Heads*, n. 11 above; P. Hogg, *Constitutional Law*, student edn. (Toronto: Carswell, 1999); and Hutchinson, n. 10 above.

[25] See F. L. Morton, P. H. Russell, and M. J. Withey, 'The Supreme Court's First 100 Charter of Rights Decisions: A Statistical Analysis', (1992) 30 *Osgoode Hall LJ* 1; and G. Hein, *Interest Group Litigation and Canadian Democracy* (Quebec: IRPP, 2000).

[26] See Hogg and Bushnell, n. 22 above.

[27] See M. Smith, *Lesbian and Gay Rights in Canada: Social Movements and Equality Seeking, 1971–95* (Toronto: University of Toronto Press, 1999); and M. McCann and H, Silverstein, 'Social Movements and the American State: Legal Mobilization as a Strategy for Democracy', in G. Albo, L. Panitch, and D. Langille (eds.), *A Different kind of State* (Oxford: Oxford University Press, 1993).

[28] Knopff and Morton, n. 18 above.

[29] L. Pal, 'Advocacy Organizations and Legislative Politics: The Effect of Charter Rights and Freedoms on Interest Group Lobbying of Federal Legislation 1989–91', in L. Seidle (ed.), *Equity and Community* (Montreal: Institute for Research in Public Policy, 1993), 119.

[30] A. Cairns, *Reconfigurations: Canadian Citizenship and Constitutional Change* (Toronto: McClelland & Stewart, 1999).

which the most prominent represent women, lesbians and gay men, and visible minorities, have won a few notable legal victories and suffered some legal defeats. They have also faced a strong backlash, mostly right wing, which is directed against the Charter and the courts, and which proposes an alternative version of equality.[31]

Nancy Fraser's distinction between different types of injustices and remedies helps to make sense of social movements' mixed experience with the Charter and its broader impact on politics.[32] She distinguishes between recognition claims asserted by groups that are subject mainly to cultural and symbolic injustice and claims for redistribution made by groups whose injustice is primarily political and economic. She is careful to point out that the distinction is analytic and that it attempts to capture the normative dimensions of different claims. In practice, the two ideal types of injustice are intertwined.[33] According to Fraser, the question of when one injustice converges with another is a historical one. The utility of the heuristic depends upon whether it is able to account for political dilemmas that arise when different types of rights claim are asserted. Moreover, these two types of claim are linked to two types of remedy. The first involves some form of political-economic restructuring, often involving redistributing income, reorganizing the division of labour, or subjecting investment to democratic decision-making.[34] The second requires some sort of cultural or symbolic change, typically dealing with the re-evaluation of social norms and identities and usually entailing a transformation in patterns of representation, interpretation, and communication.[35] Again, Fraser emphasizes that this distinction is analytic; what people are entitled to typically depends upon how they are recognized, and the choice of who to recognize for what purpose often rests on an underlying commitment to redistribution.

Fraser's conceptual spectrum of different kinds of social collectivity, with class at the redistributive pole and lesbians and gay men at the recognition end, captures some of the conspicuous contours of social movements in Canada. Lesbian and gay groups are regarded as examples of new social movements who have broken from a class- or interest-based politics to emphasize identity, equality and difference.[36] This contrasts with the politics of labour unions, which focuses on economic wrongs and distributional remedies.[37] According to Fraser, women's groups fit somewhere in between, since recognition and redistribution are so clearly and deeply intertwined through the sexual division of labour. To complicate matters further, groups which exemplify a particular form of injustice may experience the other. For example, women may want their unpaid but necessary domestic labour recognized in ways that have significant distributional impacts through the tax

---

[31] See Knopff and Morton, n. 18 above; Patten, n. 20 above; and Peacock, n. 19 above.

[32] N. Fraser, 'From Redistribution to Recognition? Dilemmas of Justice in a "Post Socialist" Age', (1995) 212 *New Left Review* 68.

[33] Ibid. 72. Fraser's article generated a great deal of debate among feminist political theorists, much of which was published in the *New Left Review*. This literature is cited in Boyd, n. 20 above, 375. See also A. Phillips, *Which Equalities Matter?* (Cambridge: Polity Press, 1999).

[34] Fraser, n. 32 above, 73.   [35] Ibid.   [36] See Smith, n. 29 above, 146.   [37] Ibid.

system.[38] Lesbians and gay men have claimed that the legal recognition of their right to equal respect and value means that they should be entitled to some of the public benefits of the welfare state.[39] Claims involving recognition often have redistributional aspects and vice versa. The question is whether Fraser's heuristic helps to sort out what kinds of claim are being made and how the courts have responded.

Some groups have had much more success with the Charter than have others, and even those groups that have enjoyed the greatest success have had more success with certain types of claim than others. The closer a rights claim is pitched to the recognition pole of the injustice spectrum, the more likely that the Supreme Court of Canada will uphold it. Claims to equal value and respect for different identities have fared well under the Charter. Lesbians and gay men and groups representing them who have used the Charter in their struggle against discrimination and for social recognition have enjoyed a remarkable degree of success before the courts.[40] In a series of cases beginning with *Canada(AG) v. Mossop*[41] and concluding with *M v. H*,[42] the majority of the Supreme Court of Canada has condemned discrimination against gays and lesbians as a violation of their right to equality under the Charter. In 1998 in *Vriend*, the Supreme Court added sexual orientation to the list of prohibited grounds of discrimination under the Alberta human rights legislation, arguing that the 'denial of access to remedial procedures for discrimination on the ground of sexual orientation must have dire and demeaning consequences for those affected.'[43] The Court went on to elaborate the consequences of failing to provide legal redress to lesbians and gays in the following terms:

Fear of discrimination will logically lead to concealment of true identity and this must be harmful to personal confidence and self-esteem. Compounding that effect is the implicit message conveyed by the exclusion that gays and lesbians, unlike other individuals, are not worthy of protection.[44]

The following year, in *M v. H*, the Supreme Court of Canada handed down another victory for lesbian and gay Charter equality claims by legally recognizing same-sex relationships for the purpose of spousal support under the Ontario Family Law Act. The Court declared the offending section of the Act that defined a spouse for the purposes of support to be of no force or effect.[45] In response, the Ontario

---

[38] See *Symes v. Canada* [1993] 4 SCR 695; and *Thibaudeau v. Canada (Minister of National Revenue)* [1995] 2 SCR 627.

[39] See *Egan v. Canada* [1995] 2 SCR 513 [hereinafter *Egan*].   [40] See Herman, n. 14 above, 200.

[41] [1993] 1 SCR 554 [hereinafter *Mossop*]. In *Mossop* a gay rights activist and federal government employee challenged his employer's denial of bereavement leave to attend the funeral of his partner's father on the ground that it violated the protection of family status under the federal Human Rights Act. The Supreme Court of Canada ruled that since Parliament had not included sexual orientation as a prohibited ground in the human rights act, it could not be imported through the family status clause. However, the Court invited Mossop to reframe his claim as a challenge to the constitutionality of the Human Rights Act exclusion of sexual orientation under s. 15 of the Charter.

[42] [1999] 2 SCR 3.   [43] [1998] 1 SCR 548.   [44] Ibid. 551.

[45] However, unlike *Vriend*, where the Court remedied the offending legislation by reading in a provision, in *M v. H* it suspended the declaration for a period of 6 months to allow the Ontario government to amend the legislation.

Conservative government grudgingly introduced legislation to ensure that same-sex couples and opposite-sex common law couples were treated equally under the province's laws.[46]

M v. H stands in striking contrast to *Egan*, in which the majority of the Supreme Court of Canada agreed that the exclusion of same-sex couples from access to social benefits in the form of old age pensions constituted a violation of equality rights, but upheld the violation as a limitation justified under section 1 of the Charter. While both decisions recognized that lesbians and gay men deserve to be treated with respect and value equal to heterosexuals, *M v. H* neither involved the expenditure of public funds nor challenged the hegemony of heterosexual marriage. In fact, in *M v. H* the majority of the Court reiterated twenty-one times in as many paragraphs that the remedy favoured reducing the expenditure of public money, and four times that it had no impact on the interests of heterosexual couples and families.[47] According to the Court, the impugned spousal support provision 'has the deleterious effect of driving a member of a same-sex couple who is in need of maintenance to the welfare system and it thereby imposes additional costs on the general taxpaying public'.[48]

Analysing the Supreme Court of Canada's evolving Charter equality jurisprudence in the context of claims made by lesbian and gay men, Lajoie, Gelineau, and Janda[49] conclude that the Court is willing to recognize the equality rights of lesbians and gay men where there is no expenditure of public funds and the traditional conceptions of marriage and the heterosexual family are not threatened. To the extent that Charter claims brought by lesbians and gay men cleave closely to the recognition pole of injustice claims and do not involve redistribution or challenge deeply held social norms and relations, they are likely to be upheld.[50] The recognition of the equal value and dignity of lesbians and gay men is an important victory. As Didi Herman[51] has argued, 'the application of de jure equality to previously excluded groups or identities is something that has been fought *for*'. But, as she acknowledges, the scope of such recognition is context-dependent. 'It is one thing to say that you support 'equal rights for lesbians and gays'; it is quite another to champion lesbians' and gay men's right to foster and adopt children.'[52]

Moreover, the courts' equality jurisprudence has had an impact on the litigation strategies and arguments of lesbian and gay organizations and their supporters. It is almost impossible for such groups to avoid making assimilationist arguments—that same-sex relationships are just the same as heterosexual ones[53]—if the goal is to win the litigation. Moreover, as Susan Boyd[54] notes, it was also impossible to avoid

---

[46] Ontario Ministry of the Attorney-General, 'Ontario protects traditional definition of spouse in legislation necessary because of the Supreme Court of Canada decision in *M v. H*', (Government of Ontario press release, Oct. 1999) Http://www.newswire.ca/government
[47] Lajoie et al., n. 3 above.   [48] *M v. H* [1999] 2 SCR 76.   [49] Lajoie et al., n. 3 above, 133.
[50] See Boyd, n. 20 above.
[51] D. Herman, 'Beyond the Rights Debate', (1993) 2 *Social and Legal Studies* 32.
[52] Herman, n. 14 above, 211.   [53] Boyd, n. 20 above, 379; and Smith, n. 27 above, 92.
[54] Ibid.

reinforcing the privatization argument: 'that part of the objective of support law is to reduce the burden on the public purse (wider community) by creating private (familial) obligations to provide spousal support.'[55] And perhaps even more importantly, the Charter had an impact on the broader politics of movement organizing. In her study of the lesbian and gay rights movement in Canada, Miriam Smith[56] concluded that Equality for Gays and Lesbians Everywhere (EGALE) focused on Charter-based rights and winning legal victories at the expense of grass-roots mobilization, class inequalities, and alternative models of family life. 'Rights talk', which she defines as equating social and political change with legal change, came to dominate EGALE's political discourse.[57] According to her, 'rights talk pulls lesbian and gay rights organizations towards an assumed lesbian and gay identity and focuses on the achievement of legal change as a primary goal'.[58] This points to 'the limits of seeking cultural recognition through law as well as the disciplining effects of engaging with law as a tool of social change'.[59]

The experience of women's groups, especially that of LEAF, the most prominent of the feminist equality litigation groups, supports the assessment that the judicial determination of Charter equality rights fosters recognition claims and supports recognition remedies, but is not very amenable to claims that either challenge pervasive social and legal norms or involve redistribution. In order to allow governments time to prepare, the equality rights in the Charter did not come into effect until 1985. As a result of audits of statutes designed to root out sexism, only a few of the explicit uses of gender-based classifications that remained did not benefit women. When LEAF went to court to challenge provisions such as the requirement that married women take their husbands' names it was successful. But the problem was that formal legal equality did nothing in itself to further substantive equality for women.[60]

Moreover, formal legal equality arguments quickly redounded to women's disadvantage as men argued in court that their equality rights were violated by statutory provisions designed to address some of the negative effects of the sexual division of labour on women. Thus, the initial results of equality litigation were very disappointing for LEAF and other groups committed to substantive notions of equality.[61] Men were bringing and winning many more Charter equality cases than

---

[55] Boyd worked with the Women's Legal Education and Action Fund (LEAF) on its intervention in *M v. H.*

[56] Smith, n. 27 above, 93.   [57] Ibid. 75.   [58] Ibid. 151.   [59] Boyd, n. 20 above, 380.

[60] See J. Fudge, 'The Public/Private Distinction: The Possibilities of and the Limits to the Use of Charter Litigation to Further Feminist Struggles', (1987) 25 *Osgoode Hall LJ* 485. A recent study of appeal court decisions affecting feminist issues found that the extent of feminist success varies among different policy fields. The closer the policy field involves redistribution and central legal norms, the less likely it is that feminist litigation will be successful. F. L. Morton and A. Allen, 'Feminists and the Courts: Measuring Success in Interest Group Litigation in Canada', (2001) 34 *Canadian Journal of Political Science* 54.

[61] See Brodsky and Day, n. 11 above; K. Ruff, 'The Canadian Charter of Rights and Freedoms: A Tool for Social Justice?', (1989) 12(2) *Perception* 19; and S. Razack, *Canadian Feminism and the Law* (Toronto: Second Story Press, 1991).

were women.[62] Eventually, the Supreme Court of Canada put a stop to this by holding that, to achieve equality, it might be necessary to treat differently placed groups unequally.[63] LEAF was instrumental in persuading the Court to develop a contextualized approach to equality that rejects the purely formalized model.[64] In subsequent cases the Supreme Court made it clear that discrimination is to be determined in terms of disadvantage.[65]

However, this equality jurisprudence was beneficial to women more as a shield against litigation brought by men than as a sword to obtain substantive equality for women. In part, this is because the Charter only directly applies to government action.[66] In order to challenge private discrimination, recourse must be made to human rights legislation. The Charter equality jurisprudence has had a salutary spillover on human rights adjudication for women as the Supreme Court of Canada demonstrated its willingness to challenge the male norm embedded in many workplace practices, standards, and entitlements.[67] The thrust of this jurisprudence is to recognize that, although women's bodies and work histories differ from men's, these differences should not be used to deny women equal value, respect, and entitlements at work.

The most important legal victory for women under the Charter did not come under the equality provisions, but under section 7, which guarantees everyone 'the right to life, liberty and security of the person and the right not to be deprived thereof except in accordance with the principles of fundamental justice'. Henry Morgentaler, a doctor who had been repeatedly convicted of, and charged with, performing abortions in violation of the criminal code provisions, which required a woman to obtain the approval of a therapeutic abortion committee established at a hospital before undergoing an abortion, challenged the constitutionality of the provisions on the ground that they violated section 7. The Supreme Court of Canada centred its analysis on the administrative unevenness of requiring the approval of therapeutic abortion committees, given that hospitals were under no legal obligation to establish a committee in the first place. The Court found that the lack of committees in some parts of the country could lead to dangerous delay or outright denial of access to safe abortions for women.[68] Except for Justice Wilson, the only

---

[62] See Brodsky and Day, n. 11 above; and K. Lahey, 'Feminist Theories of (In)Equality' in S. Martin and K. Mahoney (eds.), *Equality and Judicial Neutrality* (Toronto: Carswell, 1987).

[63] See *Law Society of British Columbia v. Andrews* [1989] 1 SCR 143.

[64] See L. Gotell, 'LEAF's Equality Approach: Foundational Past/Contingent Future?' in R. Jhappan (ed.), *Women's Legal Strategies* (Toronto: University of Toronto Press, forthcoming).

[65] See Mahoney, n. 15 above, 95; and R. Jhappan, 'The Equality Pit or the Rehabilitation of Justice', (1998) 10 *Canadian Journal of Women and the Law* 60.

[66] See T, Bateman, 'Rights Application Doctrine and the Clash of Constitutionalism in Canada', (1998) 31 *Canadian Journal of Political Science* 1; and J. Fudge, 'Lessons from Canada: the Impact of the Charter of Rights and Freedoms on Labour and Employment Law', in K. Ewing (ed.), *Human Rights at Work* (London: Institute for Employment Rights, 2000), 175–201.

[67] See *British Columbia (Public Service Employee Relations Commission) v. British Columbia Government and Service Employees Union (BCGSEU)* [1999] 3 SCR 3; and Mahone, n. 65 above.

[68] *R v. Morgentaler* [1988] 1 SCR 30 [hereinafter *Morgentaler*].

woman on the bench, who seemed to suggest that any restriction on abortion would violate a woman's Charter right, the majority of the Court emphasized that constraints could be placed on abortion. However, the majority found that the one under attack did not survive constitutional scrutiny and declared it to be void.

Although the majority decision in *Morgentaler* stopped short of recognizing a women's right to reproductive choice, it outlawed arbitrary limits on abortion. But this did not stop the federal government from attempting to enact new criminal code provisions to restrict access to abortion. When this attempt failed, Minister of Justice Kim Campbell explained her government's refusal to introduce new legislation: 'I think you will find action by the provinces . . . that will generate . . . litigation. We will have to wait for . . . the Supreme Court . . . to provide the kind of national certainly that people want.'[69] Yet, even though there is no law that criminalizes abortion, access to this procedure continues to be very uneven, depending upon the part of the country in which a woman lives and whether she has economic resources. At the same time as courts have struck down provincial legislation designed to restrict access to abortion, there has been no positive legal obligation placed on governments either to provide access to abortion or to pay for the procedure.[70] Thus, although women are formally free to choose whether or not to continue with a pregnancy, the substantive conditions (access and funding) that influence whether they can exercise that choice have not been guaranteed by law.

Subsequent rounds of litigation to protect the foetus through recognition of a constitutional entitlement to life were rebuffed by the Supreme Court, as was an attempt by a man seeking to restrain a woman with whom he had sexual relations with from having an abortion.[71] While these decisions were applauded by feminists, they proved to be a rallying point for social conservatives against the Charter and the courts.[72] The abortion-related Charter litigation confirms Ian Greene's[73] prediction that 'leaving the resolution of divisive social equality issues to the courts is likely to harm the legitimacy of the Supreme Court as a neutral arbiter of legal disputes'.

A great deal of LEAF's legal interventions have been to defend legislative changes to sexual assault offence provisions in the criminal code. These changes were designed to be more woman-friendly because they set aside judge-made law that not only made it difficult for the crown to secure convictions but that also made it an ordeal for women to lay charges and to testify. Beginning in the early 1980s, feminist activists and lobbyists had been very successful in persuading the federal

---

[69] As quoted by W. A. Bogart, *Courts and Country: Limits of Litigation and the Social and Political Life of Canada* (Toronto: Oxford University Press, 1994), 152.

[70] See ibid.; J. Brodie, S. Gavigan, and J. Jenson, *The Politics of Abortion* (Toronto: Oxford University Press, 1992); and *Morgentaler*.

[71] See Bogart, n. 69 above; Brodie et al., n. 70 above; *Borowski v. Canada (AG)* [1989] 1 SCR 342; *Tremblay v. Daigle* [1989] 2 SCR 530; Mandel, n. 6 above; F. L. Morton, *Morgentaler v. Borowski: Abortion, The Charter and the Courts* (Toronto: McClelland, 1992); and Morton and Knopff, n. 3 above.

[72] See Morton, n. 71 above; and Knopff and Morton, n. 18 above.

[73] I. Greene, *The Charter of Rights* (Toronto: Lorimer, 1989), 185.

government to provide legislative protection from judicially devised rules of evidence that allowed the accused to cross-examine complainants regarding their sexual activity.[74] But once the Charter came into effect, defendants argued that these provisions violated their Charter-protected right to a fair trial. The Supreme Court of Canada accepted this argument and struck down the legislation.[75] As a result of concerted feminist lobbying, legislation that was designed to restrict this evidence and pass Charter muster was introduced.[76] The Supreme Court of Canada upheld the new rape shield legislation, characterizing it as, in essence, a codification by Parliament of the Court's guidelines in *Seaboyer*.[77] Defence lawyers invoked the Charter again, arguing that third parties should be required to disclose the therapeutic records of sexual assault complainants. The Supreme Court of Canada agreed that this was necessary in order to provide defendants accused of sexual assault with a fair trial.[78] Once again, feminists turned to Parliament, and legislation that was shaped by deference to judicially articulated guidelines was introduced to restrict the circumstances in which such disclosure could be required.[79]

Another area of law in which equality rights arguments on behalf of women have enjoyed little success is tax. An attempt by a self-employed woman lawyer to have her child care expenses classified as a business deduction for tax purposes was rejected by the Supreme Court of Canada on the ground that, although she had demonstrated that women bore a disproportionate share of the responsibility for child care, she had not established that they bore a disproportionate share of the costs.[80] In another case, a woman used the equality rights in the Charter to challenge the provisions of the Income Tax Act that required her to pay income tax on the child support payment she received from her former husband and which allowed him to deduct those payments from his tax.[81] The all-male Supreme Court majority (the two women judges dissented) found no discrimination under section 15. The majority of the court declared that the proper unit for analysing the effect of these income tax provisions was not the individual, but the couple. Referring to the 'post-divorce "family unit"' two judges agreed that 'the fact that one member of the unit might derive a greater benefit from the legislation than the other does

---

[74] See J. Fudge, 'The Effect of Entrenching a Bill of Rights on Political Discourse: Feminist Demands and Sexual Violence in Canada', (1989) 71 *International Journal of the Sociology of Law* 445.

[75] See *R v. Seaboyer* [1991] 2 SCR 577 [hereinafter *Seaboyer*].

[76] See S. Chapman, 'Section 276 of the Criminal Code and the Admissibility of "Sexual Activity" Evidence', (1999) 25 *Queen's LJ* 121.

[77] See *R v. Darrach* [2000] SCC No. 46, 12 Oct. 2000.

[78] See L. Gotell, 'Colonization through Disclosure', Social and Legal Studies (forthcoming); and *R v. O'Connor* [1995] 4 SCR 411.

[79] See Gotell, n. 78 above; and J. Van Dieen, 'O'Connor and Bill-46: Differences in Approach', (1999) 23 *Queen's LJ* 1.

[80] *Symes v. Canada* [1993] 4 SCR 695.

[81] *Thibaudeau v. Canada (Minister of National Revenue)* [1995] 2 SCR 627.

not, in and of itself, trigger a s. 15 violation'.[82] These cases led Philipps and Young[83] to remark:

There has been tremendous resistance to seeing the *Income Tax Act* for what it is: a social policy document, influenced by notions of just distribution and ideologically-specific understanding of ideal forms of social ordering. Instead, the ITA is often viewed as a politically and morally neutral document, structured by the dictates of financial accounting, economic theory and tax principles that permit no political shades or shaping.

To address the problem of the disproportionate tax burden for child support payments falling on women, the federal government introduced guidelines for determining child support and amended the Income Tax Act to place the burden of paying tax on the child support on the payer, who in the overwhelming majority of cases is a man.[84]

Feminist arguments designed to persuade the courts to recognize women's vulnerability to sexual violence and deeply entrenched legal biases against women ran aground against firmly held legal norms and social stereotypes. What success feminists have enjoyed in court in the context of the criminal law has come when they have deployed arguments that tend to reify female sexual vulnerability and male sexual aggression. Claims for economic redistribution have met with little favour in the judicial realm. And although groups like LEAF have been able to persuade Parliament to introduce legislation that is designed to ameliorate some of the most detrimental effects of Charter decisions on women, this dialogue between the courts and the legislature has followed a script written by judges.[85]

The impact of Charter litigation on the women's movement has been less well studied than its influence on lesbian and gay rights organizations. However, the evidence available indicates that the Charter has not channelled women's organizations away from grass-roots mobilization, and that most of the prominent feminist groups have been able to distinguish between social and legal change.[86] The courts' unwillingness to compromise deeply held legal and social norms and directly engage in redistribution has kept the women's movement extremely active on the

---

[82] Ibid. 702. By contrast, the two women judges adamantly rejected the notion that the post-divorce family unit was the appropriate focus and concluded that the provisions discriminated against women.

[83] L. Phillipps and M. Young, 'Sex, Tax and the Charter: A Review of Thibaudeau v. Canada', (1995) 2 *Review of Constitutional Studies* 222.

[84] See N. Bala, 'A Report from Canada's "Gender War Zone": Reforming the Child Related Provisions of the Divorce Act', (1999) 16 *Canadian Journal of Family Law* 163.

[85] Manfredi's analysis of LEAF's experience with the Charter conforms to the preceding characterization of the kinds of cases in which LEAF has enjoyed the greatest success. See M. Manfredi, *The Canadian Feminist Movement, Constitutional Politics, and the Strategic Use of Legal Resources* (Vancouver: SFU-UBC Centre for the Study of Government and Business, 2000). See also *R v. Butler* [1992] 1 SCR 452; Fudge, n. 74 above; L. Gotell, 'Litigating Feminist "Truth": An Anti-foundational Critique', (1995) 4 *Social and Legal Studies* 99; and L. Gotell, 'Shaping *Butler*: The New Politics of Anti-Pornography', in B. Cossman, et al. (eds.), *Bad Attitude on Trial: Pornography, Feminism, and the Butler Decision* (Toronto: University of Toronto Press, 1997), 48.

[86] See A. Dobrowolsky, *The Politics of Pragmatism: Women, Representation and Constitutionalism in Canada* (Don Mills: Oxford University Press, 1999).

legislative front. Yet, when engaging in litigation, organizations like LEAF have had to recast and de-radicalize their claims in order to have any hope of influencing the court.[87]

Organized labour's demands exemplify the redistributive end of the injustice spectrum. Unlike the lesbian and gay rights and women's movements, the labour movement was not active during the Charter drafting process in lobbying for constitutional protections designed to protect its constituents' rights.[88] However, since the enactment of the Charter coincided with the most concerted attack on the collective bargaining system by the federal and provincial governments, unions were quick to resort to the courts.[89] Throughout the 1980s, the International Labour Organization validated a series of complaints lodged by Canadian unions against the federal and provincial governments on the ground that statutes imposing temporary wage restraints, permanent bans on strikes in the public sector, and back-to-work orders violated workers' freedom of association.[90] Despite this, in 1987 the Supreme Court of Canada issued three decisions, known as the Labour Trilogy, which held that the freedom of association protected in section 2(d) of the Charter did not include either the right to bargain collectively or the right to strike.[91] One judge started from the premise that the freedom of association only encompassed the freedom to join in association for a common purpose and association activities insofar as they represented the exercise of another fundamental or constitutionally protected right or freedom. Since he characterized the rights to bargain collectively and strike as modern legislative rights and not fundamental freedoms, he concluded that neither was protected by the Charter. Another judge emphasized individualism in denying a Charter-protected right to strike. He reasoned that freedom of association included all activities pursued in association with others that a person could lawfully pursue as an individual. Since an individual could not lawfully strike, he concluded that strikes were not protected by the freedom of association.

In subsequent cases, the Supreme Court of Canada confirmed its position that neither the right to bargain collectively nor the right to strike was protected by the Charter.[92] And although the Court stated that peaceful picketing was a form of expression protected under section 2(b) of the Charter, it concluded that the common law limits on the scope of picketing were demonstrably justified.[93] The labour

---

[87] See Boyd, n. 20 above; Fudge, n. 74 above; and Gotell, 'Litigating Feminist "Truth" ', n. 85 above.

[88] See L. Panitch and D. Swartz, *The Assault on Trade Union Freedoms* (Toronto: Garamond, 1993).

[89] See J. Fudge, 'Labour, the New Constitution and Old Style Liberalism', (1988) 13 *Queen's LJ* 61.

[90] See Panitch and Swartz, n. 88 above.

[91] In *PSAC v. Canada (AG)* [1987] 1 SCR 424, the union challenged wage control legislation which effectively deprived federal public service workers of collective bargaining and the right to strike for a two- to three-year period. In *RWDSU v. Saskatchewan* [1987] 1 SCR 460, the union challenged an ad hoc back-to-work law which prohibited the pending strike and substituted interest arbitration to resolve the dispute. In *Reference Re Public Service Employees Relations Act (Alta)* [1987] 1 SCR 313, unions challenged a number of Alberta statutes that placed restrictions on collective bargaining by provincial government employees, firefighters, police, and hospital workers by prohibiting strikes, restricting the scope of bargaining and imposing compulsory arbitration.

[92] See Fudge, n. 66 above.   [93] See *RWDSU Local 580 v. Dolphin Delivery Ltd* [1986] 2 SCR 573.

movement's attempts to use the Charter to liberate workers' freedom to strike and picket from legislative and common law restrictions have been an abysmal failure. In the only case that a union used the Charter to widen the scope of lawful collective action, it lost the larger ideological struggle. At the same time that the Supreme Court of Canada declared that restrictions on peaceful leafleting to inform consumers of a labour dispute violated the constitutional guarantee of freedom of expression, it depicted peaceful picketing as coercive, and thus suspect, activity.[94]

While the Supreme Court of Canada has not used the Charter to revoke rights that organized labour has already won, the decisions also signify that the pro-free enterprise ideals which had inspired the judiciary for two centuries were not to be set aside by the constitutionalization of the liberal right of association. For the courts, collectivism is still aberrational and individualism is paramount. Moreover, the denial of a constitutional right to strike by the Supreme Court of Canada provided an imprimatur of legitimacy for the anti-labour programme of severely restricting the right to strike.[95] In this context, when trade unions are allowed by the Supreme Court to keep a right they have won through struggles over the last century, such as the right to use compelled dues for political purposes, it is greeted as a Charter victory.[96]

Fraser's heuristic helps to make sense of how progressive rights claims made under the Charter have fared. Rights claims that involve the recognition and affirmation of despised or devalued social identities have enjoyed some success before the Supreme Court of Canada. By contrast, Charter claims that involve redistribution or class have enjoyed little success before the Court. This is not surprising, as history suggests that courts have not been a particularly good avenue for redistributive politics.[97] The vast majority of social democratic welfare rights, which are the rights that actively involve redistribution, have been creations of legislatures and not the courts. According to McCann and Silverstein,[98] 'legal rights strategies are more useful in framing negative demands for challenging an abusive or arbitrary state practices than in legitimatizing positive substantive demands for egalitarian social policy. This is especially true with respect to questions of altering capital investment or income redistribution.'

But does this assessment of the different judicial reception of recognition and redistribution claims mean that the political value of justiciable bills of rights must be determined at the level of 'who is claiming what and why',[99] or is it possible to make broader claims about the impact of entrenched bills of rights on political discourses and institutions? I want to argue that the Canadian experience suggests that justiciable bills of rights have a broader and generally negative impact on political

---

[94] See Fudge, n. 66 above; and *UFCW Local 1518 v. Kmart Canada Ltd* [1999] 2 SCR 1083.

[95] I. Greene, *The Charter of Rights* (Toronto: Lorimer, 1989), 88; and Panitch and Swartz, n. 88 above, 53.

[96] See P. Weiler, 'The Charter at Work: Reflection on the Constitutionalization of Labour and Employment Law', (1990) 40 *U. of Toronto LJ* 117.

[97] See Bogart, n. 69 above; and Mandel, n. 6 above.

[98] McCann and Silverstein, n. 27 above, 141.   [99] Herman, n. 14 above, 213.

struggles for social justice in advanced capitalist liberal democracies. There are two reasons for this. First, recognition claims, which are fostered by their favourable reception in the courts, tend to displace redistribution claims. Second, legal rights discourse, which reifies individualism, negative liberty, and private property, has imperialistic tendencies when it comes to political discourse and debate.

It is not inevitable that recognition claims displace struggles for redistribution. As Nancy Fraser[100] has recently argued, recognition struggles can be cast either as identity politics or as status subordination. The identity model treats recognition injustices as problems of cultural depreciation, and either ignores the social-structural underpinnings of economic inequality in capitalist societies or misunderstands the link between cultural devaluation and economic inequality. However, it is possible to treat recognition as a question of social status. On this model, misrecognition 'does not mean the depreciation and deformation of group identity, but social subordination'.[101] To redress this injustice, the affirmation of different identities is not sufficient; a politics of overcoming institutionalized relations of social subordination, which invariably includes an economic dimension, is also required.[102]

But while it is not inevitable that recognition claims are cast as a form of identity politics that displaces redistribution claims, it is precisely these sorts of claim that are the most successful in court. Litigation strategies that portray lesbian and gay men as sexual minorities seeking toleration and respect are much more successful than those that challenge the heterosexual family as the primary unit of civil society and social order.[103] Furthermore, courts are not very receptive to rights claims which challenge prevailing distributions of power and resources that result in social subordination. In part, judges claim that this is not their role, since the Charter's scope is confined to government action.[104] Moreover, the common law's imperative to focus on the individual as the primary unit of analysis influences how judges interpret the Charter. Individual choice, not social structures, explain people's actions, and government interference with this choice is inherently suspect, although justifiable.[105] Traditional forms of legal argument, legal institutions, and legal procedures all contribute to the displacement of redistributive claims by recognition demands. Moreover, depending on the scope of judicial authority and the strength of its legitimacy, legal discourse has the power to colonize other more democratic political institutions.

---

[100] See N, Fraser, 'Rethinking Recognition' (2000) 3 (2nd ser.) *New Left Review* 107.
[101] Ibid. 113.   [102] See also Phillips, n. 33 above.
[103] See L. Gotell, 'Queering Law, Not by Vriend' (on file with the author); D. Herman, 'Beyond the Rights Debate', (1993) 2 *Social and Legal Studies* 25–43; K. Lahey, *Are We 'Persons' Yet? Law and Sexuality in Canada* (Toronto: University of Toronto Press, 1999); and Lajoie et al., n. 3 above.
[104] See Bateman, n. 66 above.   [105] See Bakan, n. 10 above.

III. Legally speaking: expression, democracy, and the market

The Supreme Court of Canada's jurisprudence on the scope of the Charter's guarantee of freedom of expression exemplifies the distinctive form and key elements of liberal legal discourse. The separation of the public sphere from the realm of private activity and the emphasis on individualism, negative liberty, and commodification exert real limits on the types of rights claim that courts will recognize on a systematic basis.[106] Together, they constitute a block on the development by the judiciary of the social and collective rights necessary for redistributive policies. They can also operate, as the cases involving freedom of expression make clear, as a check on democracy.

One of the features of bills of rights is the level of abstraction at which the rights are articulated. 'Freedom of expression', for example, has a wide array of meanings. The important question is how meaning is attributed to it. The deep grammar of judicial reasoning and general legal norms shape how the courts define expression and when they will uphold restricting it. In Canada, entrenched human rights are grafted onto a legal system that promotes private property and contract.[107] The courts have a particular understanding of the relationship between human rights, the market, and democracy, and their close association with rationality and right tends to imbue their understanding with a great deal of legitimacy.

The Supreme Court of Canada has adopted a formalist approach to determine whether an activity constitutes expression as protected under the Charter. According to it, every activity short of violence is potentially expressive.[108] The form of the activity is what counts; the speaker and content are irrelevant to determining whether the activity is protected. This does not imply, however, that limitations are not justified. They may be. The question is whether the limitation can be justified in the process of balancing competing interests under section 1. Because this process is not particularly principled, judicial discussions of the limitations on expression have produced a quagmire of doctrinal inconsistency, and have given rise to calls for the court to move to a substantive understanding of expression[109] or a situated conception of communicative activity.[110]

Cases involving freedom of expression under the Charter fall into three general categories that have to do with the purpose or goal of the expressive activity: commercial, political, and criminal. These categories are not watertight. Restricting the language in which advertisements can be published is a limitation on commercial expression, but one which also has political overtones, especially in Quebec, the

---

[106] See ibid.; Hutchinson, n. 10 above; and Mandel, n. 6 above.

[107] See G. Anderson, 'Understanding Constitutional Speech: Two Theories of Expression' in Anderson, n. 12 above, 49.

[108] See *RWDSU Local 580 v. Dolphin Delivery Ltd* [1986] 2 SCR 573.

[109] Hogg, n. 24 above, 856; see also Anderson, n. 107 above.

[110] See R. Moon, *Constitutional Protection of Freedom of Expression* (Toronto: University of Toronto Press, 2001).

only province in Canada where the majority of the residents speak French.[111] Moreover, some types of claim and restriction are hybrids; picketing during a labour dispute is economic and political.[112] Solicitation for the purposes of prostitution is simultaneously commercial and criminal.[113] How the Court classifies the expression is important. Although '"content neutrality" is the norm governing interpretation of the right to expression, the Court does evaluate the substance of expression when determining whether a law found to limit that right should be upheld under s.1 of the Charter'.[114]

Freedom of expression is one of the fundamental rights of a liberal democracy, and it is valued for a number of reasons. It is justified as an instrument of democracy, truth, and personal fulfilment.[115] The marketplace of ideas is one of liberalism's strongest metaphors, and perhaps this helps to explain why commercial speech is considered as maybe even more worthy of protection than political expression under the Charter. In *Ford*, where a small corporation challenged the Quebec government's attempt to force all advertising to be exclusively in French, the Supreme Court easily held that freedom of expression protected commercial expression, since advertisers' messages assist consumers in making 'informed economic choices' which, in turn, enhances their 'individual self-fulfilment and personal autonomy'.[116] The Court also struck down legislation restricting dentists from advertising[117] and a statute requiring tobacco companies to print large health warnings on cigarette packages.[118]

The Supreme Court has upheld limitations on commercial expression. Advertising restrictions designed to protect children, the quintessential vulnerable group, were considered by the Court to be justified.[119] The Court also accepted that the criminal code restriction on soliciting for the purposes of prostitution was justified on the meagre ground that it was important to eradicate the nuisance of street solicitation.[120] Picketing, which the Supreme Court characterized as economic speech with a political overtone, is considered to be expressive activity, but legal restrictions on its scope are justified in order to protect innocent third parties from economic harm.[121] However, restrictions on leafleting consumers for the purpose of informing them about a labour dispute are not justified, since this sort of activity is more akin to the rational debate of ideas than the coercion of a picket line.[122]

---

[111] See *Ford v. Quebec (AG)* [1988] 2 SCR 712 [hereinafter *Ford*].

[112] See *RWDSU Local 580 v. Dolphin Delivery Ltd* [1986] 2 SCR 573.

[113] See *Reference re ss. 193 and 195.1(1)(c) of the Criminal Code* [1990] 1 SCR 1123.

[114] Bakan, n. 10 above, 64.   [115] Hogg, n. 24 above, 456; Moon, n. 110 above, 18.

[116] R. Bauman, 'Business, Economic Rights, and the Charter', in Schneiderman and Sutherland, n. 6 above, 83.

[117] See *Rocket v. Royal College of Dental Surgeons of Ontario* [1990] 2 SCR 232.

[118] See *RJR-MacDonald Inc v. Canada (AG)* [1995] 3 SCR 1999.

[119] See *Irwin Toy Ltd v. Quebec (AG)* [1989] 1 SCR 927.

[120] See *Reference re ss, 193 and 195.1(1)(c) of the Criminal Code* [1990] 1 SCR 1123.

[121] See *RWDSU Local 580 v. Dolphin Delivery Ltd* [1986] 2 SCR 573.

[122] See *UFCW Local 1518 v. Kmart Canada Ltd* [1999] 2 SCR 1083.

Restrictions on expressive activity are most likely to be upheld in the context of the criminal law, especially if the Court can justify the restriction by invoking the protection of members of a vulnerable group. Justifications of restrictions on the sale of pornography solely on the grounds of public morals have fallen out of favour. A nascent equality-based analysis of harm has been used on a couple of occasions by the Court to uphold prohibiting hate speech and the sale of obscene material.[123]

By a four to three majority, the Supreme Court of Canada upheld the hate propaganda provision of the criminal code, which makes it a crime wilfully to promote hatred against 'any section of the public distinguished by colour, race, religion or ethnic origin', and confirmed the conviction of Mr Keegstra, who had been found guilty of making anti-Semitic remarks to his students.[124] By contrast, by the same narrow majority the Court struck down the criminal code offence of spreading false news, which was committed by anyone who published a statement that he or she knew to be false and that caused or was likely to cause injury to public interest. Ernest Zundel's conviction of spreading false news by publishing a pamphlet that claimed that the Holocaust was a fraud by an international conspiracy of Jews was overturned on the ground that the false news provision was too general to be justified.

Much was made of the relationship between prohibiting hate propaganda and promoting social equality by the Supreme Court in *Keegstra*. In *R v. Butler*,[125] the Court unanimously upheld Canada's anti-obscenity law, which made it a crime to sell or possess in order to sell obscene material. It characterized the objective of the obscenity provision as not that of 'moral disapprobation, but rather avoidance of the type of harm which potentially victimizes women'.[126] Although the statute was vaguely drafted, the judicial gloss of harm was considered to be sufficiently precise to justify the restriction.[127] And while the decision has been hailed in some quarters as a victory for feminist equality analysis,[128] other feminists suggest that it may just be the old repressive sexual morality in a new feminist drag.[129] They point to how the obscenity law has been used to target gay and lesbian material of a sexual nature, and how the *Butler* decision supports a specific, and partial, picture of women and human sexuality.[130] Intervening in a recent case that challenges the power of Canadian customs officers to censor as obscene materials being sent to a lesbian bookstore, LEAF has attempted to distinguish heterosexual pornography, which harms women, from lesbian pornography, which does not.[131]

---

[123] See Mahoney, , n. 15 above, 95.   [124] *R v. Keegstra* [1990] 3 SCR 697 [hereinafter *Keegstra*].
[125] [1992] 1 SCR 452 [hereinafter *Butler*].   [126] Mahoney, n. 15 above, 115.
[127] Hogg, n. 24 above, 874.   [128] See Mahoney, n. 15 above.
[129] See Cossman et al., n. 85 above; and R. Moon, 'R v. *Butler*: The Limits of the Supreme Court's Feminist Re-Interpretation of Section 163', (1993) 25 *Ottawa LJ* 361.
[130] See B. Cossman, 'Feminist Fashion or Morality and Drag? Sexual Subtext of the *Butler* Decision', in Cossman et al., n. 85 above 107; Gotell, n. 85 above, and B. L. Ross, ' "It's Merely Designed for Sexual Arousal": Interrogating the Indefensibility of Lesbian Smut', in Cossman et al., n. 85 above, 152.
[131] See Gotell, n. 64 above. In *Little Sisters Book and Art Emporium v. Canada* [2000] SCC No. 69, the Supreme Court of Canada affirmed the *Butler* interpretation of obscenity in emphasizing harm, and criticized any approach to obscenity that would target gay and lesbian material.

Given that one of the primary justifications that is offered for freedom of expression within liberalism is that it promotes democracy, it may come as a bit of a surprise that only a relatively few freedom of expression cases which have reached the Supreme Court or which have attracted much public attention have dealt with political expression. But this small sample indicates that the Supreme Court of Canada perceives the primary threat to expression to be state limits on an individual's freedom rather than private constraints that bias public debate.

In *Osborne v. Canada (Treasury Board)*,[132] the Court struck down a provision in the Public Service Employment Act that prohibited federal public service employees from 'engaging in work' for or against a candidate for election to Parliament or for or against a federal political party. While the Court agreed that protecting the neutrality of the public service was an acceptable legislative objective, the total ban was too broad, and thus could not be justified. The same year, the Court supported the claim of an anti-monarchist group that a publicly controlled and owned airport's total ban on leafleting violated its freedom of expression in a manner that was not justified. The majority of the Court also made it very clear that the Charter did not apply to private property:

Freedom of expression does not, historically, imply freedom to express oneself wherever one pleases. . . . For example, it has not historically conferred a right to use another's property as a forum of expression. A proprietor has the right to determine who uses his or her property and for what purpose. Moreover, the Charter does not extend to private actions. It is therefore clear that s. 2(b) confers no right to use private property as a forum of expression.[133]

But the problem with this approach is that it ignores what is obvious: that the unequal distribution of resources countenanced by a system of private property and contract influences an individual's ability to speak and, more importantly for the political process, whether they are heard.[134] The relationship between private resources and democratic accountability is at the crux of the debate over the legitimacy and legality of state policies regarding election financing.[135]

To date, provincial legislation providing public funds to reimburse political parties for a portion of election expenses has withstood a challenge that it violates a citizen's freedom of expression.[136] However, restrictions on the amount of money that third party interest groups can spend on political advertising during an election or referendum campaign have been struck down. Some of these lower court decisions have had a dramatic short-term instrumental impact on how federal elections were conducted

In 1983, the federal government imposed a ban under the Elections Act on third party expenditures during federal elections. Just before the 1984 federal election, the National Citizens' Coalition, a right-wing lobby group financed by big business,

---

[132] [1991] 2 SCR 69.
[133] *Committee for the Commonwealth of Canada v. Canada* [1991] 1 SCR 448.
[134] See Anderson, n. 107 above and Bakan, n. 10 above.   [135] See Ewing, n. 23 above.
[136] Ibid.

persuaded the Alberta Queen's Bench that this ban on political advertising violated the Charter's guarantee of freedom of expression. Although the decision was only legally binding in Alberta, the Chief Electoral Officer, who was charged with administering the Election Act, decided not to apply the ban anywhere in the country. Since the government did not appeal the decision or amend the legislation, in the 1988 federal election the ban was not applied. That election was remarkable for the unprecedented amount of third party spending by interest groups, which overwhelmingly went to supporting free trade.[137] The Conservative Party, the only party that supported the free trade deal with the United States, was re-elected. One of the first things it did was appoint a royal commission to study and report on how the electoral process was conducted and how it could be reformed. The commission criticized the Alberta court decision striking down the ban on third party advertising as unfair and undemocratic and recommended that a modest financial limit be imposed on individual and group spending during an election campaign. In 1993, the federal government enacted a weaker version of restrictions on third party advertising during elections. Once again, the National Citizens' Coalition managed to persuade an Alberta court that the spending restriction was unconstitutional, the federal government decided not to appeal it on the eve of the federal election, and the Chief Elections Officer did not apply the legislation.[138] In 2000, the federal government made another attempt to introduce restrictions on interest group election spending. Although the National Citizens' Coalition was able to persuade two levels of superior courts in Alberta to strike down the federal legislation imposing expenditure restrictions, this time after the federal election was called, the Supreme Court of Canada ruled that, since the trial judge had been hasty in determining whether the limitation was justified, the legislation should be given effect pending the retrial of its constitutionality.[139]

The Supreme Court of Canada has indicated that it is prepared to accept limits on third party election expenses as a justified limitation on freedom of expression. Although it struck down a prohibition on third party expenditures in Quebec's Referendum Act, it went out of its way to disagree with the Alberta courts' decisions and to declare the control of election expenses to be an important and laudable legislative objective. It preferred less intrusive expenditure restrictions to outright bans on interest group election spending.[140] This battle over the legality of non-party spending restrictions on political advertising during elections has been going on for seventeen years, with the result that in three out of four federal elections no controls were enforced.

---

[137] See ibid.; J. L. Hiebert, 'Money and Elections: Can Citizens Participate on Fair Terms amidst Unrestricted Spending?', (1998) 31 *Canadian Journal of Political Science* 91; and Mandel, n. 6 above.

[138] Ibid. 292.

[139] See *Harper v. Canada (AG)* [2000] SCC no 57, 10 Nov. 2000; S. McCarthy, 'Ottawa defends limit on election advertising', *Globe and Mail*, 3 Aug. 2000; D. Walton, 'Court lifts spending limit on third-party election advertising', *Globe and Mail*, 24 Oct. 2000; and D. Walton, 'Court upholds Election Act Ruling', *Globe and Mail*, 26 Oct. 2000, A7.

[140] See *Libman v. Quebec (AG)* [1997] 3 SCR 569.

The marketplace of ideas is the metaphor that best captures the Supreme Court of Canada's vision of freedom of expression. It has liberated business from some of the strictures of advertising and packaging regulation. Each time the federal government has introduced legislation to restrict cigarette advertising and packaging, tobacco companies have threatened litigation.[141] Sometimes they have invoked the Charter, other times the Free Trade Agreement, revealing once again the close connection between fundamental rights and economic interests. In this context, it is not surprising that the supporters of free trade successfully invoked the Charter to liberate well-financed lobbyists from expenditure restrictions during federal elections. David Schniederman suggests[142] that the 'Charter's guarantee of freedom of expression can be understood . . . as a mechanism that helps to reinforce these trade agreements and that further disciplines government in an era in which democratic control and state regulation increasingly are seen as being hazardous to one's economic health'.

According to the Supreme Court of Canada, freedom of expression is not concerned with how the prevailing distribution of resources shapes how and to whom people can express themselves, but rather whether state censorship is justified.[143] It contributes to the hardening of the contemporary anti-state orthodoxy which has found expression in policies of privatization and deregulation and been reinforced by supranational free trade regimes.[144] Liberating the market from state controls does not enhance democracy. On the contrary, it transfers decision-making away from institutions that are, in theory, subject to democratic accountability to private actors who happen to enjoy private property rights. As Bakan[145] remarks, this 'evisceration of democratic authority' is 'seldom acknowledged or considered'. Not only do the courts ignore private economic power when it comes to defining or protecting Charter rights, their decisions tend to enhance it.[146]

A distinctive feature of Charter rights discourse is the extent to which it ignores class and prior distributions in defining and protecting human rights. One effect of this is that the Charter tends to reinforce the legitimacy of existing private law entitlements and thus creates a barrier to public policies of redistribution. This is because 'the Charter is imperialistic'.[147] Not only will its clientele seek to expand its jurisdiction, the courts, especially with the authority of the Charter, speak with the force of right. Although particular decisions are controversial, the judiciary's institutional legitimacy, especially when compared with its main contenders, is strong.[148] Thus, increasingly, the courts play a role in shaping the terms of political debate.

---

[141] See D. Schneiderman, 'A Comment on *RJR-MacDonald* v.*Canada*', (1996) 30 *University of British Columbia Law Review* 165; and M. MacKinnon, 'Big Tobacco backs down', *Globe and Mail*, 9 June 2000.

[142] Ibid. para. 33.   [143] See Moon, n. 110 above.

[144] Bakan, n. 10 above; Mandel, n. 6 above.   [145] Bakan, n. 10 above, 148.

[146] See Anderson, n. 107 above, 49; and R. Bauman, 'Business, Economic Rights, and the Charter', in Schneiderman and Sutherland, n. 6 above, 58.

[147] A. Cairns quoted, in F. L. Morton (ed)., *Law, Politics and the Judicial Process in Canada* (Calgary: University of Calgary Press, 1992), 233.

[148] See Lajoie et al., n. 3 above.

IV. Conclusion

Fundamental human rights are crucial to a democracy, for ideally they ensure that political authority respects individual dignity and worth despite individual and group differences. Historically, they have been claimed in the struggle for emancipation by individuals who have been subjugated on account of their social identity.[149] A truly democratic state would recognize and respect fundamental human rights. The important question is how to go about doing so.

Entrenching a bill of rights and having it enforced by the ordinary common law courts is only one mechanism for protecting human rights and enhancing democracy, and at first glance it seems an odd choice. Courts are hardly democratic in structure; in fact, they tend to be authoritarian.[150] But, as judicial democrats[151] point out, there are limits in existing political institutions that claim a more direct democratic heritage. Courts, they argue, are uniquely suited to listening to groups who lack political power, protecting vulnerable minorities, and guarding fundamental values.[152]

Ultimately, the question of whether an entrenched bill of rights enforced by the ordinary common law courts enhances respect for fundamental human rights and democracy is an empirical question.[153] I have argued that in the Canadian context, courts are disposed to recognition claims but inclined against redistribution ones. The rights claims of social movements that courts recognize under the Charter are important, but they come at quite a cost. Features of legal methodology and deeply entrenched legal norms displace redistribution claims and reinforce prevailing material inequalities. The courts are not an auspicious place to attempt to impose democratic constraints on the free market. In fact, the official legal system constitutes a formidable barrier to democratic reform.[154]

There are other ways of institutionalizing respect for human rights and enhancing democracy which involve reforming the political institutions that have a democratic heritage. Proportional representation, instead of the current system of the candidate with the largest number of votes and the party with the largest number of elected candidates winning, is likely to lead to a more representative House of Commons. Mirror representation, in which a specified number of seats are reserved for groups historically excluded from the political process, is another possibility.[155] Limits on election spending and public funding to assist parties in communicating

---

[149] W. Brown, *States of Injury: Power and Freedom in Late Modernity* (Princeton. NJ: Princeton University Press, 1995) 96.

[150] See Tushnet in this volume.

[151] G. Hein, *Interest Group Litigation and Canadian Democracy* (Quebec: IRPP, 2000), 5.

[152] See D. Beatty, 'The Canadian Charter of Rights: Lessons and Laments', in Anderson, n. 12 above, 3; Day and Brodsky, n. 11 above; Hein, n. 151 above.

[153] Mandel, n. 2 above, 256.

[154] McCann and Silverstein, n. 27 above, 138; Brown, n. 149 above, 133.

[155] See W. Kymlicka, 'Group Representation', in Seidle , n. 29 above.

their platforms would reduce the bias that economic inequality imposes on the political process. Moreover, there are a number of proposals for parliamentary reform, including reducing party discipline and registering lobbyists, that would probably enhance democracy.[156] Within a revitalized parliamentary system, standing legislative committees to evaluate bills in terms of their implications for protected rights may avoid some of the problems of using the courts.[157]

But these kinds of institutional change depend not only upon a transformation in how we view the relationship between democracy and human rights, but also upon an agent that can effect such a transformation. The common law courts are not good candidates either for such a revitalized vision of democracy or as agents of egalitarian social change. According to Madame Justice Beverly McLachlan,[158] who is now Chief Justice of the Supreme Court, 'democracy is more than mere populism; it is the lawful exercise of powers conferred by the constitution'. This understanding of democracy is very formal and legalistic. It has a tendency to ignore how differences in economic resources that influence political power are reinforced by law. One of the most troublesome aspects of relying on the ordinary courts to enforce fundamental rights is that this reinforces the view that the state poses the primary threat to human rights and that the solution is simply to reduce its power. The relationship between private and political power is not questioned. A deeper understanding of democracy and a different agency of social transformation are required in order to institutionalize respect for human rights.

[156] See F. L. Seidle, 'Proposals for Parliamentary Reform', in Seidle, n. 29 above.

[157] See J. L. Hiebert, 'Legislative Scrutiny: An Alternative Approach to Protecting Rights', in J. F. Fletcher (ed.), *Ideas in Action: Essays on Politics and Law in Honour of Peter Russell* (Toronto: University of Toronto Press, 1999), 294.

[158] B. McLachlan, 'Charter Myths', (1999) 33 *University of British Columbia Law Review* 23.

19

Scepticism about Judicial Review:
A Perspective from the United States

MARK TUSHNET

One might think that a US perspective on entrenchment of human rights would be particularly valuable for states like Great Britain beginning to develop institutions for entrenchment. The US experience with the institution of judicial review of legislation for compatibility with some norms expressed in a document, the Constitution, dates at least to *Marbury v. Madison*, decided in 1803.[1] Two hundred years' experience might provide a useful perspective on new institutions entrenching human rights.

One might be sceptical, though, about what precisely the US experience can contribute to a general understanding of entrenchment, on a number of grounds. Here I describe a few of those grounds briefly, and devote the bulk of this essay to the most fundamental sources of scepticism about the usefulness of a US perspective— the manner in which the judges who exercised the power of judicial review are chosen in the United States, and the conception they have of their role.

First, we should note that human rights can be entrenched in a number of ways. The characteristics of the US version—enforcement of entrenched human rights by judges appointed for life terms through a process that blends professional concerns with political ones—may be a unique combination. Other systems of entrenching human rights would have different effects from the US system. Human rights could be entrenched by ensuring that legislative bodies specifically attend to the human rights implications of their actions—through the creation, for example, of a legislative committee that must submit a report on the consistency of all proposed legislation with the entrenched norms.[2] Even judicial systems of entrenchment vary widely. The United States has one of the very few systems in which judges appointed in the ordinary way and with life terms enforce entrenched rights. Most other systems of constitutional review through courts give the constitutional judges defined terms, usually ranging from seven to fifteen years, and many insist that judges performing this sort of review be appointed through a process in which political concerns play a substantially larger role than professional ones.

---

[1] 5 US (1 Cranch) 137 (1803).
[2] Cf. Human Rights Act 1998, s. 19 (requiring the minister in charge of a proposed bill to make a statement that the proposal is compatible with the European Convention, or make a statement that the government wishes to proceed even though the minister cannot make a statement that the proposal is compatible with the Convention).

Someone whose perspective derives from the US experience with its form of constitutional review may have less to offer than we might initially think for those dealing with other forms of enforcing entrenched rights.

Second, the sheer *temporality* of entrenching human rights today may matter when one considers the relevance of the US experience. By this I mean that the United States developed institutions for protecting entrenched rights decades ago. Countries doing so today face a different situation. First, a worldwide culture of human rights has begun to emerge, penetrating all countries but some more than others. This culture suggests that there might be what we could call a pent-up demand for enforcement of human rights. In its simplest form, this demand seeks the elimination of egregious violations of human rights that for one reason or another—legislative inertia, indifference, or inattention—have remained on the statute books. Most of the laws that will fall when the new institutions to protect human rights respond to the pent-up demand are likely to be relatively unimportant.[3] Still, the new institutions will generate a significant number of decisions that seem clearly appropriate and that are likely to be taken as demonstrating the institutions' vitality. In short, there is likely to be a first blush of enthusiasm, validated by this early stream of decisions, about the effectiveness of entrenching human rights. As time passes that enthusiasm may diminish, but by then the institutions for protecting entrenched rights may have established their legitimacy permanently.

For example, on the enactment of the Charter of Rights and Freedoms Canada may well have faced pent-up demand, which the Canadian courts satisfied. A so-called 'Charter Party' developed, defending the Canadian Supreme Court and the Charter against challenges to their democratic legitimacy.[4] As time has passed, some members of the Charter Party have become more tempered in their enthusiasm.[5] David Beatty's position is exemplary. Beatty, an early member of the Charter Party, is more sceptical today. His conclusion in 1999 was that 'the single most important lesson to be learned from Canada's experience is that the extent to which human rights are protected in a society depends, more than anything else, on the way judges are appointed to its courts. Regrettably, Canada's contribution here must be a negative one.'[6] The new institutions, that is, may become obstacles to democratic governance that are nonetheless difficult to evade.

---

[3] The reason is that the very culture of human rights that leads to entrenchment is likely to have directed its attention to egregious human rights violations through prior political mobilization.

[4] For a sceptic's description of the Charter Party, see A. C. Hutchinson, 'Supreme Court Inc.: The Business of Democracy and Rights', in G. W. Anderson (ed.), *Rights and Democracy: Essays in UK–Canadian Constitutionalism* (London: Blackstone Press, 1999), 31–5.

[5] See e.g. D. Beatty, 'The Canadian Charter of Rights: Lessons and Laments', in Anderson, n. 4 above, 3–27.

[6] Hutchinson, n. 4 above, 34, provides the description of Beatty on which I rely (along with my own reading of Beatty's work). The quotation is from Beatty, n. 5 above, 27. For additional discussion of the role of judicial appointment, see text accompanying n. 28 below.

A second facet of temporality is revealed by considering the institutions that helped produce the cross-border culture of human rights. Non-governmental organizations (NGOs) have played a large role in producing that culture, and they typically play an equally large role in creating domestic institutions designed to protect entrenched human rights. Once such rights are entrenched, NGOs play a new role. As Charles Epp has demonstrated, successful protection of entrenched human rights seems to require the existence of a reasonably thick network of NGOs available to support challenges to existing practices as violations of entrenched rights.[7] Rights-supporting NGOs in the United States date from 1909, when the National Association for the Advancement of Colored People, and the 1920s, when the American Civil Liberties Union began actively to support constitutional litigation.[8] But the thick network that rights revolutions may require came into its own only in the 1960s. The existence of international human rights NGOs, and their domestic counterparts, makes it more likely that the networks Epp describes will be available today.

As the example of NGOs suggests, the United States has long experience with judicial review of statutes for constitutionality, but a much shorter history of review for compatibility with fundamental human rights norms. *Marbury* itself was about the constitutionality of a statute affecting the Supreme Court's jurisdiction, or, more broadly, about a question of the separation of legislative and judicial power. Separation of powers arguably promotes human rights indirectly, but even successes in enforcing the separation of powers shed little light on the question of the utility of judicial review of statutes for compatibility with human rights norms.

The US Supreme Court did enforce some individual rights nearly from the beginning, though it is worth emphasizing that it was not until 1965 that the Court found a statute enacted by the national Congress unconstitutional as a violation of the First Amendment's protection of free speech.[9] I describe the history of constitutional review in the United States with an extremely broad brush. The original Constitution contained a few protections of individual rights—a guarantee against bills of attainder and ex post facto laws, applicable to the national government and state (subnational) governments, and a ban on state government action impairing contractual obligations, for example. The Bill of Rights (1791), a classic list of first-generation liberal individual rights, contained many more such protections, although not a generalized guarantee of equality. Until the late nineteenth century, however, the US national government was hardly expansive in exercising its powers, and so it rarely enacted legislation that might fairly be characterized as

---

[7] *The Rights Revolution: Lawyers, Activists, and Supreme Courts in Comparative Perspective* (Chicago: University of Chicago Press, 1998).

[8] For histories, see C. Kellogg, *NAACP: A History of the National Association for the Advancement of Colored People* (Baltimore: Johns Hopkins University Press, 1967); S. Walker, *In Defense of American Liberties: A History of the ACLU*, 2nd edn. (Carbondale, Ill.: Southern Illinois University Press, 1999).

[9] *Lamont v. Postmaster General* 381 US 301 (1965), invalidated a law that required the post office to block Communist propaganda from being sent to anyone unless the recipient first told the post office that they did want to get it.

threatening the rights protected by the Bill of Rights. In addition, in 1833 the Supreme Court held that the provisions in the Bill of Rights did not protect individuals against rights violations by subnational governments.[10]

For the first fifty years of judicial review in the United States, then, the Supreme Court enforced constitutional limitations on state governments directed at limiting those governments' ability to regulate contractual obligations. Libertarians would see that as enforcing a fundamental human right. And, as with separation of powers, contract and property rights protect individual liberty indirectly, as even non-libertarians generally concede. But for the latter group, rights of contract and property as such are not fundamental human rights, and the experience of enforcing such rights might therefore not illuminate for them the issue of the value of entrenching what they regard as truly fundamental human rights.

The Supreme Court took the opportunity to adopt a more vigorous form of judicial review after the adoption in 1868 of the Fourteenth Amendment, which barred the states from denying people 'due process of law' and the equal protection of the laws. The Fourteenth Amendment expanded the Court's purview by allowing it to subject to judicial review not just the legislation adopted by a Congress not used to expansive exercises of power, and not just state legislation dealing with contractual rights, but the entire range of state legislation. Most of the Court's work, however, concerned property rights, as the Court interpreted the due process clause to preclude states from violating vested rights of property by adopting laws, such as minimum wage and maximum hours laws, that came to characterize twentieth-century government. The early history of judicial review for consistency with equality norms is mixed at best. The Court generally acceded to strong existing prejudices against women and African-Americans, although it occasionally invalidated statutes that were blatant attempts to preserve the racial caste system inherited from slavery, and against local laws reflecting severe prejudice against immigrants from China.[11]

The first glimpses of a serious system of judicial review based on non-property human rights norms could be seen in the opening decades of the twentieth century.[12] But the Supreme Court actually began regularly to exercise the power of judicial review for human rights violations only in the 1940s. Focusing on free

---

[10] *Barron v. City of Baltimore* 32 US (7 Pet.) 243 (1833). *Barron* involved the due process clause of the Fifth Amendment, which does not contain a literal restriction like the one in the First Amendment identifying 'Congress' as the body that may not enact laws restricting free speech.

[11] See e.g. *Plessy v. Ferguson* 163 US 537 (1896) (upholding a state law requiring the separation of races on railroads), *Strauder v. West Virginia* 100 US 303 (1879) (invalidating a state law denying African Americans the right to serve on juries), *Bradwell v. Illinois* 83 US (16 Wall.) 130 (1873) (upholding a state court's refusal to issue a licence allowing a woman to practise law), and *Yick Wo v. Hopkins* 118 US 351 (1886) (reversing a conviction for violating a local ordinance that was shown to have been enforced against Chinese laundry operators but not against equally culpable white laundry operators).

[12] *Buchanan v. Warley* 245 US 60 (1917) (invalidating a local ordinance creating segregated residential zones, primarily on the ground that the ordinance restricted property-owners' rights to dispose of their own property as they wished); *Brown v. Mississippi* 297 US 278 (1936) (overturning a conviction based on a confession extracted from the defendant by gross physical coercion).

speech law, the picture is roughly this. Initially the Supreme Court interpreted the First Amendment to provide protection for political dissidents who were not seen as serious threats to the established order. For example, it struck down restrictions on demonstrations against the political 'boss' of Jersey City, New Jersey, but upheld the convictions of the leaders of the US Communist party.[13] As the perceived threat from internal Communism receded, the Court became more generous in protecting the rights of Communists.[14] Free speech doctrine now provides a great deal of protection against efforts to imprison political dissidents,[15] and probably has contributed to a culture in which arguments against speech suppression carry a great deal of weight. That culture, and the Court's doctrine, have an underside, however. The Court has interpreted the First Amendment to provide substantial protection to the commercial activities of large media enterprises, to the point where credible doctrinal arguments can be made that restrictions on the advertising of tobacco products are unconstitutional.[16]

Similarly ambiguous stories could be told about the US experience in enforcing equality norms, and other fundamental human rights. For example, the Court's vindication of a right to racial equality has led it to invalidate affirmative action programmes.[17] It has veered from denying gay rights in upholding the constitutionality of laws making homosexual sodomy a crime[18] to protecting gays against the enactment of rules impairing their ability to secure anti-discrimination legislation,[19] and back to finding that a large private association, the Boy Scouts, could discriminate against gays in selecting leaders.[20]

The actual US experience with judicial review in the name of fundamental human rights is thus significantly shorter and more ambiguous than one might have thought. The longer view of US constitutional history is important nonetheless. The Constitution's text and structure, and some of the understandings that underlie it, provided interpretive possibilities that the Court forewent. It was open to it to adopt interpretations of the due process clause of the Fifth and Fourteenth Amendments, for example, that would have protected fundamental human rights, and yet it did not do so. One might take US constitutional history to suggest that judges will rarely seize opportunities the law gives them to protect fundamental

---

[13] *Hague v. CIO* 307 US 496 (1939); *Dennis v. United States* 341 US 494 (1951).

[14] See e.g. *Yates v. United States* 354 US 298 (1957) (overturning the convictions of second-level Communist party leaders on the ground that the evidence showed only that they advocated forcible overthrow of the government as an abstract principle, not as a guide to action); *United States v. Brown* 381 US 437 (1965) (invalidating as a bill of attainder a statute denying members of the Communist party the right to serve as a union officer).

[15] *Brandenberg v. Ohio* 395 US 444 (1969) (holding that a person can be convicted of sedition only if the evidence shows that the person incited imminent lawless conduct).

[16] See esp. *44 Liquormart, Inc. v. Rhode Island* 517 US 484 (1996) (invalidating a statute prohibiting price advertising for liquor, and suggesting that bans on factually accurate advertising may be impermissible). But see *Turner Broadcasting System, Inc. v. FCC* 520 US 180 (1997) (upholding a federal statute requiring that cable systems carry certain stations, employing 'intermediate' scrutiny).

[17] *Adarand Constructors, Inc. v. Pena* 515 US 200 (1995).

[18] *Bowers v. Hardwick* 478 US 186 (1986).   [19] *Romer v. Evans* 517 US 620 (1996).

[20] *Boy Scouts of America v. Dale* 120 S. Ct. 2446 (2000).

human rights. That view of history would support scepticism about the possibilities of judicial review generally.

But rarely does not mean never, and there are undoubtedly important occasions on which judicial review seems to have made a difference. For the present generation of progressives, *Brown v. Board of Education* and *Roe v. Wade* are the central examples.[21] They are usually taken to show that the Supreme Court can protect human rights when legislatures do not. Here too, however, some scepticism seems justified. *Brown* had quite limited effects on the actual separation of the races in the American South for about a decade, although it did provide some moral encouragement to a civil rights movement that was already in its early stages when *Brown* was decided.[22] By the early 1950s broad social trends were changing the complexion of US racial politics. In particular, the migration of African-Americans from the South to northern cities substantially enhanced their political power within the national government, and specifically within the Democratic party. It seems quite likely that some substantial civil rights statutes would have been adopted by Congress by the mid-1960s even if the Court had not decided *Brown*, although of course the content and structure of those statutes might have reflected the fact that the Court had not acted.

More important, *Brown* is best understood as the imposition on recalcitrant local governments of norms widely and strongly held by *national* political elites and less widely and more weakly held by non-Southerners. *Brown* is a success story for judicial review within the framework of US federalism, and may have few implications for the enforcement of fundamental human rights in a non-federal system whose political elites—judges as well as legislators—might *support* human rights violations.

The story of *Roe* is equally complex. As with racial segregation, so too with restrictive abortion laws, and sex-based discrimination more generally. By the early 1970s a significant political movement had begun to accomplish some legislative erosion of restrictive abortion laws. The movement's ultimate success was not guaranteed, however, because its initial achievements had begun to generate substantial opposition. The Supreme Court's decision in *Roe* extended these early legislative initiatives across the nation, and protected them against repeal. A sceptic might note, however, two characteristics of *Roe*. It came to be interpreted as a fundamentally libertarian decision. That is, it came to mean that governments could not interfere with *private* choices, of women and providers of abortion services. The Supreme Court soon decided that the government was under no obligation to

---

[21] *Brown v. Board of Education* 347 US 483 (1954); *Roe v. Wade* 410 US 113 (1973).

[22] G. Rosenberg, *The Hollow Hope: Can Courts Bring About Social Change?* (Chicago: University of Chicago Press, 1991), argues that *Brown* was ineffective until the political branches came to support desegregation, largely as a result of the increasing power of African Americans in the Democratic party. Rosenberg's specific arguments have been criticized: see e.g. D. A. Schultz and S. E. Gottlieb, 'Legal Functionalism and Social Change: A Reassessment of Rosenberg's *The Hollow Hope: Can Courts Bring About Social Change?*', (1996) 12 *Journal of Law and Politics* 63, but his work clearly demonstrates that claims for the effectiveness of the Supreme Court's decision must be temperate.

provide abortion services to women who could not afford to purchase them.[23] As Gerald Rosenberg emphasizes, the line of abortion cases made abortion services an ordinary commodity. Not all fundamental human rights can readily be treated as commodities, however, and even the right to choice is seen by some as requiring social supports that US constitutional law does not provide.

Roe's second characteristic returns us to broader themes, by providing an alternative model to *Brown* of judicial review's successes. *Brown* was a case in which the Court enforced a norm supported by a majority—of the nation's political elite, at least, and perhaps of the nation as a whole—against legislation enacted by a regional minority. In *Roe* the Court cast its vote on one side in a closely contested political battle. Neither of these models make judicial enforcement of entrenched human rights insignificant, although, as I have suggested, the conditions for success on the *Brown* model may rarely be met in a non-federal nation. Notably, however, neither is a model of judicial review acting on behalf of a true minority, one that has no real chance of success in the legislative process.

These sketches of *Brown* and *Roe* can introduce a quite general perspective on the US experience with constitutional review. Political scientist Robert Dahl, writing in 1957, offered the generalization that the Supreme Court's decisions were rarely out of line for an extended period with the policies supported by the nation's governing coalition, considered over a similarly extended period.[24] Dahl's argument has to be modified in detail to deal with developments in the half-century since he wrote, but the main thrust of his argument remains valid. If at some point one observes a gap between the Supreme Court's position and that of the rest of the nation's political elite, five or ten years later that gap will have been reduced, usually by changes in the Court's position. Or, as I have put it, Supreme Court decisions are basically 'noise around zero'.[25] Sometimes the Supreme Court's decisions are somewhat to the right of the public's (or the political elite's), sometimes they are somewhat to the left, but over time the Court's position on average tracks what is happening elsewhere in the political system.

Consider the *Brown* and *Roe* models of judicial review in this light. I have argued that *Brown* represents the triumph of a national view over a local one. Again more generally, many Supreme Court decisions strike down statutes that can fairly be described as 'outliers', far beyond the range of what reasonable people on the left or the right would think justified. For example, the foundational case for the US constitutional law of privacy, *Griswold v. Connecticut*, invalidated a law prohibiting the use of contraceptives.[26] When the Court decided the case, only one other state had a similar law on the books. I know of no compilations, but I suspect that by far the

---

[23] *Maher v. Roe* 432 US 464 (1977).

[24] 'Decision-Making in a Democracy: The Supreme Court as a National Policy-Maker', (1957) 6 *Journal of Public Law* 279.

[25] M. Tushnet, *Taking the Constitution Away from the Courts* (Princeton, NJ: Princeton University Press, 1999), 153.

[26] *Griswold v. Connecticut* 381 US 479 (1965).

largest proportion of the Supreme Court decisions invalidating statutes as violations of human rights deal with such 'outliers'. Here judicial review clearly makes a contribution to protecting human rights, and does so without seriously eroding democratic governance. But, precisely because the statutes are outliers, the contribution of judicial review is relatively small.

At first the *Roe* model may seem different. There the Court acts on behalf of one side in a controversy that sharply divides the public. Suppose the division is 55 per cent to 45 per cent, which in terms of US public policy is quite substantial. In weighing in on the side of the 45 per cent minority, the Court clearly does interfere with majoritarian politics. And yet the impairment of democratic self-government may be no larger here than in the cases dealing with outliers. For, after all, the Court is coming down on the side of the 45 per cent, a non-trivial number of people.

Considering Dahl's perspective and the two models of judicial review, I conclude that the US experience with judicial review is nothing to get excited about one way or the other. The Supreme Court has not done much that could not have been accomplished, in perhaps a slightly longer period, through ordinary political action. But what it has done has not interfered much with democratic self-governance.

Why has judicial review made so little difference? Judicial review's limited impact in the United States may arise from some structural features of the US constitutional system. The lessons of the US experience would of course be significantly limited if that experience derived from such features, in so far as other constitutional systems differed in the relevant respects. One can readily identify the relevant features of the US constitutional system. The separation of legislature and executive, and the division of the legislature into two houses of roughly equal power but different terms of service, means that large-scale changes in policy can take place only over an extended period.[27] A president can get a mandate from the people, and may carry a majority of the House of Representatives along. But in *that* election only one third of the seats in the Senate will have been contested. By the time the next election occurs, the president's mandate may have weakened, or the president's party may gain control of both houses of Congress. Further, the structure of the US party system modulates the pace of change. The so-called national political parties are more like federations of relatively independent parties centred in the states, and there can be wide divergences within a party. Politicians on the left side of the Republican party may be more liberal than politicians on the right wing of the Democratic party. These politicians can be elected to Congress because the federated national parties find it difficult to impose discipline on candidates. Finally, the electoral system itself damps down differences. Legislators are elected from single-member districts in which the candidate who wins a plurality of the votes is elected. As is well known, such an electoral system makes it likely that only two parties will be serious competitors for any district seat, and that the two parties will develop programmes appealing to the centre in each district.

[27] See B. Ackerman, 'The New Separation of Powers', (2000) 113 *Harvard LR* 633.

The overall effect of these features of the US constitutional system is to make it unlikely that legislators will enact large-scale changes in any short period. Of course, political crises sometimes occur, producing rapid and dramatic change. The pace of change in the courts is structured to be slow, however. Federal judges serve during good behaviour, meaning in practice for as long as they wish to. They are nominated by the president and must be confirmed by the Senate.[28] The normal rate of departure from the bench, through retirement, resignation, or death, ordinarily gives the political branches the opportunity to shape the federal bench over a period of four to six years. That corresponds to the ordinary rate of change in public policy. If policy change occurs more quickly, the federal courts *can* be obstructionist, acting in the service of the principles of the regime under which they were appointed but which has been decisively replaced.

These structures account for the crisis between the Supreme Court and the political branches during the early years of the New Deal. The New Deal judicial crisis was resolved only when President Franklin D. Roosevelt was able to pack the Court with new appointees as older judges retired. Notably, however, the New Deal judicial crisis, which culminated in 1937, is the last occasion on which the Supreme Court put itself in serious tension with dominant tendencies in the political branches.

The way in which US political institutions are structured makes it likely that the role of judicial review will be relatively small. Legislators are unlikely to enact programmes that seem extreme. Even more, the governing coalition will be able to gain control of the federal courts if it holds together for a reasonably extended period. The judicial appointment process is inevitably political, although the nature of the politics involved changes as the basic features of legislative politics changes. When legislation results from deals made in the backrooms of the legislature, judges will be chosen in much the same way, and when legislation results from open bargaining for votes by interest groups, judicial selection will take on the same characteristics.[29] These structures make it unlikely that, over the medium to long run, federal judges will have views about what rights are entrenched in the Constitution that differ in major ways from the views on that question held by national legislators. In addition, the slow pace of legislative change, induced by constitutional structures, suggests that federal judges will rarely be presented with policies so novel that they seem strongly at odds with long-standing statutes the judges think clearly permissible.

Dahl's conclusion about the limited impact of judicial review might not hold in systems with a political structure different from the United States. As Bruce

---

[28] The process of judicial selection in the US states is even more obviously political, because those judges typically must have the direct approval of voters in elections.

[29] D. A. Yalof, *Pursuit of Justices: Presidential Politics and the Selection of Supreme Court Nominees* (Chicago: University of Chicago Press, 1999); M. Silverstein, *Judicious Choices* (New York: Norton, 1993). Yalof deals with the processes by which presidents choose whom to nominate, Silverstein with the confirmation process.

Ackerman has emphasized, for example, purely parliamentary systems facilitate rapid and large changes in public policy.[30] Ackerman advocates what he calls a constrained parliamentary system precisely because the constraints can modulate the pace of policy change. One can defend this modulation, as Ackerman does, on the ground that rapid swings in policy may reflect immediate policy preferences but are unlikely to produce good public policy over any extended period.[31] Modulating the rate of policy change makes it possible for a nation's people to achieve more permanent changes in policy in accordance with their long-term views. In the short run, however, the constraints are likely to interfere with the immediate policy preferences of a governing majority, probably more dramatically than they do in the US system. Constrained parliamentarism thus may be prone to more judicial crises akin to the New Deal crisis than occur in the US system.

It should be obvious, as well, that the politicized nature of the judicial appointment process plays an important part in the structural explanation for the US experience as described by Dahl and the *Brown* and *Roe* models of judicial review. Judges do not get out of line for long with what the political branches want, because the judges are appointed by the political branches who act with an eye to what the judges are likely to do once in office. Entrenching human rights to be enforced by judges appointed through less political, more professionalized processes may introduce instabilities into a nation's governing processes. These more professionally oriented judges may be indifferent to politics, and so may precipitate crises that judges appointed in a more politicized way would not.

Similarly, judges with long terms may have been appointed at a time when one view of what constitutes a violation of entrenched rights prevailed in the political and judicial branches, but may be called upon to enforce such rights at a time when the legislative view has changed. 'Old-fashioned' judges may interfere with policy 'innovations' on human rights grounds that were powerful when the judges took office but whose credibility has waned substantially. For these reasons, and perhaps based on some early experience with review by such judges, systems may move in the direction of subjecting the judicial appointment process to closer political scrutiny, or creating specialized institutions of review staffed by members with defined tenure.

This account of the relation between judicial enforcement of entrenched rights and particular political structure of US institutions suggests that the relatively sanguine depiction of judicial review provided by Dahl and others may be inaccurate if rights are entrenched in systems whose political structures differ from the US structure. Another possibility, however, deserves some attention. It might be called

---

[30] N. 27 above.

[31] Ackerman suggests another reason for seeking modulation. Public-choice scholars, drawing on the work of Kenneth Arrow, suggest that one cannot coherently take immediate policy preferences to reflect a 'majority's' policy preferences because there is no such thing as *a* majority about which a person interested in democratic self-governance should be concerned. However, moving from that suggestion to the proposition that modulated policies, those that survive over a longer term than a single electoral cycle, are preferable in democratic terms seems to me to require a rather substantial argument.

materialist determinism. Here the idea is that the basic direction a society takes is determined by things like demography and economics. Law, even entrenched law, can do little in the medium or long run to affect that direction. I invoked ideas associated with materialist determinism in referring to African-American migration as part of the *Brown* model of judicial review. The difficulty with materialist determinism is that it lacks a clear mechanism by which material factors get translated into law. One can make some vague gestures in the direction of a mechanism by referring to the dissemination of ideas among political elites, including judges, and to the credibility that such ideas get from their apparent conformity to social reality. But in the end these can be only gestures; I know of no really satisfactory materialist theory of ideology or law. Yet, if the materialist determinist account of judicial review's impact is correct, the US experience might offer some instruction to other systems of entrenching rights. Because entrenchment is, on the materialist determinist view, largely epiphenomenal, entrenchment is unlikely to make much difference, either in advancing human rights or restricting democratic governance.

So far I have offered what might be called a politically based scepticism about enforcing entrenched human rights through the courts. There is of course a well-known normative scepticism as well. It is what Frank Michelman has called the paradox of constitutional democracy.[32] Sustaining a democratic system requires that certain decisions, what Michelman calls the law of lawmaking, be immune from revision lest the democratic character of the system be lost. And yet the law of lawmaking is the most basic set of decisions a people can make about how it is to govern itself. How can a system that deprives people of the power to alter the law of lawmaking possibly be described as democratic? But then, how can a system that gives people that power be described as constitutional?

For present purposes I will take the law of lawmaking to correspond reasonably well to first-generation human rights. What does the US experience suggest about the resolution of the paradox of constitutional democracy? One might take *Roe* and the decisions that followed as providing a defence of judicial review for libertarian (or perhaps more broadly, first generation) human rights, but supporting scepticism about its usefulness beyond that. Protecting first-generation human rights is undoubtedly important. Yet, the real question at issue is an institutional one. What institutions are *needed* to protect fundamental human rights? As Cass Sunstein has emphasized, constitutions are useful to the extent that they entrench rights vulnerable to violation by real political forces; there is no particular value, albeit no particular harm, in entrenching rights that no one thinks likely to be violated by government officials now or in the foreseeable future.[33]

Are threats to first-generation rights realistic? Of course they are in some nations, and entrenching them might be valuable there. Elsewhere, however, a culture of rights has arisen that makes such threats unusual. Even more, it is all well and good

---

[32] F. I. Michelman, *Brennan and Democracy* (Princeton, NJ: Princeton University Press, 1999), 4.

[33] C. R. Sunstein, 'Against Positive Rights', in A. Sajó (ed.), *Western Rights? Post-Communist Application* (The Hague: Kluwer Law International, 1996), 225–32, at 226.

to write of *first-generation rights* in the large, but in fact the precise content of each first-generation right is often a matter of reasonable disagreement. Entrenching first-generation rights and providing that 'they' may be enforced by institutions set apart from ordinary politics gives those institutions the opportunity to come down on one side of a reasonable disagreement about *what* precisely is guaranteed by fundamental human rights norms.

Here the US experience may well be illuminating. No one in the United States denies that free expression is a fundamental human right. The Supreme Court has decided that statutory restrictions on a political candidate's expenditures violate free expression. This is clearly a defensible judgment, but it is equally clearly not the only reasonable interpretation of what the fundamental human right of free expression requires.[34] Another example, also involving free expression, is that the Supreme Court has developed free-expression doctrine in a way that makes it almost impossible to enforce legislation restricting so-called hate speech.[35] What makes this example so dramatic is that the right to free expression, as entrenched in the US Constitution and interpreted by the Supreme Court, makes it a constitutional violation to enact laws that some international human rights documents say are *required* by fundamental human rights norms.[36]

The US experience illustrates one risk that cannot readily be dissociated from entrenching human rights. The precise content of a particular entrenched right—that is, whether a specific policy is consistent with that right—will frequently be subject to reasonable disagreement among people all of whom agree that the right is and should be entrenched. If *entrenchment* means that some institution will have the last word, at least in the short run, on the content of entrenched rights, that institution's choice among reasonable alternative interpretations will prevail, even though a democratic process may have selected a policy that, on some other reasonable interpretation, is consistent with the entrenched right.[37] And sometimes the short run may matter, as when a political coalition implements a policy and then loses power for reasons unrelated to that policy.

One response to this concern is to insist that the enforcement institution adopt a stance of restraint with respect to legislation challenged as violating entrenched rights. That is, the rule should be that legislation should not be found to violate entrenched rights if there is some reasonable interpretation of the entrenched rights with which the legislation is consistent. I believe that there are two difficulties with this response, one mostly technical and one mostly psychological or sociological.

---

[34] One can be sceptical about the soundness of campaign finance statutes adopted by legislators who are likely to structure the law in ways that protect incumbents from challengers, and still think that this scepticism is better expressed in politics than through interpretation of an entrenched right of free expression.

[35] *R.A.V. v. City of St. Paul* 505 US 377 (1992).

[36] The International Covenant on Civil and Political Rights, § 20(2), provides: 'Any advocacy of national, racial or religious hatred that constitutes incitement to discrimination, hostility or violence shall be prohibited by law.'

[37] For reasons suggested above, text accompanying nn. 21–5 above, it is unlikely that the institution will have the last word in the medium and long runs.

The technical difficulty has two facets. First, deferential review may miscommunicate the enforcement institution's view of what the entrenched rights truly are. Consider here a decision by the European Court of Human Rights refusing to find a violation of the Convention because the act in question fell within the margin of appreciation given to legislative choices in a diverse community. One can take such a decision in two ways. The decision might mean that the Court finds the act to embody a reasonable judgment about the content of the Convention right. Here the Court's judgment is, 'We think the act is reasonable.' But there is an alternative interpretation of such a decision. It is, roughly, 'The institutional constraints on us, particularly the importance of avoiding too overt a confrontation with member-states, lead us to refrain from finding a violation.'

A posture of restraint is ambiguous between these alternatives. Legislators ought to draw different implications from them, however. The first tells legislators that what they have done is *consistent* with the entrenched rights. The second ought to tell legislators that what they have done might well be *inconsistent* with those rights, and should lead legislators to think hard when a similar issue comes before them. More likely, however, is the complacent response that the prior legislation was not found to violate the entrenched rights, so there is nothing to worry about in connection with later proposals. A restrained form of review, that is, may paradoxically undermine legislative attention to entrenched rights.[38]

Second, and looking in the opposite direction, enforcement institutions, particularly courts, typically seek to determine not only whether a specific statute is consistent with entrenched rights but also what instructions they can give, in the form of a rule or doctrine, that will assist legislatures in avoiding similar difficulties in the future. The task of giving guidance imposes some constraints, mostly in the form of transparency or simplicity, in the rules or doctrines the enforcement institutions develop. Entrenched rights may be systematically over-enforced, even under a deferential system of review, because only simple and broad rules can give the kind of guidance the enforcement institutions wish to give while simultaneously allowing those institutions to find violations in all the cases they believe to involve unreasonable interpretations of the entrenched rights.

The psychological or sociological difficulty with the posture of restraint is that such a posture may be difficult for real people to sustain, and particularly for lawyers selected on the basis of their professional rather than political qualifications. Here Michelman's analysis is enlightening. He notes that all institutions inevitably make mistakes. A legislative mistake occurs when the legislature chooses an unreasonable interpretation of the entrenched rights; a judicial mistake occurs when the courts find unreasonable a legislative interpretation that is in fact reasonable. Michelman

---

[38] For a discussion of a related problem in the US context, see Tushnet, n. 25 above, 60–1. Geoffrey Marshall has pointed out that the interpretive direction of the Human Rights Act (1998), s. 3(1), may lead courts to find legislation compatible with the European Convention not by interpreting the legislation in ways that eliminate a conflict, but by finding the legislation as it stands consistent with the limitations on Convention rights that the Convention and the European Court's jurisprudence recognize.

concludes his tentative defence of judicial review by finding it justified, if at all, by what he calls the *reliability* of judges, the chance that they are less likely than legislators to make serious mistakes about the precise content of entrenched rights.[39] Michelman then asks under what conditions we can gain confidence that courts are reliable in this sense. His answer is that 'one condition that [may] . . . contribute greatly to reliability is the constant exposure of the interpreter . . . to the full blast of the sundry opinions on the question of the rightness of one or another interpretation, freely and uninhibitedly produced by assorted members of society listening to what the others have to say out of their diverse life histories, current situations, and perceptions of interest and need.'[40]

The final question then is: do the actual institutions of enforcement satisfy this condition? The US experience suggests scepticism here too.[41] The US Supreme Court has an authoritarian attitude toward its own role.[42] At least since 1958, and perhaps since the beginning, the Supreme Court has asserted that the people of the United States must take the Court's own decisions as the last word on what the Constitution means for all the people, not merely with respect to particular cases in which one person's legal rights are at issue.[43]

The Court's authoritarianism comes through more clearly in its occasional rhetoric than in its holdings. Here I offer three examples from recent decisions. Most recently, the Supreme Court invalidated a provision of the national Violence Against Women Act.[44] Congress had the power to enact the statute if violence against women affected interstate commerce. As Justice David Souter wrote for the dissenters, Congress assembled a 'mountain of data' demonstrating that such violence did affect interstate commerce, by deterring women from travelling and taking or keeping particular jobs.[45] The majority responded that the evidence was well and good, but irrelevant because Congress used the evidence in the service of 'a method of reasoning that *we* have already rejected as unworkable'.[46]

---

[39] Michelman, n. 32 above, 58.   [40] Ibid. 59.

[41] I should note an ambiguity, or perhaps error, in Michelman's formulation of the condition. As written, it asserts that the institution of review must be *exposed* to the full blast of positions asserted by people who themselves listen to each other. As my argument in the text indicates, I think it reasonably clear that one could have confidence in reliability only if the institution of review not only was exposed to such arguments but itself listened to them. I take the words 'full blast' to mean that the institution of review does in fact listen.

[42] I draw the term 'authoritarian' from R. West, 'The Authoritarian Impulse in Constitutional Law', (1988) 42 *University of Miami LR* 531.

[43] The clearest articulation of this authoritarianism is *Cooper v. Aaron* 358 US 1 (1958). The position is defended in L. Alexander and F. Schauer, 'On Extrajudicial Constitutional Interpretation', (1997) 110 *Harvard LR* 1359. Their position is criticized in Tushnet, n. 25 above, ch. 1, with specific discussion of their argument at pp. 26–30.

[44] *United States v. Morrison* 120 S. Ct. 1740 (2000).   [45] Ibid. 1760–2.

[46] Ibid. 1752 (emphasis added). The method the Court rejected is to aggregate the impact of *non-commercial* activities to determine whether in the aggregate they have a substantial effect on interstate commerce. According to the Court, the aggregation method is available only when Congress seeks to regulate *commercial* activities. As Justice Stephen Breyer cogently observed, '[W]hy should we give critical constitutional importance to the economic, or noneconomic, nature of an interstate-commerce-affecting *cause*? If chemical emanations through indirect environmental change cause identical, severe

A few years before, the Court had invalidated the Religious Freedom Restoration Act (RFRA).[47] The Act was passed after the Court had adopted the rule that the entrenched right of religious liberty was not violated by generally applicable laws that adversely affected religious practices along with many non-religious ones.[48] The RFRA attempted to protect religious liberty by requiring that such laws satisfy a stringent standard. Its constitutionality rested on Congress's power to 'enforce' religious liberty. But, the Court said, with no justice expressing disagreement with this analysis,[49] that Congress cannot 'enforce' religious liberty 'by *changing* what the right is'.[50] Here the Court simply denies Congress any role in offering an interpretation of the entrenched right of religious liberty that differ from the Court's interpretation. The Court's interpretation *is* what the Constitution means; anything else seeks to change, not what the Court has said the Constitution means, but the Constitution itself.[51]

Undoubtedly the most egregious recent expression of constitutional authoritarianism came in the Court's decision refusing to overrule *Roe v. Wade*, the 1973 decision finding a right to choose with respect to abortion entrenched in the Constitution.[52] Three justices wrote a joint opinion, in which they discussed, among other things, the circumstances under which overruling a prior decision could be justified. The joint opinion framed the issue in this way:

Because not every conscientious claim of principled justification will be accepted as such, the justification claimed must be beyond dispute. The Court must take care to speak and act in ways that allow people to accept its decisions on the terms the Court claims for them, as grounded truly in principle, not as compromises with social and political pressures having, as such, no bearing on the principled choices that the Court is obliged to make.[53]

The abortion rights controversy was so intense, according to the joint opinion, that a decision to overrule *Roe* would be seen as an act in which the Court succumbed to social and political pressures. The joint opinion offered a vision of the relation among the Court, the people, and the Constitution that I believe can fairly be called authoritarian: 'the Court's interpretation of the Constitution calls the contending sides of a national controversy to end their national division by accepting a common mandate rooted in the Constitution.'[54]

An authoritarian Court may be *exposed* 'to the full blast of . . . sundry opinions', but, as these excerpts suggest, it is unaffected by them. Notably, in each case legislators

commercial harm outside a State, why should it matter whether local factories or home fireplaces release them?' Ibid. 1775 (Breyer J dissenting) (emphasis original).

[47] *City of Boerne v. Flores* 521 US 507 (1997).
[48] *Employment Division, Dept. of Human Resources v. Smith* 494 US 872 (1990).
[49] The dissenters focused on what they regarded as the Court's own error in the *Smith* case.
[50] 521 US at 519 (emphasis added).
[51] See also ibid. 529 ('If Congress could define its own powers by *altering the Fourteenth Amendment's meaning*, no longer would the Constitution be "superior paramount law, unchangeable by ordinary means." It would be "on a level with ordinary legislative acts, and, like other acts, . . . alterable when the legislature shall please to alter it"' (quoting *Marbury v. Madison*) (emphasis added).
[52] *Planned Parenthood of Southeastern Pennsylvania v. Casey* 505 US 833 (1992).   [53] Ibid. 865–6.
[54] Ibid. 867.

appear to have thought seriously about whether the laws they were about to adopt were consistent with fundamental rights. The legislatures simply gave answers that the Supreme Court did not like. Michelman's account suggests that we should be sceptical of the reliability of the US Supreme Court to enforce entrenched rights.[55]

I doubt that every institution committed to enforcing entrenched rights will inevitably be authoritarian. One important condition—the asserted distinction between law and politics—may make authoritarianism more likely, however. Suppose that those who staff the enforcement institution believe (1) that there is a clear difference between law and politics, (2) that the entrenched rights are legal rather than political, (3) that legislators oriented to politics are likely to be inattentive to the legal dimensions of what they do, and (4) that the members of the enforcement institution are particularly attentive to legal matters, and relatively indifferent to political ones. I believe that authoritarianism is more likely under these conditions than under others.

The US experience suggests that those committed to constitutional democracy should be concerned about what those who enforce entrenched rights believe. Direct inquiries may sometimes be useful, particularly if there is a public process for appointing members who staff the enforcement institution. An indirect strategy may also be helpful. I think it likely that lawyers, and especially judges, are professionally committed to the four beliefs I have described. If so, one should be quite cautious about staffing enforcement institutions with lawyers and judges, at least exclusively.

In conclusion, the US experience supports scepticism about enforcing entrenched human rights through the particular institutional mechanisms in the United States. There may be an irresistible worldwide movement in the direction of entrenching human rights. But there is nothing inevitable or irresistible about adopting a particular institutional design for enforcing such entrenched rights. Here I have tried to identify some of the considerations for institutional design that emerge out of reflection on the US experience.

---

[55] Of course a full account would require a comparison between the legislatures' openness to the 'full blast of argument' and the Court's, across a wider range of issues than I have provided here. Tushnet, n. 25 above, provides my own comparison.

20

The Effect of a Statutory Bill of Rights where Parliament is Sovereign: The Lesson from New Zealand

JAMES ALLAN

Look around the world for a country whose legal and constitutional arrangements most closely resemble the United Kingdom's and you will be hard pressed to look any further than New Zealand. When it comes to some things, of course, this is hardly surprising. As with almost all former colonies, the common law legal tradition was inherited from England.[1] So too was a Westminster parliamentary system and a constitutional monarchy. But unlike Canada, Australia, or South Africa, New Zealand never got a written constitution. Instead, the UK's unwritten constitutional arrangements, with parliamentary sovereignty (and supremacy) at its heart, was passed on to New Zealand. That remains the case to this day. Indeed, only the UK, New Zealand, and Israel, of all the world's democracies, can still be said (more or less[2]) to have unwritten constitutions and sovereign parliaments.

For our purposes, these shared constitutional structures between the two countries matter, not in their own right, but because New Zealand has already travelled down the road of enacting a statutory or 'watered-down'[3] Bill of Rights *Act*.[4] If anywhere in the world is likely to prove a reliable guide to the effects of the Human Rights Act 1998, it is New Zealand. There, in 1990, a statutory Bill of Rights Act was passed and came into force, one which is if anything *less* potent (on its face) than the statutory model chosen for the UK.

How then have the New Zealand judges—judges situated very much in the English common law tradition, let us not forget, and having the Privy Council way

---

This chapter is based on a re-writing and updating of my 'Turning Clark Kent into Superman: The New Zealand Bill of Rights Act 1990', (2000) 9 *Otago LR* 613–32.

[1] See the English Laws Act 1858, which in effect transferred the then existing English body of law to New Zealand.

[2] Clearly the UK's entry into Europe has, to the extent of conflicts with European law, massively diminished parliamentary sovereignty there. See *ex parte Factortame Ltd* [1990] 2 AC 85, and *ex parte Factortame Ltd (No. 2)* [1991] 1 AC 603. For more on the extent to which these three countries lack an American-style constitution, see n. 1 of R. Kay, 'American Constitutionalism', in L. Alexander (ed.), *Constitutionalism: Philosophical Foundations* (Cambridge: Cambridge University Press, 1998).

[3] See M. Taggart, 'Tugging on Superman's Cape: Lessons from Experience with the New Zealand Bill of Rights Act 1990', [1998] *Public Law* 266 (hereinafter 'Taggart'), 267.

[4] A Bill of Rights *Act* is a statute; a Bill of Rights is not. What's in a name? Sometimes an accurate description of the status (and so powers) of the thing being described.

off in London still as their final court of appeal—treated their statutory (and seemingly not overly potent) Bill of Rights Act? This will be of interest to all those in the UK who fear the possibility that the Human Rights Act 1998 will bring with it a transfer of much social policy-making power to the unelected judiciary. After all, such doubters know that enthusiasts for this new Act can always reject comparisons with countries like Canada or the US which possess an entrenched, justiciable, 'constitutionalized' Bill of Rights. Even if these latter sort of instruments *do* hand ultimate power to an unelected judiciary to decide what the enumerated rights they contain (which are necessarily expressed in vague, amorphous and emotively attractive terms) mean in specific cases, and to strike down any Acts of the legislature which breach or infringe the specific meanings so given, that is not a worry here in the UK, these enthusiasts will say. Unelected judges here will not grow overmighty. Whatever else a statutory Bill of Rights Act is meant to do, they will point out,[5] it is clearly meant to keep the judiciary subordinate to the legislature when it comes to social policy-making.

As I suggested, however, others will be less optimistic about the deference of the judiciary to elected politicians once the Human Rights Act is in force. They will suspect there is a fair amount of scope for the judges to treat a statutory, unentrenched Bill of Rights *Act* as though it were an entrenched, constitutionalized Bill of Rights.[6] Again, the far Antipodes is a good place to look to see which side is likely to be correct.

This chapter will examine the first decade of operation of the statutory New Zealand Bill of Rights Act 1990. To start, I will review the sort of Bill of Rights adopted in New Zealand, and then consider the extent to which there have been any judicial moves to 'upgrade' it, to make it a more potent instrument than the enactors seemed to intend. Next, and related to these concerns, is the issue of certainty and the degree to which Bill of Rights Act jurisprudence in New Zealand can be said to be settled. Whatever the answer to that, there is the further but connected issue of the degree of discretion the judges have given themselves (in that case law) when it comes to applying the Bill of Rights Act. So certainty will be the second subject of this chapter. The third and final topic follows on from the first two but will be discussed in far less detail. Here I will consider the likely role and powers of unelected judges called upon to operate, apply, and interpret a statutory Bill of Rights Act. What lessons can be drawn from the New Zealand experience?

---

[5] I here imagine Bill of Rights enthusiasts somewhat alive to the dangers of unelected judges making the sort of social policy decisions they do in Canada and the US. In reality, of course, many enthusiasts will not worry about this transfer of power but welcome it. For those who are, however, alive to the potential democratic deficiency, and who thus favour the statutory alternative, the comparison with New Zealand should prove instructive.

[6] 'In the shell game of constitutional reform, however, it is often difficult to keep your eye on the pea. And once the reform is securely in place, history often is quickly forgotten, pushed down by the imperative to make the best (as judges see it) of what we have in a forward looking manner. Such is the New Zealand experience . . .' (Taggart, 268.)

I. A judicial upgrade?

It is beyond dispute that in 1990 New Zealand opted for an enervated, statutory Bill of Rights Act that on its face even lost out to past inconsistent statutes.[7] It is true, of course, that half a decade earlier the prime political mover for a Bill of Rights, Geoffrey Palmer (now Sir Geoffrey), had wanted a justiciable, constitutionalized version modelled on the Canadian Charter of Rights and Freedoms (1982). 'The Draft Bill originally proposed in the 1985 Government White Paper *A Bill of Rights for New Zealand* took the form of an entrenched supreme law that would empower the courts to strike down inconsistent legislation, and included a wide remedies clause (Article 25) authorizing the courts to redress violations of rights by granting "such remedy as the court considers appropriate and just in the circumstances." '[8] But this model 'met with overwhelming public opposition'[9] and was rejected. To be precise, the Select Committee concluded that New Zealand was not ready, if it ever would be, for a fully fledged Bill of Rights along the lines of the White Paper draft.[10] Instead, the Select Committee recommended enactment of an ordinary statute Bill of Rights Act.

But even to get this 'fall-back' model enacted was far from easy. First off, even as regards this enervated, statutory version '[t]here was no ground-swell of public support for it; indeed, it is possible that public opinion was against it'.[11] Geoffrey Palmer's Labour party colleagues were not much more enthusiastic, viewing 'even the watered-down [Bill of Rights Act] with suspicion . . . in the event [buckling] down and vot[ing] for the government measure'.[12] But not before it was further enfeebled.

The Bill's passage only took place after two major changes had been made. First, a new operative provision not present in the Draft Bill had to be added. This became section 4

---

[7] In other words, as far as the Bill of Rights Act was concerned, the doctrine of implied repeal was explicitly excluded by s. 4. See below.

[8] J. A. Smillie, 'The Allure of "Rights Talk": *Baigent's Case* in the Court of Appeal', (1994) 8 *Otago Law Review* 188, 193 (internal footnote to 'Government Printer, Wellington, 1985' omitted) [hereinafter 'Smillie'].

[9] Ibid. 194. Smillie at the same page goes on to note that '[t]he Parliamentary Select Committee to which the White Paper was referred for investigation received 431 submissions. Of these, only 35 supported the Draft Bill or even the concept of a bill of rights, while 243 were wholly opposed to the proposal.' Taggart, describing those same statistics, states that this Superman model 'was rejected in the court of elite public opinion' (266).

[10] See Smillie, 194.

[11] P. Rishworth, 'The New Zealand Bill of Rights Act 1990: The First Fifteen Months', in *Essays on the New Zealand Bill of Rights Act 1990* (Auckland: Legal Research Foundation, 1992), 7–8. For more on the history of the Bill of Rights Act, see P. Rishworth's 'The Birth and Rebirth of the Bill of Rights', in G. Huscroft and P. Rishworth (eds.), *Rights and Freedoms: The New Zealand Bill of Rights Act 1990 and the Human Rights Act 1993* (Wellington: Brooker's, 1995).

[12] Taggart, 267 (internal footnote omitted).

4. Other enactments not affected—No court shall, in relation to any enactment (whether passed or made before or after the commencement of this Bill of Rights),—

(a) Hold any provision of the enactment to be impliedly repealed or revoked, or to be in any way invalid or ineffective; or

(b) Decline to apply any provision of the enactment—by reason only that the provision is inconsistent with any provision of this Bill of Rights.

Notice that this section 4 not only makes explicit the doctrine of implied repeal (whereby later statutes that are inconsistent with the Bill of Rights Act would prevail) but, singularly, directs that even earlier inconsistent Acts should prevail. It needs to be remembered (particularly in discussions of the Act's purpose) that of the three main operative provisions (sections 4, 5, and 6[13]), section 4 was the only one that was not present in the rejected entrenched version. More importantly, its insertion prior to the second reading was a necessary price for passage of even this enfeebled version.

The second major change before passage was the removal[14] of the wide remedies clause referred to above. Indeed, to get the Bill passed in the face of continuing opposition and public concern Geoffrey Palmer, by now Prime Minister, was forced[15] to say the following in moving the second reading of the Bill which by now lacked a remedies clause:

[T]he Bill creates no new legal remedies for courts to grant. The judges will continue to have the same legal remedies as they have now, irrespective of whether the Bill of Rights is an issue.[16]

---

[13] Ss. 5 and 6 read as follows:

5. Justified limitations—Subject to section 4 of this Bill of Rights, the rights and freedoms contained in this Bill of Rights may be subject only to such reasonable limits prescribed by law as can be demonstrably justified in a free and democratic society.

6. Interpretation consistent with Bill of Rights to be preferred—Wherever an enactment can be given a meaning that is consistent with the rights and freedoms contained in this Bill of Rights, that meaning shall be preferred to any other meaning.

[14] Smillie calls it the 'deliberate omission' (195).

[15] I use the passive verb 'was forced' because of Sir Geoffrey's subsequent comments about the legislative history of the Bill, and in particular about his own statements in the House during the Bill's progress. In an editorial to Issue 5 of the 1995 *Bill of Rights Bulletin*, 78, Sir Geoffrey stated, 'I am amused at the different interpretations placed on what I said. Bills are made to pass.' I am not clear what to infer from this 1995 remark, though it certainly provides ammunition to those with a strong dislike of selective judicial recourse to legislative history in interpreting statutes. If the point is that politicians shepherding Bills through the House say whatever is necessary to get them passed, then the debates and legislative history never provide a safe indication of the enactors' purpose in enacting them and the courts should never have recourse to that history. Bills are made to pass, but in my view they are best passed by actors observing particular standards, or not at all.

As it happens, the New Zealand courts do *not*, at present, assume that the legislative history is completely unreliable. There seems to be an assumption that most legislators generally say what they mean. That is why the present New Zealand position is that the courts will sometimes—though admittedly selectively—look at the legislative history in interpreting a statute.

[16] (1990) 510 *New Zealand Parliamentary Debates* 3449, 3450. See too some of Geoffrey Palmer's other statements to the House, detailed in Smillie, 195–6. In the event the New Zealand judiciary paid no attention to these remarks uttered 'to get the Bill passed'. Or in Taggart's characterization, 'the Court of Appeal *rose above* that legislative history' (269, emphasis added).

Enough has been said, I think, to repeat the claim that Parliament intended to enact 'a parliamentary Bill of Rights'[17] which took every precaution to limit any new powers the judges might otherwise have with such an instrument and which left Parliament as the 'guardian of fundamental rights and freedoms in New Zealand'.[18] It is beyond dispute, that is, that in 1990 the New Zealand Parliament opted for an enervated, statutory Bill of Rights Act that on its face even lost out to past inconsistent statutes.

What the judges have done

Why settle for an enfeebled, statutory Bill of Rights Act if it can be turned into a more potent, constitutional-type Bill of Rights over time, bit by bit, bootstrap by bootstrap? Why, indeed, many supporters of entrenched, constitutionalized Bills of Rights might ask themselves.

The judge most keen to 'upgrade' the New Zealand Bill of Rights Act 1990 was the then President of the New Zealand Court of Appeal, Sir Robin Cooke (now Lord Cooke of Thorndon, a sitting member of the House of Lords and occasional member of panels of its Judicial Committee and of the Privy Council). In the first ever Bill of Rights Act case to reach the Court of Appeal[19] Cooke P suggested that section 6 of the Bill of Rights Act[20] may require a court to depart from a long established judicial interpretation of the meaning and intent of a particular statutory provision. Speaking for the Court, Cooke P said they saw 'force in the argument that, to give full effect to the rights . . . , [a particular statutory provision with a long-standing interpretation] . . . should now receive a wider interpretation than has prevailed hitherto'.[21]

A year later, in *R v. Butcher*,[22] Cooke P made the following comments in obiter:

---

[17] (1989) 502 *New Zealand Parliamentary Debates* 13038 *per* Rt. Hon. Geoffrey Palmer PM moving introduction of the Bill.

[18] Ibid.

[19] *Flickinger v. Crown Colony of Hong Kong* [1991] 1 NZLR 439. It is worth mentioning here that Cooke, prior to the enactment of the Bill of Rights Act, had advocated an entrenched, constitutionalized version extrajudicially. Indeed, he had claimed there was very little difference between administrative law and Bill of Rights adjudication. (See 'Synopses of Papers Presented at Legal Research Foundation Inc. seminar at the University of Auckland 20–1 February 1986: Judicial Review of Administrative Action in the 1980s—Prospects and Problems', in particular p. 3 of Cooke's synopsis of his own paper 'The Struggle for Simplicity in Administrative Law', where he states: 'While this is not a seminar on the Bill of Rights, I suspect that the present paper will not be the only one thus to bring out, directly or indirectly, the extent to which the courts have long had to make value judgments in determining issues between citizens and authorities. From the work already performed by the courts *it would be only a small step to the work under the proposed Bill of Rights* of determining whether some particular restraint on a right or freedom falls within "such reasonable limits prescribed by law as can be demonstrably justified in a full and democratic society" ' (emphasis added; this comment does not appear in the published version of the paper in Taggart (ed.), *Judicial Review of Administrative Action in the 1980s: Prospects and Problems* (Auckland and New York: Oxford University Press and Legal Research Foundation, 1986). In a sense, therefore, Cooke had been on the side that lost 'in the court of elite public opinion'.

[20] See n. 13 above.   [21] [1991] 1 NZLR 439 at 441.   [22] [1992] 2 NZLR 257.

What can and should now be said unequivocally is that a parliamentary declaration of human rights and individual freedoms, intended partly to affirm New Zealand's commitment to internationally proclaimed standards, is not to be construed narrowly or technically.[23]

Certainly the Act is not entrenched. Still it is an affirmation of the basic rights of people in New Zealand. The correct judicial response can only be normally to give it primacy, subject to the clear provisions of other legislation.[24]

And in the same year in *Noort*[25] more obiter still from Cooke P:

... the [Bill of Rights] Act requires development of the law where necessary. Such a measure is not to be approached as if it did no more than preserve the status quo. . . . The effect of the Bill of Rights Act will have to be worked out with common sense. No more in New Zealand than anywhere else in the world can detailed rules be laid down in advance. They would be contrary to the spirit of a bill of rights. . . . it is asking no more than that we in New Zealand try to live up to international standards or targets and to keep pace with civilisation.[26]

So from the beginning there was a suggestion (which was to grow and strengthen for a while) that the enervated Act actually enacted should, contrary to the clear legislative history, be treated as some sort of extra-special, half-'constitutionalized' Bill of Rights to which the judges would give primacy unless clear legislation indicated otherwise. A stronger Bill of Rights was already beginning to take shape.

From the pen of Cooke P such judicial creativity was anything but surprising. After all, this is the judge who from the early 1980s had suggested in various obiter dicta that '[s]ome common law rights presumably lie so deep that even Parliament could not override them'.[27] Were such a notion true, were it the case that the judges had (or had given themselves or could give themselves) some sort of veto on what the legislature could do then, *pace* all the received wisdom, New Zealand would *not* have a parliamentary supremacy form of government. Rather, it would be best described as a judicial supremacy. But such obiter dicta are simply nonsense. They bear no relation, and have never borne any, to an accurate factual account of New Zealand's governing rule of recognition.[28] Instead such comments must be understood as an attempt by Cooke P to change the existing rule of recognition, to bring

---

[23] [1992] 2 NZLR 264.   [24] Ibid. 267.
[25] *Ministry of Transport v. Noort* [1992] 3 NZLR 260.   [26] Ibid. 270–1.
[27] *Taylor v. New Zealand Poultry Board* [1984] 1 NZLR 394, 398. See too *Fraser v. State Services Commission* [1984] 1 NZLR 116, 121, and *New Zealand Drivers' Association v. New Zealand Road Carriers* [1982] 1 NZLR 374, 390. For more details of such obiter dicta and extrajudicial utterances by Robin Cooke to the same effect, see P. Rishworth, 'Lord Cooke and the Bill of Rights', in Rishworth (ed.), *The Struggle for Simplicity in the Law: Essays for Lord Cooke of Thorndon* (Wellington: Butterworths, 1997). For a contrary view to Lord Cooke's, in the same book, see Justice Michael Kirby of Australia's chapter, 'Lord Cooke and Fundamental Rights'.
[28] On the rule of recognition see H. L. A. Hart, *The Concept of Law*, 2nd edn. (Oxford: Clarendon Press, 1994), 94–110. For an excellent fleshing out of Hart's rule of recognition notion, see K. Greenawalt, 'Hart's Rule of Recognition and the United States', (1988) 1 *Ratio Juris* 40.

about a very quiet revolution in the power relations between Parliament and the judiciary.[29]

Accordingly, it is easy to understand why Cooke P would welcome any sort of Bill of Rights Act, however limited, and be keen to upgrade it at the first opportunity. But he was not alone. With the qualified exception of Gault J, all the justices of the Court of Appeal in the first few years after the enactment of the Bill of Rights Act seemed keen to upgrade and retool what Parliament had enacted.

[T]he Court of Appeal insisted that the [Bill of Rights Act] had to be interpreted and applied generously and purposively, rather than narrowly and technically. . . . The rights and freedoms affirmed were said to be part of the fabric of New Zealand law, and the fact that they are not constitutionally entrenched . . . does not diminish their importance or affect their meaning. . . . [T]here was enthusiasm for the [Bill of Rights Act] among some senior members of the judiciary. In the early years one intuited a sense of excitement in at last joining the pantheon of civilised societies with Bills of Rights . . .[30]

This early judicial enthusiasm manifested itself overwhelmingly in the criminal procedure realm.[31] Within three years or so the Court of Appeal had created a prima facie exclusion rule for evidence obtained improperly in breach of the Bill of Rights Act.[32]

Then came the big development in the civil law sphere. In *Baigent's Case*,[33] in a 4–1 decision by the Court of Appeal, a public law remedy sounding in the Bill of Rights Act was both created ad hoc and distinguished from the common law tort of breach of statutory duty.[34] In creating this new *sui generis* cause of action two obstacles, which

---

[29] Justice Antonin Scalia of the US Supreme Court makes a similar, if more strongly expressed, point about the sometimes heard claim that Lord Chief Justice Coke was stating orthodoxy nearly 400 years ago in *Dr. Bonham's Case*. 'Professor Wood accepts as orthodoxy Lord Chief Justice Coke's statement in *Dr. Bonham's Case* (1610) that "in many cases, the common law will controul Acts of Parliament and sometimes adjudge them to be utterly void: for when an Act of Parliament is against common right and reason, or repugnant, or impossible to be performed, the common law will controul it and adjudge such Act to be void". It was not orthodoxy at all, but an extravagant assertion of judicial power, scantily supported by the authorities cited, vehemently criticized by contemporaries, and seemingly abandoned by Coke himself in his *Institutes*.' (A. Scalia, *A Matter of Interpretation: Federal Courts and the Law* (Princeton, NJ: Princeton University Press, 1997), 129–30—4 internal footnotes omitted.) See too John Smillie's 'Introduction' to Taggart, n. 19 above. For a book-length examination of the doctrine of parliamentary sovereignty, in which the notion that judges have ever been free *not* to recognize as valid statutes enacted by Parliament is rubbished, see J. Goldsworthy, *The Sovereignty of Parliament: History and Philosophy* (Oxford: Clarendon Press, 1999). *Dr. Bonham's Case* is discussed at 111–17.

[30] Taggart, 274–5 (3 internal footnotes omitted).

[31] In this realm the judges need not strike down statutes to rewrite the law (or 'constitutionalize' new rights if you are a Bill of Rights enthusiast). Most of this area of law is a creature of executive action, judges' rules, and common law.

[32] See e.g. *R v. Kirifi* [1992] 2 NZLR 8; *R v. Butcher* [1992] 2 NZLR 257; *Ministry of Transport v. Noort* [1992] 3 NZLR 260; *R v. Goodwin (No. 2)* [1993] 2 NZLR 390. The pre-Bill of Rights Act position had been that improperly obtained evidence was admitted unless there was real unfairness to the accused. Leaving aside confessions where reliability was the main test and the hurdle for admissibility relatively high, this meant that such improperly obtained evidence had been excluded rather infrequently.

[33] *Simpson v. Attorney-General* [*Baigent's Case*] [1994] 3 NZLR 667.

[34] Taggart describes the case as 'creat[ing] a public law claim for compensation for breach of the Bill of Rights.' (269—see too a similar description at 283).

had to be overcome or got round, lay in the path of the majority justices.[35] The first was the lack of any provision in the Bill of Rights Act itself for remedies for infringement. (The reader will recall that the remedies clause was removed, seemingly to ensure the Bill's passage, and will recall also Sir Geoffrey Palmer's comments in moving the Bill's second reading.) The second was a statutory immunity provision which seemed to apply and if so, by section 4 of the Bill of Rights Act, would mean that provision prevailed.

The majority justices in the event did overcome or get round both these obstacles, though in this author's opinion 'the reasoning of the majority in [*Baigent's Case* was] sophistical'.[36] Certainly it was a clear example of the strongest sort of judicial activism, as Taggart implicitly concedes:

Baigent's Case gives some indication of the potential potency of the technique known as 'reading down' (and its travelling companion 'reading in'). My colleague, Paul Rishworth, has championed the use of these techniques in the context of the [Bill of Rights Act] from the beginning. In essence, his argument is that in respect of statutes which affirm fundamental rights *the courts are justified in departing from even clear words* by reading the statute down (or reading words in) so as not to infringe rights as long as by so doing the legislative purpose is not frustrated. This well-supported thesis opens up considerable scope for attaining rights-respecting outcomes by the judiciary.[37]

After *Baigent* the way seemed clear for an ongoing judicial upgrade and makeover of the less than potent statutory Bill of Rights Act which had actually been enacted. Following on from *Baigent*, the judges looked set to continue with their retooling. And all the while they would be cheered on by their various supporters in the legal academy and the practising Bar.[38] *Baigent* seemed to portend a continual, piecemeal 'upgrade' of New Zealand's statutory, parliamentary Bill of Rights Act. But continual it was not. *Baigent's Case* turned out to be, for a time at least, a high-water mark or apogee in the judicial upgrading process. It was some time until the tide began to flow again.

One partial explanation for this halt in judicial activism when it comes to the Bill of Rights Act is that soon after *Baigent's Case* was decided Sir Robin became Lord Cooke of Thorndon and retired from the Court of Appeal.[39] So too did Casey J and Hardie Boys J. The newly composed Court of Appeal under Richardson P took a noticeable step back in *Grayson*.[40] In that case, in a judgment of the Court, the

---

[35] I have discussed *Baigent's Case* in more detail in 'Speaking with the Tongues of Angels: The Bill of Rights, *Simpson*, and the Court Appeal', [1994] 1 *Bill of Rights Bulletin* 2.

[36] Ibid. 3. For a contrary view, though, see Rodney Harrison's replies to me in Issues No. 2 and 3 (March and June 1995) of the *Bill of Rights Bulletin*.

[37] Taggart, 284 (internal footnote omitted, emphasis added).

[38] See nn. 50 and 51 below, and related text.

[39] Lord Cooke has been less successful in the House of Lords than he was in the New Zealand Court of Appeal at carrying other judges along in his views. See e.g. *Platform Home Loans Ltd v. Oyston Shipways Ltd* [1999] 1 All ER 833; *Effort Shipping Co. Ltd. v. Linden Management SA* [1998] AC 605; and *Hunter v. Canary Wharf Ltd* [1997] AC 655.

[40] *R v. Grayson and Taylor* [1997] 1 NZLR 399.

judges decided that a police search which involved a trespass onto property without lawful justification was not unreasonable. (And as the police had been held not to have acted unreasonably under the section 21 'unreasonable search and seizure' provision of the Bill of Rights Act, the accused had no chance of any remedy.) In other words, the effect of *Grayson* was clearly and unambiguously to sever the unreasonableness determination (in s. 21) from a simple consideration of illegality.[41] Illegality could not be thought of as coextensive with or even subsumed by unreasonableness, according to the *Grayson* Court.

However, for our purposes, what is of particular note in *Grayson* are the two pages of obiter dicta at the end of the judgment in which the Justices signalled a desire to move away from the existing prima facie exclusion rule for evidence obtained in breach of the Bill of Rights Act. Indeed, the judgment finished with the explicit statement that 'on an appropriate occasion the Court would be prepared to re-examine the prima facie exclusion rule'.[42] Instead of a purely rights-centred approach the Justices indicated they were attracted to a 'broader perspective [which] also looks to the general underlying public interest'.[43] So possible remedies might include exclusion, a reduced penalty, an order for costs, police disciplinary proceedings, criminal prosecution, civil proceedings for damages, or a declaration. Indeed, the possible remedies were deliberately left open and made dependent upon all the circumstances.

My point is this: *Grayson* was a clear (albeit obiter, and, as we shall see, only temporary) step back in the bootstraps operation to mould some sort of half-constitutionalized Bill of Rights out of what was in fact enacted. What the judges had given, not least their earlier ascribing to a 'rights-centred' interpretive framework, the judges said (in obiter) they could also take away. As a result, the case was harshly criticized by commentators who prefer their Bills of Rights unshakeable and stirring.[44] That said, and despite these protestations, it was a small step back, not a giant one. To date, despite submissions having been made on the point, the Court of Appeal has yet to re-examine the prima facie exclusion rule. Indeed, there is some evidence the court may not abandon this rule after all.[45]

---

[41] I have argued in 'Hoisting *Grayson* with *Baigent's* Petard', [1997] 1 *Bill of Rights Bulletin* 13, that this standard of unreasonableness—being different from illegality and determined on a case-by-case basis according to the particular circumstances—is precisely the same standard of unreasonableness the Court of Appeal invoked in *Baigent*. What this approach means in terms of certainty I leave for Section II below.

[42] *R v. Grayson and Taylor* [1997] 1 NZLR 399, 412.   [43] Ibid. 411.

[44] See e.g. A. Butler, 'The End of Precedent and Principle in Bill of Rights Cases? A Note on *R v. Grayson*', [1997] *New Zealand LR* 274; S. Optican, 'Rolling Back s. 21 of the Bill of Rights', [1997] *New Zealand LR* 42; and all of (1996) 10 *Public Law Bulletin* (New Zealand Institute of Public Law). Taggart notes that *Grayson* has 'been harshly criticised by some commentators, who see the courts extracting the self-same teeth they had *earlier uncovered* in the [Bill of Rights Act]' (276, emphasis added). It is worth emphasizing, in response to the anti-*Grayson* commentators, that the prima facie exclusion rule had not been in existence long; certainly there was no basis for treating it as writ in stone.

[45] See R. Mahoney, 'Evidence', [1998] *New Zealand LR* 53, 83–4. See too *R v. T* (CA302/98, 2 Nov. 1998) and *R v. Reid* (CA108/98, 30 July 1998).

Another recent case which showed that there is a limit to the social policy-making the judiciary is prepared to indulge in, under the guise of upholding and giving life to the broad, amorphous rights set down in the New Zealand Bill of Rights Act, was *Quilter*.[46] All five judges in this case held that the Marriage Act 1955 was intended to confine marriages to those between a man and a woman, and that whatever the s. 19(1) 'freedom from discrimination' provision of the Bill of Rights Act might imply about discrimination for lesbian couples wanting to marry but being unable to do so, where there is clear inconsistency the Marriage Act 1955 must prevail.

So despite some differences of opinion amongst the five judges in *Quilter*,[47] a clear line was drawn—one that would not be drawn in Canada or the United States with their entrenched, constitutionalized Bills of Rights. The metamorphosis in New Zealand of a statutory, quite limited, Bill of Rights Act into something more by means of some judicial bootstraps operation had its limits. The upgrade would only go so far.

Or so it seemed until the recent Court of Appeal case of *Moonen*.[48] There, the judges say some remarkable things. Most indefensibly, in my view, they say that henceforth when some statute is found to be inconsistent with the Bill of Rights Act, although they will be bound by section 4, they may also make a declaration of inconsistency.[49] Recall, though, that there is nothing at all in the Bill of Rights Act itself to mandate, warrant, or legitimate such a course of action. Accordingly, this appears to be yet another new (and particularly gratuitous) remedy the judiciary has simply created ad hoc without, unlike as in Britain, any statutory warrant whatsoever. What new remedies and powers the judges might fashion for themselves in future is therefore anybody's guess. All that seems safe to say is that the judges are still, for now at any rate, prepared to give effect to section 4.

It needs also to be noted, in finishing this section, that most legal academics and commentators welcome this upgrading operation. Quite simply, there has been a good deal of encouragement for the judiciary from the academy[50] when the courts

---

[46] *Quilter v. Attorney-General* [1998] 1 NZLR 523.

[47] Richardson P, Gault J, and Keith J took the view that the prohibition on same-sex marriages in the Marriage Act 1955 does *not* infringe the s. 19(1) discrimination provision. For Richardson P and Gault J this was an obiter holding. For Keith J it was unclear whether it was the ratio of his decision or an obiter holding (cf. the first three paragraphs of his decision, p. 555), though probably it was the former. Thomas J and Tipping J, by contrast, both held the prohibition *did* discriminate against lesbian couples, though Tipping J appears to leave open the question whether it is justifiable discrimination. For Thomas J it is not. Strictly speaking, both Thomas and Tipping JJ's views on discrimination were obiter.

[48] *Moonen v. Film and Literature Board of Review* [2000] 2 NZLR 9.

[49] 'That purpose necessarily involves the Court having the power, and on occasions the duty, to indicate that although a statutory provision must be enforced according to its proper meaning, it is inconsistent with the Bill of Rights . . . Such judicial indication will be of value should the matter come to be examined by the Human Rights Committee. . . . New Zealand society as a whole can rightly expect that on appropriate occasions the Courts will indicate whether a particular legislative provision is or is not justified thereunder' (ibid. 17) The Court relies implicitly on an expansive view of s. 5, and indeed of s. 6, to justify this minimalist approach to s. 4. See the main text to n. 59 below.

[50] On the mutually reinforcing relationship between judges and legal academics in Canada, see F. L. Morton, 'The Charter Revolution and the Court Party', (1992) 30 *Osgoode Hall LJ* 627.

give themselves more power under the Act.[51] These cheers quickly turn to jeers if anything, however small, is removed or if the piecemeal 'upgrade' is halted. My guess is that this support is not without effect in the judges' efforts to transform an enervated, statutory Bill of Rights Act, bit by bit, into one giving them virtually the same role and powers they would have in a full-blooded, constitutionalized Bill of Rights.

II. The uncertainty principle

However much the judiciary may or may not have resisted the desire to transform a weak, parliamentary Bill of Rights Act into a strong, overriding one, there remains the separate but related issue of certainty in the law. This is best examined in two affiliated inquiries. First, to what extent can Bill of Rights Act jurisprudence be said to be settled in New Zealand over ten years after the Act's coming into force? Secondly, and whatever the answer to that, how much discretion have the judges given themselves (in that jurisprudence) when it comes to applying the Bill of Rights Act? Let us take each inquiry in turn.

It is certainly settled after *Baigent* that New Zealand law recognizes and allows public law actions sounding in the Bill of Rights Act. Having *discovered* that this sort of action and remedy were implicit all along in the Bill of Rights Act itself (with its long title reference to the International Covenant on Civil and Political Rights), whatever the actual legislative history or status of the enactment, it is near-impossible to imagine that the judges will reverse themselves. It is far less settled how common such actions will become. So far they have not been frequent—or rather, litigation has been relatively infrequent, and even where it occurs *Baigent* awards are usually concurrent with awards under existing forms of action. But there could be any number of settled *Baigent* actions which never get to court, actions which are no doubt run concurrently with other 'established' causes of action. It is difficult to assess, in other words, the actual effect the *Baigent* action and remedy is having.

Moving over to criminal procedure, and in particular to the prima facie exclusion rule for evidence obtained in breach of the Bill of Rights Act, the law is anything but settled. It is over three years since the *Grayson* decision and still the Court of Appeal has yet to take up its own invitation to re-examine the prima facie exclusion rule.[52] Uncertainty is rampant here, with entrail-reading of each case that fails to address the issue[53] adding to the doubtfulness and indeterminacy.

---

[51] See my 'Turning Clark Kent into Superman: The New Zealand Bill of Rights Act 1990', (2000) 9 *Otago LR*, 623–4.

[52] See the main text above, at nn. 40–5, and in particular n. 42. It is possible, though this is pure speculation, that the Court of Appeal has not revisited the question of admissibility of improperly obtained evidence because its members are aware that the Law Commission's proposed evidence code would be dealing with this topic. (See s. 29, at p. 84, of the Law Commission's Report 55, vol. 2, *Evidence Code and Commentary*, Wellington, Aug. 1999.)

[53] See e.g. n. 45 above. Of course I do not mean to imply that criminal procedure law before the Bill of Rights Act was a model of certainty (cf. tests such as 'unfairly' obtained evidence and 'fair' trials). The issue is whether the Bill of Rights Act has made matters worse.

Then there is the thorny problem of the operative provisions (i.e. ss. 4–6) of the
Bill of Rights Act and how they affect the interpretation of other enactments and of
the Bill of Rights Act itself. On this issue much remains in fog. One of the leading
cases on the interrelation of the three main operative provisions is *Ministry of
Transport v. Noort*.[54] What happens when there is a possible conflict or inconsistency between one of the Bill of Rights Act's Part II rights and freedoms and some
other statutory enactment? In other words, what weight are we to give to and in
what order are we to consider each of the three operative provisions? There is no
obvious answer to this, especially when one recalls that section 4 had to be added[55]
in order to get the Bill through Parliament. The five judges in *Noort* evidently
struggled in their attempts to rationalize the interrelationship. Two of the five
judges thought the correct sequence is section 5, then section 6, then section 4.
When confronted with a competing statutory provision that may be inconsistent
with the Bill of Rights Act, 'it is more consistent with the purposes of the Bill of
Rights Act to resort to s. 4 only if the challenged action cannot be justified in terms
of ss. 5 and 6. . . . [and between the latter two it] is at least arguable that [s. 6] serves
a function different from s. 5 and logically falls for consideration following the
application of s. 5 as the statutory sequence would itself also indicate'.[56] Two others disagreed. They thought that section 5 has no application in such situations, that
only sections 4 and 6 apply. And the fifth judge was of the view that sections 4, 5,
and 6 'must be read as a whole'.[57] This holistic approach will allow 'the true significance of s. 5, otherwise a difficult provision, [to become] apparent'.[58]

In fact, nothing much was apparent after *Noort*. For eight years this resulting
unsettledness and inconclusiveness gave the judiciary great scope to get on with the
upgrading task; judges simply ignored the thorny issue of how the three operative
provisions can be understood together and instead picked whichever one was useful or preferable in the circumstances. Meanwhile the litigant was left unsure of the
likely outcome of his case. And then came the recent case of *Moonen*,[59] which looked
again at the operative provisions, without any mention of *Noort*. And nothing much
changed. We learn in *Moonen* only that the judges will turn to sections 5 and 6 first,
treat them expansively (though possibly starting with section 6 now), and only
resort to section 4 if there is no alternative[60] (at which point they may also make a
declaration of inconsistency if they so decide).

The extent, therefore, to which the judges are prepared to avoid having recourse
to section 4 has obvious ramifications. One has only to compare *Baigent* (where the
judges were prepared to rely on the section 6 'prefer a consistent interpretation'

---

[54] [1992] 3 NZLR 260. I have discussed this issue at more length in 'The Operative Provisions: An
Unholy Trinity', [1995] 5 *Bill of Rights Bulletin* 79. See too P. Rishworth, 'Two Comments on *Ministry
of Transport v. Noort*: Part A—How Does the Bill of Rights Work?', [1992] *New Zealand Recent LR* 189.
[55] The text of s. 4 is given above, just after n. 12 in the main text. As for the second operative provision, s. 5, be aware that it was slightly altered when s. 4 was added in order to make it 'subject to s. 4'.
See n. 13 above.
[56] *Ministry of Transport v. Noort* [1992] 3 NZLR 260, 282.   [57] Ibid. 287.   [58] Ibid.
[59] *Moonen*, n. 48 above.   [60] Ibid. 16–17.

provision—the reliance is implicit, but crucial all the same—to circumvent a competing statutory provision) with *Quilter* (where the judges were not prepared to use section 6 to circumvent an arguably less express statutory provision and instead relied on section 4) to see that this is so.

Leave now the extent of unsettledness of Bill of Rights Act jurisprudence and turn to the second inquiry raised above, the amount of discretion the judges have given themselves when it comes to applying the Bill of Rights Act. First off, the discussion above illustrates that the section 6 interpretation power, or more accurately the manner in which the judges can use that power if they are so inclined, heaps discretion on discretion. Secondly, were the obiter dicta in *Grayson* to be picked up, the possible remedies for evidence obtained in breach of the Bill of Rights Act would be myriad and left to the discretion of the judge, all the factors and circumstances being thrown into the hopper, as it were. The earlier civil case of *Baigent* took the same line with respect to just what 'an adequate public law remedy for infringement [of the Bill of Rights Act] obtainable through the Courts'[61] would be. We were told that '[w]hat is adequate will be for the Courts to determine in the circumstances of each case'.[62] Judicial discretion, according to the judges, lies at the heart of applying the Bill of Rights Act and granting remedies. This is the uncertainty principle writ large.

Nor is the present President of the Court of Appeal immune to the charms of judicial discretion. Have regard to the implications of His Honour's comments in *Noort* on the extent of section 5 inquiries and the (implicit) desirability of Brandeis brief-type submissions to the Court:

It is worth emphasising too that in principle an abridging inquiry under s. 5 will properly involve consideration of *all economic, administrative and social implications*. In the end it is a matter of weighing:
(1) the significance in the particular case of the values underlying the Bill of Rights Act;
(2) the importance in the public interest of the intrusion on the particular right protected by the Bill of Rights Act;
(3) the limits sought to be placed on the application of the Act provision in the particular case; and
(4) the effectiveness of the intrusion in protecting the interests put forward to justify those limits.[63]

---

[61] *Baigent*, n. 33 above, 692, *per* Casey J.

[62] Ibid. Casey J continues, 'In some it may be that already obtainable under existing legislation or at common law: in others, where such remedies are unavailable or inadequate, the Court may award compensation for infringement, or settle on some non-monetary option as appropriate. . . . Selection of the remedy which will best vindicate the right infringed will be a matter best left to a Judge rather than a jury.' Cooke P, in a similar vein, says of the level of compensation for such Bill of Rights Act actions: 'In the end the Judge can only exercise judgment in the light of the particular circumstances' (678).

[63] *Noort*, n. 54 above, 283–4 (emphasis added), *per* Richardson J. Remember, too, that Richardson J would have all considerations of the operative provisions *start* with s. 5. Hence such abridging inquiries could never be avoided.

Then, of course, there is the newly pronounced power the judges have given themselves to make declarations of inconsistency. We know only that the judges now have this power, 'and on occasions the duty'[64] to use it.

The point of this section of the chapter is that the New Zealand Bill of Rights Act has substantially increased uncertainty in the law. On the one hand, the judges have given themselves much discretion in how they will apply it and the remedies they will award when they decide it has been breached. On the other hand, the law surrounding the Bill of Rights Act is itself still unsettled in various areas. The result is plenty of uncertainty. For those who value a relatively high degree of certainty in the law, this is an unfortunate state of affairs.[65]

III. The power of unelected judges: lessons from New Zealand

Many people seem to assume that the simple mention of the words 'justice' and 'fairness' or articulation of some particular right, the 'right to freedom of expression' or 'right to be secure against unreasonable searches', divides the world into good and bad—those *for* justice, fairness, and these rights on one side and those *against* on the other. Of course concessions will generally be made—'rights are not absolute, but involve some sort of balancing with other interests' can usually be heard eventually, though the concession is uttered *sotto voce*. But the underlying assumption that rights and justice are uncontentious, and only questioned by those beyond the moral pale, remains in place. This is what gives such force to the desire to make rights justiciable. The forces of good and evil are seen to be clearly demarcated and the job of the judge to ensure the triumph of the former.

As it happens, however, the world is not like that. Virtually all of us may hold our hands up high when asked if we are in favour of justice or fairness. We nod in agreement that society should ensure rights to life, freedom of religion, and expression, no undue delay before trying an accused, and no unreasonable police searches. However, all this widespread agreement occurs at the most general level where talk is in terms of free speech, privacy, equality, personal safety, or some such other emotively and rhetorically attractive—but quite unspecific—quality or trait. Unfortunately, the minute anyone moves from the plane of vague generalities to that of specific policy choices it becomes abundantly clear that consensus, even near-consensus, disappears. In other words, when we take the broad and imprecise standards embodied in the language of rights (and of 'justice' and 'fairness' for that

---

[64] *Moonen*, n. 48 above, 17 (*per* Tipping J in a judgment of the Court).

[65] For two diverging opinions on the merits of a relatively high degree of certainty in the law, cf. my 'The Invisible Hand in Justice Thomas's Philosophy of Law', [1999] *New Zealand LR* 213 with the response of Justice Thomas in 'The "Invisible Hand" Prompts a Response', [1999] *New Zealand LR* 227 and with Justice Thomas's earlier paper 'Fairness and Certainty in Adjudication: Formalism *v.* Substantialism', (1999) 9 *Otago LR* 459.

matter) and apply them to specific situations,[66] any notion of consensus or even widespread agreement disappears.

This point is crucially important. Once a constitutionalized Bill of Rights is in place, giving judges power to strike down legislation and so, undeniably, enormous social policy-making powers,[67] the judges end up deciding *controversial questions of social policy* over which sincere, intelligent, well-meaning people disagree— questions about where to draw the line when it comes to abortion, privacy, police powers, free speech, religious practices, who can marry, how refugee claimants are to be treated, and much else. The judges *do not* end up stopping vulnerable minorities from being imprisoned because of their race[68] or protecting those with (or even without) distasteful political views from being hounded into unemployment and pariah status.[69] In any imaginable scenario in which the elected legislators would contemplate the sort of things almost everyone today (in the absence of an external threat, when times are good) would consider wicked, the judges too would contemplate the same measures. There is no special moral goodness or acute ethical perspicacity inhering in judges that the rest of us lack.

So what such a Bill of Rights does is to deliver from elected politicians to unelected judges power to decide highly contestable, debatable, social policy issues (where both sides to the dispute can be seen as reasonable, sincere, and thoughtful), under the guise of upholding and protecting universally desired and uncontentious rights. It is not the 'black and white', 'good versus evil' type issues, so often used to sell a Bill of Rights to the public, that the judges will be deciding. Rather, it is the day-to-day but highly contentious political and social issues over which these unelected judges will have the first (and in all practical senses the final) say.

---

[66] For example, how long should those accused of serious criminal offences be kept waiting for trial before judges order their release? (See *R v. Askov* (1990) 74 DLR (4th) 355, and then one of the Justices of the Supreme Court of Canada's rather pathetic extra-judicial rationalization and apology for that decision in *Lawyers Weekly* (26 July 1991), followed finally by the recanting of *Askov* in *R v. Morin* (1992) 72 CCC (3d) 11 (SCC).) Similarly, what should the permissibility and extent of abortions be? (see *Roe v. Wade* 410 US 113 (1973)); when should free speech concerns trump health and safety concerns (see *RJR MacDonald Inc v. Canada* (1995) 127 DLR (4th) 1) or worries about pornography? (see *R v. Butler* (1992) 89 DLR (4th) 449); when should police misconduct trigger an exclusion of the evidence thereby obtained? (see *R v. Grayson and Taylor* [1997] 1 NZLR 399); and so on.

[67] Since the introduction of the Charter of Rights in Canada in 1982 the judges there have made a multitude of rulings with social policy implications, rulings that the elected legislature cannot (in any practical sense) ever overrule. The situation is similar in the US. For detailed argument on this, and why it is democratically deficient, see my 'Bills of Rights and Judicial Power: A Liberal's Quandary', (1996) 16 *Oxford Journal of Legal Studies* 337; *A Sceptical Theory of Morality and Law* (New York: Peter Lang, 1998), ch. 9; 'The Invisible Hand in Justice Thomas's Philosophy of Law', n. 65 above; and 'Rights, Paternalism, Constitutions and Judges', forthcoming as a chapter in G. Huscroft and P. Rishworth (eds.), *Liberty, Equality, Community: Constitutional Rights in Conflict?* (Oxford: Hart).

[68] Cf. the plight of Japanese Americans in the Second World War. (See *Korematsu v. US* 323 US 214 (1944)). See too *McClesky v. Kemp* 481 US 279 (1987), where the US Supreme Court refused to stop minorities from being executed in numbers disproportionate to race.

[69] Cf. the McCarthy hearings in the US. And recall that McCarthy was ultimately stopped by the political process.

It is not obvious, however, why any supporter of democracy[70] would wish to take power out of the hands of the elected representatives of ordinary citizens and give it to unelected judges to exercise in highly contentious matters where no side can be characterized as wicked or unjust.[71] So one respectable-looking compromise might appear to be to opt for a statutory Bill of Rights Act. This compromise seems to promise all the benefits of moderation, avoiding the danger of creating over-mighty judges of the sort who operate constitutionalized (and justiciable) Bills of Rights. Alas, if the experience of New Zealand is anything to go by, the apparent moderation is illusory. There are few differences between what judges *could accomplish* (in the way of 'giving life' to 'fundamental rights') when operating a New Zealand-type Bill of Rights Act[72] and what they *do accomplish* when operating constitutionalized and entrenched models.

In an effort to ensure that elected politicians 'live up to international standards or targets and . . . keep pace with civilisation'[73] in what is anyway, we are told, 'the shell game of constitutional reform',[74] we can expect judges to upgrade and retool their statutory model. That, at any rate, is the lesson from New Zealand.

---

[70] In New Zealand, supporters of parliamentary supremacy can note that it was elected politicians who gave women the vote there (1893) before they were given it in any other country; that elected politicians there were amongst the first to introduce social democracy; and that it is this system that in early 2001 sees the 5 top jobs in New Zealand (Prime Minister, Leader of the Opposition, Governor-General, Chief Justice, and Attorney-General) held by women (the top six if you count Head of State).

[71] Or, what amounts to the same thing, large groups of citizens on both sides will hold their view sincerely and think the other side's view is wicked and unjust.

[72] Recall, too, that the New Zealand Bill of Rights Act is, on its face, less potent than the UK version.

[73] *Noort*, n. 26 above, per Cooke P.   [74] Taggart, 268. See n. 6 above.

21

The Australian Free Speech Experiment and Scepticism about the UK Human Rights Act

ADRIENNE STONE

Australia might seem an unusual place to turn for a perspective on the likely operation of the Human Rights Act 1998 (UK). Unlike the other countries featured in this collection, Australia has no comprehensive Bill of Rights (statutory or constitutional)[1] and there appears to be no prospect of the adoption of one in the foreseeable future.[2] Nonetheless, Australia's recent constitutional history is marked by a period of rights-conscious constitutional interpretation during which the High Court of Australia went some way to filling the gap left by the constitutional reform process, reinvigorating its interpretation of the common law[3] and the Constitution. Most significantly for my purposes is the development of a limited kind of free speech right known as the freedom of political communication.[4]

In this chapter I will examine the nine-year history of the freedom of political communication. That history demonstrates the depth of the challenge presented to courts by entrenched rights. It shows just how quickly courts will be faced with

---

[1] There are a few provisions in the Australian Constitution that appear to protect rights: see s. 41 (a person who acquires the right to vote in a State shall have the right to vote in the Commonwealth); s. 80 (a trial on indictment shall be by jury); s. 116 (Commonwealth shall not make any law 'for establishing any religion, or for imposing any religious observance, or for prohibiting the free exercise of any religion'); s. 117 (States not to discriminate against the residents of any other states); s. 51(xxxi) (acquisition of property to be on just terms). For the most part these have been narrowly interpreted. See G. Williams, *Human Rights Under the Australian Constitution* (Melbourne: Oxford University Press, 1999), 96–128.

[2] There have been a number of proposals for constitutional reform to provide for greater rights protection and some proposals for the incorporation of a comprehensive Bill of Rights. See ibid. 250–7. Most recently, there was a recommendation in the Communiqué of the Constitutional Convention of 1998 (convened to develop a model for a republican constitution) for further conventions to consider *inter alia* the rights of citizens. That recommendation was, however, conditional on the acceptance of the proposed republic by referendum in 1999. See *Report of the Constitutional Convention* (1998), i: Communiqué. That referendum failed and consequently the proposal for an ongoing constitutional reform process died with it. The failure of the republican referendum may have, moreover, dampened political will for constitutional change.

[3] See e.g. *Dietrich v. The Queen* (1992) 177 CLR 292, recognizing that in most cases the right to counsel provided at the expense of the State is an indispensable element of the common law requirement of a fair trial.

[4] For a review of the freedom of political communication, see A. Stone, 'Lange, Levy and the Direction of the Freedom of Political Communication', (1999) 21 *University of New South Wales LJ* 117, Williams, n. 1 above, 155–97.

difficult choices between competing visions of rights, and thus with the challenge of defining the values on which any particular right relies.[5]

In Australia, this challenge has produced two unsatisfactory modes of decision-making. At first, the High Court showed a tendency to excessive and uncritical reliance on the model provided by the US Constitution and overlooked the role the common law might play in the resolution of some disputes. On the other hand, when the High Court reformulated the doctrine, it retreated to a more textually based approach to the implication of rights that has discouraged discussion, or even acknowledgment, of the values that underscore judicial decisions. This failure has, in turn, produced great uncertainty and undermined protection of freedom of speech in the lower courts. At the same time, the Court has begun to struggle with the difficult task of defining the limits of the freedom, in particular of determining its application to apparently private action, a task made harder by the decidedly anti-theoretical quality of the Court's most recent decisions.

The Australian experience reminds us of the enormity of the challenge before the British courts. If the Australian High Court has been so challenged by these issues in the context of a single implied right of narrow scope, these problems can only magnify and multiply as courts elaborate the comprehensive rights scheme in the Human Rights Act.

I. Freedom of speech in Australia: adventurous expansion

The judicial development of the freedom of political communication began with a period of adventurous development. Two foundational decisions of the High Court of Australia[6] striking down important federal legislation were followed by a remarkable decision,[7] adopting into Australian law a modified form of the *New York Times v. Sullivan*[8] rule.

In these cases, the High Court was confronted by the task of developing a conception of freedom of political communication and, in doing so, choosing among competing visions of the freedom. Its experience thus bears out the often-made point that, despite widespread agreement about the importance of some right when described at a high level of abstraction, disagreements, often intractable disagreements, proliferate when it comes to defining more precisely the content of that right.[9] Judges, therefore, have to make inevitably controversial decisions about the specific contents of rights.

---

[5] The tendency of rights to produce more philosophical judicial reasoning is well canvassed in J. Webber, 'Tales of the Unexpected: Intended and Unintended Consequences of the Canadian Charter of Rights and Freedoms', (1993) 5 *Canterbury LR* 207, 229: 'When deciding specific cases, courts will also be fashioning an official, enforceable, theory of society.'

[6] *Australian Capital Television v. Commonwealth* (1992) 177 CLR 104; *Nationwide News v. Wills* (1992) 177 CLR 1.

[7] *Theophanous v. Herald & Weekly Times* (1994) 182 CLR 104.   [8] 376 US 254 (1964).

[9] See J. Waldron, 'A Right-Based Critique of Constitutional Rights' (1993) 13 *Oxford Journal of Legal Studies* 18, 28–9. See also C. R. Sunstein, *Legal Reasoning and Political Conflict* (New York: Oxford University Press, 1996), 35–6. In Ch. 18 above Judy Fudge has shown how the initially popular Canadian Charter of Rights and Freedoms has become controversial as it has been applied to specific circumstances.

Freedom of speech is no exception; indeed, given the notorious complexity and controversy it has generated in other constitutional systems, it is a paradigmatic example. The problem persists in Australia even though the freedom of political communication is a limited kind of free speech right, which exists to protect only certain kinds of political speech. For even accepting that freedom of speech exists only to protect some form of democratic self-government, there are competing views as to how freedom of speech best serves that goal.

One view, best represented by the philosophy underlying the American free speech tradition, is, to state it roughly, 'the more speech the better'. This philosophy of freedom of speech places much faith in the notion that an unregulated 'marketplace of ideas',[10] in which ideas compete for dominance like competitors in a market, will produce the best discussion of public affairs.[11]

This vision of speech has been subjected to a noteworthy critique by American scholars such as Owen Fiss and Cass Sunstein, who place more emphasis on the capacity of freedom of speech to promote public deliberation. They have argued that the traditional American philosophy of freedom of speech neglects the distorting effect of existing inequalities in access to information and the capacity to communicate.[12] This critique suggests that government intervention might actually be required to ensure a fair public discussion in which all can participate, a suggestion that adherents to the former vision regard as dangerously exposing public discussion to authoritarian censorship.[13]

As it developed the freedom of political communication, the choice before the High Court was between these competing visions of the relationship between freedom of speech and democracy. Sceptics of judicial enforcement of human rights make several arguments about the capacity of courts to make these kinds of choice. Most prominently, it is said that judges have no special expertise in making what is essentially a judgment of moral and political philosophy and, indeed, that their institutional structures make them a less appropriate forum for the resolution of such issues than the other arms of government.[14] Others have sought to undermine the principal argument in favour of judicially enforced right (that the non-majoritarian nature of courts allows them to protect minorities) by pointing to the political nature of the judiciary, demonstrating that, over time, judicial decisions reflect centrist politics.[15] To criticize the High Court, however, it is not necessary to go quite so far. What is particularly disappointing about its response is that it has

---

[10] *Abrams v. United States* 250 US 616, 630 (1919) (Holmes J dissenting): 'the best test of truth is the power of the thought to get itself accepted in the competition of the market.'

[11] See generally K. Greenawalt, 'Free Speech Justifications' (1989) 89 *Columbia LR* 119, F. Schauer, *Free Speech: A Philosophical Enquiry* (New York: Cambridge University Press, 1981).

[12] See O. M. Fiss, *The Irony of Free Speech* (Cambridge, Mass.: Harvard University Press, 1996); C. R. Sunstein, *Democracy and the Problem of Freedom of Speech* (New York: Free Press, 1993), 17–51.

[13] For an argument of this kind, see R. C. Post, 'Meiklejohn's Mistake: Individual Autonomy and the Reform of Public Discourse', (1993) 64 *University of Colorado LR* 1109.

[14] J. Waldron, *Law and Disagreement* (1999); Sunstein, n. 9 above.

[15] See Mark Tushnet, Ch. 19 above.

shown a lack of awareness of, and even at times denied the existence of, this kind of choice. In the early cases, this failure manifested itself in two ways.

Failure to exercise independent judgment

First, the High Court's early decisions demonstrate an uncritical over-enthusiasm about the American law of the First Amendment and inattention to the critique to which it has been subjected. The influence of American free speech law can be seen in parts of *Australian Capital Television v. Commonwealth*, particularly in the adoption by some judges of a distinction between content-based and content-neutral laws and the application of a 'compelling' justification requirement to the former.[16] However, it is perhaps most clearly illustrated by *Theophanous v. Herald & Weekly Times*,[17] in which the majority adopted a modified form of the rule in *New York Times v. Sullivan*.[18]

New York Times might have seemed an obvious place for the High Court to turn to, as the underlying rationale of that decision (that freedom of speech serves democratic government) is related to the rationale of the freedom of political communication. However, *New York Times* is clearly imbued with the very particular 'marketplace of ideas' philosophy that dominates the American free speech tradition. The resonant passages of *New York Times v. Sullivan*, the invocation of 'a 'profound national commitment' to debate that is 'uninhibited, robust and wide-open',[19] all reflect a faith that vigour and variety in public debate, the competition and contradiction among ideas, will produce the best public discussion.[20]

In adopting the *New York Times* rule, then, the High Court aligned itself with this vision of the relationship between freedom of speech and democracy. Although the *Theophanous* Court modified this rule to accord a little more protection to reputation, the Australian rule retained the core feature of *New York Times*: the protection of false defamatory statements out of fear of the 'chilling effect'[21] of libel action.

---

[16] See *Australian Capital Television v. Commonwealth*, (1992) 177 CLR 106 at 143 per Mason CJ, at 234–5 per McHugh. It can also be seen in Mason CJ's distrust of any role government might have in improving the quality of public discourse. Ibid. 145 per Mason CJ. See also G. Rosenberg and J. M. Williams, 'Do not Go Gently into that Good Right: The First Amendment in the High Court of Australia', [1997] *Supreme Court Review* 439.

[17] (1994) 182 CLR 104. The theoretical basis of *Australian Capital Television* is actually rather unclear as some judges seem prepared to consider an argument for validity on the basis that legislation that burdens freedom of speech nonetheless promotes an appropriate political debate (ibid. 145 per Mason CJ, at 169 per Deane and Toohey JJ), a form of reasoning to which the First Amendment has proved to be hostile especially in the context of campaign finance reform (see *Buckley v. Valeo* 424 US 1, 48–9 (1976)).

[18] 254 US 367 (1964). *New York Times* established a rule limiting the power of a public official to bring actions for libel: 'a public official . . . [may not recover] damages for a defamatory falsehood relating to his official conduct unless he proves that the statement was made with "actual malice" . . . or with reckless disregard of whether it was false or not'. Ibid. 279–80.

[19] 376 US 254, 270, 279 (1964).

[20] Indeed, one form of the marketplace of ideas philosophy is evident in the Supreme Court's citation of Learned Hand's statement that the First Amendment 'presupposes that right conclusions are more likely to be gathered out of a multitude of tongues, than through any kind of authoritative selection'. 376 US 254, 270 (1964).

[21] Ibid. 279: 'A rule compelling the critic of official conduct to guarantee the truth of all his factual assertions—and to do so on pain of libel judgments virtually unlimited in amount—leads to a

The disappointment is that the High Court overlooked the critique of the American philosophy represented by scholars such as Fiss and Sunstein. Had it considered their arguments, it might have been more concerned about the accuracy or fairness of public debate. Considering this, it might have shared the concerns later expressed by the Canadian Supreme Court in *Hill v. Church of Scientology*:[22] that the *New York Times* rule would deprecate the importance of truth in public discourse[23] and deter 'sensitive and honourable men from seeking public positions of trust and responsibility'.[24] The oversight of the critical analysis of *New York Times* suggests that, blinded by the fame and the richness of the American free speech tradition, the High Court adopted *New York Times* rather hastily and perhaps without fully understanding its theoretical basis.[25]

Neglect of the common law alternative

The over-enthusiasm for American law points to a second problem with this early period. It is all the more unfortunate because, in its enthusiastic rush to approve of American law, the High Court seems to have overlooked its capacity to decide matters of common law[26] and thus neglected an alternative way of resolving the case.

Again, the problem is acutely illustrated by *Theophanous*. It should be remembered that *New York Times*, the model for the *Theophanous* decision, was partly driven by very particular features of the US legal system: the jurisdictional limitations that preclude the US Supreme Court from reviewing the decision of a lower court on matters of state law, including the general common law. Because of these limitations, there is great pressure to 'constitutionalize' an issue so that the case can be brought into the Supreme Court.[27]

Theophanous, on the other hand, could have been much more straightforward. The Australian High Court can review the application of the common law by lower courts, including state courts, and has the power to develop the common law. There

---

comparable "self-censorship" . . . Under such a rule, would-be critics of official conduct may be deterred from voicing their criticism, even though it is believed to be true and even though it is in fact true, because of doubt whether it can be proved in court or fear of the expense of having to do so.'

[22] *Hill v. Church of Scientology* [1995] 2 SCR 1130.   [23] Ibid. 1182–5.

[24] *Gatley on Libel and Slander in a Civil Action*, 4th edn. (London: Sweet & Maxwell, 1953), quoted in *Hill* [1995] 2 SCR 1130, 1174.

[25] I make this argument more fully in 'The Freedom of Political Communication, the Constitution and the Common Law', (1998) 27 *Federal LR* 219.

[26] S. 73 of the Constitution relevantly provides that the High Court shall have jurisdiction to hear appeals from 'all judgments, decrees, orders and sentences of any . . . federal court, or court exercising federal jurisdiction, or of the Supreme Court of any State'. Federal courts in the US principally exercise power over federal law, which has been taken to exclude most common law and in the limited cases where they do decide matters of the general common law, their power is limited to following or predicting state court decisions on these matters. See *Erie RR v. Tompkins* 304 US 64 (1938).

[27] The incentive was all the stronger, no doubt, in *New York Times* itself, where the decision of the Alabama state courts appeared to be inspired by Southern hostility to Northern institutions during the civil rights movement. See A. Lewis, *Make No Law* (New York: Random House, 1991), 21–35.

was no need, therefore, for the High Court to have considered the constitutional doctrine of the freedom of political communication at all. It could simply have considered whether the common law of defamation needed any alteration and, if so, developed the common law appropriately.[28] Indeed, this was the path taken by two judges who, because of a narrower interpretation of the freedom of political communication, declined to adopt even a modified *New York Times* rule.[29] Justices Brennan and McHugh extended the common law of qualified privilege, which traditionally excluded publications in newspapers or broadcasts,[30] to cover some publications of this nature.[31]

The common law alternative has a number of advantages. First, a common law decision would have avoided shutting out the majoritarian arms of government. Use of the common law therefore responds to the most traditional argument for restraint with respect to judicial review: that judicial review is counter-majoritarian.[32] Moreover, arguments that advocate restraint on the basis that courts have a limited capacity to fashion and enforce solutions[33] suggest that the entrenchment of solutions ought not to be undertaken unless the court has to. To these arguments I would add two more reasons to refrain from constitutional decision-making that apply where there is a common law alternative.

Perhaps most importantly, by using the common law, the Court might have avoided adopting a contested philosophical position, and thus escaped the criticism I have just mounted. In contrast to the majority's reasoning in *Theophanous* which (inadvertently or not) elaborated on the underlying philosophy of the freedom of political communication, use of the common law would have allowed the Court to proceed with considerable theoretical modesty. Because common law reasoning typically develops through the adjudication of individual disputes rather than

---

[28] Indeed, the possibility was explicitly put before the Court by the procedural mechanism by which the case came before it. These cases came to the High Court under s. 40 of the *Judiciary Act* 1903 (Cth) which allows a case raising a constitutional question to be removed into the High Court by its own order. The Court was faced with a number of questions stated for its consideration by the Chief Justice. The third of these questions directed the Court to consider the application of the common law defence of qualified privilege. See *Theophanous* (1994) 182 CLR 104 at 120.

[29] This part of the judges reasoning is not found in *Theophanous* but in its companion case, *Stephens v. West Australian Newspapers* (1994) 182 CLR 211 argued, and then delivered simultaneously.

[30] The classic statement of the defence of qualified privilege is that of Parke B In *Toogood v. Spyring* (1834) 1 CMR 181 at 189: 149 ER 1044.

[31] Justice Brennan and Justice McHugh both extended the traditional category of 'public interest' to include matters relating to government and the conduct of public affairs. (1994) 182 CLR 211 at 251 (Brennan J), at 265 (McHugh J).

[32] A. Bickel, *The Least Dangerous Branch*, 2nd edn. (New Haven, Conn.: Yale University Press, 1986). This argument, typically directed to the judicial review of legislative and executive action, does not apply with quite the same force to the judicial review of the common law, which is not the result of a majoritarian process. However, there is a more indirect counter-majoritarian effect. The replacement of a common law rule by a constitutional rule as in *Theophanous* excludes or at least limits the scope for future legislative (and executive) action.

[33] On the limited institutional capacity of courts, see generally G. N. Rosenberg, *The Hollow Hope* (Chicago: Chicago University Press, 1991).

reasoning from a statement of underlying principle,[34] more general propositions tend to emerge gradually as later courts apply, distinguish, develop, or even overrule previous cases. Although this incremental, case-by-case reasoning would not allow the Court entirely to avoid attention to underlying principle,[35] it could at least postpone the development or adoption of a vision or philosophy of freedom of speech. It could proceed by being relatively vague as to the overriding principle and comparatively specific as to the resolution of the particular dispute, leaving the adoption of a more ambitious set of principles to a later time.

Thus in *Stephens v. West Australian Newspapers*,[36] a companion case to *Theophanous*, Justices Brennan and McHugh developed the common law of qualified privilege without much explanation of the underlying principle of 'public interest'.[37] As the cases make clear, the parameters of this concept are set not by some overriding theory of the purpose it is to serve, but through incremental extension of individual cases.[38] The result is that these Justices were not required to explain, and did not commit the Court to, a particular understanding of the value of freedom of expression. Although a theory or theories may emerge over time, this decision formed only a step toward the formation of that theory. The virtue of an incremental approach is that a court can build up some experience, see the consequences of its more limited decisions play out in lower courts, and take into account any critical analysis of its decisions before it commits itself to any particular free speech theory. It thus avoids much of the risk that attends an ambitious decision that formulates a theory of freedom of political communication.

Of course, incremental reasoning is not necessarily confined to the common law.[39] The arguments I have just made might be taken as arguments for a cautious, incremental approach to the development of a rights guarantee rather than an argument for preference for the common law. Arguments for judicial minimalism, which can apply to judicial decision-making generally,[40] have special force with respect to the peculiarly difficult task of developing of a human rights regime. My point, however, is that the common law provides an especially attractive way of pursuing judicial minimalism. The use of the common law leaves maximum space open to the majoritarian arms of government and provides a base from which to make incremental movements. By contrast, developing a new rights guarantee with relatively few

---

[34] It could thus be described as reasoning 'from the bottom up'. See R. A. Posner, 'Legal Reasoning from the Top Down and from the Bottom Up', (1992) 59 *University of Chicago LR* 433.

[35] M. A. Eisenberg, *The Nature of the Common Law* (Cambridge, Mass.: Harvard University Press, 1988), 76–83; R. Dworkin, *Law's Empire* (Cambridge, Mass.: Belknap Press, 1986), 312.

[36] (1994) 182 CLR 211.

[37] *Gerhold v. Baker* [1918] WN 369. See also *Toogood v. Spyring* (1834) 1 CM&R 181 at 193; 149 ER 1044; *Huntley v. Ward* (1859) 6 CB(NS) 517.

[38] *Baird v. Wallace-James* (1916) 85 LJPC 193 at 198, cited with approval by Dixon J in *Guise v. Kouvelis* (1947) 74 CLR 102 at 117.

[39] Constitutional reasoning can, and in the opinion of some should, resemble the common law approach. See D. A. Strauss, 'Common Law Constitutionalism' (1996) 63 *University of Chicago LR* 877.

[40] C. R. Sunstein, 'Foreword: Leaving Things Undecided', (1996) 110 *Harvard LR* 4.

interpretive resources, courts may well be inclined toward general, underlying principle and thus to a more theorized method.

Finally, the common law alternative has the benefit of mitigating the uncertainty as to outcome that is bound to beset the development of a new rights doctrine. As the experience of American courts with the *New York Times* rule shows, judicially formulated rules may have unexpected consequences. It has been widely recognized that, despite the strength of its free speech rhetoric, the focus of the *New York Times* rule on the actions and motives of defendant journalists and editors has proved intrusive[41] and conducive to large awards of damages.[42] In turn, these features have created just the kind of chilling effect that *New York Times* was designed to prevent.

This problem persisted with the High Court's reformulated *New York Times* rule. Even though it was able to assess the practical result of the *New York Times* rule, and reformulate its own rule in response, the High Court's reformulation of the rule opened the way for the problem to repeat itself. The uncertain direction of subsequent judicial interpretation made the ultimate operation of its new rule rather unclear. The *Theophanous* test, which employs the open standards of 'recklessness' and 'reasonableness',[43] was particularly prone to this.[44]

By contrast, when a court is building upon an established system of law such as the common law it is less likely to be taken unawares by the results of its decisions. After *Theophanous*, if judges had adopted the common law approach of Justices Brennan and McHugh, they would have approached a false and allegedly libellous statement concerning a public figure with the established standard for qualified privilege and a new incremental extension of that test.

An illustration of the importance of underlying case law is found in Justice McHugh's consideration of the protection of comment. Although Justice McHugh extended the defence of qualified privilege to some statements made to the world at large, he excepted 'bare defamatory comment' (comment published without the facts on which it is based). This exception drew on the established refusal of the common law to protect such comment unless the factual basis could be proved.[45] In this light, Justice McHugh concluded that 'experience has shown that, in the absence of malice, the factual content of such publication is generally true' and consequently that '[s]ociety benefits even though some statements made on those occasions are in fact untrue'.[46] However, because Justice McHugh was not convinced of any additional benefit in protecting bare defamatory comment based on false information, it remained unprotected.[47]

---

[41] A. Lewis, '*New York Times v. Sullivan* Reconsidered: Time to Return to "The Central Meaning of the First Amendment"', (1983) 83 *Columbia LR* 603.

[42] Ibid. 614.   [43] (1994) 182 CLR 104 at 140–1.

[44] The test's novelty also left other important issues undecided, including its application to defamatory comment; see *Peterson v. Advertiser Newspapers Ltd* (1995) 64 SASR 152, and whether the test was to be applied by the judge or the jury; see *Hartley v. Nationwide News Pty Ltd* (1995) 119 FLR 124 at 129.

[45] (1994) 182 CLR 211 at 267.   [46] Ibid.   [47] Ibid.

Of course, Justice McHugh's determination that the new defence of qualified privilege did not extend to bare defamatory comment was based on his own assessment of the value of false information.[48] However, the existing law's emphasis on the truth of the facts underlying comment guided his inquiry. He accepted the existing law and sought a reason to extend the privilege to comment based on false factual information. That reason could be found with respect to comment generally, but not with respect to bare defamatory comment.

The established common law, therefore, can provide a degree of guidance and mitigate the chance that lower courts will develop the doctrine in a wholly unexpected way. That is not to say that common law method will always produce a perfect or a perfectly predictable result. However it does seem that an *unexpected, self-defeating* result, the failure of a rule to achieve its own aims, is less likely if the Court builds on an existing body of common law instead of formulating a new, freestanding rule.[49]

II. The response: the conservative retreat

Lange: the poverty of text and structure

This period of adventurous development of Australian free speech jurisprudence was brief. In part due to the retirement of some judges,[50] a more conservative mood began to take hold, culminating in the announcement of a narrower, more textual reading of the constitutional freedom of political discussion in *Lange v. Australian Broadcasting Corporation*.[51] The essence of the new approach is that any implication from the institutions of representative and responsible government (such as the freedom of political communication) is to be confined narrowly by constitutional text.[52] Thus it is only the *specific institutions* of representative and responsible government which are identifiable in the text that should be protected, rather than some fuller concept of representative and responsible government informed by political theory.

---

[48] Ibid.: '[A]lthough some champions of freedom of expression might argue otherwise, I am not convinced that society benefits by allowing persons to make defamatory comments that injure the reputations of others unless that comment is fair and based on facts that are true or . . . attract the defence of qualified privilege.'

[49] In making this argument I do not mean to deny an element of choice in the interpretation of the common law. I rely on the relatively modest point that the common law guides but, of course, does not determine the development of a doctrine.

[50] 1994 and 1995 saw the retirements of Mason CJ and Deane J, both members of the *Theophanous* majority.

[51] (1997) 189 CLR 529.

[52] Ibid. '[T]he Constitution gives effect to the institution of 'representative government' only to the extent that the text and structure of the Constitution establish it . . . the relevant question is not, 'What is required by representative and responsible government?' It is, 'What do the terms and structure of the Constitution prohibit, authorise or require?' The concept of an implication from structure in this circumstance is a narrow one limited to those 'logically or practically necessary' to the integrity of the Constitution.' *Lange* (1997) 189 CLR 520, 566–7.

The method of constitutional interpretation set down in *Lange* is notably averse to drawing on broad statements of principles or values, because these cannot be located in constitutional 'text and structure'. That is not to say that the Court denies the influences of extraconstitutional ideas altogether. Indeed, Justice McHugh, perhaps the most persistent advocate of this method of constitutional interpretation, has acknowledged that the commitment to this method is itself a commitment to a theoretical position, drawn from values external to the Constitution.[53] However, although this method of interpretation is itself based on an extraconstitutional theory, its point is to preclude other analysis of a theoretical or philosophical kind. So, except to the extent that the Court is committed to the general principle that the freedom of political communication is to be interpreted by reference to its 'text and structure', the Court has been quite emphatic that the freedom is not to be interpreted with reference to broad principle, overarching or underlying theories.[54]

This textualist interpretive method was, of course, bound to fail.[55] The failure of the *Lange* test to preclude reference to extra constitutional values or theories is evident in issues that have already been before the courts. One clear example, which I have discussed elsewhere,[56] is provided by the High Court's indecision over the nature of the standard of review to be applied to laws burdening political communication. The Court has fluctuated between adopting a European or Canadian-style 'proportionality' or balancing test and a more categorized American approach.[57] The principal difference between these tests is the degree of discretion left in the hands of a judge at the point of application of the test: the proportionality or balancing tests leaving more discretion in the hands of judges and the categorical approach confining judicial discretion. The choice between these kinds of test

---

[53] *McGinty* (1996) 186 CLR 140 at 230: 'The Constitution contains no injunction as to how it is to be interpreted. Any theory of constitutional interpretation must be a matter of conviction based on some theory external to the Constitution.'

[54] Ibid. 168 (Brennan CJ), 182–3 (Dawson J), 231–2 (McHugh), 270 (Gummow J); *Lange* (1997) 189 CLR 520, 566–7.

[55] It is probably surprising to a foreign observer to see textualism invoked as an appropriate method of constitutional interpretation. The idea that generally expressed text could determine the many specific decisions that arise over the life of a constitution has, of course, been comprehensively discredited. Nonetheless, although the High Court's approach has never been uniformly textualist, the method has had a strong hold on that Court. The reason may lie in Australia's constitutional history. An early turning point in Australian constitutional history is the decision of the High Court in *Amalgamated Society of Engineers v. Adelaide Steamship Co Ltd* (1920) 28 CLR 129, which contributed to the centralization of power to the Commonwealth through the mechanism of textual interpretation that overturned implied doctrines limiting the power of the central government. The case marked the beginning of a centralization of power that has since dominated the development of Australian constitutional law. Appeals to textualism have usually increased the power of the central government. See *Fairfax v. Federal Commissioner of Taxation* (1965) 114 CLR 1, *Tasmania v. Commonwealth* (1983) 158 CLR 1.

[56] I make this argument in detail in 'The Limits of Constitutional Text and Structure: Standards of Review and the Freedom of Political Communication', (1999) 23 *Melbourne University LR* 668.

[57] In *Lange* itself it seemed that the Court appeared to adopt a proportionality-type test to be applied in all circumstances. See *Lange* (1997) 189 CLR 520, 566–7. However, almost immediately afterwards, in *Levy v. Commonwealth* (1997) 189 CLR 579, some judges continued to apply tests that varied according to particular circumstances. See Stone, n. 56 above, 679–81.

requires the High Court to grapple with fundamental issues relating to the comparative merits of flexibility and constraint in judicial decision-making, or at least in the judicial development of free speech principles.[58] The choice, however, cannot be made by considering only the text of the Constitution. The text identifies only the institutions that the freedom exists to serve, but says nothing about the particular way in which doctrine should be applied by judges.

Other examples can easily be given. The *Lange* approach also fails to determine whether the freedom of political communication covers the discussion of the political matters of a state (or, for that matter, an Australian territory or even local government). Although some judges appear to think that *Lange* requires narrower coverage of state political discussion than the Court recognized beforehand,[59] the *Lange* method itself does not require that result. The emphasis on the textual basis of the implication does establish that a link must be drawn between the state political matters discussed and the institutions of representative and responsible government at the Commonwealth level found in the text. The problem is that it is consistent with that requirement to conclude either that state political matters will rarely be covered or that they will always be covered by the freedom or some point in between. It all depends on how readily a connection is made between matters relevant to state government and matters relevant to Commonwealth government, an issue on which the Constitution gives little guidance.

To use, by way of illustration, a case that has already been before the High Court, political communication in the form of protest against duck-hunting in the state of Victoria might appear to have no relevance to Commonwealth government.[60] The Act enabling the hunting and restricting the activities of protestors around the hunt was a Victorian Act, criticism or support of which is presumably directed to Victorian government, a matter with which the Constitution is not concerned. However, the opposite view is equally plausible if the matter is considered at a higher level of generality.[61] Although a Commonwealth law or policy was not the

---

[58] To illustrate how these kinds of consideration might assist in the choice, compare the law of the First Amendment with the protection of freedom of speech under the Canadian Charter of Rights and Freedoms. The American free speech tradition is so highly protective of speech that discretion-limiting rules are valued because the limitation on discretion is seen to protect speech from the natural human instinct to allow censorship of unpopular speech. F. Schauer, 'Fear, Risk and the First Amendment: Unravelling the "Chilling Effect" ', (1978) 58 *Boston University LR* 685. In Canada, on the other hand, the Supreme Court has been more receptive to government control and, consistently with this, the it has developed a test for invalidity that is less confining of discretion. *R v. Oakes* [1986] 1 SCR 103, 139–40; *Irwin Toy Ltd v. Quebec* [1989] 1 SCR 927, 991–1000. See Stone, n. 56 above, 696–7.

[59] *Levy* (1997) 189 CLR 579, 626 (McHugh J), 596 (Brennan J), though note that Brennan J had expressed this view in *Stephens v. West Australian Newspapers* (1994) 182 CLR 211, 235. The majority view in *Stephens v. West Australian Newspapers* was that the state matters were practically indivisible from federal political matters and thus the freedom of political communication covered political discussion of state matters generally. *Stephens* (1994) 189 CLR 211, 232 (Mason CJ, Toohey and Gaudron JJ), 257 (Deane J).

[60] As Brennan and McHugh JJ found in *Levy v. Commonwealth* (1997) 189 CLR 579.

[61] The choice here is between defining the coverage of the freedom of political communication at a low level of generality (covering perhaps the discussion of the public conduct of members of Commonwealth Parliament, the policy proposals of the Commonwealth Government, and the laws of

subject of the discussion and the Commonwealth may have no power over the particular dispute, the protestors against duck-hunting were in part concerned with environmental matters (the effect of hunting on endangered species). The Commonwealth government has considerable power over the environment,[62] and thus discussion of such matters at state level may well inspire citizens to reconsider their attitudes to the performance of the Commonwealth legislature and executive in this regard.[63] The *Lange* test thus cannot achieve the restraint it seeks, and a court minded to take a more expansive view of the freedom of political communication could do so consistently with the *Lange* test.

After Lange*: theoretical poverty and the public/private distinction*

Although the *Lange* method does not necessarily require greater restraint with respect to the freedom of political communication, it does seem to have had that effect at least for the moment. Since *Lange* there have been almost no cases raising freedom of political communication issues in the High Court,[64] and challenges in lower courts have, almost without exception, been unsuccessful.[65] However, because this restriction of the freedom is not required by the *Lange* method, the reasoning of many of these decisions is rather unconvincing. The problem is that courts are attempting to respond to the High Court's evident desire to confine the

the Commonwealth) or at a higher level of generality (encompassing the discussion of issues that could be the subject of Commonwealth legislative and executive power). Defining the level of generality of rights is an enduring problem of constitutional interpretation. Justice Scalia has suggested that the problem can be overcome by confining the right to 'the most specific level at which the relevant tradition protecting or denying protection to, the asserted right can be identified.' *Michael H v. Gerald D* 491 US 110 at 127 n. 6 (1989). Laurence Tribe and Michael Dorf have demonstrated the value-laden nature of this choice. See L. H. Tribe and M. C. Dorf, 'Levels of Generality in the Definition of Rights', (1990) 57 *University of Chicago LR* 1057. On the problem of levels of generality in implications from representative and responsible government under the Australian Constitution, see S. Evans, 'Commentary: Mr Egan, the Legislative Council and Responsible Government', in A. Stone and G. Williams (eds.), *The High Court at the Crossroads* (Leichhardt, NSW: Federation Press, 2000), 69–71.

[62] Although the environment is not the subject of a specific grant of power, the Commonwealth has been able to use other grants of power to regulate the environment, most notably its power over external affairs which allows it to implement international treaties on the environment. *Tasmania v. Commonwealth* (1983) 158 CLR 1. For another example, see the use of the trade and commerce power in *Murphyores Incorporated Pty Ltd v. Commonwealth* (1994) 136 CLR 1.

[63] This kind of argument was considered by Brennan J but rejected with little explanation: 'The plaintiff's intended protest related to the discrete State issue of the appropriateness of the relevant Victorian laws.' *Levy* (1997) 189 CLR 579, 596. Having acknowledged a potential link to federal matters, Brennan J does not explain why the protest against the duck hunt is a 'discrete' State issue. For a more expansive reading of the connection between state and Commonwealth political matters, see *John Fairfax v. Attorney General (NSW)* [2000] NSWCA 198 (Spiegelman CJ, Priestley JA agreeing).

[64] The only major case is *Levy v. Commonwealth* (1997) 189 CLR 579, argued at the same time as *Lange* and handed down shortly afterwards.

[65] *Rann v. Olsen* [2000] SASC 83, *Communications Electrical Energy Information Postal Plumbing and Allied Services Union v. Laing* (1998) 159 ALR 73; *Higgins v. The Commonwealth* (1998) 160 ALR 175; *Brown v. Classification Review Board* (1998) 154 ALR 67, 85; *Watson v. Trenerry* (1998) 122 NTR 1. For a rare successful challenge (that may yet reach the High Court), see *John Fairfax v. Attorney General (NSW)* [2000] NSWCA 198.

freedom without the necessary tools to do so. The result so far has been an unthinking conservatism.

In a number of cases judges have overlooked seemingly obvious freedom of speech points. A federal appellate court found, by majority, that a censored student newspaper article advocating shoplifting and containing a critique of capitalism[66] would not bear on the kind of choice a reader would make at a federal election and therefore had no relevantly political message.[67] Although there may well be good reason to allow this kind of speech to be regulated,[68] it is frankly difficult to deny that there is *some* political content to this message. A challenge to a political theory of this kind does invite citizens to re-think the overall direction of government and thus may (even if it is not likely to) affect their federal electoral choices.[69] Equally concerning was the Queensland Court of Appeal's failure to see *any* free speech issue implicated in the treatment of the satirical artist 'Pauline Pantsdown', whose song satirizing a controversial federal politician was subjected to an interlocutory injunction in a defamation action.[70] Both these decisions seem to represent a reflex (and as we have seen unjustified) assumption that the *Lange* test requires a narrower reading of the protection of political discussion.

However, the most striking illustration of the poverty of the High Court's current theoretical approach may be in its rather curious treatment of the relationship between the common law and the freedom of political communication. After an initial finding

---

[66] *Brown v. Classification Review Board* (1998) 154 ALR 67, 89: 'the injunction against stealing from capitalism is itself a capitalist ideology and should be spurned as such.'

[67] (1998) 154 ALR 67, 87 (Heerey J). See also the judgment of Sundberg J: '[T]he article does not relate to the exercise by the people of a free and informed choice as electors.' (1998) 154 ALR 67, 98. Sundberg J also took this view because only a small portion of the article was devoted to material that could be described as political: the article was 'overwhelmingly a manual about how successfully to steal' (ibid.).

[68] As I make clear in 'The Freedom of Political Communication since *Lange*', in A. Stone and G. Williams, n. 61 above, my argument is not so much with the decision that the law in question was valid, but with the conclusion that it did not even burden political discussion. It would have been possible for the Federal Court to have held that the law did burden political communication but was valid as a measure 'reasonably appropriate and adapted to serve a legitimate end the fulfilment of which is compatible with the maintenance of . . . the system of government prescribed by the Constitution'. See *Lange* (1997) 189 CLR 520, 567. Indeed, this was the view taken by the third member of the Court in *Brown* (1998) 154 ALR 67, 80 (French J).

[69] See French J ibid.

[70] An appeal against the granting of the injunction failed in the Queensland Court of Appeal. The Court's reasoning as to the freedom of political communication issue is strikingly brief: 'Enjoining the broadcast of this material could not possibly be said to infringe against the need for free and general discussion of public matters fundamental to our democratic society. These were grossly offensive imputations relating to the sexual orientation and preference of a Member of Parliament as part of a fairly mindless effort at cheap denigration.' *Australian Broadcasting Corporation v. Hanson* (unreported, 28 Sept. 1998). The comparison with a case like *Hustler v. Falwell* (1988) 485 US 46, 54–5, protecting a particularly offensive and obviously inaccurate satire, is particularly stark. Although the Australian court might reasonably adopt a different approach to satire, the simple assertion that there is no question that the communication might have political value is not convincing. The High Court subsequently denied special leave to appeal with no further argument about the freedom of political communication. See *Australian Broadcasting Corporation v. Hanson* transcript, 24 June 1999 (High Court of Australia).

to the contrary,[71] the Court's current position is that the Constitution is primarily addressed to legislative and executive action and thus does not apply directly to a constitutional doctrine like the freedom of political communication.[72] The elements of this argument each involve considerable theoretical confusion, and are contradicted by other aspects of the Court's doctrine.

First, the High Court attached great importance to the idea that the freedom of political communication is 'not a personal right'.[73] In part, it seems that the Court means that the freedom of political communication is primarily a negative rather than a positive right.[74] On close examination, however, this idea turns out to say nothing as to whether the freedom of political communication applies to the common law. Assuming that the freedom is negative, in the sense that it provides freedom from interference, it would still be possible that it might protect individuals from the operation of the common law. In other words, if the freedom is a negative right, why might it not be a negative right that protects from the interference of common law in so far as common law offends the principles underlying the implied freedom?

More important, then, is the Court's finding that the Constitution directs itself only to the exercise of legislative and executive power.[75] This conclusion rests on a conception of the common law as primarily[76] regulating relationships between private individuals.[77] The Constitution, on the other hand, is conceived of as a charter of government, concerned with delimiting government power and not with the (private) common law. Thus the Court seems to mean that the freedom of political communication operates 'vertically' (against governments) rather than 'horizontally' (between private parties).

---

[71] *Theophanous* (1994) 182 CLR 104 at 126 per Mason CJ, Toohey and Gaudron JJ, at 164–5 per Deane J.

[72] (1997) 189 CLR 520, 560–1.

[73] See *Lange* (1997) 189 CLR 520, 560: 'Those sections [from which the freedom of political communication is implied] do not confer personal rights on individuals. Rather they preclude the curtailment of the protected freedom by the exercise of legislative or executive power.' See also *Theophanous* (1994) 182 CLR 104, 146–8 (Brennan J), 168 (Deane J); *Cunliffe v. Commonwealth* (1992) 182 CLR 372, 327 (Brennan J); *Australian Capital Television*, n. 6 above, 150 (Brennan J).

[74] This appears to be the distinction Justice Brennan had in mind when he wrote: 'If the freedom implied in the Constitution were a personal right or immunity, it would extend to what is needed to facilitate or permit its full enjoyment'. (1994) 182 CLR 104 at 148. See also *Cunliffe v. Commonwealth* (1994) 182 CLR 272, 326; *McClure v. Australian Electoral Commission* (1999) 163 ALR 734, 741 (Hayne J). It is probably more satisfactory to speak, as international lawyers do, in terms of first-generation rights (civil and political liberties, typically negative rights) and second-generation rights (social and economic rights, typically positive rights).

[75] *Lange* (1997) 189 CLR 520, 560.

[76] This view excepts common law principles that govern the structures and powers of government, such as the common law determining the extent of executive power. See L. Zines, 'The Common Law: Its Nature and Constitutional Significance', (1999, CIPL Law and Policy Papers, Australian National University), 16.

[77] This point of view is expressed most clearly in the judgment of Justice Brennan in *Theophanous* (1994) 182 CLR 104, 153, the judgment that first advanced the idea that the freedom of political communication does not apply to the common law.

The problem with this analysis, as anyone with even a passing acquaintance with American constitutional law will instantly recognize, lies in the classification of the common law as 'private'. The distinction is challenged by the view, clearly expressed in *New York Times v. Sullivan*,[78] that judicial enforcement of the common law is government action and thus directly subject to constitutional requirements.[79]

The American doctrine accords with the realities of the exercise of governmental power. It recognizes that the involvement of the state at the point of enforcement of the common law transforms the act of an individual (which might be adequately characterized as simply a private wrong by an individual against another individual) into the governmental act of protecting the perpetrator or vindicating the injured party.[80] Further, as Canadian scholars commenting on the Canadian Supreme Court's refusal to apply the *Charter* to the common law[81] have argued, the Canadian (and therefore the Australian) position seems to rely on a pre-realist understanding of the common law as something that the courts could 'discover' and apply to cases before them rather than as something created by judges.[82] Indeed, although it might not always be easy to distinguish between public and private action, the judicial enforcement of the common law seems to be a clear example of state (rather than private) action.[83]

Finally, it seems that other aspects of the High Court's own analysis contradict this finding and implicitly recognize the governmental nature of common law enforcement. Although it has held that the freedom of political communication does not 'apply' to the common law, the Court has also found that the common law and the Constitution form 'one system of jurisprudence'[84] within which the Constitution is the 'basic law' that 'may have effect on the content of the common law'.[85] In *Lange*, therefore, although the Court abandoned the constitutional rule formulated in *Theophanous*, it altered the common law to conform to constitutional

---

[78] 254 US 367 (1964).

[79] Although the Court does not expressly say so, the decision is clearly based on an understanding that the enforcement of the common law provided the requisite state action. 376 US 254, 265 (1964): 'Although this is a civil lawsuit between private parties, the Alabama courts have applied a state rule of law which petitioners claim to impose invalid restrictions on their constitutional freedoms of speech and press. It matters not that that law has been applied in a civil action and that it is common law only . . . The test is not the form in which state power has been applied but, whatever the form, whether such power has been exercised.'

[80] This point was made as long ago as 1883, see *Civil Rights Cases* 109 US 3, 17 (1883): 'An individual cannot deprive a man of his right[s] . . . he may by force or fraud, interfere with the enjoyment of the right in a particular case; [but] unless protected in these wrongful acts by some shield of State law or state authority, he cannot destroy or injure the right.'

[81] *Retail, Wholesale & Department Store Union v. Dolphin Delivery Ltd* [1986] 2 SCR 573.

[82] B. Slattery, 'The *Charter*'s Relevance to Private Litigation: Does Dolphin Deliver?', (1987) 32 *McGill LJ* 905 at 918–19.

[83] L. H. Tribe, *American Constitutional Law*, 2nd edn. (New York: Foundation Press, 1988), 1711: 'the general proposition that common law is state action—that is, that the state "acts" when its courts create and enforce common law rules—is hardly controversial.' See H. Wechsler, 'Toward Neutral Principles of Constitutional Law', (1959) 73 *Harvard LR* 1, 29:'[t]hat the action of the court is action of the state . . . is, of course, entirely obvious.'

[84] (1997) 189 CLR 520, 564. [85] Ibid.

requirements of the freedom of political communication. As a practical matter this means that although constitutional limitations like the freedom of political communication do not 'apply' directly to the common law regulating the relationship between individuals,[86] the common law will be developed in a manner that eliminates any conflict with the Constitution.[87]

The significance of this part of the High Court's analysis for my argument is that it shows that the Court does not take seriously its own classification of the common law as private. The notion that the common law must conform to the Constitution has an intuitive appeal that points to a more explicit justification: the idea of inconsistency between the judicial enforcement of the common law and the Constitution is unappealing because we seem to be receiving conflicting instructions from the same source. This reflects our idea that the common law and the Constitution are essentially products of the same source: the state. Thus, in adopting the position that the common law must conform to the Constitution, the Court contradicted its first proposition: that the common law should be conceived of as private and consequently not subject to constitutional review. If the common law were truly private, why would there be any concern as to inconsistency between it and the charter of government set down in the Constitution?[88]

That is not to say that the freedom of political communication or any other guaranteed rights *ought* to apply to the common law or to other apparently private actions. There may be reasons not to subject some governmental action to the scrutiny of rights guarantees.[89] The point is only that in this sphere, as in others, courts cannot escape the need to make a normative judgment about the content of rights. It is not especially helpful to ask the question 'when is the government or state involved?' as whenever a dispute reaches a court, it is almost always possible to identify some state action in the matter.[90] The real question is whether the

[86] For the distinction between the common law as it regulates government and the common law as it regulates individuals, see n. 76 above.

[87] L. Zines, *The Common Law in Australia: Its Nature and Constitutional Significance* (Sydney: Butterworths, 1999), 26.

[88] Slattery makes the same point with respect to the Canadian position requiring the Court to develop the common law consistently with fundamental constitutional values: 'The problem is that any such judicial role seems inconsistent with the premise that the *Charter* does not extend to private disputes governed by the common law . . . If the Courts "ought" to develop the common law in the way suggested, this can only mean that they have some sort of duty to do so. This duty must stem from the Constitution itself, for it is difficult to see where else it might come from.' N. 82 above, 920–1.

[89] *Retail Wholesale and Department Store Union v. Dolphin Delivery Ltd* [1986] 2 SCR 573, 600–1. See also *McKinney v. University of Guelph*, [1990] SCR 229, 262–3 per La Forest J: 'To open up all private and public action to judicial review could strangle the operation of society and, as put by counsel for the universities, "diminish the area of freedom within which individuals can act".'

[90] See G. Gunther and K. M. Sullivan, *Constitutional Law*, 13th edn. (Westbury, NY: Foundation Press, 1997), 938: 'If Shelley were read at its broadest, a simple citation of the case would have disposed of most subsequent state action cases. Some seemingly "neutral" state nexus with a private actor can almost always be found at least by way of the usual state law backdrop for the exercises of private choices . . . Given the entanglement of private choices with law, a broad application of Shelley might in effect have left no private choices immune from constitutional restraints.'

policies that motivate the freedom, or the values that underlie it, require the application of the freedom to the action in question. To answer this, judges need to develop tests which reflect the judgment that really underlies a decision to subject an individual actor to government scrutiny.[91] It cannot be satisfactorily hidden behind an unconvincing distinction between private and public law.

III. Reflections on the Human Rights Act

The Australian experience with relatively limited development of rights suggests the depth of challenge a new rights regime can present. Courts will be faced with making choices about the complex value systems that underscore rights which cannot be avoided by recourse to text. If British judges, perhaps because they are more used to the comparatively concrete task of interpreting ordinary statutes, are tempted to treat the text of the Human Rights Act as determinative,[92] the Australian experience should serve as a reminder of the limitations of textualism, and that over-reliance on text tends simply to suppress the nature of the value choices the judges must make.

The Australian experience therefore counsels overt attention to underlying values. That kind of approach could considerably clarify the question of how the Human Rights Act applies to regulation of private disputes by the common law. The concerning feature of the British debate on this issue so far is that some English lawyers appear to be repeating the mistakes made by the Australian High Court. Sir Richard Buxton has argued (1) that the Convention and, therefore, the incorporation of it by the Human Rights Act creates rights only against governments (including public authorities); and (2) that as a result, the Human Rights Act has no effect on the common law.[93] Thus, the argument goes, even though section 6 of the Human Rights Act requires public authorities, including courts, to act in accordance with the incorporated Convention rights, these rights are rights against government only, and therefore the requirement does not affect the application or development of the common law in disputes between individuals.

---

[91] Alexander Bickel made this point in relation to the state action requirement in the 14th Amendment's equal protection clause: 'The question really is, what places and activities should be deemed so private that, in respect of them, the state should be allowed to protect—albeit implicitly only—voluntarily adopted policies of segregation, just as it enforces other privately made policies and protects the enjoyment of other liberties in the course of maintaining general legal order?' Bickel, n. 32 above, 175.

[92] These problems are not overcome by the fact that the rights of the Human Rights Act are expressly guaranteed and in a considerably more elaborated form than many rights guarantees. It is not hard to find concepts such as the 'right to life', 'inhuman or degrading treatment', 'private and family life' that require a considerable amount of interpretation and, in the course of that interpretation, choice between competing conceptions of the right.

[93] Sir R. Buxton, 'The Human Rights Act and Private Law', (2000) 116 *Law Quarterly Review* 48, 59. For an argument against this position, see M. Hunt 'The "Horizontal Effect" of the Human Rights Act', [1998] *Public Law* 423.

The point of my argument about the High Court's approach to the Australian common law is that, even if the first of these points is accepted, it does not lead to the conclusion contained in the second point. The inherently 'public' nature of the development and enforcement of the common law means that, even though the common law regulates relations between individuals, it is easy to see that it is the *state* that is doing the regulation.

So far I have emphasized the necessity for courts to face up to the value-laden nature of their task. The Australian experience also suggests that courts should be sensitive to the limitations on their capacity to make these decisions. This approach has particular ramifications for the treatment of the existing common law on human rights. The Human Rights Act apparently does not preclude reliance on pre-existing common law,[94] and thus the possibility of rights sensitivity in the common law, such as that seen in *Derbyshire County Council v. Times Newspapers Limited*[95] and more recently in *Reynolds v. Times Newspapers Ltd*,[96] remains.

The Australian experience with the freedom of political communication suggests both that it is likely that enthusiasm for new rights will obscure the possibility of common law solutions (some British scholars have already spoken of the role for the common law as *residual*, suggesting that review under the Human Rights Act will always be the first port of call and the common law will be a last resort where no Human Rights Act claim is available)[97] and that courts should resist the temptation to ignore the common law. Given the complexity of the task of illuminating the rights incorporated by the Human Rights Act, courts should at least consider whether the advantages of incremental, comparatively untheorized decision-making and predictability of result make the common law an appropriate alternative.

To complete my argument I must, of course, address the particular features of the Human Rights Act that distinguish it from an entrenched bill of rights. The suggestion that the Act effects only moderate change obviously relies on a 'soft' form of judicial review[98] implemented by the Human Rights Act. It is obviously significant that judicial review under the Human Rights Act does not render the law invalid but allows Parliament to respond if it chooses to do so. Given the reservations that I have expressed as to the capacity of courts to respond to the task of

[94] This much seems to be contemplated by s. 11(a), which provides that reliance on a Convention rights does not restrict 'any other right or freedom conferred by or under any law having effect in any part of the United Kingdom'.

[95] [1993] 1 All ER 1011.

[96] [1999] 4 All ER 609 (*Reynolds*). Although the Court did not adopt the special rule for criticism of political figures pressed on it by the defendant (the 'generic privilege'), it did emphasize that the classical duty and interest test that governed the defence of qualified privilege should be sensitive to free speech concerns by taking into account matters such as the nature of the publication, including its importance for public discussion.

[97] P. Craig, 'Constitutionalism, Regulation and Review', in R. Hazell (ed.), *Constitutional Futures: A History of the Next Ten Years* (Oxford: Oxford University Press, 1999), 75.

[98] The Human Rights Act allows for a declaration that an Act is incompatible with a Convention right (s. 4(4)) which does not affect the validity of that Act (s. 4(6)) but gives rise to ministerial power of amendment under s. 10.

defining human rights, it is reassuring that the Act makes declarations of incompatibility by British courts only provisional judgments as to invalidity.[99]

Nonetheless, the role of courts in developing rights will certainly be significant. First, although it remains to be seen just how Parliament will respond to declarations of incompatibility, there is some reason to suppose that declarations of incompatibility will be of great force. In particular, there seem to be structural incentives for Parliament to respond. A complainant who has exhausted her remedies in the British courts is still entitled to pursue an action in Strasbourg. Parliament may prefer to respond (and to be seen to be responding) to British courts rather than to the European Court of Human Rights.[100] Moreover, it seems likely that much of the action under the Human Rights Act will be played out under section 6, which provides that any action by a public authority (which includes any body exercising 'public functions') in contravention of an incorporated right is 'unlawful'. In any event, the real difficulty the Australian courts have faced is in making the normative judgment that legislation offends a particular right, and that problem remains even if the result of the finding is somewhat more limited.

IV. Conclusion

I have suggested that the Australian experience serves as a warning to British courts of the nature of the task before them. I hope, at the very least, to have put paid to the suggestion seen in the parliamentary debates on the Human Rights Bill that the Act would effect only moderate change quite consistent with Britain's established political traditions.[101] The enactment of the Human Rights Act is an extraordinary event in British constitutional history. Never before have judges had so much power to decide matters of high moral import and so fundamental to social and political life. The task is far more daunting than the implementation of the relatively narrow speech right developed by the Australian High Court, a sobering thought given the High Court's struggle with that right.

[99] Whether this is the *best* response to the institutional limitations of courts is another question. See M. C. Dorf, 'Foreword: The Limits of Socratic Deliberation', (1997) 112 *Harvard LR* 1.

[100] This sentiment is reflected in the title of the White Paper, *Rights Brought Home: The Human Rights Bill* (24 Oct. 1997).

[101] Naturally enough these comments rely primarily on the limited effect of a declaration of incompatibility. See e.g. Lord Irvine of Lairg: 'The Bill is carefully drafted and designed to respect our traditional understanding of the separation of powers.' HL Deb. 582, col. 1228, 3 Nov. 1997; and Lord Lester of Herne Hill, col. 1239: 'It involves no challenge to the English dogma of absolute parliamentary sovereignty . . . True to the doctrine of parliamentary sovereignty . . . the courts must defer to existing and future Acts of Parliament if it is impossible to read and give effect to them in a way which is compatible with the convention.'

Index